The Archaeology of the First Farmer-Herders in Egypt

New Insights into the Fayum Epipalaeolithic and Neolithic

Noriyuki Shirai

Leiden University Press

Archaeological Studies Leiden University
is published by Leiden University Press, the Netherlands

Series editors: C. C. Bakels and H. Kamermans

Cover Design: Joanne Porck
Layout: Noriyuki Shirai
Illustrations: Noriyuki Shirai

ISBN 9789087280796
E-ISBN 9789048512690
NUR 682

ARCHAEOLOGICAL STUDIES LEIDEN UNIVERSITY 21

The Archaeology of the First Farmer-Herders in Egypt

New Insights into the Fayum Epipalaeolithic and Neolithic

Proefschrift

ter verkrijging van
de graad van Doctor aan de Universiteit Leiden,
op gezag van Rector Magnificus prof. mr. P. F. van der Heijden,
volgens besluit van het College voor Promoties
te verdedigen op
donderdag 29 april 2010
klokke 13.45 uur

door

Noriyuki Shirai

geboren te Kyoto
in 1970

Promotiecommissie

Promotor: Prof. Dr. J. Bintliff (Universiteit Leiden)

Co-promotor: Prof. Dr. A. L. Van Gijn (Universiteit Leiden)

Referent: Prof. Dr. P. M. Vermeersch (Katholieke Universiteit Leuven)

Overige leden: Prof. Dr. P. M. M. G. Akkermans (Universiteit Leiden)
Prof. Dr. R. T. J. Cappers (Universiteit Leiden)
Prof. Dr. L. P. Louwe Kooijmans (Universiteit Leiden)
Dr. G. Van der Kooij (Universiteit Leiden)

This research was made possible with the grant of the Netherlands Organisation for Scientific Research (NWO/WOTRO file number: W52-1038).

Contents

Preface

This dissertation includes the result of my fieldwork carried out in the framework of the UCLA-RUG Fayum Project, which is directed by Willeke Wendrich and René Cappers. A full account of the work by the Fayum Project and further acknowledgements would appear in a monograph edited by them and published by the Cotsen Institute of Archaeology at University of California, Los Angeles.

1. Introduction

1.1. Present state of knowledge regarding the origins and development of farming and herding in Egypt

The beginning of farming and herding in the Eastern Mediterranean in the Early Holocene has drawn a great deal of archaeological interest. The transition from the Palaeolithic foraging way of life to the Neolithic food producing way of life and associated changes in society and culture has been regarded as a revolution, and many studies have attempted to answer how and why Palaeolithic foragers abandoned their traditional way of providing subsistence by developing or adopting farming and herding. In contrast, little is still known about the transition process in Egypt due to the lack of sufficient data.

Nevertheless, Wetterstrom has summarised the information available to her in the early 1990s about the Late Palaeolithic-Neolithic human occupations in the Egyptian Nile Valley, and has argued the transition process in detail (Wetterstrom 1993). Her article which was originally published in English was later translated into French (Wetterstrom 1996), and it is probable that her article was read by many people who were concerned with this topic. Indeed, her article has been repeatedly cited as an authentic source of information in other scholarly articles and even in some recently-published general books about the origins of food production (*e.g.*, Barker 2006; Bellwood 2005). There is little doubt that her article had a great impact on readers regarding the ideas about the transition from foraging to farming and herding in Egypt. Her article was certainly innovative in terms that she not only described a series of facts concerning Late Palaeolithic, Epipalaeolithic and Neolithic subsistence on the basis of archaeological evidence obtained in the Nile Valley, but also attempted to answer how and why farming and herding started in the Nile Valley. However, her article included many unsubstantiated assumptions.

She assumed that even though Epipalaeolithic foragers in the Nile Valley had a seemingly successful subsistence, (1) people would have continually suffered from serious food shortages caused by the annual Nile floods which could fluctuate from year to year and over time, sometimes causing disastrous inundation but other years failing and leading to equally disastrous drought, (2) people would have adopted wheat/barley farming and sheep/goat herding from Levantine farmers-herders to mitigate the food shortages and to augment the variety of staple food, (3) people would have thought that the most attractive feature of farming and herding was their predictability rather than their productivity, (4) people would have gradually rejected foraging because it was not compatible with the emerging trend toward sedentism caused by the adoption of farming. I found it hard to accept her assumptions, because she did not refer to ideas obtained through anthropological studies on foragers since the 1960s and archaeological research in other regions at that time. Therefore, I thought that the beginning of farming and herding in Egypt had to be reconsidered in the light of more sound theories and models as well as new archaeological data. This is the primary reason why I decided to embark on new research.

Ethnological research on foragers has revealed many unexpected and intriguing facts since the 1960s. Until then, it was widely believed that foragers were always starving and spent much time foraging food whereas farmers were wealthy and stable, and enjoyed much leisure time. However, ethnological studies have revealed that even foragers who inhabited marginal areas did not always suffer from food shortages because they relied on a wide variety of wild plants and animals, and could usually manage to find something edible. It is recognised that the farming and herding way of life is much less stable and subject to environmental changes because it depends on only a few domesticated plants and animals which are vulnerable to climatic fluctuations. Furthermore, it has also been recognised that foragers as a rule spent less time procuring food than farmers did (*e.g.*, Lee 1968; Sahlins 1972). Accordingly, the common belief that foragers are always starving and the farming and herding way of life is stable is no longer viable and cannot easily be applied to the past. Whereas Wetterstrom refers to the broad-spectrum subsistence strategy in Late Palaeolithic and Epipalaeolithic Egypt, she does not give convincing evidence of starvation at the end of the Epipalaeolithic period. Her assumption that Epipalaeolithic foragers in the Nile Valley would have continually suffered from food shortages caused by recurrent failures of Nile floods is doubtful given the presence of aquatic resources in the Nile as well as wild plants and animals in the Nile floodplain. She seems to overestimate the effects of the Nile flood failures.

The second question about Wetterstrom's assumptions is whether Epipalaeolithic foragers in Egypt had no means other than to adopt farming and herding to mitigate food shortages if they were actually faced with seasonal and/or long-term food shortages. In case of seasonal food shortages, they could have migrated, or have stored surplus food when available and have depended on the stored food during the season of hunger. This would have been a realistic solution in generally resource-rich environments of the Nile Valley. Although she refers to the archaeological evidence of the making of dried fish at Late Palaeolithic sites in Middle and Upper Egypt, she does not seem to regard it as important. However, the significance of food preservation and storage among ethnographic foragers has been discussed elsewhere (*e.g.*, Testart 1982), and should not be ignored even in prehistoric contexts. In case of long-term food shortages, the people could have moved on, or have curtailed their numbers by the regulation of population such as abortion, contraception and infanticide. Therefore, it can be said that the adoption of farming and herding is not the sole solution.

Wetterstrom's assumption gives rise to a question as to under what conditions farming and herding were introduced. It has been argued that wild food resources were constantly so rich and reliable in the Nile Valley that the inhabitants of the Nile Valley had failed or resisted the introduction of foreign domesticates for a long time, but it has hardly been explained why domesticates were adopted in the Nile Valley at long last (Butzer 1976: 9; Hassan 1984a: 222; Wenke 1990: 377). She seems to think that farming and herding must have been adopted under conditions of food shortages. In fact, many archaeologists working in the Near East and elsewhere concur that the food shortage caused by various reasons may have resulted in the initiation or adoption of farming and herding. However, some scholars are of the opinion that it was too risky for Epipalaeolithic foragers to attempt a new subsistence regime under conditions of starvation because if it failed, the situation would deteriorate and lead to fatalities (*e.g.*, Gould 1985: 431; Hayden 1990: 35, 57). It has been reported in Near Eastern archaeology that there was no evidence of food shortages at the transitional period from foraging to farming in the Middle Euphrates and thus the beginning of food production was not inevitable (Moore 1989: 629). In short, farming is not necessarily adopted under conditions of food shortages. Even though her assumption of occasional food shortages cannot totally be rejected, a possibility of the adoption of farming and herding under good conditions should also be considered in Egypt.

The third question about Wetterstrom's assumption is whether farming and herding are predictable. She uses the term 'predictable' as meaning that Epipalaeolithic foragers, who introduced domesticates, could control the location and size of crops and livestock and the time of sowing in response to the vagaries of the annual Nile floods. However, it does not follow from her assumption that farming and herding are predictable because the growth of crops and livestock is at the mercy of natural conditions like fluctuations in the annual Nile floods. If an unusually low flood did not supply enough water to the field of crops and pastures along the Nile in summer, or if extreme heat wave arrived in early spring, they could not thrive at all without irrigation facilities. It was not until irrigation facilities were introduced in the Predynastic or Early Dynastic period that people could somehow control the growth of crops and livestock. Therefore, it can be said that farming and herding could never be predictable at the beginning of their introduction.

On the other hand, it is widely accepted that well-developed farming and herding are far more productive per unit area than foraging. This is undoubtedly the most attractive feature of farming and herding. Thus, it seems more likely that Epipalaeolithic foragers in the Nile Valley would have introduced domesticates because of their productivity rather than their predictability. However, it is uncertain whether the human population in Epipalaeolithic Egypt had increased so excessively that it required more productive subsistence. The possibility of such a population increase in this period has been suggested without giving any archaeological evidence (Clark 1971: 71-74; Clark 1980: 578-579). Population pressure has been argued as the prime mover at the beginning of farming (*e.g.*, Cohen 1977; Rosenberg 1990) or as a favourable precondition for the beginning of farming (*e.g.*, Hassan 1981: 219; Price and Gebauer 1995: 7; Redding 1988; Keeley 1988), but it cannot presently be concluded that population increase was the sole reason for the adoption of farming in Egypt. Other reasons must also be sought.

The fourth question about Wetterstrom's assumption is whether foragers in the Nile Valley were not sedentary before the adoption of farming. She seems to repeat the idea that sedentism became common in Egypt long after the adoption of farming (Wenke 1989: 138). However, the causality between farming and sedentism has long been a focus of debate in archaeology. There are examples of sedentism before the beginning of farming in prehistory, whereas examples of sedentism after the beginning of farming are also known in archaeology and ethnography (*e.g.*, Flannery 1973; Kelly 1992; Rafferty 1985; Testart 1982). Scholars who have expertise in sedentary foragers of the Natufian in the Levant suggest that sedentism may have been realised in the Nile Valley before the introduction of farming from the Levant (Bar-Yosef and Meadow 1995: fig.3.5). Therefore, the context of the introduction of farming in Egypt deserves careful re-examination.

The last questions about Wetterstrom's argument are who were the agents of the diffusion of wheat/barley farming and sheep/goat herding from the Levant to Egypt and who was responsible for the adoption of farming and herding in Egypt. Although gradual infiltration of a small number of Levantine drifters and refugees into Egypt over hundreds of years and peaceful mix of the Levantine people and local foragers in Egypt have been suggested (Hassan 1984a: 222), she does not mention these questions as if these do not matter at all. On the other hand, the diffusion of farming and herding from the Near East to the European continent has been well studied. Already in the early 1990s, it has been argued that 1) indigenous foragers in coastal regions of Mediterranean Europe might have willingly adopted domesticated sheep from the Near East without causing any remarkable changes in the local culture of those regions, and 2) farmers might have firstly immigrated to sparsely-populated regions of Central Europe and then inhabitants of coastal regions might have gradually adopted farming from the farmers, though there seem to have been conflicts between them (Donahue 1992). It has been said that unlike modern examples of colonialism, prehistoric farmers did not invade densely-populated regions and did not displace or enslave indigenous foragers but tended to colonise sparsely-populated regions. Furthermore, it has also been suggested that farming was likely to be adopted willingly by knowledgeable indigenous foragers through direct or indirect contacts with farmers (Gebauer and Price 1992; Headland and Reid 1989; Spielmann and Eder 1994). Therefore, the scale, places, process and reasons of the contact between Levantine farmer-herders and Egyptian foragers should be important research topics, no matter what were the reasons for the adoption of farming and herding in Egypt.

1.2. Aims of research

As demonstrated above, another reason for the poor state of knowledge regarding the beginning of farming and herding in Egypt may be that Egyptian archaeology in general has traditionally lacked cross-cultural and anthropological perspectives (O'Connor 1997; Trigger 1979; 1997). As a consequence, it has failed to explain the characteristics of the beginning of farming and herding in Egypt on the basis of not only comparisons with other cases in different times and regions, but also references to anthropological perspectives and various explanatory models. It is common for scholars studying the beginning of farming in Europe, for instance, to refer to various perspectives and models regarding the beginning of farming as well as current research in the Near East and elsewhere (*e.g.*, Bogucki 1999; Gebauer and Price 1992; Hodder 1990; Price and Gebauer 1995; Price 2000; Thorpe 1996), but this has not always been the case with scholars dealing with the same topic in Egypt. In the studies of interregional contacts and dispersal of farming and herding, Egypt has been isolated even in the Eastern Mediterranean. As several proceedings of international conferences and workshops on the beginning of farming clearly demonstrate, Egyptian case studies have not appeared at all and have not contributed to the understanding and model-building of the beginning of farming in a worldwide perspective (*e.g.*, Anderson 1999; Cappers and Bottema 2002; Cowan and Watson 1992; Harris 1996; Price and Gebauer 1995).

Through the examination of previous studies on this topic, I have felt it indispensable to know more about current studies in regions other than the Nile Valley, and to compare the situations. Even within Egypt, much information regarding human occupations of desert areas far away from the Nile Valley in the Early-Middle Holocene, which was scarcely referred to by Wetterstrom, became available in the last decades. It has also been revealed that domestication of cattle began independently in Egypt and that domesticated sheep/goats were diffused from the Levant to Egypt earlier in date than previously believed. This information must be taken into consideration.

Furthermore, it is necessary to learn about theories, models and perspectives which have been employed in other regions, in order to enable their application to the study of Egypt. Although I have presented Wetterstrom's study as a first step toward developing a new idea about the beginning of farming and herding in Egypt, it is far from satisfactory in terms of the examination of various models. The adaptation model, which emphasises food shortages caused by environmental changes or population increase as the reason for the beginning of farming and herding, has been the most traditional model. In addition, the biological model, which emphasises symbiosis between humans and plants and regards farming as unintentional consequence of the symbiosis, has been put forward since the 1980s (*e.g.*, Harris 1989; O'Brien and Wilson 1988; Rindos 1980; 1984). The socioeconomic model, which focuses on the affluence and complexity of foraging societies revealed by ethnographic and ethnological studies and considers human ambition to acquire status and power by using domesticates as the reason for the beginning of farming and herding, has also been eloquently advocated (*e.g.*, Bender 1978; Hayden 1990; 1992; 1995a).

Moreover, following the recognition of the period of worldwide cooling and drying of climate called the Younger Dryas before the onset of the Holocene, attention to climatic and environmental disruptions in the argument of the beginning of farming in the Near East has revived since the early 1990s (*e.g.*, McCorriston and Hole 1991; Moore and Hillman 1992; Wright 1993). This has boosted attempts to reconstruct climatic and environmental changes in the Eastern Mediterranean and Africa by assembling various data. While climatic and environmental deterministic arguments tend to neglect to explain human motivations behind efforts to cultivate wheat and barley or to keep sheep and goats, other research has centred on evolutionary changes in the cognitive abilities of modern humans and has explained how such developments may have been related to the development of early farming and herding (Mithen 1996). Consequently, the historical contingency of the beginning of farming in the Holocene has become emphasised in association with the evolution of behaviourally modern humans (*e.g.*, Layton 1999; Richerson *et al.* 2001; Sherratt 1997). This trend seems to suggest that the application of the concept of the structural history to archaeology, which has been discussed mainly in the studies on the rise and fall of regional societies in later prehistory and history (Bintliff 1991), can also be considered in the study on the incipient social complexity of foragers and beginning of farming and herding in prehistoric Egypt.

Therefore, the first step of my research is to set out a framework which covers the long-term history of subsistence change in a wider geographic scale while putting Egypt into the Near Eastern and northeastern African context and the Early-Middle Holocene context, both of which must have offered constraints and possibilities for the beginning and diffusion of, and the adoption or rejection of farming and herding. Then, the second step is to consider how and why wheat/barley farming and sheep/goat herding were diffused and adopted in Egypt when they were from an anthropological point of view, through referring to the models regarding the beginning of farming and herding. In so doing, a new synthesis concerning the diffusion and adoption of farming and herding from the Levant may be developed, and the structure and contingency at the beginning of farming and herding in the Eastern Mediterranean may be illustrated. This would be a contribution to be made by fairly isolated Egyptian archaeology towards the understanding of world prehistory.

Whereas the contributions of archaeobotany and zooarchaeology have been significant in the debates concerning the beginning of farming and herding in Egypt, it has been observed that the study of material culture, especially lithic artefacts, has not contributed to such debates (Hassan 1986a: 73). In Egyptian archaeology, the understanding of technology from an anthropological point of view has been a neglected area of study. Therefore, my research will focus on lithic artefacts. The main body of this research will attempt to demonstrate how the study of the beginning of farming and herding in a particular region of Egypt benefits from such anthropological understandings.

The following chapter will begin by elaborating on my research orientation, and will summarise the spatial and temporal scale which is dealt with in this research. I will review recent studies on climatic changes in the Eastern Mediterranean and northeastern Africa in the Early-Middle Holocene, and mention the present state of knowledge and ignorance concerning the beginnings of farming and herding in the Near East and northeastern Africa.

Then, the focus will shift to the Fayum where the best data regarding the beginning of farming and herding have so far been obtained. Chapter 3 will describe the background to new research in the Fayum. Chapter 4 will describe explanatory and predictive models concerning the transition from foraging to farming and herding, and will examine the applicability of the models to the Fayum case study in more detail. Chapters 5, 6 and 7 are based on the latest field research in Fayum. Chapter 5 will describe a new field survey and a spatial analysis of archaeological remains, and Chapters 6 and 7 will discuss the subsistence and mobility strategies of Fayum Epipalaeolithic and Neolithic inhabitants through lithic studies. Chapter 8 will discuss the diffusion process of domesticates from the southern Levant and look for lithic evidence for the interaction between the southern Levant and Egypt. Throughout Chapters 6, 7 and 8, the data about lithic artefacts obtained through literature study, museum research, and fieldwork are the primary sources of argument. Chapter 9 will summarise the results of this research.

2. Neolithisation in Egypt in a wider context

2.1. Geographical and chronological distribution of Early-Middle Holocene cultures in Egypt

Before discussing the origins and early development of Neolithic farming and herding cultures in Egypt, the geographical and chronological range of archaeological cultures in Egypt in the Early-Middle Holocene dealt with in my research should be defined here in more detail.

Egypt refers to a present-day country located at the northeastern corner of Africa (**Fig.2.1**). Egypt abuts the Mediterranean Sea in the north and the Red Sea in the east. Egypt is bordered by Libya in the west and by Sudan in the south. The river Nile runs in the middle of the land from the East African highlands through the Second Cataract near Wadi Halfa and the First Cataract at Aswan in the southern part of Egypt into the Mediterranean Sea in the north, and forms the Nile Delta in the area between Cairo and the Mediterranean coast. Since there is no cataract between Aswan and Cairo, the river is a homogeneous stretch of water with a gentle gradient. The Nile Valley is deeply incised in the Egyptian Limestone Plateau in the northern part and in the Nubian Sandstone Plateau in the southern part, and is bounded by steep cliffs rising up to 300 m. The Nile Valley is very narrow in the sandstone terrain in the south. The floodplain in the Nile Valley widens progressively from the north of the sandstone terrain around Gebel Silsila down to the Nile Delta, but the width of the floodplain is approximately 25 km at most. The region of the upstream of the Nile between the Qena bend and the First Cataract is conventionally called Upper Egypt, whereas the region of the downstream of the Nile to the north of the Fayum is called Lower Egypt, and the region between Upper and Lower Egypt is called Middle Egypt. The region between the First Cataract and the Second Cataract is called Lower Nubia. The rocky mountainous terrain between the eastern cliffs of the Nile Valley and the Red Sea coast is called the Arabian Desert or the Eastern Desert. The relatively flat terrain between the western cliffs of the Nile Valley and the Egyptian-Libyan border is called the Libyan Desert or the Western Desert. This vast terrain is also called the Eastern Sahara. The Western Desert has five major oases including Siwa, Bahariya, Farafra, Dakhleh, and Kharga from the north to the south. These oases are rich in groundwater derived from the Nubian aquifer (Baines and Marek 2000: 12-21; Bard 2007: 47-54).

The Middle-Late Holocene saw the developments of diverse archaeological cultures in different regions of Egypt (**Table 2.1**). In the Egyptian Nile Valley in the late 5th - early 4th

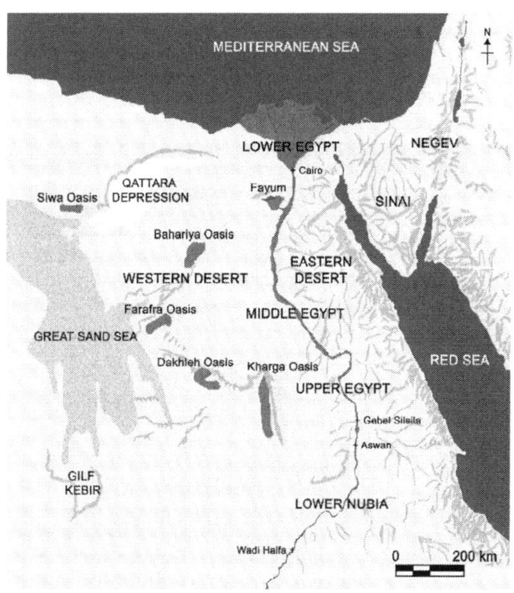

Fig.2.1. Geographical map of Egypt

	Nabta Playa	Dakhleh Oasis	Nile Valley	Fayum	Lower Egypt	Eastern Desert	Negev & Sinai	southern Levant
4000 cal.BC	Bunat El Ansam (Final Ceramic pastoral)	Sheikh Muftah (Ceramic pastoral)	Naqada (Predynastic) Badarian (Predynastic)	Moerian (Predynastic)	Maadi-Buto (Predynastic)			Ghassulian (Chalcolithic)
5000 cal.BC	Ru'at El Baqar (Late Ceramic pastoral) Ru'at El Ghanam (Middle Ceramic pastoral)	Bashendi B (Ceramic pastoral) Late Bashendi A (Ceramic pastoral)		Fayumian (Neolithic)	Merimde (Neolithic)	Tree Shelter AH 3 & Sodmein Cave (pastoral)	Timnian	Qatifian (Late Pottery Neolithic) Lodian (Jericho IX)
6000 cal.BC	El Nabta/Al Jerar (Early Ceremic pastoral)	Early Bashendi A (Ceramic pastoral)	? Tarifian ? (Ceramic)				Early Pottery Neolithic	Yarmukian (Early Pottery Neolithic)
7000 cal.BC	El Ghorab (Early Ceramic pastoral)		Elkabian (Epipalaeolithic)	Qarunian (Epipalaeolithic)		Tree Shelter AH 5 & 4 (Epipalaeolithic)	Tuwailan	PPNC LPPNB
8000 cal.BC	El Adam (Early Ceramic pastoral)	Masara (Epipalaeolithic)			? Helwan ? (Epipalaeolithic)		Desert PPNB	MPPNB EPPNB
9000 cal.BC			Arkinian (Epipalaeolithic)				PPNA	PPNA

Table 2.1. Chronology of Egypt and the Near East in the Early-Middle Holocene

millennia cal.BC, the Badarian culture developed in Middle Egypt, and subsequently, the Naqada culture appeared in Middle and Upper Egypt, and the Maadi-Buto culture appeared in Lower Egypt. They are collectively called the Predynastic cultures which mean the predecessors of the Early Dynastic culture and are actually equivalent to the Chalcolithic in more general terms. The Naqada culture eventually spread over Lower Egypt in the second half of the 4th millennium cal.BC, and culminated in the Early Dynastic state in the 3rd millennium cal.BC (Midant-Reynes 2000: 152-250). The cultures before the Predynastic have been given different names depending on technological developments and subsistence activities, as described below, and their spatial distribution is very wide and is not confined in the Nile Valley (**Fig.2.2**).

The floodplain and marginal low desert in the Egyptian Nile Valley have been the major human habitat since early prehistory, but the Nile alluviation and the expansion of modern land use activities have made it difficult to discover the remains of prehistoric human habitation beneath the present surface. Quite a few Early-Middle Holocene cultures have been found and studied. Cultures of the Egyptian Nile Valley in the Early Holocene are represented by the Arkinian and Shamarkian in Lower Nubia, the Elkabian in Upper Egypt, and the Qarunian in the Fayum. They are characterised by microlithic toolkits and are devoid of pottery and domesticates, and thus are designated as the Epipalaeolithic. An ephemeral, enigmatic culture named the Tarifian in Upper Egypt is characterised by the mixture of microlithic and flake industries and the presence of pottery but lacks domesticates, and its precise chronological position is uncertain (Close 1996b; Vermeersch 2002).

The floodplain of the Nile Delta must also have been a human habitat since prehistory, but due to the Nile alluviation and the expansion of modern land use activities, it is extremely difficult to locate the remains of prehistoric human habitation. Prehistoric remains in the alluvial plains are deeply buried and can be located only in exceptional circumstances like uncultivated natural mounds called *geziras* which have been formed between channels, or can be retrieved by deep drill augering. One of such exceptional circumstances has been seen at Sa el-Hagar (Sais) in the central Nile Delta, where surface soils have been removed to a fairly large and deep extent for *sebakh*, and drill augering and excavations yielded lithic artefacts and pottery sherds which could possibly be dated

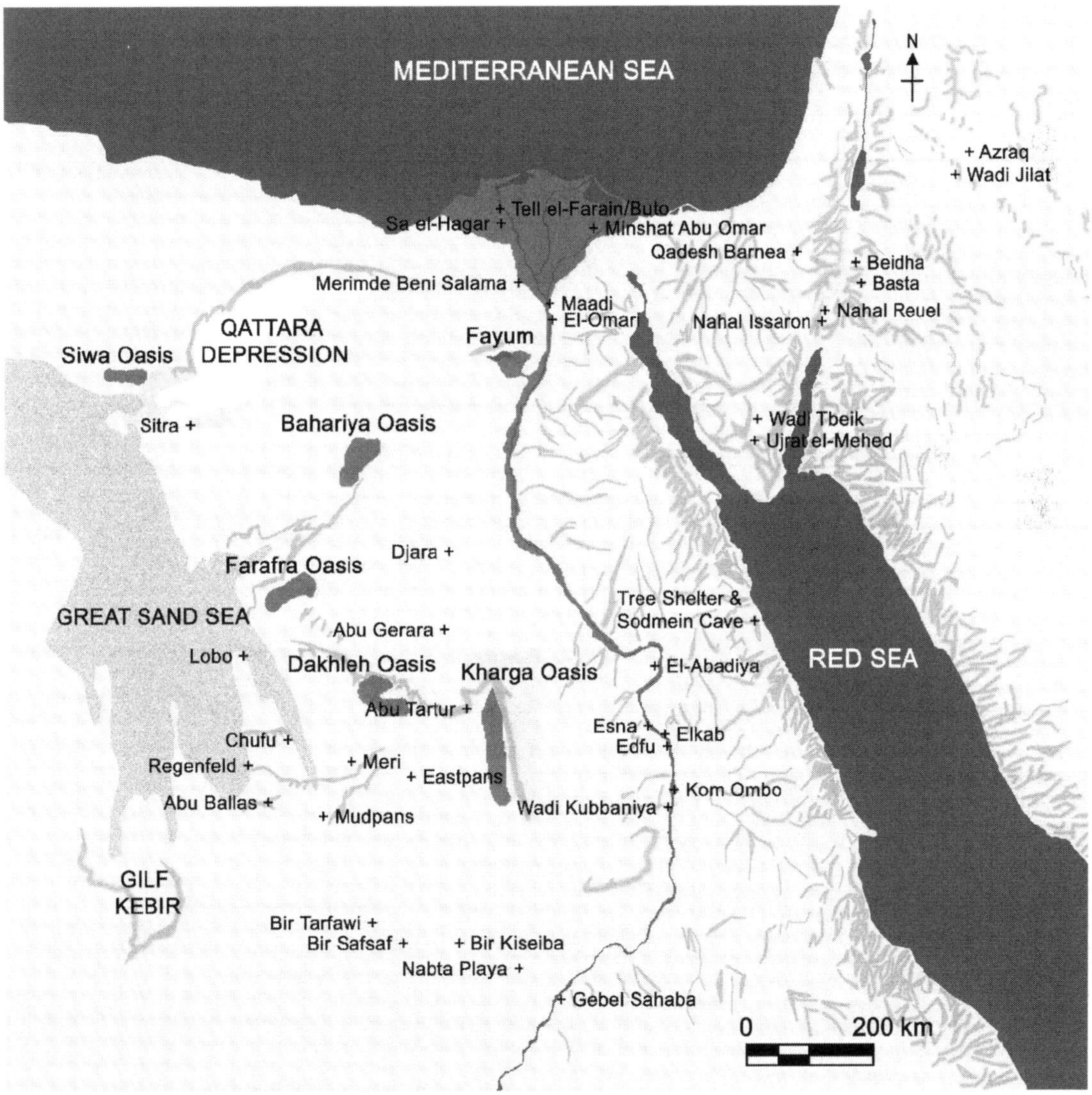

Fig.2.2. Map of the sites mentioned in this chapter

to the 6th-5th millennia cal.BC as well as the Predynastic and much later periods (Wilson 2006; Wilson and Gilbert 2002; 2003). Approximately 7 m deep drill augering at a Predynastic-Early Dynastic site of Minshat Abu Omar in the eastern Nile Delta has also retrieved pottery sherds which could probably be dated to the first half of the 5th millennium cal.BC (Krzyzaniak 1992; 1993). Although many other Predynastic-Early Dynastic sites in the central and eastern Nile Delta have not yielded artefacts which would be dated earlier than the Predynastic, it is likely that the sites in the Nile Delta where Predynastic remains have been found had been occupied before the Predynastic.

In contrast, prehistoric remains on the marginal low desert of the Nile Delta are far more visible, and have been undisturbed until modern land use activities started to expand on that terrain. Extensive survey at the western margin of the Nile Delta has revealed the presence of prehistoric cultures of the Middle Pleistocene and Early-Middle Holocene on the gravelly escarpments and low desert (Junker 1928; Menghin 1933a; 1933b; Schmidt 1980). Merimde Beni Salama is the richest in prehistoric artefacts in this area, and further excavations at the margin of the low desert of Merimde Beni Salama yielded not only numerous lithic artefacts, pottery sherds, and miscellaneous artefacts but also dwellings and tombs, all of which are regarded as the representatives of the Nile Delta culture in the Early-Middle Holocene (Eiwanger 1984; 1988; 1992; Junker 1930; 1931; 1933; 1934; 1935; 1941).

Human activities in the Eastern Desert in the Early-Middle Holocene are still poorly known. The human occupations of caves, rock shelters, wadis, and coastal plains in areas near the Red Sea coast have been revealed (Marinova *et al.* 2008; Moeyersons *et al.* 1999; Vermeersch *et al.* 1994; 1996; 2002; 2005a; 2005b; 2008). According to the data obtained from Sodmein Cave and Tree Shelter near the Red Sea coast, the area has been continually occupied since the end of the 8th millennium cal.BC when the climate became humid. The material culture of Tree Shelter in the 7th millennium cal.BC shows a marked similarity to that of the contemporaneous Elkabian in the Nile Valley, and the material culture of the 6th millennium cal.BC also bears some similarity to those in the contemporaneous Western Desert. However, little information about other parts of the Eastern Desert is available due to the lack of extensive field research, and hence cultural connections within the Eastern Desert and between the Eastern Desert and the rest of Egypt remain to be investigated further.

On the other hand, oases in the Western Desert have been major foci of human habitation in a generally semi-arid to arid environment since prehistory. Thanks to extensive field research covering the entire stretch of the Western Desert in the past decades and relatively undisturbed conditions, many archaeological remains of human activities in the Early-Middle Holocene have been studied not only in the oases but also in other seasonally rain-fed areas. Human occupation loci tend to be found around permanent water springs and rain-fed shallow lakes/ponds called playas.

The chronology of Early-Middle Holocene cultures in the Western Desert has been established on the basis of a growing number of radiocarbon dates obtained from different regions (**Table 2.1**). A particularly long-term continual human occupation sequence since the 9th millennium cal.BC has been obtained from the Nabta-Kiseiba region near the southern border of Egypt and from Dakhleh Oasis (McDonald 2001; Wendorf and Schild 2001). The Early Holocene culture in these two regions is marked by a distinct Epipalaeolithic lithic assemblage named the Masara Complex after the type site in Dakhleh Oasis. Subsequently, a new cultural entity named the El-Ghorab unit after the type site in the Nabta-Kiseiba region has spread not only in other parts of the Western Desert but also in the Nile Valley (McDonald 2003: 53-57; Wendorf and Schild 2001: 654-655; Wendorf *et al.* 1984: 412-413). The early development of pottery production and cattle domestication has been known in the Nabta-Kiseiba region since the 9th millennium cal.BC, but they did not develop in other parts of the

Western Desert until the 6th millennium cal.BC. The early 6th millennium cal.BC also saw the beginning of sheep/goat herding in some regions in the Western Desert. However, the cultures in the Western Desert have gradually vanished after the middle of the 6th millennium cal.BC, and only some have persisted in well-watered regions (Kuper 2007; McDonald 2001; Nicoll 2001).

It was not until the middle 6th millennium cal.BC that a 'typical' Neolithic culture, which is defined by the existence of wheat/barley farming and sheep/goat herding, first appeared in the Fayum. Subsequently, similar but advanced cultures appeared at Merimde Beni Salama and El Omari in Lower Egypt and the Badari region in Middle Egypt in the 5th millennium cal.BC. My research will deal with the sequence of cultural developments in the Early-Middle Holocene up to the emergence of Neolithic cultures in the northern part of Egypt in the 6th millennium cal.BC. The consequence of the development of Neolithic cultures in Egypt like the formation of state society is not the major focus of my research.

2.2. Origins and early development of Neolithic farming and herding cultures in Egypt

It is known that the natural habitat of wild emmer wheat (*Triticum turgidum* ssp. *dicoccoides*) and wild two-rowed barley (*Hordeum vulgare* ssp. *spontaneum*) is the dwarf-shrublands of the Fertile Crescent in the Near East, which has an annual precipitation of at least 300 mm. Wild einkorn wheat (*Triticum monococcum* ssp. *boeoticum*), which requires wetter conditions, does not spread to the southern Levant (van Zeist and Bottema 1991: 31-32, figs.3 and 4; Willcox 2005). There are no wild ancestors of domesticated wheat in northeastern Africa, whereas more drought-resistant and less cold-tolerant wild barley is sparsely spread along the Mediterranean coast of northeastern Africa only in weedy forms (Zohary 1989; Zohary and Hopf 1993: 13-64). This is apparently because the minimal amount of winter/spring rainfall for sustaining the natural growth of wild wheat and barley has hardly been attained in most parts of northeastern Africa. In addition, extensive research in the Near East and northeastern Africa has reached the conclusion that domesticated sheep (*Ovis ammon* f. *aries*) and domesticated goat (*Capra aegagrus* f. *hircus*) dispersed in northeastern Africa were not related to barbary sheep (*Ammotragus lervia*) and Nubian ibex (*Capra ibex nubiana*) that were indigenous to northeastern Africa (Gautier 2002: 201-202; 2007: 82-83; Uerpmann 1987: 113-132). Discussions on when and where in the Near East domesticated wheat, barley, sheep and goats first occurred are still underway, and there are hypotheses of a single event/origin in the upper Euphrates-Tigris basin and multiple events/origins in different regions of the Near East (*e.g.*, Gopher *et al.* 2001; Lev-Yadun *et al.* 2000; Nesbitt 2002; Peters *et al.* 2005; Willcox 2002; 2005). Nonetheless, there is little doubt that the domesticated emmer wheat, barley, sheep and goats found in Egypt originated from the southern Levant and most likely came from Sinai along the Red Sea coast and the Mediterranean coast.

In spite of these facts, the transition to food production through relying on wheat/barley farming and sheep/goat herding in Egypt has seldom been discussed within the framework of Near Eastern archaeology. This is firstly because Egypt is geographically separated from the Levant by the Sinai Peninsula, and secondly because Egyptian archaeology as a discipline has been isolated from Near Eastern archaeology. It seems that many scholars working in Egypt have not been willing to look beyond Egypt at data and ideas obtained from the Levant. Instead, scholars have preferred to emphasise the independent development of food production and culture in Egypt, and have obscured the context of the advent of wheat/barley and sheep/goat.

Although the claim for possible incipient barley farming in the Nile Valley in the Late Palaeolithic period was totally dismissed in the 1980s, research in the Western Desert near the southern border of Egypt during the last decades has revealed that pottery had emerged and incipient attempts at domestication of indigenous aurochs (wild cattle: *Bos primigenius*) might have begun in this region no later than the 8th millennium cal.BC (Close 1995; Close and Wendorf 1992; Gautier 2001; 2002: 198-201; 2007: 77-82; Hassan 2002a: 12-13; 2002b: 62-63, Marshall and Hildebrand 2002: 109; Wendorf and Schild 1994). This pottery-bearing pastoral culture was actually quite widespread from the Sudanese Nile Valley to the Libyan Sahara, and hence has been recognised as a distinct Saharo-Sudanese culture in the Early Holocene (Close 1995; Cremaschi and Di Lernia 1999; Garcia 2004; 2006; Jesse 2003; Mohammed-Ali and Khabir 2003). Because of the early development of pottery production and the subsequent development of cattle domestication, the sequence of this Saharo-Sudanese culture has been understood first as Mesolithic and then as Neolithic. It has been shown that the cultural sequence of the Nabta-Kiseiba region in the Early Holocene also started from the Early Neolithic of the El-Adam and then the El-Ghorab types (Wendorf and Schild 2001: 653*ff*; Wendorf *et al.* 1984: 409*ff*). On the other hand, contemporaneous cultures in other parts of the Egyptian Western Desert and the Egyptian Nile Valley, which shared a similar microlithic tradition with the Saharo-Sudanese culture but lacked pottery and domesticated cattle, have been designated as Epipalaeolithic.

However, there have been discussions in which the use of the term 'Neolithic' in Africa is really problematic because this term is defined so ambiguously in European archaeology that it is not always appropriate to describe the situation in Africa. Careless Neolithic designation has often carried different connotations to different scholars and has caused confusions in understanding the archaeological cultures under consideration (Sinclair *et al.* 1993: 3-8; Smith 2005). Some scholars have advocated that the Saharo-Sudanese pottery-bearing pastoral culture in the Egyptian Western Desert should not be called a 'Neolithic' culture but should simply be called a 'Ceramic' culture through focusing on technological development rather than subsistence, because the term 'Neolithic' carries the connotation of cereal farming (Hendrickx and Vermeersch 2000: 32; Kuper 1995: 125). Therefore, in the following, I rephrase the so-called Neolithic cultures of the Nabta-Kiseiba region as Ceramic pastoral cultures.

In Near Eastern archaeology and European archaeology, the term 'Neolithic Revolution' as first used by Childe has less commonly been used, because the simultaneous appearance of all elements of the so-called Neolithic package like domesticates, pottery, ground/polished stone tools, and sedentary villages, as defined in the arguments of the Neolithic Revolution, was disputed and the overall process of change did not look revolutionary (Barker 2006: 9-26). Instead, the term 'Neolithisation' has recently been preferred. The term 'Neolithisation' refers to the long-term process of the beginning and development of wheat/barley farming and sheep/goat/cattle/pig herding either by means of domestication of existing wild species or by means of adoption of domesticates from elsewhere as well as the associated development of new technologies, artistic or symbolic expressions in material items, complex societies, and unprecedented mortuary/religious cults in the Early-Middle Holocene. The developments of individual features which have conventionally been regarded as elements of the Neolithic package are considered as not necessarily simultaneous and as correlated to each other in more complicated ways. The difficulties of ordering the individual features in relative significance and distinguishing effects from causes are also recognised.

Furthermore, Neolithisation by adoption of the Neolithic package from elsewhere is called 'secondary Neolithisation' (Cauvin 2000a: 1-8). It is argued that the Neolithisation process in Europe, which is a typical example of secondary Neolithisation, took the stages of 1) encounter with available elements of the Neolithic package, 2) initial commitment to incorporating the elements of the package into existing socioeconomic practice, and 3) consolidation of the incorporated elements, and particularly the encounter stage often lasted many centuries or even a millennium, whereas the subsequent stages were much more short-lived (Barker 2006: 325-381; Zvelebil 1986a; 1986b; Zvelebil and Rowley-Conwy 1984). By contrast, archaeology in Egypt has failed to or has been reluctant to use the term 'Neolithisation' when it described the development of a unique Saharo-Sudanese culture in the Early-Middle Holocene as the Neolithic, probably because this development did not lead to a huge and rapid change of socioeconomic circumstances as seen in the Fertile Crescent and Europe but resulted in pastoral nomadic adaptation to harsh desert environments.

Whereas the beginning of attempts at cattle domestication occurred very early in the southernmost part of Egypt, the adoption of Levantine domesticated sheep and goats occurred at a considerably later date in several parts of Egypt, and the adoption of Levantine domesticated wheat and barley did not occur in the Egyptian Western Desert. Previous studies have often focused on the reasons for the late adoption of Levantine domesticates, citing adaptation to local climatic and environmental changes in the Early-Middle Holocene as well as the availability of domesticates in neighbouring regions during the same period. Egyptian civilisation emerged in the Nile Valley on the basis of the Levantine farming-herding way of life, and not solely on the basis of indigenous cattle herding. Therefore, although very late in date, Levantine influence on Egypt should not be underestimated.

However, this does not mean that Neolithisation in Egypt began at the time of the arrival of a Levantine Neolithic package of domesticates. In the light of general Neolithisation arguments (Midant-Reynes 2000: 69*ff*), it must be considered that Neolithisation in Egypt has already begun in the Early Holocene and was nearly completed by the arrival of Levantine domesticates, even though it is not without serious complications to designate the Saharo-Sudanese pottery-bearing pastoral culture in the Egyptian Western Desert as Neolithic. It is certainly important for archaeologists working in Egypt to understand the development of indigenous cultures in the Egyptian Western Desert and Nile Valley in the Early Holocene in their own terms and for their own sake, but it is equally significant to stress that Neolithisation in Egypt has partially been synchronous with Near Eastern Neolithisation and hence can be better understood by putting it in the wider Near Eastern context. In the following, I will elaborate on this idea by referring to supra-regional concepts in Near Eastern Neolithisation.

2.3. The relevance of supra-regional concepts for Egyptian Neolithic research

Currently, supra-regional concepts in Near Eastern Neolithisation are enthusiastically advocated, and a large workshop was recently held in order to discuss the relevance of these concepts for Near Eastern Neolithic research (Rollefson and Gebel 2004; Warburton 2004). Whereas it has been believed that most innovations in the Pre-Pottery Neolithic would have been generated in the southern Levant, early attempts of plant and animal domestication and unique socioeconomic and cultural developments in the northern Levant have also been recognised. This recognition is being increased as a result of recent spectacular discoveries of Pre-Pottery Neolithic sites in the upper Euphrates-Tigris basin and Cyprus. It is certain that these new discoveries cannot be explained by relying solely on the traditional concepts of the dispersal of people, or the diffusion of ideas, technology and items from one specific region. As a consequence, the idea of "a polycentric evolution of different environmentally conditioned socioeconomic developments that show a general tendency over several millennia" in the Near Eastern Neolithic was proposed (Gebel 2002: 314-315; 2004). This is a reasonable consequence of research, and an encouragement to understand regional developments thoroughly before discussing polycentric evolution should be welcome. Although the idea of polycentric evolution itself is obviously not a universal and comprehensive model or theory to explain diverse developments of Neolithisation in the Near East, this is significant in terms of reminding scholars to abandon the thoughts of their own regional 'centrism' or 'primacy'.

Regrettably, Egypt seems to be completely ignored or excluded from the idea of polycentric evolution. Such a tendency is also seen in studies on the dispersal of farming and herding from the Near East. Whereas the dispersal of farming and herding toward Europe has been thoroughly investigated, no mention has been made of the dispersal of farming and herding toward Egypt (*e.g.*, Colledge *et al.* 2004; Zeder 2008). From the viewpoint of archaeologists working in Egypt, this is probably because Near Eastern archaeologists, many of whom are Europeans, are still not free from Near Eastern centrism and tend to look for their own roots in the Near East. I believe that the understanding of the Neolithisation process in Egypt and related socioeconomic connections with the southern Levant, Negev and Sinai, can enrich, strengthen and diversify the idea of polycentric evolution in Near Eastern Neolithisation.

Although the dispersal of some types of Levantine PPNB and Pottery Neolithic lithic artefacts into Lower Egypt has been mentioned by some Near Eastern archaeologists (*e.g.*, Gopher 1994; Schmidt 1996), their reference to Egyptian materials has been geographically limited, and they have not paid enough attention to the Epipalaeolithic and Neolithic lithic assemblages of the Fayum and Merimde Beni Salama, which suggest some cultural relationships with contemporaneous Levantine ones. Even when the Fayum was referred to, a thorough consideration on the nature and chronology of contacts between the southern Levant and Egypt was hampered due to insufficient data (Goring-Morris 1993: 77). There was an attempt by an archaeologist working in Egypt to view the Neolithic cultures in the southern Levant, Lower Egypt and Cyrenaica as one distinct Levantine Early Neolithic culture (Eiwanger 1987: 83-86), but the lack of the presentation of material evidence on a sound chronological basis made the acceptance of this view very difficult. The cultural connection between the Levant and northeastern Africa during the Early-Middle Holocene has been argued by an Africanist archaeologist (Smith 1989; 1996), but his argument has also failed to attract the attention of either archaeologists working in Egypt or Near Eastern archaeologists. Consequently, it has been concluded by Near Eastern archaeologists that there were no extensive and regular socioeconomic connections between the southern Levant and the Nile Valley until the Pottery Neolithic or somewhat later (Kuijt and Goring-Morris 2002: 428).

Bar-Yosef is one of the exceptional Near Eastern archaeologists who have shown a keen interest in Neolithisation in Egypt. His ambitious attempt at reconstructing the socioeconomic entities or 'tribal' boundaries in the Eastern Mediterranean in the transitional period from hunting-gathering to farming-herding, based on a thorough analysis of lithic artefacts and other archaeological features, should be highly appreciated (Bar-Yosef 2001; 2003; 2004; Bar-Yosef and Meadow 1995; Bar-Yosef and Bar-Yosef Mayer 2002). But his understanding of the transition to food production in Egypt seems to be insufficient, partly because he mentions the Merimde Neolithic but does not refer to the Fayum Neolithic, another early farming-herding culture in Egypt (Bar-Yosef 2002a).

However, these omissions are understandable, because one problem is that information about the Egyptian Palaeolithic and Neolithic is not always accessible to Near Eastern archaeologists. For instance, the chronological relationship between the Fayum Neolithic and Merimde Neolithic is still unclear even for archaeologists working in Egypt because of the lack of reliable radiocarbon dates. Merimde Beni Salama is the only site where the development of the Neolithic culture was revealed in a stratigraphic context in northern Egypt, but the radiocarbon date of its earliest Neolithic layer is approximately 4900 cal.BC, which seems to be too young for the material contents of the layer (Eiwanger 1988: 53-54). In the Fayum, there is a long time gap in the archaeological record between the Epipalaeolithic and Neolithic cultures in the 6th millennium cal.BC, and hence exactly when the Fayum Neolithic began is still debatable. There is no definitive conclusion regarding which of the Merimde Neolithic and Fayum Neolithic is actually earlier in date (Eiwanger 1983: 63-65; 1992: 72-75). It may be that archaeologists working in Egypt should be criticised for not having provided information in relevant interdisciplinary meetings and publications, and for not having reacted to the ideas published by Near Eastern archaeologists. Therefore, I feel that archaeologists in Egypt now stand at a fork in the road: either they should keep walking along their own road in splendid isolation, or they could pursue common interests in Near Eastern Neolithic research in cooperation with scholars working in the Near East, thereby eliminating neighbourly ignorance.

Except for a few synthetic studies (*e.g.*, Barker 2003; 2006; Hassan 2002b; Midant-Reynes 2000), previous research in Egypt had a tendency to neglect to argue how Levantine domesticates became available to the inhabitants of Egypt and why the diffusion of the Levantine domesticates into Egypt did not occur earlier than the 6th millennium cal.BC. From the standpoint of archaeologists working in Egypt, the question as to what climatic and environmental conditions in northeastern Africa made the inhabitants of the Nile Valley and the Western Desert reject or adopt Levantine domesticates is an important research subject. Indeed, some scholars have argued that Egypt was so rich in wild food resources that the inhabitants of Egypt did not need foreign domesticates for a long time (*e.g.*, Wenke 1990: 377). Other scholars have argued that despite the overall richness in wild food resources, the inhabitants of Egypt must have occasionally suffered from food shortages, especially around the middle of the 6th millennium cal.BC, and thus they must have needed to introduce domesticates as backup food from the Levant (*e.g.*, Wetterstrom 1993: 225).

On the other hand, whether Egypt was actually outside 'the PPNB interaction sphere' (Bar-Yosef and Belfer-Cohen 1989), and who could become the agents of the diffusion of Levantine domesticates into Egypt, and under what conditions, are intriguing research topics for archaeologists working in Egypt. The idea of the expansion and intensification of a sociocultural interaction sphere with more and more communities being attracted by novel items and 'buying into' the networks regardless of the language barrier or other obstacles (Watkins 2003: 37) deserves consideration in the Neolithisation of Egypt. When the concept of 'the PPNB interaction sphere' was thoroughly re-investigated by a Near Eastern archaeologist recently, Egypt was not mentioned at all (Asouti 2006). It must be significant for Near Eastern archaeologists as well to take Egypt into account, in order to make the concept of 'the PPNB interaction sphere' viable.

It has been argued that the PPNB culture and societies in the southern Levant 'collapsed' around 6900 cal.BC, not only because of human-induced environmental degradation but also due to steady climatic deterioration related to the southward retreat of the Intertropical Convergence Zone (Rollefson and Köhler-Rollefson 1989; Simmons 1997; 2000). It is worth considering how the 'PPNB collapse' triggered a domino effect in neighbouring regions and affected Neolithisation in Egypt. Although a dramatic 'collapse' of local communities is not known in Egypt at the same time, it is evident that Egypt did experience frequent climatic fluctuations after 7600 cal.BC, and that many occupation sites in the Western Desert were temporarily abandoned several times and particularly around 6000 cal.BC (Riemer 2006: 556). Therefore, it is probable that the simultaneous climatic deterioration in northeastern Africa and the Levant in the 7th millennium cal.BC was related to a global climatic event, which is called either 'the 8.6-7.9 kyr cal.BP cooling event' or 'the 8.2 kyr cal.BP event,' or more simply 'the 8 ka cal.BP event' (Rohling *et al.*, 2002: 42-43; Rohling and Pälike 2005). This may have caused the reorganisation of human mobility strategy and territories. It has been argued that the 8.2 kyr cal.BP event would have triggered the spread of early farmer-herders out of the Levant into the Balkan (Weninger *et al.* 2006), but it is also probable that the spread of early farmer-herders occurred in different directions, and the inhabitants of Egypt may have encountered refugees from arid regions of the southern Levant, Negev and Sinai during this period.

Inevitably, research into these topics encourages scholars working in Egypt to reflect on factors which caused the Neolithisation of Egypt in a more organised way and to recognise on what timescale the factors appeared and affected each other. Following the theoretical developments as represented by processual archaeology in the 1960s and 1970s and postprocessual archaeology in the 1970s and 1980s, archaeological studies of initial and secondary Neolithisation in general have shifted their focus from ecological and demographic pressure in the Late and Terminal Pleistocene and Early Holocene, to which foragers adapted, to foragers' economic decision making which must have been subject to cultural needs, social relations and ideologies (Barker 2006: 17-41; Bellwood 2005: 19-25). Consequently, studies in Near Eastern archaeology have recently made clear how the opposed theoretical approaches would be reconciled and which factors must be investigated in further detail (*e.g.*, Hole 2003; Verhoeven 2004; Watkins 2006). What must be done is not merely to highlight the uniqueness or distinctiveness of the pathway which northeastern Africa, including Egypt, followed towards food production and then to express negative opinions about the applicability of Near Eastern models to northeastern Africa (*e.g.*, Garcea 2004), but also to describe how and why such uniqueness or distinctiveness appeared in Africa (*e.g.*, Marshall and Hildebrand 2002), and moreover to consider how archaeologists in Egypt and the Near East can work on common ground. In the following, the most critical factors for Neolithisation in Egypt will be considered.

2.4. Factors causing Neolithisation in Egypt

2.4.1. Climate, flora, and fauna

Climatic conditions in northeastern Africa are mainly determined by the locations of low pressure areas which yield rainfall (**Fig.2.3**). In general, rain falls in a belt of low pressure, like the polar front in the high latitudes around N40-60° and the Intertropical Convergence Zone (ITCZ) in the low latitudes around N0-20°. The regions under high pressure in the latitudes around N30°, which are called the horse latitudes or subtropical high, receive little precipitation, but subtropical cyclones occur there on the Mediterranean Sea under a trough of low pressure. Such a trough extends southward onto northeastern Africa in winter, and the meandering westerlies bring rain in cyclonic storms to the latitudes around N25°. The Intertropical Convergence Zone moves north-south seasonally across the equator, following the zenith point of the sun, and shifts northward to the latitudes around N15° in summer, while bringing rain. The polar front shifts southward in winter/spring while spreading rain in the Near East, but does not reach northeastern Africa. Therefore, the amount of rainfall in northeastern Africa is definitely subject to the seasonal and long-term northward-southward shifts of the subtropical trough and particularly the Intertropical Convergence Zone (Nicholson 2000; Said 1993: 82-91). This was also the case in the Pleistocene and Early-Middle Holocene, with different extents of the northward-southward shifts of the subtropical trough and the Intertropical Convergence Zone (Brookes 2003; Close 1996b; Gasse 2000; Hassan 1997a; Haynes 1987; Kuper and Kröpelin 2006; Kuper *et al.* 2007; Nicholson and Flohn 1980; Staubwasser and Weiss 2006; Sultan *et al.* 1997).

As far as the Middle Pleistocene and Early Holocene are concerned, Egypt was not necessarily a gift of the Nile. Archaeological field research and studies of faunal remains in Bir Tarfawi near the southern border of Egypt and Dakhleh Oasis have revealed that the present-day Western Desert was fairly wet enough to sustain the Sudano-Ethiopian fauna including rhinoceros (*Ceratotherium simum*), giraffe (*Giraffa camelopardalis*), buffalo (*Pelorovis antiquus* or *Syncerus caffer*), warthog (*Phacochoerus aethiopicus*), and hippopotamus (*Hippopotamus amphibius*) among others during the Middle Pleistocene but was deserted as late as 70000 years ago due to the advent of hyper-arid climate (Churcher *et al.* 1999; Churcher *et al.* 2008; Gautier 1993a; 1993b). It has been confirmed by well-dated data that the Early Holocene climate of Egypt was characterised by the return of generally wetter conditions, but with recurrent and abrupt arid intervals after a Terminal Pleistocene aridity known as the Younger Dryas (Hassan 1996; 1997; McDonald 2001; Nicoll 2001; 2004; Riemer 2006; Schild and Wendorf 2002).

Studies of marine cores obtained from the Eastern Mediterranean Sea off the shore of the Nile Delta have revealed a significant increase of freshwater inputs to the Eastern Mediterranean Sea in the Early Holocene, which must have been caused by the increase of the Nile water discharge resulting from heavy summer rainfall in the headwaters of the Nile in the Ethiopian Highlands (Ducassou *et al.* 2008; Fontugne *et al.* 1994; Rossignol-Strick 1999). Alluvial sediments observed in different parts of the entire stretch of the Nile also indicate that the Nile was generally much higher in the Early Holocene, though there were some fluctuations (Said 1993: 128-133). Studies of marine cores obtained from the Red Sea have also revealed that a considerable amount of freshwater inputs occurred in the northernmost part of the Red Sea in the late 8th - late 6th millennia cal.BC, suggesting the enhancement of rainfall in this area caused by the southward extension of low pressure areas (Arz *et al.* 2003). These have greatly affected the vegetation in northeastern Africa.

At present, the southern limit of Mediterranean flora is around the latitude of Cairo (N30°), while the northern limit of Sudano-Sahelian steppe shrubs is around the latitude of the Fifth Cataract of the Nile (N15°), and the vast area between these two distinct vegetation zones is absolute desert (Neumann 1989a; 1989b; Nicoll 2004). It has been revealed through botanical and sedimentological studies that in the Early-Middle Holocene the Sudano-Sahelian flora had spread across the Western Desert up to the latitude of Dakhleh-Kharga Oases (N25°-N26°) following the northward shift of the Intertropical Convergence Zone, and that the Mediterranean flora had also been distributed down to the same latitude following the southward expansion of the subtropical trough (Darius and Nussbaum 2007; Haynes 1987; 2001; Neumann 1989a; 1989b). Recent discoveries of both Mediterranean and Sudano-Sahelian plants at the Early-Middle Holocene sites at Djara on the Abu Muhariq Plateau and in Farafra Oasis (N27°) (Hassan *et al.*, 2001; Kindermann *et al.*, 2006) also suggest the convergence of the Intertropical Convergence Zone and the subtropical trough around this

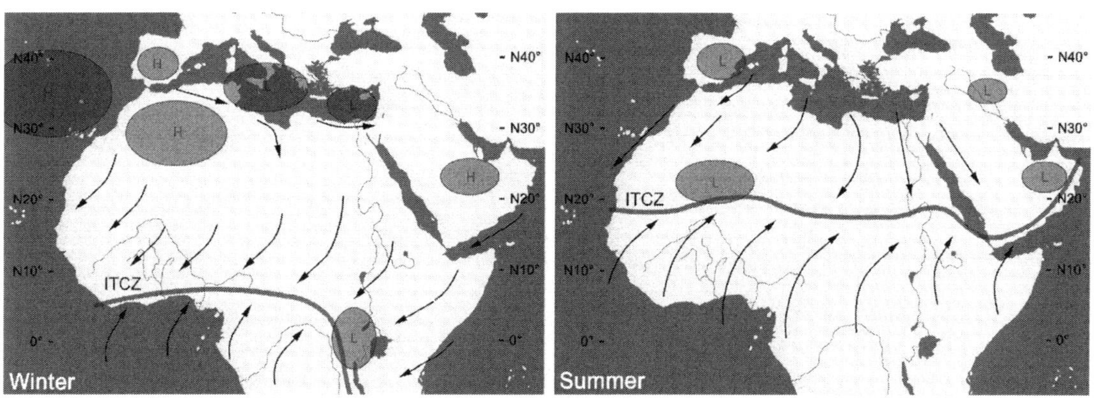

Fig.2.3. Atmospheric circulation in Africa in winter and summer

latitude in that period.

For an understanding of the rise and fall of Levantine Neolithic cultures, the importance of both the northward shift of the Intertropical Convergence Zone which may have reached the southernmost part of the Levant (**Fig.2.4**) and the southward shift of the polar front which may have reached the Negev has already been recognised by Near Eastern archaeologists (Henry 1989: 65*ff*; Simmons 1997: 313-314), but the southward retreat of the Intertropical Convergence Zone in the Middle Holocene is becoming stressed as an important key event in the beginning of the southward diffusion of Levantine winter crops in Sinai, Arabia and northeastern Africa (McCorriston 2006).

Rainfall during wet phases of the Early Holocene created grasslands and shrublands in the present-day Western Desert. This facilitated hunter-gatherers exploiting the 'green desert' as well as the Nile Valley. The most common wood flora identified at human habitation sites in the Western Desert in this period are acacia (*Acacia* sp.) and tamarisk (*Tamarix* sp.) (Neumann 1989a; 1989b; Wasylikowa *et al.* 2001), and the fauna includes oryx (*Oryx dammah*), dama gazelle (*Gazella dama*), dorcas gazelle (*Gazella dorcas*) and hare (*Lepus capensis*) (Gautier 2001; Van Neer and Uerpmann 1989). These flora and fauna indicate that the Western Desert was generally a semi-arid environment in spite of rainfall and hence was not comparable to the situation during the Middle Pleistocene, which was generally wetter. However, even in the Western Desert, regions like Dakhleh Oasis which has permanent groundwater sources have had a wider variety of flora and fauna through the Early-Middle Holocene. They were represented by more water-dependant animals like buffalo (*Pelorovis antiquus* or *Syncerus caffer*), hartebeest (*Alcelaphus buselaphus*) and zebra (*Equus* sp.), as well as desert-adapted animals like dorcas gazelle (Churcher 1999a; 1999b; Churcher *et al.* 2008).

On the other hand, the environmental situation in the contemporaneous Nile Valley is less clear. The Upper and Late Palaeolithic fauna in the Nile Valley in Upper Egypt provides a good sample of the wild animals which were present in a riverine environment under the cool and dry climatic conditions of the Late and Terminal Pleistocene. Six major mammals, including hippopotamus, wild cattle, hartebeest, wild ass (*Equus africanus*), dorcas gazelle, and barbary sheep have occurred at El Abadiya, Edfu, Esna, Kom Ombo and Wadi Kubbaniya, although hippopotamus, wild ass and barbary sheep were rare to absent (Baker and Gautier 1997; Gautier 1976a; Gautier and Van Neer 1989; Peters 1990; Vermeersch *et al.* 2007). They are actually the faunal base on which hunters of the Epipalaeolithic Elkabian culture in the same region in the 8th-7th millennia cal.BC have also depended (Gautier 1978; Vermeersch 1984; 1994; 2002). The Nile water discharge would have increased in this period, but there is little information about how the inhabitants of the Nile Valley reacted to such an increase.

These contrasting environmental situations between the Western Desert and the Nile Valley are the first factor which should be considered in the context of Neolithisation in Egypt. It is not certain which of these situations was more favourable for innovations such as the earliest pottery making and cattle domestication to take place. Presently-available data suggest that the earliest pottery and the earliest domesticated cattle (*Bos primigenius* f. *taurus*) appeared first at Bir Kiseiba and Nabta Playa near the southern border of Egypt between 9000 cal.BC and 7600 cal.BC during one of the Early Holocene wet phases named the El-Adam humid interphase (Schild and Wendorf 2002; Wendorf and Schild 1998; 2001), but this may be because of relatively better preservation of archaeological remains in the Western Desert.

A remarkable change in subsistence in the Western Desert in the Early-Middle Holocene is the beginning of intensive exploitation of wild grasses including sorghum (*Sorghum bicolor*) by hunter-gatherers at such sites as Nabta Playa, Eastpans of the Abu Ballas scarp land, Dakhleh Oasis, and Farafra Oasis (Barakat 2002; Barakat and Fahmi 1999; Barich and Lucarini 2002; 2005; 2008; Barich and Hassan 2000; Hassan

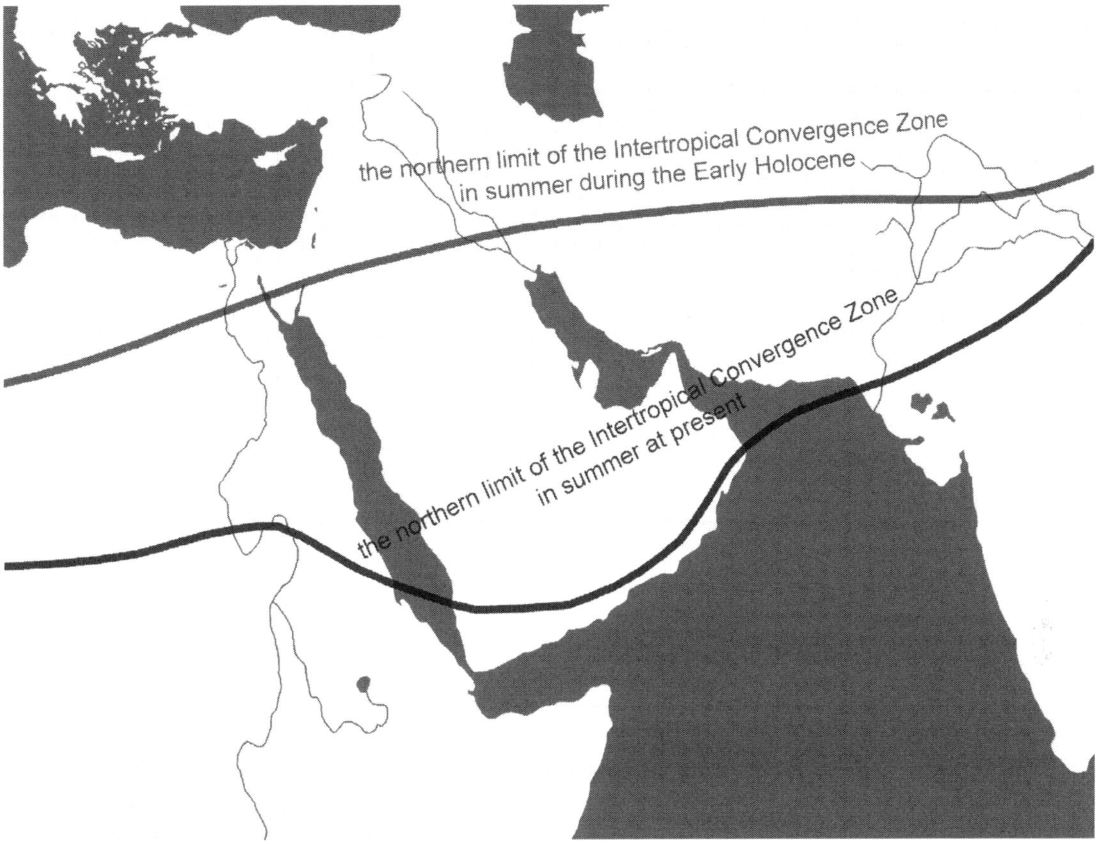

Fig.2.4. Shifting position of the Intertropical Convergence Zone on East Africa and the Near East

et al. 2001; Lucarini 2007; McDonald 2008; Wasylikowa *et al.* 1993; 1997; 1999; 2001). Although there are no botanical remains, the exploitation of wild grasses is suggested by the appearance and increase of grinding stones at Regenfeld in the Great Sand Sea, Chufu and Meri in the Abu Ballas scarp land, and Djara (Gehlen *et al.* 2002; Riemer 2007a). Another remarkable change is the beginning of cattle herding at such sites as Nabta Playa, Bir Kiseiba and Dakhleh Oasis (Close and Wendorf 1992; Gautier 2001; McDonald 1998; Wendorf *et al.* 1984; Wendorf and Schild 1994; 2001), and the beginning of sheep/goat herding at such sites as Nabta Playa, Dakhleh Oasis, Farafra Oasis and Djara (Barich and Lucarini 2002; 2005; 2008; Barich and Hassan 2000; Churcher 1999a; 1999b; Churcher *et al.* 2008; Gautier 2001; Kindermann *et al.* 2006).

One question here is why domestication of indigenous animals like buffalo did not begin under the wet conditions of the Middle Pleistocene elsewhere in Egypt and why the domestication of wild cattle developed in the Early Holocene in a semi-arid environment of the Western Desert, which was not the natural habitat of wild cattle. The natural habitat of wild cattle must have been the Nile Valley, and there seems to have been no ecological corridor linking the Nile Valley and the Nabta-Kiseiba region in the middle of the Western Desert (Gautier 2002: 198-201; 2007: 77-82). Hence, it is assumed that amelioration of desert environments in the Early Holocene due to the return of humidity may not have been the sole sufficient precondition for the autonomous development of cattle domestication.

Recent palaeoclimatological studies have revealed that Pleistocene wet phases were totally different from Holocene wet phases in terms of temperature, density of carbon dioxide in the atmosphere, and degree of fluctuations, all of which greatly affected the growth and spread of plants, and it has been argued that agriculture was impossible under Pleistocene conditions (Richerson *et al.* 2001). It has been argued that Holocene plants were more productive, nutrient-rich, and cold/drought tolerant than Pleistocene plants due to the improvement of the atmosphere for plant growth, and hence it was almost inevitable for Holocene hunter-gatherers to become increasingly dependent on plant food (Bettinger 2001: 148-149). The beginning of intensive plant exploitation in the Egyptian Western Desert in the Early Holocene is a quite reasonable phenomenon. Therefore, it can be presumed that the beginning of intensive exploitation of wild grasses by hunter-gatherers in Nabta Playa around 7000 cal.BC (Barakat and Fahmy 1999) was related to the spread of new vegetation caused by the advent of the Early Holocene climatic optimum called the El Nabta/Al Jerar humid interphase (Schild and Wendorf 2002; Wendorf and Schild 1998; 2001), and would not have been realised in the Pleistocene. In addition, wild grasses in the Western Desert must not only have attracted wild game animals but also have become good fodder plants for livestock (Wasylikowa *et al.* 1997: 940; 2001: 561-562). It was not until hunter-gatherers became aware of the economic importance of wild grasses that they could use the wild grasses for feeding animals. This may be an important environmental reason why the domestication of cattle in an environment which was not the natural habitat of cattle occurred in the Early Holocene.

The second question here is why domesticated wheat/barley and sheep/goats did not diffuse from the southern Levant to Egypt under favourable Early Holocene climatic conditions. The Middle PPNB period in the Levant was the time of great farming dispersal under Early Holocene wet conditions, and domesticated wheat/barley did diffuse beyond the fertile Levantine Corridor to semi-arid regions. However, it was not until the Middle Holocene arid intervals that domesticated sheep/goats and wheat/barley reached the Red Sea coast and the Fayum in Egypt respectively. Therefore, the direct reason for the delay of the diffusion of Levantine domesticates to Egypt may be something other than wet climatic conditions, though it seems probable that the desiccation at the onset of the Middle Holocene was the initial driving force behind the diffusion.

It has been argued that domesticated sheep/goats came from the Sinai Peninsula to the mountainous terrain of the Egyptian Eastern Desert near the Red Sea coast in the early 6th millennium cal.BC, and then diffused from the Eastern Desert to the Western Desert across the Nile Valley (Close 2002b; Riemer 2007b). The arrival of Levantine sheep/goats in the Egyptian Western Desert is a consequence of the southward dispersal of sheep/goat herding in the southern Levant which started no later than the PPNC period, but this description of the diffusion process does not explain how and why the Levantine domesticates were adopted in Egypt when they became available to the inhabitants of Egypt. This question must be answered by asking whether any other unprecedented things were happening in Egypt at that time, and will be discussed in more detail below.

2.4.2. Population aggregation and sedentism

Although the Western Desert of Egypt became inhabitable in the Early Holocene wet phases, not all parts of the Western Desert have been equally occupied. For instance, vast areas like the inner Great Sand Sea have not yielded evidence of human occupations. There is no doubt that people had to aggregate around permanent water sources like oases and ephemeral lakes/ponds fed by rainfall, while moving radially from a water source or moving between water sources. Even though the people could dig wells and they actually did in the Nabta-Kiseiba region (Kobusiewicz 2003), groundwater could not be found everywhere in the Western Desert (Riemer 2005: fig.4). Field research in combination with the studies of satellite images, digital elevation data and geological maps has illustrated that archaeological sites of the Early-Middle Holocene in the southern part of the Western Desert were related to depressions in the foreland of escarpments and palaeodrainage systems with intermediate/terminal pans or dune barriers (Bolten and Bubenzer 2007; Bubenzer and Riemer 2007). It is apparent that the availability of sufficient surface water was the essential condition for the choice of habitation location.

A degree of sedentism must have been a necessary solution to maintain a close link to water sources and accompanying food resources, and the necessity of sedentism must have been recognised more seriously by the inhabitants of the Western Desert than it had been by those who inhabited the Nile Valley, because the number of water sources was limited in the Western Desert. Even in the Nile Valley, many human bodies which show the evidence of violent death at Late Palaeolithic sites of Wadi Kubbaniya and Gebel Sahaba (Wendorf 1968; Wendorf and Schild 1986) suggest that fierce conflicts between human groups were not uncommon in the Late and Terminal Pleistocene. It seems likely that such conflicts were caused by claims for access to essential resources. It may be said that stressful situations and some degree of conflict between different human groups were features of life during the Late and Terminal Pleistocene. Improvement of climate and resultant resource abundance in the Early Holocene may not immediately have led to human population increase, but must have increased its chances. No evidence of violence in the Early-Middle Holocene Western Desert may suggest the appearance of a new set of social relationships which reduced bloody conflicts.

A tendency toward a certain degree of sedentism has been inferred in Nabta Playa and Dakhleh Oasis as early as the Early Holocene on the basis of lithic assemblages, site distribution, and the existence of water wells and storage pits for harvested wild grass seeds (Kobusiewicz 2003; McDonald 1991b; 1998; Wendorf and Schild 1998; 2001; 2002b; 2003). According to arguments about the emergence of territoriality (Rosenberg 1990; 1998), as more people aggregated around a limited number of water sources perennially or seasonally, the right to the water sources and accompanying food resources may have become more specific and rigid, and the notion of territoriality may have been generated. In such circumstances, freedom of movement for food quests must have become gradually hampered, even though the right to visit each other's territory was ensured by socioeconomic ties like reciprocity and exogamy. Consequently, stressful situations or conflicts within and between territories must have occasionally occurred. In the case of the Western Desert in the Early-Middle Holocene, recurrent arid intervals could be another cause of stressful situations, and population/resource imbalances must have continually taken place in the short term. It has been argued that in such circumstances much labour may have become increasingly invested to ensure sufficient yield from one's own territory, because it might be burdensome to visit and exploit another's territory. Procuring and storing as many food resources as possible while they were abundantly available would become key subsistence strategies, no matter how time-consuming and labour-intensive the foraging and processing of the food resources were (Bettinger 2001). It has also been argued that such an intensification of food procurement in circumscribed habitats had the potential to lead to the beginning of food production, especially if predictable, relocatable and tameable food resources were available and if technological innovations which would permit efficient utilisation of the resources occurred (Rosenberg 1990; 1998). It would be possible that such moderately stressful situations over the procurement of water and food took place at particularly favourable regions for human occupation in the Western Desert like Nabta Playa and Dakhleh Oasis. Digging water wells and storing surplus food would have been viable solutions to stay in one's own territory as long as possible and to avoid unnecessary conflicts with people inhabiting neighbouring areas.

It has been suggested that the beginning of intensive exploitation of wild sorghum in Nabta

Playa would probably be an indication that the inhabitants attempted to augment the amount of food resources in circumscribed habitats by harvesting previously less-exploited plants (Wendorf and Schild 2002). Nabta Playa was completely abandoned around 6000 cal.BC due to a short hyper-arid interval known as the Post-Al Jerar arid phase (Schild and Wendorf 2002; Wendorf and Schild 1998; 2001), but when people returned there to settle down again after 5900 cal.BC, they brought domesticated goats with them. Domesticated goats were rapidly diffused to other places such as Dakhleh Oasis, Farafra Oasis, and Djara in the same period (Riemer 2007b). The exploitation of wild sorghum also became common, as evidenced by botanical remains and grinding implements in Farafra Oasis, Dakhleh Oasis, and Eastpans of the Abu Ballas scarp land (Barakat and Fahmy 1999; McDonald 2008). There appears evidence for increasingly sedentary occupation as well as exploitation of sorghum and domesticated goats at some particular localities of Farafra Oasis and Dakhleh Oasis in the early 6th millennium cal.BC (Barich and Lucarini 2002; 2005; 2008; Hassan *et al.*, 2001; Lucarini 2007; McDonald 2008). It can be suggested that domesticated goats were another solution to augment the amount of available food resources, thereby adjusting population/resource imbalances in circumscribed habitats.

2.4.3. Population movements and expansion of sociocultural and socioeconomic networks

Long distance population movements between the Western Desert and the Nile Valley, and between the southern Levant and the Nile Valley via the Negev and Sinai, should not be ignored as a factor that enabled access to domesticates, even though a certain degree of sedentism in circumscribed habitats seems to have been one reason why domesticates were introduced.

As evidenced by recurrent abandonment and reoccupation of sites in the Western Desert in the Early-Middle Holocene, population movements were not uncommon. The appearance and disappearance of settlements were not always coincident between oases and other occasionally well-watered regions such as the Fayum, Siwa Oasis, Farafra Oasis, Djara, Kharga Oasis, Dakhleh Oasis, Abu Ballas, Nabta Playa, and the Gilf Kebir (Gehlen *et al.* 2002; Kuper 1995; 2002; McDonald 2001; Nicoll 2001). Therefore, it is supposed that an entire population sometimes moved long distances from water source to water source within the Western Desert, probably following the northward-southward shifts of the Intertropical Convergence Zone or the subtropical trough. It has been pointed out that lithic artefacts of the Fayum Neolithic culture were very similar to those of the Bashendi A and B cultures in Dakhleh Oasis and those of the Djara B culture in Djara, and thus one of the origins of the Fayum Neolithic culture must have been located far to the south of the Fayum (Kindermann 2003; 2004; McDonald 1991a; 1996; Warfe 2003). The coincidence of the reoccupation of the Fayum with the temporary abandonment and subsequent reoccupation of Dakhleh Oasis and with the final abandonment of Djara around the middle of the 6th millennium cal.BC suggests that a certain number of people moved from this region to the Fayum.

In contrast to the north-south population movements, the east-west population movements are less clear. Especially at the time of unexpected, long-lasting aridity, movements of an entire population toward permanent water sources like the Nile must have been the ultimate solution. However, it is difficult to trace precisely the immigration of people into the Nile Valley from different directions and the outflow of people from the Nile Valley, because there is little information about the situation in the Nile Valley in the Early-Middle Holocene due to the problems of site preservation (Close 1996b; Vermeersch 2002).

As mentioned earlier, only a few Epipalaeolithic cultures of the Early Holocene are known in the Nile Valley. It seems certain that around the 9th-8th millennia cal.BC, people of the El-Adam Early Ceramic pastoral culture in the Nabta-Kiseiba region had contacts with the Nile Valley, as evidenced by the presence of

Nilotic freshwater bivalves at El-Adam sites and the similarity in lithic assemblages to the Epipalaeolithic Arkinian culture near the Second Cataract of the Nile Valley (Schild *et al.* 1968; Wendorf and Schild 2001). Based on the fact that there are many similarities in lithic assemblages between the Epipalaeolithic Elkabian culture in the Nile Valley and the El-Ghorab Early Ceramic pastoral culture in the Western Desert, it has been assumed that around the 8th-7th millennia cal.BC, people of the Elkabian culture were moving seasonally between the Nile Valley and the Western Desert (Vermeersch 1984). However, it turned out recently that the El-Ghorab culture is earlier in radiocarbon date than the Elkabian culture, and thus it seems better to consider that people of the El-Ghorab culture may have migrated to the Nile Valley at the onset of the Post El-Ghorab arid phase in the Western Desert around 7200-7100 cal.BC. On the other hand, many similarities in lithic assemblages are observed between the Epipalaeolithic Elkabian culture in the Nile Valley and its variant at Tree Shelter on the Red Sea coast, and their contemporaneity is demonstrated by radiocarbon dates. A Nilotic freshwater bivalve was also found at Tree Shelter. Therefore, it is argued that in the 7th millennium cal.BC, people of the Elkabian culture were moving seasonally between the Nile Valley and the Red Sea coast (Vermeersch 2002: 36; 2008: 89-94; Vermeersch *et al.* 2002).

As for the cultures of the Middle Holocene, few archaeological sites are known in the Nile Valley, and only some material items like Nilotic freshwater bivalves found at sites in the Western Desert have been used as evidence for contacts between the Nile Valley and the Western Desert (Kindermann and Bubenzer 2007; Kindermann *et al.* 2006; Riemer and Kindermann 2008). The earliest domesticated sheep/goats in Egypt were found in Sodmein Cave near the Red Sea coast and were dated to around 6200-5300 cal.BC, and the presence of domesticated goats that are dated to around 5600 cal.BC are confirmed at the nearby site of Tree Shelter (Vermeersch *et al.* 1994; 1996; 2002; 2008). The second earliest domesticated sheep/goats were found in Djara and Farafra Oasis and were dated to around 5900-5500 cal.BC (**Fig.2.5**). Sheep/goats identified in Nabta Playa also fall in this time range. Therefore, it seems that domesticated sheep/goats were diffused to the Western Desert immediately after their first arrival at Sodmein Cave (Close 2002b: 459-461 and 467-468; Riemer 2007b: 107-113). It can be supposed that there were constant movements of people between the Red Sea coast and the Western Desert behind the diffusion of domesticated sheep/goats.

In addition to population movements, the expansion of exchange networks within Egypt must have been a critical factor for the Neolithisation in Egypt. Some similarities in material culture across different parts of the Western Desert can probably be explained by the expansion of exchange networks as well. But what seems more important for the Neolithisation of Egypt is a further expansion of the exchange networks beyond Egypt with the Near East. Remarkably wide distributions of peculiar types of projectile points in the Near East in the Pre-Pottery Neolithic are well known, and they are presumed to be the results of extensive exchange/sharing of finished items as well as the expansion of local production facilitated by the diffusion of technical knowledge. As mentioned earlier, some types of Levantine PPNB and Pottery Neolithic projectile points actually appeared in Lower Egypt, though they were small in number and their raw materials are not certain. Thus the reasons for and the context of the appearance of these projectile points must be explained. Since large scale migration of Levantine people in these periods has not been attested archaeologically and linguistically (Barker 2003; Bar-Yosef 2003; Bellwood 2005: 207-210; Hassan 2003), it is more probable that the Levantine projectile points were accepted and thereafter imitated as novel and prestigious items in Egypt through socioeconomic networks. This manner of acceptance may also be the case with Levantine wheat/barley and sheep/goats.

Moreover, the spread of minor items must not be overlooked. The spread of stone bead making has a curious coincidence with the beginning of food production and sedentary life in the southern Levant (Wright and Garrard 2003). This is worth examining in the Egyptian context in terms of the development of social identities and boundaries on the one hand and the development of exchange networks regarding the demand and supply of raw materials and finished items on the other, because similar stone beads are known in Egypt as well. The spread of Red Sea shell ornaments in the southern Levant in the Middle-Late PPNB is also noteworthy. This suggest that there were some exchange networks between farmers in the southern Levant and hunter-gatherers who wandered around the Red Sea coasts of southern Sinai (Bar-Yosef Mayer 1997). The late diffusion of Levantine domesticates to Egypt must have something to do with the development of such socioeconomic networks.

2.4.4. Dispersal of farming and herding in the Levant and the availability of domesticated wheat/barley and sheep/goats for Egypt

In addition to the development of extensive socioeconomic networks across the Near East and Egypt, another reason for the late diffusion of wheat/barley farming and sheep/goat herding to Egypt may possibly be the late advent of domesticated sheep and goats in the southern Levant. Since the first wheat/barley farming culture in the Fayum was accompanied by sheep/goat herding from the beginning, it is reasonable to presume that the diffusion of wheat/barley farming to Egypt was closely tied to the advent of sheep/goat herding.

The domestication of goats seems to have been attempted elsewhere in the Near East. Whereas the earliest attempt of goat domestication would have started in the Zagros Mountains, Beidha in the southern Levant is supposed to be the southernmost place where goat domestication was attempted in the Middle PPNB period. On the other hand, the domestication of sheep was evidently achieved in the Anti-Taurus Mountains and the upper Euphrates-Tigris basin, and then domesticated sheep was introduced into the southern Levant no earlier than the Late PPNB period (Horwitz *et al.* 2000; Horwitz 2003; Martin 2000; Peters *et al.* 2000; 2005; Zeder 2000; 2005; 2008).

Before discussing further the context of the diffusion of Levantine domesticates into Egypt, it is important to look at the beginning of the dispersal of farming in the marginal areas of the fertile Levantine Corridor or outside the Levantine Corridor (**Fig.2.5**). The spread of farming had occurred in the Jilat-Azraq Basin of Transjordan no later than the Middle PPNB period. People in this area still relied heavily on hunting, but as game animals like equids went extinct and small animals like hares had to be hunted, a farming-hunting way of life was first enhanced by the adoption of goat herding for meat around the Late PPNB period. The farming-herding way of life was further enhanced by the introduction of sheep in the PPNC period (Betts 2008; Byrd 1992: 54*ff*; Garrard 1998; Garrard *et al.* 1996: 218*ff*; Martin 2000).

While similar adaptations seem to have occurred in the southernmost part of the Levantine Corridor as evidenced by the Middle PPNB site at Beidha and the Late PPNB site at Basta in southern Jordan, most of the contemporary or slightly later sites in the Negev and Sinai, such as Nahal Reuel, Nahal Issaron, Wadi Tbeik and Ujrat el Mehed suggest that hunting of wild animals and collecting of wild plants were still the dominant subsistence activities in these areas (Bar-Yosef 1984; Dayan *et al.* 1986; Goring-Morris 1993; Goring-Morris and Gopher 1983; Ronen *et al.* 2001; Tchernov and Bar-Yosef 1982). For this reason, the culture in the Negev and Sinai in this period is called the Desert PPNB, and it has been argued that the Negev and Sinai were the autonomous territories of mobile hunter-gatherers (Rosen 2002), even though they may have had contact with farmer-herders in more fertile areas of the southern Levant and may have possibly obtained wheat/barley and sheep/goat in exchange for other resources or goods like Red Sea shells (Bar-Yosef 2001; Bar-Yosef Mayer 1997;

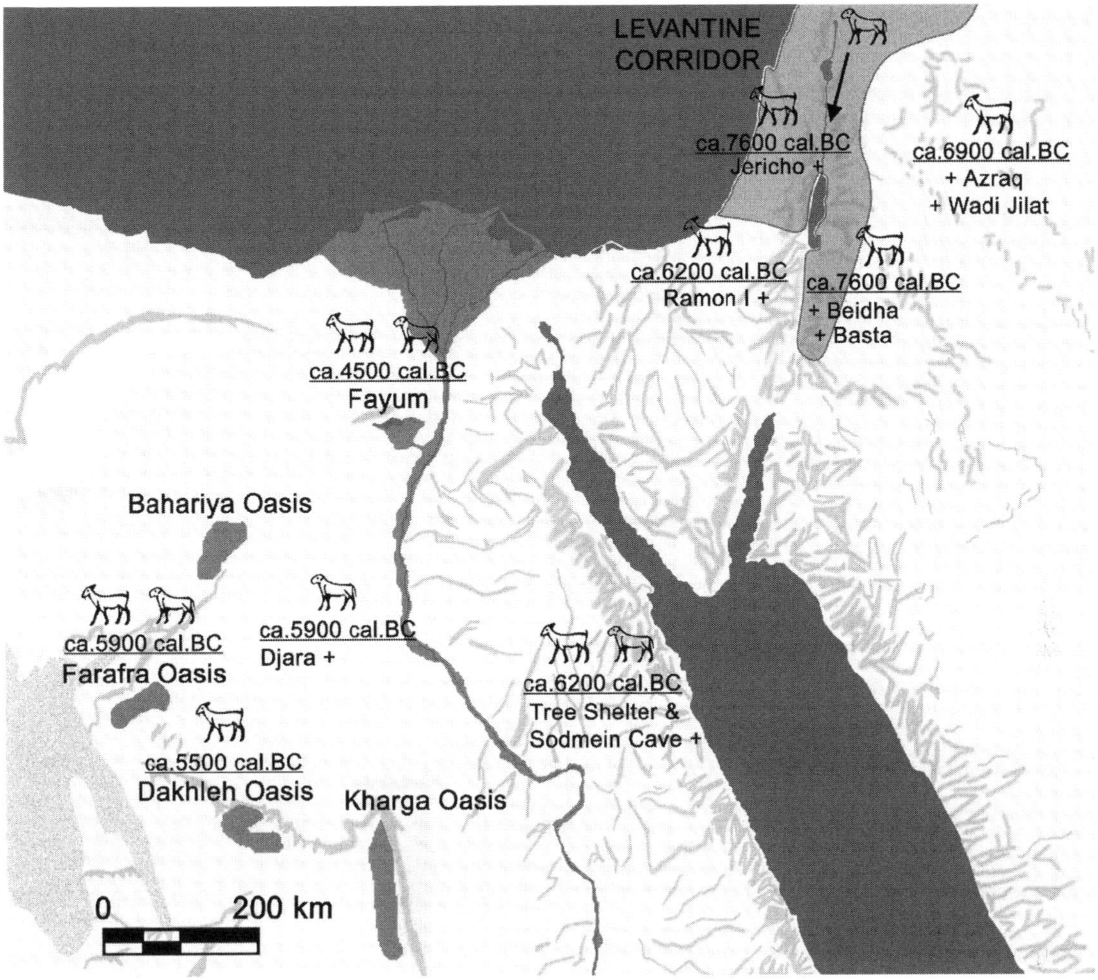

Fig.2.5. The earliest dates of domesticated sheep/goats in Egypt, the Negev and southern Levant

Hassan 2002b). This argument is supported by the fact that Late PPNB people in southern Sinai were morphologically unique and different from contemporaneous Levantine and North African people (Hershkovitz *et al.* 1994). Therefore, it seems unlikely that southern Levantine farmer-herders infiltrated into southern Sinai while establishing new settlements in the Late PPNB period, eventually moving on into Egypt.

Even though direct colonisation of Sinai by southern Levantine people is unlikely, one question is why farming did not diffuse across the Negev and Sinai into Egypt in the Middle PPNB period. As mentioned above, farming did diffuse outside the fertile areas onto the arid Jordanian Plateau in the same period. In other words, the question is why the diffusion of farming to Egypt had to wait until the Pottery Neolithic period. Thus it is necessary to consider what prevented the spread of farming from the southern Levant to Egypt in the Middle PPNB period. Physical distance between the southern Levant and Egypt may be one reason why the diffusion of farming was prevented and retarded. However, it has been argued that the distance between the two regions could have been easily traversed in a matter of days (Kuijt and Goring-Morris 2002: 428), though the mountainous terrain of Sinai could be a considerable geographic barrier. It may be concluded that the distance of approximately 500 km between the southern Levant and Lower Egypt was not a serious problem for the diffusion of farming. Therefore, it must be made clear whether the present lack of evidence for the diffusion of farming to Egypt in the Middle PPNB reflects the past reality.

As suggested by submerged PPNC and Pottery Neolithic sites along the Carmel coast of Israel, the Eastern Mediterranean coastline in the Early-Middle Holocene was positioned around 10-15 m below the present sea level and a few hundred metres off the present coast, and the sea level was even lower in the Middle PPNB period (Galili *et al.* 1988; 2005). Furthermore, large parts of the northwestern Negev and northern Sinai are presently covered by huge dunes and alluvial deposits (Goldberg 1995: 46-50; Goring-Morris and Goldberg 1990; Stanley 2002: 104-114). Therefore, even if contacts between the southern Levant and Lower Egypt in the Early-Middle Holocene took place on the Mediterranean coastal plain (Goring-Morris 1993: 77), it is possible that their archaeological remains are submerged or covered, and hence invisible.

There is another possibility that the contacts were realised through seafaring off the coast of northern Sinai and the Nile Delta (Bar-Yosef 2002a: 54-55; Bar-Yosef 2003: figs.10.3 and 4; Bar-Yosef and Bar-Yosef Mayer 2002: fig.8), but convincing evidence to support such a possibility has not been obtained. It has been suggested by the sum of various studies that the prominent current flow along the coast of the southern Levant, northern Sinai and the Nile Delta in the Early Holocene was clockwise from the east and northeast to the west and southwest, but this became counter-clockwise from the west to the east and northeast in the Middle Holocene due to changes in climate and atmospheric circulation (Stanley 2002: 98-100). Such a change in the current flow along the coast may have made the navigation from the Levant to Egypt difficult. Therefore, it may be said that the seafaring diffusion of farming from the southern Levant to Egypt would have been much easier in the Middle PPNB than that in later periods.

If the present lack of evidence for the diffusion of farming to Egypt in the Middle PPNB reflects the past reality, climatic conditions in the Negev and Sinai may be more likely reason why the diffusion of farming to Egypt had been interrupted. It has been argued that the advent of the Early Holocene climatic optimum and the following northward shift of the polar front caused desiccation in the southern Levant in the Middle to Late PPNB periods. This may have in turn resulted in an earlier decrease of rainfall in the Negev and Sinai, and made rain-fed farming impossible. This seems to be a reasonable explanation. However, if climatic conditions in the Negev and Sinai were actually the major reason why the diffusion of farming to Egypt had been interrupted, the question is whether a subsequent climatic amelioration in the Negev and Sinai is the reason why the diffusion of farming to Egypt became possible. Some scholars argued that such dramatic improvement of the climate has not been well attested in the Negev and Sinai in the 7th and 6th millennia cal.BC (Tchernov 1998; *cf.* Rossignol-Strick 2002). On the basis of the study of land snails, other scholars insist that precipitation in the Negev might have generally increased in the Middle Holocene and particularly around 5500-5000 cal.BC (Goodfriend 1990; 1999). The sedimentary record of the Dead Sea also demonstrate that the water level of the Dead Sea dropped rapidly around 6700 cal.BC, and after temporal recoveries, it dropped rapidly again around 6200 cal.BC and remained the lowest in the Early-Middle Holocene until it started to rise around 5600 cal.BC. This suggests that there was almost no precipitation in this region during this period (Migowski *et al.* 2006). Therefore, the reason for the diffusion of farming to Egypt must be looked for not only in possible changes in climatic conditions but also in changes in human adaptation to such conditions.

One dramatic change in subsistence activities in the Negev and Sinai is the possible introduction of sheep/goat herding around the PPNC or Tuwailan period, though the transition from the PPNB to Pottery Neolithic and Chalcolithic periods in the Negev and Sinai is not well known because of the paucity of archaeological data (Goring-Morris 1993; Rosen 2002). The initial introduction of sheep/goat herding into the Negev and Sinai has not yet been demonstrated by faunal remains, but merely suggested by changes in the lithic assemblage and the appearance of stone structures which look like animal pens (Goring-Morris 1993: 77*ff*). The penning of domesticated sheep/goats by using rock shelters, as suggested by concentrations of dung, was present at Ramon I in the Negev no later than 6000 cal.BC (Rosen *et al.* 2005) (**Fig.2.5**).

As exemplified by the emergence of a farming-herding way of life in Transjordan after the Late PPNB period, farming in arid areas outside the fertile Levantine Corridor had to be complemented by hunting and sheep/goat herding as a buffer against the risks of bad harvests (Garrard 1998: 145-146; Garrard *et al.* 1996). One reason why farming did not diffuse to Egypt across the Negev and Sinai in the Middle PPNB period may be because domesticated sheep and goats were not yet available in the Negev and Sinai and thus intensive exploitation of arid regions with the aid of farming alone was a risky business. Consequently, extensive exploitation of wild plants and animals based on seasonal movement remained the most successful subsistence in the Negev and Sinai until the Pottery Neolithic period.

The possibility that wheat/barley farming diffused to the Negev and Sinai well in advance of sheep/goat herding cannot be ruled out, but there is no evidence for farming in the Negev and Sinai in the Middle PPNB period (Rosen 1988; 2002). If farming actually did not diffuse to the Negev and Sinai in the Middle PPNB period, another reason may be because of different climatic regimes rather than the total amount of rainfall per year. Palynological records and other paleoclimatological data suggest that the amount of summer rainfall increased in the Arabian Peninsula and the southernmost part of the Fertile Crescent during the Early Holocene, due to the northward shift of the Intertropical Convergence Zone and weakening of the subtropical ridge which brought drought over these regions (El-Moslimany 1994; Staubwasser and Weiss 2006). This means that the Negev and Sinai were included in the Intertropical Convergence Zone in the Early Holocene (**Fig.2.4**), and thus Levantine wheat and barley, which had grown with winter/spring rainfall and relied on long daylight hours through spring and summer, could not grow under the monsoonal climatic regime of high spring-summer humidity and temperature (McCorriston 2006). In other words, it can be considered that as long as the monsoonal climate predominated in the Negev and Sinai, wheat and barley could not spread into this region. It may not have been until the Intertropical Convergence Zone retreated to the south that the southwestward diffusion of wheat and barley across the Negev and Sinai became possible.

Secure establishment of sheep/goat herding in combination with wheat/barley farming in the southern Levant in the Pottery Neolithic period could have made possible a more intensive exploitation of the Negev and Sinai. A farming-herding way of life is well attested in the southern Levant after the PPNC period, and sedentary farming and herding communities started to be segregated into a sedentary farming part and a mobile herding part, in order to keep the herds of sheep and goats away from farmland and to exploit nearby steppes and deserts which are unsuitable for farming (Gopher and Gophna 1993; Rollefson and Köhler-Rollefson 1993). It is in this context that peculiar small projectile points of the Pottery Neolithic appeared. These peculiar Pottery Neolithic projectile points have been found in some sites in the Negev as well, like Qadesh Barnea and Nahal Issaron, and it is supposed that these sites were hunter-herders' seasonal camps (Gopher 1994; Gopher *et al.* 1994). It is not clear whether these hunter-herders in the Negev were special task groups coming from sedentary farming settlements in the Mediterranean coastal plain of the southern Levant, or autonomous nomadic people who inhabited the steppes and deserts of the Negev and Sinai and had regular or occasional contact with farmers. However, the latter is more likely, because they gradually developed a distinct nomadic pastoral culture named the Timnian since the middle 6th millennium cal.BC (Rosen 2008a; 2008b). No matter what their identity, it is assumed that the diffusion of domesticated wheat/barley and sheep/goats to Egypt became possible in this context.

As mentioned, the earliest domesticated sheep/goats in Egypt were found at Sodmein Cave in the Red Sea Mountains and are dated to the early 6th millennium cal.BC, and there is little doubt that they came from Sinai. The reason why the southwestward diffusion of sheep/goats to Egypt was slightly earlier than that of wheat/barley is because sheep/goats were not affected by the difference in the climatic regime and could easily be adapted to the rocky mountainous environment of the coastal area of the Egyptian Eastern Desert, which might be similar to their homeland in the Negev and Sinai. It is likely that herders from Sinai infiltrated into the coastal area of the Egyptian Eastern Desert to some extent. Due to insufficient information about socioeconomic circumstances, however, it is difficult to say exactly at which point sheep/goats were passed on to the people who were indigenous to this area and why the indigenous people adopted sheep/goats. Moreover, although the first domesticated sheep/goats were not accompanied by domesticated wheat/barley, the role of sheep/goat herders, who carried with them a limited amount of grain, as the possible agents of the diffusion of wheat/barley farming to the northern part of Egypt at a later date must be considered (Hassan 2002b: 61).

2.4.5. Human cognitive development and human agency

While external reasons such as climatic and environmental changes and population/resource imbalances for the beginning and development of Neolithisation have long been argued in Near Eastern archaeology, internal reasons such as human mentality and decision making for the Neolithisation have recently been emphasised. From a general evolutionary point of view, Mithen has elaborated an idea that the development of the complex cognitive abilities of behaviourally modern humans played a significant role in the beginning of food production. He has argued that the development of human cognitive abilities to establish 'social' relations with wild plants and animals, to manipulate their lives, and to use the plants and animals not merely as food resources but also as tools for socioeconomic negotiation and competition was essential for the development of domestication. Modern humans had already exhibited complex cognitive and symbolising abilities as exemplified by rock art, bone/ivory sculptures, and personal ornaments like beads made in the Late Pleistocene, but it was not until the Terminal Pleistocene that modern humans seemed to have acquired the ability to think about controlling nature by domesticating wild plants and animals, and not necessarily for subsistence, as evidenced by the domestication of dog in the Natufian in the Levant. Food production must have been impossible before the development of such a cognitive ability (Mithen 1996).

It follows from this argument that the complex cognitive ability of modern humans which was ultimately critical for the beginning of food production has developed earlier regardless of ecological and demographic pressure at the transition between the Pleistocene and Holocene (Cauvin 2000a; 2000b; Watkins 2006). In the Near East, the remarkable appearance of various artistic or symbolic items and remains of symbolic behaviour, which is called the 'revolution of symbols' by Cauvin, started around the transition between the Upper Palaeolithic and Epipalaeolithic in the Terminal Pleistocene. Since the Neolithisation in the Near East ultimately derived from this 'revolution of symbols' particularly in the Natufian, Neolithisation can be considered as essentially a restructuring of human mentality rather than of subsistence, in order to cope with changing demands in the symbolic realm (Cauvin 2000a; 2000b; Goring-Morris and Belfer-Cohen 2002; Watkins 2006).

In contrast, artistic or symbolic items are poor in Egypt in the Late and Terminal Pleistocene and Early Holocene. No personal ornaments have been offered to Late Palaeolithic burials in Upper Egypt and Lower Nubia (Wendorf 1968; Wendorf and Schild 1986). The date of some rock art in Upper Egypt is not yet certain but is probably no earlier than the Late Palaeolithic (*ca.*15000 BP). Various animal motifs of the rock art certainly reflect people's view of wildlife and particularly their special concern with wild cattle, but the interpretation of abstract motifs and strange depictions of animals is still debatable (Huyge 1998; 2002; Huyge *et al.* 2001; 2007). Decorated pottery vessels in the Saharo-Sudanese culture are examples in which the artistic or symbolising skills of makers in the Early Holocene were exhibited. But the meanings of various wavy line patterns are unclear, and the variety of the decoration patterns may simply be regarded as a regional marker (Close 1995; Jesse 2003; Mohammed-Ali and Khabir 2003). Despite the early development of pottery making in the Western Desert, it was not until the Merimde Neolithic that clay figurines became common (Eiwanger 1992: 59*ff*). Apart from tiny ostrich eggshell beads and incised fragments, decorative carved bone or stone items are rare to absent in Early Holocene cultures in the Nile Valley and the Western Desert. Such items flourished well after the Early Holocene, as represented by those of the Bashendi culture in Dakhleh Oasis in the 6th millennium cal.BC (McDonald 2008). The appearance of cattle burials and associated megalithic complex in the Nabta-Kiseiba region was in the Late Ceramic pastoral culture in the Middle Holocene, which is much later than the initial attempts of cattle domestication (Wendorf and Schild 2001).

Therefore, it is hard to imagine through looking at these things the mentality or cognition in general and the ambition or intention in particular of the people who first attempted food production in Egypt. Nonetheless, it seems that the 'revolution of symbols' should be a factor which deserves serious consideration in future Neolithic research in Egypt. Ongoing arguments concerning symbolic aspects of Near Eastern Neolithisation would be of great help for such a consideration. For instance, as has been argued in Near Eastern Neolithic research (*e.g.*, Goring-Morris and Belfer-Cohen 2001), the symbolic aspects of seemingly utilitarian material culture like stone tools should not be ignored for a better understanding of the dynamics of prehistoric societies. This topic will be discussed further in Chapter 4.

Human agency should also be considered in the sociocultural/socioeconomic networks between the southern Levant, Negev, Sinai, and Egypt. The reasons why a very limited number of Levantine Neolithic items, such as specific projectile points, reached Egypt and why nothing seems to have gone out of Egypt in return, must be related to intentional choices of the people involved, and may probably be explained by a sort of prestige economy in which ambitious individuals tried to obtain novel items for status display. A social model for the origins of food production suggests that ambitious individuals in complex forager societies would have been under pressure to maintain prestige among their followers and may have been attracted to food production as a way of securing exotic and high-status food or increasing surplus food to sustain their competitive activities (Hayden 1990; 1992; 1995). The introduction of domesticated wheat/barley and sheep/goats into Egypt may also be in part attributed to such ambitious individuals' eagerness for raising their status through the distribution of novel food. This topic will also be discussed in more detail in Chapter 4.

2.5. Areas of cooperative research

An overview of factors causing Neolithisation in Egypt reveals more differences than similarities between the Near East and Egypt. Nevertheless, I insist that cooperative research between archaeologists working in Egypt and Near Eastern archaeologists is essential.

As for the similarities in cultural, economic and social development in the Levantine PPNB interaction sphere, if Near Eastern archaeologists agree that more attention should be paid to such topics as the colonisation of the isolated island of Cyprus for a better understanding of unprecedented human territorial behaviours which may have caused the similarities in different regions (*e.g.*, Kuijt 2004; Peltenburg 2004), there seems to be no reason to ignore Egypt which is connected to the Levant by the land bridge of Sinai and must have been more easily accessible. Given that Neolithic people had fewer physical difficulties in moving across seas and deserts than previously believed, demographic trends across the Near East in the Early-Middle Holocene should be reconsidered not only by Near Eastern archaeologists (*e.g.*, Bar-Yosef 2003; Bar-Yosef and Bar-Yosef Mayer 2002; Kuijt 2000) but also by archaeologists in Egypt. Special attention must be paid to the population expansion into arid regions like the Negev and Sinai, in which sedentary farming-herding adaptations did not become prevalent despite a certain degree of similarity in material culture. In particular, social crowding and subsequent social fragmentation in the south-central Levant around the end of the Late PPNB period (Kuijt 2002) must have made a considerable impact on the Negev and Sinai, and this may have eventually affected Neolithisation in Egypt. What seems most interesting is that the Negev and Sinai can be studied not only in terms of the heartland-hinterland or heartland-periphery relationship with the Levant (Rosen 1988: 503; 2002: 24), but also in terms of the mediator of cultural transmission between the Levant and Egypt. The expansion of exchange networks between the Near East and Egypt over time can be re-examined through exchanges of information between archaeologists working in the Near East and Egypt.

As for the differences in cultural, economic and social development, Egypt definitely provides extreme examples. In order to develop a new explanatory framework that is applicable to the entire Near East including Egypt, one has to take into account the fact that cattle herding and pottery making were quite normal in the Egyptian Western Desert before crop farming. Archaeologists working in Egypt are responsible for explaining these contrasting phenomena in terms not only of the distribution of resources but also of the medium-term developments of technology and demographic changes that are unique to northeastern Africa. Compared with the core area of the Near East, more frequent population expansion/contraction phenomena and more sparsely distributed resources were characteristics of northeastern Africa except for the Nile Valley, and these characteristics are obviously related to the pace of developments of different technologies, subsistence practices and social organisation in the Western Desert.

2.6. Structural history of Neolithisation

Finally, the argument so far can also be considered in terms of Structural History, an Annaliste mode of thought which explicitly focuses on multiple processes of events which mutually interact on different timescale (Bintliff 1991; 2004). There is no doubt that the Neolithisation process in the Near East and Egypt went on during the long-term climatic trend of reaction to and recovery from the Younger Dryas cooling and drying event and subsequent increasing aridity between 10000 cal.BC and 5000 cal.BC. This climatic trend gave possibilities and constraints for the Neolithisation process in terms of the selection of human habitats, the timing of domestication and the selection of potential domesticates (Bar-Yosef 2002b; Bar-Yosef and Belfer-Cohen 2002; Bar-Yosef and Meadow 1995; McCorriston and Hole 1991; Moore and Hillman 1992; Rossignol-Strick 2002; Wright 1993). In addition, the development of the complex cognitive ability of behaviourally modern humans, which can also be regarded as a part of long-term human evolution since the emergence of anatomically modern humans more than one hundred thousand years ago, must also have given great possibilities for the Neolithisation process elsewhere. Therefore, it seems quite reasonable to conclude from the long-term perspective that the beginning of food production in the Early Holocene is a contingent event at the conjuncture of rare climatic changes and the steady evolution of human cognition (Layton 1999; Sherratt 1997), even though the exact timing of climatic changes varied by latitude and elevation.

The above-mentioned idea of polycentric

evolution in Near Eastern Neolithisation seems to focus solely on the medium-term developments of culture, economy and society in different environments and to argue the reasons for regional differences as well as similarities, without making clear the long-term climatic trends and human evolutionary trends behind developments and short-term events that are constrained and enabled by these medium-term developments. It is necessary to distinguish long-term trends from medium-term events and to recognise on what timescale the trends and events under consideration occurred and how they converged or diverged at a certain point of time, for a more comprehensive understanding of Neolithisation in the entire Near East including Egypt.

The emergence of knowledgeable and ambitious individuals who have the potential to change things on the short timescale within the medium-term developments of societies or sociocultural networks is the most unpredictable factor in the Neolithisation process. According to structuration theory and complexity theory, individuals cannot be freed from the existing cultural, economic and social structure which is unique to each region and constrains individual behaviour, but they can create subtle changes in the structure. Although the role of active individuals should not be overestimated (Bintliff 2003), such a series of subtle changes may radically alter the trajectory of the developments of entire cultural, economic and social structure ultimately (Layton 2003). Therefore, archaeologists must be careful when looking at subtle changes in material culture that do not necessarily seem to be adaptive or functional while exploring the socioeconomic context in which such changes appeared. Subtle changes in material culture or the appearance of new features in material culture may be clues to recognise the emergence of socially-prominent individuals. In the case of Egypt, the late emergence of bifacial technology within the traditional lithic technology in the 7th-6th millennia cal.BC may be interpreted as a sign of the appearance of such individuals, who eventually adopted foreign domesticates. This topic will be discussed in more detail in Chapter 4.

In short, the Neolithisation process in Egypt can probably be explained as the convergence of 1) long-term Holocene climatic changes and human cognitive development, 2) medium-term demographic changes and the accompanying unprecedented expansion and intensification of sociocultural/socioeconomic networks, and 3) the unpredictable emergence of socially-prominent individuals on a short-term basis.

2.7. Summary

As demonstrated in this chapter, the theoretical framework concerning the Neolithisation process remains under construction, while many critical elements including the timescale are under the research focus. What seems clear is that archaeologists in Egypt and Near Eastern archaeologists can work on a common ground and provide information to each other for mutual benefits. Further discussions about supra-regional concepts in Near Eastern Neolithisation will trigger a change in relations between Egyptian archaeology and Near Eastern archaeology, thereby eliminating neighbourly ignorance.

Following this research orientation, the next chapter will focus on the Fayum where the supposedly earliest evidence for wheat/barley farming in combination with sheep/goat herding in Egypt was found, and will examine the Neolithisation process on a more local level.

3. Background to research in the Fayum

3.1. Introduction

The Fayum has been a focus of scholarly research for a hundred years, and the sequence of human occupation ranging from the Palaeolithic to the Roman period has been revealed. Among the periods, the Epipalaeolithic and Neolithic are of great importance not only in terms of regional history but also in terms of the history of Egypt. The beginning of wheat/barley farming was attested first in the Fayum, in association with other new elements like cattle herding and pottery production, which may have derived from the Western Desert, and sheep/goat herding, which surely derived from the southern Levant but may have arrived in the Western Desert earlier than it did in the Fayum. Therefore, the Fayum Neolithic must be viewed as a unique culture at the intersection of one route from the southwest, and another from the northeast (Midant-Reynes 2000: 106). Any arguments concerning the beginning of wheat/barley farming in combination with animal herding in Egypt must rely on the Fayum data.

This chapter will firstly summarise the Fayum geography and geology and will review the history of academic research on the prehistoric Fayum and current discussions on the Epipalaeolithic-Neolithic sequence there. Secondly, on the basis of ecological and archaeological data obtained by previous research, local factors for the transition to food production in the Neolithic will be investigated in detail. Lastly, following these investigations, strategies for new research will be presented.

3.2. The Fayum geography and geology

The Fayum is located approximately 60 km to the southwest of Cairo. The Fayum Depression, covering an area of approximately 12000 km^2, is a circular depression carved out of the Middle-Upper Eocene bedrock of the Western Desert, and is bounded by cliffs on all sides (**Fig.3.1**). In particular, the northern ridge of the depression is marked by a huge, vertical scarp, and it attains the highest elevation above the floor of the depression. Most of the scarp face and the low-lying pediplain surface in the northern part of the Depression are the Upper Eocene bedrock.

According to geology (**Fig.3.2**), the Upper Eocene bedrock consists of the Birket Qarun Formation and the overlying Qasr el-Sagha Formation. The Birket Qarun Formation is composed mainly of calcareous sandstone and sandy limestone and is approximately 50 m thick, whereas the Qasr el-Sagha Formation is made up of four interfingering fossiliferous limestone-shale-sandstone facies and is approximately 180 m thick. The Oligocene beds of the Gebel Qatrani Formation are also exposed in the north of the Depression, overlying the Qasr el-Sagha Formation, and are formed of variegated sandstone with alternating shale and calcareous grit beds. The top of the Oligocene formation at the northern ridge of the Depression is capped by extensive basalt sheets. Overlying the basalt sheet, there is a series of Miocene red sand and gravel containing petrified wood trunks (Gingerich 1993; Issawi 1976: 152-153; Said 1993: 78-81; Van Couvering and Harris 1991; Wanas 2008: 41-43).

The western and southern scarps are much lower in height and are more dissected than the northern scarp, and the Middle Eocene bedrock is widely exposed. The terminology and divisions of the Middle Eocene formations in the Fayum have been changed due to the development of geological and palaeontological research in the last hundred years, and there still seems to be no agreement in the usage of terms among geologists and palaeontologists. The

Middle Eocene bedrock in the western and southern scarps consists of the Wadi Rayan Formation and the overlying Gehannam Formation. The Wadi Rayan Formation consists of hard limestone and is approximately 130 m thick, whereas the Gehannam Formation consists of gypseous shale, marl and limestone, and is approximately 50 m thick (Issawi 1976: 152-153; Said 1990: 451-486; Said 1993: 78-81; Wanas 2008: 41-43). The eastern ridge of the depression, which is formed of the Gehannam Formation and is called the Nile-Fayum Divide, is covered by Pliocene and Pleistocene gravel and gypseous deposits (Aref 2003; Bussemer *et al.* 2006; Mohamed 2003; Sandford and Arkell 1929: 5-10).

The Nile-Fayum Divide is approximately 5-15 km away from the Nile, and is breached by the Hawara Channel. Through this channel, the Nile water has flown to the depression and converted it into a lake. But the water could not flow back to the Nile, because the bottom of the depression is much lower than the Nile bed. Due to its proximity to the Nile and its reliance on Nile water and mud supply, the Fayum has had almost the same natural environment as the Nile

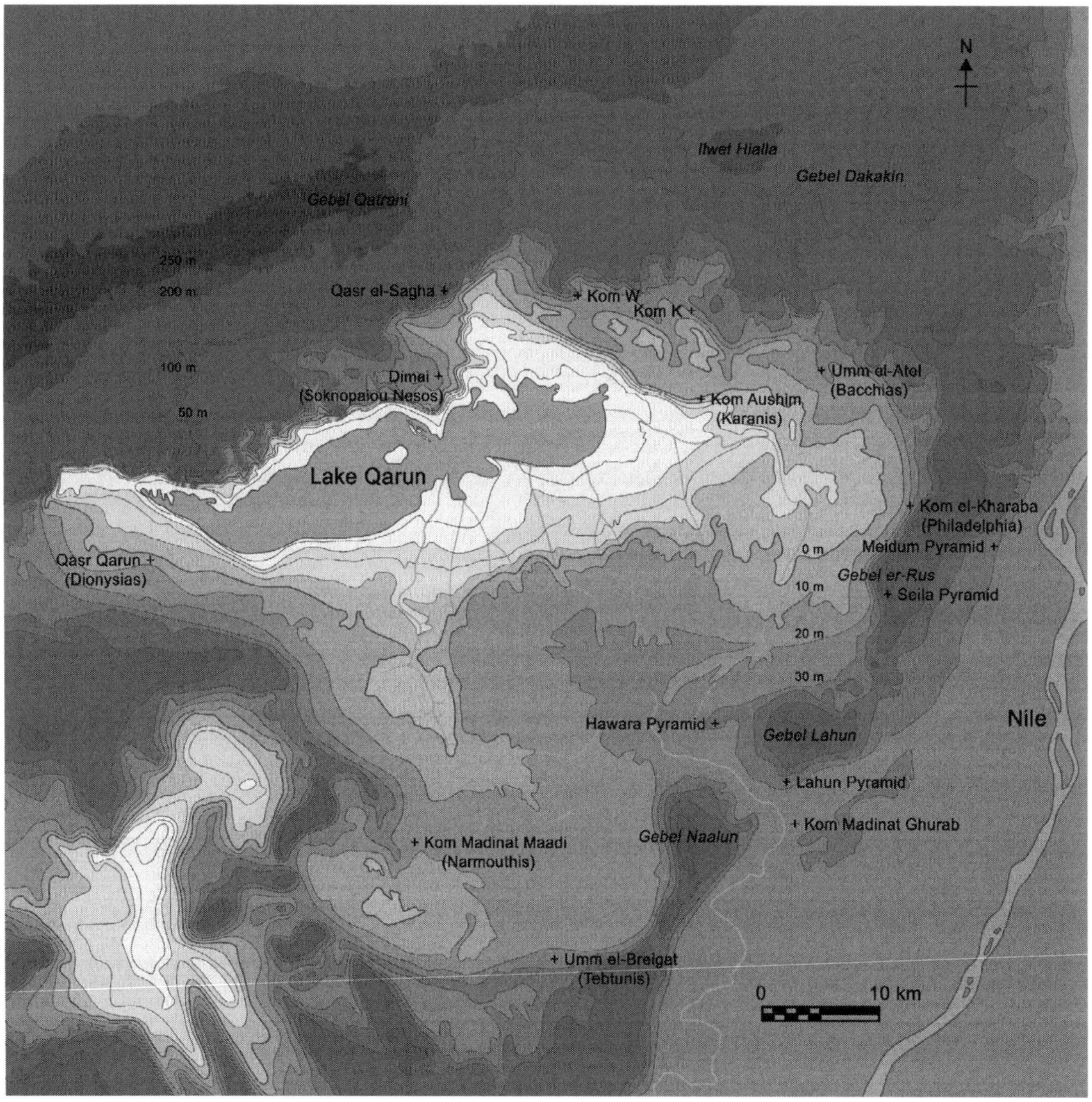

Fig.3.1. Geographical map of the Fayum

Fig.3.2. Geological map of the Fayum

Valley. The floor of the depression forms an undulating plain and its elevation ranges from 0 m up to 30 m above sea level. The surface of the plain is covered by Quaternary deposits like freshwater lacustrine sediments, diatomites, silt, gravel sheets, and deflated sand. They were deposited for the most part in the form of a lake-delta spreading out fan-wise from the point where the Nile water entered the Fayum Depression. The thickness of the deposits above the bedrock is approximately 8 m. The plain rises gradually toward its periphery and forms a series of terraces at various heights, ranging up to more than 40 m above sea level. These terraces mark the shorelines of an inland freshwater lake which was fed by the Nile and stood at different levels at different times. Studies of the various terraces have indicated that the Fayum Depression had already been hollowed out to its full depth before the Nile obtained access to it, and that the breaking of the Nile into the Fayum Depression and the consequent formation of the lake took place after the Pliocene. Thereafter, the level, area, and volume of the lake underwent a complicated succession of variations due to changes in the level of the Nile (Ball 1939: 33-35; Said 1993: 80-81).

At present, the Fayum is a large depression, and its lowest northwestern part is occupied by a brackish lake called Lake Qarun or Birket el-Qarun, which is 44 m below sea level and is approximately 200 km^2 in area. While the fertile southern half of the depression, which is approximately 1700 km^2, has been irrigated by canals and heavily cultivated, marginal desert and rocky terrains of the depression, which are the major natural features particularly on the north side of the lake, have remained undisturbed. Many archaeological sites dating from the Epipalaeolithic to the Ptolemaic and Roman periods have been better preserved on the north side of the lake, and hence research has concentrated on this terrain.

3.3. History of archaeological field research in the Fayum

3.3.1. The age of the antiquarians

The marginal desert plains of the Fayum Depression have been well known for the surface scatter of beautifully-made flint tools. Such tools had been collected and sold at antiquities markets by local people since the 19th century. Due to these circumstances, French and British antiquarians and early archaeologists had been drawn to the Fayum with curiosity, but they started to collect flint tools on the north side of Lake Qarun in a rather scholarly manner.

De Morgan, Reygasse and Seymour de Ricci are amongst French antiquarians who were active in the late 19th - early 20th centuries, and many of their collections are presently housed in the National Antiquities Museum of Saint-Germain en Laye near Paris (Beck and Amiet 1982: 78-95). Petrie, Randall-McIver, John Evans (father of Arthur Evans), Seton-Karr, Ruffer and Gayer-Anderson are among British people who were active in the late 19th - early 20th centuries, and they proudly donated their collections of flint tools to museums in Britain such as the Pitt-Rivers Museum and the Ashmolean Museum in Oxford. Seton-Karr was the most generous person, and after he left part of his collection to the Egyptian Museum in Cairo, the rest of his collection was distributed not only in Britain but also all over the world.

These early antiquarians had already recognised that carefully-retouched flint tools in their collections probably dated to the Neolithic period by analogy with the stone tools of the European stone age, and they published these flint tools as Neolithic artefacts. De Morgan's Fayum collection was published in a large volume as early as the 1890s and republished later (de Morgan 1896; 1926). Seton-Karr's Fayum collection was published in an authentic scholarly journal and the general catalogue of the Egyptian Museum in Cairo in the 1900s and 1910s (Seton-Karr 1904; 1905; Currelly 1913). However, it was not until the 1920s that the first modern academic investigations were carried out by British scholars in the Fayum.

3.3.2. The first modern academic research in the 1920s and 1930s

Since it had already been recognised that geological information was essential for understanding the remote past of the Fayum, it was logical that the first comprehensive academic investigations in the Fayum were carried out by geologically-oriented archaeologists. A pioneering survey was conducted by a British geologist Beadnell of the Geological Survey of Egypt between 1898 and 1902 (Beadnell 1905). Thereafter, Caton-Thompson and Gardner focused on the Holocene geology and Neolithic human activities on the northern shore and southwestern shore of Lake Qarun, and carried out fieldwork under the auspices of the British School of Archaeology in Egypt and the Royal Anthropological Institute of Great Britain and Ireland (Caton-Thompson and Gardner 1934). Almost simultaneously, Sandford and Arkell were employed by the Oriental Institute of the University of Chicago and were asked to survey the eastern ridge of the Fayum Depression, which is called the Nile-Fayum Divide. They focused primarily on the Pliocene-Pleistocene geology and the earliest human activities (Sandford and Arkell 1929). As a result, the basic sequence of the Pleistocene and Holocene of the Fayum Depression in relation to the rise and fall of the lake level and the Nile level was reconstructed.

The fluctuations of the lake level have been a major focus of research since the initial work by Caton-Thompson and Gardner. Immediately after the publication of Caton-Thompson and Gardner's report, their ideas were re-examined at different locations of the Fayum by a geologist Little of the Geological Survey of Egypt (Little 1936). A further re-examination was attempted at different locations of the Fayum by Caton-Thompson and Gardner themselves with the help of a local geologist (Caton-Thompson *et al.* 1937). These works were later reviewed and reconsidered by a geologist Ball (1939).

While the survey by Sandford and Arkell has not yielded many archaeological finds, Caton-Thompson and Gardner carried out extensive surface survey and made good results in terms of the discovery of various archaeological sites dated from the Palaeolithic to the Roman period. While the southwest side of the lake was only briefly investigated, the north side of the lake was quite intensively investigated. Caton-Thompson and Gardner located a number of prehistoric artefact concentrations on the desert surface and gave them alphabetical site names, though they left several prehistoric sites unnamed but merely indicated them on their survey map.

The named and unnamed prehistoric sites on the northern shore of the lake are geographically divided into two clusters by a very large erosional basin named Moeris Bay (**Fig.3.3**). One cluster on the west side of Moeris Bay includes Site F, Site G, Site H, Site M, Site N, Site O, Site R, Site S, and Site T. It must be noted that Site N, Site O, Site R, Site S, and Site T are all located around the northern margin of a basin named the N Basin at the foot of the escarpment of Qasr el-Sagha, whereas Site F, Site G and Site H are located in a narrow strip of sandy beach farther to the southwest of the N Basin. Another cluster on the east side of Moeris Bay includes Kom K, Site K, Site L, Site V, Kom W, Site X, Site Z, Site ZI, Moeris I and Camp II. Many of these sites are also associated with basins in this area. Kom K and Site K are located at the northern margin of a basin named the K Basin. Site L is located at the northern margin of the L Basin. Site V, Kom W, Site Z, and Camp II are located at the northern and northeastern margins of the Z Basin. Site ZI and Moeris I are located on the northeast and eastern shores of Moeris Bay.

The most important discoveries on a desert ridge named the K Ridge to the north of the K Basin were two concentrations of storage pits named the Upper and Lower K Pits. Many of the pits were lined with matting, and some pits contained grains of domesticated wheat and barley. This is the sole place where grains of domesticated wheat and barley were found in a prehistoric context in the Fayum. Other important discoveries are a concentration of

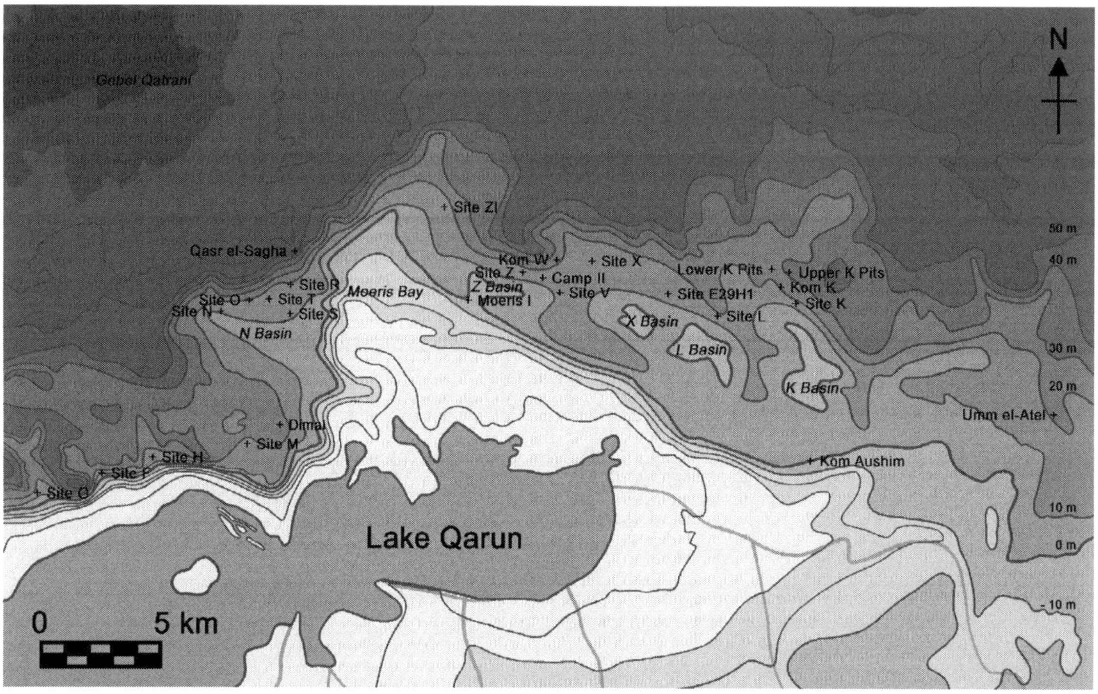

Fig.3.3. Map of Caton-Thompson's sites on the northern shore of Lake Qarun

fireholes excavated on a low, oval mound named Kom K in the vicinity of the K Ridge, and a similar site excavated at another low, oval mound named Kom W, which is 8 km to the west of Kom K. Both excavations yielded a large number of various pottery vessels, lithic artefacts and other categories of objects.

The study of artefacts obtained not only through excavations at Kom W, Kom K, and the Upper and Lower K Pits but also through surface collection at many other named and unnamed sites mentioned above helped Caton-Thompson recognise that the artefacts could be divided into two distinct prehistoric culture groups. One culture group, namely 'the Neolithic A group', is characterised by the presence of pottery vessels and bifacially-retouched flint tools and is associated with domesticates and granaries. Kom K and Kom W were regarded as the type sites of the Neolithic A group. Another culture group, namely 'the Neolithic B group', is characterised by the predominance of microlithic artefacts and the absence of pottery vessels and is not associated with domesticates. Therefore, the Neolithic B group was regarded as an impoverished culture.

It was also recognised that apart from the type sites of the A group culture, most other named sites often yielded mixed assemblages of the A group and B group artefacts, but that some unnamed and named sites at lower elevations of the lakeshore did not yield the A group artefacts. Since Caton-Thompson and Gardner assumed that the lake kept lowering through the Neolithic period, it followed that the sites located at lower elevations of the lakeshore should be later in date than those located at higher elevations. They concluded that the A group culture preceded the B group culture and that the A group people who had settled around the shores of the high lake had moved to lower elevations following the receding lake water and had culturally degenerated. Concerning the dating, Caton-Thompson speculated that the Fayum Neolithic culture would perhaps be dated to before 5000 BC and a total time span of the A group and B group cultures would be 800 years (Caton-Thompson and Gardner 1934: 93).

3.3.3. Resumption of research in the 1960s

There was a long interruption of scholarly research in the Fayum between the 1940s and the 1960s. According to my museum research, the Fayum was visited by renowned British anthropologists like Seligman and Evans-Pritchard during this period, and their stone tool collections are presently housed in the Pitt-Rivers Museum in Oxford. Even when Caton-Thompson and Gardner were still active in the Fayum in the 1920s-1930s, the Fayum was visited by a renowned American explorer De Prorok. He collected lithic artefacts at Kom Aushim and Qasr el-Sagha, and part of his collection is presently housed in the Egyptian Museum in Cairo. This means that the Fayum has been a popular flint hunting ground and thus has been plundered constantly.

Scholarly research in the Fayum was resumed in the late 1960s by the Sapienza University of Rome team led by Puglisi. He revisited not only the Nile-Fayum Divide surveyed by Sandford and Arkell but also several named and unnamed sites investigated by Caton-Thompson on the northeast side of the lake, and carried out surface collection of Palaeolithic, Neolithic and Predynastic stone tools (Puglisi 1967). Parts of his collection were later studied in detail by his fellow scholars (Casini 1984; Mussi *et al.* 1984). According to sketch maps (Casini 1984: fig.2; Mussi *et al.* 1984: fig.1), it seems that Puglisi visited Caton-Thompson's Kom K, Kom W, Site V, Site Z, Site ZI, Site M and other unnamed sites at lower elevations that are close to the present lakeshore, and gave them new names. For instance, Kom K was indicated as V, and Kom W was indicated as KW, and Site V was indicated as KI. Site Z was re-named as S4, and Site ZI was re-named as MB, and Site Moeris I was re-named as MOE.

Puglisi was soon followed by the Combined Prehistoric Expedition led by Wendorf and Schild. After the rescue campaign in Lower Nubia, Wendorf and Schild changed their direction to the downstream of the Nile, in order to strengthen their knowledge of the Pleistocene-Holocene archaeology and geology of the Nile Valley obtained in Lower Nubia, and took a trip to the Fayum for a geoarchaeological investigation in 1969. Although their fieldwork was short in time and their research area on the north side of the lake overlapped Caton-Thompson's survey area, this new research contributed to an important revision of the succession of the two prehistoric cultures identified by Caton-Thompson (Said *et al.* 1970; 1972; Wendorf and Schild 1976).

They revealed that the lacustrine deposits and shore features recorded at least four successive episodes of lake transgression in the Late Pleistocene and the Early-Middle Holocene. Lake Qarun, which presently occupies the northwestern part of the Fayum Depression, is the remnant of a larger lake called the Moeris Lake in the Ptolemaic period, and it has been known that the lake was much larger before the Ptolemaic period. According to the reconstruction by the Combined Prehistoric Expedition, the lake started its largest in the Pleistocene, and then has undergone repeated shrinking and expanding through the Holocene. The first highest lake in the Early Holocene is named the Paleomoeris Lake. The second highest is named the Premoeris Lake, and the third highest is named the Protomoeris Lake. The name of the Moeris Lake is assigned to the lake which has been present since the beginning of the Middle Holocene (**Fig.3.4**). These four successive lake stages are divided by sudden drops of water level. Contrary to Caton-Thompson's assumption that the lake kept lowering, their idea is that the lake level has risen and fallen repeatedly. Caton-Thompson's Neolithic B group culture was associated with the Premoeris and Protomoeris Lakes which were relatively low, and the Neolithic A group culture was associated with the Moeris Lake which was relatively high, suggesting that the Neolithic B group culture preceded the Neolithic A group culture. Subsequently, the Moeris Lake lowered temporarily, probably causing the decline of the Neolithic A group culture (Wendorf and Schild 1976: 222-226).

In addition, they excavated *in situ* flint tools at sites such as Site E29G1 (Caton-Thompson's

Site ZI), Site E29G3 (Caton-Thompson's Site R) and Site E29H1 (Caton-Thompson's unnamed site at the northeastern margin of the X Basin) (**Fig.3.3**), and concluded from the study of the assemblages that Caton-Thompson's Neolithic B group culture included mixed associations of Epipalaeolithic and Neolithic stone tools, and thus the B group culture was an invalid entity. They identified a purely Epipalaeolithic assemblage, and proposed to name it the Qarunian. On the basis of radiocarbon dates, they also argued a gap of approximately 1000 years between the Qarunian and the A group cultures. It was assumed that Qarunian people abandoned the Fayum due to the drying-up of the Protomoeris Lake, and new people with domesticates and new material items like pottery vessels migrated to occupy the Fayum as the Moeris Lake began to appear (Wendorf and Schild 1976: 311-319).

3.3.4. New research after the 1970s

The investigation by the Combined Prehistoric Expedition was followed by a joint team of the Jagiellonian University in Cracow and the

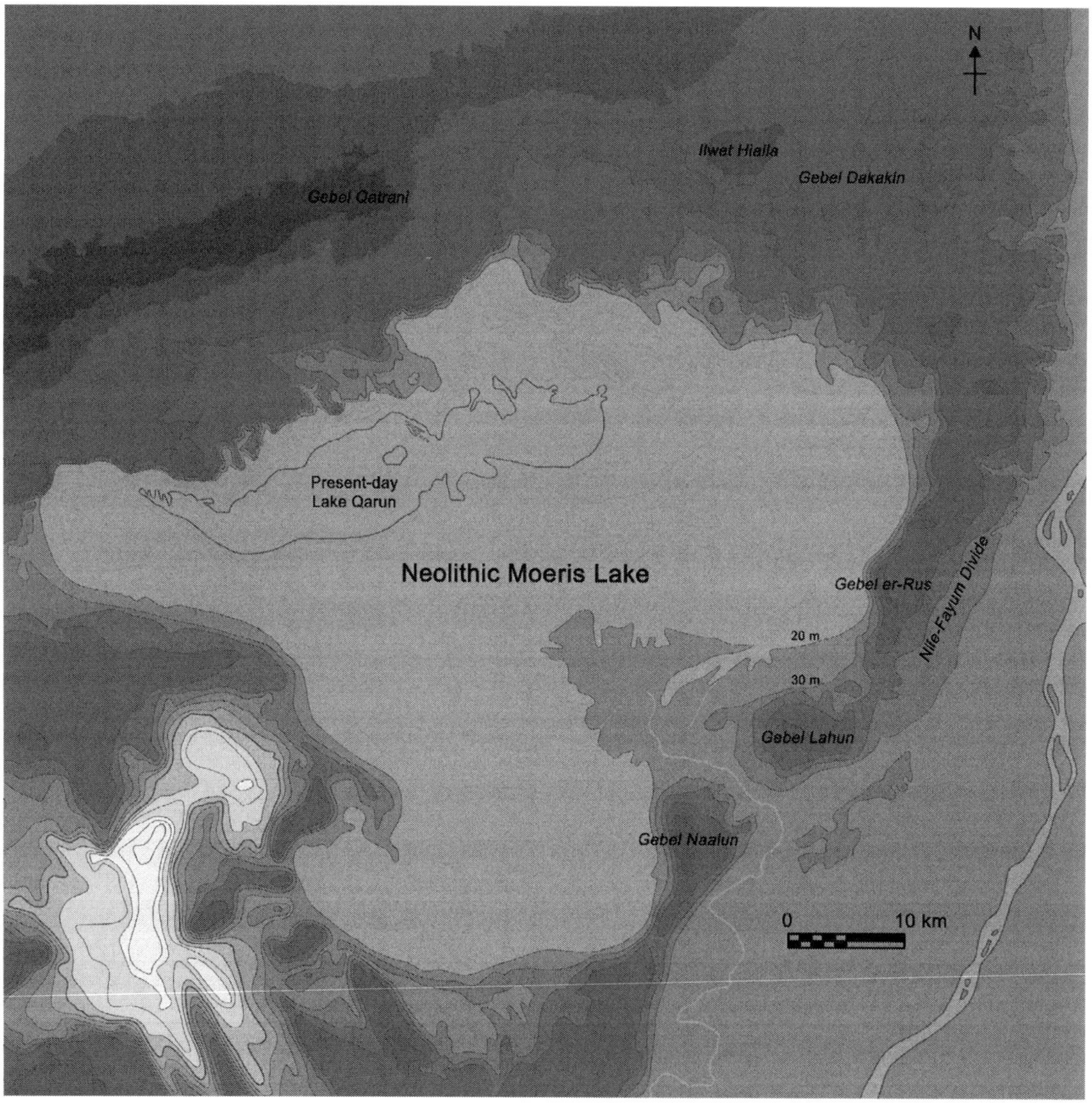

Fig.3.4. The maximum extent of Neolithic Moeris Lake in the Middle Holocene

German Archaeological Institute in Cairo led by Ginter and Kozlowski (Dagnan-Ginter *et al.* 1984; Ginter and Kozlowski 1983; 1986; Ginter *et al.* 1980). They conducted geological surveys and excavations around Qasr el-Sagha on the north side of Lake Qarun. Their sites, including QS I/79, QS V/79, QS VII/80, QS IX/81, QS XI/81 among others, are all located in the area named the N Basin which has intensively been investigated by Caton-Thompson and the Combined Prehistoric Expedition.

Based on the examination of stratigraphy and the associated inventories of stone tools and pottery types, they distinguished two phases of Neolithic culture and designated the earlier as the Fayumian culture and the later as the Moerian culture. While the Fayumian was associated with the episode of lake transgression and was equivalent to Caton-Thompson's Neolithic A group, the Moerian was associated with the episode of lake recession and was discerned from Caton-Thompson's Neolithic A and B group cultures. They also revealed that the previously-accepted view on the stone tool inventory of Caton-Thompson's Neolithic A group culture had been distorted by her selective collection of bifacial and core tools, and that the true Neolithic culture of the earlier phase included many flake tools as well. As for the Moerian, they revealed the occurrence of blade tools that showed affiliations with Epipalaeolithic techniques, and suggested the invasion of Saharan people with an Epipalaeolithic tradition into the Fayum after the decline of the Fayumian due to the lake recession.

They also reconstructed the lake level fluctuations in the Early-Middle Holocene based on the data obtained around Qasr el-Sagha (Kozlowski and Ginter 1989; 1993), but their reconstruction does not agree with the reconstruction published by Wendorf and Schild at many points, and gives the impression that the reconstruction by Wendorf and Schild was rather simplistic. For instance, while Wendorf and Schild's reconstruction suggested that the Neolithic A or Fayumian culture appeared and flourished when the lake was on a constantly rising trend, Ginter and Kozlowski's reconstruction indicated that the Fayumian culture appeared when the lake was on a lowering trend, and that it was in the middle of the Fayumian period when the lake level started to rise. Such disagreements clearly show the difficulty of reconstructing a general long-term fluctuation pattern on the basis of fragmented data obtained at a limited number of locations.

While previous scholars concentrated mainly on the north side or northeast side of Lake Qarun, the University of Washington team led by Wenke focused on the southwest side of the lake (Wenke 1984; Wenke and Casini 1989; Wenke *et al.* 1983; 1988), for the reason that there had been few reports of early sites on this side except for Caton-Thompson's Site J (**Fig.3.5**). Wenke's research was the second attempt to locate prehistoric sites on the south side of the lake since the first survey by Caton-Thompson. Wenke had been interested in general questions regarding the transition from hunting and gathering to farming and herding in a worldwide perspective, and had a strong motive to answer these questions by using the data obtained from the relatively undisturbed area of the Fayum.

His general questions about the beginning of farming and herding in Egypt include 1) when and how the first domesticates appeared in Egypt, 2) what kind of subsistence preceded farming and herding there, 3) whether Egyptian hunter-gatherers were converted to farmer-herders or were simply replaced by farmer-herders moving into Egypt from outside. Concerning the Fayum evidence, the foreign origin of farming and herding in the Fayum had already been suggested by Caton-Thompson. The reason for the late appearance of domesticates in the Fayum in contrast to the early use of domesticates in the Levant as well as the place of the ultimate origin of the Fayum culture had been the focus of debate. However, previous investigations in the Fayum had not clearly demonstrated what kind of resources other than domesticates were actually exploited by the inhabitants of the Fayum. Therefore, the research by Wenke and his associates in the Fayum was devoted to revealing subsistence changes, based mainly on the analysis of the distribution of

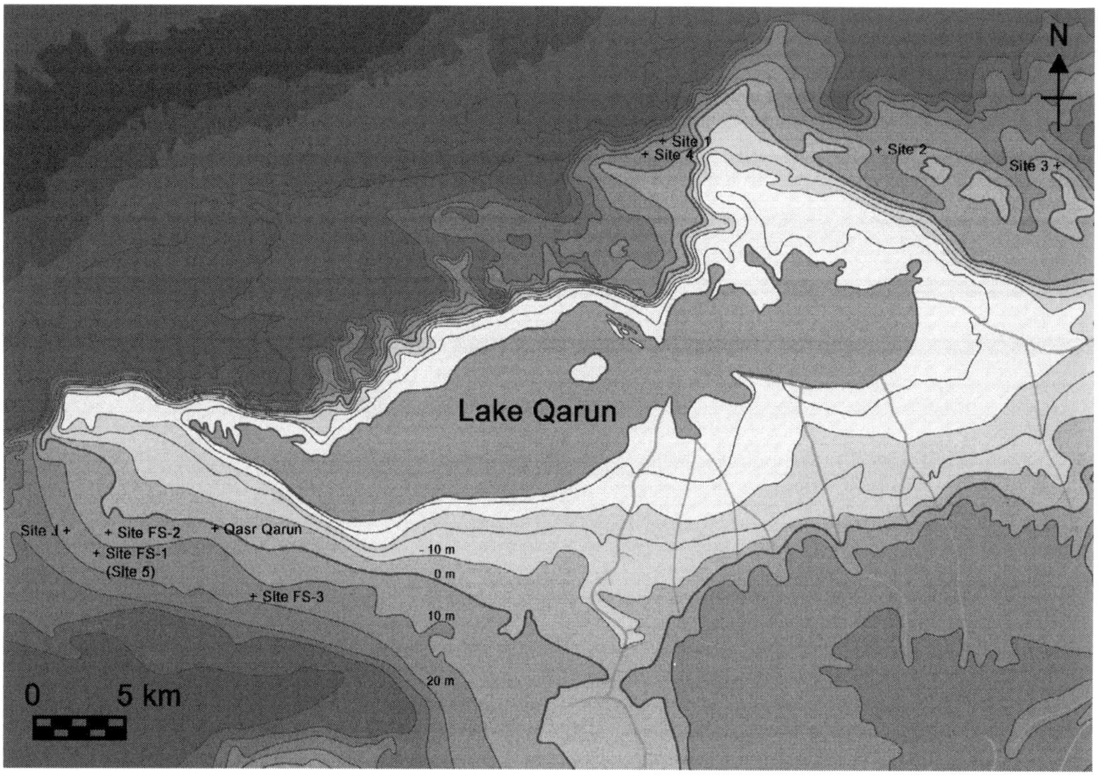

Fig.3.5. Map of Wenke's and Brewer's sites on the northern and southern shores of Lake Qarun

faunal remains and artefacts at Site FS-1, which was dated to the Neolithic, at Site FS-2, which was dated to the Epipalaeolithic, and at Site FS-3, which was dated to the Predynastic (Wenke 1984; Wenke *et al.* 1983) (**Fig.3.5**).

It was reported that in both the Epipalaeolithic and Neolithic periods, massive quantities of fish as well as mammals and waterfowl had been exploited, and that the exploited species had been almost the same in Epipalaeolithic and Neolithic sites. As for the use of domesticates in the Neolithic period, the evidence was scarce. Small quantities of domesticated cattle, sheep and goats indicated that these animals played a minor role in subsistence. Like previous investigations, they also could not find evidence for substantial dwellings in either period. In the end, they reached the same conclusion as their predecessors, that there was no direct cultural relationship between Epipalaeolithic and Neolithic inhabitants of the Fayum, and that it was difficult to trace a gradual change of subsistence besides the sudden addition of domesticates in the Neolithic period. Their theoretically-oriented investigation is remarkable, but their research was suspended, and their final report remains to be published. They did not answer clearly the questions they raised above, even though they discussed several possible reasons for the disruption between the Epipalaeolithic and Neolithic periods, and suggested several possible places of origin of the Fayum Neolithic (Wenke *et al.* 1988; Wenke and Casini 1989; Wenke and Brewer 1992).

Hassan, who was a geoarchaeologist in Wenke's team, published a reconstruction of lake level fluctuations in the Holocene, based mainly on the data obtained from the southwest side of the lake (Hassan 1986b). However, his reconstruction is even more schematic than those by the Combined Prehistoric Expedition and the Polish-German team mentioned earlier. The only agreement between these three different reconstructions is a remarkable drop of lake level around 6000-5800 cal.BC. Therefore, it is not easy to understand precisely the long-term pattern of lake level fluctuations. Hassan's reconstruction of lake level fluctuations was recently reviewed and visualised through his new research in the Fayum, but there is no considerable modification to his previous reconstruction (Hassan *et al.* 2006).

A field survey which had especially focused on faunal remains on the surface was carried out by the zooarchaeologist Brewer in the late 1980s (Brewer 1989a; 1989b). Prehistoric faunal remains in the Fayum have long been a neglected area of study since Caton-Thompson briefly mentioned the discovery of the bones of pig, sheep or goat, ox, hippopotamus, canine, crocodile, turtle and Nile perch at Kom W (Caton-Thompson and Gardner 1934: 34). Faunal remains were also studied by a zooarchaeologist of the Combined Prehistoric Expedition (Gautier 1976b), but the sample studied was very small, and fish remains were not published. Brewer's research was more comprehensive in terms of the wider area coverage and the study of fish as well as terrestrial animals.

Brewer's survey was conducted independently on the north side of the lake and partially in cooperation with Wenke's team on the southwest side of the lake. Brewer studied five sites named Site 1 to Site 5, including four sites (Site 1 to Site 4) on the north side of the lake and one site (Site 5) on the southwest side of the lake (**Fig.3.5**). Site 4 in the N Basin is identical to Caton-Thompson's Site T which had been investigated by one of Wenke's associates but had not been published. Site 5 is identical to Wenke's Site FS-1 which had already been surface-collected. Therefore, faunal remains from Site 4 and Site 5 were used only in a supportive role. Site 3 at the northern margin of the K Basin yielded a very small sample. On the other hand, Site 1, which is identical to Caton-Thompson's Site R and the Combined Prehistoric Expedition's Site E29G3 at the northern margin of the N Basin and is dated to the Neolithic, and Site 2, which seems to be identical to the southernmost part of Caton-Thompson's Site V and is dated to the Epipalaeolithic, yielded a considerable number of faunal remains for a substantial analysis. Brewer revealed that fishing was the dominant subsistence activity throughout the Fayum Epipalaeolithic and Neolithic periods, and that both Epipalaeolithic and Neolithic people exploited the same species of fish and migratory waterfowl in similar relative abundances, using similar strategies during the same time of year. Considerable differences in lithic technology between the Fayum Epipalaeolithic and Neolithic despite the similar exploitative strategies for wild food resources in these two cultural groups made him agree with the idea suggested by Wendorf and Schild that the Fayum Neolithic represented an immigrant group possessing different cultural affinities than the Fayum Epipalaeolithic inhabitants (Brewer 1989b: 170).

Except for a short survey at three locations in the rocky and gravely terrains of the Fayum Depression for a lithic sourcing study along with an analysis of lithic artefacts which were surface-collected at Wenke's Site FS-1 and Site FS-2 on the southwest side of the lake by one of Wenke's associates in the early 1990s (Cagle 1994), archaeological field research that focuses on the prehistory of the Fayum has not been conducted in the last decade. Some excellent summaries of the prehistory of the Fayum have been published (*e.g.*, Hendrickx and Vermeersch 2000; Midant-Reynes 2000; Wetterstrom 1993), but many questions have remained unanswered.

3.4. Holocene chronology and cultures of the Fayum

As mentioned, early investigators had already recognised that bifacial stone tools collected on the desert surface in the Fayum should be dated to the Neolithic period by analogy with the stone tools of the European stone age. However, it was not until the 1960s that radiocarbon dating in combination with stratigraphy was applied to the Fayum materials. Since then, the chronology and cultural development of prehistoric Fayum have been revised.

It must be stressed that Caton-Thompson's definition of the Fayum Neolithic A and B cultures is no longer valid, though still in use in many general books. The sequence of Early-Middle Holocene cultures in the Fayum is presently understood as; 1) the Qarunian (Fayum Epipalaeolithic), 2) the Fayumian (early Fayum Neolithic), and 3) the Moerian (late Fayum Neolithic), and 4) the Fayum Predynastic. It has been argued that the Fayumian should be regarded as the period when the first manifestation of a farming-herding culture appeared in Egypt, and that there was a hiatus between each period and no cultural connection with each other. Therefore, the emergence of each culture has generally been explained as the arrival of a new population caused by environmental amelioration in the Fayum, or desiccation in its surroundings, and the main focus of study has been on the ultimate origin of each culture. In the following, the features and radiocarbon dates of each culture are summarised.

3.4.1. The Qarunian

Qarunian sites have been located on the southwest side of the lake as well as on the north side of the lake. There are relatively many sites which are exclusively attributed to this culture, but some other sites which yielded the artefacts of the Qarunian also yielded the artefacts of later cultures. The elevation of Qarunian sites or the sites which yielded Qarunian artefacts ranges from approximately 5 m asl to 20 m asl. Qarunian sites have generally been reported as surface scatters of artefacts and animal/fish bone fragments, but the spatial extent and density of the artefact scatters are not equal between sites.

Among the sites on the north side of the lake, Site E29H1 in the X Basin exhibits a vast scatter of Epipalaeolithic artefacts on the gently sloping expanse of lacustrine sediments and occupies an elongated oval area of approximately 300 m by 100 m and of 15-17 m asl, overlain by a larger oval area of Neolithic artefact scatters. Site E29H1 seems to be the largest single scatter of Epipalaeolithic artefacts in the Fayum. Within the elongated oval area, Epipalaeolithic artifacts have been excavated *in situ* in small portions named Areas A and C, and surface-collected in Area B (Wendorf and Schild 1976: 182-199).

Site E29G1 (Caton-Thompson's Site ZI) on the east side of Moeris Bay comprises more than six artifact concentrations of around 20 m in diameter, which have been named Areas A to F respectively. The site occupies an area of approximately 700 m long and 120 m wide in total on the east slope of two deflated basins, and its elevation ranges from 10 m to 19 m asl. While Area D at high elevation exhibits a surface scatter of Neolithic artifacts, Epipalaeolithic artifacts have been excavated *in situ* in Areas A, B, E and F. An isolated human burial, which was supposed to be dated to the Epipalaeolithic, has been found near Area C (Henneberg *et al.* 1989; Wendorf and Schild 1976: 162-182). Site E29G3 (Caton-Thompson's Site R) in the N Basin exhibits a scatter of Epipalaeolithic artifacts on an eroded area of approximately 30 m in diameter and 10 m asl surrounded by a rock-capped L-shaped mound, which has been named Area A. Epipalaeolithic artifacts have been excavated *in situ* in Area A (Wendorf and Schild 1976: 199-208).

More sites on the north side of the lake include Site S4 (Caton-Thompson's Site Z) in the north of the Z Basin, Site MOE (Caton-Thompson's Moeris I) in the south of the Z Basin, and Site MB (Caton-Thompson's Site ZI, and Combined Prehistoric Expedition's Site E29G1) on the east side of Moeris Bay. A considerable number of Epipalaeolithic lithic artefacts were surface-collected at these sites (Mussi *et al.* 1984).

In contrast to the situation on the north side of the lake, only one site named Site FS-2 has been known on the southwest side of the lake. Site FS-2 is an area of vast artefact scatter at lower elevations of below 10 m asl on the gentle slope of lakeshore, and is separated from an area of Neolithic artefact scatter named Site FS-1 at higher elevations by a broad beach ridge. Site FS-2 covers the area of 600 m x 1200 m, but the density of surface artefacts and other archaeological remains in this entire area is not clear from the incomplete publications. According to the publications, the surface of Site FS-2 is less severely deflated and hence better preserved than that of Site FS-1, but no structural remains have been found. An isolated human burial, which was supposed to be dated to the Epipalaeolithic, has been discovered in one excavation square of Site FS-2 (Wenke *et al.* 1983; 1988).

Although poorly published by the Combined Prehistoric Expedition, the lithic artefacts collected at Site E29G1, Site E29G3 and Site E29H1 are characterised by a very high frequency of various backed bladelets. It has been claimed that the lithic artefacts collected by Puglisi at Site S4, Site MOE and Site MB were different from those found at Site E29G1, Site E29G3 and Site E29H1 in terms of the tool type frequency. It has been supposed that the observed differences might reflect a different chronological position or a different range of tool-using activities (Mussi *et al.* 1984: 189). On the other hand, it has been argued that the Qarunian stone tool inventory has many features in common with those of the contemporaneous cultures in the Western Desert of Egypt but there are differences in tool type frequencies. Such differences are said to be because the Qarunian was especially adapted to the exploitation of lacustrine resources (Wenke *et al.* 1988: 37).

It has been revealed that the preferred lithic raw material utilised in Qarunian sites was small, rounded pebbles from the Oligocene conglomerate of the Gebel Qatrani Formation, which was extensively exposed on the plateau above Qasr el-Sagha (Wendorf and Schild 1976: 311). For the people who resided in the N Basin, this source area is certainly within an easy walking distance. However, it is far away from the Z Basin and X Basin, and no convincing evidence for the utilisation of the Gebel Qatrani pebbles by the people who resided at Site E29H1 in the X Basin has been provided. The Qarunian lithic artefacts will be described and discussed in more detail in Chapter 6.

The Qarunian has simple bone projectile points, but has no ground stone tools and no pottery vessels (Wenke *et al.* 1988: 34-38; Wendorf and Schild 1976: 311-319). A considerable amount of faunal remains has been found at Brewer's Site 2 and Wenke's Site FS-2. The faunal data strongly suggest that Qarunian people were mobile hunter-fishers particularly relying on fishing. On the other hand, there is scarce evidence of their exploitation of wild plants (Wetterstrom 1993: 186-191). The ecology and subsistence of the Qarunian will be described below in more detail.

As for the radiocarbon dates of the Qarunian, the following dates have been obtained from several sites. Most of the dated samples are charcoal, except for I-4129 which is said to be burnt shell, and Beta-4180 which is said to be bone. They have been calibrated by using the calibration curve available at that time and published (Hassan 1986b: 487*ff*; 1988: table II; Hendrickx 1999: 34; Pazdur 1983: table 18; Wendorf and Schild 1976: 162-207; Wenke *et al.* 1983: table 1). Based on the dates, the time span of the Qarunian has previously been understood as 7100-6000 cal.BC (Hassan 1988: 142-143 and fig.2). These dates can be re-calibrated by using the latest calibration software OxCal ver.4.0 (Bronk Lamsey 1995; 2001) (**Table 3.1**).

Taking the 95.4 % probability (2 sigma), the possible latest date of the Qarunian is 5749 cal.BC on the sample I-4129. However, as mentioned above, this sample is burnt shell. It is well known that shell is a problematic material for radiocarbon dating, and that it can provide too old radiocarbon ages due to reservoir effects and/or carbon isotope fractionation (Rapp and Hill 1998: 166-168). Therefore, it is highly probable that the calibrated age estimate of the sample I-4129 is wrong. It is safe to take the second latest calibrated date on charcoal (I-4130) and to presume that the time span of the Qarunian is approximately 7530-6090 cal.BC.

3.4.2. The Fayumian

Fayumian sites have also been located on the southwest side of the lake as well as the northeast side of the lake. There are only a few sites which are exclusively attributed to this culture, and

Site E29H1, Area A, Trench 1, layer 2	**8070±115 BP (I-4126)**	7347 cal.BC (95.4%) 6656 cal.BC	OxCal <IntCal04>
Site E29G1, Area A, Trench 1, layer 3	**8100±130 BP (I-4128)**	7382 cal.BC (91.8%) 6684 cal.BC	OxCal <IntCal04>
Site E29G1, Area E, Trench 4, layer 2	**7140±120 BP (I-4129)**	6238 cal.BC (95.4%) 5749 cal.BC	OxCal <IntCal04>
Site E29G3, Area A, Trench 5	**7500±125 BP (I-4130)**	6592 cal.BC (95.4%) 6094 cal.BC	OxCal <IntCal04>
Site QS II/79, Hearth No.2	**7440±60 BP (Bln-2336)**	6438 cal.BC (95.4%) 6213 cal.BC	OxCal <IntCal04>
Site FS-2, TS-8, level 2	**8220±105 BP (Beta-4871)**	7531 cal.BC (95.2%) 7031 cal.BC	OxCal <IntCal04>
Site FS-2, TS-12, level 4	**7720±70 BP (Beta-4872)**	6680 cal.BC (95.4%) 6441 cal.BC	OxCal <IntCal04>
Site FS-2	**7600±70 BP (Beta-4180)**	6600 cal.BC (91.8%) 6352 cal.BC	OxCal <IntCal04>

Table 3.1. Radiocarbon dates of the Qarunian

many other sites which yielded the artefacts of the Fayumian often yielded the artefacts of earlier or later cultures as well. The elevation of Fayumian sites or the sites which yielded Fayumian artefacts ranges from approximately 13 m asl to 20 m asl.

The largest habitation site of the Fayumian is Kom W, which is a low, oval mound of approximately 90 m by 150 m, and its top elevation is approximately 22 m asl (**Fig.3.6**). Its cultural deposit was 1.5 m thick at most beneath the surface and was not well stratified. Hundreds of fireholes and a variety of artefacts were excavated in high density, but the artefacts were uniform from the top to bottom of the deposit (Caton-Thompson and Gardner 1934: 22-25). A similar habitation site is Kom K, which is also a low, oval mound of approximately 50 m by 80 m, and its top elevation is approximately 20 m asl (**Fig.3.7**). Its cultural deposit was only 30 cm think beneath the surface. Kom K was not thoroughly excavated, and hence only 16 fireholes were found. The artefacts found at Kom K are quite similar to those at Kom W (Caton-Thompson and Gardner 1934: 37-41). No substantial dwellings have been found at these Kom sites, and thus scholars have been reluctant to call them sedentary settlements and have assumed that they were more than just seasonal encampments (Hassan 1988: 149-150; Wenke *et al.* 1988: 44*ff*). It remains uncertain whether Fayumian people were sedentary. In the neighbourhood of Kom K, a cluster of pits containing grains of domesticated wheat and barley at the Upper and Lower K Pits were located, and one pit contained a complete sickle (Caton-Thompson and Gardner 1934: 41-54 and pls.XXIV-XXXI). The grains and the sickle are the most obvious evidence for farming in the Fayum. Grains of domesticated wheat and barley have not been found at any other Fayumian sites so far.

By contrast, most of the other sites on the east side of Moeris Bay have been reported as scatters of stone tools, pottery sherds and animal/fish bone fragments on the deflated plain desert surface and as not exhibiting features like mounds of cultural deposits. However, their spatial extent tends to be comparable to or wider than Kom W. For instance, Caton-Thompson's Site X is located on the west side of a wadi mouth draining to the X Basin and seems to occupy an area of approximately 300 m in diameter at elevations from 15 m to 18 m asl. It was littered with stone tools and grinding stones, but no structural remains like hearths or pits were found (Caton-Thompson and Gardner 1934: 74-75). Caton-Thompson's Site V is located on a peninsula-like natural mound of approximately 17 m asl and seems to occupy an elongated area of approximately 200 m x 400 m. It was strewn with pottery sherds and ostrich eggshell chips, and some sunken pottery vessels *in situ* were found, but no structural remains like hearths were noted (Caton-Thompson and Gardner 1934: 75-76).

The conditions of surface sites seem to be almost the same on the west side of Moeris Bay. Site E29G3 Area B is approximately 80 m to the west of an Epipalaeolithic site named Site E29G3 Area A. The Area B occupies a roughly oval area of approximately 100 m x 60 m at elevations from 13 m to 15 m asl, and exhibits an extensive concentration of Neolithic lithic

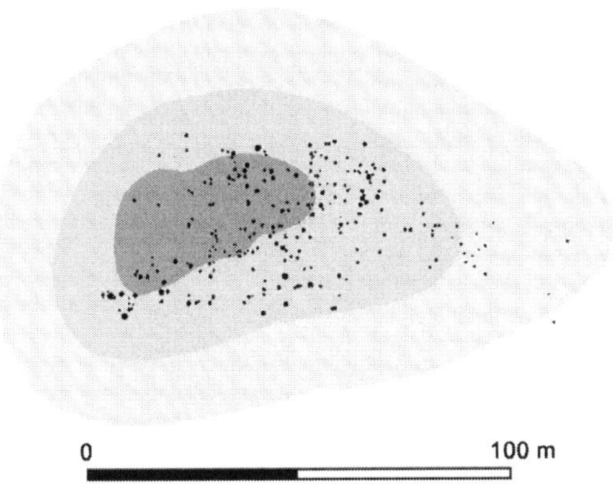

Fig.3.6. Kom W (Black dots indicate fireholes. The vertical interval is 1.8 m)

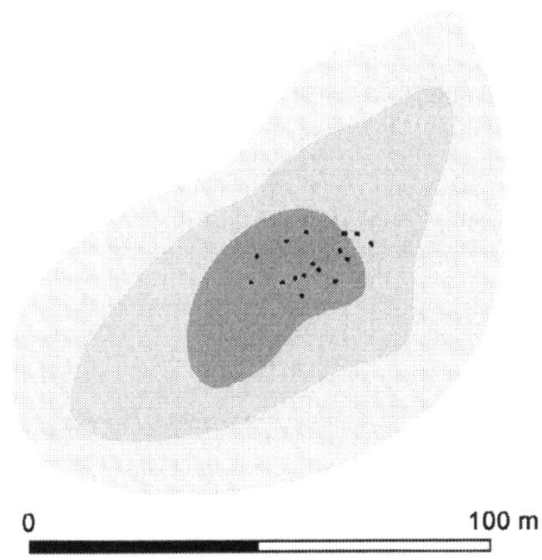

Fig.3.7. Kom K (Black dots indicate fireholes. The vertical interval is 0.6 m)

artefacts, pottery sherds and bone fragments as well as at least 17 hearths in two or three clusters on the deflated surface (Wendorf and Schild 1976: 199-211). Site QS I/79, Site QS V/79, Site QS IX/81, Site QS X/81 and Site QS XI/81 are all located in the neighbourhood of Site E29G3 in the N Basin at the foot of the Qasr el-Sagha escarpment, and their elevation is approximately 14-16 m asl. These sites were exposed in excavation trenches and were marked by the presence of hearths accompanied by lithic artefacts, pottery sherds and animal/fish bones and their fragments, but the spatial extent of individual sites is not clear due to the limited scale of excavations. There is no evidence for farming activities, whereas domesticated sheep and goats were certainly present (Dagnan-Ginter *et al.* 1984; Ginter and Kozlowski 1986: 14-19; Ginter *et al.* 1980; Kozlowski and Ginter 1989: 163*ff*).

Site FS-1 is the sole Neolithic site known on the southwest side of the lake. It was an area of vast artefact scatter at higher elevations of above 14 m asl on the gentle slope of the lakeshore, and was separated from an area of Epipalaeolithic artefact scatter named Site FS-2 at lower elevations by a broad beach ridge. Site FS-1 covers an area of 900 m x 1100 m, and the spatial distribution of surface artefacts like grinding stones, sickle blades, projectile points and pottery sherds in this entire area was made clear by an intensive transect survey. According to the publications, the surface of Site FS-1 was severely deflated. However, in some areas, the surface was littered with tiny, fragile fish bone fragments, and lithic artefacts and stone-built hearths with ash and charcoal were found embedded in diatomaceous lake sediments. Furthermore, the surface exhibited several remarkable artefact concentrations, and these were interpreted as residential areas, cereal processing areas, and hunting areas (Wenke *et al.* 1983; 1988).

The appearance of bifacially-retouched, formal flint tools like axes, serrated sickle blades and concave-based arrowheads is a hallmark of the Fayumian culture. While it has been described by Caton-Thompson that bifacially-retouched, formal flint tools were predominant in the Fayum Neolithic, it has been argued later that such tools were minor components of the Fayum Neolithic lithic assemblage and that the majority of lithic artefacts were actually crude flake tools (Kozlowski and Ginter 1989: 170-173). Nevertheless, bifacially-retouched, formal flint tools are certainly characteristics of the Fayumian culture, and they are quite distinct from the preceding Qarunian lithic artefacts in terms of raw material use, knapping and retouching techniques, and tool size and morphology.

Besides flint tools, bone tools were also used.

In addition to simple bone projectile points, double-pointed ones which seem to be used as bevelled self-barbed projectile points, and bone harpoons with several barbs are included in the findings (Caton-Thompson and Gardner 1934: 22, 33, 78, pls.XII and XLVII). They show a remarkable development from Epipalaeolithic bone tools. It is evident from the tool inventory and faunal assemblages that Fayumian people still relied heavily on hunting and fishing. The ecology and subsistence of the Fayumian will be described below in more detail.

The appearance of pottery vessels is another hallmark of the Fayumian culture. The pottery is made from local clay and shale, and fibre-tempered. It is handmade and is usually very thick. The rims are simple and direct, and the bases are flat or rounded. Hemispherical bowls and tall bag-shaped jars are the most common pottery types at Kom K, Kom W and the K Pits, and flat plates and miniature vessels with pedestals are also noticeable. No pottery with incised or painted decoration has been found, though a limited number of pieces were red-slipped and burnished (Caton-Thompson and Gardner 1934: 35-37, 41, 44-45 and pls.XIII-XX). It is argued that the pottery from Site E29G3 Area B is not identical to that excavated at Kom K and Kom W because the pottery vessels are small and sand-tempered (Wendorf and Schild 1976: 199), whereas another study of pottery sherds collected in the N Basin area revealed that the mineral composition of the fabric and the method and temperature of firing were various though the basic shapes of vessels were similar to those at Kom K, Kom W and the K Pits (Kozlowski and Ginter 1989: 166).

The appearance of grinding stones and grinders is a further hallmark of the Fayumian culture. It has been reported that many of these found at Kom W were made of limestone and grit. There is no detailed description of the morphology of grinding stones, but it seems that one face of a large slab is usually depressed due to heavy use (Caton-Thompson and Gardner 1934: 31-32 and pl.VII). Similar grinding stones and grinders seem to have been found sporadically at surface sites around the Z Basin and in the N Basin on the northern shore, and they were numerous at Site FS-1 on the southwestern shore (Caton-Thompson and Gardner 1934: 71-86; Wenke *et al.*, 1983: 27*ff*; 1988: 39-40). Although grinding stones have not been found in association with any plant remains, grinding stones tend to be associated with cereal processing (Wenke *et al.*, 1988: 39).

The appearance of non-local material items is also noticeable in the Fayumian culture. Caton-Thompson has described various material items and their possible sources. Particularly exotic materials include diorite from Nubia, which was used for making axes and palettes, feldspar from the Eastern Desert, which was used for making beads, unworked turquoise pebble from Sinai, and marine shells from the Red Sea and Mediterranean Sea, which were used as ornaments (Caton-Thompson and Gardner 1934: 87-88). They suggest that long distance exchange/trade networks developed in this period. Other raw materials which were commonly used by Fayum Neolithic people and were said to be local by Caton-Thompson include dolerite, flint, grit, petrified wood, limestone, and volcanic ash (Caton-Thompson and Gardner 1934: 87). However, these materials actually occur in the gravelly and rocky terrains in the periphery of the Fayum Depression. Hence it is certain that the Fayum Neolithic people who resided in the sites near former lakeshores had to walk a distance of 10-40 km to procure these materials. The Neolithic people's effort to procure raw materials from distant source areas shows a sharp contrast to the behaviour of Epipalaeolithic people, who did not leave clear evidence for long distance trips and exchange/trade networks.

As for the radiocarbon dates of the Fayumian, the following dates have been obtained from several sites, excluding the dates which contain the uncertainty of more than ±200 radiocarbon years. The dated samples are all charcoal, except for C-550 which is said to be grain. They have been calibrated by using the calibration curve available at that time and published (Hassan 1985: table 1; 1986b: table 1; Hendrickx 1999: 58-59; Pazdur 1983: table 18; Wendorf and

Upper K Pit 59	**6391±180 BP (C-550)**	5666 cal.BC (95.4%) 4935 cal.BC	OxCal <IntCal04>
Site E29H2 (Kom W), Trench 1, layer 4	**5810±115 BP (I-4127)**	4946 cal.BC (93.8%) 4444 cal.BC	OxCal <IntCal04>
Site E29G3, Area B, Trench 4, layer 2	**5860±115 BP (I-4131)**	5006 cal.BC (95.4%) 4457 cal.BC	OxCal <IntCal04>
Site QS I/79, sandy layer 1.45-1.50 m	**5555±60 BP (Bln-2333)**	4520 cal.BC (93.7%) 4325 cal.BC	OxCal <IntCal04>
Site QS I/79, sandy layer 1.70-1.75 m	**5540±70 BP (Gd-1140)**	4526 cal.BC (95.4%) 4258 cal.BC	OxCal <IntCal04>
Site QS I/79, sandy layer 1.75-1.85 m	**5645±55 BP (Bln-2334)**	4606 cal.BC (95.4%) 4355 cal.BC	OxCal <IntCal04>
Site QS V/79, Hearth No.1/AB/47	**5990±60 BP (Gd-693)**	5021 cal.BC (95.4%) 4726 cal.BC	OxCal <IntCal04>
Site QS IX/81, Hearth No.1	**6380±60 BP (Gd-1499)**	5476 cal.BC (88.4%) 5291 cal.BC	OxCal <IntCal04>
Site QS X/81, Hearth No.1	**6320±60 BP (Gd-1497)**	5472 cal.BC (94.1%) 5206 cal.BC	OxCal <IntCal04>
Site QS X/81, Hearth No.2	**6290±100 BP (Gd-979)**	5474 cal.BC (95.4%) 5022 cal.BC	OxCal <IntCal04>
Site QS X/81, Hearth No.5	**6290±110 BP (Gd-980)**	5478 cal.BC (95.4%) 4998 cal.BC	OxCal <IntCal04>
Site QS XI/81, Hearth No.2	**6480±170 BP (Gd-2021)**	5722 cal.BC (95.4%) 5056 cal.BC	OxCal <IntCal04>

Table 3.2. Radiocarbon dates of the Fayumian

Schild 1976: 199-213). Based on these dates, the time span of the Fayumian has been understood as either 5200-4500 cal.BC (Hassan 1985: 105-106; 1988: 141 and fig.2) or 5400-4400 cal.BC (Hendrickx 1999: 18). These dates can be re-calibrated by using the latest calibration software OxCal ver.4.0 (**Table 3.2**).

Taking the 95.4 % probability (2 sigma), the earliest possible date of the Fayumian is 5722 cal.BC on the sample Gd-2021 or 5666 cal.BC on the sample C-550. However, these calibrated dates contain great uncertainty, and thus it may be safe to take the third earliest calibrated date (5478 cal.BC) on the sample of Gd-980 and to assume that the possible time span of the Fayumian is approximately 5480-4260 cal.BC. The sample C-550 is actually the earliest dated evidence for farming in the Fayum, but because of its great uncertainty, exactly when the first attempt at farming started during the possible time span of the Fayumian remains a big question. It may be natural to suppose that farming started at the beginning of the Fayumian occupation in the second half of the 6th millennium cal.BC, but it is also possible that the advent of farming was earlier or later than the beginning of the Fayumian occupation.

3.4.3. The Moerian

The sites which are exclusively attributed to the Moerian have been located mainly around the N Basin at the foot of the Qasr el-Sagha escarpment on the north side of the lake, and are represented by Site QS VID/80, Site QS VIE/80, Site QS VIIA/80, and QS XII/81. Their elevation is approximately 16-18 m asl. Site QS VID/80 and Site QS VIE/80 have only a single stone-built hearth respectively. Site QS VIIA/80 covers an area of 14 m x 8 m, having several hearths and a scatter of postholes that must be the remains of windbreaks, and Site QS XII/81 covers a small, partially damaged area of approximately 2 m x 3 m, having some patches of charcoal and ash and a scatter of lithic artefacts, pottery sherds and fish/animal bone fragments (Dagnan-Ginter *et al.* 1984: 60-65; Ginter and Kozlowski 1983: 38-43). However, there is no evidence of more substantial dwellings in these sites. There is also no evidence of farming and scarce evidence of sheep/goat herding. Faunal remains suggest that fishing was the major subsistence. Therefore, Moerian people are thought to have been mobile hunter-fishers (Ginter and Kozlowski 1986: 19-22; Kozlowski and Ginter 1989: 166-169; Wetterstrom 1993: 211). Apart from the N Basin area, the sporadic occurrence of Moerian artefacts has been claimed at Kom W (Kozlowski and Ginter 1989: 174).

The Moerian has been defined as the later phase of the Fayum Neolithic, based on stratigraphic sequence and radiocarbon dates. The Moerian culture is characterised by the predominance of blade technology. The most numerous are backed blades, micro-retouched blades and bladelets, retouched blades and perforators, whereas there are few scrapers,

Site E29G3	**5160±110 BP(I-3469)**	4242 cal.BC (95.4%) 3708 cal.BC	OxCal <IntCal04>
Site QS VID/80, Hearth No.1	**5410±110 BP(Gd-903)**	4454 cal.BC (92.2%) 4032 cal.BC	OxCal <IntCal04>
Site QS VIE/80, Hearth	**5650±70 BP(Gd-1495)**	4620 cal.BC (90.4%) 4352 cal.BC	OxCal <IntCal04>
Site QS VIIA/80, Hearth No.5	**5070±110 BP(Gd-895)**	4071 cal.BC (93.1%) 3641 cal.BC	OxCal <IntCal04>
Site QS VIIA/80, Hearth No.5	**5160±110 BP(Gd-915)**	4242 cal.BC (95.4%) 3708 cal.BC	OxCal <IntCal04>
Site QS VIIA/80	**5080±110 BP(Gd-916)**	4072 cal.BC (92.1%) 3646 cal.BC	OxCal <IntCal04>
Site QS VIIA/80, locus 6	**5160±110 BP(Gd-917)**	4242 cal.BC (95.4%) 3708 cal.BC	OxCal <IntCal04>
Site QS VIIA/80, locus 6	**5080±110 BP(Gd-918)**	4072 cal.BC (92.1%) 3646 cal.BC	OxCal <IntCal04>
Site QS VIIA/80	**5480±100 BP(Gd-977)**	4504 cal.BC (95.0%) 4050 cal.BC	OxCal <IntCal04>
Site QS VIIA/81	**5000±60 BP(Gd-1496)**	3948 cal.BC (90.8%) 3692 cal.BC	OxCal <IntCal04>
Site QS X/81, Hearth No.6	**5330±100 BP(Gd-978)**	4349 cal.BC (95.4%) 3966 cal.BC	OxCal <IntCal04>

Table 3.3. Radiocarbon dates of the Moerian

notched and denticulated tools, and bifacial tools. On the basis of this lithic assemblage, it has been argued that the Moerian people would have been immigrants who retained the Epipalaeolithic tradition in the Western Desert (Ginter and Kozlowski 1983: 70; Kozlowski and Ginter 1989: 176). However, such a lithic assemblage is common in a contemporaneous Predynastic culture known at Maadi and Buto in Lower Egypt, and hence it seems better to assume that the Moerian also exhibits a similar line of the development of lithic technology, and that the Moerian is included in the Maadi-Buto culture (Schmidt 1993: 273).

Moerian pottery was made from local clay and shale, and had fibre and sand temper. Pottery vessels are represented by a variety of types including hemispherical bowls with rounded walls, vessels with hemispherical and spherical bellies and everted rims, S-profile vessels, pots with cylindrical necks and everted or thickened rims, deep vessels with rounded bottoms, and vessels with conical bottoms (Ginter and Kozlowski 1983: 53-67; Kozlowski and Ginter 1989: 169).

As for the radiocarbon dates of the Moerian, the following dates have been obtained from several sites, excluding the dates which contain the uncertainty of more than ±200 radiocarbon years. Since Site QS VIIA/80 gave a stratigraphic sequence and provided the richest artefacts and samples for radiocarbon dating, the time span of the Moerian has been based on this site. The dated samples are all charcoal. They have been calibrated by using the latest calibration curve available at that time and published (Hassan 1985: table 1; 1986b: table 1; Hendrickx 1999: 59-60; Pazdur 1983: table 18; Wendorf and Schild 1976: 199-213; Wenke *et al.* 1983: table 1). Based on these dates, the time span of the Moerian has been understood as either 4300-4000 cal.BC (Hassan 1985: 105-106; 1988: 141 and fig.2) or 4500-3800 cal.BC (Hendrickx 1999: 18). These dates can be re-calibrated by using the latest calibration software OxCal ver.4.0 (**Table 3.3**).

Taking the 95.4 % probability (2 sigma), the possible latest date of the Moerian at Site QS VIIA/80 is 3641 cal.BC on the sample of Gd-895, and the possible time span of the Moerian is approximately 4620-3640 cal.BC.

3.4.4. The Fayum Predynastic

Caton-Thompson found that lithic artefacts of the Nile Valley Predynastic type were distributed over the north and southwest sides of the lake, though in fairly small numbers. Sporadic occurrences of Predynastic artefacts have been reported at Kom K, Site L, Site V and Camp II (Caton-Thompson and Gardner 1934: 38 and 73-77). She roughly dated the most substantial lithic and pottery assemblage at Qasr Qarun on the southwest side of the lake to the Predynastic, based on the similarity to the finds from Predynastic sites at Maadi in Lower Egypt and Badari in Middle Egypt (Caton-Thompson and Gardner 1934: 69-71). Sparse scatters of Predynastic artefacts have been recognised by later researchers at sites like Wenke's Site FS-3

Site FS-1	**5160±70 BP (Beta-4181)**	4080 cal.BC (86.6%) 3785 cal.BC	OxCal <IntCal04>
Site FS-3	**4960±160 BP (Beta-4182)**	4070 cal.BC (88.6%) 3484 cal.BC	OxCal <IntCal04>
Site QS VIIG/80, Hearth No.2	**5120±110 BP (Gd-874)**	4175 cal.BC (91.6%) 3694 cal.BC	OxCal <IntCal04>
Site QS VIII/80, Trench 1, 250-255cm	**5010±120 BP (Gd-904)**	4052 cal.BC (92.4%) 3626 cal.BC	OxCal <IntCal04>
Site QS VIIA/81	**4820±100 BP (Gd-976)**	3800 cal.BC (94.8%) 3366 cal.BC	OxCal <IntCal04>
Site QS VIIA/81	**4580±180 BP (Gd-973)**	3711 cal.BC (95.4%) 2878 cal.BC	OxCal <IntCal04>

Table 3.4. Radiocarbon dates of the Fayum Predynastic

on the southwest side of the lake and the Combined Prehistoric Expedition's Site E29G4 in the N Basin on the north side of the lake (Wendorf and Schild 1976: 215-216; Wenke and Brewer 1992). Site QS VIIG/80, Site QS VIII/80 and Site QS VIIA/81 were exposed in excavation trenches in the N Basin, but the artefacts were generally scarce and hence the site function was unclear (Kozlowski 1983).

Due to the scarcity of diagnostic artefacts, the association of the Fayum Predynastic with a specific cultural group in the Nile Valley remains uncertain (Kozlowski 1983: 79). Although Caton-Thompson had initially argued that the pottery vessels of the Fayum Predynastic were comparable to those of the Maadi Predynastic (Caton-Thompson and Gardner 1934: 70-71), it was reconsidered on the basis of differences between the pottery vessels of these two cultures that the Fayum Predynastic might rather be associated with the Naqada culture of Middle and Upper Egypt (Rizkana and Seeher 1987: 61). An U-shaped fishtail flint blade seen in the Qasr Qarun assemblage (Caton-Thompson and Gardner 1934: pl.LIII-34) is a typical item in the Naqada culture (Holmes 1989: 408-412), and its rarity in the Fayum and Maadi suggests that it derived from Middle and Upper Egypt (Schmidt 1993: 272; Watrin 2003: 568). Considering that the Fayum is located in the border between Upper Egypt and Lower Egypt and that the cultural contacts between these two regions gradually increased in the 4th millennium cal.BC (Guyot 2008; Watrin 2003), it is not easy to associate the poor data of the Fayum Predynastic with either the Maadi culture or the Naqada culture. It would suffice to say that people have continually inhabited the Fayum after the Neolithic.

As for the radiocarbon dates of the Fayum Predynastic, only a few dates have been obtained from limited areas of the Fayum. The dated samples are all charcoal. They have been calibrated by using the latest calibration curve available at that time and published (Hassan 1985: table 1; Hendrickx 1999: 59-60; Pazdur 1983: table 18; Wendorf and Schild 1976: 199-213; Wenke *et al.* 1983: table 1). These dates can be re-calibrated by using the latest calibration software OxCal ver.4.0 (**Table 3.4**).

Taking the 95.4 % probability (2 sigma), the possible earliest date of the Fayum Predynastic is 4175 cal.BC on the sample Gd-874. The latest date of the Fayum Predynastic is 2878 cal.BC on the sample of Gd-973. However, this calibrated date contains great uncertainty, and thus it may be safe to take the second latest calibrated date (Gd-976) and to presume that the latest date is 3366 cal.BC. The possible time span of the Fayum Predynastic is thus approximately 4170-3360 cal.BC. It has been suggested that the Moerian and Fayum Predynastic cultures were partially contemporaneous (Kozlowski 1983: 76), but this sounds fairly unlikely. Given a poor understanding of these two cultures, it seems more probable that these two cultures were actually a single culture and different aspects of a single culture were misinterpreted.

Based on the data presented, the Early-Middle Holocene chronology of the Fayum is summarised as follows (**Fig.3.8**);

Qarunian (Fayum Epipalaeolithic):
ca. 7530-6090 cal.BC
Fayumian (Fayum Neolithic):
ca. 5480-4260 cal.BC
Moerian (Fayum Predynastic):
ca. 4170-3360 cal.BC

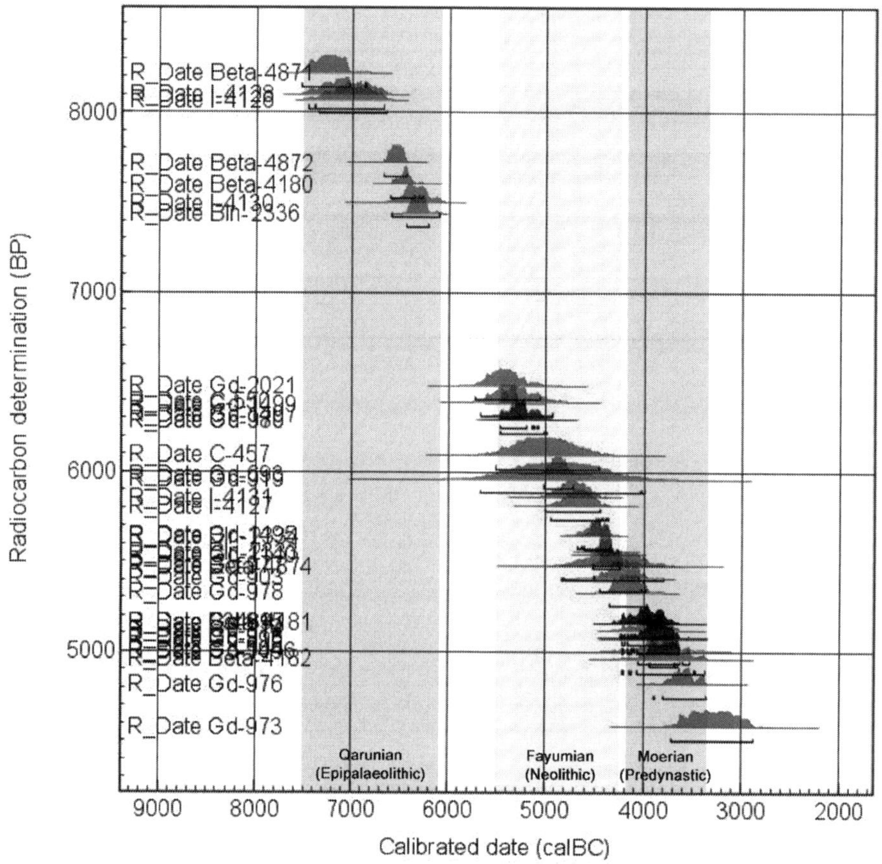

Fig.3.8. Radiocarbon chronology of the Fayum

3.5. Some consideration on the sequence of the Fayum Epipalaeolithic and Neolithic and the controversial time gap between them

As mentioned earlier, the duration of the remarkable drop of lake level between the Fayum Epipalaeolithic and Neolithic periods has been assumed to be either a few hundred years or at least eight hundred years in the 6th millennium cal.BC. Since such a disagreement significantly influences the interpretation about the sequence between these two periods, it must be made clear which presumed duration of the drop of lake level would be more likely. This problem would be considered in terms of 1) climatic and environmental conditions, 2) radiocarbon chronology, and 3) changes in lithic artefacts at the Epipalaeolithic-Neolithic transition.

3.5.1. Climatic and environmental conditions at the Epipalaeolithic-Neolithic transition

The gap between the Fayum Epipalaeolithic and Neolithic periods was argued on the basis of the lack of data on the lake level in the period in question. However, the lack of data does not necessarily mean that the lake dried up for this entire period and people were forced to abandon the Fayum. In order to better understand what may have caused lake level fluctuations and occasionally caused a remarkable drop of lake level, the climatic and environmental conditions of the Fayum in the Early-Middle Holocene have to be reviewed in more detail.

As described in the preceding chapter, the major determinants of Early-Middle Holocene climatic conditions in northeastern Africa were the subtropical trough that came from the north and spread winter rain, and the Intertropical Convergence Zone that came from the south and deposited summer rain. As for the Fayum, it is located around the latitude of N29°30‘, and this is approximately 300 km to the north of the zone where the subtropical trough and the Intertropical Convergence Zone are presumed to have converged during wet periods in the Early-Middle Holocene.

According to a rough reconstruction of rainfall zones and annual precipitation in Egypt (Kuper and Kröpelin 2006: fig.3; Kuper *et al.* 2007: fig.1), the annual precipitation around the latitude of the Fayum was no more than 150 mm, even during the wettest period between 8500 and 7000 cal.BC. Thereafter it dropped to 50 mm between 7000 and 5300 cal.BC, and dropped further to nearly 0 mm between 5300 and 3500 cal.BC (**Fig.3.9**). Local palaeoclimatic indicators also give some clue to precipitation in the Fayum. According to geomorphological studies on extensive gypsum crusts seen at the eastern and southern ridges of the Fayum Depression, their formation must have occurred under the conditions of several cycles of wetting and drying and an annual precipitation between 50 mm and 250 mm during the Late Pleistocene and Early-Middle Holocene (Aref 2003; Bussemer *et al.* 2006; Mohamed 2003). At present, the average annual precipitation in the Fayum is between 5 mm and 20 mm and the rain falls mostly in the winter months, but there is no rainfall in the summer months (Ball 1939: 225; Bornkamm and Kehl 1990: fig.2; Mohamed 2003: fig.9; Soliman and Koopmans 1992: 5-7). Therefore, while winter rain has surely fallen in the Fayum, it is not certain that the Fayum had summer rain in the Early-Middle Holocene.

However, despite the lack or scarcity of summer rainfall, the Fayum could have greatly benefited from summer rain in the far south, in the form of the influx of overflow water from the Nile into the Fayum lake basin through the Hawara Channel in the Nile-Fayum Divide. The Fayum could have contained considerable amounts of water in the lake basin from summer to autumn, unless the flood water level of the Nile was too low to flow into the lake basin. Since it is known that the record of low Nile floods coincides with the record of reductions in the water level of lakes in Ethiopia and its neighbouring countries in the Equatorial zone (Hassan 1997a: 220*ff*), it is quite probable that the decrease of rainfall in the headwaters of the Nile reduced the amount of floodwater which reached Lower Egypt, and led to the remarkable drop of lake level in the Fayum.

Recent research in the Western Desert and the resultant radiocarbon chronology have indicated that there was apparently a short hiatus of human occupation almost simultaneously around 6000 cal.BC at Djara, Dakhleh Oasis and Nabta Playa (McDonald 2001; Nicoll 2001). There is no doubt that this hiatus was caused by

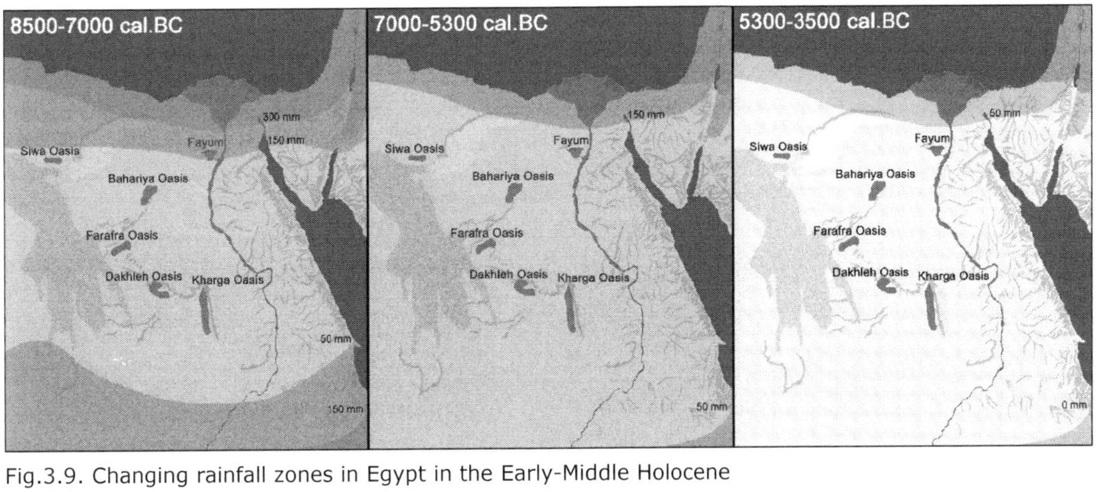

Fig.3.9. Changing rainfall zones in Egypt in the Early-Middle Holocene

a sudden decrease of summer rainfall due to the waning and southward retreat of the Intertropical Convergence Zone. Such a retreat of the Intertropical Convergence Zone may have caused less summer rainfall in the headwaters of the Nile. It has actually been revealed that the water level of many lakes in Ethiopia dropped around 6600-6000 cal.BC (Hassan 1997a: 218-219). However, Djara, Dakhleh Oasis and Nabta Playa were reoccupied around 5800 cal.BC, and this suggests that summer rain came back to these regions immediately after the short hiatus. Considering this phenomenon in the southern half of Egypt, it is difficult to believe that the water supply to Lower Egypt by annual Nile floods remained deficient after 5800 cal.BC and that the Fayum remained very dry and totally uninhabitable until the supposed beginning of the Neolithic occupation around 5480 cal.BC. Although it may be possible that the inflow of the Nile water to the Fayum Depression was blocked due to some local factor in the Hawara Channel during the period in question, it is more likely that the water supply to the Fayum by annual Nile floods resumed after 5800 cal.BC and as a consequence the Fayum gradually became inhabitable.

3.5.2. Radiocarbon chronology of Epipalaeolithic and Neolithic sites

The lack of radiocarbon dates for the archaeological sites which fill the gap between the possibly latest Fayum Epipalaeolithic site and the possibly earliest Fayum Neolithic site has also been argued as evidence for the lack of human occupation in the Fayum and as consistent with the supposed dry-up of the lake (Wendorf and Schild 1976: 222-226 and 317-318). As demonstrated, the calibration of presently-available radiocarbon dates of the sites in the Fayum, by using the latest calibration curve, could not dramatically reduce the gap between the Fayum Epipalaeolithic and Neolithic, and there is still at least a 600 calendar year gap between 6090 cal.BC and 5480 cal.BC. In addition, it has never been considered that previous surveys in the Fayum by different research teams might miss sites that were dated to this blank period in question (Wenke *et al.*1988: 38).

However, it is unimaginable that the entire Fayum has been completely investigated without missing anything. The facts are that many prehistoric sites in the Fayum were surveyed and excavated before the 1950s when the radiocarbon dating technique was invented and improved, and that the sites investigated after the 1960s were quite limited in number and tended to be concentrated in small parts of the Fayum. Indeed, most of the presently-available radiocarbon dates of the Fayum Neolithic came from around the N Basin. Therefore, the presently-available radiocarbon dates of the Fayum Epipalaeolithic and Neolithic must be viewed as merely a small sample and hence potentially biased. It would not be surprising if the undated sites which have been investigated before the 1950s actually represent human occupations in the blank period in question. It is still possible that the re-investigation of Caton-Thompson's undated sites would provide radiocarbon dates which reduce the gap of 600 calendar years between the Epipalaeolithic and Neolithic.

3.5.3. Lithic artefacts at the Epipalaeolithic-Neolithic transition

A comparative study of lithic artefacts may also demonstrate that the gap between the Fayum Epipalaeolithic and Neolithic is not very large, and the transition between them may have been gradual. Previous studies on Fayum lithic artefacts did not have enough data for comparisons outside the Fayum, and tended to focus on extremely different tool classes like Epipalaeolithic backed bladelets on the one hand and Neolithic bifacially-retouched knives on the other, and to argue that there was no cultural relationship between them (Wenke and Casini 1989; Wenke *et al.* 1988: 38). At present, however, more lithic artefacts of contemporaneous periods are being found in the surrounding regions of the Fayum, and they are quite comparable to the Fayum artefacts.

Therefore, a thorough re-study of Caton-Thompson's Fayum tool classes is worthwhile.

Caton-Thompson roughly classified all Fayum prehistoric tools into 25 classes (Caton-Thompson and Gardner 1934: 19-22). Except for rare tool classes, examples of Caton-Thompson's tool collection presently housed in the Egyptian Museum in Cairo are presented in **Fig.3.10-Fig.3.27**. Although the names and sequence of her tool classes are definitely not logical, they are presented here without change. Her tool classes are;

1) ground and polished axes
2) polished and flaked axes
3) flaked axes
4) adzes
5) gouges
6) planes
7) knife blades
8) daggers, spears, or javelin heads
9) halberds
10) chisels
11) ground points
12) triangular or slightly hollow-based arrowheads
13) concave-based arrowheads
14) sickle blades
15) leaf-shaped points
16) partially retouched, leaf-shaped points
17) pebble-butted points/knives
18) pebble-backed knives/scrapers
19) side-blow flakes
20) celtiforms
21) scrapers
22) backed blades
23) trihedral rods
24) tanged arrowheads
25) leaf-shaped arrowheads

A meticulous study on the vertical distribution of tools at many surface sites and the excavations of *in situ* tools at Kom K and Kom W allowed Caton-Thompson to understand which tool classes were distributed at which elevations and to recognise two distinct groups of tool classes according to elevations. For instance, axes and sickle blades occurred only at higher elevations, and their occurrence at a high elevation was confirmed at Kom K and Kom W. The number of backed blades gradually decreased as the elevation rose. Pebble-butted or backed tools were most numerous at middle elevations though they were sparsely seen at lower and higher elevations. Based on such observations, one group of tool classes frequently found at higher elevation was named 'the Neolithic A group', and another group of tool classes at lower elevation was named 'the Neolithic B group', and the co-occurrence of several A group tool classes and B group tool classes at middle elevations was also observed. Since Caton-Thompson assumed that the lake level kept lowering through the Neolithic period, she related the vertical distribution pattern of the A group and B group tools to the lowering lake level, and concluded that cultural changes were at work on the slope of the lakeshore, and that elaborate A group tools degenerated into crude B group tools (Caton-Thompson and Gardner 1934: 55-67).

According to her, 1) ground and polished axes, 2) polished and flaked axes, 4) adzes, 7) knife blades, 8) daggers, spears, or javelin heads, 9) halberds, 10) chisels, 11) ground points, 12) triangular or slightly hollow-based arrowheads, 13) concave-based arrowheads, 14) sickle blades, certainly belong to the A group, whereas 22) backed blades exclusively belong to the B group, and 24) tanged arrowheads are likely to belong to the B group. She speculated that 3) flaked axes, 5) gouges, 6) planes, 15) leaf-shaped points, 16) partially retouched, leaf-shaped points, 17) pebble-butted points/knives, 18) pebble-backed knives/scrapers, 19) side-blow flakes, 20) celtiforms, 23) trihedral rods might probably belong to both A and B groups, because they have been found at middle elevations. She also suggested that some of 21) scrapers and some of 25) leaf-shaped arrowheads might be dated to the post-Neolithic. On the other hand, she left the date of the majority of 24) tanged arrowheads and 25) leaf-shaped arrowheads uncertain (Caton-Thompson and Gardner 1934: 19-22).

As described earlier, Caton-Thompson's B

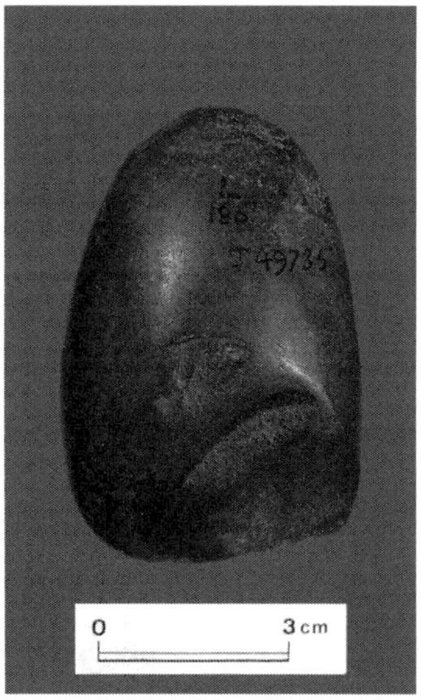

Fig.3.10. Ground and polished axe (JE49735 from Site L)

Fig.3.11. Polished and flaked axe (JE52299 from Lower K Pit 87)

Fig.3.12. Flaked axe (JE49745 from Camp II)

Fig.3.13. Plane (JE49747 from the Camp II Basin)

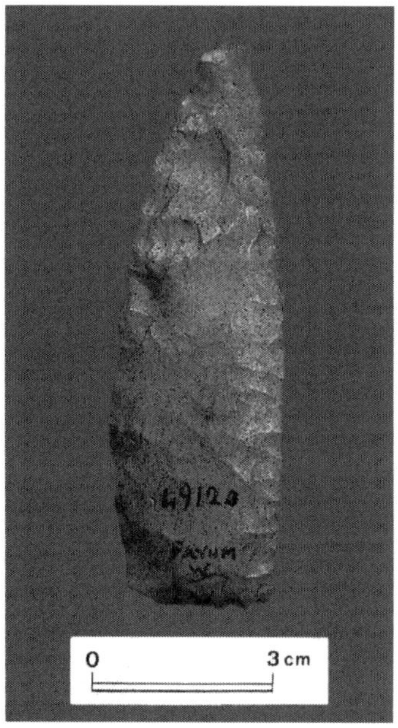

Fig.3.14. Knife blade (JE49120 from Kom W)

Fig.3.15. Triangular or slightly hollow-based arrowhead (JE52320 from Site ZI)

group should be dated to the Epipalaeolithic and is renamed as the Qarunian, and the A group could definitely be dated to the Neolithic and is renamed as the Fayumian. It has been argued that the Fayum Epipalaeolithic assemblage falls within the general Nilotic and North African microlithic tradition, and that there was a considerable chronological and technological hiatus between the Fayum Epipalaeolithic and Neolithic cultures (Wendorf and Schild 1976: 317*ff*). If this argument is true, it must be considered that some of the tool classes which

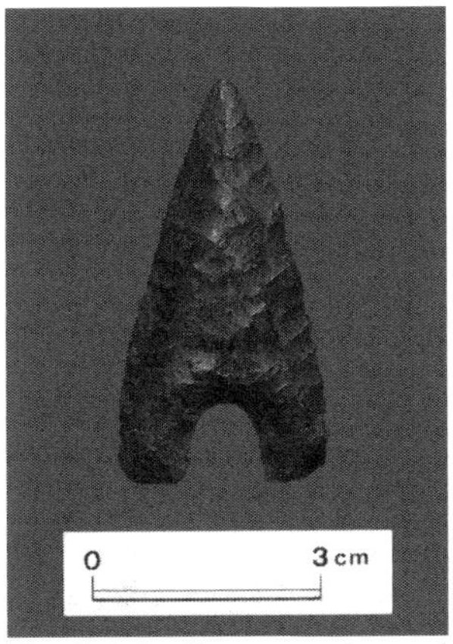

Fig.3.16. Concave-based arrowhead (JE49703 from Camp II)

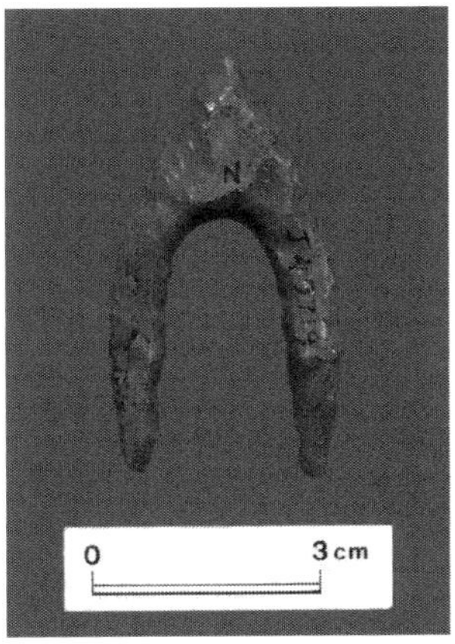

Fig.3.17. Concave-based arrowhead (JE49719 from Site N)

Fig.3.18. Sickle blade (JE49733 from Camp II)

Fig.3.19. Leaf-shaped point (JE49764 from Camp II)

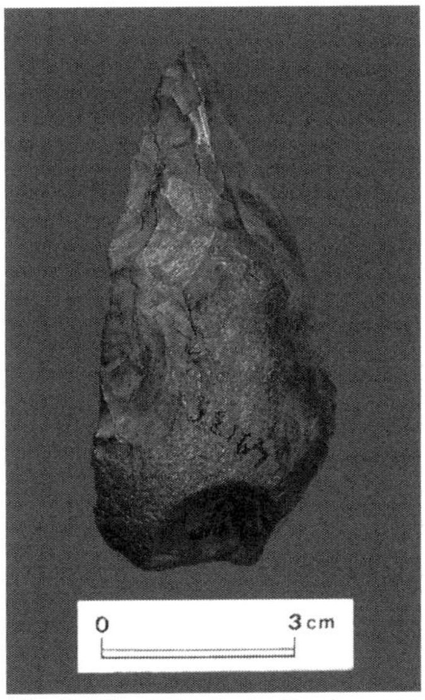

Fig.3.20. Pebble-butted point (JE49133 from Site V)

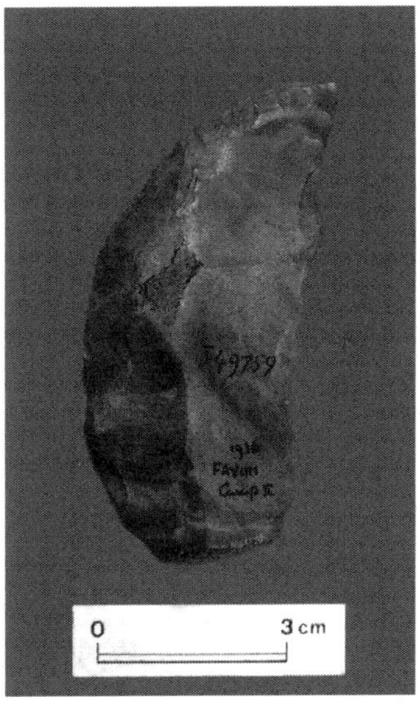

Fig.3.21. Pebble-butted knife (JE49759 from Camp II)

were assumed by Caton-Thompson to belong to both the A group and B group must belong to either the Qarunian or Fayumian. The tool classes which have not been found in the Qarunian assemblages through excavations by the Combined Prehistoric Expedition should belong to the Fayumian, or later cultures. Alternatively, the tool classes which were assumed by Caton-Thompson to belong to both the A group and B group may possibly belong to the transitional period between the Qarunian and the Fayumian.

Many new data about lithic assemblages in Egypt in the Early Holocene have been published

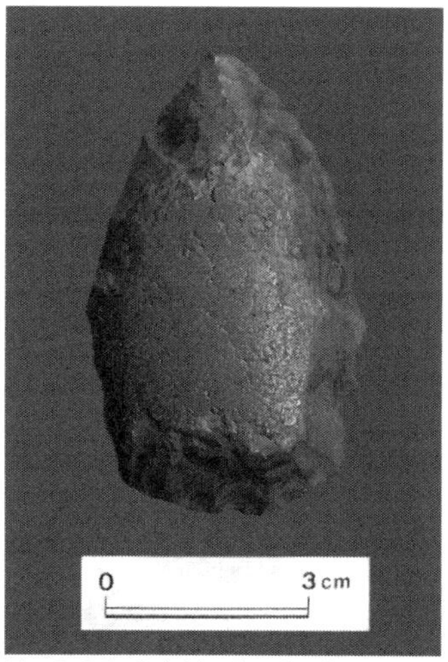

Fig.3.22. Pebble-backed scraper (JE49760 from the Z Basin)

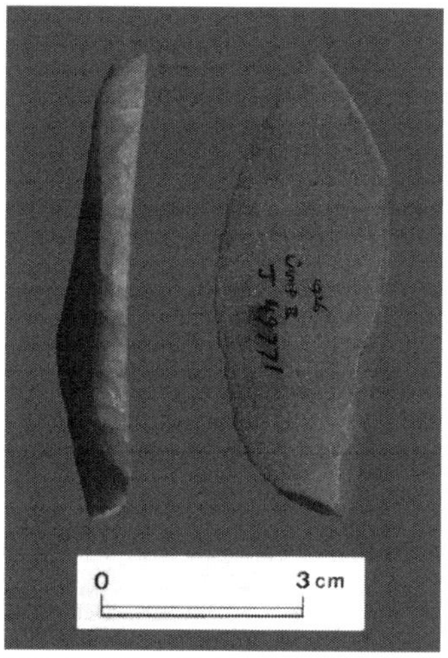

Fig.3.23. Side-blow flake (JE49771 from Camp II)

Fig.3.24. Celtiform (JE49761 from Camp II)

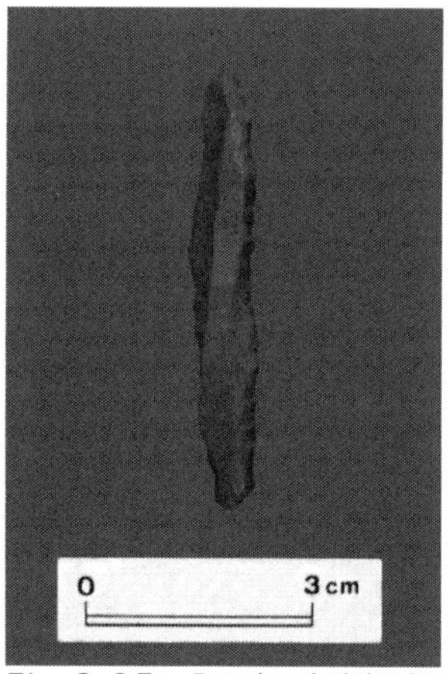

Fig.3.25. Backed blade (JE49714 from Camp II)

Fig.3.26. Tanged arrowhead (JE49707 from Site V)

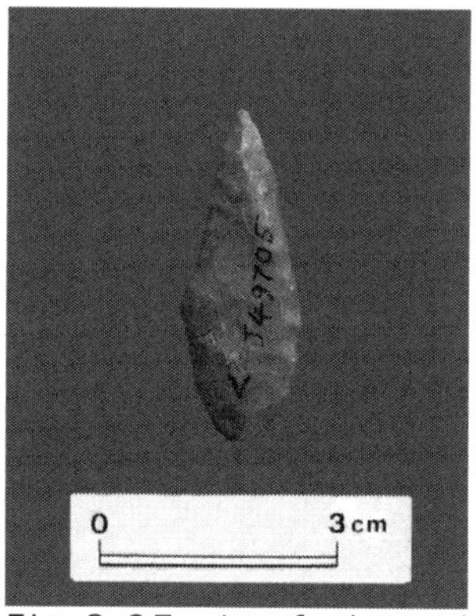

Fig.3.27. Leaf-shaped arrowhead (JE49705 from Site V)

in the past decades, and some synthetic studies on the Early Holocene lithic assemblages in Egypt have also been attempted (Kobusiewicz 1996; Vermeersch 1992). For example, comparable materials like the Elkabian assemblage in the Nile Valley of Upper Egypt (Vermeersch 1978), the Shamarkian assemblage in the Nile Valley of Lower Nubia (Schild *et al.* 1968), the Siwan assemblage in the Siwa Oasis region close to the western border of Egypt (Cziesla 1989; Hassan and Gross 1987), the Lobo assemblage in the east of the Great Sand Sea (Klees 1989), the 'Bedouin Microlithic' assemblage and other Epipalaeolithic assemblage in Kharga Oasis of the Egyptian Western Desert (Caton-Thompson 1952; Wendorf and Schild 1980), and the Early Ceramic El Nabta/Al Jerar assemblage in the Nabta-Kiseiba region close to the southern border of Egypt (Wendorf and Schild 2001; Wendorf *et al.* 1984) became available after the publication of Caton-Thompson's report on her Fayum research. Therefore, comparisons of Fayum artefacts with contemporary lithic assemblages from all over Egypt, while referring to the Tixier typology of Epipalaeolithic tools in North Africa (Tixier 1963), would be useful to determine the attribution of several undated Fayum tool classes to the Qarunian. Furthermore, the comprehensive catalogues of Neolithic lithic artefacts from Merimde Beni Salama and El Omari, which are contemporaneous with the second half of the Fayum Neolithic according to radiocarbon dates, were recently published (Debono and Mortensen 1990; Eiwanger 1984; 1988; 1992; Hendrickx 1999: 18-19 and 60-61). In particular, Merimde Beni Salama provides a sequence of technological development of Neolithic lithic artefacts obtained from a stratigraphic context. Therefore, they provide good comparable examples to determine the attribution of several undated Fayum tool classes to the Fayumian.

It may be said that 23) trihedral rods would be dated to the Qarunian and somewhat later, because they look identical to Tixier's Type 16, and indeed this type of tools often appears in the Epipalaeolithic assemblages mentioned above. The latest example of trihedral rods has been found in the earliest level (*Urschicht*) of Merimde Beni Salama, which still bears the microlithic tradition and would be dated to the early-middle 6th millennium cal.BC, but they disappeared in the subsequent level (*Schicht II*) which was dated to the first half of the 5th millennium cal.BC (Eiwanger 1984; 1988).

Other tool classes under consideration are not easy to date because of the limited number of good comparable examples. It is doubtful that 3) flaked axes, 5) gouges, 6) planes, 15) leaf-shaped points, 16) partially retouched, leaf-shaped points, 19) side-blow flakes, 20) celtiforms, and 21) scrapers were present in the Qarunian. As far as we know, these tool classes first appeared in the northern half of the Egyptian Western Desert including Kharga, Dakhleh, Farafra Oases and Djara around 5800-5400 cal.BC (Barich and Hassan 1987; Caton-Thompson 1952; Gehlen *et al.* 2002; Kindermann 2003; 2004; McDonald 1991a; Riemer 2003), which is precisely the transitional period between the Qarunian and the Fayumian, and they have never appeared in the prior period which is contemporaneous with the Qarunian. Furthermore, 1) ground and polished axes are also sporadically included in the same assemblage of this region (Gehlen *et al.* 2002; Riemer 2003). If 'the 5300 cal.BC exodus event' in Djara (Kindermann 2004: 39) did actually take place, these tools would probably have come to the Fayum at the onset of the depopulation of the Western Desert, and hence, it is likely that they are dated to the second half of the 6th millennium cal.BC. Alternatively, it is possible that these tools had already been dispersed into the Fayum around 5800-5400 cal.BC without delay.

As for 24) tanged arrowheads and 25) leaf-shaped arrowheads, Caton-Thompson could not make clear their date. Such arrowheads have scarcely been found in any stratigraphic levels of the Merimde Neolithic (Eiwanger 1984; 1988; 1992) as well as in the Maadi Predynastic (Rizkana and Seeher 1988). In the Fayum, these classes of arrowheads are quite abundant at such sites as Site V, Camp II, and the Z Basin slopes but are extremely rare at Kom K and Kom W (Caton-Thompson and Gardner 1934: 22, 75-79 and pl.LI). The Fayum tanged arrowheads and leaf-shaped arrowheads are unifacially or bifacially retouched, and they are fairly similar not only to those from Djara, Lobo, Farafra Oasis, Dakhleh Oasis and their vicinities which are well dated (Barich and Hassan 1987: figs.15 and 17; Barich and Lucarini 2002: fig.7; Barich and Lucarini 2005: fig.8; Barich *et al.* 1996: fig.2; Kindermann 2004: fig.11; Klees 1989: figs. 2 and 4; Kuper 1996: fig.3; McDonald 1991a: fig.3; McDonald 1996: fig.2; Riemer 2003: fig.8; Riemer 2007a: fig.9) but also to those from Siwa and Kharga Oases which are roughly dated (Caton-Thompson 1952: pl.100; Hassan and Gross 1987: fig.5.4). Most of these Western Desert examples surely fall in the first half of the 6th millennium cal.BC and some may be dated back to the late 7th millennium cal.BC. In addition, the tanged arrowheads and leaf-shaped arrowheads similar to the Fayum examples are well-known in the Pottery Neolithic culture of the southern Levant in the late 7th-early 6th millennia cal.BC (Gopher 1994: 41). It has also been known that the production of bifacially-retouched, tanged arrowheads started in Cyrenaica as represented by the site of Haua Fteah in the first half of the 6th millennium cal.BC, though it is not certain whether it derived from Egypt or the Maghreb (McBurney 1967: 295*ff*). It has recently been proposed that unifacially/bifacially retouched, tanged or leaf-shaped small arrowheads in the northern half of the Egyptian Western Desert in the late 7th - early 6th millennia cal.BC should be collectively called the '(bi)facial techno-complex' (Riemer 2007a; 2007b), but the appearance of such arrowheads was actually a quite widespread phenomenon from the southern Levant to North Africa along the Mediterranean coast in the late 7th-early 6th millennia cal.BC. Therefore, it is strongly suggested that most of 24) tanged arrowheads and 25) leaf-shaped arrowheads in the Fayum can be attributed to either the later half of the Qarunian, or, more likely, the transitional period between the Qarunian and the Fayumian.

Caton-Thompson described that 17) pebble-butted points/knives and 18) pebble-backed knives/scrapers were made on rounded and weathered flat pebbles, and were the most various and numerous classes. It is not certain whether they really existed in the Qarunian. Some tools in these classes seem to be identical to Tixier's Type 15 and 106, and thus it is no wonder if they existed in the Qarunian. However, tools of these classes are not well known in other Epipalaeolithic assemblages of the 9th-7th millennia cal.BC in Egypt. Some pebble-butted/backed knives or scrapers seen in Siwa Oasis (Hassan and Gross 1987: fig.5.2-i and fig.5.3-c) are similar to Fayum examples, and seem to be dated to the Early-Middle Holocene. Moreover, pebble-butted/backed knives and scrapers are numerous in the earliest level (*Urschicht*) of Merimde Beni Salama, which would probably be dated to the early-middle 6th millennium cal.BC, but they decreased in later levels (*Schichten II-V*) which were dated to the first half of the 5th millennium cal.BC (Eiwanger 1984; 1988; 1992). Therefore, it may be said that these tool classes do not belong to the 'typical' Early Holocene North African technological tradition, but rather appeared in the northern half of the Egyptian Western Desert in the Early-Middle Holocene.

Even apparently Neolithic tool classes like 13) concave-based arrowheads may have appeared earlier. It has been suggested that the first appearance of concave-based arrowheads in Dakhleh Oasis would be dated back to the Bashendi A period, which is dated to the late 7th-early 6th millennia cal.BC and hence is contemporaneous with the transitional period between the Qarunian and the Fayumian. A supposedly primitive form of concave-based arrowheads in Dakhleh Oasis has no pointed barbs but has square-ended barbs (McDonald 1991a: fig.3-a). Therefore, it is no wonder if such a primitive form of this tool class already appeared in the Fayum in the transitional period between the Qarunian and the Fayumian. Indeed, such concave-based arrowheads have been found among Caton-Thompson's B group assemblages at Site G and Site H in the Fayum (Caton-Thompson and Gardner 1934: 62, 67 and pl.L), though she suggested that those concave-based arrowheads might be stray items (Caton-Thompson and Gardner 1934: 21). In addition, Caton-Thompson found concave-based arrowheads along with backed blades in an excavated context at Site Z, and considered them to be attributable to the intermediate A-B group (Caton-Thompson and Gardner 1934: 59-60). Therefore, it is possible that even in the Fayum, concave-based arrowheads appeared prior to the Fayumian.

There is no doubt that concave-based arrowheads evolved dramatically and flourished during the Fayumian. Without any chronological considerations, it has been said that there was a virtually infinite variety of concave-based arrowheads in the Fayum (Holmes 1989: 416). However, the Neolithic lithic assemblages found in a stratigraphic context at Merimde Beni Salama show that concave-based arrowheads with square-ended barbs appeared first and predominated in earlier levels (*Schichten II-IV*) whereas concave-based arrowheads with pointed

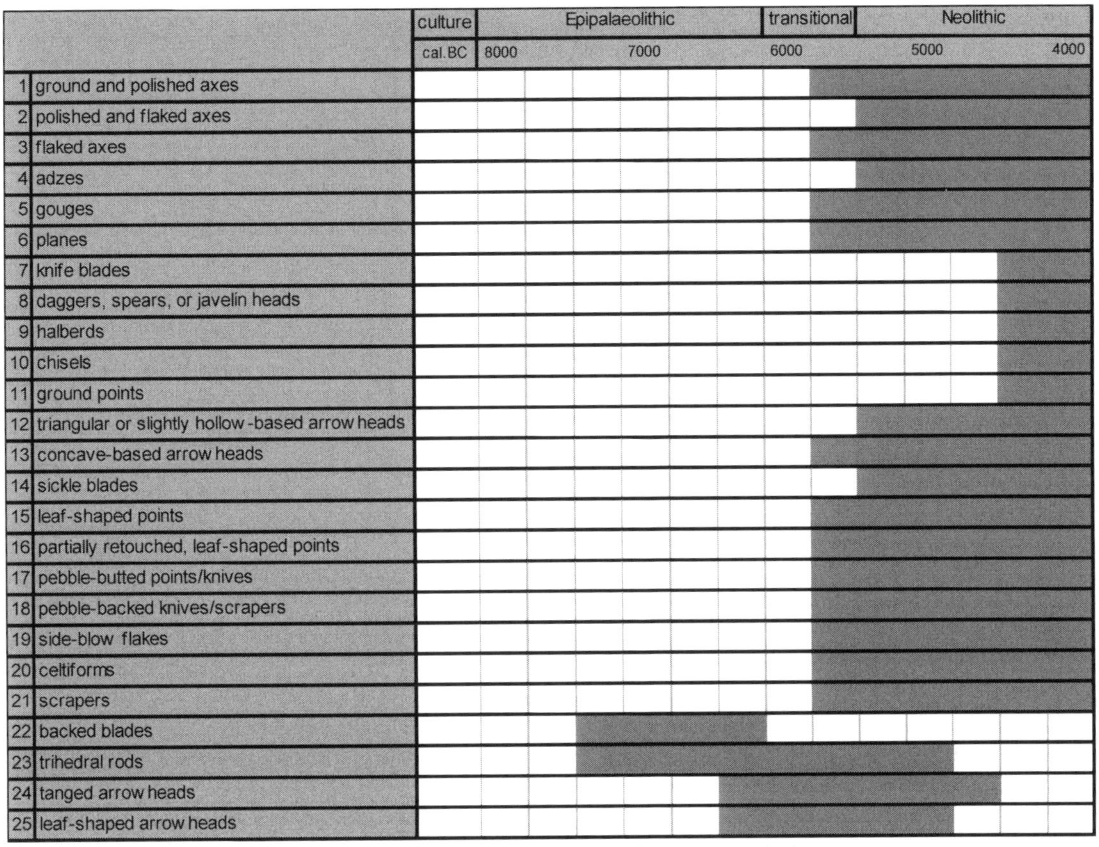

Table 3.5. Chronological reconsideration of Caton-Thompson's Fayum tool classes

barbs appeared only in later levels (*Schichten IV-V*) (Eiwanger 1983: 64-65; 1992: 44-45, pls.50 and 51). Given this observation, it is probable that the appearance of concave-based arrowheads with pointed barbs in the Fayum was also later in date in the Fayumian.

A tentative chronological reconsideration of Caton-Thompson's tool classes is summarised in **Table 3.5**.

Although in very general term, a comparison with other tool assemblages outside the Fayum suggests that a number of the Fayum tool classes may be relatively dated to the period which has been believed to be a hiatus of human habitation in the first half of the 6th millennium cal.BC. However, it must be kept in mind that this tool-class-based chronology still contains many ambiguities. A remaining problem is how to prove this suggestion within the Fayum context itself. It is hoped that new artefacts and radiocarbon dates obtained from well-preserved, stratified sites in the Fayum by future fieldwork would fill the hiatus, thereby substantiating the gradual transition from the Epipalaeolithic to Neolithic cultures without a considerable break.

3.6. The Epipalaeolithic-Neolithic transition and the beginning of farming and herding in the Fayum

The significance of the Fayum as a centre of incipient food production was first recognised by Childe, who advocated the Oasis Hypothesis in the first half of the 20th century, but after the 1950s, the Fayum lost its primary position as the place of origin of food production, because food producing cultures far earlier in date than the Fayum Neolithic were unearthed in rapid succession in the Near East. Since then, early food production in the Fayum has been regarded as relatively late in emergence and foreign in origin, and thus not relevant to the study of the ultimate origin of food production. As a consequence, the Fayum data have rarely been taken into consideration in most studies formulating general explanations of the origins of food production. Even in studies of the diffusion of food production from the Near East, the diffusion to northeastern Africa has been neglected, while the diffusion to Europe has been very popular.

Some scholars have noted that Neolithic culture in Egypt would have originated from the southern Levant. However, they have not made it clear whether food production had begun in Egypt from the adoption of domesticates and knowledge by indigenous people or from the intrusion of Levantine farmer-herders, though adoption by indigenous people has been implicitly mentioned. They have explained that extremely rich natural resources in the Nile Valley would have prevented the inhabitants from adopting foreign domesticates for a long time and that this would be the reason for the late beginning of food production in Egypt, without saying why the inhabitants of the Nile Valley nevertheless adopted domesticates at long last (*e.g.*, Butzer 1976: 10-11; Hassan 1984a: 222).

As described before, previous research in the Fayum has argued that there might be a hiatus of human habitation between the Epipalaeolithic and Neolithic periods, on the basis of the problematic reconstruction of lake level fluctuations and the superficial or insufficient comparisons of material culture. Since domesticates and new material items like pottery vessels seem to have appeared suddenly in the Fayum at the beginning of the Neolithic occupation in the second half of the 6th millennium cal.BC, it has also been argued that the Neolithic inhabitants of the Fayum must have migrated from the Nile Delta and the Nile Valley, where farming must have first arrived from the southern Levant and must have been established many centuries before it appeared in the Fayum (Wenke *et al.* 1988: 38 and 47). It has further been asserted that in addition to the Neolithic site of Merimde Beni Salama in the western Nile Delta which might be slightly later in date than the Fayum Neolithic, archaeological evidence for earlier Neolithic cultures would be buried under the alluvium in both the Nile Delta and the Nile Valley, and hence the Fayum Neolithic culture could be understood as a later marginal adaptation (Midant-Reynes 2000: 106-108; Wetterstrom 1993: 201*ff*).

However, as demonstrated, it is highly probable that the duration of climatic and environmental deterioration in the Fayum in the blank period in question is shorter than previously argued, and there seems to be continuity in the development of lithic technology. It is clear that fishing was still the dominant subsistence activity during the Fayum Neolithic as this activity is well attested archaeologically, and it has been revealed that both the Epipalaeolithic and Neolithic peoples exploited the same species of fish and migratory waterfowl in similar relative abundances, using similar strategies during the same time of year (Brewer 1989a; 1989b). As mentioned in the preceding chapter, new evidence obtained from the Western Desert of Egypt indicates that cattle domestication and pottery production developed in southern Egypt as early as the 9th millennium cal.BC. Even sheep and goats that had been domesticated first in the Near East arrived in the Western Desert as well as on the Red Sea coast in the first half of the 6th millennium cal.BC. It is no wonder if all of them were available to the inhabitants of the Fayum in the same period, and it is rather difficult to explain why it was not until the supposed beginning of the Neolithic occupation in the second half of the 6th millennium cal.BC that all of them were surely attested in the Fayum. It seems more likely that domesticates and new material cultures continually diffused into the Fayum from different directions without delay, and enabled gradual transition in subsistence and material culture through the Epipalaeolithic and Neolithic periods.

It is very easy to explain the appearance of the Fayum Neolithic culture as the complete replacement of the preceding culture caused by the arrival of a new population. However, such an explanation lacks the viewpoint of adaptation and avoids investigations into human motivation and adaptive behaviour. A possibility of sudden invasion or colonisation of the Fayum by the Nile Valley settlers who already became farmer-herders cannot totally be denied. However, it is fair to consider another possibility of gradual transition to food production by indigenous Fayum people, who attempted to adapt to the natural resources in and around the lake and to adapt the lake and its vicinity to their needs by introducing not only domesticates like cattle and new material items like pottery vessels from the Western Desert but also domesticates like wheat and barley from the Nile Valley. If so, the reasons for, and the processes of, the incorporation of farming and herding into local subsistence require explanations within a unique Fayum context. Questions must be raised as to why domesticates were needed by the Fayum inhabitants in spite of a seemingly successful way of life based on hunting and fishing, and how Neolithic people adapted these new subsistence activities to the annual resource scheduling.

Even though Egypt is not the place of origin of food production, as far as the Fayum is concerned, its significance as the place of incipient food producing experiments, or as an intriguing middle-ground society with low-level reliance on food production (Smith 2001), is still not lost. More importantly, it is apparent that all human life in the Fayum has directly relied on the lake, and this bounded and relatively undisturbed depression offers an ideal place to study human adaptation through time. The Fayum data have the potential to contribute to formulating general explanations about the adoption of food production. In the following, local factors which may have caused, affected or conditioned the transition from foraging to farming and herding in the Fayum are overviewed.

3.7. Local factors for the transition to food production in the Fayum

3.7.1. Flora

Very few data on the Fayum flora in the Early-Middle Holocene have been recovered from archaeological sites in the Fayum, and some archaeobotanical data obtained from a Fayum Epipalaeolithic site named FS-2 remain to be better published (Wetterstrom 1993: 189-190). However, given the location of the Fayum, it can be logically presumed that the Fayum flora has generally consisted of annual and perennial plants of the Mediterranean flora, that needed low temperatures and water in winter for germination and flowered and bore seeds under long daylight hour conditions in spring and early summer, as well as the Saharo-Arabian trees/shrubs that were also resistant to low temperatures in winter. Even in Farafra Oasis and Djara which are approximately 300 km to the south of the latitude of the Fayum, some plant remains of the Mediterranean flora, which were dated to the Early-Middle Holocene, have been recovered (Fahmy 2001: table 5; Kindermann *et al.* 2006: table 3), and hence there is little doubt that the climatic conditions in the Fayum in this period were much better for the spread of the Mediterranean flora. Therefore, for a tentative reconstruction of the Early-Middle Holocene Fayum flora, it may be useful to refer to the studies on archaeobotanical remains collected at a Neolithic site in El Omari (Barakat 1990) and a Predynastic site in Maadi (van Zeist and de Roller 1993; van Zeist *et al.* 2003) along the Nile approximately 60 km to the northeast of the Fayum, as well as the data on the present-day and recent-past Fayum flora (Boulos 1992; Cappers 2006; Zahran and Willis 1992: 78*ff*) and the present-day flora and their ethnobotanical accounts in Siwa Oasis and its surroundings (Bornkamm and Kehl 1990; Hassan and Gross 1987; Zahran and Willis 1992: 69-78), which is on the same latitude as the Fayum but is located approximately 500 km to its west.

A large part of the present-day Fayum flora is not in an original state. The original vegetation in arable areas of the Fayum Depression has been modified not only by the introduction of crops, fruit trees and associated weeds from outside but also by the expansion of water channels. The original vegetation along the lakeshore has been changed due to increasing salinity of lake water. However, the marginal arid areas which have not been affected by agricultural developments still retain natural vegetation that adapts to dry environments. Therefore, the present distribution and variability of wild plants can be viewed as an analogy of the situation in prehistory at least to some extent and with due caution.

According to the present-day ecological zonation of Egypt, the Fayum is included in 'extreme desert 1', which stretches between the latitude N28° and N30° and is characterised by drought-tolerant, contracted vegetation (Bornkamm and Kehl 1990: fig.20, 222-223). However, the Fayum flora is apparently much richer due to the presence of a large body of water in Lake Qarun. Since the Fayum Depression is close to the Nile Valley and there has been a water supply to Lake Qarun by the Nile, the Fayum has been considered as a part of the Nile region, and its flora has also been considered as that of the Nile region (Zahran and Willis 1992: 307*ff*).

The present-day Fayum flora can be divided into aquatic flora and terrestrial flora, and the terrestrial flora can be subdivided according to their habitats. Sedges like nutgrass (*Cyperus rotundus*), bulrush (*Typha domingensis*) and clubrush (*Scirpus tuberosus*) are quite common plants in the swampy habitat along the lakeshore and water channels. Trees/shrubs like date palm (*Phoenix dactylifera*) and willow (*Salix subserrata*), and grasses/herbs like common reed (*Phragmites australis*), ryegrass (*Lolium temulentum*), lesser canary grass (*Phalaris minor*), halfa grass (*Desmostachya bipinnata*), common vetch (*Vicia sativa*), hairy vetchling (*Lathyrus hirsutus*), fat hen (*Chenopodium album*), dented dock (*Rumex dentatus*) and prichly douch (*Emex spinosus*) flourish in relatively moist areas like the banks of water channels. Common reed has a particularly wide range of habitats from deep water swamp to channel banks, due to its deep rooting and its tolerance to a high salt concentration in soil and water. Trees/shrubs like Nile acacia (*Acacia nilotica*), tamarisk (*Tamarix nilotica*), lotus tree (*Nitraria retusa*), cocklebur (*Zygophyllum album*) and camel's thorn (*Alhagi maurorum*) are better adapted to dry and saline environments due to their deep root system, and thrive in semi-arid areas between moist areas and barren desert. In particular, lotus tree can tolerate and stabilise drift sand, building sand hummocks (Boulos 1992: tables 8-12; Zahran and Willis 1992: 321*ff*).

The occurrence of edible wild plants at archaeological sites is not necessarily evidence of their harvest. Therefore, seeds of clubrush, fat hen and dented dock found through the flotation of soil samples collected at an Epipalaeolithic site FS-2 in the Fayum (Wetterstrom 1993: 189-190) simply indicate that they were available in the area. However, seeds of a sedge species (*Cyperus conglomeratus*) and an unidentified species of knotweed (*Polygonum* sp.) found in Neolithic granary pits at the Upper K Pits (Caton-Thompson and Gardner 1934: 49; Wetterstrom 1993: 208-209) do indicate that Fayum Neolithic people have harvested them for seeds. The lack of edible wild plants at archaeological sites is also not necessarily the proof of their absence or the evidence that they have not been harvested, because plant remains are not always preserved in the archaeological record, and even if preserved, they are not always in identifiable form. Therefore, referring to ecological data about the availability of wild plants in a specific environment as well as ethnographic data about the plant food preferences among hunter-gatherers living in similar environments is vital (Hillman 1989: 218*ff*).

Carbohydrate-rich tubers of nutgrass and clubrush have been abundantly collected, and ground or pounded on grinding stones for consumption by people at the Late Palaeolithic sites of Wadi Kubbaniya in Upper Egypt (Hillman 1989). It has also been reported that nutgrass tubers were collected at a Predynastic site of Hierakonpolis approximately 50 km to the north of Wadi Kubbaniya not only for consumption but also for their use as perfume (Fahmy 2005). Nutgrass and clubrush have been recovered at a Predynastic site of Maadi (van Zeist and de Roller 1993; van Zeist *et al.* 2003), and hence it is certain that they thrived in Lower Egypt as well. It is known in ethnographic accounts that the seeds of clubrush have been eaten after roasting (Hillman *et al.* 1989: 196). Starchy rhizomes of bulrush and common reed can be eaten while still young after baking, steaming and roasting (Hillman 1989: 219; Hillman *et al.* 1989).

Seeds of dented dock and prichly douch have been found in El Omari (Barakat 1990: 112) and Maadi (van Zeist *et al.* 2003: 180), and hence it is certain that dented dock and prichly douch were common in Lower Egypt in prehistory. Leaves and rhizomes of prichly douch are known to be edible (Barakat 1990: 112). Young shoots and seeds of fat hen and dented dock are also known to have been eaten in ethnographic accounts (Wetterstrom 1993: 189). The presence of ryegrass and vetch has been reported at Maadi (van Zeist *et al.* 2003: 178), and abundantly at El Omari in particular (Barakat 1990: 111-112). Ryegrass and vetch are known as good pasture plants, and it has been suggested that they might have been cultivated as fodder in El Omari (Barakat 1990: 110-111), but it is also probable that their seeds were collected for human consumption. Fruits of date palm and sycamore fig (*Ficus sycomorus*) have been reported in El Omari (Greiss 1955: 229; 1957: 107; Täckholm 1990: 116) and Maadi (van Zeist *et al.* 2003: 173), but it is not certain whether these plants grew locally, and it is probable that only the fruits were brought there from elsewhere.

If the edible wild plants described above actually thrived in the Fayum in the Early-Middle Holocene, it may be that they were harvested and eaten by the Fayum inhabitants. Moreover, it is also probable that the Fayum Neolithic people who harvested unidentified sedges and herbs for seeds recognised the value of the leaves, rhizomes and tubers of these plants.

As for the seasonality of harvesting wild plants, the stands of marsh plants like nutgrass, bulrush and clubrush would have partially been inundated due to high lake water caused by the influx of the annual Nile flood water in summer, and hence would have become inaccessible. However, it is known that the starch content of the tubers of nutgrass and clubrush and the rhizomes of bulrush and common reed increases through autumn to winter, and that some of the sedges start to produce edible seeds in winter. As the high lake water receded in autumn, harvesting these plants would have become possible (Hillman 1989: 230*ff*). When these plants grew in extensive stands, uprooting or digging tubers and rhizomes from moist soils would not have required too much labour, and hence it must have been a worthwhile and profitable subsistence activity. An excessive amount of tubers could have been stored for later consumption (Wetterstrom 1993: 178-179). On the other hand, after spring, the tubers and rhizomes of sedges become old and woody, and hence are unpalatable or inedible. Annual wild grasses/herbs of the Mediterranean flora finish their growth cycle before summer (Wetterstrom 1993: 195-196). Therefore, it can be said that harvesting various parts of wild plants has mainly been done from autumn to early spring, and that late spring and early summer are the most unproductive seasons.

As for the reliability of harvesting wild plants, it has been noted that nutgrass was particularly stimulated into more active tuber production by soil disturbance like digging, and hence heavy annual harvesting of tubers guaranteed an equally heavy harvest of freshly-formed tubers in each ensuing year, and that the same phenomena were also seen in other wild plants which produced tubers (Hillman 1989: 226-227; Hillman *et al.* 1989: 180-181). Tolerance to exploitation is definitely an asset of tuber-producing sedges as a reliable source of carbohydrate. Therefore, if sedges had actually been harvested by Fayum Epipalaeolithic and Neolithic people, they would probably have been dietary staples. There are no positive data about the tolerance of annual and perennial wild grasses/herbs to exploitation, but it is obvious that wild grasses/herbs are vulnerable to drought in early/late spring and may die before harvest, and thus it is unlikely that their reliability is greater than that of sedges which are supposed to have been harvested earlier in the year.

In addition to their value as food items, other economic advantages of wild plants should not be overlooked. Trees/shrubs must have provided timber and firewood for the Fayum inhabitants, and leaves and culms of sedges could have provided materials for roofing and fencing, and fibres of grasses could have been used for making ropes, mats and baskets. All of the wood charcoal collected at a Fayum Epipalaeolithic site has actually been identified as tamarisk (Wetterstrom 1993: 187), and wooden sticks and shafts found in Neolithic granary pits at the Upper K Pits are all made of tamarisk (Caton-Thompson and Gardner 1934: 45-46). The lining of granary pits at the Upper K Pits is made of reed (Caton-Thompson and Gardner 1934: 88). A study on ropes and mats from El Omari has revealed that ropes were made from halfa grass, and mats were made from common reed (Greiss 1955: 227-230; 1957: 106-107).

As mentioned above, since very few data on the Fayum flora in the Early-Middle Holocene have been recovered from archaeological sites in the Fayum, it is impossible to say whether there was a dramatic disappearance of some local plant taxa caused by climatic and environmental changes or human overexploitation. Therefore, the only recognisable vegetation change at the beginning of the Neolithic in the Fayum is the appearance of wheat, barley, and flax.

The wheat and barley found in Neolithic granary pits of the Upper K Pits are all domesticated forms, and include emmer wheat (*Triticum turgidum* ssp. *dicoccon*), two-rowed barley (*Hordeum vulgare* ssp. *distichon*), and six-rowed barley (*Hordeum vulgare* ssp. *vulgare*) (Caton-Thompson and Gardner 1934: 46-49; Schepers *et al.* 2006). As mentioned in the preceding chapter, the absence of wild wheat and the rarity of wild barley in northeastern Africa are apparently because the minimal amount of winter rainfall for sustaining their natural growth has hardly been attained in most regions. There is little doubt that the domesticated wheat and barley found in the Fayum originated from the southern Levant. It can be said that although necessary conditions for the growth of domesticated wheat and barley like low temperatures in winter and long daylight hour and less severe heat conditions in spring and summer were met in the Fayum, an adequate supply of water in winter was the sole critical requirement for the introduction of domesticated wheat and barley from the southern Levant into the Fayum. It was probably not difficult for those who had once learned sowing or transplanting wherever moist soils were available to fulfil this requirement. This may be the reason why it took much more time for the southward diffusion of domesticated wheat and barley to occur along the Nile to Middle and Upper Egypt, where climatic conditions were rather different from those of the original habitat of wheat and barley.

Questions about wheat/barley farming in the Fayum are concerned with the seasons of sowing and the location of farmland. In Pharaonic times, farming in the Nile Valley was fed by annual floods of the Nile. The floodplain of the Nile Valley was entirely inundated in late summer, and then the water receded in middle/late autumn. Sowing was done on moist soils after the recession of flood water, and harvesting was done in late spring before the summer heat and flood came. This annual cycle is essentially the case with present-day farming in the Nile Valley, though the Nile flood is replaced by irrigation. If flood-fed farming was the case in the Fayum Neolithic, farmland would have been located on the receding lakeshore where moist soils were exposed, but this may not be the case.

Farming was essentially fed by rain in the original habitat of wheat and barley in the southern Levant. The present-day Bedouins in southern Jordan are occasionally cultivating drought-resistant, saline soil-tolerant barley in the stony desert valley areas of less than 100 mm annual precipitation (Cordova 2007: 90-92). Rain-fed farming in Egypt is presently restricted to the winter and spring months, and is confined to a narrow strip of land that runs parallel to the Mediterranean coast and has approximately 100 mm annual precipitation (Zahran and Willis

1992: 337). In the Fayum in the Neolithic period, however, there seems to have been more winter rainfall than at present, as mentioned earlier. Therefore, when farming was introduced to Egypt from the southern Levant via the Negev and Sinai, Egyptian people may have learned the idea of rain-fed farming in the first place, and then managed to adapt the farming to the unique environment of Egypt. If the first farming experiment in the Fayum was rain-fed farming, it may be that farmland was not necessarily located on the lakeshore, and that sowing was attempted in desert wadis, when winter rain started to fall and the wadi bed became wet due to surface runoff water.

The appearance of flax (*Linum usitatissimum*) in the Fayum Neolithic can also be argued in the same context of the appearance of domesticated wheat and barley. Seeds of flax were found in a granary pit of the Upper K Pits (Caton-Thompson and Gardner 1934: 49). Since no wild ancestors of flax have been known in northeastern Africa, there is little doubt that the flax of the Fayum Neolithic came from the southern Levant as a part of the Levantine domesticates package or in a weedy form.

It seems that the influx of the Nile flood water into the Fayum lake basin and the resultant high ground moisture content through summer and autumn had the potential to sustain the growth of African summer crops like wild sorghum (*Sorghum bicolor*), which was abundantly found in Farafra Oasis, Abu Ballas and Nabta Playa in the Early-Middle Holocene (Barakat and Fahmy 1999), but such plant remains have never been reported in Lower Egypt in prehistory (Wetterstrom 1998). Therefore, it may be said that even if there was enough ground moisture in summer and autumn in the Fayum and even though sorghum is fairly drought-tolerant due to its deep rooting system, the gradually lowering temperature and decreasing daylight hours from summer to autumn in the Fayum did not meet the conditions of high light intensity and high temperature which are ideal for the C4 photosynthesis of sorghum, and it was impossible to meet these conditions in any way.

3.7.2. Fauna

The Fayum fauna in the Early-Middle Holocene has been studied on the basis of faunal remains collected at many surface sites and some excavated sites, and a considerable number of species has been identified (**Table 3.6**). The mammalian fauna adapted to the dry semi-desert environment extending from the Sahara through the Levant into northwestern India is called the Saharo-Sindian fauna, and the Fayum mammalian fauna definitely belongs to the Saharo-Sindian one (Brewer 1989b: 91*ff*). Since the northward-southward shift of the Intertropical Convergence Zone appears to correspond to the spread of the Sudano-Ethiopian fauna including giraffe (*Giraffa camelopardalis*) and elephant (*Loxodonta africana*), it is reasonable that these large mammals were spread in the southern half of Egypt but were absent in the Fayum in the Early-Middle Holocene (Van Neer and Uerpmann 1989: 320-321), though an alleged elephant has been reported at a Neolithic site in the Fayum (Caton-Thompson and Gardner 1934: 72 and pl.II).

Major medium to large-sized mammals which were surely the prey of the Fayum Epipalaeolithic and Neolithic inhabitants include hippopotamus (*Hippopotamus amphibius*), aurochs (*Bos primigenius*), hartebeest (*Alcelaphus buselaphus*), and dorcas gazelle (*Gazella dorcas*) (Brewer 1989b: table 4; Gautier 1976b: table I-7; von den Driesch 1986: table 1; Wenke *et al.* 1998: table 1). The habitat, food requirements, and behavioural patterns of these mammals give indirect information about the local environment in these periods.

It seems that dorcas gazelle were predominant through the Fayum Epipalaeolithic and Neolithic periods. Dorcas gazelle live in small herds and inhabit sand dunes and stony terrains, and wander quite widely. They can survive without drinking water, though they drink water wherever available, and do not feed on grasses but on leaves, flowers, pods and seeds of trees like acacia, and leaves and fruits of shrubs like the lotus tree, both of which are usually seen in

species	live weight (kg)	habitat requirement	feeding behaviour	food	herd	move
gerbil *Gerbillus gerbillus*	up to 0.025	sandy desert	herbivorous	seeds, fruits and leaves	live solitarily or in pairs	wander around own burrows
hedgehog *Hemiechinus auritus*	up to 0.5	semi-desert	omnivorous	insects, small rodents, bird's eggs and fruits	live solitarily	wander around own burrows
mongoose *Herpestes ichneumon*	up to 4	savannas near water	carnivorous	birds, small animals, and fish	live solitarily or in pairs	wander around own burrows
hare *Lepus capensis*	up to 5	open grassy flats with scattered scrub	herbivorous	seeds, fruits and leaves	live solitarily or in pairs	wander in a small range
wild cat *Felis silvestris*	up to 6	savannas	carnivorous	birds, small animals and insects	live solitarily	wander in a small range
red fox *Vulpes vulpes*	up to 5	stony desert	carnivorous	small animals and insects	live in small family parties	wander around several dens
jackal *Canis aureus*	up to 10	savannas	omnivorous	small animals, insects and fruits. Scavenge carcasses	live solitarily or in pairs	wander in a small range
striped hyena *Hyaena hyaena*	up to 55	arid savannas	omnivorous	small animals, insects and fruits. Scavenge carcasses	live solitarily or in pairs	wander long distances
wild boar *Sus scrofa*	up tp 90	thick undergrowth	omnivorous	grasses, leaves, tubers and fruits. Small animals and insects	live in small family parties	wander in a small range
barbary sheep *Ammotragus lervia*	up to 110	rocky mountains and broken country	herbivorous	grasses, acacia leaves and pods, and succulents	live in herds of 3-6 head	wander in a small range
dorcas gazelle *Gazella dorcas*	up to 22	sandy and stony desert	herbivorous	acacia leaves and pods	live in herds up to 20 head	wander long distances
addax *Addax nasomaculatus*	up to 120	sandy and stony desert	herbivorous	grasses, acacia leaves and pods, and succulents	live in herds up to 20 head	wander long distances
oryx *Oryx dammah*	up to 200	semi-desert	herbivorous	grasses, acacia leaves and pods, and succulents	live in herds up to 12 head	wander long distances
hartebeest *Alcelaphus buselaphus*	up to 200	open country and light bush	herbivorous	grasses	live in herds of 4-15 head	wander in a small range
aurochs *Bos primigenius*	up to 500	open country and light bush	herbivorous	grasses		
hippopotamus *Hippopotamus amphibius*	up to 2500	streams and lakes with permanent water	herbivorous	grasses and aquatic plants	live in herds of 5-15 head	wander in a small range
soft-shelled turtle *Trionyx triunguis*	up to 10	streams and lakes with permanent water	omnivorous	crustaceans, insects, worms, and aquatic plants		wander in a small range
crocodile *Crocodylus niloticus*	up to 500	streams and lakes with permanent water	carnivorous	fish and almost any animals	live in herds	wander in a small range

Table 3.6. Biology of major Fayum animals

the semi-desert (Dorst and Dandelot 1970: 239-242). Hartebeest are the second most commonly hunted mammals through the Fayum Epipalaeolithic and Neolithic periods, but the behaviour of hartebeest is different from that of dorcas gazelle. Hartebeest are social animals living in large herds, and inhabit open grassland, and feed entirely on grasses/herbs, and like to drink water regularly, though they can survive without drinking for long periods. Where water and pastures are adequate, hartebeest are the most sedentary of all major antelopes (Dorst and Dandelot 1970: 218-221). Their presence is a good indication of the occurrence of short to tall grassland and permanent water in the Fayum in the Early-Middle Holocene. Aurochs were also common in the Fayum Epipalaeolithic, and those which were found at Neolithic sites may have been domesticated. Little is known about the food requirements and behavioural patterns of aurochs because they are extinct. However, since aurochs are known to occur consistently with hartebeest in the Nile Valley in the prehistoric archaeological record, it is suggested that aurochs were tolerant herd animals and had the same food requirements as those of hartebeest (Gautier and Van Neer 1989: 135-136).

The locations of, and strategies for, hunting dorcas gazelle must have been totally different from those for hunting hartebeest and aurochs, but such differences have not been attested in the archaeological record of the Fayum. The ease of hunting dorcas gazelle and hartebeest by means of spears or traps, or even by hand without any weapons has been described elsewhere (Hassan and Gross 1987: 97; Wetterstrom 1993: 172-173), and thus it is understandable that they became the major prey of the Fayum Epipalaeolithic and Neolithic hunters. However, it is not certain whether dorcas gazelle, hartebeest and aurochs were a reliable source of meat for Fayum people, because the carrying capacity of the circumscribed lake environment of the Fayum is apparently not very high, and thus their herds could have easily been depleted if there was no hunting control.

Although not numerous, the presence of hippopotamus in the Fayum Epipalaeolithic and Neolithic faunal assemblages also indicates the occurrence of open stretches of permanent water with submerged, gently sloping sandy banks surrounded by open grassland. Hippopotamus is gregarious and sedentary, and usually stays in pools during the daytime but feeds preferentially on terrestrial grasses rather than aquatic plants and wanders on land for grasses widely at night (Dorst and Dandelot 1970: 171-172). Hippopotamus is very aggressive and is definitely not easy prey, and it has been described in ethnographic accounts that successful hippopotamus hunting is an extraordinary occurrence (Gifford-Gonzalez *et al.* 1999: 402).

Medium to large-sized mammals which have scarcely appeared in the archaeological record in the Fayum but are reported to have recently gone extinct in the Fayum include oryx (*Oryx dammah*), addax (*Addax nasomaculatus*), wild boar (*Sus scrofa*), barbary sheep (*Ammotragus lervia*) and striped hyena (*Hyaena hyaena*) (Atta and Verheugt 1992: table 14; Wenke *et al.* 1998: table 1). Other smaller mammals which have not surely been hunted and eaten by the Fayum inhabitants but have certainly existed in the Early-Middle Holocene and still exist at present in the Fayum include jackal (*Canis aureus*), red fox (*Vulpes vulpes*), wild cat (*Felis silvestris*), hare (*Lepus capensis*), mongoose (*Herpestes ichneumon*), hedgehog (*Hemiechinus auritus*), and gerbil (*Gerbillus gerbillus*) amongst others (Atta and Verheugt 1992: table 13; Brewer 1989b: table 4; Gautier 1976b: table I-7; von den Driesch 1986: table 1; Wenke *et al.* 1988: table 1).

Hare was the most commonly hunted game animal in Nabta Playa in the Early-Middle Holocene, and particularly when Nabta Playa became increasingly dry and other desert-adapted animals like dorcas gazelle were vanishing (Gautier 2001). There is an ethnographic account that jackals, foxes and gerbils have been caught by trapping and eaten by local people in Siwa Oasis (Hassan and Gross 1987: 93). It is also known that hedgehogs have been captured and used for tomb offerings in Pharaonic times, though it is not certain whether they were eaten (Osborn 1998: 21-23).

Therefore, the presence of these small mammals as potential food resources in the Fayum Epipalaeolithic and Neolithic diet should not be ignored.

In general, mammals are active throughout the entire year. It has been assumed in the Nile Valley that medium to large-sized terrestrial mammals dispersed more widely during high water in late summer and early autumn, and aggregated around the Nile during dry months in late spring and early summer, and that hunting of the mammals may have been easier in dry months when they were highly aggregated around water (Gautier 1988: 24-25; Van Neer 2004: 265). Such a behavioural pattern of the mammals may have generally been the case in the Fayum, and the Fayum mammals may have remained dispersed also during the rainy months in winter in order to look for pastures and other edible plants in semi-desert areas.

As for reptiles, several species of desert-adapted, terrestrial lizards and snakes are presently known in the Fayum (Atta and Verheugt 1992: 30-31), but it is not clear whether they were caught and eaten by Fayum inhabitants in prehistory. Aquatic reptiles which were surely the prey of the Fayum Epipalaeolithic and Neolithic inhabitants include soft-shelled turtle (*Trionyx triunguis*) and crocodile (*Crocodylus niloticus*) (von den Driesch 1986: table 1; Wenke *et al.* 1998: table 1). The presence of these aquatic reptiles suggests that there were open sand bars on the lakeshore suitable for their basking. In general, cold-blooded reptiles become less active when the temperature is low, and therefore, it may have been easier for people to catch them in winter.

It is very difficult to know from the published faunal assemblages of the Fayum Epipalaeolithic and Neolithic whether there were changes in the relative abundance of wild mammals and reptiles between these two periods. However, according to the data obtained on the southwest side of the lake (Wenke *et al.* 1988: table 1), it looks as if hippopotamus and crocodile did not exist in the Epipalaeolithic but appeared in the Neolithic and Predynastic. Although the data are very poor, a slight increase of hippopotamus and crocodile through the Epipalaeolithic and Neolithic periods is observed on the north side of the lake (Gautier 1976b: table I-7). In addition, although not in the Fayum, a similar increasing trend of the abundance of hippopotamus and crocodile in the faunal assemblages has been observed through the early to late Neolithic period in Merimde Beni Salama (von den Driesch and Boessneck 1985: tables 15, 43, 51 and 52). Since it is unlikely that large populations of hippopotamus and crocodile migrated to the Fayum for the first time in Fayum history after the rise of the Neolithic Moeris Lake, it can be inferred that hippopotamus and crocodile were not usually exploited in the Epipalaeolithic even though they did exist. Rather, the tactics or technologies of hunting these dangerous animals improved after the Neolithic, and consequently, their remains were included in the archaeological record more frequently in later periods.

Apart from hippopotamus and crocodile, the most recognisable change at the beginning of the Neolithic in the Fayum is the appearance of sheep and goat. The sheep and goat found in the Fayum Neolithic are all domesticated forms, and they have often been described as *Ovis/Capra*, because it is difficult to distinguish sheep from goat (Boessneck 1969; Brewer 1989b: 101-102). As mentioned in the preceding chapter, since there were no wild ancestors of domesticated sheep and goat in northeastern Africa, there is little doubt that the domesticated sheep and goat found in the Fayum originated from the southern Levant. Since these animals are more tolerant to different climates and environments than plants, the introduction of domesticated sheep and goat to the Fayum must have been easier than the introduction of domesticated wheat and barley. The appearance of domesticated sheep and goat and the simultaneous increase of hippopotamus and crocodile in the Fayum Neolithic faunal assemblages stand in contrast with the situation in the contemporaneous Central Sudanese Nile Valley, where not only hippopotamus and crocodile but also other terrestrial wild mammals seem to have decreased as domesticated sheep and goat increased in the faunal assemblages (Gautier 1989: table 1).

It is known that varieties of migratory waterfowl visit the Fayum in winter and inhabit the shallow water of the lake fringed with vegetation (Brewer 1989b: 86-91). Those that have been found abundantly in Epipalaeolithic and Neolithic faunal assemblages include grebe (*Podiceps cristatus*), duck (*Anas acuta/clypeata/ penelope/strepera*) and coot (*Fulica atra*) (Brewer 1989b: table 6). Therefore, it is certain that fowling was essentially a winter activity. Another important bird that appeared in the archaeological record in the Fayum is ostrich (*Struthio camelus*) (Brewer 1989b: 87-88). It is not certain whether it was hunted by the Fayum Epipalaeolithic and Neolithic inhabitants for meat or feathers, but ostrich eggshell fragments have been used for making beads in the Fayum, and thus the Fayum people would have stolen eggs from their nests in their breeding season between spring and summer.

The ichthyofauna comprises the largest group in the Early-Middle Holocene faunal assemblages at all sites in the Fayum. The Fayum is included in the Nilo-Sudan ichthyofaunal province, which is affected by the annual rise and fall of the Nile water level due to rainfall in the headwaters of the Ethiopian Highlands in summer. Approximately 70 fish species have been known in the Lower Nile, but the diversity of fish exploited in prehistory in the Fayum and other parts of the Lower Nile is very limited (Brewer 1989b: 68*ff*; Van Neer 2004: 252*ff*).

The fish that have been identified in the Fayum Epipalaeolithic and Neolithic assemblages include a few species of catfish (*Clarias* sp., *Bagrus* sp., and *Synodontis* sp.), tilapia (Tilapiini), cyprinid (*Barbus bynni*), and Nile perch (*Lates niloticus*), among others (Brewer 1989b: 68-85; von den Driesch 1986: table 1; Wenke *et al.* 1988: table 1). These six species have been most commonly found in the Fayum. They can be divided into two ecological groups. The shallow water dwellers are those that preferentially inhabit shallow water and spawn there, and are tolerant to fluctuations in water and salinity level and oxygen concentration. Clariid catfish, tilapia and cyprinid are included in this group. The deep water dwellers are those that spend most of their life in open, deep, oxygenated water and spawn there. Bagrid catfish, synodontis catfish, and Nile perch are included in this group (Van Neer 1989: 49-52; 2004: 252-256). Clariid catfish predominated among these six species in the Fayum (Brewer 1989b: 113-116). The predominance of clariid catfish in the Fayum ichthyofaunal assemblages clearly indicates a Fayum physical environment with shallow water, long sandy beaches and submerged plants on the water margin, all of which are suitable for them. The presence of Nile puffer (*Tetraodon fahaka*) has been reported elsewhere in the Fayum Epipalaeolithic and Neolithic ichthyofaunal assemblages, but puffer is poisonous, and hence its presence may not be considered as the evidence of consumption (Brewer 1989b: 85 and 106) and may perhaps be the evidence of netting or angling for non-selective catching. However, if the Fayum fishers knew how to remove the poisonous liver of puffer, it is probable that puffer was eaten.

For an understanding of the seasonality of fishing in the Fayum, growth increment studies on fish remains as well as ecological data on the behaviour of fish have served. A study on the growth rings of the pectoral fin spines of clariid catfish as well as the ecological data has revealed that this fish might have been caught during two seasons of a year throughout the Fayum Epipalaeolithic and Neolithic periods. The first fishing season was late summer, when the lake level started to rise due to the influx of annual Nile flood water. It is known that at the beginning of annual flood, large adult clariid catfish rush to shallow marginal areas of rising water in the floodplain for spawning, and congregate there in great masses, and then migrate back to deeper parts of the water as the floodwater starts to lower. Therefore, large adult clariid catfish on beaches during their spawning could have been easily caught with spears or even by hand. The second fishing season was late spring, when the lake reached its lowest level due to gradual evaporation. It was suggested that clariid catfish were caught when they aggregated in large numbers during late spring to take advantage of some prey species which spawned at this time. Accordingly, it is probable that the Fayum Epipalaeolithic and Neolithic people stayed near the lake during at least these two possible fishing seasons (Brewer 1989b: 119-144 and 166-169).

However, it has been pointed out that pectoral fin spines are less reliable as indicators of the seasonality of capture than otoliths and vertebrae, and it is argued that a comprehensive understanding of the general behavioural patterns of the fish species under study and the ratio of adult fish and juvenile fish in the assemblages, which would indicate the seasons of their capture, as well as osteological analyses, are vital (Van Neer 2004; Gautier and Van Neer 1989: 141-153; Van Neer *et al.* 1999; 2000: 282-285). It is known that small juvenile clariid catfish that grow up in the floodplain are trapped in residual pools after the flood water receded, and hence are easily caught. It is also known that tilapia and cyprinid have behavioural patterns similar to those of clariid catfish, though tilapia continues to spawn for a longer period in shallow, inshore nests, and hence they would also have been easy prey (Van Neer 1989: 52-54; 2004: 252*ff*). The ratio of adult fish and juvenile fish in the Fayum Epipalaeolithic and Neolithic ichthyofaunal assemblages has not been studied, but a future study of the age distribution of fish across different sites would elucidate the seasons of their capture more clearly.

Moreover, this easy manner of shallow water fishing must have yielded more fish than those could be consumed immediately. Thus it is probable that an excessive amount of fish have been processed and sun-dried or smoked for later consumption, as is known in African ethnography and also has been attested at Late Palaeolithic sites in the Nile Valley (Van Neer *et al.* 2000). However, sun-dried or smoked fish would not have lasted very long due to the problem of insect infestation (Gautier and Van Neer 1989: 151-152). If such fish preservation was actually practised in the Fayum, sun-dried or smoked fish enabled people to stay in the Fayum during lean seasons.

On the other hand, deep water fish do not migrate to shallow water for spawning. Their spawning takes place near the banks of open water, and the fry migrate toward shallow water and spend their first growth period there, and then return to deeper water (Van Neer 1989: 52; 2004: 256). There is no direct clue to know the seasons for fishing deep water dwellers in the Fayum, but it is clear from this general behavioural pattern that only juveniles of deep water fish could be caught in shallow water during the annual high water season. It is probable that adult deep water fish were caught in late spring when the water reached its lowest level and was less turbulent (Van Neer 1989: 54; 2004: 256 and 266; Wetterstrom 1993: 196).

As for the reliability of fishing, it can be said that fish are generally tolerant to exploitation, and are not easily depleted. Furthermore, as described above, the habitat and behavioural pattern of shallow water fish show clear seasonality, and hence they are predictable and make the fish easy prey. Therefore, shallow water fishing would have been a quite reliable subsistence activity, and shallow water fish must have been the most essential source of meat.

Freshwater shellfish collecting was not uncommon in the Nile Valley since the Late Palaeolithic period, and it has been argued that some shellfish like Nile oyster (*Etheria elliptica*) that inhabits the main Nile were most likely collected when the water level of the Nile was at its lowest in spring and early summer (Van Neer 2004: 265). There is much information about the availability and possible use of lacustrine shellfish in the Fayum in the Early-Middle Holocene (Alexandrowicz 1986; Gardner 1932). It has been reported by Gardner that whereas Nile oyster was rare, large bivalves of around 10 cm wide like *Aspatharia rubens* (*Spatha cailliaudi*) and *Mutela nilotica* (*Mutela dubia*), which inhabit sandy areas and can survive in the floodplain even after water recession, occurred plentifully in the sandy deposits of the Neolithic lake, and were found also at Kom K and Kom W (Caton-Thompson and Gardner 1934: 34 and 40; Gardner 1932: 53-58 and 80-84). However, the remains of mass disposal of shells after consumption, which should be called shell middens, have never been seen in the Fayum, and hence there is no evidence of intensive mass collecting of shellfish.

At Kom W, several *Aspatharia* shells were found with fish bones and splintered animal bones in a firehole and in pottery vessels. These bivalves may have been cooked and eaten. In another case, a single *Aspatharia* shell and hippopotamus tusks lay in a pottery vessel and the shell seems to have been used as a soup ladle or scoop. Apart from these, *Aspatharia* shells with serrated edges were also found, and such examples indicate that they were probably used for scaling fish (Caton-Thompson and Gardner 1934: 34 and 40). Furthermore, several unmodified *Aspatharia* shells have been found in the Upper and Lower K Pits, though the reason for such deposits is unclear (Caton-Thompson and Gardner 1934: 46 and 53). Therefore, even though not numerous, it is certain that shellfish were collected in the Fayum Neolithic not only as food items but also as raw materials for making tools like scrapers and smootheners.

3.7.3. Climatic and environmental fluctuations and resource scheduling

Reconstructions of the resource scheduling in the Nile Valley in prehistory have been attempted elsewhere (Gautier 1988: fig.1; Hassan 1974: fig.60; 1984b: fig.3; Peters 1996: fig.3; Van Neer 2004: figs.10 and 11; Wendorf and Schild 1989: fig.44.8). It is possible to consider the resource scheduling in the Fayum in the Epipalaeolithic (**Table 3.7**) and the Neolithic (**Table 3.8**) on the basis of these reconstructions with some modification, because the variability and predictability of available wild food resources in the Fayum were generally the same as those in the Nile Valley. Since the seasonality of several subsistence activities in the Fayum has been revealed archaeologically or inferred logically on the basis of ecological data, it seems possible that early autumn, in which high lake water reached its peak and prevented many activities, was a lean season in the Fayum, as long as the Fayum people relied on wild food resources only and also pursued an immediate return type of resource exploitation without preserving and storing spare food resources.

As mentioned earlier, however, tubers and seeds of wild plants can be stored for a short while after harvest. Moreover, it has been suggested that sun-dried or smoked fish would most likely have been consumed in early autumn, which was the intermediate period between the first and second fishing seasons (Van Neer 2004: 264). If such possible practices are taken into consideration, it seems that there was no severe lean season in the subsistence calendar in the Fayum throughout the Epipalaeolithic and Neolithic periods, under stable climatic and environmental conditions.

In reality, however, it is known from historical records that the onset, duration and vertical/horizontal extent of annual Nile floods, which were the most important factors enabling plants and animals in the Nile Valley to grow and flourish, have fluctuated considerably from year to year and in the longer term (Butzer 1984; 1998; Hassan 1997b). The delay of the rise of water would have retarded the start of the first fishing season, and have also retarded the growth of wild plants that relied on ground moisture supplied by rising water. Extremely low flood water would have reduced the extent of submerged areas, and this would have led to the decrease of the stands of wild plants that relied on ground moisture after the recession of water in autumn (Wetterstrom 1993: 193*ff*).

Therefore, even though the growth cycle of various wild plants and the behavioural patterns of different animals are generally predictable, when a flood comes, how much water arrives and how long it lasts would be totally unpredictable. If people stayed at the same location all the year around, it must have been necessary for them to buffer the risk of food shortages through early/late summer and autumn caused by unusual floods. If unusual floods lasted over many years or decades, the annual resource scheduling which was established under stable climatic and environmental conditions would have no longer been viable, and it would have had to be reorganised and optimised.

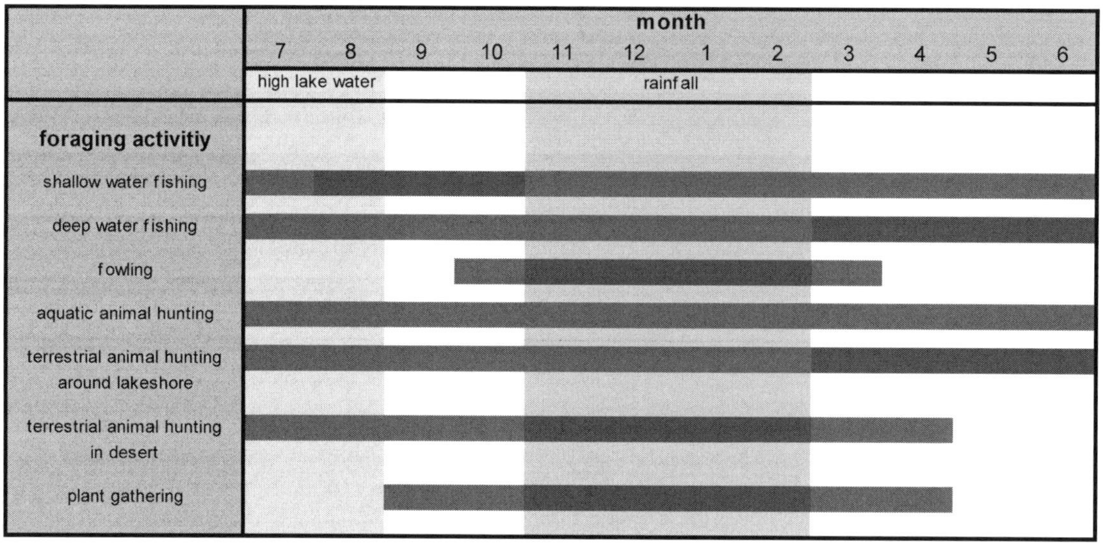

Table 3.7. Resource scheduling in the Fayum Epipalaeolithic

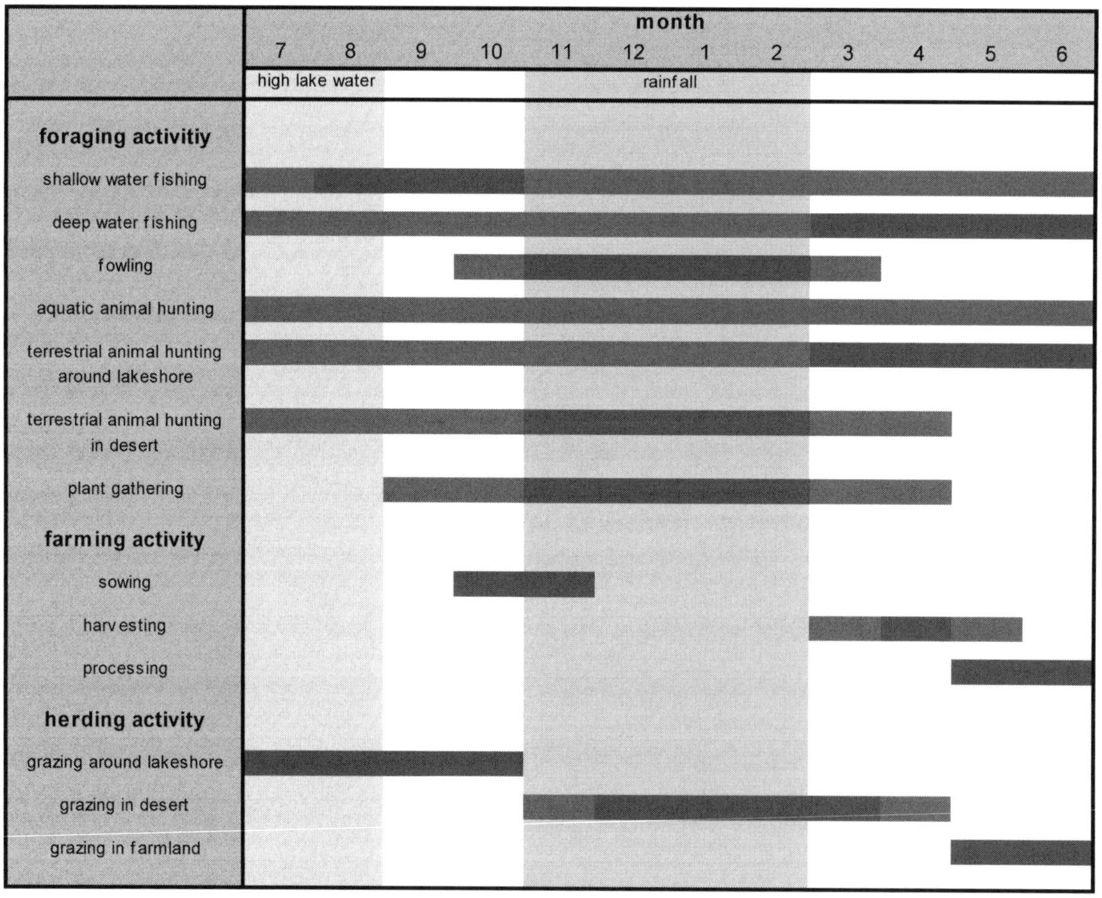

Table 3.8. Resource scheduling in the Fayum Neolithic

In the Fayum, the fluctuations in annual Nile floods have directly affected the water level of the lake, and the water supply to the Fayum lake basin may have been cut off during particularly low Nile floods (Hassan 1986b: 494). Therefore, the situation in the Fayum would have tended to be worse than that in the Nile Valley floodplain. There is little doubt that the Epipalaeolithic and Neolithic inhabitants of the Fayum have almost constantly been forced to react and adapt to changing situations by adjusting different subsistence and mobility strategies. As described earlier, some reconstructions of long-term lake level fluctuations have been attempted, and even though there are disagreements at many points between these reconstructions, some general trends have been understood. Whereas the Fayum Epipalaeolithic corresponded to the Premoeris and Protomoeris Lake stages and hence the period of generally low water level, the Fayum Neolithic corresponded to the Moeris Lake stage and hence the period of generally high water level, although the lake level may have dropped for a considerable length of time between the Protomoeris Lake and Moeris Lake stages, or only around 6000-5800 cal.BC. Therefore, it is essential to take these general trends into consideration, when assessing the productivity of fishing and the availability of wild plants that grow in the moist soils of lakeshore and the animals that feed on them in the Fayum.

Furthermore, although there are no year-to-year data regarding the amount of winter rainfall in the Fayum in the Early-Middle Holocene, it must also have fluctuated from year to year despite a generally decreasing trend in the long term. It is highly probable that fluctuations in the amount of winter rainfall greatly affected the life of some or many species of annual plants that grew in winter and spring, and consequently affected the life of animals that fed on the plants. Therefore, as is the case with Nile flood fluctuations, even though the growth cycle of annual wild plants that rely on winter rainfall and the behavioural patterns of wild animals that feed on winter plants are generally predictable, when rain starts to fall, how much rain falls, and how long it lasts would be totally unpredictable. It must have been necessary for people to buffer the risk of bad harvest and poor catch of animals through winter and spring caused by few or no rainfall.

It has been revealed on the basis of various palaeoclimatic data in the Eastern Mediterranean that there was a remarkable cooling and drying event in the Levant between 6700 cal.BC and 5900 cal.BC centring around 6200 cal.BC (Robinson *et al.* 2006; Rohling *et al.* 2002; Rohling and Pälike 2005; Rossignol-Strick 1999), and that precipitation in the Negev also seems to have decreased around this period (Goodfriend 1991). It can be interpreted that the polar front which spread winter rain in the entire Levant and the subtropical trough which spread winter rain in northern Egypt might have waned and have retreated northwards during this period. The effects of this climatic event have been well recognised in the archaeological record as the 'collapse' and restructuring of Neolithic communities in the entire Levant and particularly in the southern Levent (Bar-Yosef 2003: 120*ff*). Such dramatic changes in the size and distribution of occupation sites have not clearly been seen in the archaeological record in northern Egypt in this period, probably because most sites in northern Egypt were not as large and not as sedentary as the Levantine ones.

It has also been argued that precipitation in the Negev might have generally increased in the Middle Holocene (Goodfriend 1990; 1999) and that a particular increase around 5500-5000 cal.BC might have been caused by the northward shift of the Intertropical Convergence Zone (Goodfriend 1991). However, considering a recent study that illustrates the rapid southward shift of the Intertropical Convergence Zone after 5300 cal.BC as suggested by the southward shifting of the depopulation trend of the Western Desert (Kuper 2007; Kuper and Kröpelin 2006: figs.1 and 2), it is unlikely that the increase of rainfall in the Negev was caused by the effect of the Intertropical Convergence Zone. It is more likely that the return of the polar front near the Negev caused such a phenomenon. Since it is difficult to explain the relatively higher water level of the Neolithic Moeris Lake in the Fayum by assuming the increased discharge of the Nile water alone, it is probable that the increased winter rainfall contributed to the recharge of the groundwater table and the maintenance of the high lake level.

This probability seems to contradict the assumed constant decrease of annual precipitation from the Early to Middle Holocene in the Fayum as mentioned before. However, it is possible that whereas the annual precipitation of 50 mm between 7000 and 5300 cal.BC had mainly been supplied by the African monsoonal rain because of the waning of the subtropical trough, the rapid decrease of summer rainfall due to the southward retreat of the Intertropical Convergence Zone offset the increase of winter rainfall due to the re-occurrence of the subtropical trough, leading to the overall decrease of the annual precipitation after 5300 cal.BC.

On the whole, it can be said that the estimation of the constant decrease of annual precipitation from the Early to Middle Holocene in the Fayum is rather simplistic. Instead, it may be presumed that whereas the Fayum Epipalaeolithic corresponded to the period of temporal recovery from sudden decrease of winter rainfall around 6700 cal.BC, the earlier half of the Fayum Neolithic corresponded to the period of increased winter rainfall and the later half of the Fayum Neolithic corresponded to the period of another cooling and drying event in the Eastern Mediterranean which started around 4900 cal.BC (Rohling *et al.* 2002). The effects of the waning or shifting of the subtropical trough on the general habitation pattern of people in the Fayum may have been small, but slight increases or decreases in precipitation may have made some or great differences in vegetation in the Fayum, and have affected the subsistence activities of the Fayum inhabitants. Therefore, it is important to take these possible climatic trends into consideration when the availability of annual wild plants that grow in winter and the animals that feed on them in the Fayum is assessed.

3.7.4. Population aggregation and the emergence of sedentism

All Epipalaeolithic sites found on the north and southwest sides of the lake are nothing more than surface concentrations of faunal remains and lithic artefacts, and hearths have not been reported at sites on the north side of the lake, whereas they have been reported at a site on the southwest side of the lake. As a consequence, it has been argued that these sites were the remains of several overlapping encampments that had been used perhaps seasonally over a long period of time (Hassan 1986b: 496; Wetterstrom 1993: 187). It has also been speculated that people might have spent several months of the year away from the lake, when lakeshore resources became scarce or when the lakeshore became inaccessible (Wetterstrom 1993: 191), and that there must have been other types of sites occupied by the same people in different places, which represented different subsistence activities (Wendorf and Schild 1976: 317).

Concerning the evidence for the life of the Fayum Neolithic people on the northern shore of the lake, previous field research has found three distinct types of archaeological sites. They are: (1) extraordinary concentrations of fireholes and artefacts on two natural mounds named Kom W and Kom K, the latter of which seems to be associated with granary pits at the Lower K Pits and Upper K Pits in the neighbourhood, (2) dense and extensive surface concentrations of artefacts accompanied by grinding stones and remains of butchering at lower elevations near the lake, (3) numerous sparse scatters of artefacts which sometimes accompany hearths. On the basis of these observations, it has been argued that different types of sites represented different subsistence activities, and that Kom K and Kom W must have been associated with farming and herding and were occupied all the year round and particularly when the lake level was high, whereas sparse scatters of artefacts must have been left by single persons or smaller components of the larger group that split up and visited there for hunting, fishing or plant gathering for one or a few days during dry seasons when resources were scarce (Kozlowski and Ginter 1989: 177; Wetterstrom 1993: 209-210).

The interpretation of Kom K and Kom W must be the key to understand the residential patterns of Neolithic people. Apart from many fireholes dug into the ground, no trace of floors, postholes, or any other structural remains has so far been found at these sites. However, according to publications, the number and variety of artefacts are enormous at these two sites and particularly at Kom W. Such a wide variety of numerous artefacts suggests that a greater diversity of activities took place there. Faunal remains are also rich at Kom W, and they include sheep and goats, but the dung of sheep and goats has not been found there (Caton-Thompson and Gardner 1934: 34 and 89). Therefore, it seems probable that these sites were densely inhabited for a length of time or occupied repeatedly in the long-term, but it is difficult to say on this basis only that these sites were occupied all the year round. As mentioned earlier, some scholars' argument that Kom K and Kom W must have had more than just short-term occupations (Hassan 1998: 149-150; Wenke *et al.* 1998: 44*ff*) would not be wrong, but such an argument is not sufficient to understand the situation.

In order to better describe this situation, it is useful first to mention the distinction between site sedentariness and permanence, and the definition of sedentism, because these terms mean different things to different scholars. Sedentariness refers to the number of months per year people stay at one habitation, whereas permanence refers to the geographic stability of habitation sites from year to year as well as the persistence of a specific mobility strategy from year to year. The most widely agreed definitions of sedentism are that human groups reduce their mobility to the point where they remain residentially stationary year-round, or that at least part of the population stays at the same location all the year around. Sedentism is a relative difference rather than a static condition, and hence a term like 'sedentary settlement systems' merely implies less mobile than previously, or becoming increasingly sedentary over time (Chatters 1987: 347-348; Kelly 1995: 148-149; Rafferty 1985: 113-116).

Kom K and Kom W were located on lakeshores which have transgressed and regressed seasonally and also over years. Previous research has found traces of inundation in the stratigraphy of Kom W (Wendorf and Schild 1976: 212). Even if the inhabitants could be sedentary in one year, they needed to displace an entire residential system in another year of unusually high or low lake water. This unpredictable nature of lake level fluctuations may be one reason why the inhabitants dispensed with substantial dwelling structures. Nonetheless, the inhabitants' obsession with Kom W is evident from the cultural deposit whose time span seems to be a few hundred years, despite the difficulty of continuous sedentary habitation. It can be assumed that Kom W was a geographically and strategically advantageous site over other locations in the surroundings and hence has been inhabited as a permanent residential base. Another reason for the lack of substantial structural remains may simply be because durable building materials like rocks are not abundantly available in a generally sandy lakeshore environment of the Fayum and hence people had to be satisfied with perishable wooden materials.

One problem of previous arguments about the residential patterns of the Fayum inhabitants is that they have implicitly and explicitly suggested population aggregation in resource-rich seasons and dispersal or migration in resource-poor seasons, but have never mentioned the band composition of the local population, and have rarely estimated the size, density, and growth of the population on the whole. Therefore, a question arises as to how many people actually lived in the Fayum in these periods. Since no cemetery has been found, there is no direct evidence for the size and sex composition of the population. The health and life expectancy of individuals have been known only from two isolated burials of the Epipalaeolithic period (Henneberg *et al.* 1989; Wenke *et al.* 1983). Other circumstantial evidence has to be utilised to estimate the population size and density.

Carrying capacity is a fundamental notion in the study of prehistoric populations, and it refers to the maximum population that can be supported by available food resources in a given area under given conditions. The relation between human population and the carrying capacity of a given area is not static. Carrying capacity is increased or decreased as the yield changes due to natural causes, or as people change the conditions by new technology, labour force and management. It also depends on the rates of resource consumption by people (Hassan 1999: 679-680).

There has been an attempt to estimate the human population density of Siwa Oasis in the Early Holocene from the estimates of precipitation and biomass of herbivores (Hassan and Gross 1987: 99). Since the precipitation and biomass of herbivores in Siwa Oasis in the Early Holocene are assumed to be similar to those of the Fayum in the same period, the estimate of human population density of Siwa Oasis as 0.05 persons per km^2 would be applicable to the Fayum as a baseline. However, considering the far larger body of water in the lake and the great abundance of aquatic resources there in the Fayum, the carrying capacity of the Fayum must have been much larger under the same climatic condition, and the maximum potential population density of the Fayum would have been much higher than 0.05 persons per km^2. Therefore, the estimate of human population density of the Nile Valley in the Terminal Pleistocene as 0.11-0.27 persons per km^2 (Hassan 1981: 37) would be much closer to the situation in the Fayum. But again, this figure assumes a population that depends on terrestrial mammal hunting only and does not consider fishing, fowling and wild plant harvesting. Hence the population density estimate must become much higher when the exploitation of aquatic and plant resources is taken into account.

Assuming that terrestrial wild food resources in the Fayum would have been distributed no more than 5 km away from the lakeshore and that the total usable land on the northern shore of the present lake was approximately 175 km^2 and using the population density estimate of 0.11-0.27 persons per km^2, it can be estimated that the human population of the northern shore of the present lake in the Fayum before the beginning of food production in the Neolithic was approximately 19-47 persons. However, this number is not large enough for the people to find mates and to maintain their population within the Fayum only, and hence this number should be taken as a very minimal estimate.

Based on the data of granary pits found at the Upper K Pits in the neighbourhood of Kom K, it has been calculated how many kilograms of wheat/barley grains could be stored in those pits in total, and how large farmland was needed for the production of the grains (Caton-Thompson and Gardner 1934: 48-49). Furthermore, comparing with the diet of present-day farmers and considering other factors, there has been an attempt to estimate how many people could live on the calculated amount of grain storage (Hassan 1988: 148-149). However, this attempt had to be based on the unsubstantiated assumptions that one granary pit belonged to one family and grains were stored for a year, and that the Neolithic people's dependence on grains might have been less than that of present-day farmers and would have been 40 % of all diet. Therefore, the resultant estimate that the size of the group that lived on the stored grains at the Upper K Pits would be approximately 200 persons sounds fairly large against a nearby habitation site of Kom K which is approximately 50 m by 80 m in area and had only 16 sunken fireholes without any other traces of dwellings. But this estimate certainly shows the potential of farming to increase the carrying capacity of the Fayum lakeshore habitat and to sustain larger population.

3.7.5. Mobility

Another problem with previous arguments about the residential patterns of the Fayum inhabitants is that their mobility patterns have not clearly been explained, despite the likelihood that they not only moved short distances within the Fayum Depression but also travelled very long distances out of the Fayum Depression in a group as well as individually. The expansion of sociocultural/socioeconomic networks made by individual moves and group moves between the Fayum and the rest of the Western Desert, between the Fayum and the Nile Valley, and between the Fayum and the southern Levant via the Negev and Sinai, should not be ignored as a factor that enabled access to domesticates and novel material items, even though a certain degree of sedentism in the circumscribed lake basin seems to have been one reason why domesticates were introduced to the Fayum.

As for long distance individual and group moves beyond the Fayum, the presence of similar material culture and subsistence in Lower Egypt suggests some contacts. The Epipalaeolithic sites at Helwan are located only 60 km to the northeast of the Fayum across the Nile, and it is no wonder that there were regular sociocultural/socioeconomic contacts between Helwan and the Fayum, though the Helwan Epipalaeolithic is not well dated. The Neolithic sites of El Omari are located in the vicinity of Helwan, and the Neolithic sites of Merimde Beni Salama are located approximately 100 km to the north of the Fayum, but these Neolithic sites are contemporaneous with the second half of the Fayum Neolithic. Thus it is unlikely that contacts with the Nile Valley inhabitants and Nile Delta inhabitants gave an incentive to the Fayum inhabitants and initiated the Neolithisation of the Fayum. It is more likely that this situation reflects the almost simultaneous developments of Neolithisation in Lower Egypt through mutual influence.

As for very long distance individual and group moves, it has been pointed out that lithic artefacts of the Fayum Neolithic culture were very similar to those of the Bashendi A and B cultures in Dakhleh Oasis and those of the Djara B culture in Djara, which are located approximately 450 km and 250 km respectively to the south of the Fayum. The coincidence of the supposed beginning of the Fayum Neolithic with the temporary abandonment of Dakhleh Oasis and the final abandonment of Djara around 5300 cal.BC may perhaps suggest that the similarities in material culture occurred not only by exchange/trade between these regions but also by the movements of entire populations to the Fayum. As mentioned earlier, since exotic items like marine shells from the Red Sea and Mediterranean Sea are seen in the Neolithic finds at Kom K and Kom W (Caton-Thompson and Gardner 1934: 34, 40 and 87-88), there is no doubt that very long distance exchange/trade networks of a 300-400 km radius had surely been established in the Fayum Neolithic. In addition, some similarities between the material culture of the Fayum and that of the Siwa Oasis region in the Early Holocene have been pointed out (Hassan and Gross 1987), and Nubian diorite is seen in the Neolithic finds at Kom W (Caton-Thompson and Gardner 1934: 87-88). These suggest that there were contacts between the Fayum and remote places across a distance of more than 500 km. Therefore, it is not surprising that the exchange/trade networks had expanded further beyond Egypt with Sinai, the Negev and the southern Levant.

3.8. Strategies for new research

It is suggested that early autumn, in which rising lake water reached its peak and prevented many activities, and late spring and early summer, in which receding lake water reached its lowest level, would have been lean seasons in the Fayum subsistence calendar before the beginning of food production, though preserved food items like tubers and sun-dried or smoked fish may have been consumed in such lean seasons. Therefore, it is probable that storable food items provided by farming and herding were favourably adopted to fill gaps in the annual food supply, and that farming and herding were not intended to replace foraging. However, the explanation that Fayum Neolithic people had a wider resource base than Fayum Epipalaeolithic people in order to better adapt to the unpredictable environment of the Fayum (Brewer 1989b: 171; Wetterstrom 1993: 225-226) does not sound satisfactory, because the Epipalaeolithic people did not practise farming and herding in spite of similar or even slightly worse environmental and climatic conditions. Therefore, the timing, process and causality of adaptation must be examined in more detail, and the word 'adaptation' must be defined more clearly on a sound theoretical basis.

Enigmatic granary sites named the Lower K Pits and Upper K Pits have been found on a desert ridge to the north of Kom K, but the implications for the subsistence and mobility strategies of Neolithic people have yet to be well understood. One question is to what extent the Neolithic people actually relied on the stored grains. In other words, the question is whether the stored grains were an indispensable part of Neolithic diet for the survival of the Fayum inhabitants. These granary sites are separated from habitation sites, and there is no trace of habitation on the ridge where these granary pits were located. The nearest habitation site is approximately 1 km away. Thus it is unclear that these granaries were closely associated with everyday life and were taken care of as a part of household activities. The fact that Kom K was equipped with granaries whereas Kom W was not equipped with similar granaries also gives rise to the question as to whether stored grains really helped people to secure a stable supply of food and to survive lean seasons, and to abandon foraging. Therefore, it is worthwhile to look at the practice of food production in the Fayum not only from a purely economic point of view but also from a social point of view, and to consider the possibility that stored grains and livestock were surplus food that could be used for special occasions like feasting or trade.

Given the history of plundering and scholarly research in the Fayum in the past hundred years, a problem is whether the Fayum still deserves intensive field research in order to answer the remaining questions. It is evident that much important archaeological data have been lost from the field, and any future field research is likely to be scavenging what has been neglected or overlooked by previous visitors. Remaining artefacts in the field provide biased information about artefact assemblages. On the other hand, thousands of artefacts taken out of the Fayum are presently housed in museums around the world, although many of them are bifacially-retouched beautiful stone tools of the Neolithic period and lack the information about the context of discovery. Therefore, any study of them has no other choice but to focus on purely technological aspects of individual artefacts.

In these difficult circumstances, possible strategies of new research are two-fold. Firstly, internal reasons for the adoption of domesticates at the transition from the Epipalaeolithic to the Neolithic and the changes in residential patterns and subsistence technologies at this transition in the Fayum will be studied through fieldwork in the Fayum, while following several lines of explanatory and predictive models. The fieldwork will focus on the topics which were neglected by previous culture-historically-oriented research, and will attempt to understand land use patterns by Epipalaeolithic and Neolithic people. One principal model employed is the adaptive model, and another is the socioeconomic model, which will be described in detail in the next chapter.

Secondly, external reasons for the transition from the Epipalaeolithic to the Neolithic and the adoption of domesticates at this transition in the Fayum will be studied, while surveying the published data regarding the southern Levant and the Egyptian Western Desert. The origins of Fayum Neolithic material culture are still unclear. As mentioned, parallels with typical Fayum lithic artefacts have been abundantly found in the Western Desert but are poorly known in the southern Levant, and thus it is not an easy task to determine the origins of the Fayum lithic artefacts. Even though Levantine subsistence practices are attested in the Fayum, given the differences in material culture, it seems unlikely that Levantine people colonised the Fayum directly, bringing their domesticates with them. A further study of the distribution of characteristic artefacts throughout northeastern Africa and the southern Levant is needed in order to make clearer their possible origins. This topic will be dealt with in Chapter 8.

4. Explanatory and predictive models for the beginning of farming and herding in the Fayum

4.1. Introduction

Previous field research on the prehistoric Fayum carried out until the 1980s has principally employed a culture-historical approach, and has tended to explain the changes in subsistence and material culture by the arrival of a new farming and herding population from outside the Fayum, rather than by indigenous, autonomous development. Therefore, whereas several explanatory models of the beginning of food production, like the environmental stress model and the population pressure model, have been advocated by different schools of archaeology at that time in other parts of the world, there was little room in the Fayum for such models to be applied.

During the past few decades, a new discipline called evolutionary ecology has developed, and the adaptive design in the behaviour and morphology of organisms has been studied. According to evolutionary ecology, behaviour is adaptive when it tracks environmental variability in ways that enhance an individual's fitness. The subset of evolutionary ecology called human behavioural ecology studies the fitness-related behavioural trade-offs that humans face in particular environments by asking why certain patterns of behaviour have emerged and continued and by looking at their socioecological context. The transition between foraging and farming/herding and associated technological changes have increasingly been seen not as a progression from one subsistence type to another but as a set of alternative adaptive strategies with selective advantages and disadvantages that varied with socioecological circumstances (Bettinger 2006; Bird and O'Connell 2006; Hawkes and O'Connell 1992; Kaplan and Hill 1992: 198; Layton *et al.* 1991; Smith and Winterhalder 1992; Winterhalder and Kennett 2006; Winterhalder and Smith 1992; 2000).

Optimal foraging models are the core of human behavioural ecology, and attempt to explain the changes in subsistence activities and related technologies in terms of increasing fitness to fluctuating situations. In this chapter, the basic ideas, implications, and related concepts of optimal foraging models are summarised and employed to refine the inductive, common-sense understanding of the ecological and archaeological data of the Fayum which were described in the preceding chapter. Moreover, it is also demonstrated in this chapter that the socioeconomic model and its related ideas would give some additional explanations about the economic and technological transition between the Fayum Epipalaeolithic and Neolithic.

4.2. Adaptive model

4.2.1. Optimal foraging models

Optimal foraging models consider a goal, a currency, and a set of constraints and options or alternatives when a forager exploits different resources. The goal refers to the improvement of foraging efficiency in terms of the maximisation of yield, and/or the minimisation of time and energy spent, and/or the avoidance and minimisation of risks. The currency refers to the measure to assess the costs and benefits of a resource that gives it value. The most commonly used currency is calories used up or taken in by foragers through foraging. Constraints refer to the socioecological circumstances that structure resource selection opportunities and prevent foragers from continuing to forage, like the density and distribution of potential resources in an environment, the dangers associated with exploiting resources, the residential/mobility patterns of the foragers, and the foragers' knowledge of the environment. Constraints refer also to the foragers' technological abilities to forage and process resources and physical capabilities to survive in a given environment and to digest certain food items. Options or alternatives refer to the variability of potential resources available to foragers, and the range of possible behavioural actions, and choices of time spared for other activities. Optimal foraging models propose how a variety of resources would be used in given circumstances while considering the costs and benefits of procuring the resources, and aim to reconstruct the decision-making process of foraging. Although human foragers do not always behave optimally, the models have been substantiated by ethnographic observations (Bird and O'Connell 2006: 146*ff*; Kaplan and Hill 1992: 168-169; Kelly 1995: 73 and 97; Winterhalder and Kennett 2006: 11*ff*).

4.2.1.1. Prey choice model (Diet breadth model)

Optimal foraging models consist of two general models for practical application. The prey choice model or diet breadth model considers foraging individual resources (prey) in homogeneous environments, whereas the patch choice model considers procuring from clusters of resources in spatially heterogeneous environments. These models measure costs of foraging in terms of time expended on searching and handling. Search costs are the time spent looking for resources and patches, and are also understood as encounter rates. Handling costs are the time spent not only harvesting plants, pursuing/killing animals, and processing the plants and animals, but also making necessary tools and facilities. Foraging returns are measured in terms of calories obtained from resources, and are often described as a return per unit time like kCal/hr. Such measures are usually based on ethnographic field data or experiments. For example, according to ethnographically and experimentally derived return rates of various resources from around the world, seeds and roots normally have lower return rates than small, medium or even large-sized animals, due to high handling costs. Search costs may change with changing resource densities depending on the seasons, and can lower with new technologies or information used to locate resources easier. Although new technologies may accompany additional costs, handling costs can lower and subsequently return rates can rise with the new technologies. Return rates can change with changing nutrition contents of plants and animals depending on the seasons. Return rates may also be different from person to person depending on their age and sex, their physical and mental condition, and their experience and skills of searching, hunting/harvesting and processing. Therefore, ethnographically and experimentally derived return rates of various resources should be referred to as relative measures (Kaplan and Hill 1992: 172*ff*; Kelly 1995: 78*ff* and 98-99).

The prey choice model assumes that foragers attempt to maximise overall returns with least effort while comparing the costs and yields of various resources based on their knowledge. Potential resources for a foraging group are ranked from high to low profitability, and profitability is determined by the quality, size, density, distribution of each resource, and the time spent and the tactics and technologies used to exploit the resource. The total number of resources in the diet counting from the top of the ranking is referred to as diet breadth. The model assumes that foragers exploit the most profitable resources first, and then add less profitable resources to their diet at a given moment. If high-ranked resources are abundant, search costs are low and the diet is relatively narrow. As high-ranked resources become less abundant, search costs increase such that lower-ranked resources are added. When foragers add new resources to their diet, the time spent for searching declines due to higher resource encounter rates, but handling costs required for different resources may rise. At some point, declining search costs are balanced by rising handling costs, and the addition of a new resource would decrease the net foraging efficiency and return rate rather than increase them (**Fig.4.1**). This balancing point is an optimal diet, and it is assumed that foragers attempt to optimise their diet by choosing and combining the most profitable resources and ignoring the less profitable resources even if they are more frequently encountered than more profitable resources. The model predicts whether a resource should be taken or ignored by foragers when they encounter it during foraging trips based on this assumption. The decision to pursue one particular resource depends on foragers' perception or intuition about the improbability of encountering something else with a higher return rate during their trips (Bettinger 1991: 84-87; Bousman 1993: 61*ff*; Gremillion 1996: 185*ff*; Kaplan and Hill 1992: 169*ff*; Kelly 1995: 83*ff*; Winterhalder and Kennett 2006: 14-15).

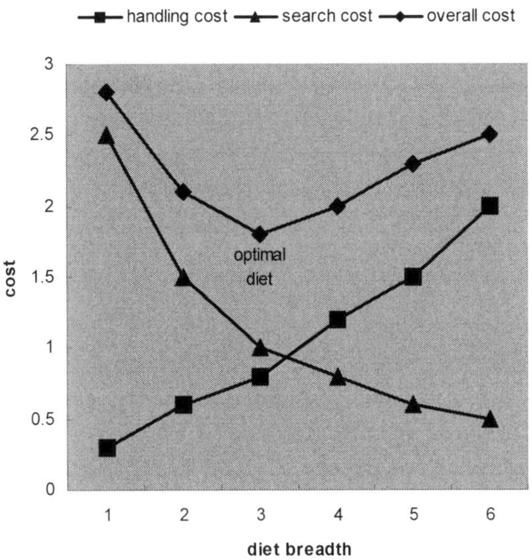

Fig.4.1. A model of foraging decision-making about diet breadth

It follows that the abundance of a resource cannot solely be used to predict whether it would be exploited, and that the decision to include a resource in an optimal diet depends on the relative abundance of high-ranked profitable resources. A decrease in the number of a high-ranked profitable resource and a subsequent increase in the search costs of the high-ranked profitable resource would diminish the net foraging efficiency and return rate, and would cause the diet breadth to expand to include lower-ranked, less profitable resources, regardless of their abundance. Conversely, if a higher-ranked, more profitable resource becomes available, lower-ranked, less profitable resources would fall out of the diet regardless of their abundance. Therefore, if climatic and environmental changes cause temporal scarcity of high-ranked resources and force the foragers to increase search time, then the diet on the whole should become more diverse, while including usually less-favoured resources which are regarded as famine food or starvation food. Although the less-favoured resources would temporarily become high-ranked and become worth pursuing when encountered, they would drop out of the diet as soon as higher-ranked, more profitable resources become available again. A seasonal increase of nutrition contents may raise the profitability of a particular resource, and such a resource can be temporarily high-ranked and pursued. The model does not predict how frequently a high-ranked resource would be included in the diet, and only proposes that all high-ranked profitable resources would be pursued and taken when encountered, but if they are rarely encountered, they would make up only a small portion of the diet (Bettinger 1991: 87; Bousman 1993: 61-62; Kaplan and Hill 1992: 171-172; Kelly 1995: 86*ff*; Winterhalder and Kennett 2006: 14-15).

4.2.1.2. Patch choice model

The diet breadth model is based on the premises that resources are homogeneously distributed, and that foragers search their environment randomly and encounter resources in direct proportion to their density in the environment. However, such premises are rarely the case with many situations. Spatial distributions of resources are usually patchy and not sequential. Foragers normally embark on foraging while bearing in mind a particular goal, which is based on their knowledge of the present climatic and environmental conditions and the likelihood of encountering resources, and hence rarely move at random. Therefore, the patch choice model serves to model other situations.

The patch choice model deals with foraging in spatially heterogeneous environments where resources are found in clusters described as patches. Patches are isolated areas of resource exploiting opportunities on such a scale that foragers may encounter several to several dozen in a daily foraging trip. A matrix of resource abundance, temporal availability, and dispersion in space characterise the resource structure in patches. Resource abundance is often regarded as edible resource density, but the size and bulkiness of resources are also important for subsistence decision-making, because these can influence search costs and handling costs.

The patch choice model is similar to the diet breadth model in that patches are ranked from high to low in terms of a return per unit time like kCal/hr, and it is predicted which resource patches are more profitable than others and thus should be included in a foraging trip. The model assumes that foragers choose the highest return rate patches at a given moment on the basis of their knowledge. The model also assumes that the net return rate is the highest when foragers first enter a patch, but the net return rate diminishes as foraging time in a patch increases, because plants are harvested to depletion and game animals become wary of foragers' presence and disperse. Since a long stay at a patch incurs low net return rates, at some point the foragers have to move on to another patch which offers higher returns in order to maintain high return rates even though temporarily. However, since moving on to another patch takes much time and energy, the cost of moving and encountering another patch must be balanced against the benefit of continuing to exploit resources in the present patch. The marginal value theorem specifies that foragers should move out of a patch when the net return rate in the patch falls below the average rate obtainable in the entire environment, rather than when all resources in the patch are completely depleted. The patch choice model also presumes that foragers do not return to a patch until its diminished resources are recovered, and that travel time between patches is non-productive. Therefore, as travel time between patches increases, then the time spent foraging in a patch may increase in order to offset the increased search costs. As patch density increases, resource return rates rise, because foragers spend less time moving between patches and more time exploiting resource patches during the initial period of patch use when return rates are at the highest (Bettinger 1991: 87-93; Bousman 1993: 61-62; Kaplan and Hill 1992: 178-184; Kelly 1995: 90*ff*; Winterhalder and Kennett 2006: 15-16).

4.2.2. Related concepts of optimal foraging models

As described above, a focus of optimal foraging models is the profitability of different resources and resource patches. However, the value of resources and resource patches is actually to a large extent affected and conditioned by various costs, constraints, and other considerations. Such affecting and conditioning factors are summarised below.

4.2.2.1. Time allocation

A central idea in optimal foraging models is time allocation. Since the time spent pursuing one resource prohibits searching for other resources simultaneously, there is a potential loss of time and energy entailed in choosing to pursue one resource when another resource offering a higher return rate may be available. The time spent for one resource exploitation is regarded as the cost of activity, or in other words, opportunity cost. The allocation of time and scheduling of activities are important concerns for foragers. Optimal allocation of time makes foragers stand on a continuum with maximising resource exploitation at one end and minimising the time spent for resource exploitation at the other. Resource maximising foragers attempt to obtain food resources at the highest rate at all costs, whereas time minimising foragers attempt to spend as little time as possible in an activity, while still getting necessary amount of food (Bousman 1993: 62*ff*; Hames 1992; Kelly 1995:

83).

Resource maximisation and time minimisation are strategies which provide solutions to different resource problems and scheduling problems. Although foraging is a means of enhancing fitness, this goal is also achieved by non-foraging activities like seeking mates and allies, protecting mates and offspring, and monitoring resources and potential allies. Therefore, foraging and non-foraging activities compete for time and energy, but it is possible that losses in foraging are offset by fitness gains in non-foraging. Consequently, it is assumed that where resources are abundant, foragers would not maximise resource exploitation but would instead increasingly minimise the time spent on foraging and would spend more time on non-foraging activities that enhance overall fitness. Conversely, as resources become scarce, foragers would tend to increase foraging time (Bettinger 2006: 312*ff*; Bousman 1993: 62*ff*).

4.2.2.2. Responses to risks

Resources are usually not constantly available, but fluctuate from season to season and from year to year, or due to occasional catastrophic climatic and environmental events. Unpredictable variations in ecological variables are defined as risks, and the probability of the loss or failure of resources is called economic risk. Resource fluctuations and scarcity are the most serious problems for foragers, and the variability and predictability of food resources are important considerations in foragers' optimal diet. As mentioned, the prey choice model addresses how foragers add a new resource to their diet, and this can be understood in terms of risk-sensitive behaviour or risk management. Food scarcity is determined by local conditions and is relative to need. If the resource procurement by a forager group meets their daily requirement and they would like to reduce the expected variation in returns, they would choose risk-averse behaviour and exploit less variable resources. However, during food shortages, they would choose risk-prone behaviour, and exploit resources and resource patches with greater variability, because the chances of getting sufficient resources are greater than those which are less variable and do not provide the minimum requirement. In fluctuating situations, foragers can shift from a risk-prone strategy to a risk-averse strategy or vice versa, according to the availability of resources. Division of labour in a foraging group and direct resource sharing between different foraging groups would also enable the foragers to combine the risk-averse exploitation of predictable and less variable resources like plants and fish and the risk-prone exploitation of unpredictable and variable resources like terrestrial mammals and to make a balance between them (Bousman 1993: 64-65; Kaplan and Hill 1992: 187-188; Kelly 1995: 99-100).

Risk is not a simple variable, but different levels of risk are related to variations in the structure of resources and to the predictability of those resources. Resource predictability is determined by varying multiple interacting temporal and spatial cycles of resource availability. In other words, resource predictability consists of constancy and contingency. If a resource is constantly available in known amounts at certain locations throughout the year and year after year, this resource has an extreme amount of constancy. By contrast, if a resource is available at a certain location and in known amounts during a specific season but totally absent in other seasons, then that resource exhibits a high degree of contingency. In terms of the economic risks of foragers, resources may be low-risk even if their seasonal availability is very cyclical as long as they are highly predictable from year to year, but risks are much greater if resource availability is highly unpredictable. Individual resources and sets of resources can be measured for their consistency and contingency. When viewed as an optimal set, the whole of the resources exploited by foragers should exhibit a high degree of constancy with few gaps in availability throughout the year (Bousman 1993: 66-67).

Economic risks among foragers can be divided into different components, and adaptive responses or strategies would be different depending on the nature of the risk. In other words, different strategies employed by an individual group of foragers should reflect the nature and structure of the socioecological risks that it encounters. For example, the locations of resource patches may change from season to season and from year to year, and this stimulates foragers to move their residential base between locations. Resource storage is also an important strategy employed by those who depend on highly contingent resources with seasonal variations and gaps in availability. Whereas mobility and storage are responses to resource fluctuations and hence passive strategies, other strategies are more oriented to prevent economic risk. Changes and improvements in hunting weapons or collecting tools, invention or introduction of transportation aides, better organisation of labour force for cooperative resource exploitation, information sharing and exchange with other groups all can help prevent economic risk. It can be said that risk prevention strategies are linked directly with variations in resource structure, whereas risk responsive strategies are mediated to a larger extent by social variables and hence would not be realised by an individual's effort only (Bousman 1993: 68-69).

4.2.2.3. Central place foraging and mobility strategies

Mobility is an essential component of optimal foraging, because searching for resources or resource patches and exploiting them are impossible without foragers' physical moves across the foraging area. Most foraging can be regarded as individual moves, whereas moves in a group are regarded as residential moves. Both types of moves are subject to cost-benefit considerations by the foragers.

When humans forage, they usually locate a sleeping or activity place which is used also by other members of a residential group in an attractive and comfortable area, and then start foraging in a radial pattern from the place and return to the place. Such a place is called a central place in optimal foraging models. Central place foraging varies between a random search and encounter and a targeted search and pursuit, and most foraging situations can be viewed as a continuum between these two extremes. Although it is ideal to locate a central place at the point which minimises foraging travel time to all accessible resource locations in all directions, finding a safe place to set up a camp would occasionally be more important than simply minimising foraging travel time. In deserts, both residential and individual foraging moves are constrained by the distribution of water sources and the sources of other essential items like wood for fuel and toolmaking. Foraging efficiency could be sacrificed in favour of remaining close to a water source, and water-tethered people would exploit all available resources within a foraging radius of the water source and leave only when net foraging returns reach nearly zero (Cashdan 1992: 250; Kelly 1992: 46-48; 1995: 126-127).

The central place foraging model adds travel time to the overall cost of foraging. When there is no travel time, a resource that requires one hour foraging would be preferred to another resource of the same or slightly higher caloric return that requires two hour foraging. However, with two hours of travel time, the latter would be preferred due to higher caloric return per hour. In other cases, increasing travel time can make a resource of low caloric return near at hand more attractive than resources of high caloric return at a distance, and hence such resources at a distance would drop out of the diet (Bettinger 1991: 96-97; 2006: 317-318).

Furthermore, in addition to the cost of going from and returning to a central place, the cost of carrying resources that are exploited at a distant location back to a central place for consumption must be considered. Since carrying a bulk of resources may decrease or preclude the foragers' possibility or ability to exploit more resources when encountered during their return trip, central place foraging apparently affects the choice of, search for, and handling of resources. The central place foraging model has shown that as the distance from a central place to the locations of encounter decrease, the diet breadth increases and includes both more and less profitable resources, whereas longer distances narrow the diet breadth. It has also been suggested that when travel cost is high relative to handling cost and the capacity of transport aids like bags limits the maximum load, foragers would choose the resources that provide the highest return rates per the transportable load rather than the most profitable resources. It has further been suggested that when the costs of transporting a procured resource to a central place are high, foragers would remove low-utility parts of the resource in the field rather than transport the bulky resource intact even if the removed parts have some utility (Bird and O'Connell 2006: 153-155; Kaplan and Hill 1992: 184-186; Kelly 1995: 133-135; Lupo 2006; Metcalfe and Barlow 1992; Winterhalder and Kennett 2006: 16-17).

When the costs of travelling long distances for foraging and transporting procured resources back to a central place do not meet the benefits of maintaining the central place at a particular location, or simply when foraging returns within a foraging radius of a central place fall below acceptable levels, foragers would consider the costs of breaking down the present central place, travelling, and setting up a new central place, and would decide to move the central place to another location which makes foraging more efficient and makes higher return rates possible. Unless the anticipated return rates of the next location minus the costs of moving is greater than the anticipated return rate of the present location, the foragers would remain at the present location and give up moving residentially. Therefore, sedentism emerges under a condition of local resource abundance in a context of regional scarcity (Kelly 1992: 46-48 and 51-54; 1995: 135*ff*, 152 and 160).

Foragers' mobility strategies can be viewed as a continuum between moving resources exploited at distant locations to stable residential bases and moving residential bases close to resource locations, or between individual move and group move. These two extreme ends of a continuum of moves are not mutually exclusive, and a reduction in movement as a group generally requires increased movement as individuals. In other words, sedentism does not emerge as people move less and less until they do not move at all. Sedentism may not reduce mobility, and no society is wholly sedentary (Kelly 1992: 49-52; 1995: 132*ff* and 160). Moving resources to residential bases by individuals is called logistical mobility and moving residential bases by groups is called residential mobility. For a descriptive purpose, the people who principally adopt a logistical mobility strategy and make few residential moves have particularly been called collectors and have been distinguished from foragers who are defined as people often moving their residential bases (Binford 1980: 5-12).

As for the manifestation of mobility in the form of material remains, it has been argued through ethnoarchaeological studies that different types of sites would be generated in relation to either the forager type of mobility or the collector type of mobility (**Fig.4.2**). Foragers generate two types of site: the residential base and the location. The location is where resource procuring and processing tasks like plant harvesting and animal hunting/butchering take place, and people leave for the residential base after the completion of their tasks. Therefore, the visibility of locations depends on the use condition and use frequency of the locations. On the other hand, due to the logistical character of resource procurement, collectors generate three additional types of sites; the field camp, the station, and the cache. A field camp is a temporary operational centre where a task group sleeps, eats, and maintains itself while far away from the residential base. A station is where a special-purpose task group is localised when engaged in ambushing and watching. A cache is where the large bulk of resources and raw materials obtained through foraging is temporarily stored, before it is transported to the residential base or task location. Such field storage is done in regular facilities (Binford 1980: 5-12).

As for the different levels of mobility, the economic zonation around a residential base has been argued on the basis of ethnographic studies

(**Fig.4.3**). The immediate surroundings of a residential base should be called the play radius for the children who reside in the residential base. Beyond the play radius, there is the foraging radius, which rarely extends beyond 10 km of the residential base. This is the zone searched and exploited by task parties that leave the residential base and return in a single day. Beyond the foraging radius is the logistical radius. This zone is exploited by special task groups that stay away from the residential base at least one night before returning. Beyond the logistical range lies an area which people are generally familiar with and attempt to monitor and to keep informed about resource distributions and changes in abundance, though they may not exploit the area at the time of monitoring. This regularly monitored area is called the extended range. Beyond the logistical or extended zone, there is the visiting zone. This is the area contemporaneously occupied by relatives and exchange partners, and hence within the foraging or logistical radius of another residential group. Trade, mating, information exchange and aggression take place there between different individuals and groups. Exploitation of resources in such a zone is generally dependent on establishing temporary residence at another people's place, and the visitors may participate in foraging by the host group (Binford 1982: 6-8; MacDonald and Hewlett 1999).

The difference in the frequency of residential moves between foragers and collectors is mainly related to the density and availability of resources in their respective environments. Three patterns of residential moves are recognised (**Fig.4.4**). Where resources are homogeneously distributed and the resources are abundant and available all the year around, a forager's residential mobility strategy would predominate, because it is most efficient to disperse and not to be tethered at one place for a long period. The residential move in the environment of very dense resource patches could be a half-radius continuous pattern, in which the residential base is continuously moved to the outer perimeter of the foraging radius previously covered with no development of a logistical zone. On the other hand, the residential move in the environment of relatively dense resource patches could be a complete-radius leapfrog pattern, in which the residential base is moved to a distant place but the logistical zones of each residential base partially overlap. Where

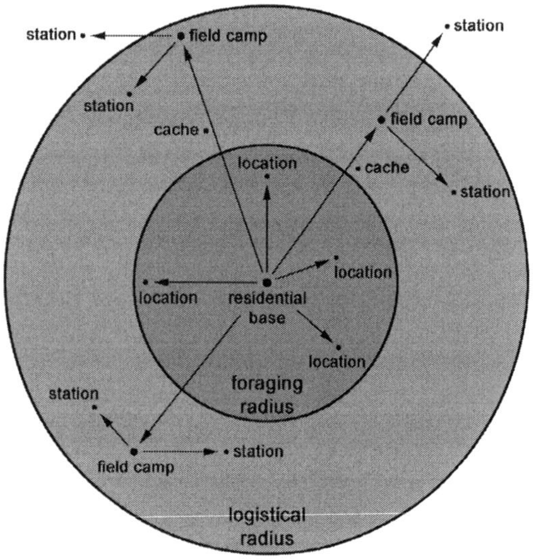

Fig.4.2. Manifestation of mobility in the form of different types of site

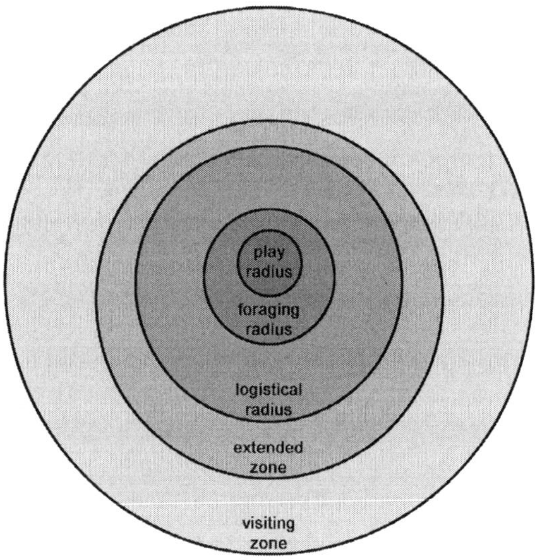

Fig.4.3. Economic zonation

resources are heterogeneously and patchily distributed and the resources are available only in specific periods of year, a collector's logistical mobility strategy would predominate, because it is most efficient to aggregate in a central place which is close to the primary resource location and to send out logistical task parties to the secondary and other lower-ranked resource locations. The residential move in the environment of sparse resource patches could be a point-to-point pattern, in which the residential base is moved to a fairly distant place with no overlap of the logistical zones of each residential base (Bettinger 2001: 154-156; Binford 1982: 8-11; Kelly 1995: 116-120).

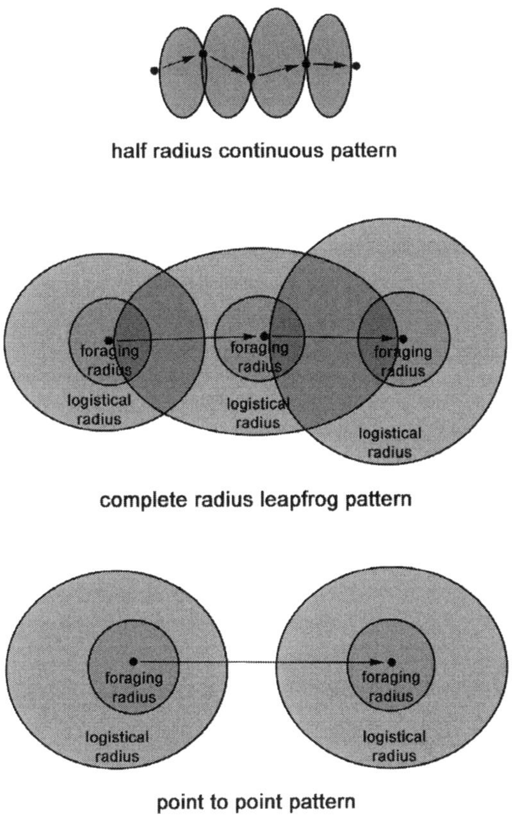

Fig.4.4. Different patterns of residential move

4.2.2.4. Information acquisition and maintenance of kin networks

Optimal foraging models are based on assumptions that foragers always have good information about the distribution and yield of resources. However, the variability of foragers' diet is actually subject to the extent to which complete information regarding potential resources can be acquired. It has been known from ethnography that it is not uncommon for foragers to make information-acquiring or monitoring trips specifically to determine the location of resources or resource patches and when and where to move camp, and to travel very long distances. This kind of mobility has recently been termed informational mobility. Such non-foraging activities apparently diminish return rates at a given moment because other resource exploiting opportunities are precluded, but can provide information that ensures the procurement of resources later. In other words, information acquisition entails opportunity costs and may reduce short-term return rates, but provides benefits through increasing long-term return rates. Alternatively, such informational moves can be embedded in other kinds of moves, thereby reducing opportunity costs. It is difficult to assess how much effort made by foragers in information acquisition would be worthwhile, but it has been suggested that patchy environments which vary temporarily at an intermediate rate but in large scale should be where foragers expend the greatest effort in information acquisition (Kaplan and Hill 1992: 186-187; Kelly 1995: 97-98; Whallon 2006: 260-264).

Another non-foraging activity which often entails trips is visiting relatives and exchange partners in distant places. The trip itself is apparently non-productive, and hence it seems to diminish return rates at a given moment, because other resource exploiting opportunities are precluded. However, ethnographic studies have shown that foragers usually maintain a network of kin ties across wide regions and use a variety of mechanisms to reinforce reciprocity, and that the objective of visiting relatives and exchange partners in distant places is often to beg for food at times of local food shortages. This kind of mobility has recently been termed network mobility. Maintaining large kin networks and allowing mutual visits entail some opportunity costs on the visitor side and resource losses on the host side, but provide both sides with benefits in the long run, because the favour will be reciprocated when circumstances change. Moreover, visitors can benefit by learning about resource locations from the hosts, and both can benefit from sharing information and considering the others' foraging plans (Cashdan 1992: 248 and 255; Whallon 2006: 260-264).

4.2.2.5. Time investment in subsistence technology

Resource exploitation does not necessarily require special tools and facilities, but many human foraging activities need them. The diet breadth model has implicitly predicted that the changes in search and handling costs due to improvements of tools, facilities and vehicles would result in changes in diet breadth. New technological items which shorten the time for searching and handling high-ranked resources could increase foraging efficiency and return rate, and thus could decrease diet breadth while encouraging the foragers to ignore lower-ranked resources (Kelly 1995: 89).

An important point which must be stressed here is that subsistence technologies are not invariables. As foraging-related investment decisions like prey choice and patch choice vary with changes in the time available to forage and the nature of available resources, investment in subsistence technologies is also a decision variable. Technological decisions are motivated by the single important goal of improving return rates by reducing handling time, but there is always a trade-off in spending more time making a tool/facility in order to reduce the time spent for collecting/catching and processing a resource, or spending less or no time making a tool/facility while being satisfied with less efficient, time-consuming collecting/catching and processing the resource (Bright *et al.* 2002: 165-166; Ugan *et al.* 2003: 1315*ff*).

Following the idea of optimal allocation of time, it has already been suggested that foragers would switch either to maximising resource exploitation by means of productive but time-consuming technologies, or, to minimising the time spent for resource exploitation by means of less time-consuming technologies. Different technologies would be chosen on the basis of their time-efficiency and used for varying combinations of resource maximisation and time minimisation strategies. Accordingly, it has also been argued that exploitation of one resource or one patch would continue until the decline of a return rate reached the least time-efficient point. Below that point, particularly those who use time-consuming technologies should switch to another more productive resource or patch, or should change their technological strategies. However, those who employ less time-consuming technologies could continue to exploit the resource for a longer time after a return rate started to decline.

One implication for the interpretation of subsistence technologies in the archaeological record is that if handling costs are generally low due to less time-consuming technologies, the diet should be broader. In contrast, if more time-consuming technologies are employed and handling costs are high, then the diet should be narrower. Another implication is that foragers using time-consuming technologies would have needed to exploit resources whose return rates were high, although foragers exploiting high return rate resources would not necessarily employ time-consuming technologies (Bird and O'Connell 2006: 153; Bousman 1993: 63-64).

The tech investment model improves this intuitive argument and addresses the time trade-off in foraging more formally by formulating the relationship between time investments in technology and handling time. A forager's goal when making subsistence tools/facilities is to acquire resources in the most efficient way, either by maximising the calories gained in some fixed time or minimising the time required to meet a fixed caloric need. Both of these ways would be realised by maximising the net caloric return rate.

The time available to forage is fixed by constraints like resource availability, foraging schedule, or the use life of the tools/facilities. When the tools/facilities are tied to particular locations and thus immobile, foraging time would depend not only on the use life but also on the duration and redundancy of site occupation. Grinding stones, pottery vessels, hunting blinds and game drives are examples of such immobile tools/facilities.

The model assumes that total foraging time (total time available to forage) consists of search time, handling time, and the making and maintaining time of technology. The amount of time spent handling a resource in the absence of an associated technology is called the total handling time. A unit of time invested in tool/facility making and maintaining, which is called the tech time, cannot be invested simultaneously in another foraging-related activity such as searching for resources. The model also assumes that each resource has a unique piece of technology associated with it, and that there are no versatile tools/facilities. It further assumes that each unit of time invested in technology decreases the total handling time of a resource by an equal or larger amount, because it makes no sense to invest in a technology that increases handling time. The optimal amount of time to invest in tool/facility making is determined by such variables as the search time, encounter rate, and intrinsic handling time of a resource. Intrinsic handling times may vary with inherent abilities of foragers like physical size and strength or with the context in which resources are procured, and are thus the most difficult to measure (Bright *et al.* 2002: 167; Ugan *et al.* 2003: 1316*ff*).

A simple prediction of the model is that where technologies serve to reduce the effort spent handling resources, the time invested in technologies should increase with the total time spent handling a resource. Another prediction is that the increased emphasis on a particular resource should be accompanied by an increase of time investment in making tools/facilities which facilitate efficient exploitation of the resource through reducing either the processing component or the collecting/catching component of handling time. Conversely, the decreased emphasis on other resources should be accompanied by a decrease of time investment in making tools/facilities for exploiting the resources. Such relationships between investments in technology and handling time in this model have an implication for the prey choice. Namely, the handling time and ranking of profitable resources depend on the efforts expended on subsistence technologies, and the efforts are subject to the amount of resources being handled. Thus, search time and encounter rates, which do not matter in the prey choice model, may become important components of prey choice decisions (Bright *et al.* 2002: 172-177; Ugan *et al.* 2003: 1321*ff*).

As has been known in ethnography, however, making and maintaining tools for foraging usually occur when the foragers stay at residential bases or field camps and not when they are on the move. Making and maintaining tools are possible while people are engaged in socialising activities like chatting, and in the evening when foraging is impractical. Therefore, the time trade-off assumption in the tech investment model has to take such non-foraging time into account. Nevertheless, foragers cannot make and maintain tools while sleeping, and thus the total time available to the foragers is certainly longer than the total foraging time but not infinitely long. Therefore, the time trade-off is still true in any case. Moreover, contrary to the model assumption, there are many subsistence technologies that are used to procure and handle more than one resource. The optimal time to invest in such a versatile technology would be subject to different encounter rates and intrinsic handling time of various resources, and thus would reflect the relative contributions of the various resources to the diet (Ugan *et al.* 2003: 1323-1324).

4.2.2.6. Foraging and technological organisation

Although the tech investment model assumes that foraging time depends on the use life of the tools/facilities, investments in making and maintaining tools/facilities can clearly affect the use life. Here is another trade-off of either making and maintaining an elaborate tool/facility that costs very much in terms of time and labour to procure and transport raw materials and to work on them meticulously but achieves the foraging goals without failure and/or lasts for a long period, or, making a crude, ephemeral tool/facility quickly by using readily-available raw materials and replacing it frequently or regularly by new ones. These technological trade-offs have been discussed as the expediency-curation alternatives in technological organisation and the reliability-maintainability alternatives in technological risk management (*e.g.*, Bamforth 1986; Bleed 1986; Parry and Kelly 1987), and also in terms of design theory (Hayden 1998: 3*ff*; Hayden *et al.* 1996).

The concepts of technological organisation and curation have gained popularity in archaeology since the rise of ethnoarchaeological studies in the 1970s (Odell 2001). Although not derived from optimal foraging models, the concepts of technological organisation and curation have a number of ideas in common with optimal foraging models. It has been understood that the designs of tools/facilities and the strategies for procuring raw materials, making, using, repairing/recycling and discarding/abandoning tools/facilities are considered and selected by makers/users depending on environmental, socioeconomic, technological, and task constraints (**Fig.4.5**). It has been emphasised that the sequence from raw material procurement to tool discard is closely related to and is particularly affected by the mobility of makers/users, and most arguments have centred on the difference between curated and expedient technologies in relation to the difference in mobility strategies. It has been argued that curated tools are made at residential bases in advance of expected tasks at distant locations, transported from location to location, resharpened and used repeatedly, whereas expedient tools are made at task locations at the time of need, used and then discarded upon completion of the task. Such differences in technology have been explained in terms of the foragers' mobility patterns and access to raw materials, the transport costs which are measured by the weight of raw materials or tools, the utility which is defined by the potential of different raw material/tool forms to serve the arising needs, and the predictability and bulkiness of the resources which foragers exploited (Binford 1979; 1980; Kuhn 1994; Nelson 1991; Shott 1986).

The reliability-maintainability alternatives are important elements of design consideration and curation. Foragers who are characterised by a residential mobility strategy are concerned with the risk that tools may break very badly and cannot be used on the next occasion, especially while they are moving in an environment where lithic raw materials are not readily available. Hence tool maintainability is very important for them. In contrast, collectors who are characterised by a logistical mobility strategy are more concerned with the risk that tools may fail to serve expected tasks on specific occasions. Hence tool reliability as well as tool maintainability is critical. Therefore, highly specialised tools tend to develop among collectors in the context of logistical moves at the expense of maintainability or versatility (Bettinger 2001: 156-157; Bleed 1986; Torrence 1989).

4.2.2.7. Habitat selection and territoriality

The prey choice model and patch choice model simply assume that foragers can move from patch to patch in an infinitely large area and are free to move, but the mobility range of a forager group is usually limited not only by geographic barriers but also by the presence of competitors who do not welcome strangers. A habitat is a much larger unit than a patch and is defined by its aggregate resource base at a regional scale. Therefore, foragers reside in a habitat, make residential and logistical moves in the habitat,

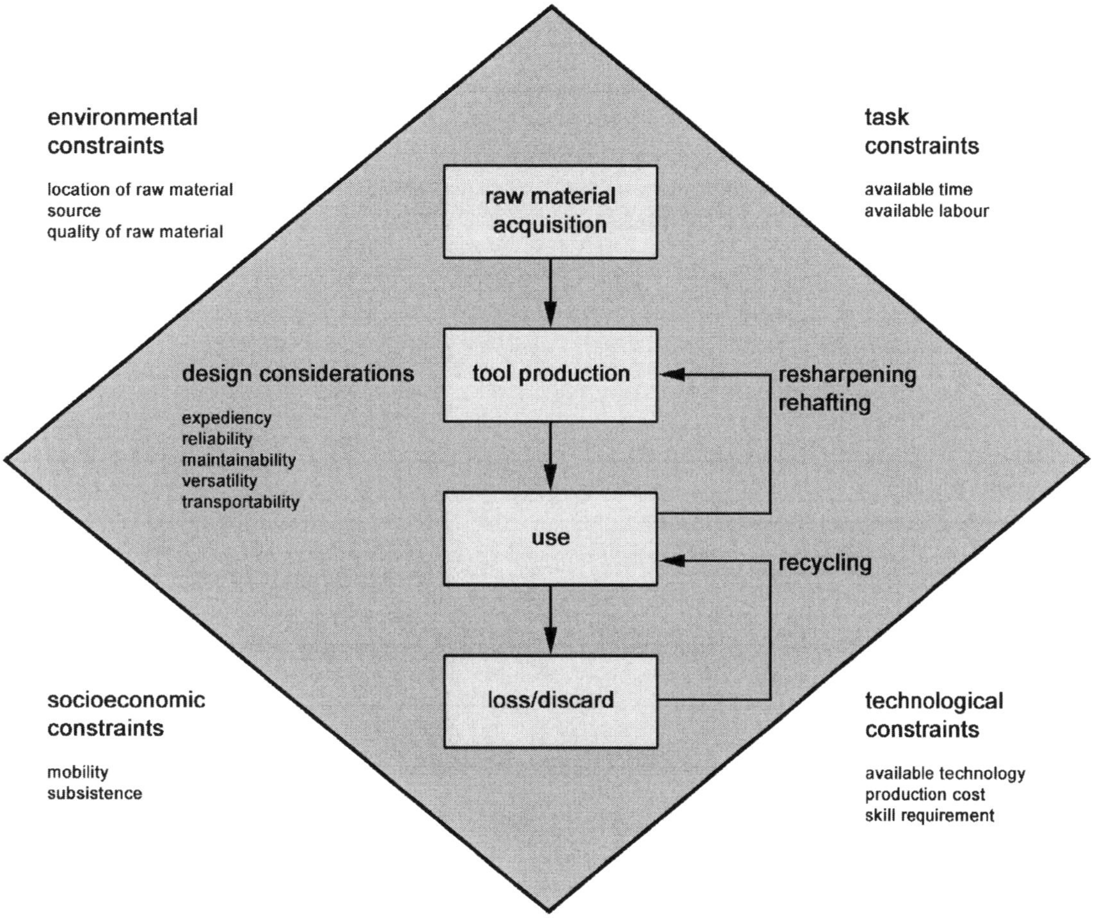

Fig.4.5. Technological organisation and various constraints

increase their population in the habitat, and migrate from a habitat to other habitats. The quality of a habitat depends not only on the abundance of resources but also on the density of the population that inhabit it and use the resources.

A significant question is what determines the size and location of residential groups. It has been known in ethnography that human foragers tend to live in large aggregated residential bases when they are exploiting highly-aggregated resources and to disperse into smaller groups when exploiting more solitary resources. It has been argued in other words that if the variance in total caloric returns between habitats was large, people should be aggregated in large groups at rich locations, but if the variance was small, people should be more uniformly distributed in small groups. In addition to resource abundance, there are more circumstances to encourage people to aggregate, to the extent that co-residents increase the fitness of the entire group. Living in large aggregated residential bases has benefits such as enhanced reproductive opportunities, better predator avoidance, reduced risk of starvation due to food sharing, increased foraging efficiency through information sharing about resource locations, and cooperative group collecting and hunting that outweigh the costs of competition and increase return rates or success rates (Cashdan 1992: 249-252 and 255-256).

However, if a habitat is rich in resources but is crowded with too many people, a poorer but empty area may be more desirable. Declining foraging efficiency due to an imbalance between population size and resource amount and increasing tension and fights between co-residents encourage the residential group to fission. After an optimal residential group size against the total amount of available resources is reached in a habitat and the habitat is no longer the most suitable and profitable in the region, then the second best habitat in the neighbourhood would be occupied. According to the ideal free distribution model, if future emigrants and immigrants who are all equal in competitive ability continue to select freely the best unoccupied habitat at the time of their fission or arrival, all occupied habitats would eventually become almost equal in profitability. On the other hand, the ideal despotic distribution model predicts that the best habitat would be occupied by people who are superior in competitive ability and would continue to be the best in profitability, and the residents of the best habitat would defend it against intruders from inferior habitats (Cashdan 1992: 252*ff*).

The difference between the ideal free distribution and ideal despotic distribution depends on whether the resources in given habitats are defendable, and whether the costs of defending the resources meet the benefits. An area which contains defendable resources and is defended against outsiders is defined as a territory. The major benefit of territorial defence is reducing competition for resources, but defending a territory entails costs in time and energy for monitoring and patrolling, and risks of being involved in fights against intruders. As the size of territory increases, the costs and risks of monitoring and patrolling increase and the benefits of exploiting more resources also increase as long as the resources are existent when needed and until the territory has more resources than the residents are capable of exploiting them efficiently. Therefore, territoriality would not be found where resources are mobile or transient but would be found only where critical resources are abundant, dense, predictable in time and space, and defendable. If a resource is so abundant that its availability or rate of capture is not limited to a population, there is no benefit to be gained by its defence and hence territoriality is not expected to occur. An optimal territorial size is determined by the balance between the costs and benefits of defence as well as the balance between population size and resource abundance. Territoriality is also subject to the characteristics and behaviour of competitors outside one's territory, and the difference in the extent to which residents and intruders value access to the territory. The access to a territory by outsiders can be tolerated when they are relatives or reciprocal partners of the residents, or when the theft of some resources by outsiders does not significantly affect the foraging returns of the residents and the avoidance of fight over the resources is more beneficial (Cashdan 1992: 259-266; Dyson-Hudson and Smith 1978).

4.2.2.8. Traveller-processor model

The forager-collector distinction described earlier was developed to understand their response to environmental variations and the temporal and spatial distributions of resources. Resource shortages in given locations are caused by overexploitation and environmental fluctuations, and people respond to such resource shortages by mobility and storage. However, resource shortages are caused by imbalance between available amount of resources and increasing population that consume the resources. Whereas resource shortages due to environmental fluctuations are seasonal or temporal, resource shortages due to population growth are not temporal and hence are not easily mitigated. Furthermore, population increase reduces opportunities for both residential and logistical mobility because a given habitat is densely occupied. Therefore, population is an important variable when foragers' adaptation is considered.

Based on the premise that human population has an increasing tendency from low densities to high densities, the traveller-processor model modifies the forager-collector distinction through uniting the prey choice and patch choice models, in order to clarify how population increase and resource depletion affect the way foragers allocate time, use a habitat, and acquire sufficient resources. When high-ranked, profitable resources are abundant and the population is small in a habitat, relatively more time is spent travelling between rich resource patches and searching for high-ranked, profitable resources within the patches, than is spent procuring and processing less profitable resources. As resources become locally scarce under these conditions, people move their residential base to richer patches. This is defined as the traveller strategy. Moving a residential base is less effective as more people compete for the same resources, because distant resource patches may already be occupied or their resources may be depleted. As an increasing population in a habitat reduces the advantages of moving residential base in the habitat, it makes foraging within a given patch increasingly less costly relative to other opportunities that require travelling. As a consequence, people should spend less time travelling between patches and expand patch choice to include low-ranked, less profitable patches where search cost and handling cost are higher. Furthermore, since more resources must be obtained in one large patch or a set of closely spaced patches, the diet breadth must expand to include lower-ranked, less profitable resources which require more handling time. Accordingly, less time is spent searching for high-ranked, profitable resources within the patch, and more time is spent procuring and processing low-ranked, less profitable resources. As these conditions grow more severely, logistical resource procurement becomes less economical, because resource procuring and processing are increasingly directed to low-ranked, less profitable resources. In the end, it becomes least costly to stay and consume resources within the patch despite their high handling cost. This is defined as the processor strategy (Bettinger 1991: 100-103; 2001: 164-166).

According to the model, the transition from the traveller to processor strategies is the transition from the time minimisation to resource maximisation strategies. Since resources are relatively abundant for travellers, they tend to minimise the amount of time invested in subsistence activities and to devote more time to other social activities. However, when they are gradually pressed by increasing population density, they initially maintain existing patterns of resource use and patch use and intensify through time minimizing strategies like more specialised division of labour, logistical procurement, and making and using of more specialised tools in ways that waste raw materials but save time. When population densities rise further, it becomes difficult to procure resources logistically because free access to distant patches diminishes. Therefore, maximising resources that can be obtained from fixed amounts of space becomes far more critical than minimising time devoted to subsistence activities. Consequently, low-ranked, costly resources are added to the optimal diet and an overall increase follows in the size and elaboration of assemblages of tools that enable mass processing of the resources by the hands of many people (Bettinger 1991: 101; 2001: 166).

4.2.2.9. Showing-off behaviour and costly signalling

Whereas the value of a resource has been measured in terms of caloric returns in the prey choice model, it has increasingly been realised and emphasised that caloric returns are not the sole measure of resource value, because there are ethnographic observations of foragers' behaviour that deviates from the predictions of the prey choice model.

Ethnographic foragers sometimes ignore plant foods when the plants increase overall caloric return rates, but exploit animals even when the pursuit of the animals decreases foraging return rates. It has been widely known that foragers prefer and desire animal meat and highly value the act of hunting even though hunting frequently provides meagre returns and plant foods are very important in their diet. One reason why meat is highly preferred is because meat contains high quality protein and fat, which are essential nutrients and sources of energy for the human body. Foragers' obsessions with animal meat and horticulturalists' special efforts to obtain meat by trade are well known in ethnography. Since fat is particularly valuable, animals that have little body fat are often considered as secondary resources or even famine food by ethnographic foragers. Another reason why animals are pursued at the expense of collecting plants is related to a gender-based division of labour. Even though men and women would do better by exploiting the same set of resources, in ethnography, men sometimes specialise on large game hunting and women specialise on plant collecting at the expense of increasing overall foraging efficiency. It can be said that since women are collecting carbohydrates, men may select resources for protein and fat rather than calories, thereby complementing food collected by women. It must be considered that foragers make trade-offs between carbohydrate, protein and fat acquisition (Kaplan and Hill 1992: 176; Kelly 1995: 101-107).

A further reason why protein/fat-rich animals are preferentially pursued by men foragers in spite of diminishing return rates may be because men can occasionally bring such a great nutritional and caloric package as large animal meat through risky hunting, thereby acquiring high status or prestige as excellent hunters and gaining great reproductive and social benefits. Hunters can signal through hunting physical quality such as strength, stamina, perception and risk taking, and cognitive skills involving the ecological and ethological knowledge needed to locate and capture game animals, as well as leadership skills including charisma and organisational abilities. The hunters who successfully exhibit their quality and skills acquire more and better mating opportunities and allies. Competitive display through hunting by men may play an important role in preferentially choosing the pursuit of animals. Such a showing-off behaviour in men's hunting has been commonly observed in ethnography and known to be quite unique to humans. Showing-off entails costs and risks, but it certainly brings benefits of increasing fitness in the social realm. Therefore, it is understood as costly signalling (Bird and O'Connell 2006: 164-166; Hawkes and Bliege Bird 2002; Smith *et al.* 2003).

Seemingly wasteful and uneconomical farming activities of ethnographic foragers are also known. Among Melanesian societies, men often concentrate on growing a few yams which are as large as possible. Yams can become extremely large depending on the depth and quality of soil, but such large yams are woody and inedible. Men tend to devote time to taking care of yams in special gardens, and the yams are grown primarily for display at feasts, for gift giving, and for trade, whereas women plant yams for daily consumption. Since considerable time investment, skill and esoteric knowledge are needed for growing large yams, men gain through growing large yams not only a reputation as skilled and knowledgeable men but also much social attention and a measure of influence in public decision making processes (Bliege Bird and Smith 2005).

It can be concluded that the choice of which resources are exploited depends not only on their caloric returns and ecological constraints but also on risk and prestige associated with their capture and use. This conclusion lets the narrow economic concern of optimal foraging models turn to social issues like gender, prestige and power that structure and affect economic activities (Kelly 1995: 107-108; Winterhalder and Kennett 2006: 17-18). An interesting question is not whether men consistently favour costly signalling over maximisation of caloric return rates while foraging, but under what conditions men tend to prefer one or the other (Bird and O'Connell 2006: 166).

4.2.2.10. Reproductive interests

As already mentioned in the description of how foragers allocate their time to foraging and non-foraging activities, seeking mates as well as foraging food resources is vital for fertile adult individuals to reproduce themselves and to ensure the prosperity of their kin groups. According to a life-history model, individual life effort consists of somatic effort and reproductive effort. Somatic effort refers to ensuring one's physical survival through securing shelter and protection from predators and obtaining food. Reproductive effort refers to getting one's copies into subsequent generations, and includes mating effort, parental effort and nepotistic effort. Therefore, the reproductive interests of foragers may affect the purely subsistence concerns of foraging activities, but may also be constrained by the spatial range and time allocation of foraging activities. In other words, there are trade-offs between somatic and reproductive efforts. However, there are no ethnographic data to show how and to what extent foragers' subsistence is influenced by their parental and nepotistic efforts.

A cross-cultural study has revealed that mating distances tend to be longer among mobile foragers whose population density is low and much shorter among sedentary horticulturalists whose population density is high, and that adult males tend to travel farther than adult females. However, it has seldom been made clear how these facts are linked to the reproductive interests of the people in question, because people travel for multiple reasons. On the other hand, some ethnographic data have shown that there is a significant relationship between foraging and mating ranges for males but not for females, and that young adult male foragers tend to travel farther and more frequently than females and other age groups. Evolutionary theory has also suggested that there is competition among men for mates and hence men tend to take risks in order to find and obtain mates. Therefore, it is argued that the foraging range of males is in part a function of their search for mates, though reproductive interests may not replace subsistence interests and may not constitute the prime mover of the travels. It is also argued that most individuals of foragers find mates in the logistical radius, but some other individuals of foragers with few close kinsmen are likely to travel long distances to the extended or visiting zone in order to find mates (MacDonald and Hewlett 1999).

4.3. Some considerations on the Fayum data in the light of optimal foraging models

In the light of optimal foraging models and related concepts, it is necessary to re-evaluate the ecological and archaeological data of the Fayum. Firstly, it is possible to assess to some extent the relative value of food resources which were available or are supposed to have been available in the Fayum. However, it is very difficult to estimate encounter rates and the net return rates, because it is often unclear by what means and under what conditions a given resource was procured, and because modern experiments cannot replicate all the factors which must have affected foraging efficiency and foraging decisions in the past (Bettinger 1991: 103-104). Thus, the relative value of the Fayum food resources would be assessed mainly in terms of their nutrients and potential risk. In addition, it is worth reconsidering the mobility patterns of the Fayum inhabitants in terms of residential/logistical moves, emergent sedentism and territoriality. Moreover, lithic technological changes at the transition between the Fayum Epipalaeolithic and Neolithic should not necessarily be understood as the evidence of population replacement but could alternatively be considered as an indication of optimisation in technology.

4.3.1. Optimal diet of the Fayum inhabitants

Concerning plant foods in the Fayum, as described earlier, seeds and roots normally have lower return rates than small, medium or even large-sized animals due to high handling costs. Although not explicitly based on the diet breadth model, a cross-cultural, statistical study of the proportions of terrestrial animals, aquatic animals and plants in the diet of ethnographic foragers has found that the availability of aquatic resources is clearly of prime importance in determining the role of plants in the diet. The reliance on aquatic resources is negatively correlated with the reliance on plants, and where there are severe constraints on the availability of aquatic resources, the proportion of plants is maximised accordingly (Keeley 1995; 1999). Therefore, no matter how abundant and how rich in carbohydrate the tubers of nutgrass and clubrush and the rhizomes of catstail and reed were in the Fayum, it may be that they were not usually or preferentially exploited because of time-consuming and labour-intensive peeling, grinding/pounding and grating in order to render them edible, especially when there were other sources of calorie or carbohydrate that provide higher returns.

The rarity of grinding stones at Epipalaeolithic sites in the Fayum stands in sharp contrast to the abundance of grinding stones at Late Palaeolithic sites in Wadi Kubbaniya, where tuber grinding/pounding by using grinding stones has been well attested (Hillman *et al.* 1989: 190-191). Hence the exploitation of tubers in the Fayum Epipalaeolithic is not certain, though reusing of Epipalaeolithic grinding stones by Neolithic people has been suggested (Wetterstrom 1993: 190). If the Fayum inhabitants had actually been accustomed to spend time and energy grinding/pounding tubers since the Epipalaeolithic, they would not have felt reluctant to adopt wheat and barley which also required grinding.

However, adding domesticated wheat and barley to the diet is not as simple as harvesting other previously-ignored wild plants. Wheat/barley farming certainly reduces search time within the total foraging time but instead requires investments of time and labour for sowing, weeding and protecting as well as threshing. In the light of cost-benefit considerations, the increase in handling costs and the risks of bad harvest due to droughts, pests and infectious diseases must be rewarded by the increase in yield, but the high crop yield requires extremely time-consuming and labour-intensive grain processing. In this sense, it can be said that domesticated wheat and barley were not very profitable initially, and it is probable that they were fairly low-ranked in the diet breadth.

The diet breadth model has suggested that the adoption of novel resources could be expected to occur under conditions of either scarcity or abundance with different goals. In a resource-rich environment where high-ranked resources are abundant and a narrow diet maximises efficiency, a new resource is likely to replace one or more existing resources only if it is profitable. Also in a resource-rich environment where the required minimum return rate is much lower than the expected average and the minimisation of risks is a goal, the adoption of a new resource is less contingent on its profitability and should occur by addition rather than replacement. In a resource-poor environment where a narrow diet composed of high-quality resources minimises risks, a new resource should be ignored unless it is highly profitable. In a resource-poor environment where a broad diet maximises efficiency, a new resource is likely to be added even if it is of low quality (Gremillion 1996: 189 and 199-200).

Therefore, according to the diet breadth model, it is assumed that the initial adoption of domesticated wheat and barley in the Fayum Neolithic was intended either for replacement of more costly sources of carbohydrate or for substitution for some temporarily-unavailable sources of carbohydrate, thereby optimising the diet. Considering that no other possible sources of carbohydrate in the Fayum seem to be more costly than domesticated wheat and barley, it is most likely that when the Fayum people introduced wheat and barley, they were eager to minimise risk under a basically resource-rich condition while knowing that opportunity costs of farming were low. Alternatively, it is also probable that people were put in the situation where they had no other choice but to take such less profitable resources for survival. However, optimal allocation of time to producing wheat and barley would have remained low until its profitability was enhanced, and/or constraints on the benefits of additional time allocation were removed by technological innovations to reduce handling time. From a long-term perspective, it may be said that the introduction of domesticated wheat and barley was a moment to shift to a strategy that reduced the expected variation in returns, or a strategy that maximised the yield of less profitable resources.

Concerning the sources of protein and fat, wheat and barley provide some protein, and legumes like vetch could have provided rich protein if they had actually been harvested, but oily seeds like olives are not known in the prehistory of Egypt. Thus it is likely that protein and fat were obtained from animal and fish meat. In the Fayum, examples of resources with high measures of constancy include aquatic resources like fish and shellfish. Resources with high measures of contingency include migratory waterfowl. Resources with low predictability due to both low constancy and contingency include terrestrial mammals like gazelle. Therefore, as mentioned in Chapter 3, fish in general seem to have been the most reliable resource for the Fayum inhabitants throughout the Epipalaeolithic and Neolithic periods.

According to a comparison of nutritional returns from different fish species, catfish species offer substantially more fat returns than perch species (Gifford-Gonzalez *et al.* 1999: 407-408). If this was also the case with the Fayum ichthyofauna, clariid catfish could have been preferred to, and higher-ranked, than Nile perch. Given these assets of catfish, it may be assumed that catching deep water fish was fortuitous in nature during the two possible fishing seasons, and was supplementary in nature during low lake water. In addition, according to a comparison of nutritional returns from other aquatic resources, crocodile offers relatively high fat returns and far more calories per unit of flesh than turtle and fish like catfish and perch do (Gifford-Gonzalez *et al.* 1999: 407-408). Therefore, crocodile may have been the highest-ranked prey in the Fayum where all these aquatic resources were available to hunter-fishers.

Although the presence of small mammals like hares as potential food resources in the Fayum Epipalaeolithic and Neolithic diet should not be ignored, it is not certain whether such small mammals occupied a permanent position in the diet breadth of the Fayum inhabitants, firstly because small mammals are generally not rich in fat and hence are not preferred, and secondly because exploiting small mammals is usually not cost-efficient, as mentioned earlier. According to a comparison of the amount of edible meat obtained from various Nilotic mammals on the premise that the percentage of edible meat is approximately 50 percent of live weight (Hassan 1974: 152-154 and table 44), whereas a hare weighing 1.5 kg provides only 0.75 kg meat, a dorcas gazelle weighing 22 kg provides 11 kg meat and a hartebeest weighing 165 kg provides 82.50 kg meat. An aurochs weighing 300 kg provides 150 kg meat, and a hippopotamus weighing 1500 kg provides 750 kg meat. As described in ethnography, the reward of successful hippopotamus hunting is extremely great, and its nutritional contribution eclipses those from all other taxa available in a lacustrine environment (Gifford-Gonzalez *et al.* 1999: 402). Therefore, it is reasonable to assume that small mammals may have been ignored no matter how often they were encountered around a camp, and that they may perhaps have been added to the diet only when other most commonly-hunted animals like dorcas gazelle and hartebeest were not readily available.

It is difficult to know whether the introduction of domesticated sheep and goats in the Fayum Neolithic was intended as substitution for some vanishing wild animals. However, adding domesticated sheep and goats to the diet is also not as simple as catching other usually-ignored wild animals. Sheep/goat herding certainly reduces search time within the total foraging time, but instead requires investments of time and labour for feeding and protecting. In the light of cost-benefit considerations, the increase in handling costs and the risks of loss due to disease or accidents must be rewarded by the increase in meat yield. In this sense, domesticated sheep and goats do not seem to be more profitable than other medium to small-sized wild animals.

As mentioned in Chapter 3, another notable change in the animal resource exploitation in the Fayum Neolithic is slightly more frequent exploitation of crocodile and hippopotamus. It can be said on these grounds that the Fayum Neolithic people attempted to ensure the procurement of protein and fat from animals other than dorcas gazelle and hartebeest, regardless of the advent of domesticated sheep and goats. The reason for the introduction of domesticated sheep and goats may thus be not necessarily to obtain meat but to obtain nutrient-rich dairy products and wool/hair, which are definitely the additional and special value of these animals. However, since it was recently revealed that sheep and goats had actually been slaughtered at a young age at Kom K and Kom W (Van Neer and Linseele 2007), it must be assumed that obtaining meat was the primary reason for the adoption of sheep and goats by at least the inhabitants of Kom K and Kom W in the Fayum Neolithic. It may be considered that whereas sheep and goats have been kept for the stable supply of meat, hunting of crocodile and hippopotamus has developed as a kind of showing-off behaviour by male hunters who wanted to acquire prestige as brave hunters and good providers of meat.

The possible rank or position of wheat/barley and sheep/goat in the Fayum Neolithic diet in the light of the diet breadth model is illustrated in **Fig.4.6**.

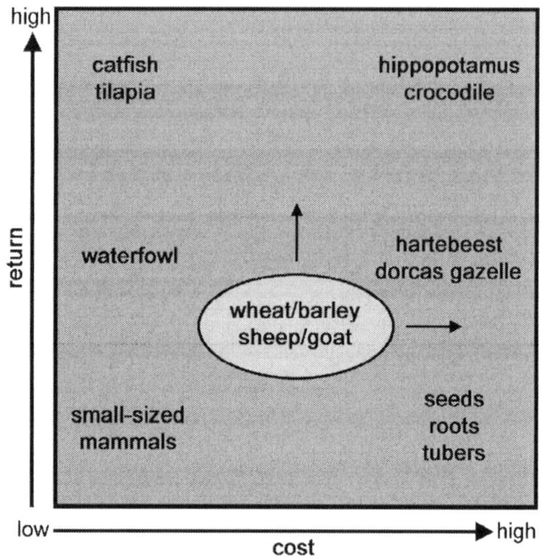

Fig.4.6. The possible rank or position of wheat/barley and sheep/goat in the Fayum Neolithic diet in the light of the diet breadth model

4.3.2. Risk prevention/responsive strategies of the Fayum inhabitants

Given the difficulty of evaluating the value or asset of domesticates in terms of nutrition and handling costs, the study of the introduction of wheat/barley farming and sheep/goat herding in the Fayum Neolithic would have to consider how variations in resource structure occurred when they arrived in terms of risk prevention and risk responsive strategies of Fayum inhabitants. An asset of wheat and barley is apparently that they provide seeds which are storable for a longer period, and an asset of sheep and goats is also that fresh meat can be kept alive for a long period. If the Fayum Epipalaeolithic people had actually preserved and stored an excessive amount of fish and tubers for the consumption in lean seasons, it can be assumed that the subsequent Neolithic people enhanced such a risk responsive strategy and diversified the food storage by introducing wheat/barley and sheep/goats, because it is unclear whether fish and particularly tubers consequently dropped out of the stored food items.

On the other hand, the drawbacks of wheat/barley farming and sheep/goat herding are undoubtedly that people had to pay more attention to preventing risks of wasting their time and labour investment by losing or failing these resources due to droughts, pests and infectious diseases. Therefore, dividing the herds of sheep and goats and keeping them separately at different places, and sowing/planting wheat and barley at different places at different times, for instance, are necessary strategies to diversify investment risks and to average losses (Cashdan 1992: 247). Such strategies also make farming and herding quite costly.

The introduction of foreign domesticates must have made a new infector-infected relationship in the Fayum pathology and a new predator-prey relationship in the Fayum ecology, and the losses of the farming/herding yield could have been occasionally caused by infectious organisms and predators other than humans. The Fayum people may have seen their crops and herds killed by bacteria, fungi, viruses and predators in the early stage of adoption. It must have taken extra time for people to let the crops and herds gain resistance/immunity against infectious organisms and to get rid of predators before making farming and herding a reliable subsistence. For instance, red fox, jackal and striped hyena could be predators of lambs and kids, though such predation has not been attested archaeologically. The interesting coincidence of the increase of crocodile and hippopotamus in the faunal assemblages with the beginning of wheat/barley farming and sheep/goat herding in the Fayum Neolithic may be explained from a viewpoint of risk prevention. That is, crocodile may have been hunted because crocodile attacks and eats almost any animals that come to take a drink at the edge of the water and hence was one of the dangerous predators of sheep and goats in the Fayum. Hippopotamus may have been hunted because hippopotamus was a voracious eater of grasses, devastating farmland which is supposed to have been near the lakeshore. Hunting hippopotamus not only for meat but also for protecting farmland has been argued on the basis of numerous hippopotamus bones at Neolithic sites of Merimde Beni Salama and El Omari (Boessneck and von den Driesch 1990: 100-101; von den Driesch and Boessneck 1985: 41), and this may also be the case in the Fayum.

4.3.3. The mobility and residential patterns of the Fayum inhabitants

It has been argued that the diet breadth of a group of people in the archaeological record can be an indicator of their occupation intensity of a locus or a resource patch (Stiner and Munro 2002). The intensity of the occupation of a locus or a patch is a combined function of the length of stay, the frequency of visits, and the size of inhabitant population at a locus or a patch per unit time. As any or all of these factors increase, the intensity of inhabitants' resource exploitation must also increase, and they have to include more lower-ranked resources in their diet in order to substitute for decreasing high-ranked resources. Therefore, it is assumed that high intensity occupations should create assemblages with high proportions of low-ranked resources whereas low intensity occupations should create assemblages with high proportion of high-ranked resources. Following this assumption, it can be considered that most Fayum Epipalaeolithic and Neolithic sites which yielded faunal assemblages with high proportions of high-ranked prey like catfish and medium to large-sized mammals and with very low proportions of low-ranked prey like small mammals were not occupied intensively. However, such a consideration does not sufficiently explain the residential patterns of the Fayum inhabitants.

One problem of previous arguments about the residential patterns of the Fayum inhabitants is that the mobility patterns of the Fayum inhabitants have not explicitly been considered. As described earlier, mobility strategies for resource procurement can be chosen between moving residential bases to the resource locations and moving resources exploited at distant locations to stable residential bases, and mobility patterns can be viewed as a continuum between these two extreme strategies. There is little doubt that the Fayum inhabitants had to aggregate around the lake and pools fed by Nile floods in summer and rainfall in winter, in order to maintain a close link to drinking water. Therefore, a certain degree of water-tethered sedentary life should have been quite natural in the Fayum Epipalaeolithic and Neolithic. It is quite likely that the Fayum inhabitants first located their residential bases near water sources and then started foraging around residential bases, even though no substantial dwelling structures of the Epipalaeolithic and Neolithic periods have so far been found in the Fayum.

It is not easy to understand the occurrence, spatial scale, and frequency of the foraging, logistical, and residential moves by the Fayum Epipalaeolithic and Neolithic inhabitants through looking at the known archaeological sites on the north and southwest sides of the lake in the Fayum, because the contemporaneity of the sites is not always clear. However, the site distribution pattern seen in the archaeological record certainly shows a repetitive long-term pattern in the positioning of adaptive systems in a given geographic space by its inhabitants (Binford 1982: 6). Therefore, it is not irrelevant to read site patterning which has been maintained for a length of time by referring to sound theoretical models. An important question is which location was favoured when a residential base was established. In the light of the central place foraging model (Bird and O'Connell 2006: 154), this question can be answered by (1) identifying the resources or resource patches potentially available to Fayum people, (2) isolating those which were most likely to be exploited, (3) plotting their distribution across the landscape, and then (4) determining which location maximised the flow of resources to the people on a daily basis. Alternatively, it is possible to assume intuitionally that Fayum Epipalaeolithic people maintained large sites like Site E29H1 as a residential base and visited nearby locations in a radial pattern for procuring resources on a daily basis. Likewise, Fayum Neolithic people may have maintained large sites like Kom K, Kom W and Site E29G3 as residential bases and visited nearby locations in a radial pattern for procuring resources on a daily basis. It must be worthwhile to draw 1-10 km foraging radii around a possible residential base and to see which geographical features and resource localities are included in the radii. Such a spatial analysis may give a clue to better understand the mobility and residential patterns of the Fayum inhabitants.

Considering the very short distance between the known sites around each Basin and the short distance between the Basins on the northern shore, it can be speculated that the situation in the Fayum Neolithic as represented by some large sites with high artefact density like Kom K, Kom W and Site E29G3 and many small, supposedly temporary sites in their surroundings does not indicate frequent residential moves on a daily or weekly basis but suggests individual foraging moves from residential bases. The residential bases may have been moved depending not only on transgressing and regressing lake margins but also on the changing distribution and profitability of resource patches and the changing comfort of the bases on a seasonal and annual basis. As mentioned in Chapter 3, previous researchers have described that three different types of Fayum Neolithic sites might represent different subsistence activities and different durations of stay (Kozlowski and Ginter 1989: 177; Wetterstrom 1993: 209-210). However, this description lacks an explanation of mobility patterns in relation to a principal residential pattern, which must be subject to the availability of resources and desirable localities for farming and herding. Likewise, the situation in the Fayum Epipalaeolithic as represented by some large sites like Site E29H1 and other small, supposedly ephemeral sites in their surroundings may also not indicate frequent residential moves on a daily or weekly basis but suggest individual foraging moves from residential bases. The residential bases may have been moved for the same reasons. Previous researchers' descriptions that all Fayum Epipalaeolithic sites were the remains of occasional or seasonal encampments (Hassan 1986b: 496; Wetterstrom 1993: 187) are rather simplistic.

Moreover, the occurrence of either logistical moves or long distance residential moves can surely be detected by focusing on the presence of locally-unavailable material items. As mentioned in Chapter 3, long distance moves of Fayum Epipalaeolithic people to Gebel Qatrani for lithic raw material and to the Nile Valley for some seasonally-available resources have been suggested (Wendorf and Schild 1976: 311 and 317; Wetterstrom 1993: 191), with a connotation that the former was a logistical move whereas the latter was a seasonal residential move. However, this suggestion has not been substantiated. In contrast, there is clear evidence for very long distance moves of people, such as the presence of non-local material items at Neolithic sites. The spatial scale of their moves ranges from at least 10 km to more than 100 km. The non-local material items could arrive in the Fayum either through return trip by the Fayum inhabitants or through outsiders' visit to the Fayum. Therefore, it is necessary to elucidate whether the transport of non-local material items to the Fayum Neolithic habitat was likely to be realised by logistical moves by individuals, residential moves in groups, or outsiders' visit in individuals or in groups, through studying the

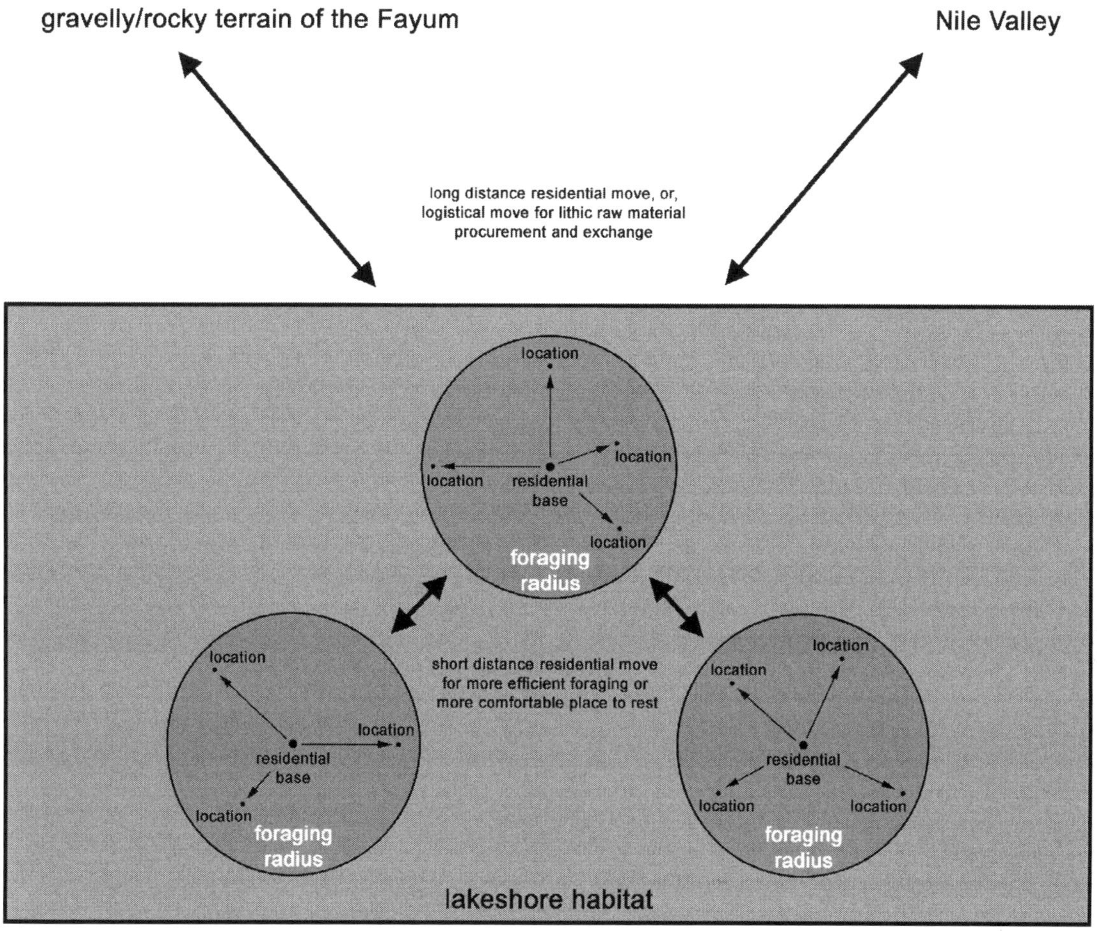

Fig.4.7. The possible mobility patterns of the Fayum inhabitants

non-local material items. Such a study may give a further clue for understanding the mobility patterns of the Fayum Neolithic people.

The possible mobility patterns of the Fayum inhabitants are illustrated in **Fig.4.7.**

4.3.4. Habitat selection and territoriality of the Fayum inhabitants

Although many prehistoric sites found to date in the Fayum show the traces of overlapping occupations by Epipalaeolithic and Neolithic people, there seems to be an increase in the number of occupation sites in the Neolithic period. Thus it is possible to assume that population in the Fayum was gradually growing, or grew suddenly due to the inflow of new populations from outside the Fayum caused by the desiccation of the Western Desert around the onset of the Middle Holocene.

If more strangers aggregated around a large body of water in the Fayum perennially or seasonally, the right to critical resources may have become more specific and rigid, and the notion of territoriality may perhaps have been generated. It is uncertain which resources were actually defendable, and how large an area could be recognised as one territory owned by one band of foragers in the Fayum, but patches of dense and predictable resources like good fisheries and natural stands of edible marsh plants could be defended against strangers. In such circumstances, freedom of foraging activities elsewhere must have become gradually hampered, even though the right to visit each other's territory were ensured by socioeconomic ties like marriage and reciprocity, and permission to enter other's territory would not be refused. Consequently, stressful situations within and between territories must have occasionally occurred. In the case of the Fayum, annual and long-term fluctuations of lake level and the subsequent appearance and disappearance of edible plant stands could be another cause of such stressful situations.

As described in Chapter 2 and also suggested by the traveller-processor model, in such circumstances, much labour may have become increasingly invested to ensure sufficient yield from one's own territory and to increase the storage of the harvest, because it was burdensome to visit and exploit another's territory. Such an intensification of food procurement in circumscribed habitats has the potential to lead to the beginning of food production and sedentism, especially if predictable, relocatable and tameable food resources are available and if technological innovations which would permit efficient utilisation of the resources arise. It is important to assume such a situation as a reason for the introduction of farming and herding in the Fayum.

4.3.5. Changes in subsistence technology at the Fayum Epipalaeolithic-Neolithic transition

Given that technological decisions are motivated by the single goal of improving return rates by reducing handling time, lithic technological changes at the transition between the Fayum Epipalaeolithic and Neolithic may be understood not only as changes in raw material availability, mobility, and gender roles, for instance, but also as the shifting focus on resources and resultant change in time invested to handle the resources. As described in Chapter 3, the most obvious change in lithic technology in the Fayum is the shift from the microlithic industry in the Epipalaeolithic to the retouched flake industry in the Neolithic.

The increasing predominance of microlithic artefacts during the Late-Terminal Pleistocene and Early Holocene, which is called microlithisation, and the deviation from this tendency after the Early Holocene are global phenomena (Kuhn and Elston 2002). Lithic industries of North Africa have also been dominated by backed bladelets through the Late Pleistocene and Early Holocene. Backed bladelets appeared suddenly out of nowhere all across North Africa from Morocco to Egypt about 21000-22000 years ago, and endured for at least ten thousand years (Close 2002a: 31-34). It has been argued that decreased seasonality under glacial conditions and low human population density allowed foragers to minimise the time spent on foraging and toolmaking and to be satisfied with expedient, simple microliths for composite tools, whereas increased seasonality and human population density after the Early Holocene forced foragers to maximise the exploitation of seasonally-abundant resources and costly resources either by more time-saving, expendable tools/facilities or by more specialised tools/facilities (Bettinger 2001: 158-166). This argument must generally be the case with the Fayum.

The idea of risk prevention must also have played a role in developing new technologies to handle resources. In this case, avoiding or reducing the risk of failure at the time of tool/facility using activity was the motive to invest time and energy to make specialised, reliable tools/facilities. There is little doubt that more frequent exploitation of crocodile and hippopotamus in the Fayum Neolithic was not made possible without lowering the high risk of exploiting these aggressive animals. The high nutritional value of crocodile and hippopotamus may perhaps have already been recognised by the Fayum inhabitants through scavenging their carcasses fortuitously, but it is probably not until innovations in hunting tactics and technologies occurred that the Fayum hunters could exploit these most profitable animals whenever encountered alive on the lakeshore. Such innovations may include not only more tactical hunting by a group rather than an individual but also hunting weapons which have better killing power. This topic will be discussed further in Chapter 7.

4.4. Socioeconomic model

As exemplified by men's showing-off behaviour mentioned earlier, foragers' behaviours cannot always be explained in terms of the optimisation of diet. Considering that increasing fitness is the ultimate biological goal of life, it is understandable that social interaction between individuals and between groups through food resources may play an important role in achieving reproductive success. Apart from anthropological studies that particularly focus on foragers living in harmony with nature and optimising their diet by various adaptive strategies, it has been gradually recognised that some ethnographic forager groups around the world have developed complex societies characterised by sedentary settlements with food storage facilities, a large number of people, the presence of social ranks and outstanding leaders, and the occurrence of lavish feasts. Such seemingly extraordinary examples have drawn special attentions from anthropologists, and have been classified as a distinctive type of society through the studies on the background of the emergence of such phenomena.

4.4.1. The socioeconomic competition model

According to Hayden, who studied many ethnographic examples (Hayden 1995b; 2001), socioeconomic equality and reciprocity tend to be dominant in regions where wild food resources are generally poor. Conversely, socioeconomic competition using food resources tends to occur in regions where wild food resources are abundant. In such regions, ambitious individuals acquire control of food resources, creating reciprocal relationships with others, and eventually generate debt relationships with members of the community. Any ethic of sharing and equality is weakened and status quests through food provisioning do not need to be repressed. Ambitious individuals may distribute food generously and competitively on occasions such as feasts, thereby raising their status. Such an act facilitates the ambitious individuals to find mates and allies. Recipients become indebted to providers such that they become subordinate to the providers, and this leads to the emergence of fixed socioeconomic inequality.

An implication of such anthropological observations for the study of social developments in prehistory is that only in such complex, trans-egalitarian forager societies, emerging socioeconomic competition between ambitious individuals could drive them to gain exclusive control of rich wild food resources and give them motives to start food production, either by domestication of indigenous plants and animals or by adoption of domesticates from others. In other words, ambitious leaders in societies would have been competitively willing to adopt novel things in order to interest their followers, to check their rivals and eventually to consolidate their positions, and such leaders would also have first adopted domesticates in order to please people by serving a large amount of crops, meat and dairy products on occasions such as feasts, rather than to compensate for the shortage of food provided by foraging. This argument has been formulated as the socioeconomic competition model for the beginning of food production (Hayden 1990; 1992). It must be noted that although this model has developed through cross-cultural anthropological observations, its theoretical basis is actually very close to the idea of costly signalling in human behavioural ecology described earlier (Bliege Bird and Smith 2005; Bird and O'Connell 2006: 167-168).

What is new about this socioeconomic competition model for the study of the beginning of food production is that it pays explicit attention to the motives of foragers to attempt farming and herding for acquiring prestige and high social status through the distribution of the farming and herding products as luxury or costly foods. Another notable thing is that this model is claimed to be applicable to most cases of the beginning of food production around the world. However, it has been pointed out that in many cases in world prehistory initial attempts of food production actually began long before ample evidence of population increase and social complexity appeared in the archaeological record. Therefore, the socioeconomic competition model might be applicable to the later stages of social development, and would better explain the intensification of food production or initial adoption of food production as a coherent system from others (Bettinger 2006: 309-310; Keeley 1995: 268*ff*; Winterhalder and Kennett 2006: 6-7).

An important question is under what conditions costly and status-related food production and distribution may be expected to develop. Most scholars concur with the assertion that a baseline of richness in wild food resources is essential for the concentration of population which is associated with increasing social complexity. However, controversy remains whether constant rich conditions or occasional stressful conditions provided the primary stimulus for socioeconomic competition and the emergence of ambitious food providers. Based on the assumption that there must have been periods when overall resource richness was occasionally diminished by temporary climatic or environmental events, some have asserted that such periods were never times of emerging socioeconomic competition. Others have been of the opinion that such periods were precisely the times that inequality increased and consequently certain members of society were able to stimulate the reorganisation of labour (Arnold 1993: 82-89; Arnold 1996: 96-101). Although it is difficult to determine which conditions may have indeed prompted the socioeconomic competition, it is possible that climatic fluctuations under generally mild Early-Middle Holocene conditions may have occasionally provided certain persons in societies with opportunities to reorganise subsistence, and eventually, ambitious and competitive persons who were willing to display their status appeared.

4.4.2. The social meaning of technology and the emergence of prestige technologies

As described earlier, the study of subsistence technologies has been preoccupied with the idea of optimal technological organisation that was subject to environmental, economic and social variables, and the mobility of tool/facility makers/users has been regarded as the most important factor to determine the choice of technology and design. However, there is a growing interest in the anthropology of technology within archaeology. Ideas obtained from anthropology have illuminated the study of cognitive and behavioural processes of tool/facility making and their social contexts (*e.g.*, Lemonnier 1992; Pfaffenberger 1992). Anthropologists have advocated that technological activities are a fundamental medium through which social relationships, power structures, world views and other social productions are represented and defined. They have focused on the role of agents in the continuity and transformation of social structures which enabled and constrained individual actions. Consequently, a number of archaeologists have begun to highlight human agency in technological activities and to discuss how technology was structured within culturally and historically specific contexts of dynamic social interaction and meaning-making. Thus, it is stressed that the goal of technological studies is not only to describe tool/facility using activities in the past, but also to understand these activities in relation to social processes involving individuals and groups (*e.g.*, Dobres and Hoffman 1994: 211-235; Hegmon 1998: 264-271; Sinclair 1990; 1995; 2000).

An interesting archaeological and ethnographic observation is that technological advances like pottery production and metal working have occurred first in the non-subsistence realm among complex, trans-egalitarian forager societies that resided in resource-rich environments, and later evolved into more practical, subsistence applications. Another observation in such societies is that inherently practical tools have sometimes been made in so elaborate forms that they seemed to lose their utility in the realm of subsistence activities. Thus the presence of outstanding persons who used novel technologies for non-subsistence goals has been argued for the technological advances. Following a recent trend of technological studies, it has been proposed that the technologies for showing-off or status display should be defined as prestige technologies and should be separated from practical technologies (Hayden 1998; 2001). Furthermore, such technologies can also be considered as a sort of costly signalling (Bird and O'Connell 2006: 163-164; Bliege Bird and Smith 2005). It can be said on the ground of the latter observation that competition for prestige or high social status would be represented not only by acts controlling food resources like domestication and generous distribution but also by the technologies that do not necessarily enable efficient foraging but rather impress other people by the visible elaborateness and make them want to possess such items, thereby creating reciprocal or debt relationships with others, and eventually enhancing fitness in an evolutionary sense.

Even in socially and technologically less complex forager societies, similar things would have occurred in the realm of seemingly practical technology. Toolmakers usually determine the form of their tools for daily use by closely imitating the ways in which their parents and close relatives make them, but individual needs also lead to new forms of tool (Hitchcock and Bleed 1997: 350). Therefore, variation in the form of tool derives from necessity as well as convention. Such convention has often been called 'style' in archaeology, and the conception of style has been one of critical issues for understanding past human behaviour (*e.g.*, David and Kramer 2001: 168-224; Hegmon 1998; Thomas 1999). Wiessner (1983), discussing how variation in the form of material culture carries with it a message concerning the identity of a certain person or group, termed the variation to be style, and subdivided style into the emblemic style and the assertive style. The emblemic style carries a message of conscious affiliation to or identity with a certain group and would likely appear in a limited area when the solidarity of a group must be emphasized. On the other hand, the assertive style carries the message that the maker or owner is different from others and that the maker or owner is concerned with new things beyond his or her descent group or ethnic group. Such styles would likely appear randomly and change quickly. Style does not always appear in every material culture but is likely to appear in artefacts which are difficult to manufacture, used for a long time, and exposed to the public.

Archaeologists have accepted that styles in archaeological material culture could carry information about the identity of individuals or groups while marking the division of age and/or gender groups, the social stratification within a group, or the social boundaries between groups. They have also understood that style did not simply carry information about personal or group identity but also functioned as an active tool used in social strategies. Therefore, in addition to taking into consideration the shape or decoration of artefacts, a crucial question deals with the circumstances under which artefacts were made and used in such social strategies (Lemonnier 1992: 91-103).

As an interesting example of the recognition of artefact style, ethnological research on the Kalahari Bushmen has revealed that they used the projectile points of a common style in a band cluster and regarded the projectile points which were made by unknown person but shared the common style with theirs as the products of affiliated people while they regarded the projectile points which did not share the common style as made by alien and felt uneasy if they encountered a dead animal with such strange projectile points in their own area. Furthermore, it was also revealed that projectile points were frequently exchanged in the circle of a band cluster, sometimes travelling over 100 km, in order to solidify socioeconomic ties between bands so that stylistic variation in projectile points became apparent between language groups. It was concluded that the mixing and blending of styles in border areas would be minimal in spite of frequent interaction, and that the mixing of styles would simply result from wounded animals crossing the border and dying in another area (Wiessner 1983: 259-269).

Such an example can be used to help an interpretation of archaeological data. The Ceramic Late Stone Age culture in Ghana is known to have a very small number of bifacially-retouched formal projectile points among basically expedient tool assemblages. It is interpreted that the bifacially-retouched formal projectile points may probably have been made by male hunters who had sometimes gone out of their own territory. The hunters may have encoded some messages regarding their personal and group identity in the uniquely-made projectile points, expecting that people living in neighbouring territories would happen to pick up stray projectile points on the ground and know about the presence of neighbours. In a sense, widely-distributed and visible items like projectile points would have functioned as business cards and occasionally claimed territorial expansion (Casey 1998).

Another ethnographic example relating to the social significance of technology demonstrates that when Inuit hunters carve 'tourist art', they try to embody boldness, perseverance and exactitude in their carvings. The choice of a complicated design means boldness, while the care which carvers take in rendering the carvings stresses exactitude and the hardness of the stone material emphasises perseverance. The reason why they engage in such craft activities is that showing these qualities is considered to be important for the success of an Inuit hunter, and indeed, the Inuit hunters attain personal status through possession of these qualities (Sinclair 1990: 77; 1995: 58; 2000: 205).

This Inuit example of the relationship between practical activities and social qualities has been considered in the interpretation of bifacial lithic technology in Upper Palaeolithic Europe. Based on the fact that elaborate Solutrean bifacial stone tools are exclusively associated with hunting and butchering, it is argued that personal qualities, such as carefulness, perseverance and exactitude, were important for both successful hunting and successful bifacial tool making so that a correspondence may have been created between similar skills exercised in different activities. Consequently, those tools became not only utilitarian objects but also symbolic items which communicated meanings about both the nature of the tasks for which they were used and the persons who undertook the tasks. The reason why symbolic meanings were explicitly given to bifacial stone tools would be because people were living in the severe environment of the Last Glacial Maximum, where personal qualities such as carefulness, perseverance and exactitude displayed in hunting were very much appreciated (Sinclair 1995; 2000). It has also been argued that the reason why anatomically pre-modern Acheulian hominids made fine symmetrical handaxes would be because of attracting mates by showing their ability to make high quality tools and proving themselves intelligent and physically healthy. They were living in large, complex and competitive societies in which sexual selection pressures and inter-male competition for mates were intense. Therefore, handaxes would have played an important role in the social realm as well (Kohn and Mithen 1999).

Ethnological research has found more reasons why toolmakers were enthusiastic about acquiring good appreciation. The Kalahari Bushmen greatly enjoy discussing their arrows and evaluating the makers. Skilled arrow makers, who are admired as 'professionals' by member of the community, express pride in their abilities. They tend to be much more enthusiastic than other community members in discussing the details of their craft not in terms of the making of specific shapes but in terms of precision and quality within a common style. The skilled arrow makers are not necessarily the best hunters. The reason why they are very much concerned with arrow making is because excellent arrow makers either receive a large portion of meat procured by bow hunters or are responsible for the distribution of the meat. The arrows are widely exchanged in order to fill the need of meat sharing and to solidify socioeconomic ties

(Wiessner 1983). The food quest can provide not only hunters but also toolmakers with great opportunities to raise their status through procuring and distributing food (Wiessner 1996). In this sense, it is no wonder that bifacial technology was applied to butchering tools like large knives in the Solutrean as mentioned above, because butchering was another important concern of ambitious food providers. Butchering knives are quite visible to many people waiting for the distribution of meat, and hence some symbolic meanings are likely to be given to the knives.

All of these examples strongly suggest that innovations in seemingly practical technology do not necessarily appear as a consequence of gradual technological developments but are closely related to socioeconomic circumstances. In other words, innovations in seemingly practical technology may reflect changing socioeconomic circumstances. Furthermore, it can also be suggested that differences in the extent of time/energy investment in the technologies for showing-off or status display in different places and time periods may reflect differences in the intensity of interpersonal and intergroup competition as a function of differences in population density. The appearance and development of symbolic items may be driven not only by an increase in human cognitive capability but by increases in human population density and competition. The absence of the technologies for showing-off or status display in certain places and time periods may be related to demography rather than the cognitive or behavioural capabilities of people (Bird and O'Connell 2006: 164). These suggestions are important when technological developments in the period of the adoption of farming and herding in Egypt are studied.

4.5. Some considerations on the Fayum data in the light of the socioeconomic model

Despite apparent problems in its applicability to the cases of the initial attempts of domestication, the socioeconomic competition model certainly gives some interesting assumptions which can be tested using archaeological data. An assumption of the model that an environment with rich wild food resources is definitely a precondition for the emergence of complex, trans-egalitarian forager societies and the subsequent beginning of food production, may be applicable to regions like the Fayum. It is significant to examine whether the beginning of food production in the Fayum can be better explained by using this model as well as optimal foraging models. A problem here is how the presence of complex, trans-egalitarian forager societies is reflected in the archaeological record. Many material features of such societies listed by the proponent of the socioeconomic model, such as cult-related objects, ritual or feasting facilities, elaborate burials and violent deaths (Hayden 1995b: table 1 and fig.6; 2001: fig.7.10), did not exist, or have not yet been found in the Fayum. On this basis, it is very difficult to say that domesticates were adopted in the Fayum in order to serve at feasts. The reinterpretation of old data and the discovery of new evidence in the field are vital.

Regarding prestige technologies, as mentioned in the preceding chapters, it has been observed that decorative elements were generally quite few in the material cultures in Egypt before the Predynastic period. The material cultures of Epipalaeolithic and Neolithic Fayum are not exceptional in terms of their general crudeness. Therefore, it is difficult to find items which may represent some social meanings in the Fayum. Nevertheless, it is significant to keep such a perspective in mind when subtle changes or variations in supposedly practical technologies are studied. In the following, in order to understand the changes and variations in subsistence technology at the Fayum Epipalaeolithic-Neolithic transition from this perspective in a wider geographical and chronological context, the environmental and socioeconomic circumstances in the Egyptian Western Desert in the Early-Middle Holocene, which have been described in Chapter 2, will be reinvestigated with special reference to lithic technology.

4.5.1. Bifacial lithic technology in the Western Desert in the Early-Middle Holocene

A curious thing about microlithisation in North Africa is that although there were some interregional variations, the basic form of backed bladelets was so standardised across the continent and millennia, irrespective of the availability and variability of raw materials and the purposes of use. Therefore, one is even tempted to assume some social factors behind this extreme consistency of backed bladelet (Close 2002a: 38-39). Given this historical and geographical background, a question arises as to why the toolmakers in Egypt in the Early-Middle Holocene gave up their obsession with backed bladelets and started to make a variety of bifacially-retouched stone tools.

As far as we know, the earliest bifacially-retouched formal projectile points appeared in regions such as Dakhleh Oasis, Abu Tartur, Djara and Farafra Oasis after 6500 cal.BC (Barich and Lucarini 2002; 2005; Bubenzer *et al.* 2007; Gehlen *et al.* 2002; Hassan *et al.* 2001; Kindermann 2002; 2003; 2004; McDonald 1991a; 2008; Riemer 2007b). The specimens from the Bashendi A (around 6400-5600 cal.BC) of Dakhleh Oasis include concave-based, tanged, and leaf-shaped points of various sizes. The Abu Tartur specimens consist mainly of small points with only a few large (more than 5 cm long) concave-based or tanged points throughout the phases named the Abu Tartur B (around 6500-6000 cal.BC) and the Abu Tartur C (around 6000-5200 cal.BC). The Djara specimens do not include large points at all in the earlier phase named the Djara A (around 6400-6100 cal.BC), but large tanged ones appeared in the later phase named the Djara B (around 5800-5400 cal.BC) after a short interval around 6000-5900 cal.BC. The specimens from the Phase B (around 6200-5800 cal.BC) and Phase C (around 5500-5200 cal.BC) of Farafra Oasis include small leaf-shaped points, and it was not until the Phase D (around 5200-4800 cal.BC) that small tanged points appeared there. Other bifacially-retouched items like large knives are also notable in Dakhleh Oasis and Djara, and their date seems to be the Late Bashendi A (around 5900-5600 cal.BC) and the Djara B respectively.

Bifacially-retouched formal projectile points flourished after 5900 cal.BC in neighbouring regions such as Abu Gerara and Kharga Oasis (Caton-Thompson 1952; Holmes 1992a; Reimer 2003; Smith *et al.* 2004). Surface surveys at sites along the margin of the Great Sand Sea such as Siwa Oasis, Sitra and Lobo, and sites around the Abu Ballas scarp land such as Mudpans, Eastpans, Chufu and Meri also yielded small bifacially-retouched, leaf-shaped or tanged projectile points which could be dated to around this period (Cziesla 1989; Gehlen *et al.* 2002; Hassan and Gross 1987; Klees 1989; Riemer 2007a; 2007b). All of them are collectively named the '(bi)facial techno-complex' of the northern half of the Western Desert in the late 7th - early 6th millennia cal.BC (Riemer 2007a; 2007b).

Further to the east, an investigation at Sodmein Cave in the mountainous terrain near the Red Sea coast yielded a certain number of bifacially-retouched, leaf-shaped projectile points which could be dated to around 6000-5300 cal.BC (Vermeersch *et al.* 1994; 1996). Further to the south, intensive surveys and excavations in the Nabta-Kiseiba region revealed that the first appearance of bifacially-retouched formal projectile points was in the Middle Ceramic Period (5900-5500 cal.BC) though they were quite rare, and that the number and variety of bifacially-retouched formal projectile points slightly increased in the subsequent Late Ceramic period (5400-4600 cal.BC) (Wendorf and Schild 2001; 2004).

It seems that the elaboration of bifacially-retouched tools culminated in the Fayum in the middle of the 5th millennium cal.BC. Large projectile points, axes, knives, and sickle blades were made by bifacial technology. Slightly after that, similar items appeared in neighbouring sites like Merimde Beni Salama and El-Omari, and this lithic tradition persisted in the Badarian culture of the 5th-4th millennia cal.BC in the Nile Valley of Middle Egypt.

In summary, given the present data, the

origins of bifacially-retouched formal tools seem to be somewhere in the middle of the Western Desert between the Great Sand Sea and the Nile Valley around the end of the Early Holocene, and the development and dispersal of bifacially-retouched formal tools continued through the Middle Holocene. It is noted that studies so far have tended to treat bifacially-retouched formal tools and particularly projectile points as cultural markers or subsistence markers, and that the frequencies of projectile points of whatever sizes and shapes in a tool assemblage at a specific site has been considered as reflecting the relative importance of hunting activity at the site (*e.g.*, Holmes 1992a; Riemer 2007b). However, the question as to why a limited percentage of stone tools started to be made in different sizes and shapes by employing bifacial technology within basically flake tool industries in this particular area at that particular time have not been answered.

As archaeology has recently come to be concerned with elucidating what kind of human behaviour had left artefacts rather than simply putting artefacts in temporal and spatial order, various studies of projectile points have appeared (Knecht 1997; Nelson 1997). Consequently, differences in shape of projectile points are presently interpreted not only as indicators of specific places and time periods but also as delineating differences in technology, function, and style. Since it is difficult to suppose the function and style of prehistoric projectile points, experimental methods and ethnological data are employed to mitigate this difficulty. Experimental methods include examining flying distance and killing power by using a variety of replica projectile points with various arrows and shafts. While experiment makes it possible to compare the function of projectile points of various size and shape, it cannot explain why such a wide variety of projectile points existed. Ethnological data are not sufficiently concrete evidence to explain the functions and styles of prehistoric projectile points. However, ethnological data can provide many otherwise unanticipated suggestions concerning the reasons for the size and shape of projectile points and insights into what people think about the projectile points as well as under what conditions and how the projectile points are used. With the aid of ethnological data, the archaeologist can gain a deep understanding of the functions and uses of projectile points, provide better interpretation of prehistoric projectile points, and make suppositions as to how prehistoric people thought about their projectile points. Keeping these perspectives in mind, the environmental and socioeconomic circumstances of the Western Desert will be overviewed.

4.5.1.1. Natural preconditions for the appearance of bifacial stone tools in the Western Desert

The first point to be explained is why such a new set of bifacial stone tools as those observed in the above-mentioned sites in the Western Desert had not appeared in the Late Pleistocene but developed in the Early-Middle Holocene. It is assumed that something was different between the Pleistocene and the Holocene, and that the difference gave the possibility for the development of such unprecedented tools. As described in Chapter 2, there was a considerable change in the vegetation cover of the Western Desert in the Early Holocene due to the improvement of atmosphere and pluvial regime, and it is likely that the fauna also changed accordingly. Therefore, the explanation of the appearance of unprecedented bifacial stone tools in the Western Desert in the Early-Middle Holocene must take account of the spread of new vegetation. It may be assumed that the development of bifacial projectile points was triggered by the beginning of the hunting of previously less-encountered animals which were attracted by the spread of pasture plants, or the beginning of more intensive hunting of familiar animals in the Western Desert.

Major game animals in the Nabta-Kiseiba region in the Early-Middle Holocene were dorcas gazelle and hare, both of which are desert-adapted and water-independent species, and it seems that the Nabta-Kiseiba region was never wet enough to attract more water-dependent animals like hartebeest and hippopotamus even in the Early Holocene climatic optimum (Gautier 1984; 2001). Therefore, the former assumption that the beginning of the hunting of previously less-encountered animals triggered the development of bifacial projectile points is apparently not the case in the Nabta-Kiseiba region. An important fact is that the number of dorcas gazelle in the archaeological record of the Nabta-Kiseiba region decreased through the Early-Middle Holocene while the number of hare increased. This may possibly imply that bifacial projectile points were inventions to raise the success rate of the hunting of dorcas gazelle which were going extinct. In the Nabta-Kiseiba region, it has been reported that the first appearance of bifacially-retouched projectile points was in the Middle Ceramic period (*ca.* 5800 cal.BC onward), and this is almost coincident with the decrease in the number of dorcas gazelle.

However, flake points are not necessarily inferior to bifacially-retouched points in terms of flying distance and killing power, especially if other attributes such as shape and weight are equal. In the Middle and Late Ceramic periods, bifacially-retouched points seem to have been very few, and less-retouched flake points were never replaced by bifacially-retouched points. Therefore, the appearance of bifacial points in this region cannot be explained in terms of functional superiority but rather in terms of differences in hunting strategy as to whether it is on a stalk basis or an ambush basis, and such differences may have affected the time spent to make and repair points.

In Dakhleh Oasis, there is very scarce evidence for the fauna in the Early Holocene, but it has shown the presence of common ungulate species like dorcas gazelle and hartebeest. The presence of the Sudano-Ethiopian fauna including elephant and giraffe has also been suggested in the Middle Holocene (Churcher 1999a; 1999b; Churcher *et al.* 2008). There is some doubt as to whether the remains of the Sudano-Ethiopian fauna derived from the Middle Palaeolithic context and were accidentally associated with the Holocene artefacts, because both of them are surface finds (Close 1992: 171). If the Sudano-Ethiopian fauna in question was actually associated with the Middle Holocene environment, it was certainly a new addition to the fauna in this part of Egypt and hence previously less-encountered. Although it is not certain whether these new large animals became the prey of hunters in Dakhleh Oasis in the Middle Holocene, the number, variety and size of bifacial projectile points became large through the Bashendi A and B (McDonald 1991a; 2008), and interestingly, it seems that elephant and giraffe went extinct during the Middle Holocene. It is possible that their extinction was caused not only by increasing aridity but also by overhunting. It can be assumed that large bifacial projectile points which first appeared in the Bashendi A played a role in this, because hunting large and tough animals must have required special tactics and technologies.

Ethnographic data show that there are few examples of hunters changing the size and shape of projectile points according to the size and species of hunted game. It is more typical for hunters to take spears tipped by large and heavy projectile points that cannot fly long distances but have greater killing power, as well as arrows tipped by small and light projectile points that can fly long distances but have lesser killing power, and to choose according to the conditions of their encounter with specific game (Christenson 1997; Ellis 1997). It is well known that spears are able to impart a knock-down force and to open severe wounds and hence are superior for killing large, slow-moving animals, though spears must be delivered at closer range. On the other hand, arrows are suitable for shooting at cautious, fast-moving animals from a distance, though arrows are not able to kill the animals immediately even if the arrows are poisoned (Hitchcock and Bleed 1997). It follows that any variation of projectile points that cannot be explained as resulting from the conditions of specific encounters with certain types of game animals should be interpreted as arising for other reasons.

As for possible targets, one important question is why there were large concave-based or tanged bifacial projectile points in the sites of Djara and the Nabta-Kiseiba region, where the existence of large game animals like elephant and hippopotamus has not been attested. Large and heavy concave-based or tanged bifacial projectile points are apparently not suitable for tipping arrows, because arrows tipped by such heavy points would be seriously unbalanced and their flying performance would not be good. Even though such large projectile points did tip hand-held spears or throwing spears, spears would not be suitable for hunting fast-moving animals like dorcas gazelle, which were the most common in those sites, but would be most effective against large aggressive animals which tend to counterattack rather than flee. Therefore, different explanations about the targets of large bifacial projectile points are necessary. One possible explanation is that those large projectile points were designed to kill humans and not game animals. This possibility will be discussed later in relation to social circumstances.

The second point to be explained is why such a new set of bifacial tools had not appeared first in the Nile Valley but developed first in the middle of the Western Desert. It is assumed that something was different between the Nile Valley and the Western Desert, and that the difference gave the possibility for the development of such unprecedented tools. It is widely recognised that procurement of lithic raw materials is absolutely essential for making stone tools, and the availability and quality of lithic raw materials critically affect and condition the making of stone tools (*e.g.*, Andrefsky 1994; Bamforth 1986). Therefore, the distribution of sources of lithic raw materials in the Western Desert and the Nile Valley must have offered possibilities and constraints for tool making.

The main area where bifacially-retouched formal tools developed in the Early-Middle Holocene is a vast rocky plain on the Limestone Plateau which abuts the Nile Valley to its east, between the latitude of Esna in the south and the Fayum in the north. Extensive scarps of the Limestone Plateau are seen in the southwest, and major oases are located at the foot of the scarps. Wherever bifacially-retouched formal tools appeared in the Early-Middle Holocene, such as in Siwa Oasis, Farafra Oasis, Dakhleh Oasis, Kharga Oasis, Djara, Abu Gerara, Sitra and Lobo, good quality lithic raw materials like flint in nodular form were abundant locally or available in the vicinity, and there is no evidence for long distance transport of exotic raw materials. It must be noted that the remains of lithic workshops have been reported in some of these regions (Barich 1996; Caton-Thompson 1952; Cziesla 1989; Hassan and Gross 1987; Kindermann 2002; 2003; 2004; Klees 1989; Kuper 1996; 2002). They indicate that lithic raw material procurement and subsequent reduction took place locally and tools were also made locally.

In contrast, the Nabta-Kiseiba region, which was another major centre of Early-Middle Holocene cultures, is characterised by a flat or undulating desert plain on the Nubian sandstone bedrock with a number of playas, a series of sandstone escarpments capped by thin flint layers, named the Kiseiba Scarp, and some sandstone outcrops like the Gebel Nabta. The vast area next to the Kiseiba Scarp is dominated by the Selima Sand Sheet. It has been revealed that it was not uncommon for the inhabitants of playa sites in the Nabta-Kiseiba region in the Early-Middle Holocene to bring good quality lithic raw materials like flint from remote scarps, even though they exploited locally-available, coarse-grained raw materials like quartzitic sandstone, and there were few bifacially-retouched formal tools (Wendorf and Schild 2001; Wendorf *et al.* 1984). In the sites of Bir Safsaf, where the ground surface is completely covered by sand and no rock outcrops are readily available, people who used this area seasonally while harvesting wild grasses and herding cattle in the Early-Middle Holocene, had no other choice but to bring all lithic raw materials and tools with them from outside the area, and no elaborate tools developed (Close 1990; 1996a).

On the basis of these contrasting geographical and geological conditions between the north and south of the Western Desert, it may be assumed that easy access to the sources of fine-grained flint on and around the Limestone Plateau in the north of the Western Desert could be an advantage for the development of bifacially-retouched formal tools earlier than that in the south, where the sandstone bedrock predominates. Since there are few comparable contemporaneous archaeological sites in the Nile Valley, it is hard to argue whether accessibility to good quality nodules or cobbles of flint in the Nile Valley affected the development of bifacially-retouched formal tools. In the Nile Valley, flint nodules occur not only on the upland surface but also in consolidated deposits exposed at the rock wall of the valley. In addition, it is also possible to exploit secondary deposits of rolled flint cobbles which were eroded out from the valley wall and transported downslope to the streambed. It seems that this situation was favourable enough for the development of bifacially-retouched formal tools which require fine-grained raw material of a certain size. Therefore, it may be that the lack of such tools in the Nile Valley in the Early-Middle Holocene is simply due to the problem of site preservation, but other possible reasons will be discussed later.

4.5.1.2. Interpretations of bifacially-retouched stone tools in the Western Desert

Given these natural preconditions, the next step is to investigate and interpret the appearance and development of bifacial stone tools in the Western Desert in the Early-Middle Holocene in terms of adaptive strategy and emergent social complexity.

Raw material economy is the first concern of the adaptive strategy of forager-herders. According to the idea of economising behaviour (Odell 1996), toolmakers make the most of hard-to-obtain or scarce lithic raw materials not only by obtaining as many usable flakes as possible from a lithic core but also by making tools and then using, resharpening, and recycling them repeatedly, in case the raw materials at hand are depleted and access to the sources is unpredictable. Such behaviour may foster the ability to make labour-intensive bifacial tools. An important observation is that bifacial tools tend to develop among highly mobile people who forage in environments where the availability of good lithic raw materials is occasionally limited. In contrast, it has been argued that in environments where good lithic raw materials are everywhere and readily available, toolmakers tend to waste the materials and to prefer expedient cores and tools, and thus time-consuming and labour-intensive stone tools do not always develop. Such contrasting situations have been discussed as the tool expediency-curation alternatives, and the economising behaviour mentioned above is also one of curatorial adaptation.

However, the cases of the Nabta-Kiseiba region and Bir Safsaf seem to contradict the idea of economising behaviour. It has been considered that Early-Middle Holocene people would have visited the sites of the Nabta-Kiseiba region and Bir Safsaf after summer rainfall and stayed there for a short length of time, and hence that they would have been quite nomadic. One study in a playa site in the Nabta-Kiseiba region has revealed that more than half of all lithic raw materials used there derived from source areas some 100 km away from the site. The preferred raw material, flint, was brought there in the form of unworked cobble as well as partly decortificated core, but no bifacially-retouched formal tools developed there (Kobusiewicz 1984). Another study in some playa sites in the Nabta-Kiseiba region has revealed that people used flint cores in a rather wasteful manner, despite a burden of obtaining flint from distant source areas (Close 1999). In Bir Safsaf, people not only carried large flakes as blanks for making partly-retouched tools but also carried cores and struck off a series of flakes when the occasion arose, and they sometimes brought unimaginably heavy unworked blocks of quartzitic sandstone, presumably for future use (Close 1990; 1996a). Although they made a certain variety of tools, most tools remained simple, and no bifacially-retouched formal tools developed.

These facts seem to suggest that making bifacial tools in advance and resharpening during use and move are not necessarily the only means to economise the use of hard-to-obtain or scarce raw materials. Toolmakers could find it better to carry lithic cores than to carry completed tools, probably because they adopted a circulating mobility strategy on a seasonal basis and their lithic raw material procurement had been embedded in their routine move. It may also be concluded that the abundance of good quality lithic raw materials was a necessary but not a sufficient condition for the development of bifacial stone tools in the Western Desert. In addition to toolmakers' consideration on raw material economy, some other socioeconomic circumstances must have required or allowed the development of bifacial stone tools.

In the Western Desert in the Early-Middle Holocene, informal flake tools include sickles, scrapers, perforators, notches and denticulates, which seem to be related to food gathering and craft working tasks, whereas bifacially-retouched formal tools include arrowheads, spearheads and large knives, and they seem to be related to hunting and butchering. This suggests that curation was mainly applied to hunting and butchering tools, and that hunting and butchering were logistically organised. In other words, the development of highly-specialised tools like bifacially-retouched projectile points and knives in basically expediently-made tool assemblages in such regions as Dakhleh Oasis, Farafra Oasis and Djara in the Early-Middle Holocene may indicate the decline of encounter hunting and the emergence of a certain degree of sedentism combined with logistical mobility.

It must be noted that the people in Nabta Playa and Farafra Oasis were equipped with bifacial stone tools just before, or by a curious coincidence with, the adoption of domesticated sheep/goats. A similar phenomenon is observed in Djara and Dakhleh Oasis as well, though the time gap between the appearance of bifacial tools and the adoption of domesticated sheep/goats seems to be a little wider. Therefore, the explanation of why bifacial stone tools first appeared and developed in the Western Desert in the Early-Middle Holocene must take into account the possibility of increasing unprecedented socioeconomic stress, which may have been caused by growing population and emerging rigid territoriality and may have somehow been mitigated by the adoption of domesticated sheep/goats. Considering such possible socioeconomic circumstances, the presence of unreasonably large bifacial projectile points and the absence of probable target animals in Djara and the Nabta-Kiseiba region may imply that those projectile points were designed to kill enemy humans, as mentioned earlier. However, since there is no clear evidence for the violent death of humans in the Western Desert in the Early-Middle Holocene, it is hard to know whether large projectile points were actually used to attack people. No evidence of violence seems to suggest that people became smart enough to reconcile territorial conflicts in different ways.

An alternative interpretation about the development of bifacial stone tools in such possible socioeconomic circumstances is that the bifacial stone tools had some symbolic meanings and some significance for the establishment and maintenance of intra/inter-group relationships. As discussed earlier, it may be said that both less-retouched informal flake tools and bifacially-retouched formal tools can serve for cutting or thrusting tasks in almost the same manner. The question is why toolmakers took the trouble to make time-consuming bifacial tools even if informal flake tools were able to serve the same purpose. The toolmakers' concern about the tool reliability-maintainability alternatives must be one reason, but the non-utilitarian function of bifacial stone tools must also be taken into consideration.

As described at length, it can be said that essential tools for survival are likely to become the media for the representation of personal or group identity. Using Wiessner's terms, the assertive style, which carries the message that the maker or owner is different from others, as well as the emblemic style, which stresses conscious affiliation to a certain group, can appear in such tools. It should be noted that bifacial technology was initially applied exclusively to hunting and butchering tools in the Egyptian Western Desert in the Early-Middle

Holocene. Therefore, it can be assumed that bifacial stone tools in the Western Desert in the Early-Middle Holocene were not merely utilitarian objects but also symbolic items, which represented personal or group identity and delivered social messages to other people in and outside their community. In other words, the appearance and development of elaborate bifacial stone tools in the Western Desert in the Early-Middle Holocene may be interpreted as a reflection of internally and externally stressful circumstances and the resultant competitive aestheticism among toolmakers.

It has also been known in ethnological studies that the Kalahari Bushmen liked to obtain projectile points that varied in material, size and shape from experienced hunters and skilled toolmakers of other group because they believed that well-made projectile points could kill game animals more easily, even though the knowledge of locations where certain species of game animals live is much more important than the quality of projectile points, and actually the success or failure of hunting is dependent on how a hunter encounters game animals. Hence the projectile points could move over long distances by inter-group exchange (Hitchcock and Bleed 1997). If such an ethnological example was the case in the Egyptian Western Desert in the Early-Middle Holocene, the presence of unreasonably large and elaborate formal stone tools without possible target animals may be explained in terms of symbolic and stylistic behaviours by hunters who wished the success of hunting and satisfied their vanity, rather than bloody conflicts between aggressive men.

4.5.1.3. The implications of the development of bifacial stone tools for the beginning of animal herding in the Egyptian Western Desert

As described earlier, whereas most scholars are coming to agree that a resource-rich environment is an essential condition for the emergence of social complexity and the beginnings of food production, there is still controversy over what conditions could drive prehistoric people to intensify food procurement and to compete with each other. In the case of Egypt, it seems plausible that moderately stressful and circumscribed situations under periodically or seasonally resource-rich conditions in the Western Desert in the Early-Middle Holocene caused recurrent population/resource imbalances on an unprecedented scale and drove the inhabitants to enhance food security through storage, sedentism and territoriality. In contrast, the Nile Valley seems to have escaped such stressful and circumscribed situations and failed to encourage its inhabitants to intensify their subsistence, even though a degree of inflow of refugees from the Western Desert may have caused some social tensions and reorganisation of territories.

If bifacial stone tools in the Western Desert in the Early-Middle Holocene were a reflection of emerging socioeconomic competition among individuals, who were enthusiastic about raising their status by procuring and providing food through using elaborate stone tools, then the introduction of domesticated sheep/goats into several regions may also be interpreted to have been motivated by such competition as well as a need for reliable back-up food. The lack of elaborate stone tools in the Nile Valley in the Early Holocene may also probably be interpreted as an indication that less stressful situations retarded the adoption of domesticates. Novel food like the meat of domesticates and their dairy products may have enabled ambitious food providers to get ahead of the competition. The reasons why elaboration of bifacial projectile points and knives continued after the period of the initial adoption of domesticates, may be because hunting was still a prestigious task in most regions regardless of the availability of domesticates, and because bifacial stone tools did not easily lose their value as the media of social representation or the means of status display.

4.5.2. The origin and development of bifacially-retouched stone tools in the Fayum Neolithic and their implications for the beginning of farming and herding in the Fayum

Following the observation and interpretation of the appearance of bifacial stone tools in the Western Desert, the next focus is on bifacial stone tools in the Fayum. As mentioned earlier, the appearance of bifacial stone tools in the Fayum seems to be later in date, but the elaboration and sophistication of bifacial stone tools culminated in the Fayum Neolithic. As described in Chapter 3, during the Fayum Neolithic, bifacial technology was employed mainly to make arrowheads, spearheads, knives, sickle blades and axes, all of which are related to hunting, butchering, harvesting, wood carving and probably ploughing. There is little doubt that these bifacial tools were first and foremost invented according to arising needs to perform a new variety of tasks in the Neolithic period and hence can be viewed as a part of adaptive strategies. However, considering that some classes of bifacial tools like arrowheads, spearheads and knives seem to be overdesigned against functional requirements, it should be assumed that those Fayum Neolithic bifacial stone tools were not merely utilitarian, but should also be considered that their manufacture involved additional meanings.

If the Fayum Neolithic data are considered in the light of ethnological examples of social meanings attributed to artefacts, it is possible to suggest that Fayum Neolithic bifacial tools embodied similar personal characteristics and skills, such as carefulness, perseverance and exactitude. Indeed, all of these attributes are essential for successfully undertaking subsistence activities, including the making of the tools used in these activities. Therefore, it may be argued that such characteristics and skills would have been recognised socially as favourable for the survival of individuals and groups. Individuals who were engaged in subsistence activities in the Fayum Neolithic may have acquired personal status by emphasising their skills in making good quality stone tools.

Considering that minimal tool morphological requirement for a specific task may be fulfilled with marginal retouching or unifacial retouching, Fayum Neolithic toolmakers would not necessarily have taken the trouble to make such elaborate bifacially-retouched tools. However, it can be argued that the cost of making and maintaining elaborate bifacial tools did meet the benefit of increasing one's status. For instance, if the Kalahari Bushmen example is taken into consideration, the elaboration of bifacial tools in the Fayum Neolithic may reflect competitive aestheticism among individuals in obtaining prestige as excellent toolmakers, rather than the pursuit of a purely functional improvement. In this sense, Fayum Neolithic bifacial technology may be regarded as prestige technology, as well as practical technology.

The coincidence of the florescence of bifacial technology with the advent of wheat/barley farming and sheep/goat herding in the Fayum Neolithic may imply a relationship between them. According to the socioeconomic competition model, provided that the circumstances became favourable for the abandonment of the ethic of socioeconomic equality and novel food resources became available, ambitious food providers would have had various motives for attempting farming and herding which could provide a large amount of novel food, in order to impress other people and to wage competition. If some classes of Fayum Neolithic bifacial stone tools reflect competitive aestheticism in the quest for higher social status, it is suggested that the first step toward the adoption of farming and herding as part of subsistence activities may also probably have been motivated by competition in the quest for increased status among individuals. The socioeconomic competition model for the beginning of food production does not make clear who could become an ambitious food provider, but it is plausible that these might be exceptionally skilled toolmakers, or persons who used their exceptional ability to please others who were ambitious. It remains possible that these processes initially occurred at an earlier date among social groups in neighbouring regions, which, led by ambitious persons, came to the Fayum with domesticates.

A further study of the processes which led to the emergence of skilled toolmakers as possibly represented in the development of Fayum Neolithic bifacial technology and the emergence of ambitious food providers is necessary in order to support the interpretation proposed above. Although it may not always be possible to discover the intentions of Neolithic toolmakers, consideration of the social implications of the development of bifacial technology is able to offer further perspectives on the beginning of farming and herding in the Fayum. Emergent social complexity in the Western Desert in the Early-Middle Holocene has been inferred on the basis of the spread of a limited number of pottery vessels after the 9th millennium cal.BC (Close 1995) and the appearance of monumental stone structures after the 6th millennium cal.BC (Wendorf and Schild 1998; 2001; 2002a; 2004). The innovation in lithic technology after the middle of the 7th millennium cal.BC must also be considered as a symptom of incipient socioeconomic complexity, which eventually led to the adoption of foreign domesticates.

4.6. Summary

It has been demonstrated in this chapter that optimal foraging models and related concepts have better explanatory power than intuitive arguments and are useful to better understand the Fayum archaeological and ecological data obtained by previous research. These models and concepts also give some predictions about foragers' responses to environmental and demographic changes and their consequences, and future archaeological research is expected to see whether such predictions are really the case. Moreover, the socioeconomic model and related ideas give a further insight into the possible socioeconomic circumstances in which food production would be needed and the motives of foragers who eventually adopted farming and herding. In the following chapters, the optimal land uses by Fayum Epipalaeolithic and Neolithic people will be described on the basis of new field survey results, and the adaptive technological behaviour of Fayum Epipalaeolithic and Neolithic people will be illustrated by focusing on their lithic technological organisation. Through these studies, it is expected that the reasons for, and the process of, subsistence change from foraging to farming and herding at the Epipalaeolithic-Neolithic transition can be revealed.

5. The Fayum Epipalaeolithic and Neolithic in the light of new survey results

5.1. Introduction

Since 2003, the UCLA-RUG Fayum Project has obtained permission to carry out archaeological fieldwork in the northeastern part of the Fayum Depression. The concession area of the project runs between Kom Aushim (the ancient Karanis) in the east and Qasr el-Sagha in the west, and includes the northeastern shore of Lake Qarun in the south and the rocky terrain in the north which marks the northern fringe of the Fayum Depression. Given the limited time for fieldwork and logistical difficulties, the 2003-2006 seasons' fieldwork concentrated on the eastern half of the concession area. It is 12 km wide east-west, and 20 km long north-south (**Fig.5.1**, **Fig.5.2** and **Fig.5.3**).

It must be stressed that this fieldwork project is not the first attempt made in this part of the Fayum. Several research teams have conducted archaeological and geological fieldwork in this area in the last century, and valuable information about the archaeological site distribution and material culture of different periods has been obtained. In particular, this concession area has been known to contain a number of Epipalaeolithic and Neolithic sites, and has provided evidence for the earliest wheat/barley farming combined with sheep/goat herding in Egypt. The 2003-2006 survey area included two remarkable Neolithic occupation loci named Kom K and Kom W, as well as clusters of Neolithic granary pits named the Upper and Lower K Pits in the proximity of Kom K (Caton-Thompson and Gardner 1934: 22-54). Notably, based on the lack of substantial dwelling remains, it has been argued that there was no clear evidence for year-round occupations in these loci, despite the fact that the inhabitants relied on farming and herding at least as part of their subsistence. Therefore, a question remains as to how the Fayum people organised their residence and subsistence. Another question is what type of mobility strategy enabled people to continue traditional foraging on the one hand, and to introduce farming and herding on the other, at the transition from the Epipalaeolithic to the Neolithic period.

It was expected that these questions might be partially answered through re-investigating the well-known Neolithic occupation loci, finding more Epipalaeolithic and Neolithic remains in their surroundings, and considering the patterns of land use and natural resource exploitation by Epipalaeolithic and Neolithic people in a wider environmental context. In other words, this field survey aimed to know what has been overlooked or neglected by previous researchers and to re-examine old information, not in terms of culture history but in terms of human adaptive behaviour, by using new data obtained in the field, and then to better understand the patterns of various land uses by people in prehistoric times.

5.2. The survey area

The Fayum Depression has been formed through long geological history since the Eocene, but the surface of Tertiary rocks and lacustrine deposits has not only been carved and polished due to intense aeolian action but also been washed and covered due to the erosive and sedimentary action of surface runoff water. Erosive aeolian action on rocks results in the formation of sand dunes near cliffs (Issawi 1976; Pawlikowski 1983). Furthermore, recurrent climatic cycles of wetting and drying have caused the formation of crusts of soluble minerals on the land surface deposited by evaporation of subsurface moisture. The development of crusts over the land surface has consolidated its surface layers and has protected it from further aeolian erosion (Aref 2003). The geomorphology of the survey area has been understood through looking at various surface features. The major geomorphic indicators of natural forces which have caused the erosion of the surface of rocks and deposits and the subsequent redeposition of clastic materials and sand as well as the formation of surface crusts in the survey area include beaches, yardangs, dunes, escarpments, and wadis.

The low desert between the contour line of 40 m above sea level (abbreviated as asl) and the present lakeshore which is around 40 m below sea level (abbreviated as bsl) is where most of the archaeological remains from the Epipalaeolithic to Ptolemaic and Roman periods have been found. This low desert records erosional and depositional events on the past lakeshores caused by oscillating lake water and wind. According to a reconstruction of lake level fluctuations in the Pleistocene and Holocene (Hassan *et al.* 2006), the water margin of the lake has moved within this vertical range, while the lake level dropped drastically and remained lower than 0 m bsl after the Ptolemaic period.

In general, the low desert is covered by fine-

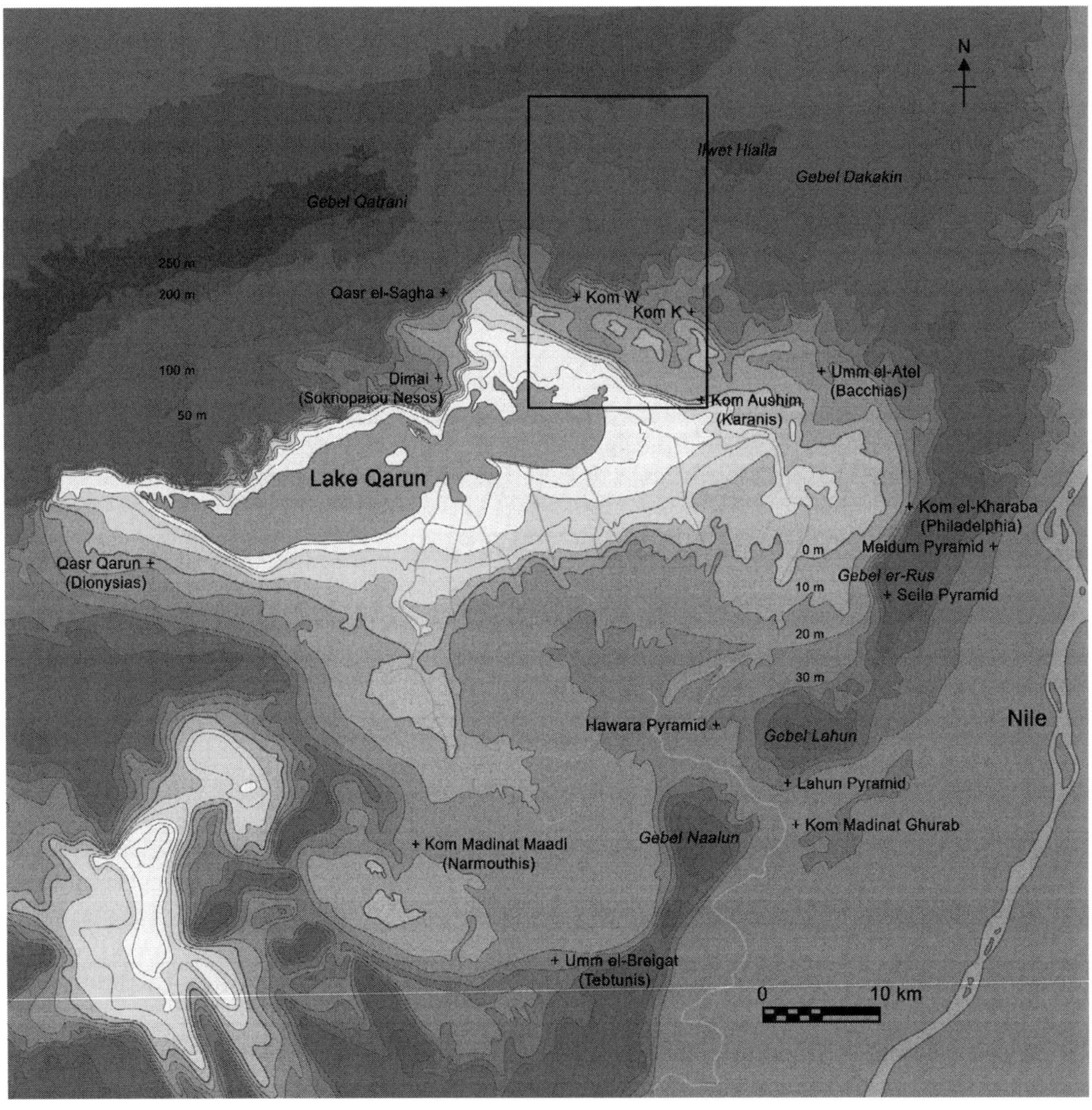

Fig.5.1. Location of the 2003-2006 season's survey area

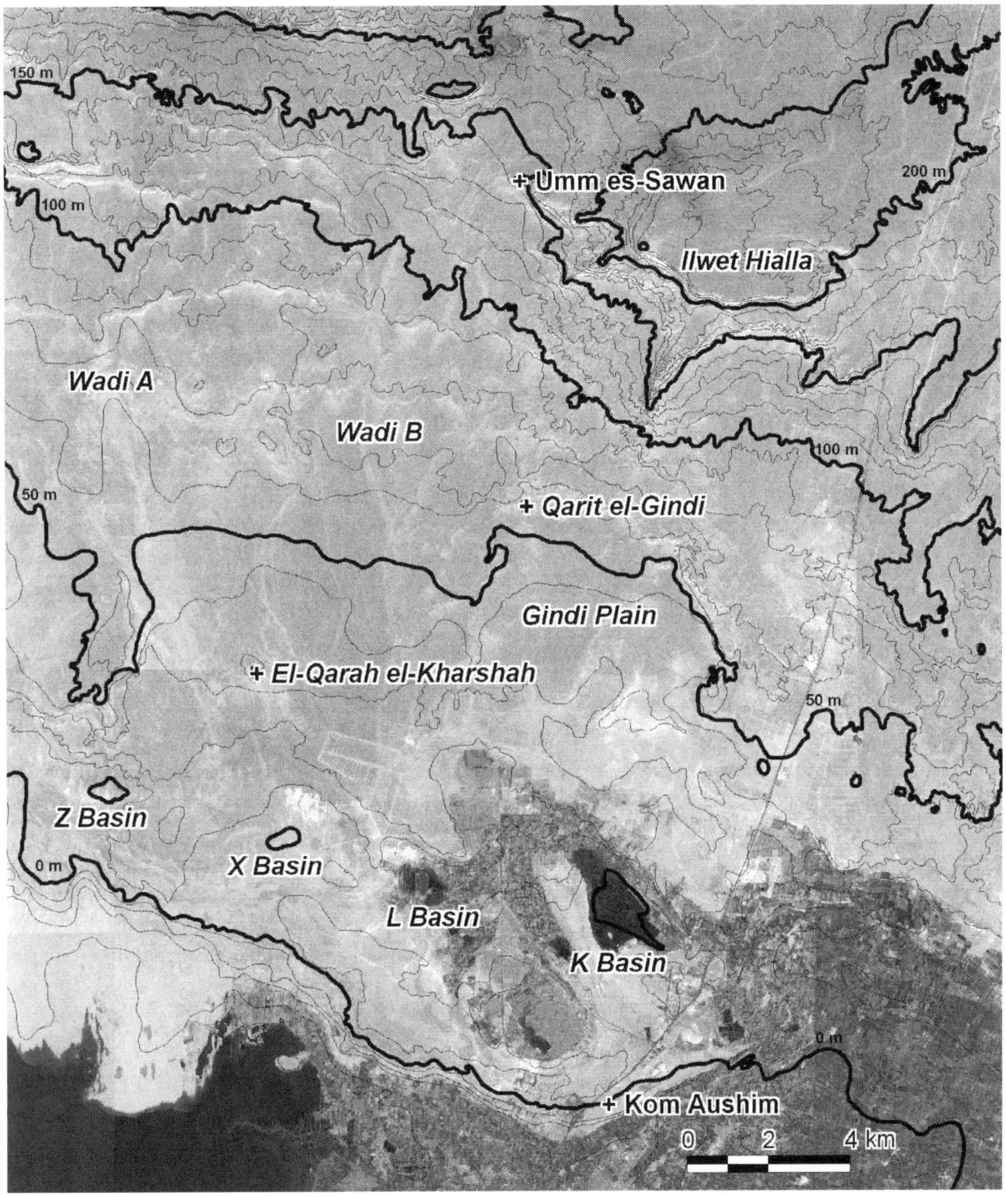

Fig.5.2. Contour map of the survey area on satellite photo

grained alluvial and aeolian sand, but many parts of the low desert actually lack aeolian deposition of loose sand due to deflation. In places where deflation has been severe, fine-grained loose sand is blown away, leaving a residual deposit of heavier and larger objects like flint fragments on the consolidated surface of alluvial sand deposits with calcified nodules of sand clast. Extensive scatters of subrounded flint fragments are noticeable in the area of the 10 m asl contour line from the northern and western shores of the X Basin to the southern shore of the Z Basin, and they seem to have been washed by oscillating lake water. The area around the 40 m asl contour line is also marked by dense flint gravels, which are supposed to be the shingle beach of the Pleistocene lake (Caton-Thompson and Gardner 1934: pl.CIX; Sandford and Arkell 1929: folding map). The bedrock of the low desert is Upper Eocene limestone of the Qasr

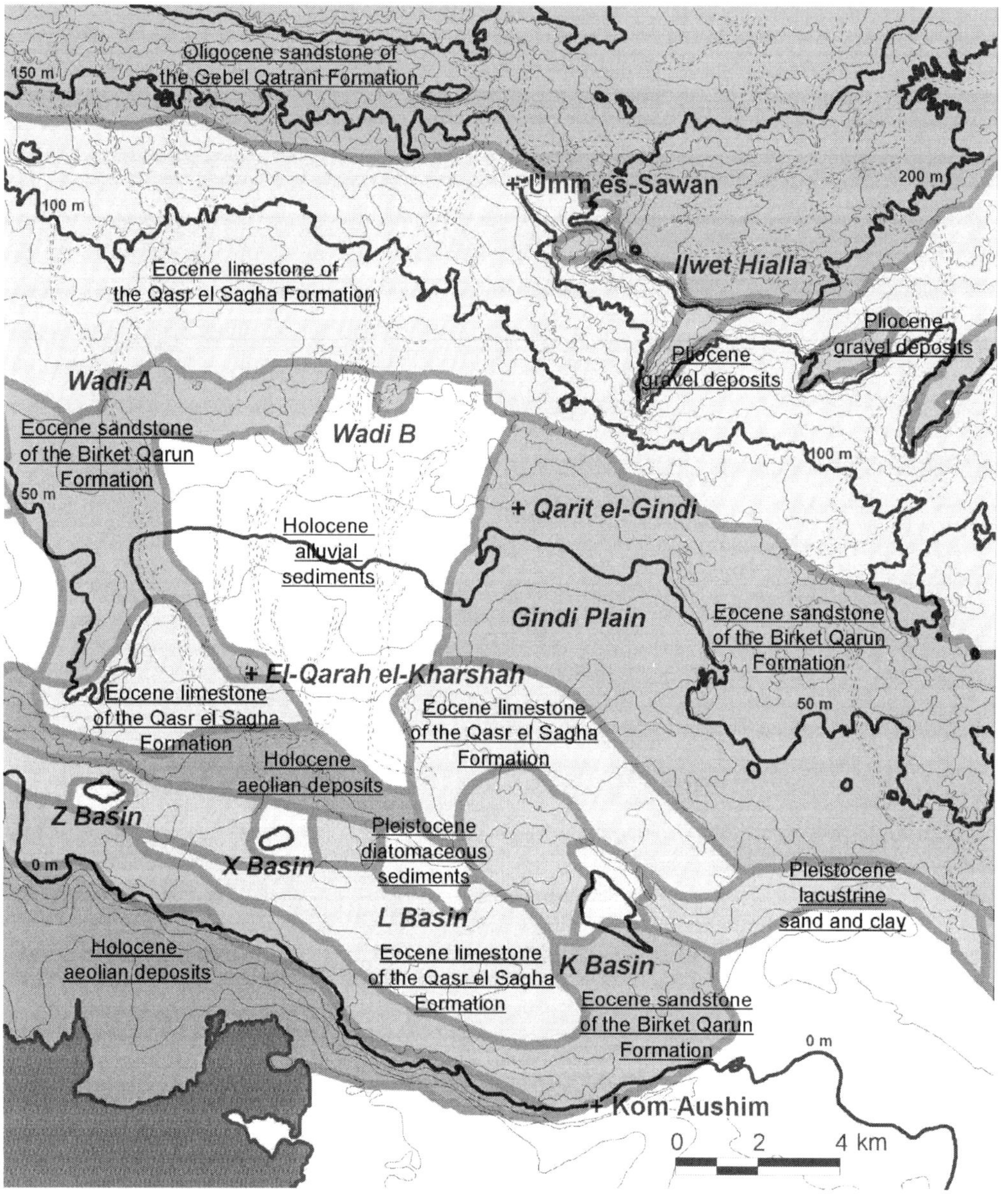

Fig.5.3. Geological map of the survey area

el-Sagha Formation, and it is sporadically exposed on the surface, with the cover of limestone fragments and fossil shells which have eroded out of highly fossiliferous bed. A particularly extensive exposure of the bedrock is seen around the 10-15 m asl contour line a few kilometres to the north of the present lakeshore.

Major topographic features in this low desert are four large basins which are aligned approximately 4-5 km away from the present lakeshore. They have been named by Caton-Thompson from the west to the east as the Z Basin, X Basin, L Basin, and K Basin respectively (Caton-Thompson and Gardner 1934: pl.CIX). These basins were probably huge residual pools off the shore of the perennial lake, and would have been filled with water as long as the lake level was higher than 10-15 m asl. Light yellow to orange silty sediments with numerous white calcium carbonate pellets as well as mottled dark grey silty sediments, which mark the water margins or beaches in the past, are seen at many locations on the gentle slopes of the northern shores of the L Basin, X Basin and Z Basin (**Fig.5.4**). In addition, the peripheries of the Basin shores are often capped by white to light grey calcrete duricrusts of a few centimetres thick (**Fig.5.5**), which are indicative of the accumulation of calcium carbonate deposited by evaporation of moisture in the shore sediments, and there are also many calcified plant root casts in the duricrusts. Most archaeological remains of the Early-Middle Holocene have been found at elevations of approximately 10-20 m asl around the Basin shores and have been associated with these features. The Basins are filled with diatomaceous earth, and its white colour is quite visible from a distance (**Fig.5.6**). The Basin bottom is thinly covered by fine-grained aeolian sand, and the accumulation of fine-grained loose sand is thicker near the foot of the Basin slope.

Yardangs on the low desert show the traces of severe wind erosion and thus record wind directions in the past. Dunes on the low desert also suggest wind directions when the dunes were formed. In the present-day Fayum, the wind predominantly blows from the north or northwest (Mohamed 2003: Fig.16), and sand ripples seen elsewhere on the terrains of loose sand expand east-west and perpendicularly to the prevailing wind from the north (**Fig.5.7**). This is because the trade winds blow in the low latitudes towards

Fig.5.4. Calcium carbonate pellets on the northern shore of the Z Basin (looking southwest)

Fig.5.6. Diatomaceous sediments in the L Basin (looking southwest)

Fig.5.5. Calcrete duricrusts on the eastern shore of the Z Basin (looking south)

Fig.5.7. Sand ripples in the Z Basin area (looking northwest)

the Intertropical Convergence Zone, which is shifting north-south near the equator (Nicholson and Flohn 1980; Said 1993: 82-91). However, yardangs on the northeastern shore of the Z Basin (**Fig.5.8**) are eroded not only on their north side but also on their west side. Furthermore, several large dunes of the transverse type extend parallel from the northeast to the southwest in the area between the X Basin and Z Basin. According to general dune formation patterns (Goldberg and Macphail 2006: 130*ff*), the fact that these dunes have a slip face on their east side suggests that they have been formed by the wind from the west. It has been revealed by geomorphological studies in other parts of Egypt that although the wind from the north is dominant in Egypt at present, the wind from the west or northwest has predominated in the Early-Middle Holocene (Brookes 2003). This is because the westerlies, which presently blow in the middle latitudes to the north of Cairo, have migrated southward following the overall shift of atmospheric circulation, and/or because the westerlies meandered extremely reaching as far south as the low latitudes due to a large difference in air temperature between the north pole and the equator (Nicholson and Flohn 1980). It is highly probable that the erosion of yardangs and formation of dunes by the intensification of the westerlies in the Fayum took place during arid periods known in northeastern Africa in the Early-Middle Holocene.

Sporadic limestone outcrops exist everywhere irrespective of elevation, but more terrace-like extensive escarpments of a few metres high are exposed at elevations between 20 m and 30 m asl in the north of the K Basin, L Basin and Z Basin. The surface of these escarpments is littered with flint and limestone pebbles and their fragments. These escarpments are interpreted as prehistoric shorelines representing fluctuating lake levels. The escarpments exhibit irregular, discontinuous ridges, and hence seem to have been severely modified by wind and water erosion.

Another topographic feature in the survey area higher than 30 m asl is the Gindi Plain. It is a vast plain named after an isolated sandstone outcrop of approximately 50 m high which is called Qarit el-Gindi (**Fig.5.9**). The Gindi Plain is located on the Upper Eocene sandstone bed of the Birket Qarun Formation and is covered by coarse-grained aeolian sand, relatively large rounded flint pebbles, and subangular flint

Fig.5.8. Yardangs in the Z Basin area (looking west)

Fig.5.9. Qarit el-Gindi (looking west)

Fig.5.10. A very shallow part of Wadi B (looking northeast)

fragments. Therefore, the area is regarded as gravel desert which is conventionally called *serir* in the local terminology, and is far from rough stony desert which is called *hamada*.

Further topographic features in the survey area are two large wadis which run with a very gentle gradient from the rocky fringe of the Fayum Depression in the north towards the lake in the south through the Gindi Plain. Wadi refers to a gully, valley, or any dry stream bed which is formed by erosion due to occasional surface water flow, but the two wadis mentioned here are dry stream beds which are for the most part only slightly lower than the surrounding terrain (**Fig.5.10**). These wadis are approximately 15 km long. The western wadi named Wadi A by the UCLA-RUG Fayum Project runs from the northwest diagonally between the X Basin and L Basin, and the eastern wadi named Wadi B runs straight and bends southeastwards between the L Basin and K Basin, though the southern extent of both wadis is obscured by modern surface disturbance. The floor of the wadis is covered by fine-grained sand with few flint fragments and the edges of the wadis are quite visible. But at some places, the wadi edges are obscured by accumulations of aeolian sand. Dried plants are sporadically seen in the wadi floor. It is not known exactly how heavily rain fell in the past, but secondary deposits of eroded surface soils of desert origin, which were most likely caused by periodical torrential rain, have been observed in between Middle Holocene lacustrine sediment layers at Qasr el-Sagha (Kozlowski and Ginter 1993: 330*ff*). Therefore, it is probable that a certain amount of winter rainfall in the Early-Middle Holocene caused occasional surface runoff and played a role in creating and maintaining this drainage system.

5.3. The cultural heritage management orientation

Remarkably, the expansion of irrigation canals and farmland into the low desert and the mining of hard clay outcrops around the K Basin and L Basin, and the quarrying of basalt outcrops in the northeastern ridge of the Fayum Depression are rapidly destroying the environment. Therefore, the survey had to be undertaken with an explicit objective of cultural heritage management.

Cultural heritage management is an idea which has developed particularly in the United States since the 1970s, and its principle is that all cultural heritages which survived a long period of time have potential value or use in the present or future, and hence must be preserved wherever feasible or must be investigated as much as possible if destruction is unavoidable (Banning 2002: 177-196; Tainter 2004). This principle has been understood and practised in Europe and other developed countries as well.

Cultural heritage management orientation is gradually becoming common in the archaeology of Egypt. However, the principle of cultural heritage management is generally not well appreciated in the case of prehistoric sites. This is firstly because there are very few monumental structures or other visible features on sites, and hence it is difficult for non-specialists to understand their historical value or significance. A second reason is rapid population increase in Egypt in the past decades and growing demands for more cultivable areas and for more places for the living and the dead. As a consequence, most prehistoric sites on the alluvial plain and low desert adjacent to modern villages, farmlands and cemeteries are doomed to be cultivated, or levelled and built over by villages and cemeteries. Such unfortunate situations have been repeatedly reported by archaeologists working at prehistoric sites in the Nile Delta (van den Brink 1987), the Nile Valley (Bard 1989; Holmes 1992b; Vermeersch 2000) and the Western Desert (Simmons and Mandel 1986), but their efforts to let the local antiquities inspectorate and local people know about the significance of prehistoric sites and to protect the sites were not always successful.

Therefore, even though special attention was paid to prehistoric archaeological remains, this fieldwork project started from knowing the present condition of the concession area and the spatial distribution of archaeological remains by means of a walking survey, while locating previously-published sites and recording any other archaeological and geological features that were encountered. Then, the significance of recorded archaeological remains and the impact of modern land use activities on their preservation were assessed, and the priority for further archaeological investigations in the later stage of the research project was determined.

5.4. Artefact collecting by previous visitors

Since the late 19th century, the Fayum has been well known for the vast scatters of beautifully-shaped flint tools, and local people and European antiquarians have collected such artefacts on the surface over the past hundred years. While archaeologists have made clear the provenance of surface artefacts which they collected, most of the surface artefacts collected by non-archaeologists and presently housed in museums in Egypt and Europe have no information about their provenance. It is impossible to know which sites have been surface-collected and consequently have been severely altered or have become almost invisible. Even at present, the Fayum is a popular place for foreign tourists and the inhabitants of Cairo to visit on holidays, and it is difficult to prevent them from collecting surface artefacts. Present artefact scatters on sites are not in an original, undisturbed state. Therefore, it is essential to take into account the past artefact collecting by antiquarians and archaeologists when the spatial distribution of sites is studied and the state of their preservation is accessed.

French antiquarians in the late 19th century started their flint tool collecting at prominent Pharaonic and Greco-Roman sites in the Fayum such as Umm el-Atel (the ancient Bacchias), Kom Aushim, Qasr el-Sagha, and Dimai (the ancient Soknopaiou Nesos), according to the publications of their collections (de Morgan 1896: 72-75; 1926: 54-68). Since Umm el-Atel, Qasr el-Sagha and Dimai are out of the UCLA/RUG concession and Kom Aushim is not included in the area of ongoing survey (**Fig.5.1**), the past artefact collecting at these sites is unproblematic.

Seton-Karr, who is one of the earliest British antiquarians wandering in the Fayum around the turn of the 19th century, published sketch maps of where he collected hundreds of flint tools and a number of heavy grinding stones. According to his sketch maps (Seton-Karr 1904: fig.1; 1905: plate I) and Caton-Thompson's account (Caton-Thompson and Gardner 1934: 23, 31, 75, and 78-79), it is highly probable that one area of Seton-Karr's intensive collecting was Kom W and its vicinity including Site V and Site Z, and another area was Caton-Thompson's Site ZI, which is identical to Puglisi's Site MB and the Combined Prehistoric Expedition's Site E29G1. Moreover, it seems that Seton-Karr already recognised more sites which were later named by Caton-Thompson as Kom K and Site L, and by the Combined Prehistoric Expedition as Site E29H1. However, it is not clear from Seton-Karr's writings whether he collected flint tools at these sites.

It is also not certain where in the Fayum the followers of Seton-Karr and Caton-Thompson visited, and how many flint tools they collected. For instance, Puglisi, who came to the Fayum in the 1960s, did not publish all artefact collections in detail, except for some Epipalaeolithic artefact assemblages (Mussi *et al.* 1984). Therefore, it is impossible to know whether Puglisi altered the state of sites by collecting surface artefacts when he visited Kom K, Kom W and its vicinity including Site Z.

It is likely that non-archaeologists firstly came to the area around Kom Aushim, because this is the most prominent and most easily accessible place. It seems that the area around Qasr el-Sagha was also a popular flint collecting place, judging from many flint tools which were collected by non-archaeologists and labelled as 'from Qasr el-Sagha' and are presently housed in museums in Egypt and Britain. Kom W is at present located near an asphalt road and a desert track which go to Qasr el-Sagha, and hence it is quite accessible to tourists who have some knowledge of Fayum prehistory. Therefore, there is little doubt that the areas around Kom W and Qasr el-Sagha are still being plundered. In contrast, other areas which are far from desert tracks or edges of farmland are not easily accessible, and thus the probability of being plundered by tourists or local people may be much lower. Keeping these probabilities in mind, the state of preservation of individual sites is assessed.

5.5. The definition of an archaeological site

In archaeology, the meaning of the 'site' has long remained implicit. Any small occupation locus of hunter-gatherers and a town in an early state can be equally called a 'site'. On the other hand, there have been discussions among field surveyors and geographers over the recognition and delineation of 'site' during survey and in the analysis of the subtle variation in surface artefact density across the landscape, and they have been aware that distinguishing a 'site' and setting its boundaries was merely an act of decision or interpretation and not observation (*e.g.*, Bintliff 2000: 200; Dunnell and Dancey 1983: 271-274; Wagstaff 1991). Especially after the advent of cultural heritage management, it has been required that site conceptions should be explicit and consistent, because management decisions like registration and protection are entirely dependent on the perceived nature of the archaeological remains being managed (Dunnell and Dancey 1983: 281-282). This has encouraged archaeologists to reflect on site conceptions for academic research as well. Consequently, a number of site definitions have appeared, but there is still no consensus, and some of the site definitions are arbitrary and thus problematic (Tainter 2004: 438*ff*).

As described below, previous researchers in the Fayum have found a number of archaeological remains, and have named them 'sites'. However, the spatial extent of the 'sites' and the thickness, density and diversity of cultural and faunal deposits at the 'sites' are considerably different. As for prehistoric 'sites', the most salient Neolithic occupation loci like Kom K and Kom W are low mounds of more or less than 100 m in basal diameter, covered by dense artefact scatters of less than 1.5 m thick with no substantial stratigraphy, and contain structural remains like firepits and sunken storage jars. On the other hand, most of the other published 'sites' are merely scatters of artefacts or faunal remains on the desert surface, and their spatial extent and density are varied, from a few metres in diameter to more than a few hundred metres wide. In other cases, individual excavation trenches of a few square metres have been named 'sites', even though the trenches were opened in a vast area of dense artefact scatter, which may otherwise be called a single 'site'. Inconsistency in the manner of 'site' naming is quite obvious.

The problems in delineating 'sites' must be considered in terms of their state of preservation. Most of the known archaeological 'sites' in the northeastern part of the Fayum are concentrated around the Basins in the low desert adjacent to the present lakeshore. These Basins were filled with water when the lake level was much higher in the past, and thus it is reasonable that the Basin shores were the loci of past human activities. However, this situation causes difficulties in identifying discrete archaeological entities or 'sites'.

Even those who survey ethnographic sites of a few days or a few decades old would face the problem of defining the outer limits of a site, because human activities may disperse rare artefacts far away from the densest concentrations of artefacts (Gifford-Gonzalez *et al.* 1999: 403-404). The archaeologist studies the spatial artefact distributions on the surface that have accumulated through prolonged human activities. Therefore, an archaeological 'site', defined as a high density cluster of archaeological remains, does not necessarily correspond with a discrete settlement or other locus of activity, but may present a set of overlapping distributions, each representing a different activity or set of activities at different times. 'Sites' in the sense of high artefact densities can occur where there was no cultural activity at any time in the past, simply because the peripheries of several artefact clusters overlap there (Banning 2002: 18-19).

It has also been known that post-depositional processes might affect surface artefact distributions and their visibility. Archaeological remains on a slope can be removed downslope by soil movement caused by sheetwash and small rills (Allen 1991). Recurrent wave action on a beach and occasional surface runoff in a dry stream bed, for example, can create a high density cluster of sorted artefacts which might look like a discrete 'site' (Banning 2002: 72-73; Morton 2004: 45-54; Rapp and Hill 1998: 56-59). There is no doubt that archaeological remains on Basin shores and on wadi beds and terraces in the Fayum have suffered from water erosion and subsequent wind erosion and the redeposition of aeolian sand. On the other hand, it is said that under rapidly rising calm water, archaeological remains on lake margins can be buried and well protected by the cover of lacustrine silty sediments which tend to deposit in deeper parts of lakes (Goldberg and Macphail 2006: 114; Rapp and Hill 1998: 57-59).

Moreover, the effects of deflation on surface artefact distributions cannot be underestimated. In aeolian environments, fine-grained loose sand is blown away, leaving a residual deposit of heavier and larger objects like lithic artefacts on a consolidated surface, and consequently, lithic artefacts originally contained in different deposits from successive occupations can be found together within the seemingly same assemblage (Goldberg and Macphail 2006: 122-129). Therefore, this new survey aimed to understand natural alternation to the morphology and distribution of archaeological remains in alluvial, colluvial and aeolian environments. Considering the problems of delineating 'sites' in this situation, the term 'locality' was used by this survey for recording and documenting a high density cluster of archaeological remains. However, concerning the localities which have been studied and named as 'sites' by previous researchers but actually do not deserve the designation of 'site', the previous names were adopted without change by this survey, in order to avoid confusion caused by giving new names.

Remarkable archaeological remains which drew the attention of archaeologists who had special research interests or specific expertise have tended to be recognised as 'sites' and given site names or site numbers. On the other hand, it has been uncertain whether there were more archaeological remains which failed to draw archaeologists' attention. It is understandable that low density surface artefact scatters were prone to be overlooked by previous surveys. However, as described below, even though not thoroughly surveyed, it was revealed that the survey area contains a number of more salient and hence easily-recognisable occupation loci like hearths which have never been published before. For the study of the land use patterns by prehistoric people, such occupation loci must be taken into account. Therefore, it was attempted to record carefully previously-overlooked archaeological remains.

The 'hearths' mentioned here in the Fayum look like heaps or circles of sandstone and fossil shell-bearing limestone cobbles, and the concentrations of the rocks are generally 1-2 m in diameter. Such rock concentrations have been conventionally called 'stone places' or *Steinplätze* in Saharan archaeology (Gabriel 1987; 2002). According to Wright (2005), the term 'hearth' which usually refers to any evidence for repeated use of fire must be more clearly defined, and seven types of ancient fire features can be distinguished on the basis of their construction and the frequency of their use. The seven types are; (1) firepatches, (2) fireplaces, (3) firepits, (4) stone-bordered fireplaces, (5) stone-filled pit hearths, (6) stone-bordered pit hearths, and (7) stone-lined pit hearths. Most heaps or circles of rocks seen in the Fayum look identical to either stone-filled or stone-lined pit hearths, but it is not certain whether all of such heaps or circles of rocks are really hearths if no trace of the use of fire is found. A previous survey report has drawn concentrations of rocks on the desert surface as 'hearths' on a sketch map of a Neolithic site E29G3 Area B near Qasr el-Sagha (Wendorf and Schild 1976: fig.147), but the reason why they were considered to be hearths was not explained. On the other hand, an excavation of a concentration of rocks at a Neolithic site QS VIE/80 near Qasr el-Sagha to the west of the survey area revealed that it was definitely a hearth and that rocks were put together in a shallow depression for distributing heat or supporting items to be heated (Dagnan-Ginter *et al.* 1984: fig.21).

Given these previous research reports, it is necessary to investigate whether every single 'stone place' found during the new survey is really a hearth, but such an investigation was not always feasible and no careful excavation could be carried out during the survey. In many cases, rocks are fire-cracked, or the underside of rocks is blackened and charcoal still remains beneath the rocks. Hence such cases are considered to be hearths. In the other cases, however, rocks sit on the sandy surface and there is no trace of the use of fire, even though there are sparse scatters of artefacts around the rocks. In a desert environment, stone-filled or stone-lined hearths could be denuded and deflated, and lighter materials like charcoal and ashes could be washed or blown away, leaving weathered rocks alone (Gabriel 2002: 52-53). Therefore, no trace of the use of fire does not necessarily indicate that a 'stone place' under investigation is not a hearth. The new survey in the Fayum found no example of 'stone place' which suggests other purposes like a landmark, burial marker, or stockpiling of rocks. Therefore, in the following, all 'stone places' are tentatively described as hearths.

The variety, size, and number of rocks for making hearths seen in the survey area are not equal between the hearths, and the degree of discreteness of features like rock layout and artefact scatter in their proximity are also not the same. Such various degrees of feature discreteness should be indicators of the duration and repetition of hearth use (Chatters 1987). During the first use of a hearth, the rock layout is distinct and encompasses charcoal and refuse. If people remained several weeks, the hearth size might grow, and its position might be shifted, and parts of the original hearth might be removed and used to make a new one while disrupting the original feature, according to the changes of wind direction and needs of shelter. Between the first occupation and subsequent visits, vegetation and water distributions over the site might change, necessitating a repositioning of activities. During subsequent visits, the rock layout might be moved, while leaving a lens of ashes and trash to be trampled by users, scavenged by wild animals, or scattered by wind, or washed away by rising lake water or surface runoff of rain water. New hearths might be made from parts of one or more old hearths, and the older hearths might be obliterated. In other words, hearth stones should be regarded as features of site furniture, and should be considered as reused repeatedly by visitors (Binford 1979). After several seasons, there is a general scatter of rocks, ashes, and hearth trash with one or more rock circles in various states of repair. Repeated occupations would be more disruptive to feature integrity, due to the greater probability of spatial nonconformity of activities between habitation events than would be expected of longer-term single occupation. As the duration of occupation increased to permanence, it might become indistinguishable from repeated site use (Chatters 1987: 346). Keeping these assumptions in mind, all hearths encountered during the survey were recorded for the interpretation of how long or how repeatedly individual hearths were used and how many hearths were operational at one time.

Other supposedly immobile items which were often encountered in isolation or in association with artefact scatters include heavy grinding stones made of limestone and sandstone blocks/slabs. They have a shallow depression on one face of a block/slab and hence can easily be understood as items for grinding or mashing/pounding something on them. Such heavy items may be regarded as site furniture, which is usually not transported from place to place but rather left at one place by mobile people in anticipation of a future revisit (Binford 1979; Nelson and Lippmeier 1993), and should be considered to have been used repeatedly by visitors. In other words, the place where heavy grinding stones were found may be a locus of subsistence activities where people visited regularly or fortuitously for grinding cultivated crop grains or mashing/pounding sedge tubers.

Previous researchers who surveyed on the north side of the lake in the Fayum have mentioned the sporadic occurrence of grinding stones, but have not thoroughly recorded their findspots, number and details. Hence it is not known how many grinding stones have actually been found at which sites and thereafter taken away, except for ten grinding stones taken from Kom W by Seton-Karr and presently housed in the Egyptian Museum in Cairo, and another six grinding stones excavated at Kom W by Caton-Thompson (Caton-Thompson and Gardner 1934: 31-32; Seton-Karr 1905: 186). Therefore, during this survey, special attention was paid to grinding stones, and their findspots were recorded. The term 'site' was principally given by this survey to a concentration of substantial and immobile remains like hearths and grinding stones. As will be described below, however, such concentrations are not common and hence only a few 'sites' were newly recognised by this survey.

Furthermore, another attempt by this survey was a sort of off-site or non-site survey. Previous 'salient site oriented' surveys in the Fayum have found several remarkable occupation loci, but the catchment analysis of such loci has not been sufficiently attempted. Although the patterns of fish and animal exploitation in prehistory have been studied at several selected localities in the Fayum (Brewer 1989a; 1989b; Gautier 1976b), it has not been thoroughly investigated what varieties of wild food resources were available around salient occupation loci, where the inhabitants of the salient occupation loci procured raw materials for tool making and clay for pottery making, where they went out for animal hunting and herding, and where they cultivated crops. Not only high density surface artefact scatters but also low density surface artefact scatters around salient occupation loci and in between salient occupation loci could give clues to know the locations visited or passed by people over some length of time.

High or low density scatters of animal/fish bones and their fragments are frequently encountered during the off-site or non-site survey, but it is difficult to interpret their scatter or concentration patterns especially when there are few artefacts around. How a scatter or concentration of bones and bone fragments is formed at one place depends firstly on how the sequence from catch to consumption took place. Removing inedible or low-utility portions of animals and fish upon catch prior to their transport back to field camp or residential base is quite common among foragers in African ethnographic records (*e.g.*, Gifford-Gonzalez *et al.* 1999; Kent 1993; O'Connell *et al.* 1988), and this behaviour could leave a scatter or concentration of the bones of specific body parts at the place of catching and butchering. When the animals and fish were eaten immediately after catching at one place, bones would have been dropped around the place of catching, cooking and eating by people who dined there, or collectively dumped away from the place. Therefore, it has been argued that concentrations of bones and bone fragments would not necessarily indicate the exact place of catching, butchering, cooking, or eating (*e.g.*, Gifford-Gonzalez 1991). Furthermore, bones are likely to be disturbed by scavenging acts of carnivores like jackals and vultures, and hence it is less possible for them to remain intact (*e.g.*, Lupo 1995). It was attempted to understand the implications of such bone scatters, thereby identifying the loci of subsistence activities.

In addition to these problems of displacement and disturbance, the preservation of bones is dependent on how long and whether they remained exposed on the desert surface or were buried under lacustrine silty sediments or aeolian sand, because bones are weathered and fragmented by various natural forces and reduced to unidentifiable splinters. Some empirical data have suggested that the preservation of bones must be understood as essentially fortuitous in the harsh desert environments of Egypt (Van Neer and Uerpmann 1989: 311). Furthermore, the differences in resistance to weathering and fragmentation between bones of different animals and their different body parts are not well known in the prehistoric archaeological record in Egypt (Gautier and Van Neer 1989: 138). The scatters or concentrations of bones and bone fragments on the present surface in the Fayum can only be considered as indicating that they have been well protected beneath the past surface and were exposed on the present surface very recently by deflation. In other words, if scatters or concentrations of bone fragments are not sporadic but are widespread in a large area, then the archaeological remains in the entire area may be regarded as having been well preserved and retaining to some extent the primary context.

Off-site or non-site surveys were particularly necessary in the northern half of the concession area. It is virtually barren desert fringed by terrace-like escarpments in the north and also marked by Wadi A and Wadi B running from the rocky terrain through the barren desert. Except for Old Kingdom gypsum quarrying workshops found at Umm el-Sawan at a northern fringe of the Fayum Depression, no archaeological remains have been reported in this terrain. Therefore, it was expected to know whether the lack of information actually meant the lack of human activities in this terrain in the past.

5.6. Method of survey and recording

A modern topographical map of the northeastern part of the Fayum, which was produced on a 1:50000 scale by the Irrigation Management Systems Projects and was issued as 'Kawm Ushim NH36-E5b' by the Egyptian General Survey Authority in 1995, was used as a base map for the field survey. The archaeological site maps made and published by Caton-Thompson and Gardner (1934: pl.CIX), Wendorf and Schild (1976: fig.95), Mussi, Caneva and Zarattini (1984: fig.1) and Brewer (1989b: fig.18) were also used as references in order to locate the sites which they have investigated.

A grid system was set up in order to cover the survey area, following the true north-south axis. The survey area was divided into 60 squares, each of which is 2 km (east-west) x 2 km (north-south), just for the convenience of walking and recording in the field. Within each square, the same manner of transect walking could not equally been employed, because the physical condition of each square was different from each other, and it was not practical to apply the same setup of transects. In the case of squares covering the K Basin and L Basin, the area is severely disturbed by modern land use activities, and it was difficult to go straight across farmland following transects. Therefore, the survey was limited to accessible margins of farmland and undisturbed terrains. In the case of squares covering the X Basin and Z Basin, the area is not severely disturbed. Thus a series of parallel transects were firstly walked, and then a second set of transects at right angles to the first were walked at a different time of the same day or on a different day, in order to increase the probability of encountering archaeological remains.

Artefact concentrations and other archaeological remains were generally quite visible on the desert surface, marking a sharp contrast with the barren parts of the desert completely covered by aeolian sand. The presence of artefact concentrations and other archaeological remains was often quite predictable in relation to the natural relief and depressions of the desert. Considering the demand of large area coverage by a few persons within limited time periods, it was impossible to employ meticulous transect walking with a rigid, equally-spaced interval in a given square and to collect or count every single artefact on the surface in order to see the density of artefact scatters over the land. Therefore, the direction and interval of parallel transects were flexible and were based on the surface conditions. It must be stressed that due to this flexible manner, the resultant record of the spatial distribution of artefact scatters and other archaeological remains is different from an objective sample obtained through a well-controlled survey, and hence has no statistical meaning. Less visible artefacts and other archaeological remains in sandy parts of the desert may have been missed. In the case of squares covering Wadi A and Wadi B, assuming that the remains of past human activities would be located along the Wadis, it was not cost-effective to employ transect walking in the entire square, and hence, the survey transect was not extended more than 500 m far away from the terraces of the Wadis.

The rough dating of localities/sites is based on diagnostic artefacts seen on the surface. The strengths and weaknesses of archaeological survey and study of surface-collected artefacts have been discussed elsewhere in comparison with the strengths and weaknesses of archaeological excavation and the study of excavated subsurface artefacts (*e.g.*, Dunnell and Dancey 1983; Millett 2000). While a survey enables broad spatial coverage of the area under study, a weakness of surface-collected artefacts is apparently that they lack precise chronological information. Surface artefacts are loosely spatially associated with each other, and it cannot simply be assumed that all artefacts or structural remains found on the same surface of a particular spot were deposited at broadly the same time. Therefore, well-dated lithic sequences or pottery sequences produced through controlled excavations are necessary to date the surface artefacts, but such artefact sequences are not yet available in the Fayum.

Pottery sherds seen on the surface of the survey area are dated to either the Neolithic, Old Kingdom, or Greco-Roman. As described in Chapter 3, Neolithic pottery of the Fayum is made from local clay and shale, and is handmade and coarse. Hemispherical bowls and tall bag-shaped jars are the most common pottery types. Most of Neolithic pottery sherds seen on the surface of the survey area are heavily-worn porous body sherds of such vessels. They are easily distinguishable from Old Kingdom pottery sherds which have much finer fabric and are well-fired, and Greco-Roman pottery sherds which are often made from hard marl clay and are better preserved. Actually, the occurrence of Old Kingdom and Greco-Roman pottery sherds is sporadic in the survey area. The presence of Neolithic pottery sherds on a locality/site can be used as an indicator of Neolithic occupation, but it does not indicate at which time within the long span of the Fayum Neolithic period the locality/site was occupied. Poorly-published Epipalaeolithic lithic assemblages obtained through controlled excavations at Site E29G1 and Site E29G3 by the Combined Prehistoric Expedition as well as the Epipalaeolithic-Neolithic tool class sequence proposed in Chapter 3 are presently usable as references to roughly date quite diagnostic Epipalaeolithic and Neolithic lithic artefacts on the surface of the survey area. A Predynastic lithic assemblage obtained at Qasr Qarun by Caton-Thompson (Caton-Thompson and Gardner 1934: 69-70 and pls.LII-LIII) and an Old Kingdom lithic assemblage obtained at Kom IV by Caton-Thompson (Caton-Thompson and Gardner 1934: 97-101 and pls.LIV-LV) are also usable as references to roughly date quite diagnostic Predynastic and Old Kingdom lithic artefacts on the surface of the survey area. As Caton-Thompson recognised when she investigated her surface sites (Caton-Thompson and Gardner 1934: 71-87), mixed assemblages of Epipalaeolithic, Neolithic, Predynastic, Old Kingdom and Greco-Roman artefacts on the present surface are not unusual in the Fayum due to overlapping occupations and severe surface deflation. Such situations were repeatedly encountered during this survey. Therefore, the possible date(s) of occupation of a locality/site encountered often had to be recorded for instance as 'Epipalaeolithic/Neolithic' or 'Neolithic/Old Kingdom'.

All information about individual locations with archaeological remains and their possible date(s) was recorded by using the record sheet, with the aid of a hand-held Garmin GPS receiver to obtain their coordinates. The datum is 'Old Egyptian', and the grid is described as latitude/longitude hddd.ddddd°. The information was processed on the Garmin MapSource ver.6.8 and the GIS software MapInfo Professional ver.7.0, and was graphically displayed. A contour map made by using this GIS software on the basis of the above-mentioned topographical map 'Kawm Ushim NH36-E5b' is superimposed on a satellite picture obtained from Google Earth. While the coordinates of individual locations were recorded by using the GPS receiver without difficulty, it was difficult to obtain their elevations, because this device is not suitable for measuring accurate elevations. Approximate elevations of most archaeological localities/sites and topographic features described below were obtained after they were plotted on the contour map. These GIS data are the basis for gaining a general overview of the large concession area, and for subsequently carrying out more intensive and systematic investigations including excavations at promising localities/sites in later stage of research.

5.7. Field observations of the survey area

5.7.1. The K Basin-L Basin area

The K Basin-L Basin area is defined as the area centring on the K Basin and L Basin (**Fig.5.11**). At present, the K Basin and L Basin are transformed into reservoir and farmland, and their surroundings are actively cultivated, whereas the plots more than 1 km to the north of both Basins have been cultivated once but are abandoned due to the failure of water supply and subsequent soil deterioration through salination. In spite of such a severe situation, dry canals and ditches are still being extended a further few kilometres northwards beyond the abandoned farmland and destroying desert environments. The access to this area is facilitated by an asphalt road which extends westwards from the Cairo-Fayum Road No.22, and many dirt tracks extend northwards and southwards from the asphalt road.

5.7.1.1. Kom K

Kom K (N29.58737° E30.87825° in the centre) is located in the low desert to the northwest of the K Basin, and its top elevation is approximately 20 m asl. The surface of this low desert is covered by fine alluvial silty sand, but this area has extensively been cultivated, and other kinds of soils and flint pebbles seem to have been brought from somewhere else as fertiliser or paving stones. At present, Kom K is in the middle of farmland, but still retains its shape as a very low mound (**Fig.5.12**). Many plough tracks and remains of plants are visible on the Kom (**Fig.5.13**), and scatters of artefacts including large flint cobbles, flint debitage products, and pottery sherds are seen in between the tracks around the highest elevation in its centre. These artefact scatters are apparently those that were excavated and left there by Caton-Thompson and thereafter ploughed. Therefore, they do not retain their original context at all but nonetheless can roughly be viewed as the representatives of this site, which has kept cultural deposits of approximately 30 cm thick (Caton-Thompson and Gardner 1934: 38*ff*). The study of the artefacts collected here will be described in Chapter 7.

5.7.1.2. Site K

Site K, which was indicated on a map and briefly described by Caton-Thompson (Caton-Thompson and Gardner 1934: 72) and Site 3, which was surveyed by Brewer in the 1980s (Brewer 1989a; 1989b), must be located somewhere in the modern farmland to the southeast of Kom K, but that area is at present actively cultivated, and hence is not accessible. It is highly probable that these sites are completely buried or destroyed.

5.7.1.3. The Upper K Pits and Lower K Pits

Approximately 1 km to the northeast of Kom K, an extensive ridge built of hard clay runs over 3 km from the northwest to the southeast. Presently an asphalt road and concrete and stone-built canals run parallel at the foot of this ridge. The surface of the ridge is covered by coarse-grained aeolian sand with many abraded flint gravels, many small lacustrine shells and fossilised shells. Some abraded flint flakes found among the gravels seem to be Levallois flakes and hence to be dated to the Middle Palaeolithic. It has been suggested that this ridge was a part of the Pleistocene lakeshore (Caton-Thompson and Gardner 1934: 41). The stratigraphic profile of the ridge on the walls of another modern canal dug deeply in the middle of the ridge perpendicularly show that surface flint gravels and hard clay overlie bands of Tertiary indurated shales and conglomerates.

Caton-Thompson and Gardner reported that

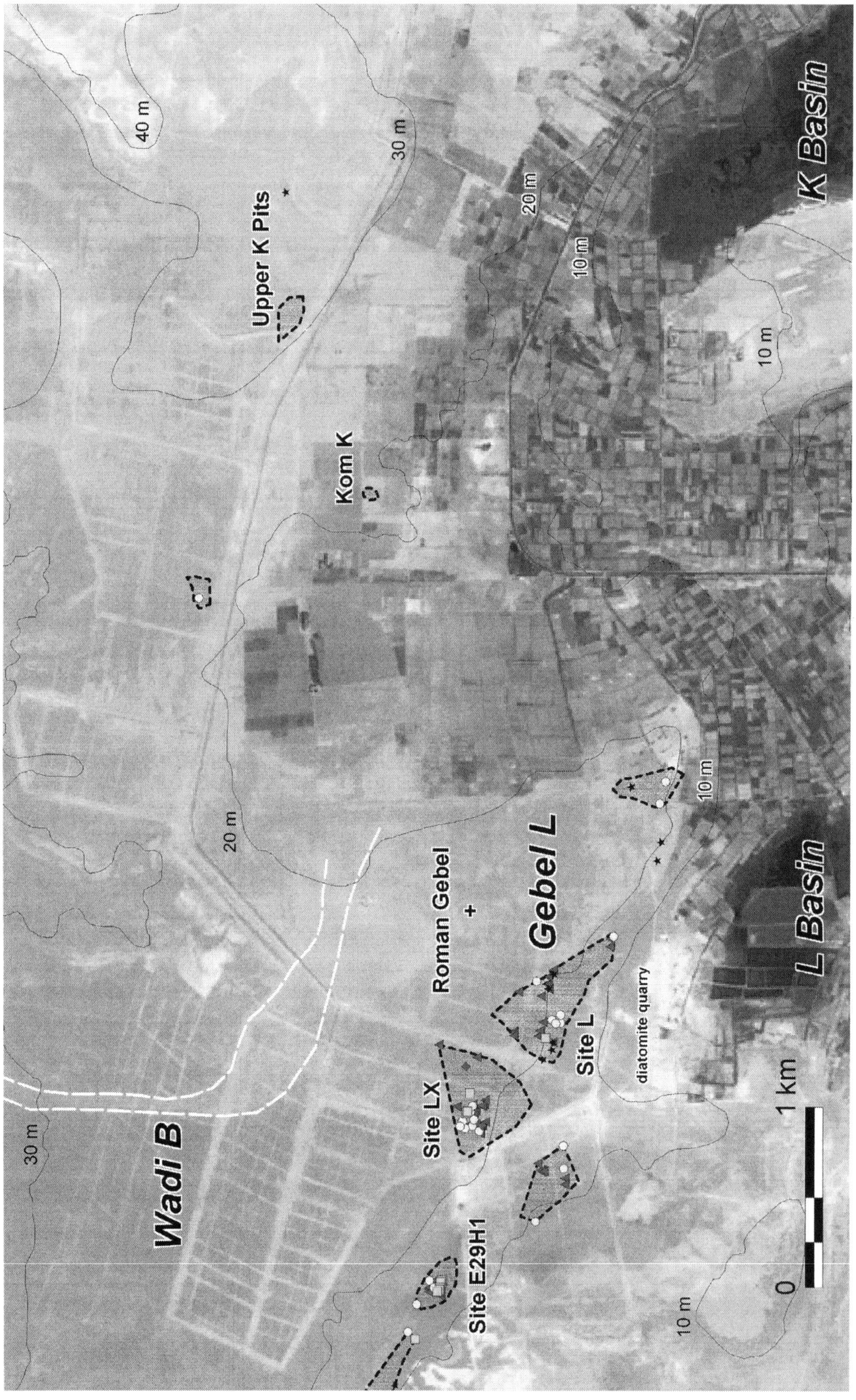

Fig.5.11. The K Basin - L Basin area (triangle: hearth, circle: grinding stone, square: animal bone, star: Neolithic projectile point, diamond: Neolithic sickle blade)

Fig.5.12. Present state of Kom K in the middle of farmland (looking southwest)

Fig.5.14. Present state of the Upper K Pits (looking west)

Fig.5.13. Kom K from a distance (looking northeast)

Fig.5.15. Supposed location of the Lower K Pits (looking south)

the Upper K Pits were spread in an area of approximately 180 m long by 45 m wide on top of a projecting northwestern spur of this ridge named the K Ridge at an elevation of approximately 30 m asl at its highest, whereas the Lower K Pits were distributed further westwards at lower elevations of around 20 m asl (Caton-Thompson and Gardner 1934: 41). A number of circular shallow depressions of less than 1 m in diameter are still visible on the surface of the higher ridge (N29.59089° E30.88955° in the centre), and a bifacially-retouched, serrated sickle blade was collected on the surface. Therefore, this locality is certainly the Upper K Pits. Comparison of the present topography with the map of the Upper K Pits made by Caton-Thompson and Gardner (Caton-Thompson and Gardner 1934: pl.XXIV) showed that a concentration of shallow depressions presently seen on the ridge corresponds to a major concentration of pits on their map. However, it is also recognised that the most obvious of those depressions are not Neolithic granary pits but are probably later robbers' pits. The location of Neolithic granary pits is often indicated only by a circular clearance which has a lower density of flint gravels.

The K Ridge is at present in the early stage of development by the Egyptian government, and is being destroyed by activities such as digging deep canals, scraping surface gravels, and paving roads with flint cobbles which are transported from elsewhere. The Upper K Pits locality is presently divided into two (the eastern part and westernmost part) by a deep canal running north-south (**Fig.5.14**). The eastern part which contains the major concentration of pits mentioned above is not severely disturbed by modern activities, because this part is higher and more undulating than surrounding areas and thus less suitable for cultivation. The westernmost part is the place where an isolated pit numbered 67 has been found by Caton-Thompson. In this westernmost part, many intact pits which had been overlooked by Caton-Thompson were found and partially excavated (Schepers *et al.* 2006; Wendrich and Cappers 2005). Surface loose sand is not thick on this ground, and most pits have been dug through compact sand into hard clay.

On the other hand, the exact location of the Lower K Pits is not clear, because Caton-Thompson did not publish the map and plan of the Lower K Pits but described them only briefly (Caton-Thompson and Gardner 1934: 52-54). The supposed location of the Lower K Pits (**Fig.5.15**), which was said to be approximately 800 m to the north of Kom K and to the northwest of the Upper K Pits, is presently covered by flint gravels and loose sand, and seems to be more heavily eroded than the area of the Upper K Pits, as Caton-Thompson has already noted. No depressions of a granary pit size can be found on the surface. It is also probable that the supposed location of the Lower K Pits has been mostly destroyed by the canals mentioned above.

Most of the area to the north of both the Lower and Upper K Pits is severely disturbed by recent expanding dry canals and ditches. Some undisturbed parts were barren, and no archaeological remains were found in this area except for a stray Neolithic concave-based arrowhead found on the side of a dirt track. The areas to the southwest and northwest of the supposed location of the Lower K Pits are also severely disturbed by recent land use activities, and no archaeological remains were found. In the area to the west of the Lower K Pits, a low desert ridge extends from the east to the west, and on the north of the ridge, a number of sandstone cobble clusters accompanied by pottery sherds were seen on the desert surface. Lithic artefacts are few, and they look different from those of prehistory. Some pottery sherds are apparently later than the Neolithic period. Therefore, it may be presumed that this locality was occupied in later periods. Since most occupation loci in later periods have been found at lower elevations to the south, the nature of this curious locality must be considered further.

5.7.1.4. Gebel L

The northern shore of the L Basin is marked by a flat brownish limestone escarpment, which was named Gebel L by Caton-Thompson (Caton-Thompson and Gardner 1934: 73). She has reported that there were one Neolithic surface site named Site L on the southern spur of Gebel L, one Old Kingdom site named Kom IV, and one Roman site named the Roman Gebel on the flat top of Gebel L (Caton-Thompson and Gardner 1934: 73-74, 97-100, and 158). The eastern half of the northern spur of Gebel L is at present occupied by modern farmland, and an archaeological survey was not possible. The southwestern part of Gebel L is occupied by two large military hangars, which were abandoned many years ago and are presently not in use. Its surroundings are flattened, and military rubbish is widely scattered. To the north of the military hangars are presently uncultivated plots divided by dry ditches (**Fig.5.16**). A noticeable limestone outcrop in the middle of the uncultivated plots is the Roman Gebel (N29.58217° E30.85390° in the centre) (**Fig.5.17**). Several supposedly rock-cut graves are present, but they are badly damaged by robbers' pits and shelters made by local people as watching stands for illegal falcon hunting. Scatters of Roman pottery sherds are seen around the outcrop.

At the southeastern end of the limestone escarpment approximately 500 m to the east of the military hangars, wide scatters of lithic artefacts were located on the flat surface. The southern spur of this flat area is covered by lithic artefacts as well as pottery sherds not only of the Neolithic but also of later periods, though there are no pottery sherds on top of the flat area.

It is likely that this area was flattened by military bulldozers and surface artefacts were removed downslope to the south. Kom IV must be located somewhere around here, but it seems to be destroyed by this activity. Surface scatters of lithic artefacts and pottery sherds are spread further toward modern farmland in the south. The surface of one locality of artefact concentration seems to have been burnt very recently, and Neolithic flint tools and relatively well-preserved pottery sherds as well as a typical Old Kingdom flint crescent drill were collected on the surface. Close proximity to Kom IV may be an explanation for the presence of an Old Kingdom artefact. Another locality of surface artefact concentration next to the first one is more chaotic, and pottery sherds of obviously later periods are mixed with Neolithic pottery sherds and Neolithic flint tools in fine-grained aeolian sand. All of these surface artefact scatters may be included in the eastern end of Caton-Thompson's Site L. However, it was also reported by Gardner that there was a Ptolemaic settlement around there (Caton-Thompson and Gardner 1934: 145-149). Therefore, a part of the pottery sherd scatters may belong to this Ptolemaic settlement.

Fig.5.16. Present state of Gebel L (looking south from Roman Gebel)

Fig.5.17. Roman Gebel (looking northeast)

5.7.1.5. Site L

According to Caton-Thompson, Site L is located on the southern slope of Gebel L, and it extends more than 1 km wide, and between 10 m asl and 20 m asl. The area at the foot of this limestone escarpment is covered by limestone slabs and blocks which fell down from the edge of the escarpment, and thus, few archaeological remains can be seen. In contrast, the areas to the east and west of these limestone slabs and blocks are not much disturbed, though the entire area is covered by thick accumulations of fine-grained aeolian sand. Surface scatters of artefacts are sparsely seen on this sand, where Caton-Thompson collected a number of Epipalaeolithic and Neolithic tools. The area further downslope of the scatter of limestone slabs and blocks exhibits light yellow to orange silty sediments which are supposed to be beach sediments and lacks aeolian deposition of sand. The artefact scatters extend on these silty sediments, and it is difficult to discern between Epipalaeolithic and Neolithic lithic artefacts. The southern end of this area is occupied by two large conical limestone buttes. Sparse scatters of supposedly Roman pottery sherds are seen around these buttes.

The slope surface of the western half of Site L is thinly covered by coarse/fine-grained aeolian sand with few flint fragments (**Fig.5.18**). As can be observed on the walls of a deep canal dug north-south, there is a lamination of very fine-grained alluvial sand and silty sediments of different colours and different extent of induration accumulated beneath the surface. It shows that this slope has repeatedly experienced inundation and desiccation events caused by fluctuating basin water levels, though the age and duration of each event cannot be understood by the visual observation of stratigraphy alone. The ground at lower elevations of the slope is very soft, and many cracks are seen on the surface and some parts are sunken or collapsed. At one location, a large band of silty sediments runs from a higher elevation downwards, and it seems to be a trace of surface runoff water of unknown age.

Most archaeological remains in the western half of Site L such as scatters of lithic artefacts and pottery sherds, and clusters of sandstone/shell-bearing limestone cobbles which are supposed to be hearths, are spread between 15 m asl and 20 m asl, but they are also observed above 20 m asl. At the lower elevation, there are several patches of deflated light yellow silty sediments, and scatters of lithic artefacts and pottery sherds are seen on these silty sediments, and many of them are embedded in the sediments. Below 10 m asl, the desert surface is covered by fine-grained aeolian sand and a sparse growth of camel's thorn (*Alhagi maurorum*) and lotus trees (*Nitraria retusa*), and few artefacts are seen.

The density of archaeological remains is relatively low in the slope area, whereas it is very high in the flat area above 20 m asl. There seems to be a tendency that Epipalaeolithic artefacts are scattered at lower elevations whereas Neolithic artefacts are more densely scattered at higher elevations. At the middle elevation, both Epipalaeolithic and Neolithic artefacts seem to be mixed, due to either taphonomic processes or overlapping areas of activities, or both. Since Neolithic flint tools are sometimes seen at lower elevations, it is difficult to locate purely Epipalaeolithic artefact scatters. Sparse scatters of unworked flint cobbles are also noticed in these areas. Since these cobbles are apparently not local ones, they must have been transported from elsewhere as lithic raw materials by toolmakers. Neolithic pottery sherds are not numerous in these areas.

A cluster of four hearths accompanied by Neolithic pottery sherds and lithic artefacts were found on the deflated surface of a high flat area

Fig.5.18. Slope of the western half of Site L (looking west)

Fig.5.19. Hearths in Site L (looking south)

of 20 m asl, overlooking the L Basin in the southeast (**Fig.5.19** and **Fig.5.20**). It is noticeable that charcoal still remains beneath hearth stones. Lithic artefacts include a number of large flint cores and debitage products, and some of them could be refitted. These facts suggest that this location has not been disturbed severely, and it was assessed that this location might represent a well-preserved Neolithic occupation locus at a high elevation in this area. The study of the lithic artefacts collected here will be described in Chapter 7.

5.7.1.6. L Basin reservoir and clay mines

Although not indicated on the modern topographical map issued in 1995, a large part of the L Basin is presently transformed into a

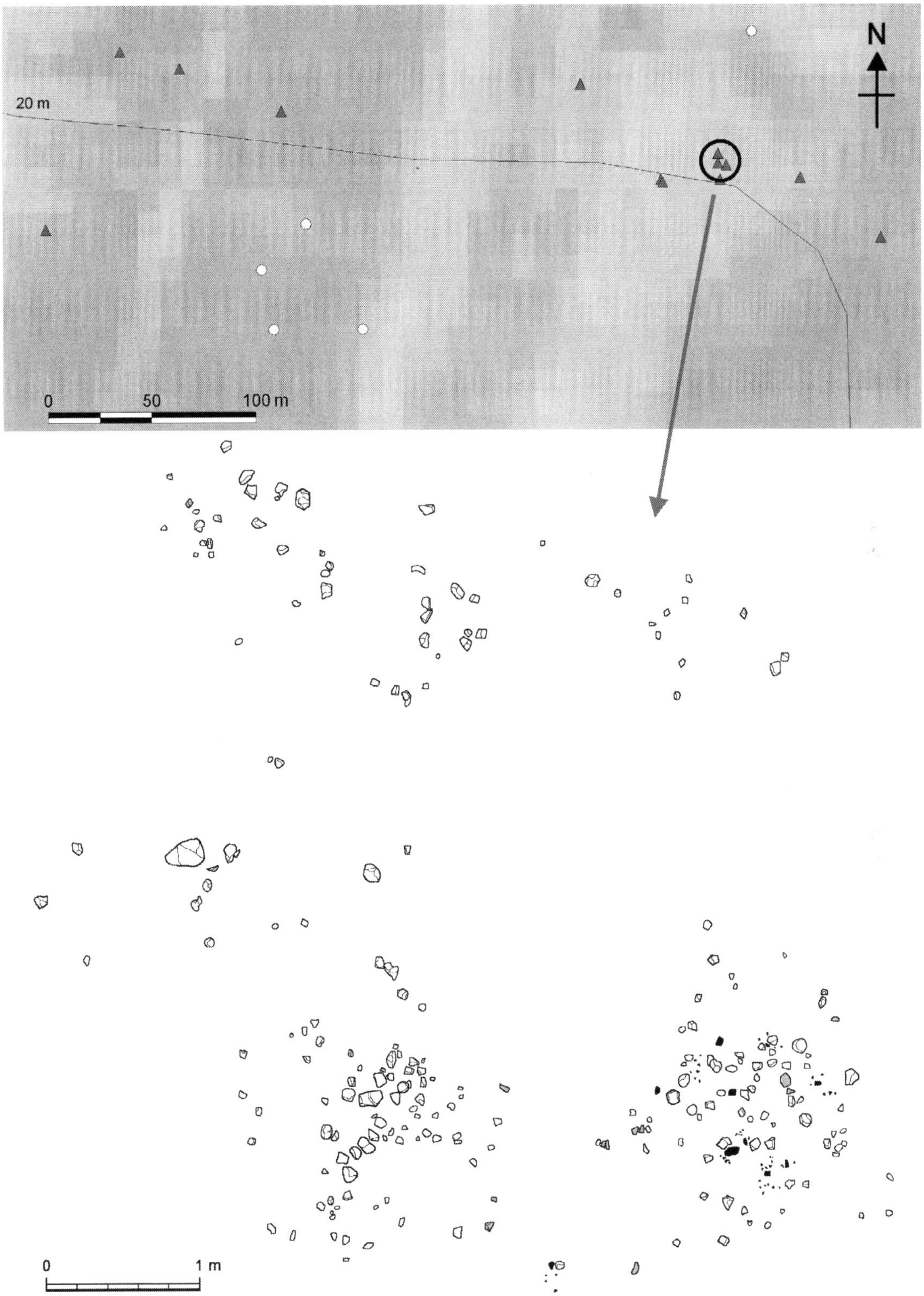

Fig.5.20. Site L (triangle: hearth, circle: grinding stone) and four hearths (sandstone in grey and pottery sherds in black)

Fig.5.21. Diatomite quarry at the northern fringe of the L Basin (looking northwest)

reservoir, and its surroundings are marshland and farmland, and are cultivated. The northern fringe of the L Basin exhibits the extensive exposure of diatomaceous earth, and blocks of diatomite are being quarried by mining machines. The accumulation of diatomaceous earth as seen on the walls of the quarry is more than 2 m thick (**Fig.5.21**), and this suggests that the bottom of the L Basin has been filled with water for a considerable length of time. Caton-Thompson has recorded an unnamed Epipalaeolithic locality on the southern shore of the L Basin (Caton-Thompson and Gardner 1934: 74, pls. CXII and CXIII), but this locality is probably in the middle of modern farmland, and could not be found.

Further to the south of the L Basin reservoir are large mining sites. Bulldozers and mining machines are levelling and digging outcrops of hard clay and shale, and dumper trucks are transporting tons of rubble on dirt tracks to nearby ceramic factories along the Cairo-Fayum Road. There is no hope of finding archaeological remains in this area.

5.7.1.7. Summary of the K Basin-L Basin area

The K Basin-L Basin area is disturbed or destroyed so severely by modern land use activities that it is difficult to imagine the original environment. Therefore, this area is not suitable for understanding the spatial distribution of past human occupation loci and natural resources and for considering human behavioural patterns in the given environment in prehistory. However, individual prehistoric localities/sites which survived recent surface disturbance but are presently under threat of destruction still deserve further study.

5.7.2. The L Basin-X Basin area

The L Basin-X Basin area is defined as the area centring on the L Basin and X Basin (**Fig.5.22**). This area has been known to include a large prehistoric locality on the northeastern shore of the X Basin. This locality has been indicated on a map and described briefly by Caton-Thompson (Caton-Thompson and Gardner 1934: 74 and pl.CX), and has later been investigated and named Site E29H1 by the Combined Prehistoric Expedition (Wendorf and Schild 1976: 182-199). On the other hand, little has been known about other parts of the area. Therefore, the entire stretch of the Basin shores was surveyed.

At present, this area is extensively disturbed by modern dry canals and ditches running east-west and north-south. Along the canals and ditches, there are many electric poles and small brick houses containing motor-powered water pumps, which are not yet in use. However, the plots divided by the canals and ditches are still intact, and natural depositional features and scatters of artefacts are clearly seen on the flat area around 20 m asl as well as on the gentle slope.

A linear band of rounded/subrounded pellets of calcium carbonate stretches northwest-southeast on the flat sandy surface along the 20 m asl contour line. As can be seen in the profiles of shallow ditches dug everywhere in this area, the accumulation of calcium carbonate pellets is not thick, and it seems to indicate a shoreline at certain times of high water of the X Basin. The surface of other parts of the flat area is covered by coarse-grained aeolian sand, and many patches of indurated light yellow silty sediments are seen. However, as can be seen in the profiles of shallow ditches dug everywhere, there are indurated light yellow to white silty

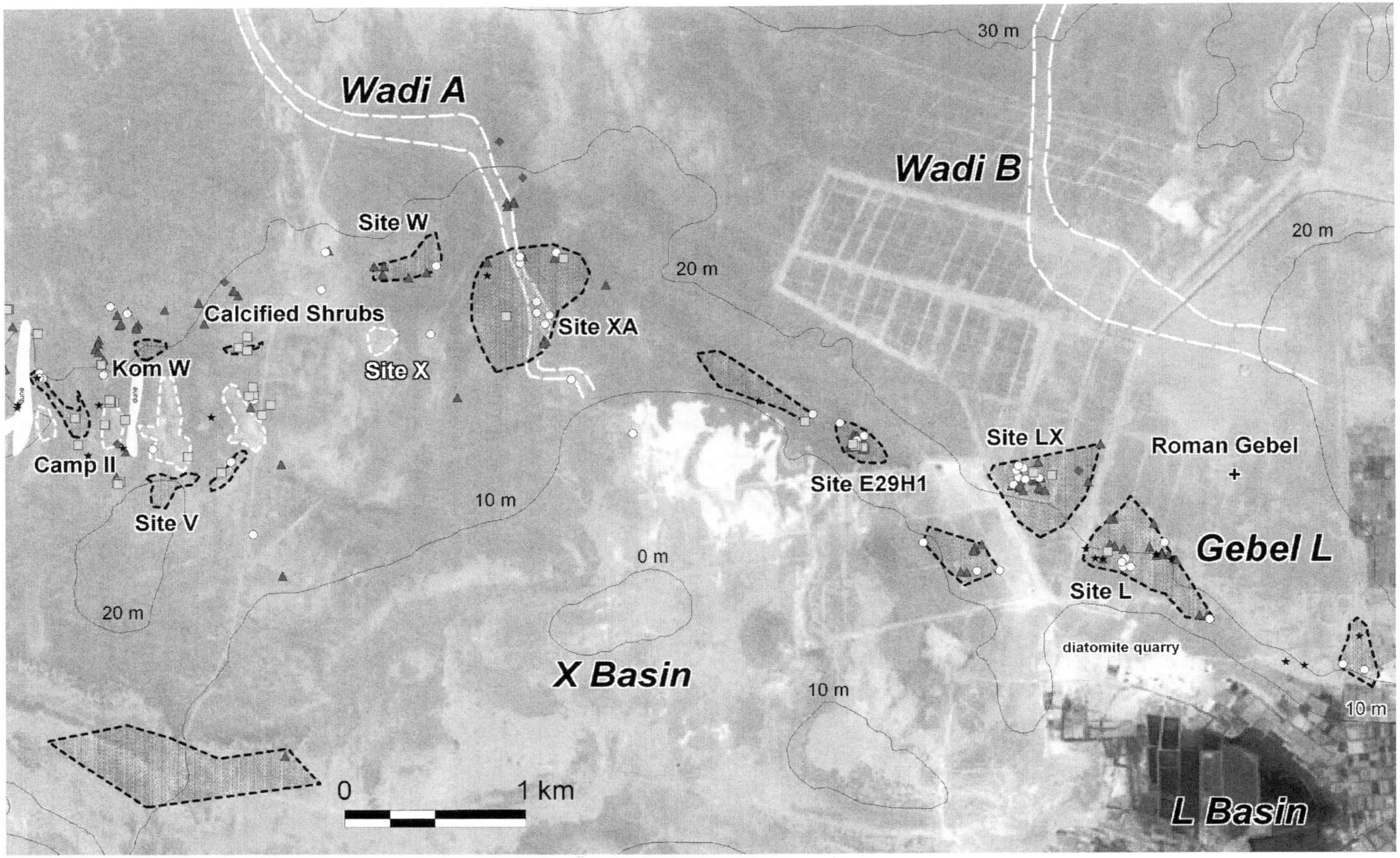

Fig.5.22. The L Basin - X Basin area (triangle: hearth, circle: grinding stone, square: animal bone, star: Neolithic projectile point, diamond: Neolithic sickle blade)

sediments beneath the surface, and beneath these silty sediments, there are thick dark grey sediments which must be rich in organic matter and are supposed to have been deposited under shallow water in a swampy environment (**Fig.5.23**). Usually, such organic matter undergoes biochemical decay or is destroyed by oxidation (Rapp and Hill 1998: 29). Good preservation of these dark grey sediments beneath the crust of silty sediments suggests a trend of rapidly rising basin water in a certain period. In other words, the swampy margins of a stagnant basin suddenly fell under deep water, thereby being buried by lacustrine silty sediments. This may also suggest that this high flat area has not repeatedly suffered from inundations and desiccations.

5.7.2.1. Site LX

At a high elevation of above 20 m asl a few hundred metres to the northwest of Site L, the deflated flat desert surface is thinly covered by fine-grained loose sand, calcified nodules of sand clast, porous calcrete duricrusts, calcium carbonate pellets, and calcified plant roots. A sparse growth of camel's thorn and lotus trees was also seen. Curious concentrations of burnt clay nodules (**Fig.5.24**), concentrations of lithic artefacts, curious scatters of ostrich eggshells as well as hearths (**Fig.5.25**) and grinding stones (**Fig.5.26**) were seen on the surface of the flat area. Lithic artefacts include a variety of typical Neolithic bifacially-retouched tools such as knives, scrapers, and sickle blades. Several lithic

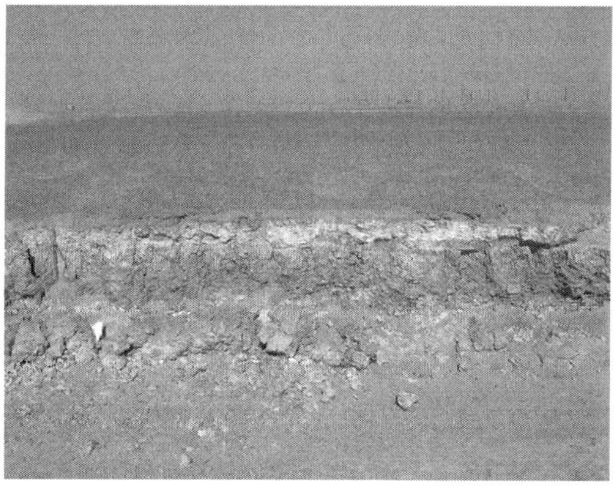

Fig.5.23. Section of a ditch dug in Site LX (looking north)

Fig.5.25. A hearth in Site LX (looking north)

Fig.5.24. A concentration of burnt clay nodules in Site LX (looking east)

Fig.5.26. Two grinding stones in Site LX (looking north)

concentrations include cores, debitage products, and hammer stones. Elongated petrified wood splinters are sometimes accompanied by lithic concentrations, and hence, the petrified wood splinters may be related to toolmaking, and may have been used as soft hammers or punches. The dense concentration of such occupational features in a circular area of approximately 200 m in diameter indicates that various activities took place there. The concentration of hearths and grinding stones in this area (**Fig.5.27**) deserves the designation of 'site'. This remarkable area has never been reported by any previous researchers, although Caton-Thompson's L Basin Bench Mark for her survey may probably be located somewhere in this area and she mentions that she collected some Neolithic artefacts around the Bench Mark (Caton-Thompson and Gardner 1934: 74). Therefore, this area (N29.58210° E30.84314° in the centre) was designated as Site LX.

Part of the largest concentration of burnt clay nodules and fragments, whose diameter was approximately 3 m, were excavated. It was revealed that the accumulation of the burnt clay nodules and fragments was very thin on an indurated mud surface with many desiccation cracks, and that few charcoal and ashes remained. Therefore, it is difficult to say with certainty that these are the remains of a bonfire for pottery firing, even though it is possible. Given that some of hearths in this area still

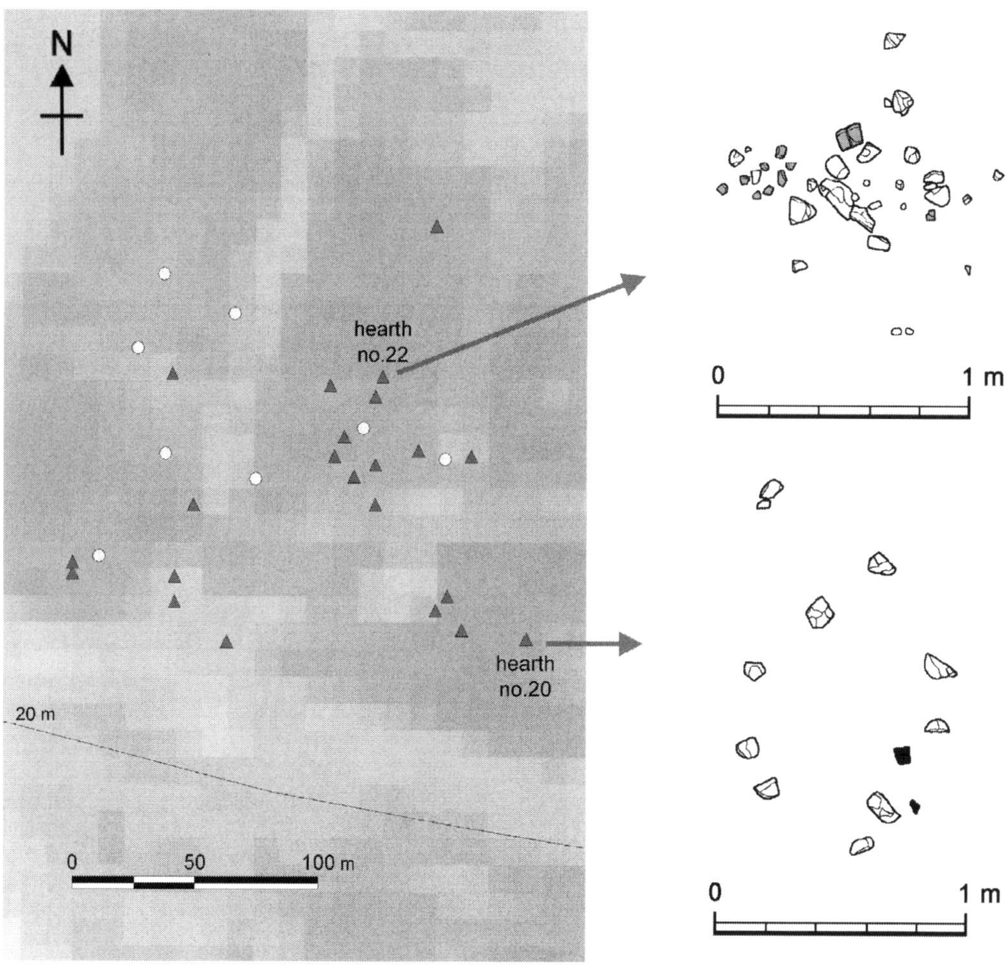

Fig.5.27. Site LX (triangle: hearth, circle: grinding stone) and two hearths (sandstone in grey and pottery sherds in black)

contained charcoal beneath hearth stones, differential effects of surface deflation and washing on varied material remains in this area must be considered.

5.7.2.2. Surroundings of Site LX

The condition of the surface is totally different at the same high elevation of above 20 m asl approximately 500 m to the northwest of Site LX. The surface is covered by coarse-grained aeolian sand with many inclusions of flint fragments and fossil shells, and a number of badly abraded flint flakes and Levallois cores were found among the fragments. They are apparently datable to the Middle Palaeolithic. Neolithic artefacts are not seen at all on this gravel surface. Stratigraphic profiles on the walls of a modern canal dug deeply in the middle of this area also show the transition from the accumulations of a series of aeolian and lacustrine sand in the southeast to bands of hard clay and shale in the northwest, indicating that this high elevation is built of deposits similar to those seen at the K Ridge. This high elevation looks high enough to escape from inundation during the Neolithic period, and thus it must have been an ideal place for the permanent habitation of Neolithic people. However, judging from the spatial distribution of Neolithic structural remains and artefacts in this area, it can be concluded that Neolithic people avoided gravel ground and preferred sandy ground for their habitation.

5.7.2.3. Site E29H1

Site E29H1 is even at present a quite visible wide distribution of numerous archaeological remains. There are many concentrations of sandstone/shell-bearing limestone cobbles, which are supposed to be hearths (**Fig.5.28**), as well as several distinct concentrations of lithic cores and debitage products and sporadic concentrations of large animal bones and their fragments. These numerous archaeological remains are spread on the gentle slope of light yellow silty sediments thinly covered by fine-grained aeolian sand,

Fig.5.28. Hearths in Site E29H1 (looking south)

mostly around 10-13 m asl. The spatial extent of this distribution is approximately 100 m by 300 m in an oval, extending from the northwest to the southeast, and both the northwestern and southeastern ends are marked by narrow colluvial fans. Judging from the location of two hillocks and a colluvial fan (described as a wadi) indicated on the sketch map made by the Combined Prehistoric Expedition (Wendorf and Schild 1976: fig.121), there is no doubt that Site E29H1 corresponds to this area (N29.58393° E30.83304° in the centre), although the elevation of the area in question is almost the same as indicated on Caton-Thompson's map but is approximately 5 m lower than that indicated on the Combined Prehistoric Expedition's map. The traces of a series of 18 trenches dug by the Combined Prehistoric Expedition in the centre of Site E29H1 are not presently seen on the surface.

Concentrations of archaeological remains are particularly dense in the eastern part of Site E29H1, but strangely, many of these remains have not at all been mentioned by Wendorf and Schild. As they reported, the majority of lithic artefacts presently scattered in Site E29H1 seem to be Epipalaeolithic and look fresh, whereas more heavily abraded Neolithic lithic artefacts are sparsely scattered in the periphery (Wendorf and Schild 1976: 182*ff*). No Neolithic pottery sherds are seen on the surface. Considering the extraordinary surface features of the eastern part of Site E29H1, surface collecting of artefacts and faunal remains and surface recording of hearths were carried out in the 2004 and 2005 seasons. Unfortunately, this work has drawn the attention of local people, and a part of the site was severely destroyed by someone's random digging after the 2005 season. The study of artefacts collected here will be described in Chapter 6.

5.7.2.4. Surroundings of Site E29H1

Another relatively sparse scatter of Epipalaeolithic and Neolithic artefacts with occupational features such as hearths and grinding stones was found approximately 500 m to the southeast of Site E29H1 and at the same elevation. Heavily abraded lithic artefacts and seemingly fresh lithic artefacts are mixed up in coarse-grained sand with many flint fragments. The lithic artefacts include both Epipalaeolithic and Neolithic, but it is hard to discern the boundaries between Epipalaeolithic and Neolithic artefact scatters. This locality seems to have suffered from complex alluvial and colluvial events, and is divided from Site E29H1 by a narrow colluvial fan, which stretches from the higher elevation where Site LX is located. This colluvium is apparently a consequence of the erosion of gravels at the higher elevation mentioned above. A further relatively sparse scatter of Epipalaeolithic and Neolithic artefacts without occupational features was found approximately 200 m to the northwest of Site E29H1 across a narrow colluvial fan and at the same elevation. This area is covered by thicker accumulations of fine-grained aeolian sand, and hence surface archaeological remains are obscured.

On the whole, the northern-northeastern margin of the X Basin on the contour line of around 10-15 m asl is occupied by these three large archaeological localities/sites, separated by colluvial fans or wadis. The total width of the three localities/sites is approximately 2 km. It may be said that the entire stretch of the shore has been densely inhabited or repeatedly visited by both Epipalaeolithic and Neolithic people.

5.7.2.5. Intersection of the X Basin and Wadi A

The landscape rises from the 15 m contour line of the northern margin of the X Basin towards the north, and is dominated by a series of gentle desert ridges, which extend from a rocky summit called Gebel Abyad or El-Qarah el-Kharshah approximately 3 km to the north of the X Basin shore. Wadi A and its meandering branches run between the ridges. The surface of the ridges is covered by coarse-grained aeolian sand with many flint pebbles and fragments. Archaeological remains are rare to absent. One apparently Neolithic flint axe and one large worked flint flake of unknown date were found on a gentle slope overlooking the wadi, but no other archaeological remains were found. On another desert ridge closer to the X Basin, many shallow depressions whose diameter is around 50 cm were found. This cluster of small depressions does not look like granary pits of the Neolithic period, but rather seems to be created by rain water or wild animals.

A remarkable modern disturbance in this area is an asphalt road made by the military many years ago. It comes from the Sixth October City in Giza, and ends in this area. This road is still in use not only by the military in order to come here for exercises but also by tourists coming from Cairo and going to Qasr el-Sagha to the west.

In the desert around the intersection of Wadi A and the asphalt road, there are sparse scatters of Neolithic lithic artefacts and pottery sherds without any structural remains. To the east of the asphalt road, there are many clusters of sandstone/shell-bearing limestone cobbles accompanied by lithic artefacts and Neolithic pottery sherds. In some cases, charcoal still remains beneath the surface sand cover of the cobble clusters, suggesting that these were hearths and were not severely deflated.

5.7.2.6. Site XA

A few hundred metres to the south of this hearth field, there are other scatters of artefacts. The elevation is approximately 15 m asl, and the surface is covered by fine-grained aeolian sand, but nevertheless, a number of Neolithic pottery sherds, lithic artefacts and structural remains are quite visible (**Fig.5.29**). Epipalaeolithic flint tools are also seen, but they are apparently quite few. Many shells of large lacustrine bivalves (*Mutela nilotica*), some of which had traces of use on the edge as a side-scraper or knife, were noticed in this area. Many grain rubbers and grinding stones made of sandstone were also found. Circular clusters of sandstone/shell-bearing limestone cobbles, which are presumably hearths, are also seen in this area. In addition to them, strange arrangements of sandstone and shell-bearing limestone cobbles were seen. One is S-shaped or keyhole-shaped, and another is square. Since one grooved limestone block which looks like a tethering stone (Gabriel 2002; Pachur 1991) was found nearby (**Fig.5.30**), these stone structures may be a sort of pen for domesticated animals. All of these are spread along the eastern terrace of Wadi A which runs to the southeast into the X Basin.

There are other wide scatters of Neolithic lithic artefacts and pottery sherds on the western terrace of Wadi A. The surface is very thinly covered by aeolian loose sand, and the crust of silty sediments, which is broken into polygons, is exposed. There are scatters of transparent gypsum crystals and so-called desert roses (aggregates of gypsum crystals with sand grains) on and around this crust surface. At one particular locality marked by several hillocks of less than two metres high, a dense concentration of unworked non-local flint cobbles, large lithic cores and blanks was noticed (**Fig.5.31**). They were accompanied by several elongated petrified wood splinters and some large basalt and sandstone blocks which may be anvil stones. The surface features suggest that this locality has been inundated, but this unusual concentration of non-local flint cobbles and lithic artefacts does not seem to be caused by torrential runoff water. It is more likely that this particular locality was a kind of flint knapping workshop, and that the cobbles were transported from elsewhere. The study of artefacts collected here will be described in Chapter 7.

Fig.5.29. Site XA (looking southeast)

Fig.5.30. A tethering stone found in Site XA

Fig.5.31. Site XA (looking northwest)

All of these features spreading on both sides of Wadi A, which have never been reported by previous researchers, seem to represent a habitation locus at an elevation of 15 m asl at some time during the Neolithic period. The diversity and moderate spatial scale of the features within an area of a few hundred metres in width and length deserve to be called a 'site'. Therefore, this area (N29.58978° E30.81465° in the centre) was named Site XA after the abuttal of the X Basin and Wadi A.

5.7.2.7. Other features

The locality approximately 500 m to the south of Site XA is a mound whose northeastern side is eroded by meandering Wadi A running into the X Basin. The surface of this mound is covered by abraded flint gravels containing a number of Levallois cores and points as well as some Epipalaeolithic flint tools. The floor of Wadi A which abuts this mound at this elevation (around 10 m asl) exhibits a wide scatter of Epipalaeolithic and Neolithic artefacts without any structural remains on the sandy surface. Considering its location and elevation, it seems probable that such a mixed artefact scatter was a consequence of the disturbance of an Epipalaeolithic occupation locus by runoff water coming from upstream of Wadi A and by rising water from the X Basin. In the periphery of the wadi floor, many patches of dark grey silty sediments are exposed beneath the surface coarse-grained sand, and one heavily-eroded human skeleton of an unknown date was found embedded in the dark grey sediments.

The bottom of the X Basin (below 10 m asl) is filled with diatomaceous earth, and desiccation cracks are everywhere. There are several trial pits dug by someone, probably for checking the quality and thickness of diatomite. Stratigraphic profiles on the walls of the trial pits show continuous accumulations of diatomite without breaks. This suggests that the bottom of the X Basin has also perennially been full of water. Since the trial pits are not deep, the stratigraphic history of the X Basin must be examined in more detail by deeper boring. Scatters of flint cobbles, cores and debitage products of unknown date are sporadically seen on the surface of the diatomaceous earth, but it is unlikely that they are in primary context.

5.7.2.8. Summary of the L Basin-X Basin area

Modern disturbances in the L Basin-X Basin area have not severely affected the preservation of archaeological remains on the surface. The archaeological remains in this area have not sufficiently been recorded by Caton-Thompson and other researchers, or have never been investigated and published. Therefore, this area is presumed to be less disturbed by scholarly activities, and it is worthwhile to study these features in more detail for a better understanding of land use patterns in prehistory.

5.7.3. The X Basin-Z Basin area

The X Basin-Z Basin area is defined as the area centring on the X Basin and Z Basin (**Fig.5.32**). This area includes a number of Epipalaeolithic and Neolithic localities/sites such as Site X, Kom W, Site V, Camp II and Site Z, which have been thoroughly reported by Caton-Thompson, and has been considered as the most densely occupied area in the prehistory of the Fayum (Caton-Thompson and Gardner 1934: 22-36 and 74-79). However, little has been reported about other parts of the area. Therefore, the entire area was surveyed. Although this area is partially disturbed by modern dirt tracks as well as the asphalt road mentioned earlier, it seems that these disturbances do not severely affect the preservation of archaeological remains.

5.7.3.1. Site X and Site W

Approximately 500 m to the west of Site XA, there is a wide and dense scatter of Neolithic lithic artefacts and pottery sherds. This artefact scatter is located on and around a shallow, circular depression of approximately 150 m in diameter and at an elevation of 15 m asl, which is surrounded on the northwest and the west by a sand dune which has a slip face on the east side and hence looks like a cove (**Fig.5.33**). The surface of this locality exhibits the deflated crust of silty sediments which is broken into polygons,

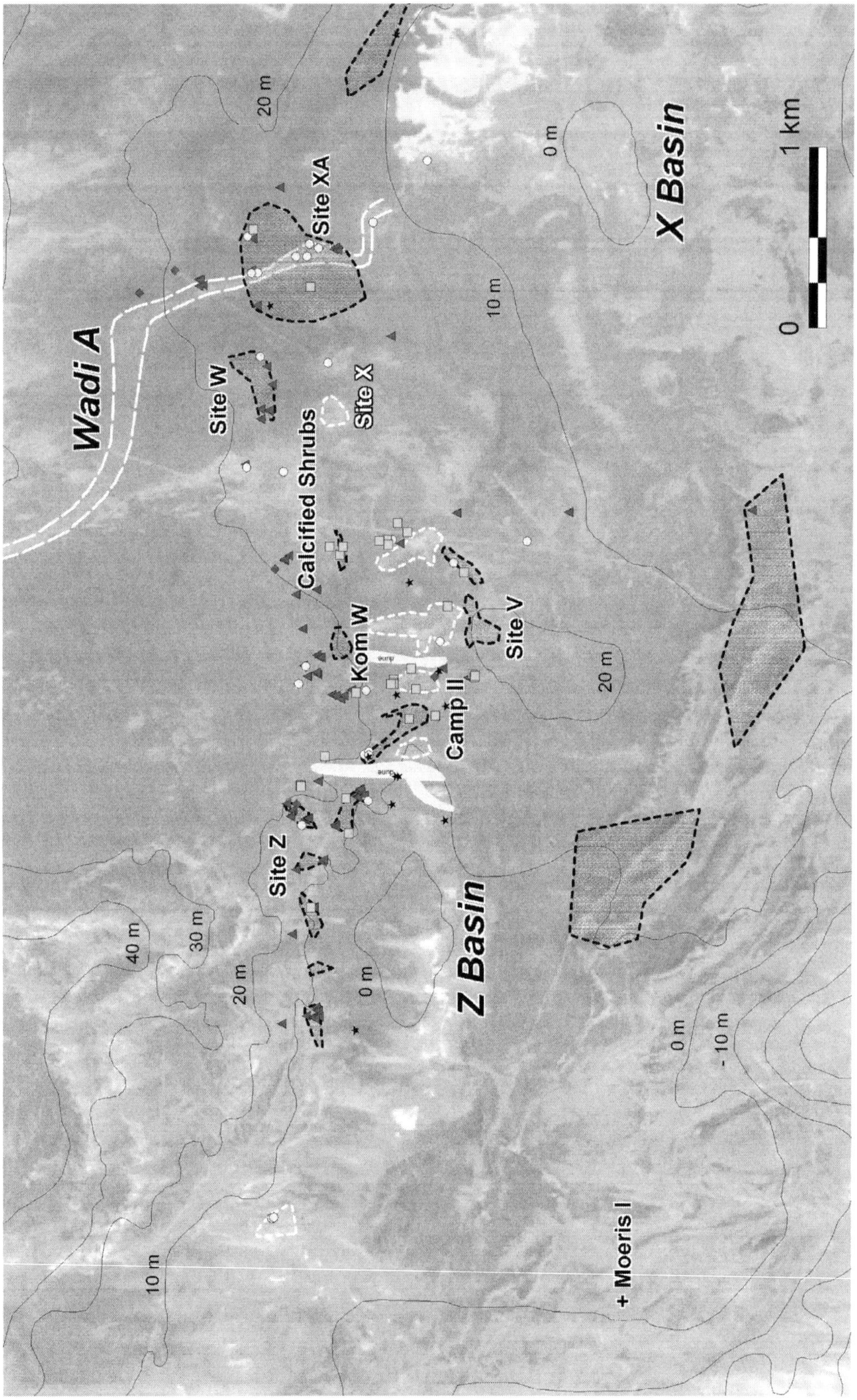

Fig.5.32. The X Basin - Z Basin area (triangle: hearth, circle: grinding stone, square: animal bone, star: Neolithic projectile point, diamond: Neolithic sickle blade)

and there are scatters of transparent gypsum crystals and desert roses on and around this crust surface. Several large lacustrine bivalves (*Aspatharia rubens*) which were embedded in the silty sediments were also noticed. These suggest the presence of water for a considerable length of time in the past. This cove-like locality (N29.58924° E30.80651° in the centre) is certainly identical to Caton-Thompson's Site X (Caton-Thompson and Gardner 1934: 74-75).

As Caton-Thompson has reported, there are no structural remains like hearths and no artefacts of the Epipalaeolithic, Predynastic and Old Kingdom in this locality. On the other hand, the scatter of Neolithic pottery sherds and non-local large flint cobbles, lithic cores and blanks is enormously wide and dense, and in particular, numerous large flint cobbles and lithic cores are quite noticeable. Although Caton-Thompson collected hundreds of formal Neolithic flint tools at Site X, she did not mention the presence of these cobbles and cores. Therefore, these neglected cobbles and cores can be a good clue to know more about Neolithic tool making. The study of cobbles and cores collected here will be described in Chapter 7.

Another notable wide scatter of artefacts was located on the higher flat area approximately 300 m to the north of Site X beyond the dune. Although the artefact scatter is not as dense as that of Site X, it is quite widespread, and some concentrations of Neolithic pottery sherds and lithic artefacts were noted. There are also some stone-built hearths and the rock scatters which may have been hearths. The diversity and moderate spatial scale of the features within an area of a few hundred metres in width deserve to be called a 'site'. Therefore, this area (N29.59331° E30.80759° in the centre) was named Site W.

5.7.3.2. Other features

The middle of the X Basin-Z Basin area is marked by a high dune which extends from the northeast to the southwest and has a slip face on the east side. No artefact scatter is seen on the dune, but there are a number of surface artefact scatters on the lower flat area at the foot of this high dune.

In the area to the southwest of the X Basin and to the south of the high dune, which is around 5-10 m asl, the environment is generally flat with some surface undulation, and gently falls southwards. Deflated concentrations of cobbles which may be hearths or workshops were observed sporadically, and scatters of Neolithic lithic artefacts were sparsely seen, but Neolithic pottery sherds were rare to absent. Further to the southwest of the X Basin, the ground surface is covered by coarse-grained aeolian sand with many inclusions of flint fragments and fossil shells, and a number of badly abraded flint flakes and Levallois cores and points and some Epipalaeolithic tools were noticeable. Neolithic artefacts are not seen on this gravel surface.

5.7.3.3. Kom W and its vicinities

Kom W (N29.58894° E30.79248° in the centre) is presently an isolated, huge excavation dump surrounded by flat desert (**Fig.5.34**), and its top elevation is approximately 22 m asl. The surface of Kom W is thinly covered by fine-grained aeolian sand, but the traces of Caton-Thompson's excavation trenches (Strips A-T; Caton-Thompson and Gardner 1934: pls.III, IV and V) are still clearly visible (**Fig.5.35**), and a great number of lithic artefacts and pottery sherds discarded by Caton-Thompson remain scattered on the surface (**Fig.5.36**). The thick accumulation of fine-grained sand on the south side of the Kom obscures the scatter of artefacts on this side. Although a small number of lithic artefacts in the neighbourhood of Strip E have been collected and studied by Kozlowski and Ginter in the 1980s (Kozlowski and Ginter 1989), lithic scatters are still enormous. One small trench dug just outside of the south end of Strip Q and another small trench dug at the southwest corner of Strip T by the Combined Prehistoric Expedition in 1969 (Wendorf and Schild 1976: 211*ff*) are not visible on the surface at all.

The area to the north of Kom W is virtually

Fig.5.33. Site X (looking northwest)

Fig.5.34. Kom W from a distance (looking southwest)

Fig.5.35. Traces of Caton-Thompson's excavation trenches on Kom W (looking north)

Fig.5.36. Scatter of lithic artefacts and pottery sherds on Kom W

Fig.5.37. A sickle blade found to the northeast of Kom W (looking southwest)

Fig.5.38. A flaked axe found to the northeast of Kom W (looking southwest)

flat desert covered by coarse-grained aeolian sand and transparent gypsum crystals, but many patches of light yellow silty sediments beneath the sand and dried plants are seen. These suggest that this area has been inundated in the past. A number of isolated hearths consisting of burnt pale limestone fragments are seen in this area, but they are accompanied by very few artefacts, and thus it is hard to date them. One hearth is accompanied by probably Old Kingdom pottery sherds, and the rest of the hearths may also perhaps be dated to the Old Kingdom. An apparently Neolithic bifacially-retouched knife was collected close to a trace of surface runoff water which is approximately 400 m to the north of Kom W, and this is the northernmost findspot of Neolithic artefacts in this area. To the north farther than this findspot, it is definitely barren desert covered by flint gravels, and no more archaeological features were found. Approximately 900 m to the north of Kom W, there are several isolated conical buttes and terrace-like low ridges covered by flint pebbles and transparent gypsum crystals. It may be concluded that this area was out of the range of major human activities when Kom W and other nearby localities were occupied in prehistoric and historic times, though flint pebbles on the ridges may possibly have been exploited by people for tool making. Remarkably, there are remains of modern military camps on and around the ridges. There are several large circles made by sand bags, and the ground is dug up and levelled, while rusty metal fragments are scattered widely. They cause severe disturbance of the environment.

At a distance of approximately 100-200 m to the west of Kom W, there are two remarkable concentrations of Neolithic pottery sherds and lithic artefacts. They are scattered on and around the patches of light yellow silty sediments, and some are embedded in the sediments. Apart from them, other archaeological remains to the west of Kom W are isolated hearths consisting of pale limestone fragments. These hearths are accompanied by very few artefacts, and hence it is difficult to date them. However, lithic artefacts among sparse scatters in this area include several Neolithic bifacially-retouched knives, and the hearths may be dated to the Neolithic. Alternatively, their close proximity to other supposedly Old Kingdom hearths mentioned above may suggest that all of these hearths were made in the Neolithic habitation during the Old Kingdom period.

A large area approximately 200-300 m to the northwest of Kom W is covered by pale limestone fragments and fossil shells, and few artefacts are seen on this shelly surface. It seems that the stones of the hearths mentioned above were obtained from this area. Further to the west and northwest of this shelly area, the ground is completely covered by a well-developed dune which runs north-south and forms the eastern edge of the Z Basin. There are no artefacts and no archaeological features on this vast dune.

The area to the northeast of Kom W is very gently rising, and is characterised by some meandering traces of surface runoff water which come from the north to the south, though the southern end is not clear. Several hearths consisting of pale limestone cobbles were seen, but some of them are accompanied by Old Kingdom flint tools as well as Neolithic flint tools. Therefore, it is presumed that Neolithic hearths were reoccupied by Old Kingdom people or hearth stones were reused by Old Kingdom people.

Regardless of whether the date of artefacts is the Neolithic or the Old Kingdom, the scatter of artefacts is quite sparse in this area, but these few artefacts were often found close to the traces of surface runoff at the elevation of 20 m asl. The artefacts include a bifacially-retouched sickle blade (**Fig.5.37**), bifacially-retouched knife blades, a flaked axe (**Fig.5.38**), a bifacially-retouched hoe of the Neolithic period, and a serrated blade of the Old Kingdom. There are no arrowheads and no animal bone scatters in this area. To the north of this elevation towards the highest point in this area which is approximately 600-700 m away from Kom W, the surface is covered by flint gravels, and no more artefacts and structural remains are seen. Judging from this situation, possible subsistence activities in this area both in the Neolithic and

Old Kingdom periods were not hunting, but are something else dependent on surface runoff water which must have become available through winter rainfall. A few flint tools suggest harvesting activities relying on seasonally available water. Contrary to the assumption that farming was practised close to the shores of permanent water bodies like large basins and small depressions, it seems probable that farming was practised in other locations where surface runoff water was collected by natural drainage and remained in ephemeral ponds. Considering that farming of wheat and barley was basically rain-fed farming in their original habitat in the Levant and that there must have been more winter rainfall in the Fayum in the Early-Middle Holocene than that at present, it is probable that the area which collected surface runoff water in the northeast of Kom W was used as a farming plot. Alternatively, it is necessary to consider the possibility that the flint sickle blades mentioned above were not used for harvesting domesticated wheat and barley but for harvesting other wild plants which thrived with surface water.

In the east of Kom W, there are wide scatters of Neolithic pottery sherds and lithic debitage products. These artefact scatters expand northeastwards, and it seems that they derived from Kom W. It is possible that these artefacts were transported and spread out by rising lake water coming from the south in the past. Another large scatter of artefacts was located 100 m to the northeast of the artefact scatter mentioned above. In contrast to the low mound of Kom W, this area is generally flat, and covered by coarse-grained sand and flint pebbles/fragments. Some surface undulations caused by sand ripples are seen. The artefact scatter consists of a large number of small Neolithic coarse pottery sherds as well as unworked flint cobbles and lithic artefacts. Such a wide scatter of pottery sherds has not been seen in the surroundings, and hence it makes this area quite remarkable.

Approximately 300 m to the east of Kom W, there is a wide scatter of calcified plant roots (**Fig.5.39**). In contrast to its surroundings characterised by fine-grained loose sand sheet and well-developed sand ripples, this dense scatter of calcified plant roots is quite remarkable, and it is approximately 200 m wide. To the north of this calcified plant field, several isolated concentrations of large animal bones and their fragments, including those of hippopotamus, were noticed.

At many places in this calcified plant field, the bottom parts of the trunk still remain standing (**Fig.5.40**). A large number of unworked and worked flint cobbles and flakes deriving from them are scattered only on and around this calcified plant field. Many worked globular flint cobbles are undoubtedly single platform cores. As for other worked flat, oval cobbles, one end of the cobbles is struck once from one face, and by using the flake scar as a platform, a few flakes are struck off from the other face. Therefore, they look like choppers, which have been seen frequently at other Neolithic localities including Kom W during this survey. Except for one presumably Neolithic bifacially-retouched knife, no formal tool was encountered in this calcified plant field. Although there is no concrete clue to determine how old these calcified plant roots are and what species they are, the scatters of choppers on and around this field may suggest that these plants are not sedges but shrubs, and that these tools were used for cutting the plants in the Neolithic period, probably by the inhabitants of Kom W. Therefore, this remarkable locality (N29.58880° E30.79805° in the centre) was designated as Locality 'Calcified Shrubs'. The study of flint cobbles and lithic cores collected here will be described in more detail in Chapter 7.

The area in the southeast of Kom W is almost barren, and the surface is covered by fine-grained aeolian sand. Farther to the southeast of Kom W, the ground gradually becomes gravelly, and from around 500 m to the southeast of Kom W, the ground is slightly depressed and covered by calcareous white silty sediments. A number of lacustrine gastropods (*Bithynia* sp. and/or *Cleopatra* sp.) of approximately 2 cm tall are scattered on the surface of this depression, and many lacustrine bivalves (*Aspatharia rubens*) of more than 10 cm wide remain embedded vertically in the sediments. These suggest the

Fig.5.39. A concentration of calcified plant roots (looking west)

Fig.5.41. A concentration of animal bones (looking west)

Fig.5.40. Calcified plant field (looking southwest)

presence of water for a considerable length of time in certain periods. On this shallow depression, which is named the CS Depression after Locality 'Calcified Shrubs', artefacts are only sparsely scattered, and they include Old Kingdom flint tools like a bifacially-retouched knife with handle and Old Kingdom pottery sherds as well as some supposedly Neolithic flint tools. Neolithic pottery sherds are rare to absent. Several large animal bone concentrations were seen in the northeastern margin of the CS Depression (**Fig.5.41**), and they may be dated to the Old Kingdom, because some of them were accompanied by Old Kingdom artefacts. Major modern disturbances around this depression are some large craters made by bombing exercises of the military and a dirt track running north-south.

The southern end of this depression, which is approximately 700 m away from Kom W, is marked not only by an extensive linear exposure of pale limestone bedrock but also by a high ridge which stretches southwest. Wind-eroded outcrops of indurated white calcareous clay sediments are seen elsewhere in the northern margin of this high ridge. The surface of the ridge is covered by porous calcrete duricrusts and fine-grained loose sand. Artefact scatters on this ridge are quite dense, and concentrations of Neolithic pottery sherds are seen everywhere.

Neolithic flint tools found there include concave-based arrowheads, all of which are broken, and tiny arrowheads of the types which have been abundantly found at Camp II by Caton-Thompson. Many broken blades/bladelets were collected among these lithic scatters, but except for one piece, none of them have backing retouch, and hence it is not certain whether they are dated to the Epipalaeolithic. It has been reported that blades/bladelets without backing retouch were common in the Old Kingdom in the Fayum (Caton-Thompson and Gardner 1934: pls.LIV and LXXXI), and indeed, one Old Kingdom handled knife was found there. However, none of those blades/bladelets have basal notches which are the characteristics of the Old Kingdom blades/bladelets. Therefore, even though it is certain that Old Kingdom people visited this high ridge, it is not certain whether those blades/bladelets belong to them. There are a number of unworked and worked flint cobbles, and cubic core fragments deriving from flint cobbles apparently for bladelet production. Therefore, it can be said that the people of the Epipalaeolithic, Neolithic and possibly Old Kingdom have brought flint cobbles to this ridge and made tools there. The absence of animal bone concentrations and hearths on this ridge may suggest that the people visited and stayed there shortly for some tasks.

5.7.3.4. Site V and the Site V Depression

To the south of Kom W, there is a dune which stretches southwards. On the east of this dune, there is a large, oval, shallow depression of approximately 500 m north-south and 300 m east-west, and the northern shore of the depression is approximately 150 m to the south of Kom W. The surface of this depression is covered by white calcareous silty sediments and scatters of transparent gypsum crystals and desert roses (**Fig.5.42**), and beneath the surface, there is a thin layer of dark grey fine-grained sand. A number of lacustrine gastropods (*Bithynia* sp. and/or *Cleopatra* sp.) of approximately 2 cm tall are scattered on this surface, and also many bivalves (*Aspatharia rubens*) of more than 10 cm wide remain intact and embedded vertically in this silty sediments (**Fig.5.43**). These suggest that this depression has been filled with water permanently or has been inundated repeatedly at certain periods of time.

Scatters of lithic artefacts and pottery sherds are seen on and around this depression, but particularly dense scatters of artefacts are seen on slightly higher mounds to its west. The surface of these higher mounds is also covered by silty sediments and tiny fragments of indurated calcium carbonate, but no lacustrine gastropods and bivalves are seen on the mounds. This may mean that inundations of the mounds were not long enough for lacustrine gastropods and bivalves to inhabit there and to grow up. As for the dense scatters of artefacts on the mounds, the pottery sherds are undoubtedly dated to the Neolithic, and most lithic artefacts seem to be dated to the Neolithic, but several lithic artefacts can be dated to the Predynastic and Old Kingdom periods. Epipalaeolithic tools are rare to absent. This artefact scatter pattern suggests that there has been permanent water in this depression at some times during the Neolithic-Old Kingdom periods, and people had visited the shores of this pond. Many concentrations of bones of catfish and large mammals including hartebeest are also seen on and around the depression, and hence it is highly likely that people came here for hunting and shallow water fishing. There are clusters of pale limestone cobbles and fragments on and around the depression, but it is not certain whether they are deflated stone-built hearths.

Caton-Thompson has speculated that this depression with marginal loams has been used as an agricultural field by the inhabitants of Kom W (Caton-Thompson and Gardner 1934: 75). As she has noted, several grinding stones made of sandstone and basalt were found in this locality. However, grinding stones are not necessarily related to domesticated wheat/barley grains, and no other material evidence for agricultural activities was found around this depression by this survey.

The southern end of this depression, which is approximately 700 m away from Kom W, is marked by a number of eroded mudstone yardangs. These yardangs are located on a ridge, which is actually the western extension of the ridge mentioned earlier and stretches further westwards. This ridge is much higher than the depression to the north. This entire ridge (N29.58182° E30.79320° in the centre) seems to be identical to Caton-Thompson's Site V (Caton-Thompson and Gardner 1934: 75-76), and therefore, the depression to the north is provisionally designated as the Site V Depression. The surface of the Site V Ridge is densely covered by porous calcrete duricrusts, calcified nodules of sand clast and calcified plant roots (**Fig.5.44**), and particularly in the eastern half, scatters of Neolithic pottery sherds and lithic artefacts were seen. While there are several concentrations of pottery sherds (**Fig.5.45**), scatters of lithic artefacts are rather sparse. Scatters of animal/fish bones and their fragments are not as numerous as those on and around the depression to the north. According to Caton-Thompson, Site V has been plundered by local and other casual flint collectors for years, and she also collected a large number of formal Neolithic flint tools at Site V (Caton-Thompson and Gardner 1934: 75). Therefore, the present scarcity of Neolithic flint tools is apparently the result of surface collecting by previous visitors.

To the south of the Site V Ridge, the ground gently falls southwards, and the surface is covered by moderately sorted small flint pebbles and fragments, and there are several large hillocks. Caton-Thompson recognised this gentle slope area as a southern extension of Site V, and noted that the area was dominated by Epipalaeolithic lithic artefact scatters (Caton-Thompson and Gardner 1934: 75). However, Epipalaeolithic artefacts are presently quite rare to absent in this area. Instead, Neolithic pottery sherds and lithic artefacts are sparsely scattered on the surface. In this area, there must be another Epipalaeolithic locality named Site 2, where faunal remains have been intensively collected (Brewer 1989a; 1989b), but it could not be located. Therefore, the present rarity of Epipalaeolithic artefacts in this area may be a consequence of previous research endeavours.

5.7.3.5. Camp II, the Camp II Depression, and the Camp II Basin

Approximately 500 m to the southwest of Kom W, there is a low ridge. This is probably a part

Fig.5.42. The Site V Depression (looking west)

Fig.5.43. A bivalve embedded in silty sediments of the Site V Depression (looking north)

Fig.5.44. Surface of the Site V Ridge (looking east)

Fig.5.45. A concentration of pottery sherds on the Site V Ridge (looking west)

of Caton-Thompson's Camp II (Caton-Thompson and Gardner 1934: 75*ff*). The ridge stretches northwest-southeast, and the width of the ridge is approximately 100 m at most. This peninsular low ridge is marked by several yardangs of laminated siltstone, and the surface of the entire ridge is undulating and covered by porous calcrete duricrusts, calcified plant roots, and rounded/subrounded pellets of calcium carbonate. Hence, it forms a remarkably wide white strip, and shows a striking contrast to the flat desert area to the east (**Fig.5.46**). Some outcrops of laminated siltstone along the western edge of the ridge are heavily eroded from the west. Therefore, it can be concluded that this ridge was actually the eastern beach of the Z Basin, and that the beach has been eroded by high energy waves caused by the wind coming from the west, which is presumed to have blown in the Early-Middle Holocene (Brookes 2003).

Lithic artefact scatters are seen all over this peninsular low ridge, which is named the Camp II Ridge, but probably because of both intensive surface collecting by Caton-Thompson and severe erosion, there are few noticeable concentrations of artefacts. There are no Neolithic pottery sherds, and Neolithic lithic artefacts are not numerous in the northern half of the ridge. Some exceptionally high density concentrations of lithic artefacts were found in the eastern margin of the ridge, and they include a number of typical Epipalaeolithic cores and bladelets. The study of the artefacts collected here will be described in Chapter 6.

The Camp II Ridge, which is characterised by the above-mentioned white beach sediments, stretches further south toward the presumed southeast corner of the Z Basin, but artefacts and other features on the ridge are not evenly distributed. Neolithic pottery sherds and unworked/worked flint cobbles are seen only in the southernmost part of the ridge, and there are no Epipalaeolithic artefacts. Some supposedly hearths found in the southernmost part of the ridge consist of pale limestone fragments and are accompanied by Old Kingdom flint tools and pottery sherds.

According to Caton-Thompson, the area between Camp II and Kom W and between Camp II and Site V has been most intensively surface-collected by her (Caton-Thompson and Gardner 1934: 76), and probably for this reason, lithic artefacts scatters are sparse. A surface observation of this area revealed that there were wide patches of white calcareous silty sediments in which intact large lacustrine bivalves (*Aspatharia rubens*) remained embedded and on which transparent gypsum crystals were scattered (**Fig.5.47**). In the northern and northeasternmost margin of these silty sediment patches, there are many concentrations of animal bones, which belong to hippopotamus (**Fig.5.48**), soft-shelled turtle (**Fig.5.49**) and crocodile (**Fig.5.50**). Such concentrations of animal bones have not been described by Caton-Thompson. The western and southwesternmost margins of these silty sediment patches is marked by high density scatters of tiny carbonised fish bone fragments, most of which seem to belong to catfish. These fish bone scatters touch the eastern margin of the Camp II Ridge, and spread onto the middle of the ridge. Therefore, it seems certain that there was a water-containing depression which is similar to the Site V Depression to the east. This area, provisionally designated as the Camp II Depression, is presently separated from the Site V Depression by a dune which stretches from the south of Kom W southwards, but it is probable that the Site V Depression has been connected to the Camp II Depression and formed one large pond.

To the west of the Camp II Ridge, the ground falls steeply westwards, and leads to the bottom of a basin (**Fig.5.51**). The west and northwest sides of the basin are surrounded by a huge dune, and the basin is open to the south only. This deep and triangular depression (N29.58504° E30.78658° in the centre) seems to be the Camp II Basin, judging from Caton-Thompson's location map and description of topography (Caton-Thompson and Gardner 1934: 75*ff*). However, no trace of her camp was found, except for an unnatural concentration of unifacially/bifacially-retouched flint tools accompanied by several rocks, which may have been left by her. The basin floor is covered by fine-grained

Fig.5.46. The Camp II Ridge (looking northwest)

Fig.5.47. Silty sediments in the Camp II Depression (looking north)

Fig.5.48. A concentration of hippopotamus bones (looking northwest)

Fig.5.49. A concentration of soft-shelled turtle bones (looking northeast)

Fig.5.50. A concentration of crocodile bones (looking west)

Fig.5.51. The Camp II Ridge and Camp II Basin (looking south)

aeolian sand. Artefact scatters on the basin floor are not quite visible, but this may be because artefacts were already intensively collected by Caton-Thompson. There are many dried plants on the basin floor, and several patches of white calcareous silty sediments are seen particularly in the south. As she described, many lithic artefacts seem to be washed down on the steep slope from the Camp II Ridge to the basin floor, and as a result, artefact scatters are the densest around the margin of the basin at the foot of this slope. Several tiny arrowheads of the types which she found at Camp II abundantly and whose dates are uncertain (Caton-Thompson and Gardner 1934: pl.LI) were collected on top of the easternmost edge of the peninsular ridge as well as at the foot of the basin slope.

On the slope between the Camp II Ridge and the Camp II Basin, curious concentrations of large lacustrine gastropods called apple snails (*Pila ovata*) of approximately 5 cm long and 4 cm wide were found to the west of Epipalaeolithic artefact concentrations on the Camp II Ridge (**Fig.5.52**). Each concentration includes at least 30 pieces of snails of various sizes, and some concentrations are partly embedded in mottled dark grey silty sediments, which are indicative of the accumulation of organic matter and hence a swampy environment (Rapp and Hill 1998: 37-38). No diagnostic artefact was found within this locality, and hence it is difficult to date these features, but it seems likely that those snails were intensively collected on the beach, and eaten, and then discarded there collectively by Epipalaeolithic or Neolithic people.

At an approximately 150 m distance to the southeast from these snail concentrations on the slope, there are dense concentrations of animal bones and lithic artefacts including unworked/worked flint cobbles and both Epipalaeolithic and Neolithic flint tools. Some concentrations of pale limestone fragments may probably be hearths. Further to the southeast of these artefact concentrations on the slope, there seems to be a colluvial deposit which runs east-west from the Camp II Ridge to the bottom of the Camp II Basin. Only in this strip of the colluvial deposit,

Fig.5.52. A concentration of apple snails on the Camp II Ridge (looking west)

there are Neolithic pottery sherds and bivalve shells which have otherwise not been seen on the slope. This may suggest a water outflow between the Camp II Depression and the Camp II Basin across the Camp II Ridge.

5.7.3.6. The dune on the west and northwest sides of the Camp II Basin

The dune which forms the western and northwestern sides of the Camp II Basin (**Fig.5.32**) is a key to understanding the environmental history of this area. This dune has a slip face on its east side and stretches from the north while overlying the northeastern beach of the Z Basin to the south, and reaches the gravelly southern shore of the Z Basin, thereby making a rectangular cove, namely the Camp II Basin, in the easternmost part of the Z Basin. The question is when this dune was formed. The northeastern beach of the Z Basin which is overlain by the dune is rich in Epipalaeolithic artefacts, and therefore, it is safely concluded that the dune was formed after the Epipalaeolithic period. If the assumptions that there was a hiatus of many hundreds of years between the Epipalaeolithic and Neolithic periods due to a severe desiccation, and that the Z Basin dried up during this hiatus, then it is reasonable to think that the dune was formed during this arid period by the westerly wind that transported a huge amount of sand. Accordingly, it is possible to suppose that the

Camp II Basin existed when Neolithic people reoccupied the eastern beach of the Z Basin after the Epipalaeolithic period.

On the west side of the dune around the intersection of the dune and the northeast beach of the Z Basin, there are a number of hearths accompanied by scatters of fish bone fragments, Neolithic lithic artefacts and pottery sherds. These Neolithic artefact scatters are spread over the slope down to the bottom of the Z Basin to the southwest. Around the foot of the slope, patches of indurated and wind-eroded light yellow silty sediments and a sparse growth of lotus trees are seen. These indicate that water stayed there in the Neolithic period and that underground water still remains. Neolithic artefact scatters are spread further to the south on this west side of the dune. Another dune stretches from the middle of this dune diagonally southwestwards, overlying the Neolithic artefact scatters on the west side of the first dune. Around the middle of the first dune, scatters of small lacustrine bivalves (*Mutela nilotica*) and Neolithic artefacts are still seen at higher elevations which are not overlain by the second dune, and the artefacts include Neolithic concave-based arrowheads. In the southern half of the first dune, no more Neolithic artefacts are seen. It can be said from these field observations that the dune which forms the western and northwestern sides of the Camp II Basin became the new eastern shore of the Z Basin after the Epipalaeolithic period, and the west side of the new eastern shore of the Z Basin was visited by Neolithic hunter-fishers. However, even after this new eastern shore of the Z Basin was formed, it seems probable that the original eastern shore of the Z Basin was still visited by Neolithic people, judging from the presence of Neolithic artefact scatters. This may suggest that the Camp II Basin had been inundated by the inflow of high-rising lake water coming from the south during the Neolithic period.

The dune which stretches diagonally from the first dune also reaches the gravelly southern shore of the Z Basin, while overlying an oval depression filled with indurated calcareous white clay sediments. The first dune, which became the new eastern shore of the Z Basin, and the second dune, and the southern shore of the Z Basin form there a triangular cove. Around this white clay-filled depression, there are numerous concentrations of animal/fish bones and their fragments, and scatters of artefacts include pottery sherds of apparently not Neolithic, and several typical Predynastic-Old Kingdom flint tools as well as some Epipalaeolithic and Neolithic flint tools.

5.7.3.7. The southern shore of the Z Basin

The southern shore of the Z Basin is covered by flint gravels, and at some places, extensive linear deposits of transparent gypsum crystals are seen along it. Several large depressions which are filled with indurated calcareous white clay sediments are distributed along the southern shore. Some complete skeletons of catfish and Nile perch are still embedded in the sediments, but there is no trace of human consumption. Lithic artefact scatters on the flint gravels of the southern shore are quite sparse and sporadic, and except for some Levallois flakes, there is no datable, diagnostic artefact. Therefore, it is probable that the southern shore of the Z Basin had seldom been visited by people, or else that any traces of human activities were washed away by oscillating water.

5.7.3.8. The northern shore of the Z Basin

The eastern half of the northern shore of the Z Basin is covered not only by rounded/subrounded pellets of calcium carbonate but also by porous calcrete duricrusts. Therefore, it forms a remarkably wide white beach at an elevation of approximately 15 m asl. A concentration of hearths was found at the easternmost part. It is located approximately 800 m to the west of Kom W. The hearths are accompanied by Neolithic pottery sherds, lithic artefacts, and animal/fish bone fragments, suggesting temporary Neolithic occupations. To the west of this location on the northern shore of the Z Basin, no more Neolithic pottery sherds were encountered.

Another remarkable feature of the eastern half

of the northern shore is the presence of two clusters of many wind-eroded yardangs of various sizes still standing 1-3 m high, in the north of the white beach at an elevation of 20 m asl. The extent of one cluster in the east is approximately 120 m x 160 m, and the extent of another in the west is approximately 250 m x 160 m. These two clusters are separated by an open, flat space of approximately 120 m wide, and its surface is covered by coarse-grained aeolian sand. These yardangs are composed of indurated lacustrine silty sand, and are heavily eroded by wind not only from the north but also from the west. Erosion on the western face of the yardangs indicates that the dominant wind was from the west in the Early-Middle Holocene (Brookes 2003), and hence it is assumed that the silty sand was deposited and indurated before the Holocene. The ground surface of the area exhibits indurated silty sediments and is undulating. The surface lacks aeolian deposition of sand. No artefact is embedded in these silty sediments. Although sparse artefact scatters are seen on the surface, no datable diagnostic artefact was noticed. This locality (N29.59061° E30.78256° in the approximate centre) seems to be identical to a part of Caton-Thompson's Site Z, which has yielded intact hearths with Epipalaeolithic and Neolithic artefacts beneath a collapsed yardang (Caton-Thompson and Gardner 1934: 77*ff*), and also identical to Puglisi's Site S4 (SS-4 and SES-4), where a number of Epipalaeolithic artefacts were collected and part of them were published (Casini 1984; Mussi *et al.* 1984: Puglisi 1967).

According to Caton-Thompson, surface artefacts at her Site Z were scattered between 6 m asl and 18 m asl, and the width of the artefact scatters was approximately 700 m (Caton-Thompson and Gardner 1934: 59-60, 77-78 and pl.CX). The intact hearths beneath a collapsed yardang mentioned above seem to have been located at the northeastern part of Site Z. At present, artefact scatters are actually spread on the gentle slope of 10-15 m asl over the entire stretch of the northern shore of approximately 1300 m wide (**Fig.5.53**). The eastern half of the slope surface is covered by two wide bands of coarse/fine-grained aeolian sand which stretch north-south, and very few artefacts are seen on these sand bands. The slope surface which is not covered by the bands of sand exhibits many indurated patches of light yellow, orange and dark grey silty sediments. The orange colour of the silty sediments can result from oxidation due to good drainage and aeration (Rapp and Hill 1998: 38), and is indicative of constantly fluctuating water levels in a basin margin environment. It is difficult to call such wide artefact scatters on the northern shore a 'site', but the name Site Z is adopted in order to avoid a confusion caused by giving new site names to individual clusters divided by sand bands.

The majority of the finds on the deflated slope surface are Epipalaeolithic lithic artefacts. Noteworthy Epipalaeolithic artefact concentrations tend to be located at relatively lower elevations. The study of the Epipalaeolithic artefacts collected at one concentration will be described in Chapter 6. Neolithic bifacially-retouched flint tools were very rarely found. The rarity of Neolithic flint tools on the northern shore of the Z Basin may perhaps be a consequence not only of plundering by antiquarians since the late 19th century, as Caton-Thompson mentions, but also of collecting by Caton-Thompson herself (Caton-Thompson and Gardner 1934: 77*ff*). However, the complete lack of Neolithic pottery sherds may suggest that this slope area was actually not frequently visited and occupied by the pottery-

Fig.5.53. Site Z on the northern shore of the Z Basin (looking west)

using people of the Neolithic.

The western half of the northern shore of the Z Basin is covered by pale limestone and fossil shell fragments, and this shelly beach is more heavily deflated, and consequently, more widely spread in the west. The surface of the gentle slope of the northern shore toward the bottom of the Basin is covered by several wide bands of coarse/fine-grained sand or limestone/shell fragments which flow north-south, and no artefact was seen on these bands. Apart from such obscured and disturbed areas of the slope, Epipalaeolithic artefacts are quite widespread over the slope, and they exhibit several concentrations, one of which seems to be the remains of tool production. The study of the artefacts collected from there will be described in Chapter 6.

The westernmost part of the northern shore of the Z Basin is dominated by an extensive exposure of water/wind-eroded pale limestone beds which stretch east-west approximately 1 km in length. A number of fossil shell-bearing limestone slabs and fragments are scattered downslope to the south. Epipalaeolithic artefact scatters were observed on the parts of the slope which are not disturbed by the flow of limestone slabs and fragments, and a concentration of many supposedly Epipalaeolithic hearths which consisted of limestone cobbles and were accompanied by Epipalaeolithic artefacts was found near the easternmost edge of the exposure. Another concentration of Epipalaeolithic artefacts was found on the southern end of the limestone exposure. The area to the west of this Epipalaeolithic artefact concentration is barren, and is covered by fine-grained aeolian sand.

The western end of the Z Basin area is marked by a heap of limestone slabs, and few artefacts are seen. In the north of this heap of limestone slabs, there is a large depression. It is approximately 200 m in diameter, and is filled with white clay sediments and marked by a sparse growth of lotus trees. It seems that there is a colluvial deposit from the northwestern part of the Z Basin into the southeastern corner of this depression, and an extensive scatter of Epipalaeolithic artefacts is seen on the southern shore of this depression. The western and eastern shores of the depression look almost barren due to the cover of fine-grained aeolian sand, but the northern shore of the depression is marked by an extensive exposure of limestone beds, and a number of Epipalaeolithic artefacts are scattered on the surface.

5.7.3.9. The barren terrain to the north of the northern shore of the Z Basin

The area to the north of the northern shore of the Z Basin is barren flat desert. The surface is generally flat, and is covered by flint gravels and gypsum fragments which must have derived from the Pleistocene beach terraces further to the north, and pale limestone fossil shell fragments which spread from the shelly northern shore of the Z Basin. The nearest Pleistocene escarpment, whose elevation is around 25 m asl, is approximately 400 m to the north of the northern shore of the Z Basin. The surface of this first escarpment is covered by small, angular flint gravels which are absolutely not suitable for any kind of tool making. The second and the third escarpments which are located approximately 800-1000 m away from the northern shore of the Z Basin and whose elevations are above 30 m asl, are covered by flint pebbles and cobbles. They are large enough to be used as lithic raw materials, and they are quite similar to those which were used by the Epipalaeolithic toolmakers in the Z Basin.

5.7.3.10. The terrain to the south of the southern shore of the Z Basin

Caton-Thompson located one Epipalaeolithic locality named Moeris I to the southwest of the Z Basin and studied the artefacts collected there (Caton-Thompson and Gardner 1934: 67-69). This locality is undoubtedly identical to Site MOE which was visited and surface-collected by Puglisi in the late 1960s (Mussi *et al.* 1984). This locality was located but could not be investigated in detail due to the lack of time.

Caton-Thompson indicates another unnamed Epipalaeolithic locality to the southeast of the Z

Basin on her map (Caton-Thompson and Gardner 1934: pl.CXIII), but the nature and date of this locality remain unclear. This locality and its vicinities were investigated in some detail. Around the contour line of 10-15 m asl, several continuous linear outcrops of pale limestone bed are seen on an undulating sandy surface. This limestone bed extends northwest-southeast, and seems to mark a lake bank at certain times in the past. The surface of this limestone bed is severely deflated by water and wind, and fragile limestone flakes are scattered on it. Lotus trees grow sparsely in the surface cracks. Artefact scatters in this area are located not only on these linear outcrops of limestone bed but also on the gentle slope and flat area adjacent to it. A modern dirt track, which is used mainly by tourists going to Qasr el-Sagha, runs northwest-southeast a few hundred metres to the south of these linear outcrops, and hence, surface artefact scatters are obscured.

Dense scatters of flint tools and debitage products, many of which are heavily abraded, were encountered at several places to the north and south of the dirt track, and their spatial distribution is approximately 2 km in width. This is much wider than that indicated by Caton-Thompson. No Neolithic pottery sherds, no faunal remains and few structural remains like hearths were found on the sandy and gravelly surface of this area, though some supposedly Roman pottery sherds are sparsely seen. Heavily abraded lithic artefacts suggest that archaeological remains in this area have not been protected by a cover of lacustrine sediments but have suffered severely from water rolling and wind erosion.

Many of the flint tools were backed bladelets, which are characteristics of the Epipalaeolithic culture. However, some unusually large pointed blades, retouched pieces and core tools collected at these localities have no parallel in other Fayum Epipalaeolithic assemblages, and it is not certain whether such odd pieces are dated to the Epipalaeolithic, or earlier, or later. One fragment of a bifacially-retouched, pointed knife or spearhead seems to be dated to the Predynastic, and a heavily abraded, perforated limestone ball,

Fig.5.54. Mushroom-like rocks near the present lakeshore (looking southeast)

which looks like a macehead, also suggests the presence of a Predynastic locality in this area. Some large retouched pieces and core tools in question may also perhaps be dated to the Predynastic.

To the south of these wide artefact scatters is undulating desert covered by sandstone and flint fragments and is marked by sporadic lotus trees. Sandstone/siltstone bedrock of the Birket Qarun Formation is exposed everywhere, and at some locations, there are numerous mushroom-like rounded rocks of more than 1 m in basal diameter (**Fig.5.54**), which are cemented concretions eroded out of the bedrock (Wanas 2008). The area around the 0 m asl contour line falls gently southwards, but also has steep cliffs at some places. On the slope below the 0 m asl contour line, there are scatters of stone slabs and flint fragments, but lithic artefacts are quite rare to absent.

5.7.3.11. Summary of the X Basin-Z Basin area

Archaeological remains of the X Basin-Z Basin area are not disturbed severely by modern destructive activities such as canal/ditch digging, although there are dirt tracks made at the eastern and southern ends of the area and still used by the military and tourists, some craters made by bombing exercises of the military at the eastern end, and a huge amount of rubbish left by the military at the northern end. As described, most of the previously investigated archaeological localities/sites are still easily identifiable in their primary context. More importantly, there are many surface archaeological remains which have never been studied and published. Therefore, the X Basin-Z Basin area is an ideal place for the study of the palaeoenvironment and prehistoric human land use activities.

5.7.4. Wadi A and Wadi B in the Gindi Plain

Wadi A and Wadi B are very shallow wadis, and the wadi terraces are not notably developed, particularly in the south (**Fig.5.55**). The environment is generally flat with slight surface undulations, and the wadi bed is slightly lower than the surrounding terrain. Therefore, it is hard to see the width of the wadis at many places. The wadi bed is usually covered by fine-grained aeolian sand, and colluvial sediments consisting of pebbles and fragments of flint, quartz, and petrified wood are not always seen on the surface. Such sediments are better seen on the gentle slope of well-developed wadi terraces (**Fig.5.56**). Some parts of the wadi bed are also marked by a dense growth of lotus trees, suggesting the presence of underground water.

Particularly to the north of 70 m asl contour line, the environment is hilly with a number of large and small hillocks, and wadi banks which consist of limestone become more salient. It seems that the east bank is more severely eroded than the west bank. This may suggest that the wind came from the west in the past.

Wadi B bends northeastwards from around the area approximately 12 km to the northwest of Kom K, and around the location approximately 14 km to the northwest of Kom K, Wadi B runs further northeastwards while diverging and cutting through a remarkably high sandstone plateau of approximately 120-150 m asl (**Fig.5.57**). A plateau on the east side of Wadi B is called Umm es-Sawan (**Fig.5.58**). Umm es-Sawan is the western extension of the highest elevation in this area called Ilwet Hialla (Sandford and Arkell 1929: folding map). Ilwet Hialla is a plateau of the Oligocene Gebel Qatrani Formation which marks the northeastern boundary of the Fayum Depression, and stretches east-west. It forms steep cliffs and slopes on its southern face. The surface on top of the plateau of Umm es-Sawan is covered by enormous scatters of large petrified wood nodules and their splinters (**Fig.5.59**), fine/coarse-grained black sandstone slabs and cobbles as well as flint pebbles of elongated or irregular shape. Many circular depressions of a few metres in diameter fringed by black sandstone slabs on this plateau, which were interpreted by Caton-Thompson as hut circles used in the Old Kingdom (Caton-Thompson and Gardner 1934: 120-122, pl.LXIII-1 and 2), still exist. These depressions were recently reinterpreted as shallow quarries of sandstone slabs for the production of grinding stones (Bloxam and Heldal 2007; Heldal *et al.* 2006). In the lakeshore habitat in the Neolithic and Old Kingdom, sandstone slabs have commonly been utilised as raw materials for making grinding stones, and petrified wood nodules and splinters seem to have been used as grinders and hammers. It is probable that this plateau was the major source of these materials.

The southern face of the plateau of Umm es-Sawan is marked by three Old Kingdom gypsum quarrying workshops, which have been investigated by Caton-Thompson and designated as Workshop A (N29.71392° E30.87826°), Workshop B (N29.71340° E30.87966°), and Workshop C (N29.71244° E30.88125°) respectively (Caton-Thompson and Gardner 1934: 103-120), and they are still easily identifiable. The rock wall of the workshops exhibits relatively fresh, bright white gypsum deposits, and scatters of Old Kingdom pottery vessels and their sherds, unworked and worked flint cobbles, and quarried gypsum nodules are quite dense around these workshops. The surface of the flat area in the south of the plateau is an extensive exposure of deflated gypsum deposits (**Fig.5.60**), and artefacts are sparsely scattered.

On the opposite side of Umm es-Sawan across Wadi B, there is another sandstone plateau overlying limestone beds. It is approximately 2 km to the northwest of Umm es-Sawan, and is approximately 17 km to the northwest of Kom

Fig.5.55. Wadi A and El-Qarah el-Kharshah (looking east)

Fig.5.56. Wadi B (looking north)

Fig.5.57. Wadi B running beside the plateau of Umm es-Sawan (looking north)

Fig.5.58. Plateau of Umm es-Sawan (looking east)

Fig.5.59. A concentration of petrified wood on the plateau of Umm es-Sawan (looking south)

Fig.5.60. Gypsum outcrop at Umm es-Sawan (looking northwest)

K, and its elevation is higher than 150 m asl. This plateau is partly capped by thick layers of basalt nodules. There is an abandoned modern quarry of basalt on this plateau, and demolished brick and concrete buildings and wide scatters of rusty old drums and truck tyres still remain. The ground is dug up everywhere, and hence, the original environment seems to have been severely altered. To the north of this abandoned basalt quarry, there are some enigmatic rock tumuli on undisturbed desert slopes. To the west of the basalt quarry, a huge outcrop of quartzitic sandstone was found. There are some enigmatic rock tumuli around the quartzitic sandstone outcrop, and sparse scatters of Roman pottery sherds are noticed, though Roman activities in this remote area have not been known previously.

As described, Wadi B runs northeastwards while cutting through the high sandstone plateau which forms the northern boundary of the Fayum Depression. Hence it is probable that the wide dissection of the sandstone plateau at this location was used by people as a gate out of the Fayum Depression in the direction of Dahshur to the northeast, by way of a dirt track recognised by Caton-Thompson and Gardner and named as the Dahshur Road (Caton-Thompson and Gardner 1934: 109-110). Despite the lack of dating evidence, they discussed the probability that the Dahshur Road was used by Old Kingdom quarry workers for transporting the Fayum natural resources to Dahshur. This probability would explain the reason why the traces of not only Old Kingdom but also Roman human activities are concentrated on the sides of the dissection of the sandstone plateau.

The bed of Wadi B in the dissection of the sandstone plateau is marked by wide scatters of well-rounded black sandstone and basalt blocks. It is apparent that they derive from the top of sandstone plateau on both sides. A sparse growth of lotus trees is also seen on the wadi bed, but few artefacts were found.

At a locality in Wadi A, which is approximately 2 km to the northwest of Site XA and whose elevation is around 25 m asl, some isolated Neolithic flint tools and pottery sherds were collected, though no occupational feature was found. It is possible that these isolated Neolithic artefacts were transported there from the upstream of this wadi by surface runoff water, though these artefacts do not have clear traces of water rolling. In any case, this finding suggests that Neolithic people reached such a distant place via the wadi for some purposes, without leaving any material remains in between. It seems likely that the Neolithic people used this wadi as a track to go further northward to the rocky terrain of the Fayum Depression.

Isolated pottery sherds are not rare in the upstream of both wadis. Many of the sherds are so fragmentary and so abraded that it is difficult to date them. Some are made of fine-grained marl clay, and are wheel-made and well-fired. Therefore, they are apparently not Neolithic but probably Roman. There is no sherd of Islamic pottery.

Lithic artefact scatters were quite rare in the upstream of Wadi A, and several lithic artefacts including retouched tools of unknown date were collected only around the area of the 60-70 m asl contour line, which is approximately 7-9 km to the north of Kom W. In contrast, a number of lithic artefacts including cores, flakes and retouched tools which seem to range from the Middle Palaeolithic to the Neolithic were collected continually along Wadi B at elevations between 50 m asl and 150 m asl. Most of them are isolated finds, and there is no associated occupational feature around the findspots. Some lithic artefacts were found on high and low wadi terraces. But others were found on the wadi bed, and hence they may have probably flowed from the upstream of the wadi. The raw material of those lithic artefacts is flint, but it is apparently different from the one scattered in the wadi area in terms of colour, texture and size. Flint pebbles which naturally occur in the wadi area are too small to be used for toolmaking, but most lithic artefacts are made of larger flint cobbles which are not seen in the wadi area. Therefore, it is presumed that those lithic artefacts were brought from somewhere outside the wadis in the form of unworked cobbles, worked cores, blanks, or finished tools.

The most important discovery in Wadi B is a

concentration of Epipalaeolithic lithic artefacts on a high wadi bank, which is located approximately 14 km to the north of Kom K and approximately 1 km to the southwest of Umm es-Sawan. The findspot (N29.71137° E30.86858°) is located on the edge of the eastern bank overlooking the wadi bed to the northwest. The surface of the bank is covered by flint gravels and fine-grained aeolian sand. On this surface, 105 pieces of lithic artefacts, including a number of bladelet cores but few retouched tools, were concentrated within an approximately 5 m radius. Neither structural remains such as hearths or hut circles nor faunal remains were found in the surroundings. Considering such an odd situation and the location with a fine view, it is presumed that this was a watching station or hunting stand where Epipalaeolithic hunters sat down and made tools while watching for game animals in the wadi. The study of artefacts collected here will be described in Chapter 6.

In summary, the Gindi Plain and two wadis are definitely understudied areas, and their potential importance for a better understanding of the Fayum inhabitants' mobility and land use activities is very high. In particular, it is quite likely that Wadi B was used as a track which connected the lake and the northern rocky terrain of the Fayum Depression and furthermore the Nile Valley by way of the Dahshur Road. It must be considered that not only Old Kingdom and Roman people but also Epipalaeolithic and Neolithic people walked between the Fayum and the Nile Valley on this track.

5.8. Radiocarbon dates

Because of the few amounts of collected samples, only one radiocarbon date for a sample from a Neolithic surface site was obtained by this survey, and no radiocarbon dates of Epipalaeolithic localities/sites were obtained. Except for samples from the Upper K Pits, all other dated samples are charcoal. The radiocarbon dates were calibrated by using the latest calibration software OxCal ver.4.0 (Bronk Lamsey 1995; 2001), and the 95.4 % probability (2 sigma) was taken (**Table 5.1**).

As mentioned in Chapter 3, the radiocarbon dates of the Upper K Pits and Kom W have been obtained by previous researchers. The newly-obtained radiocarbon dates of the Upper K Pits and Kom W do not contradict them, and enhance the probability that both the Upper K Pits and Kom W are dated to approximately 4600-4200 cal.BC and that the previously-obtained dates of the Upper K Pits and Kom W are not reliable because they contain great uncertainty. In addition, the contemporaneity of the Upper K Pits and Kom K, which has been discussed only on the ground of their close proximity to each other and their similarity in material items, is proved by the newly-obtained radiocarbon dates of the Upper K Pits and Kom K. These dates indicate that these prominent Neolithic sites have been used or occupied for a few hundred years or less in the second half of the Fayum Neolithic, which is supposed to be approximately 5480-4260 cal.BC. Furthermore, the dates of the Upper K Pits are actually the earliest dates of clear evidence for farming in the Fayum, but these dates give rise to the question as to exactly when farming started during the supposed time span of the Fayum Neolithic. It can be assumed that the first attempt of farming in the Fayum may have started much earlier, but given the presently-available data, it is not easy to substantiate this assumption.

One radiocarbon date from Site LX is slightly older than the supposed time span of the Fayum Neolithic. It is difficult to assess the preciseness or reliability of such an isolated radiocarbon date within the chronology of the Fayum. However, considering that most radiocarbon dates of the first half of the Fayum Neolithic have been obtained only in the N Basin area at the foot of the Qasr el-Sagha escarpments, the significance of the probability of such old habitation in the L Basin-X Basin area, which is comparable to that in the N Basin area, should not be underestimated. It would not be surprising if more localities/sites in the vicinity of Site LX are dated to the supposed first half of the Fayum Neolithic or even earlier. It suggests that the time span of the Fayum Neolithic can be extended

Upper K Pits, pit 68 (basket)	**5440±35 BP (GrA-31247)**	4348 cal.BC (95.4%) 4240 cal.BC	OxCal <IntCal04>
Upper K Pits, pit 75 (chaff)	**5640±35 BP (GrA-31248)**	4544cal.BC (74.4%) 4436 cal.BC	OxCal <IntCal04>
Kom K trench 202. unit 025	**5620±20 BP (UCIAMS-34422)**	4499 cal.BC (95.4%) 4368 cal.BC	OxCal <IntCal04>
Kom K trench 202. unit 018	**5680±20 BP (UCIAMS-33840)**	4546 cal.BC (95.4%) 4460 cal.BC	OxCal <IntCal04>
Kom K trench 202. unit 019	**5640±15 BP (UCIAMS-33841)**	4526 cal.BC (93.0%) 4447 cal.BC	OxCal <IntCal04>
Kom W trench 01.unit 031	**5710±20 BP (UCIAMS-33835)**	4612 cal.BC (94.5%) 4486 cal.BC	OxCal <IntCal04>
Kom W trench 01.unit 037	**5665±20 BP (UCIAMS-33836)**	4541 cal.BC (95.4%) 4456 cal.BC	OxCal <IntCal04>
Kom W trench 01.unit 013 hearth	**5660±20 BP (UCIAMS-33838)**	4538 cal.BC (95.4%) 4456 cal.BC	OxCal <IntCal04>
Kom W trench 01.unit 018 hearth	**5670±15 BP (UCIAMS-33839)**	4537 cal.BC (95.4%) 4460 cal.BC	OxCal <IntCal04>
Site LX hearth no.22	**6600±100 BP (UCIAMS-33842)**	5708 cal.BC (95.4%) 5372 cal.BC	OxCal <IntCal04>

Table 5.1. Recent radiocarbon dates

earlier, thereby reducing the controversial time gap between the Fayum Epipalaeolithic and Neolithic, which was discussed in Chapter 3. Therefore, it is tentatively redefined that the time span of the Fayum Neolithic could be approximately 5700-4240 cal.BC.

5.9. The spatial distribution of hearths and its implication for the land use pattern

About 150 hearths were recorded at localities/sites in the survey area, and no hearth was found far from the basin shores (**Table 5.2**). Hearths are not evenly distributed across the land. It is rare that a hearth is located in complete isolation, and hearths were often found in a cluster. It is not certain whether multiple hearths were used by a group of people at one time or were a consequence of repeated visits by different people at some time intervals. In either case, it is considered that the localities where hearths were made were favourable places to stay in certain periods. If the latter was the case, it is also probable that in a basically sandy basin shore environment, people tended to be drawn to the places where hearth stones of suitable size already existed for reuse, and consequently, a cluster of hearths was formed over a long time. Although not a few hearths yielded charcoal, radiocarbon dating of the charcoal samples could not sufficiently be conducted. Therefore, how a cluster of hearths was actually formed remains to be further investigated.

In the L Basin-X Basin area, clusters of hearths were found at Site L and Site LX, whose elevations are above 20 m asl, whereas clusters of hearths at Site E29H1 and its southeastern annex are below 15 m asl. In the X Basin-Z Basin area, hearth clusters at Site XA and Site W are located between 15 m asl and 20 m asl. Most of the hearths around Kom W are above 20 m asl. Site Z has three clusters of hearths. Two clusters in the northeastern and eastern localities of Site Z are located between 10 m asl and 20 m asl, whereas one cluster in the western locality is located below 10 m asl. There seems to be no preservation bias for certain topographic locations within the vertical range from ±10 m asl to ±20 m asl. Therefore, the elevations of these immobile structural remains are the most reliable indicators of lake levels when the loci were occupied. Hearth clusters which would be dated to the Epipalaeolithic are located at lower elevations, whereas those which would be dated to the Neolithic and Old Kingdom are located at higher elevations. These facts confirm the previous idea that the lake level was generally low in the Epipalaeolithic and rose up in the Neolithic and Old Kingdom.

5.10. The spatial distribution and nature of Epipalaeolithic localities/sites in the L Basin, X Basin and Z Basin areas

As described, a number of known and unknown Epipalaeolithic localities/sites were visited during this survey, and it was revealed how Epipalaeolithic localities/sites look like at present.

Area	Locality/site name	hearth number	Date	burnt/cracked stone	charcoal	Northing	Easting
L Basin	Site L	1	Neolithic	+	+	29.57819	030.85027
L Basin	Site L	2	Neolithic	+	+	29.57824	030.85023
L Basin	Site L	3	Neolithic			29.57820	030.85023
L Basin	Site L	4	Neolithic			29.57813	030.85024
L Basin	Site L	5	Neolithic			29.57813	030.84994
L Basin	Site L	6	Neolithic			29.57793	030.84689
L Basin	Site L	7	Neolithic			29.57789	030.85105
L Basin	Site L	8	Unknown			29.57814	030.85065
L Basin	Site L	9	Unknown			29.57812	030.84995
L Basin	Site L	10	Neolithic			29.57867	030.84726
L Basin	Site L	11	Neolithic			29.57860	030.84756
L Basin	Site L	12	Unknown			29.57842	030.84806
L Basin	Site L	13	Neolithic			29.57853	030.84954
L Basin	Site L	14	Epipalaeolithic/Neolithic			29.57502	030.85238
L Basin	Site L	15	Epipalaeolithic/Neolithic			29.57499	030.85281
L Basin	Site L	16	Neolithic			29.57994	030.84752
L Basin	Site L	17	Neolithic			29.57993	030.84741
L Basin	Site L	18	Neolithic			29.57995	030.84727
L Basin	Site L	19	Unknown			29.57970	030.84978
X Basin	Site E29H1	1	Epipalaeolithic			29.58370	030.83239
X Basin	Site E29H1	2	Epipalaeolithic		+	29.58383	030.83260
X Basin	Site E29H1	3	Epipalaeolithic			29.58390	030.83257
X Basin	Site E29H1	4	Epipalaeolithic			29.58398	030.83254
X Basin	Site E29H1	5	Epipalaeolithic			29.58403	030.83260
X Basin	Site E29H1	6	Epipalaeolithic			29.58406	030.83271
X Basin	Site E29H1	7	Epipalaeolithic			29.58417	030.83265
X Basin	Site E29H1	8	Epipalaeolithic			29.58434	030.83263
X Basin	Site E29H1	9	Epipalaeolithic			29.58433	030.83278
X Basin	Site E29H1	10	Epipalaeolithic			29.58430	030.83286
X Basin	Site E29H1	11	Epipalaeolithic		+	29.58410	030.83314
X Basin	Site E29H1	12	Epipalaeolithic			29.58402	030.83326
X Basin	Site E29H1	13	Epipalaeolithic			29.58394	030.83330
X Basin	Site E29H1	14	Epipalaeolithic			29.58390	030.83299
X Basin	Site E29H1	15	Epipalaeolithic			29.58385	030.83290
X Basin	Site E29H1	16	Epipalaeolithic			29.58390	030.83317
X Basin	Site E29H1	17	Epipalaeolithic			29.58379	030.83316
X Basin	Site E29H1	18	Epipalaeolithic			29.58380	030.83322
X Basin	Site E29H1	*19*	Epipalaeolithic			29.58381	030.83271
X Basin	Site E29H1	*20*	Epipalaeolithic			29.58393	030.83304
X Basin	Site E29H1	*21*	Epipalaeolithic			29.58411	030.83296
X Basin	Site E29H1	*22*	Epipalaeolithic			29.58380	030.83277
X Basin	Site E29H1 SE-annex	1	Unknown			29.57728	030.83911
X Basin	Site E29H1 SE-annex	2	Unknown			29.57730	030.83877
X Basin	Site E29H1 SE-annex	3	Unknown			29.57846	030.83959
X Basin	Site E29H1 SE-annex	4	Unknown			29.57855	030.83958
X Basin	Site E29H1 SE-annex	5	Unknown			29.57845	030.83949
X Basin	Site E29H1 SE-annex	6	Unknown			29.57837	030.83952
X Basin	Site E29H1 SE-annex	7	Neolithic			29.57869	030.83997
X Basin	Site LX	1	Unknown			29.58233	030.84277
X Basin	Site LX	2	Neolithic			29.58157	030.84212
X Basin	Site LX	3	Neolithic			29.58166	030.84212
X Basin	Site LX	4	Neolithic			29.58191	030.84220
X Basin	Site LX	5	Unknown			29.58167	030.84169
X Basin	Site LX	6	Unknown			29.58171	030.84169
X Basin	Site LX	7	Unknown			29.58237	030.84211
X Basin	Site LX	8	Neolithic			29.58147	030.84332
X Basin	Site LX	9	Unknown			29.58143	030.84234
X Basin	Site LX	10	Unknown			29.58191	030.84296
X Basin	Site LX	11	Unknown			29.58205	030.84296
X Basin	Site LX	12	Unknown			29.58215	030.84283
X Basin	Site LX	13	Unknown			29.58208	030.84279
X Basin	Site LX	14	Unknown			29.58201	030.84287
X Basin	Site LX	15	Unknown			29.58210	030.84314
X Basin	Site LX	16	Unknown			29.58208	030.84336
X Basin	Site LX	17	Unknown			29.58289	030.84321

Table 5.2. The list of hearths found during the survey

Area	Locality/site name	hearth number	Date	burnt/cracked stone	charcoal	Northing	Easting
X Basin	Site LX	18	Neolithic			29.58154	030.84321
X Basin	Site LX	19	Neolithic			29.58159	030.84326
X Basin	Site LX	20	Neolithic			29.58144	030.84359
X Basin	Site LX	21	Neolithic			29.58229	030.84296
X Basin	Site LX	22	Neolithic		+	29.58236	030.84299
X Basin	Site LX	23	Neolithic			29.58186	030.84604
X Basin	Site LX	24	Neolithic			29.58380	030.84675
X Basin	Site XA	1	Unknown			29.58930	030.81502
X Basin	Site XA	2	Unknown			29.58922	030.81513
X Basin	Site XA	3	Unknown			29.58911	030.81498
X Basin	Site XA	4	Unknown			29.59354	030.81384
X Basin	Site XA	5	Unknown			29.59327	030.81179
X Basin	Site XA	6	Neolithic			29.59348	030.81563
X Basin	Site XA-sw	1	Unknown			29.58636	030.81006
X Basin	Site XA-e	1	Unknown			29.59210	030.81854
X Basin	Site XA-n	1	Neolithic			29.59634	030.81329
X Basin	Site XA-n	2	Unknown			29.59627	030.81327
X Basin	Site XA-n	3	Unknown		+	29.59632	030.81292
X Basin	Site XA-n	4	Neolithic		+	29.59610	030.81295
X Basin	Site W	1	Neolithic			29.59275	030.80834
X Basin	Site W	2	Neolithic			29.59249	030.80730
X Basin	Site W	3	Neolithic			29.59307	030.80590
X Basin	Site W	4	Neolithic			29.59267	030.80579
X Basin	Site W	5	Neolithic			29.59262	030.80584
X Basin	Site W	6	Neolithic			29.59306	030.80533
X Basin	Site V-se	1	Greco-Roman			29.57722	030.80003
X Basin	Site V-se	2	Unknown			29.58294	030.79998
X Basin	Loc. SV-s	1	Greco-Roman?		+	29.56788	030.80016
Z Basin	CS Depression	1	Greco-Roman?			29.58586	030.79824
Z Basin	CS-n	1	Neolithic?			29.59018	030.79561
Z Basin	CS-n	2	Old Kingdom			29.59124	030.79531
Z Basin	CS-n	3	Neolithic			29.59161	030.79754
Z Basin	CS-n	4	Neolithic	+	+	29.59183	030.79727
Z Basin	CS-n	5	Neolithic	+		29.59181	030.79734
Z Basin	CS-Site W	1	Unknown			29.59389	030.80274
Z Basin	Kom W-n	1	Unknown			29.59082	030.79126
Z Basin	Kom W-n	2	Unknown			29.59063	030.79066
Z Basin	Kom W-n	3	Neolithic			29,59010	030.79077
Z Basin	Kom W-n	4	Neolithic			29.59017	030.79088
Z Basin	Kom W-n	5	Neolithic	+		29.59088	030.79336
Z Basin	Kom W-n	6	Old Kingdom?			29.59013	030.79186
Z Basin	Kom W-n	7	Old Kingdom?			29.59003	030.79174
Z Basin	Kom W-n	8	Old Kingdom?	+		29.58993	030.79173
Z Basin	Kom W-w	1	Neolithic			29.58833	030.78988
Z Basin	Kom W-w	2	Neolithic			29.58936	030.78960
Z Basin	Kom W-w	3	Neolithic			29.58915	030.78956
Z Basin	Kom W-w	4	Neolithic			29.58888	030.78936
Z Basin	Kom W-w	5	Neolithic			29.58872	030.78957
Z Basin	Camp II-Site V	1	Old Kingdom	+		29.58362	030.79111
Z Basin	Camp II-Site V	2	Old Kingdom			29.58233	030.79058
Z Basin	Site Z-e	1	Unknown			29.59006	030.78467
Z Basin	Site Z eastern hearth field	1	Neolithic	+		29.58816	030.78384
Z Basin	Site Z eastern hearth field	2	Neolithic	+		29.58806	030.78379
Z Basin	Site Z eastern hearth field	3	Neolithic	+		29.58801	030.78377
Z Basin	Site Z eastern hearth field	4	Neolithic	+		29.58799	030.78411
Z Basin	Site Z eastern hearth field	5	Neolithic	+		29.58784	030.78404
Z Basin	Site Z eastern hearth field	6	Neolithic	+		29.58787	030.78425
Z Basin	Site Z eastern hearth field	7	Neolithic	+		29.58787	030.78420
Z Basin	Site Z eastern hearth field	8	Neolithic	+		29.58767	030.78388
Z Basin	Site Z eastern hearth field	9	Neolithic	+		29.58918	030.78219
Z Basin	Site Z eastern hearth field	10	Neolithic			29.58915	030.78209
Z Basin	Site Z northeastern hearth field	1	Neolithic	+		29.59170	030.78340
Z Basin	Site Z northeastern hearth field	2	Neolithic	+		29.59145	030.78300
Z Basin	Site Z northeastern hearth field	3	Neolithic	+		29.59138	030.78302
Z Basin	Site Z northeastern hearth field	4	Neolithic	+		29.59148	030.78269

Table 5.2. The list of hearths found during the survey (continued)

Area	Locality/site name	hearth number	Date	burnt/cracked stone	charcoal	Northing	Easting
Z Basin	Site Z northeastern hearth field	5	Epipalaeolithic?	+		29.59072	030.78247
Z Basin	Site Z northeastern hearth field	6	Epipalaeolithic?	+		29.59072	030.78253
Z Basin	Site Z northeastern hearth field	7	Epipalaeolithic?	+		29.59061	030.78256
Z Basin	Site Z northeastern hearth field	8	Epipalaeolithic?	+		29.59056	030.78256
Z Basin	Site Z	1	Epipalaeolithic/Neolithic			29.58983	030.78009
Z Basin	Site Z	2	Epipalaeolithic/Neolithic			29.58978	030.78021
Z Basin	Site Z	3	Unknown	+	+	29.59122	030.77964
Z Basin	Site Z	4	Epipalaeolithic/Neolithic			29.59032	030.77749
Z Basin	Site Z	5	Epipalaeolithic/Neolithic			29.59027	030.77750
Z Basin	Site Z	6	Unknown			29.59194	030.77086
Z Basin	Site Z	7	Unknown	+		29.59142	030.77597
Z Basin	Site Z western hearth field	1	Epipalaeolithic			29.59019	030.77180
Z Basin	Site Z western hearth field	2	Epipalaeolithic			29.59015	030.77165
Z Basin	Site Z western hearth field	3	Epipalaeolithic	+		29.59008	030.77161
Z Basin	Site Z western hearth field	4	Epipalaeolithic			29.59007	030.77158
Z Basin	Site Z western hearth field	5	Epipalaeolithic			29.59007	030.77138
Z Basin	Site Z western hearth field	6	Epipalaeolithic		+	29.59002	030.77125
Z Basin	Site Z western hearth field	7	Epipalaeolithic		+	29.59069	030.77130
Z Basin	Site Z western hearth field	8	Epipalaeolithic			29.59034	030.77125
Z Basin	Site Z western hearth field	9	Epipalaeolithic			29.59031	030.77119
Z Basin	Site Z western hearth field	10	Epipalaeolithic			29.59023	030.77115

Table 5.2. The list of hearths found during the survey (continued)

It has been known that the spatial distribution of Epipalaeolithic localities/sites around major basins on the northeastern shore of the lake was limited to the 5-19 m asl contour lines, and was not expanded to higher elevations. As long as one looks at this situation, it is hard to imagine frequent vertical movements of Epipalaeolithic people according to the annual rise and fall of the lake level. Since all the localities/sites are not far from each other but are located within easy walking distance, the differences in density and extent between localities/sites around the basins seem to imply horizontal dispersal and aggregation of small groups of people within the narrow strip of aquatic resource-rich basin shores.

However, based on the fact that most Epipalaeolithic localities/sites are nothing more than surface scatters of lithic artefacts without clear structural remains, it has been suggested that these localities/sites were occasional or seasonal encampments, and that there must have been other residential bases or task locations occupied by the same people in different places, which represent different subsistence activities (Hassan 1986b: 496; Wendorf and Schild 1976: 317). It has also been suggested that Epipalaeolithic people were quite mobile and may have spent several months of the year away from the Fayum when lakeshore resources became scarce or when the lakeshore became inaccessible (Wetterstrom 1993: 191). According to the study of lake level fluctuations in the Early Holocene (Wendorf and Schild 1976: 222-226), during the long span of the Fayum Epipalaeolithic period, there were two peaks of high water which are named the Premoeris Lake and Protomoeris Lake respectively, and there was a considerable drop of the water level between these peaks. Therefore, it is certain that Epipalaeolithic people were subjected to long-term fluctuations of the lake water level. On the other hand, the suggestion concerning the seasonal migration of Fayum Epipalaeolithic people has never been substantiated by archaeological data, and hence sounds like mere speculation.

Most Epipalaeolithic localities visited during this survey were certainly just surface scatters of lithic artefacts with no structural remains. On the other hand, Site E29H1 in the X Basin and Site Z in the Z Basin are remarkable in terms of the presence of structural remains like hearths and supposedly lithic debitage dumping spots as well as clear concentrations of animal bones. They surely deserve the designation of 'sites', and may represent the occupation loci of Fayum Epipalaeolithic people. Therefore, some

Epipalaeolithic localities/sites are probably the remains of either residential bases for daily dining and resting or task locations for daily foraging. It would be too simplistic to regard all the Epipalaeolithic localities/sites equally as occasional or seasonal encampments. One is even tempted to suppose that the water level of the lake was fairly stable in the short term, and that people were quite sedentary, relying on aquatic resources in this environment in certain periods during the Fayum Epipalaeolithic.

However, such differences in the appearance of sites/localities may simply be the consequence of different degrees of taphonomic processes caused by natural forces as well as by overlapping occupations of later peoples. As mentioned above, the spatial distribution of Epipalaeolithic localities/sites in the L Basin, X Basin and Z Basin is limited to lower elevations, and it is certain that all Epipalaeolithic localities/ sites were underwater when the lake level was generally higher during the Neolithic and Old Kingdom periods. Therefore, the Epipalaeolithic localities/sites on lake margins must have been either eroded by oscillating water or well protected by the cover of lacustrine silty sediments. The latter would particularly be the case with Site E29H1 and Site Z, both of which are located on the northern shores of the X Basin and Z Basin respectively and hence must have been under calm water coming from the south. They may not have severely suffered from high energy waves caused by the wind coming from the west. It is probable that Site E29H1 and Site Z have been protected by fine-grained lacustrine sediments which tend to deposit in deeper waters while the lake level was rapidly and calmly rising after their last occupation. Such a rapid rising trend of lake level, which may have reached 24 m asl, has indeed been observed at Site E29H1 in the Protomoeris lake stage that corresponds to the second half of the Fayum Epipalaeolithic period (Wendorf and Schild 1976: 225, fig.159). Then, these sites would have gradually been exposed on the present surface by water recession and wind erosion. In contrast, it is quite likely that the Camp II Ridge, an Epipalaeolithic locality on the eastern shore of the Z Basin which exhibits a remarkably dense concentration of Epipalaeolithic artefacts but lacks structural remains, was heavily washed and eroded by high energy waves caused by the wind coming from the west.

Given this likelihood, it may be assumed that the present surface situation of Epipalaeolithic localities/sites on the northern shores of the X Basin and Z Basin reflects the reality of a certain period in the past fairly better than those on the eastern shores of the Basins. That is, hearths, faunal remains and lithic debitage dumps tended to concentrate on one or two particular places on the northern shores of the Basins, whereas the entire northern shores of approximately 2 km wide were almost evenly exploited, as indicated by vast scatters of artefacts. This may perhaps suggest that a group of Epipalaeolithic foragers habitually located a residential base on the basin shore and walked from the residential base for daily foraging along the entire shoreline. This suggestion requires a reconsideration of the general image of the mobility and sedentariness of Fayum Epipalaeolithic foragers.

Faunal data have strongly suggested that Fayum Epipalaeolithic people could have heavily relied on fishing and fowling on the lakeshore almost all the year around (Wetterstrom 1993: 190-191). Indeed, aquatic resources like fish are not sparsely distributed but concentrated on basin shores, and they are abundant and not easily depleted. Moreover, they have predictable seasonality as exemplified by the seasons of spawning, aggregating and migrating. Considering these resource assets and the need for drinking water, it would not be surprising if the Fayum Epipalaeolithic foragers were tethered at residential bases on the basin shores even though seasonally and if they returned to the same residential base cyclically.

It is not certain whether the dense concentrations of hearths at Site E29H1 in the X Basin and at Site Z in the Z Basin reflect continuity of occupation by one group of people who stayed at the sites exclusively for a certain period of time, or show the consequence of regularly or irregularly repeated occupations of the same residential bases by one or many groups of people for a length of time. The questions about the social organisation and mobility of the Epipalaeolithic people and the duration of site occupation are difficult to answer as long as one relies on the surface observations of sites without radiocarbon dates. Therefore, different approaches to these questions are needed. Since the basin shore localities/sites are quite sandy and devoid not only of flint pebbles suitable for making tools but also of rocks suitable for making hearths, these materials must have been transported from somewhere else. The study of the sources of pebbles and rocks found at these occupation loci can give a clue to gauge at least the mobility range of the people. This study will be dealt with in Chapter 6.

Although not sufficiently investigated, Epipalaeolithic localities far to the south of the L Basin, X Basin and Z Basin are distributed below 10 m asl, and this indicates rising and lowering lake water during the Epipalaeolithic period. If the localities below 10 m asl are contemporaneous with the localities/sites on the northern shores of the L Basin, X Basin and Z Basin, it is possible to suggest that the Epipalaeolithic people moved following the seasonal rise and fall of the lake water level within the vertical range of 0-15 m asl and the distance of no more than 2 km. It follows that the localities/sites on the northern shores of the L Basin, X Basin and Z Basin were occupied in the season of the highest basin water, that is, in late summer to autumn. However, if the localities below 10 m asl are not contemporaneous with the localities/sites on the northern shores of the L Basin, X Basin and Z Basin, then it must be considered that the different elevation of Epipalaeolithic localities/sites reflects changing levels of lake water and people's adaptation to it in the long term.

5.11. The spatial distribution of sickle blades and grinding stones and its implication for the land use pattern in the Fayum Neolithic

5.11.1. Sickle Blades

Given that sickle blades of the Fayum Neolithic were held firmly in a groove of a wooden shaft by resin (Caton-Thompson and Gardner 1934: 45, pls.XXVIII and XXX), it is unlikely that blades were frequently replaced by new ones during a sickle-using task at the location of their use, because blade replacement requires a fire to melt resin, and this is complicated and time-consuming work. A study of the distributional effects of hafting suggests that hafted tools are likely to be resharpened or replaced when it is convenient to do so rather than when it is necessary (Keeley 1982: 799*ff*). Therefore, it can be assumed that worn sickle blades were more frequently discarded and replaced at residential bases than they were at use locations. It can also be assumed that the findspots of sickle blades in the Fayum Neolithic indicate either residential bases or use locations.

According to the reports of the surface collection and excavations by Caton-Thompson, bifacially-retouched, pointed or square-ended sickle blades of complete shape have been collected or excavated at the following sites within the concession of the UCLA-RUG survey.

13 (9 pointed and 4 square-ended) from Site K
10 (8 pointed and 2 square-ended) from Kom K
10 (9 pointed and 1 square-ended) from Site L
5 (4 pointed and 1 square-ended) from Area L-X
15 (10 pointed and 5 square-ended) from Site X
12 (11 pointed and 1 square-ended) from Site V
31 (28 pointed and 3 square-ended) from Kom W
4 (2 pointed and 2 square-ended) from Triangle Area of Camp II-Kom W-Site V
20 (9 pointed and 11 square-ended) from the Camp II Basin
4 (2 pointed and 2 square-ended) from Site Z
4 (4 pointed) from the Z Basin

Despite the fact that Kom W and its vicinities have been most intensively surface-collected by antiquarians before Caton-Thompson visited, sickle blades were most numerously found at Kom W by her. This suggests that sickle blades tended to be made and discarded more frequently at habitation loci like Kom W than at use locations. Sporadic occurrence of sickle blades at other localities which do not seem to be associated with habitation, such as Caton-Thompson's Area L-X and Triangle Area of Camp II-Kom W-Site V, may indicate their use locations.

During the new survey, a small number of Neolithic bifacially-retouched sickle blades were found at different localities (**Fig.5.61**).

1 (pointed) from the surface of the Upper K Pits
2 (1 pointed and bilaterally-serrated and 1 square-ended) from the east terrace of Wadi A
2 (2 square-ended) from Site LX
1 (1 pointed) from a hilly terrain to the northeast of Kom W
1 (1 pointed) from the western shore of the Camp II Depression
1 (1 pointed) from Site Z

Fig.5.61. Three pointed sickle blades collected at different localities

Two square-ended sickle blades found at Site LX may be understood as supporting the probability that Site LX was a residential base where tools were resharpened or replaced. On the other hand, other sickle blades were collected in isolation at unexpected places, such as the terraces of desert wadi and surface runoff which are far from the water margins of the lake. Therefore, it is highly probable that these findspots were the use locations of the sickles and thus where plant harvesting took place. Although it is possible that wild plants were harvested there by sickles, it is significant to consider another possibility that wheat/barley farming has been attempted in places which became wet due to winter rainfall. These isolated sickle blades give a clue to understand the diversity of the subsistence and land use of Fayum Neolithic people.

5.11.2. Grinding stones

Although it was expected that the findspots of grinding stones might indicate the locations of plant grinding/mashing activity, it turned out that the use of grinding stones as a clue to know Neolithic activity loci was not easy. This is firstly because there is no direct means to date grinding stones, and other diagnostic artefacts around the grinding stones are the only clues to speculate the possible date of the grinding stones. Based on such a manner of speculation, very few grinding stone could be dated solely to the Epipalaeolithic, and many grinding stones could be dated either to the Epipalaeolithic or more likely to the Neolithic. Moreover, the grinding stones encountered during the survey do not always seem to retain their original positions, and some have apparently been moved for reuse very recently by local people or other visitors. Nonetheless, apart from such recently-moved grinding stones, it is assumed that many of grinding stones indicate their last use locations, even though they might have been reused and/or recycled and moved in the Neolithic, Predynastic, Old Kingdom and even Greco-Roman periods.

About 50 grinding stones were found at

Area	Locality/site name	grinding stone number	Date	Northing	Easting
K Basin	Loc. LKP-w	1	Old Kingdom? Greco-Roman?	29.59631	030.87230
L Basin	Site L	1	Neolithic	29.57875	030.85040
L Basin	Site L	2	Neolithic?	29.57751	030.84802
L Basin	Site L	3	Neolithic?	29.57751	030.84846
L Basin	Site L	4	Neolithic?	29.57795	030.84818
L Basin	Site L	5	Neolithic?	29.57776	030.84796
L Basin	Site L	6	Epipalaeolithic/Neolithic	29.57482	030.85296
L Basin	Site L SE-annex	1	Neolithic/Old Kingdom/Greco-Roman?	29.57216	030.86180
L Basin	Site L SE-annex	2	Neolithic/Old Kingdom/Greco-Roman?	29.57246	030.86056
X Basin	Site E29H1	1	Unknown	29.58429	030.83325
X Basin	Site E29H1	2	Epipalaeolithic/Neolithic	29.58496	030.83189
X Basin	Site E29H1	3	Epipalaeolithic/Neolithic	29.58496	030.83189
X Basin	Site E29H1	4	Unknown	29.58405	030.83284
X Basin	Site E29H1	5	Epipalaeolithic	29.58377	030.83268
X Basin	Site E29H1 NW-annex	1	Unknown	29.58541	030.83033
X Basin	Site E29H1 SE-annex	1	Unknown	29.57880	030.83663
X Basin	Site E29H1 SE-annex	2	Unknown	29.57734	030.83967
X Basin	Site E29H1 SE-annex	3	Unknown	29.57736	030.84098
X Basin	Site LX	1	Unknown	29.58173	030.84180
X Basin	Site LX	2	Unknown	29.58209	030.84208
X Basin	Site LX	3	Unknown	29.58246	030.84196
X Basin	Site LX	4	Unknown	29.58246	030.84196
X Basin	Site LX	5	Unknown	29.58258	030.84237
X Basin	Site LX	6	Unknown	29.58272	030.84207
X Basin	Site LX	7	Unknown	29.58200	030.84246
X Basin	Site LX	8	Neolithic	29.58218	030.84291
X Basin	Site LX	9	Neolithic	29.58218	030.84291
X Basin	Site LX	10	Unknown	29.58207	030.84325
X Basin	Site XA	1	Neolithic	29.59069	030.81461
X Basin	Site XA	2	Neolithic	29.59010	030.81508
X Basin	Site XA	3	Neolithic	29.59055	030.81533
X Basin	Site XA	4	Neolithic	29.59125	030.81460
X Basin	Site XA	5	Unknown	29.59320	030.81367
X Basin	Site XA	6	Unknown	29.59354	030.81365
X Basin	Site XA	7	Unknown	29.59375	030.81575
X Basin	Site XA-s	1	Unknown	29.58448	030.82006
X Basin	Site XA-s	2	Epipalaeolithic/Neolithic	29.58728	030.81655
X Basin	Site W	1	Neolithic	29.59309	030.80889
X Basin	Site W	2	Neolithic	29.59309	030.80889
X Basin	CS-Site W	1	Neolithic	29.59379	030.80256
X Basin	CS-Site W	2	Epipalaeolithic/Neolithic?	29.59188	030.80231
X Basin	Site X-Site XA	1	Epipalaeolithic/Neolithic?	29.58960	030.80854
X Basin	Site V-se	1	Unknown	29.57933	030.79836
Z Basin	Site V Depression-w	1	Neolithic/Predynastic	29.58375	030.79264
Z Basin	Kom W-n	1	Unknown	29.59070	030.79123
Z Basin	Kom W-n	2	Neolithic	29.59105	030.79024
Z Basin	Kom W-w	1	Neolithic	29.58758	030.78985
Z Basin	CS Depression	1	Old Kingdom	29.58625	030.79843
Z Basin	Site V-e	1	Epipalaeolithic/Neolithic	29.58307	030.79713
Z Basin	Camp II Ridge	1	Epipalaeolithic/Neolithic	29.58767	030.78620
Z Basin	Camp II Ridge	2	Epipalaeolithic/Neolithic	29.58741	030.78637
Z Basin	Camp II Ridge	3	Epipalaeolithic/Neolithic	29.58741	030.78617
Z Basin	Site Z eastern hearth field	1	Neolithic	29.58745	030.78355
Z Basin	Site Z northeastern hearth field	1	Epipalaeolithic?	29.59090	030.78217
Z Basin	NW depression E shore	1	Neolithic?	29.59246	030.75978
Z Basin	NW depression E shore	2	Neolithic?	29.59235	030.75982

Table 5.3. The list of grinding stones found during the survey

localities/sites on basin shores, and no grinding stone was found far from the basin shores (**Table 5.3**). Many of them are in their original shapes even though partly broken, but some are fragmentary. While sporadic occurrence of grinding stones was certainly seen at or around Kom W, Site V, Site X and Site Z as already mentioned by Caton-Thompson, two remarkable concentrations of more than a few grinding stones, which have never been reported before, were noticed in other areas. One concentration of grinding stones was seen in Site LX, and another concentration of grinding stones was seen in Site XA. Such concentrations of grinding stones are comparable to that at Kom W, which was reported by Caton-Thompson (Caton-Thompson and Gardner 1934: 31-32). It is assumed that these concentrations indicate the regularity or continuity of site occupation and the mass processing of grains or tubers.

The difference in their environments is interesting to note. Site LX and Kom W are located at an elevation of slightly higher than 20 m asl, which is supposed to be around the margin of the highest-rising lake water in late summer in the higher stage of the Moeris Lake. On the other hand, Site XA is located at the abuttal of the X Basin and Wadi A at elevations of around 15 m asl. This location is supposed to be around the margin of high-rising lake water in late summer in the relatively lower stage of the Moeris Lake, and is supposed to become wet due to surface runoff caused by rainfall in winter. These two distinct locations with a supposedly similar subsistence activity imply either different seasons of occupation within the same time period according to the seasonal rise and fall of lake water level, or different time periods of occupation in the longer term.

5.12. The spatial distribution and nature of Neolithic localities/sites in the L Basin-X Basin area

The new field survey revealed that the area to the north of the L Basin and X Basin had some interesting Neolithic sites like Site L and Site LX (**Fig.5.62**). Despite the surface disturbance caused by natural erosion and recent expansion of dry canals and ditches, these sites seem to retain an original context to some degree, judging from the presence of immobile remains like hearths and fragile materials like charcoal beneath the hearth stones. Such well-preserved Neolithic remains can serve to reconstruct the land use patterns of the Neolithic people in this area.

As described earlier, this area consists of the high flat desert (above 20 m asl), the gentle slope (15-20 m asl), and the low flat desert (below 15 m asl). Neolithic artefact scatters are spread in this entire area. There seems to be no significant difference in the basic structure of individual hearths between elevations. The density of the distribution of hearths accompanied by other occupational features is particularly high at higher elevations above 20 m asl, whereas the distributions of artefacts on the gentle slope is relatively sparse. This gives the impression that the high flat area was a major Neolithic habitation area, which has been occupied for a certain length of time or has been visited and stayed at routinely or frequently, and that many different kinds of tasks were performed there. In particular, the location, variety and spatial extent of archaeological remains at higher elevations of Site LX are comparable to those of other well-investigated occupation loci like Kom K and Kom W.

However, differences in the appearance of localities/sites according to elevation in this area may again simply be the consequences of different degrees of taphonomic processes caused by natural forces. That is, undurable and fragile archaeological remains at lower elevations may have been prone to be eroded and washed away by oscillating water near the beaches of later times, whereas archaeological remains at higher elevations may have escaped from such erosional events. A field observation at Site E29H1 by the Combined Prehistoric Expedition and this survey that Neolithic lithic artefacts seen at this site are heavily abraded clearly suggests that Neolithic remains on the northeastern beach at an elevation below 15 m asl tended to suffer from oscillating water for a considerable length of time and to be lost, instead of being buried by lacustrine sediments under deep water and protected.

On the other hand, although not comprehensively studied, Neolithic artefact assemblages appear to be slightly different from elevation to elevation, and thus the differences in artefact assemblages may give not only clues to understand the function of localities but also some ideas about the mobility and subsistence strategy of the Neolithic people in this basin shore environment. Localities at lower elevations were marked by the presence of bifacially-retouched arrowheads and spearheads, whereas localities above 20 m asl were noted for the absence of such hunting weapons and the presence of numerous grinding stones and pottery sherds, and some bifacially-retouched sickle blades and knife blades. These differences may perhaps reflect a general difference in subsistence activities and land use. The localities at lower elevations are obviously related to hunting or fishing on the receding basin shores. The sporadic presence of crude knives and denticulates at lower elevations may suggest that butchering or scaling were also performed there, and that large portions of meat were taken away to occupation loci at higher elevations. The low elevation localities must have been occupied or visited from winter to late spring when the water level of the basins was low and the flock of migratory waterfowl came. In contrast, artefact assemblages in the localities above 20 m asl suggest subsistence activities other than hunting and fishing. In addition, the existence of curious remains like the concentrations of burnt clay nodules and the supposedly stockpiles of flint cobbles and quartz cobbles at higher elevations of Site LX suggest craft working activities.

It is hard to say through a surface observation of artefacts and structural remains how many people inhabited the high flat desert of the L Basin-X Basin area at one time and how long they stayed there. This is related to a larger question as to the sedentariness of people in this habitation area. As is the case with Epipalaeolithic sites mentioned earlier, it is not certain whether a number of various archaeological remains on the high flat desert reflect continuity of occupation by one group of people for a certain period of time, or suggest the regularly or irregularly repeated occupations of the same place by one or different groups of people for a length of time. Only a single radiocarbon date for Site LX suggests that it has been occupied earlier in date in the Fayum Neolithic, but does not tell the duration of occupation. It can only logically be considered that the high flat desert would have been occupied at least in summer because it was high enough to escape from high-rising basin water in summer.

In order to answer the questions about the sedentariness of the Neolithic inhabitants of Site L and Site LX and the duration of site occupation, different approaches must be considered. Since the high flat desert of the L Basin-X Basin area is sandy or gravelly and is devoid not only of flint cobbles suitable for making tools but also of blocks/slabs suitable for making hearths and grinding stones, these materials must have been transported from somewhere else. The presence of a number of apparently non-local cobbles and blocks/slabs in Site L and Site LX suggests that the mobility range of Neolithic people was not limited to this basin shore environment. The fact that the mouth of Wadi B is located less than 1 km to the north of Site LX is important in this context. Although the mouth of Wadi B could not be surveyed due to the lack of time, it is probable that the Neolithic inhabitants of Site L and Site LX used Wadi B as a track when they walked to the sources of blocks/slabs in the rocky terrain of the Fayum Depression in the north. Given this probability, the location of Site L and Site LX is considered to be strategically quite favourable, because it could benefit from aquatic resource-rich basin shores in the south as well as a wadi in the north which may have brought runoff water caused by winter rainfall. It is possible that either wild or domesticated plants were harvested around the wadi when it became moist in winter. If this was really the case, year-round habitation in Site L and Site LX would not have

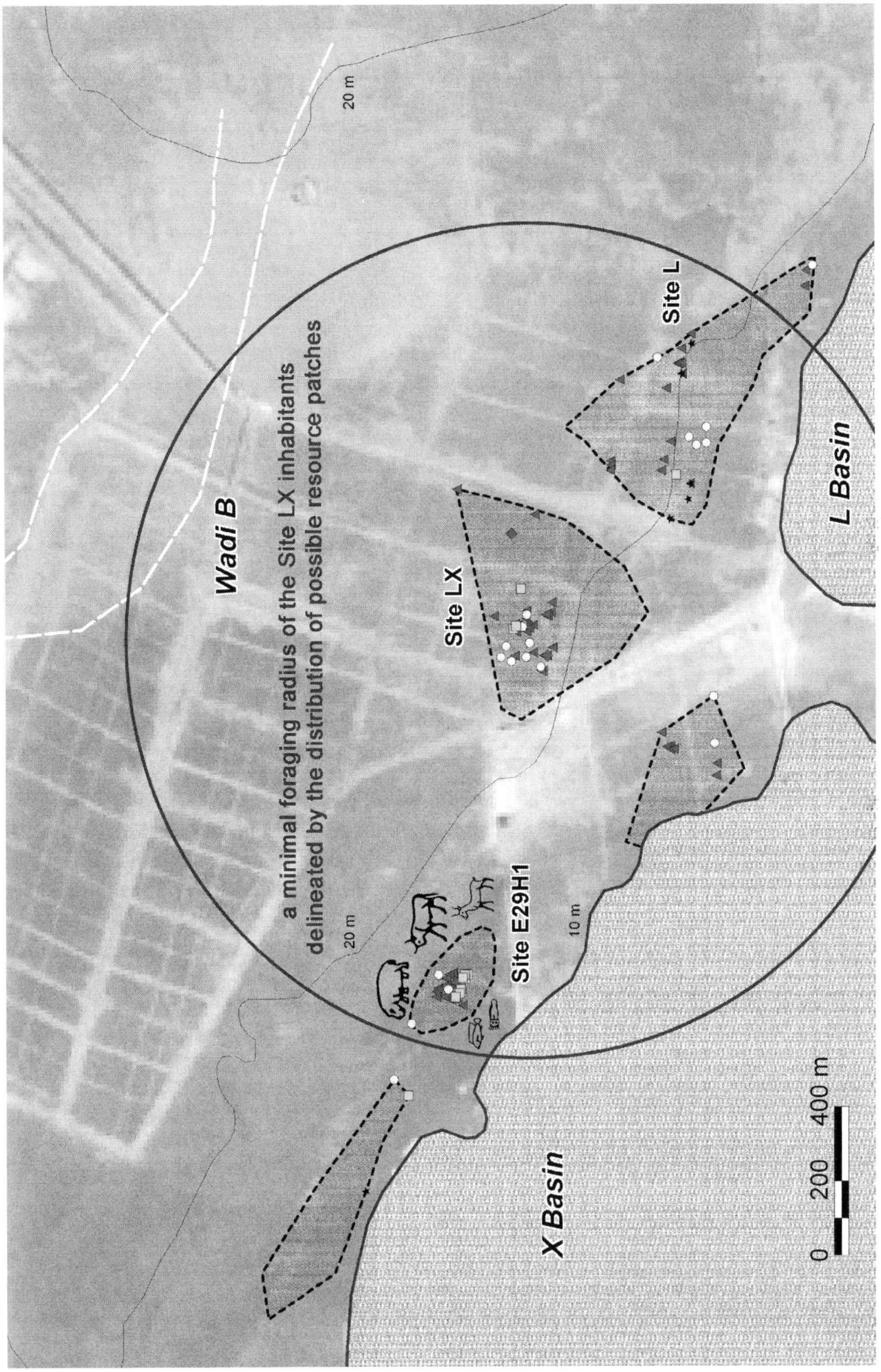

Fig.5.62. Palaeoenvironment of the L Basin - X Basin area

been unlikely.

Another habitation area to the north of the X Basin is interesting in terms of the natural environment. This habitation area named Site XA is where Wadi A drains into the X Basin, and it exhibits a different land use pattern from those around Site L and Site LX. Neolithic artefacts and other remains in this habitation area concentrate at elevations between 15 m asl and 20 m asl and overlie sparse Epipalaeolithic artefact scatters. Very few archaeological remains were encountered above the 20 m asl contour line. A vast mixed scatter of Epipalaeolithic and Neolithic artefacts is seen around the abuttal of Wadi A and the X Basin at elevations between 10 m asl and 15 m asl, and such a scatter may probably be caused by the combination of alluvial and colluvial events.

Hearths and other occupational features at elevations between 15 m asl and 20 m asl are distributed on both sides of Wadi A, and it is assumed that they were related to subsistence activities along the wadi. Hearths and enigmatic stone structures as well as a supposedly tethering stone suggest that this area was a herders' camp. If this was really the case, it is probable that the wadi was used as a track by the herders to go northwards for pastures. The finds like bifacially-retouched arrowheads and spearheads suggest that this area was a hunting ground at other times. On the other hand, the presence of sickle blades and grinding stones suggests that plant harvesting was also one of the subsistence activities along this wadi. It can be presumed on the basis of elevation that the occupation of this locality and the harvest of either wild or domesticated plants took place in winter and spring, when the water of the X Basin lowered and the wadi bed became wet due to runoff water caused by rainfall. Hunting may also have been practised when wild game animals were attracted by water and plants in the wadi in winter and spring.

5.13. The palaeoenvironment of the X Basin-Z Basin area and the foraging radius of the Kom W inhabitants in the Neolithic

The field survey in the X Basin-Z Basin area (**Fig.5.63**) revealed that the scatters or concentrations of relatively large animal bones and their fragments on the present surface is particularly dense in a wide area around Kom W at elevations of 15-20 m asl, whereas few or no animal bones were encountered at elevations lower than 15 m asl and higher than 20 m asl. This suggests that the archaeological remains in the surroundings of Kom W may be regarded as having been well preserved, and that recurrent lacustrine sedimentation events at elevations of 15-20 m asl have played a significant role in the protection of fragile faunal remains.

Apart from a small surface concentration of animal bones at Site E29H1 in the X Basin, the surface scatters of animal bones are sporadic to absent in the other areas even at elevations of 15-20 m asl. This suggests that taphonomic processes have not been homogeneous between areas even at the same elevation. The area around Kom W at elevations of 15-20 m asl is wide and relatively flat with little surface relief, whereas the area around other occupation loci like Site LX at elevations of 15-20 m asl is fairly narrow and is relatively steeply inclined. Such a difference in topography must have caused a different rate of lacustrine sedimentation in water margin environments, and have favourably affected the protection of archaeological remains in the flat area around Kom W.

It was also recognised through the survey that Kom W was quite strategically located. Although Kom W is approximately 600 m away from the Z Basin shore to the southwest, the vast flat area between Kom W and the Z Basin shore would have been inundated in summer, as suggested by large lacustrine bivalves embedded in the silty sediments of the Site V Depression and Camp II Depression, and the wadable area of seasonally rising water could have been good fishing grounds from summer to autumn. It is probable that part of this vast flat area contained water in

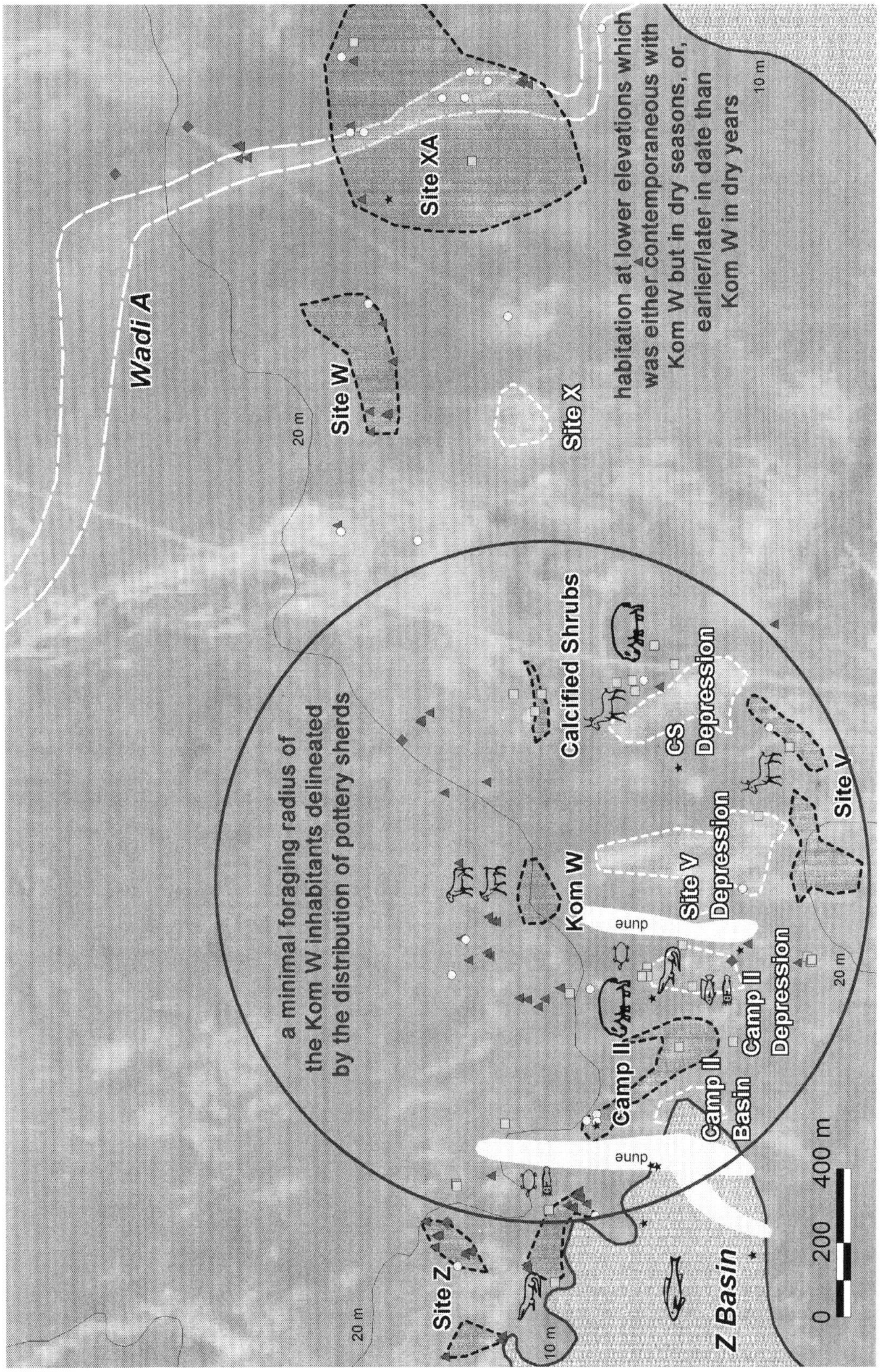

Fig.5.63. Palaeoenvironment of the X Basin - Z Basin area

residual pools for some length of time even after the seasonal high water receded from the flat area in autumn, and that some residual pools persisted until the next high water season. The residual pools must have given extra opportunities of catching fish trapped there. Even when the seasonal high water completely receded, given the depth of the Camp II Basin and the Z Basin, it is probable that these Basins contained a large body of water throughout the year and provided the Kom W inhabitants with drinking water and the opportunities for sedge/reed harvesting, fishing, shellfish collecting, fowling, and crocodile/hippopotamus hunting from winter to spring.

As evidenced by concentrations of calcified plant roots, the margins of seasonally rising basin water near Kom W must have been fringed with sedges and shrubs. These must have provided shade and shelter to wildlife as well as humans, and must have provided the Kom W inhabitants with not only edible rhizomes and seeds but also timbers and fibres for building and craft working, and fuels for warming, cooking and pottery firing. Also as suggested by the surface finds of the bones of hartebeest and hippopotamus, this flat area would have become grassland from autumn to spring, and large sedentary herbivores would have wandered and have been hunted there, though it is probable that some other mammals were wary of human presence and hence did not come close to the human habitat. Part of this vast flat area may have been used for farming, as speculated by Caton-Thompson (Caton-Thompson and Gardner 1934: 75). As suggested earlier, however, there is another area which may possibly have become moist due to winter rainfall and may have been used for farming to the northeast of Kom W. Considering the presence of wild and domesticated animals, special care to prevent them from eating crops before harvest must have been necessary, and it is no wonder if a farming plot was located far from the Z Basin shore where voracious hippopotamus inhabited.

In short, apart from rock materials for making various tools, vital natural resources like drinking water and fuels, as well as wild food resources which are aggregated seasonally and are renewed yearly, seem to have been almost constantly available within easy walking distance of Kom W. As has been argued regarding the reason for the choice of site location in the Nile Valley in the Late Palaeolithic (Van Neer *et al.* 2000: 282), the location of residence at Kom W may also have been chosen not only because it was just above the seasonally highest water level but because it was close to a large area which had been inundated but wadable. Given these conditions, it is considered that Kom W was certainly a residential base which may have been occupied for most of the year, and that the daily foraging of the Kom W inhabitants was in a radial pattern, though with little interest in the barren flat area to the north of Kom W.

Moreover, it may be possible to delineate more clearly the mobility range of pottery-using people in the Kom W area by focusing on the spatial distribution of Neolithic pottery sherd scatters on the surface, because the scatter of pottery sherds is the densest and widest at Kom W and its immediate vicinity, and tends to be sparse and small in the periphery of the Kom W area. A field observation that scatters of Neolithic pottery sherds continually spread westwards from Kom W to the northeastern shore of the Z Basin, which is 800 m away from Kom W, but no more pottery sherds are seen from there to the western end of the survey area, which is 3.5 km far away from Kom W, suggests that the vanishing point of pottery sherds on the northeastern shore of the Z Basin was the western end of the mobility range of pottery-using people in the Kom W area. Likewise, another field observation that scatters of Neolithic pottery sherds continually spread southwards and show some high density concentrations on the Site V Ridge but become rare to absent in the south of the Site V Ridge, which is approximately 800 m to the south of Kom W, suggests that this vanishing point was the southern end of the mobility range of pottery-using people in the Kom W area. Moreover, the Neolithic pottery sherd scatter does not continuously spread far to the east of Locality 'Calcified Shrubs', whose eastern end is approximately 500 m away from Kom W, but the next remarkable concentration of pottery sherds is seen at Site X, which is approximately 1 km far from Kom W, whereas further scatters of pottery sherds are seen at Site XA, which is approximately 2 km far away from Kom W.

In terms of the economic zonation of foragers/collectors described in Chapter 4, a 800 m radius from Kom W delineated by the spatial distribution of Neolithic pottery sherd scatters may be considered as a play radius and a minimal foraging radius of the Kom W inhabitants. However, since the contemporaneity of localities/sites within this radius is not certain, it is difficult to assume that Kom W has always been the sole residential base or the central place within this radius and that all other localities/ sites within this radius were left by people coming from Kom W. The spatial distribution of Neolithic pottery sherd scatters may simply suggest that this entire area have been permanently inhabited by Neolithic people and Kom W became an outstanding residential base at a certain time.

In order to substantiate the assumption about the foraging radius of the Kom W inhabitants and to answer the question as to whether this foraging radius expanded farther, it is necessary to find other possible residential bases and to elucidate whether the other possible residential bases were used by the people who moved from Kom W sequentially or by another group of people simultaneously. If the former was the case under conditions of low population density and high density distribution of resource patches, then the mobility pattern could have been either a half-radius continuous pattern, in which the residential base was continuously moved to the outer perimeter of the foraging radius previously covered with no development of logistical zones, or a complete-radius leapfrog pattern in which the residential base was moved to a distant place but the logistical zones of each residential base partially overlapped. If the latter was the case under conditions of high population density, it means that the foraging range of the Kom W inhabitants was determined and constrained by the presence of the foraging radius of another group of people, even though there was some overlap at the peripheries of the two foraging radii, and the necessary resources which were not obtained within the foraging radius of Kom W could be procured through logistical trips. Numerous stone tools made on raw materials which are not available within easy walking distance of Kom W indicate that the raw materials have been transported from distant sources either through logistical trips by task parties sent from Kom W or through residential moves by a group of people who went to and came back from the source area cyclically. This topic will be dealt with in Chapter 7.

Other possible residential bases which are comparable to Kom W in terms of the spatial scale of locality and the diversity and density of artefacts and structural remains are Site LX and Kom K. According to the radiocarbon dates, the contemporaneity of Kom W and Kom K is obvious, whereas Site LX is older in date. Given the 8 km distance between Kom W and Kom K, it may be possible that the Kom W inhabitants routinely moved to Kom K in a half-radius continuous pattern. However, considering the similar water margin environment at almost the same elevation of Kom W and Kom K and the supposedly similar seasonally-fluctuating availability of food resources in their surroundings which is naturally subject to the transgression and regression of lake water, it does not seem to have been beneficial for the Kom W inhabitants to move to Kom K on a seasonal basis after the seasonally-available resources around Kom W were depleted. Even when residential moves from Kom W on a seasonal basis had taken place, the moves should have been oriented toward more profitable resource patches close to receding water margins at elevations lower than that of Kom W. On this basis, it is reasonable and likely that the inhabitants of Kom W moved their residential base to the Site V Ridge to the south of Kom W or Site XA to the east of Kom W. The lack of grinding stones and hearths on the Site V Ridge is a weak point for arguing that Site V was a residential base, and some sunken pottery vessels found *in situ* on the Site V Ridge by Caton-

Thompson (Caton-Thompson and Gardner 1934: 75-76) are also not good evidence to support such an argument. Site XA is a more likely location to which the Kom W inhabitants moved after the seasonal high water receded.

It is tentatively concluded that in the second half of the Fayum Neolithic in the middle 5th millennium cal.BC, at least two distinct groups of people simultaneously occupied Kom W and Kom K respectively. It is assumed that Kom W and Kom K had their own foraging radius, with some possible overlap at the peripheries of the two foraging radii. This means that each foraging radius was around 4-5 km. It is also assumed that Kom W and Kom K developed their own logistical zones by using Wadi A and Wadi B respectively.

5.14. The distribution and nature of Epipalaeolithic and Neolithic localities in Wadi A and Wadi B in the Gindi Plain

A survey in the previously uninvestigated wadis in the Gindi Plain revealed that there were certainly Epipalaeolithic and Neolithic human activities in the wadis, and that the mobility range of the Epipalaeolithic and Neolithic people was not limited to the basin shores but was widely extended far away from the lake. The most unexpected thing is the discovery of a remarkable concentration of Epipalaeolithic artefacts at a particular spot in Wadi B. It was revealed by previous research that Epipalaeolithic people were heavily dependent on aquatic resources on the basin shores. Furthermore, it has also been suggested that most Fayum Epipalaeolithic localities might reflect seasonal fishing occupations, and that a very different economic emphasis might possibly be indicated for the same group when they utilised a different microenvironmental situation or in the base camps wherever they were located (Wendorf and Schild 1976: 317). However, this suggestion has never been substantiated. Several isolated Epipalaeolithic finds along Wadi B indicate that Epipalaeolithic people passed through the wadi while making and using flint tools, but a concentration of lithic debitage products at a particular spot on the wadi bank very far to the north of the lake suggests that Epipalaeolithic foragers visited such a distant place and stayed there for a while, perhaps overnight. These findings require a reconsideration of the subsistence and mobility strategies of the Fayum Epipalaeolithic people. These topics will be discussed in more detail in Chapter 6.

As for the Neolithic finds, although there were no clear concentrations of artefacts, sparse scatters of artefacts are not surprising. Neolithic people started to use sandstone blocks and slabs which were not available in their habitat on the basin shores but were available in the gravelly and rocky terrains of the Fayum Depression. Hence there is little doubt that they have visited these terrains. Furthermore, Neolithic people introduced wheat/barley farming and sheep/goat herding, which must have required them to organise pasturing trips in wider areas beyond the basin shore habitat, in order to feed sheep and goats, and more importantly, to keep them away from farming plots while crops were growing. The interpretation of the Neolithic localities or artefact scatters found along these large wadis must be a clue to understand the mobility of Neolithic people. However, the mobility type and mobility frequency of the Neolithic people are still not clear from the spatial distribution of finds. Given that the sources of flint for Neolithic tools could not be located by this survey, the mobility range of the Neolithic people must be far beyond the northern and northeastern ridges of the Fayum Depression. This topic will be discussed in more detail in Chapter 7.

6. Lithic technological organisation and mobility in the Fayum Epipalaeolithic

6.1. Introduction

The Fayum Epipalaeolithic culture is the predecessor of the Fayum Neolithic culture that adopted wheat/barley farming and sheep/goat herding for the first time in the history of Egypt. Previous studies by different research teams have provided information about the site location, material culture, subsistence activities, and burial custom of the Fayum Epipalaeolithic. However, its lithic assemblage has been poorly published. In addition, although great attention has been paid to the description of tools, such a description has not very much served to explain the actual tool making/using activities of Fayum Epipalaeolithic people. Such a descriptive approach has merely regarded lithic technological changes at the transition from the Fayum Epipalaeolithic to Neolithic as the evidence of population replacement (Wendorf and Schild 1976: 317*ff*; Wenke *et al.* 1988: 38), rather than as an indication of adaptation or optimisation in technology in response to changing environments and subsistence needs.

Reconstructing the whole sequence of lithic reduction in terms of purely technical aspects and understanding how this reduction sequence is closely associated with the general subsistence and mobility strategies of prehistoric and ethnographic foragers have been popular as the studies of lithic technological organisation since the late 1970s (Binford 1979; Odell 2001: 62-69). This kind of approach is relevant to know to what extent the tool making/using activities of Fayum Epipalaeolithic people were affected by the mobility or sedentariness of the people and how people adapted their lithic technological organisation to their needs in subsistence activities.

This study aims to reconsider the Fayum Epipalaeolithic culture in terms of its mobility and subsistence strategies through focusing on lithic artefacts collected at several localities/sites, which were visited and studied during the survey. Therefore, a particular consideration is given to the possible sources of lithic raw materials used. The lithic sourcing study may reveal where in the Fayum the lithic raw materials derived from, and this could be direct evidence for the mobility range of the Epipalaeolithic people. If the people had usually exploited non-local lithic raw materials, it would be possible to assume that they left the Fayum and migrated seasonally to other places or often took hunting trips to distant places, and that their lithic raw material procurement was embedded in seasonal migrations or hunting trips. It has been asserted that the preferred lithic raw materials utilised at Fayum Epipalaeolithic sites were small, rounded pebbles from the Oligocene conglomerate of the Gebel Qatrani Formation, which is extensively exposed on the plateau above Qasr el-Sagha (Wendorf and Schild 1976: 311), but it has not been explained how this source was identified and specified so surely. It would be worth considering other possible sources, and such possibilities would give further clues to the mobility and subsistence of Fayum Epipalaeolithic people. Another consideration is given to the sequence from the raw material procurement and the manufacture and use of tools to the discard of debitage products and worn/broken tools. The study of debitage products may reveal where in the Fayum core reduction started and continued, and this is an important clue to speculate on the function and occupation duration of the localities/sites in the Fayum Epipalaeolithic.

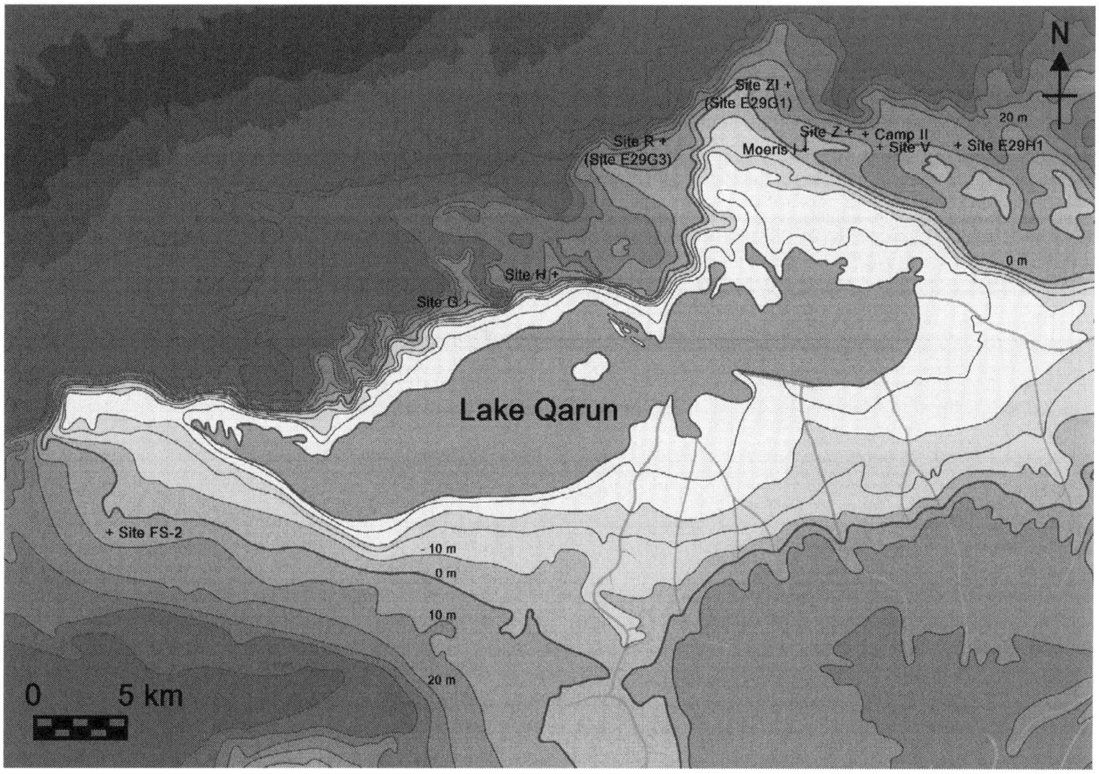

Fig.6.1. Map of Epipalaeolithic sites

6.2. The locations and features of Fayum Epipalaeolithic localities/sites

In the Fayum, whereas only one Epipalaeolithic site named Site FS-2 is known on the southwest side of the lake, a considerable number of Epipalaeolithic lithic artefacts have been found on the north side of the lake at the following localities/sites (**Fig.6.1**).

1) Combined Prehistoric Expedition's Site E29H1 (Caton-Thompson's unnamed site) in the northeast of the X Basin (Wendorf and Schild 1976: 182-199)
2) Caton-Thompson's Camp II in the east of the Z Basin (Caton-Thompson and Gardner 1934: 76-77)
3) Caton-Thompson's Site V (identical to Seton-Karr's unnamed site and Brewer's Site 2) in the east of the Z Basin (Brewer 1989a; 1989b; Caton-Thompson and Gardner 1934: 75-76; Seton-Karr 1904: fig.1; 1905: plate I)
4) Caton-Thompson's Site Z (identical to Seton-Karr's unnamed site and Puglisi's Site S4) in the northeast of the Z Basin (Caton-Thompson and Gardner 1934: 77-78; Mussi *et al.* 1984; Puglisi 1967; Seton-Karr 1904: fig.1; 1905: plate I)
5) Caton-Thompson's Moeris I (identical to Puglisi's Site MOE) in the southwest of the Z Basin (Caton-Thompson and Gardner 1934: 67-68; Mussi *et al.* 1984; Puglisi 1967)
6) Caton-Thompson's Site ZI (identical to Seton-Karr's unnamed site, Puglisi's Site MB, and Combined Prehistoric Expedition's Site E29G1) in Moeris Bay (Caton-Thompson and Gardner 1934: 79-80; Mussi *et al.* 1984; Puglisi 1967; Seton-Karr 1904: fig.1; 1905: plate I; Wendorf and Schild 1976: 162-182)
7) Caton-Thompson's Site R (identical to Combined Prehistoric Expedition's Site E29G3) in the north of the N Basin (Caton-Thompson and Gardner 1934: 81-82; Wendorf and Schild 1976: 199-211)
8) Caton-Thompson's Site G and Site H to the west of Dimai (Caton-Thompson and Gardner

1934: 61*ff*).

In addition, there are some unnamed Epipalaeolithic sites around the L Basin and X Basin, but they were merely indicated on a map, and few descriptions of the sites and finds were published (Caton-Thompson and Gardner 1934: pl.CXIII).

In this study, Site Z, Camp II, and Site E29H1 were selected among the major eight Epipalaeolithic localities/sites on the north side of the lake as listed above, and the lithic artefacts on their surface were collected for a new study on how the procurement of lithic raw materials and the manufacture of tools were organised in relation to the mobility strategies of the people who resided there. Possible sources of raw materials were considered on the basis of the survey results. Furthermore, a previously-unknown locality in Wadi B gave a clue to know the mobility range of the people (**Fig.6.2**).

6.3. Previous studies of Fayum Epipalaeolithic lithic assemblages

The beginning of serious studies on the Fayum Epipalaeolithic lithic artefacts is dated back to the time of Caton-Thompson. Besides a variety of bifacially-retouched, formal Neolithic tools which were frequently found at higher elevations, she found concentrations of various backed bladelets at several surface sites at lower elevations. She recognised that those backed bladelets, which she named 'the Neolithic B group', were technologically and chronologically apart from the assemblages of various bifacially-retouched Neolithic tools which she named 'the Neolithic A group', but she could not say which tools other than various backed bladelets certainly belonged to the B group. Even though she assumed that these two groups were distinguished according to their vertical distribution pattern, she could not exclude the possibilities that stray tools of the A group had accidentally been included in the supposedly B group artefact scatters at lower elevations or that the distribution of the A group tools and B group tools had overlapped at some middle elevations. She should have checked her assumption about the grouping of tools according to elevation by finding more tools from *in situ* contexts elsewhere, but she had no other choice but to depend mostly on surface artefact scatters. Furthermore, she did not realise that the B group as represented by various backed bladelets was later in date than the A group, due to her incorrect correlation of the lake transgression and regression against the vertical distribution of artefacts (Caton-Thompson and Gardner 1934: 55-69).

Some more systematic collections and typological analyses of Epipalaeolithic lithic artefacts have been undertaken in the 1970s and 1980s by three different research teams at the sites where Caton-Thompson has visited and studied. The Combined Prehistoric Expedition led by Wendorf and Schild studied artefacts which were surface collected and excavated at Site E29H1, Site E29G1 and Site E29G3 (Wendorf and Schild 1976). The Sapienza University of Rome team led by Puglisi has studied artefacts which were surface collected at Site S4, Site MB, and Site MOE (Mussi *et al.* 1984). The University of Washington team led by Wenke has studied artefacts which were surface collected and excavated at Site FS-2 (Wenke *et al.* 1983; 1988). All of them have studied their collections in the same manner, which was actually the standard approach at that time, and as a consequence, they have the same problems in publishing their data.

The main objectives of their lithic studies were to understand the tool typology and frequency in the assemblages of individual sites in the Fayum, and to present to what extent the Fayum Epipalaeolithic tool assemblages were similar or dissimilar to each other and were different from contemporaneous tool assemblages in other parts of North Africa. For these objectives, they referred to the Tixier typology of Epipalaeolithic tools in the Maghreb (Tixier 1963), and presented the main typological indices in percentages with the actual number of tools and the cumulative graphs of tool type frequencies (Mussi *et al.* 1984: Fig.3 and Table 3; Wendorf and Schild 1976: Fig.210 and Table 17; Wenke *et al.* 1988: Fig.6). By using

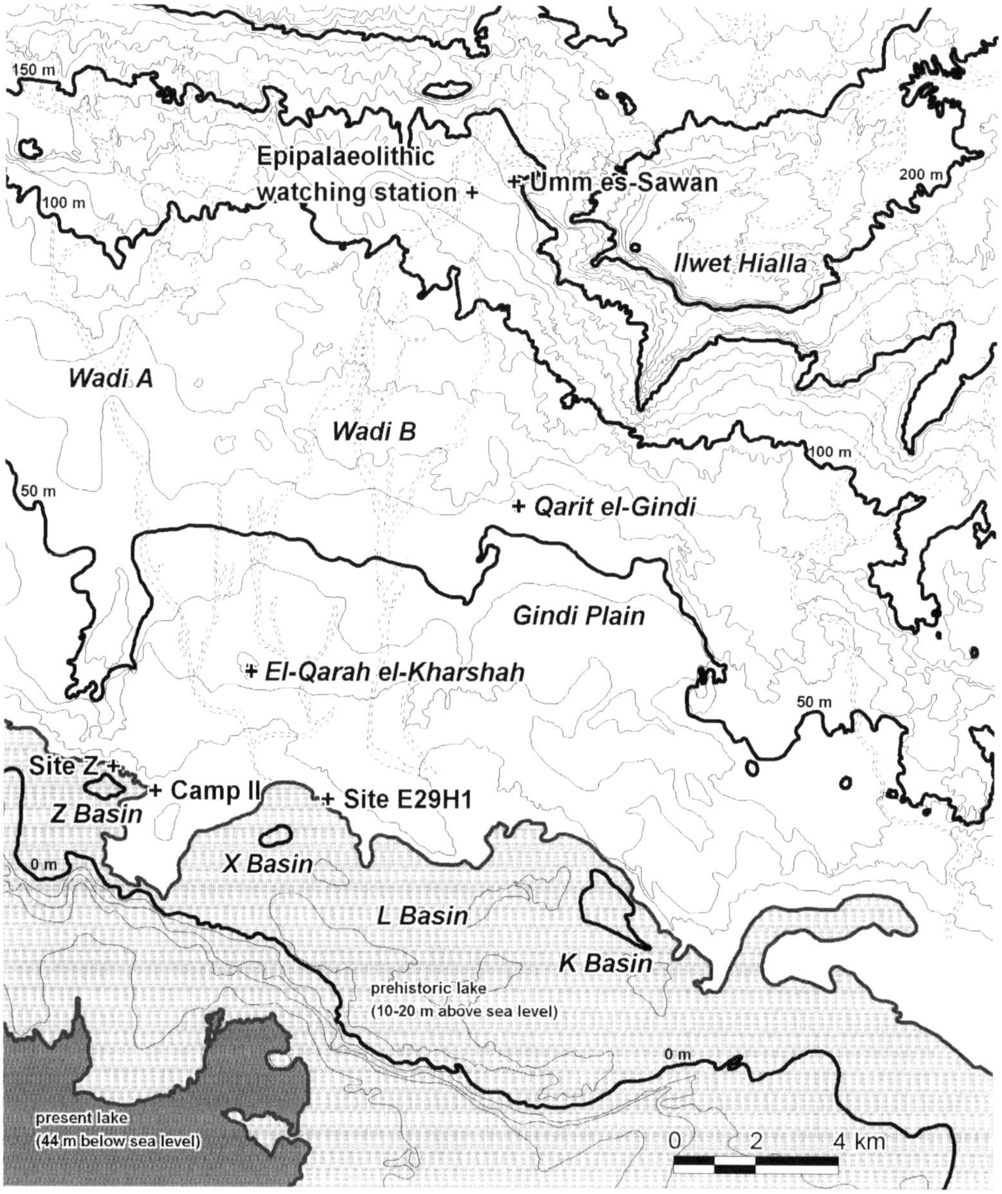

Fig.6.2. Map of Epipalaeolithic sites studied in this chapter

the cumulative graphs, they presented not only the comparison of the tool assemblages from different Fayum sites, but also the comparison of the Fayum tool assemblages with the Shamarkian tool assemblage in the Nile Valley of Lower Nubia (Schild *et al.* 1968) and the El-Ghorab Playa tool assemblage in the Western Desert of Egypt (Kobusiewicz 1984), and graphically showed the overall similarity between these assemblages. Although the cumulative graphs were not presented, the Fayum tool assemblages from Site S4, Site MB, and Site MOE were also compared with the Elkabian assemblage in the Nile Valley of Upper Egypt (Vermeersch 1978: 125-134), and the noticeable features like the rarity of microburins and the high frequency of backed bladelets in the Fayum were highlighted (Mussi *et al.* 1984: 190).

On the basis of these comparisons, it has been

argued that, in spite of the overall similarity, functional and stylistic differences in tools did exist between the Fayum sites. Although insufficiently published by the Combined Prehistoric Expedition, the lithic artefacts collected at Site E29G1, Site E29G3 and Site E29H1 are characterised by extremely high percentages of various backed bladelets, which account for more than 50 % of all tools (Wendorf and Schild 1976: 311). In contrast, the lithic artefacts collected at Site S4, Site MOE and Site MB are different from those found at Site E29G1, Site E29G3 and Site E29H1 in terms of the tool type frequency. It has been argued that the observed differences like the slightly lower frequency of backed bladelets and the relative abundance of scrapers, perforators, notches and denticulates at Site S4, Site MOE and Site MB might reflect a different chronological position or a different range of tool-using activities (Mussi *et al.* 1984: 189).

However, the argument has focused on subtle differences in the frequency of tool types, and such differences do not seem to reflect a significant difference in tool-using activities, especially if one considers the almost same environmental situation of the Fayum sites, which are very close to each other, as well as the presumably same range of available wild food resources. More importantly, Site S4, Site MOE and Site MB have been intensively surface collected by Seton-Karr and Caton-Thompson before Puglisi visited, and thus it is highly probable that Puglisi's collection is distorted. This probability has not been mentioned at all by the researchers who studied Puglisi's collection, but it is no wonder if nice-looking artefacts like backed bladelets and projectile points had already been taken away, and Puglisi collected what had been ignored and left by previous visitors. Therefore, it must be said that the argument on a different range of tool-using activities has no sound ground. It is likely that the lithic artefacts collected at Site E29G1, Site E29G3 and Site E29H1 represent intact Fayum Epipalaeolithic lithic assemblages, and it is possible that the frequency of tool types at Site S4, Site MOE and Site MB was previously the same as that at Site E29G1, Site E29G3 and Site E29H1.

On the other hand, the claimed similarity between the Fayum tool assemblage and the El-Ghorab Playa tool assemblage in the Egyptian Western Desert sounds fairly unreasonable, given the apparent difference in environmental situation, subsistence, and available lithic raw materials between these two regions. El-Ghorab Playa was a rain-fed shallow lake with no fish, and the major subsistence activity around the ephemeral lake is considered to be hunting of dorcas gazelle and hare. Lithic raw materials used there are local chert and petrified wood as well as flint brought from sources which are some 100 km away (Kobusiewicz 1984: 145 and 159). El-Ghorab Playa is not comparable to the Fayum, in which the major subsistence activity was fishing around the shores of a permanent lake fed by the Nile and the major lithic raw material was locally-available flint.

It must be noted that the account of tool type frequencies based on the Tixier typology and the resultant cumulative graphs are subject to variability in sampling and typological identification. In addition, as long as one is dependent on the Tixier typology, a number of unique local tools which do not exist in the Tixier type list tend to be underestimated, though they are classified as *varia*. As a consequence, comparisons based on the Tixier typology can only say whether tool assemblages under consideration are relatively more similar or less similar to each other, and the uniqueness beyond such similarity is hardly revealed. Furthermore, the Tixier typology conflates both functional and stylistic variability, and hence it is not easy to say on the whole whether similarity in tool assemblages reflects style or function.

Despite the similar high frequency of backed bladelets in general, a difference has been recognised in the type frequency of backed bladelets between the tool collection by Wendorf and Schild and the tool collection by Puglisi. Straight-backed and pointed bladelets (Tixier's Type 45), arch-ended bladelets (Tixier's Type 55) and arch-backed bladelets (Tixier's Type 56) predominate in both collections, but straight-backed and pointed bladelets with truncated base (Tixier's Type 47) are numerous in Puglisi's collection but are poor in Wendorf and Schild's collection. Accordingly, it is assumed that stylistic differences in tools may have existed within the Fayum Epipalaeolithic, and that such subtle differences may possibly represent different chronological positions (Mussi *et al.* 1984: 189). However, the chronological aspect of different backed bladelet types is not clear in the Tixier typology. Therefore, this assumption has to be substantiated not only by the discoveries of well-preserved and well-dated tool assemblages at more localities/sites in the Fayum but also by further comparisons with well-dated tool assemblages found outside the Fayum. New data on almost contemporaneous Epipalaeolithic tool assemblages in other parts of Egypt like Siwa Oasis (Hassan and Gross 1987), Kharga Oasis (McDonald 2003; Simmons and Mandel 1986; Wendorf and Schild 1980), Dakhleh Oasis (McDonald 1991b; 2003) and the Nabta-Kiseiba region (Wendorf and Schild 2001; Wendorf *et al.* 1984) were published after the above-mentioned studies on the Fayum Epipalaeolithic tool assemblages, and some syntheses of these assemblages are presently available (*e.g.*, Kobusiewicz 1996; Vermeersch 1992). They provide good comparable examples with the Fayum tools.

Another problem in the studies of the Fayum Epipalaeolithic lithic assemblages in the 1970s and 1980s is that cores and debitage products were neglected. The researchers seem to have collected not only tools but also other artefacts, and briefly mentioned how the predominant cores looked like, and published some drawings of the cores (Mussi *et al.* 1984: 185; Wendorf and Schild 1976: 311 and Figs.206-208). However, no quantitative data on cores have been presented, and there has been no mention of debitage products at all. My visit to the Wendorf collection presently housed in the British Museum in London and the study of documents in the collection revealed that the cores and debitage products collected at Site E29G1, Site E29G3 and Site E29H1 by the Combined Prehistoric Expedition had actually been studied quite thoroughly in the 1970s and quantitative data exist, but these data have not been published for some unknown reason. As a result, little has been known about raw material economy, knapping techniques, and reduction sequences.

In short, the present knowledge of Fayum Epipalaeolithic lithic assemblages is more or less biased and distorted because of 1) the possible inclusion of artefacts from later periods into purely Epipalaeolithic assemblages 2) the study of already-plundered assemblages, 3) the misleading presentation of tool type frequencies in percentages and cumulative graphs, and 4) the insufficient publication of data on the entire lithic assemblages including cores and debitage products. In the following study, more emphasis is placed on the description of cores and debitage products and the reconstruction of reduction sequences. As for formal tools, the Tixier typology is always referred to, in order to describe the tools, but the tool type frequencies are not presented, due to the general paucity of tools in the studied assemblages and my insufficient ability to identify tool types. Some tools in the assemblages studied may or may not have been overlooked and included in the category of debitage products.

6.4. Epipalaeolithic lithic assemblages on the northern shore of the Z Basin

6.4.1. Introduction

Site Z is located on the northern slope of the Z Basin. The entire site was already surveyed by Caton-Thompson in the 1920s, and surface scatters of the A and B group lithic artefacts have been reported in the area between 6 m asl and 18 m asl (Caton-Thompson and Gardner 1934: 59-60, 77-78 and pl.CX). While the lower elevation of the northern slope of the Z Basin is covered by fine-grained aeolian sand, the higher ridges, which are supposed to be old beaches, are covered by pale limestone fragments and fossil shells. The width of artefact scatters reported at Site Z by Caton-Thompson was approximately 700 m. It is probable that Puglisi's

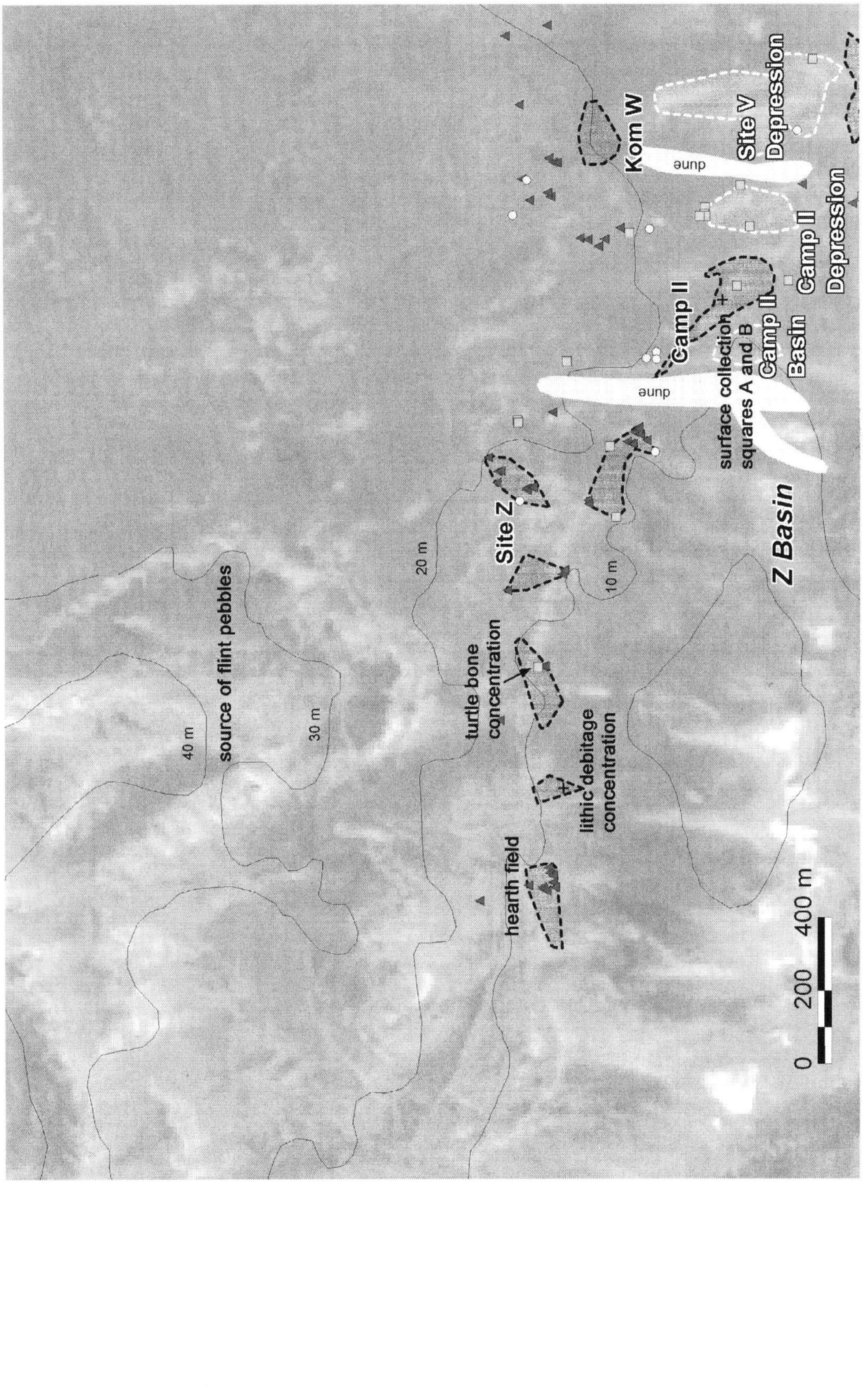

Fig.6.3. Map of Site Z and Camp II

Site S4 was located around the easternmost part of Site Z and is beyond the old beaches at higher elevations. According to my field observation, artefact scatters on the northern slope of the Z Basin at lower elevations are spread over the entire stretch of approximately 1300 m wide, but are disrupted by strips of fine-grained aeolian sand or colluvial deposits of limestone fragments and fossil shells extending north-south at several locations. Concentrations of sandstone and fossil shell-bearing limestone cobbles which seemed to be hearths, and concentrations of bone fragments, are observed on the slope surface in the areas which are not disturbed and obscured by natural features mentioned above. The majority of the finds on the deflated slope surface are Epipalaeolithic lithic artefacts. Apparently Neolithic artefacts were very rarely found. In the following, noteworthy archaeological remains found in Site Z are called localities (**Fig.6.3**).

6.4.2. A concentration of turtle bones

One locality of Site Z was chosen for surface artefact collection. This locality (N29.59044° E30.77747°) is located in the eastern half of Site Z and on the gentle slope of approximately 13-15 m asl. It is marked by a concentration of turtle bones surrounded by sandstone and fossil shell-bearing limestone cobbles in a circle (**Fig.6.4**). It is probable that these archaeological remains have been protected beneath lacustrine sediments, and were recently exposed on the surface by wind erosion. A 5 m x 5 m square was set up to contain this concentration, and 153 pieces of lithic artefacts were surface collected and studied (**Table 6.1**).

6.4.2.1. Lithic raw materials

The most popular raw material for Epipalaeolithic tools at this locality is subangular or rounded, globular or irregularly-shaped flint pebble of various colours from light to dark brown. The surface of the pebble is smooth and well polished. Another raw material is light brown flint cobble of unknown original shape. They do not naturally occur in this basin environment, and hence must have been transported from elsewhere.

Fig.6.4. A concentration of turtle bones in Site Z (looking south)

	n
single platform core	14
opposed platform core	1
multiple platform core	7
discoidal core	1
primary chunk	2
chip/chunk	13
primary flake	10
flake from single platform core	40
flake from opposed platform core	5
flakes from ninety-degree core	6
flake from multiple platform core	7
flake from discoidal core	1
unidentifiable flake	15
primary blade/bladelet	3
blade/bladelet from single platform core	5
blade/bladelet from opposed platform core	3
blade/bladelet from multiple platform core	1
blade/bladelet	11
notch	1
denticulate	2
endscraper	2
sidescraper	2
winged and tanged projectile point	1
total	153

Table.6.1. Inventory of finds at Site Z turtle bone concentration

	n	%
single platform core	14	60.87
opposed platform core	1	4.35
multiple platform core	7	30.43
discoidal core	1	4.35
total	23	100.00

Table.6.2. Cores at Site Z turtle bone concentration

	n	mean (cm)	st.dev
length	22	1.87	0.68
width	22	2.71	0.74
thickness	22	2.43	1.29

Table.6.3. Metrical data of measured cores on pebbles at Site Z turtle bone concentration

6.4.2.2. Cores

Cores are not numerous in the collection (**Table 6.2**), and they are small (**Table 6.3**). There are 14 single platform cores, followed by seven multiple platform cores. There are only one opposed platform core and one discoidal core. Only one multiple platform core is made on a fragment of large cobble, and the rest are made on pebbles of various shapes.

6.4.2.3. Debitage products

Although the sample size is small, debitage products are dominated by flakes rather than blades/bladelets (**Table 6.4**). They are small (**Table 6.5**), as already suggested by cores.

6.4.2.4. Tools

Tools are not numerous, and they are all made on flakes. One small unifacially-retouched projectile point with barbs and broken tang is noted. It resembles those which have been found numerously at other sites in the Fayum like Site N, Site V, and Camp II but have remained undated (Caton-Thompson and Gardner 1934: 75-77, 84-85, and pl.LI).

	n	%
primary chunk	2	1.80
chip/chunk	13	11.71
primary flake	10	9.01
flake from single platform core	40	36.04
flake from opposed platform core	5	4.50
flakes from ninety-degree core	6	5.41
flake from multiple platform core	7	6.31
flake from discoidal core	1	0.90
unidentifiable flake	15	13.51
primary blade/bladelet	3	2.70
blade/bladelet from single platform core	5	4.50
blade/bladelet from opposed platform core	3	2.70
blade/bladelet from multiple platform core	1	0.90
total	111	100.00

Table.6.4. Debitage products at Site Z turtle bone concentration

	n	mean (cm)	st.dev
length	68	2.02	0.92
width	68	1.80	0.81
thickness	68	0.50	0.30

Table.6.5. Metrical data of measured debitage products at Site Z turtle bone concentration

6.4.3. A gentle slope next to the turtle bone concentration

Since the size of sample from around the turtle bone concentration is small, a 5 m x 25 m square was set up longitudinally along the north-south axis 10 m to the east of the 5 m x 5 m square, in order to cover the slope of the northern shore of the Z Basin which gently rises northwards. 960 pieces of lithic artefacts were surface collected in the 5 m x 25 m square and studied (**Table 6.6**).

6.4.3.1. Lithic raw materials

The most popular raw material for Epipalaeolithic tools at this locality is subangular or rounded, globular or irregularly-shaped flint pebbles of various colours from light to dark brown. The surface of the pebbles is quite smooth and well polished. Another raw material is globular flint cobble of various colours from light to dark brown. The cortical surface of

	n
single platform core	18
opposed platform core	4
multiple platform core	11
discoidal core	2
primary chunk	15
chip/chunk	66
primary flake	73
flake from single platform core	341
flake from opposed platform core	33
flakes from ninety-degree core	33
flake from multiple platform core	29
unidentifiable flake	99
primary blade/bladelet	25
blade/bladelet from single platform core	51
blade/bladelet from opposed platform core	5
blade/bladelet from ninety-degree core	5
blade/bladelet from multiple platform core	1
blade/bladelet	116
backed bladelet	14
double-backed bladelet	1
notch	3
denticulate	3
endscraper	2
sidescraper	6
leaf-shaped projectile point	1
winged and tanged projectile point	1
Neolithic knife blade	2
total	960

Table.6.6. Inventory of finds at the Site Z slope

	n	%
single platform core	18	51.43
opposed platform core	4	11.43
multiple platform core	11	31.43
discoidal core	2	5.71
total	35	100.00

Table.6.7. Cores at the Site Z slope

	n	mean (cm)	st.dev
length	7	2.41	0.86
width	7	3.11	0.81
thickness	7	2.69	0.64

Table.6.8. Metrical data of measured cores on pebbles at the Site Z slope

	n	mean (cm)	st.dev
length	19	1.69	0.70
width	19	2.35	0.32
thickness	19	1.67	0.59

Table.6.9. Metrical data of measured cores on conical or hemispherical chunks of pebbles at the Site Z slope

	n	mean (cm)	st.dev
length	6	2.43	0.83
width	6	2.72	0.82
thickness	6	1.77	0.70

Table.6.10. Metrical data of measured cores on fragments of cobbles at the Site Z slope

cobble is commonly weathered and exhibits a dark brown colour. A further variety of raw material is translucent brown chert of uncertain original shape. All of them do not naturally occur in this basin environment, and hence must have been transported from elsewhere.

6.4.3.2. Cores

Cores are not numerous in the collection (**Table 6.7**). Cores can be divided into three different categories based on their original shape. The first is made on pebbles of various shapes (**Table 6.8**). The second is made on conical or hemispherical chunks with almost 100 % cortex, which derived from elongated or globular pebbles, and the ventral face of the chunks were flaked (**Table 6.9**). The third is made on fragments of cobbles (**Table 6.10**). There are 18 single platform cores, which make up more than a half of all. Except for one single platform core made on an angular fragment of a weathered cobble, the rest are made on pebbles of various shapes (**Fig.6.5**-1) and conical or hemispherical chunks which derived from pebbles. All of these single platform cores are for flake or microbladelet production. There are four opposed cores made on pebbles and chunks. There are 11 multiple platform cores, five of which are made on fragments of cobbles and the rest are made on chunks and pebbles.

	n	%
primary chunk	15	1.93
chip/chunk	66	8.51
primary flake	73	9.41
flake from single platform core	341	43.94
flake from opposed platform core	33	4.25
flakes from ninety-degree core	33	4.25
flake from multiple platform core	29	3.74
unidentifiable flake	99	12.76
primary blade/bladelet	25	3.22
blade/bladelet from single platform core	51	6.57
blade/bladelet from opposed platform core	5	0.64
blade/bladelet from ninety-degree core	5	0.64
blade/bladelet from multiple platform core	1	0.13
total	776	100.00

Table.6.11. Debitage products at the Site Z slope

	n	mean (cm)	st.dev
length	466	1.74	0.67
width	466	1.51	0.61
thickness	466	0.41	0.24

Table.6.12. Metrical data of measured debitage products at the Site Z slope

6.4.3.3. Debitage products

As already suggested by the presence of flake cores, debitage products are dominated by flakes rather than blades/bladelets (**Table 6.11**), and they are quite small (**Table 6.12**). The most numerous kind of flakes are from single platform cores, and they amount to 341. There are 73 primary flakes, 33 flakes from opposed platform cores, another 33 flakes from ninety-degree cores, and 29 flakes from multiple platform cores. There are 99 unidentifiable flakes.

Blades/bladelets are not numerous. The most numerous kind of blades/bladelets are from single platform cores, and they amount to 51. Primary blades/bladelets are 25. There are only five blades/bladelets from opposed platform cores, another five blades/bladelets from ninety-degree cores, and only one blade/bladelet from multiple platform core.

Other notable debitage products are primary chunks, and they amount to 15. Apparently such a chunk was obtained by striking one end of an elongated pebble.

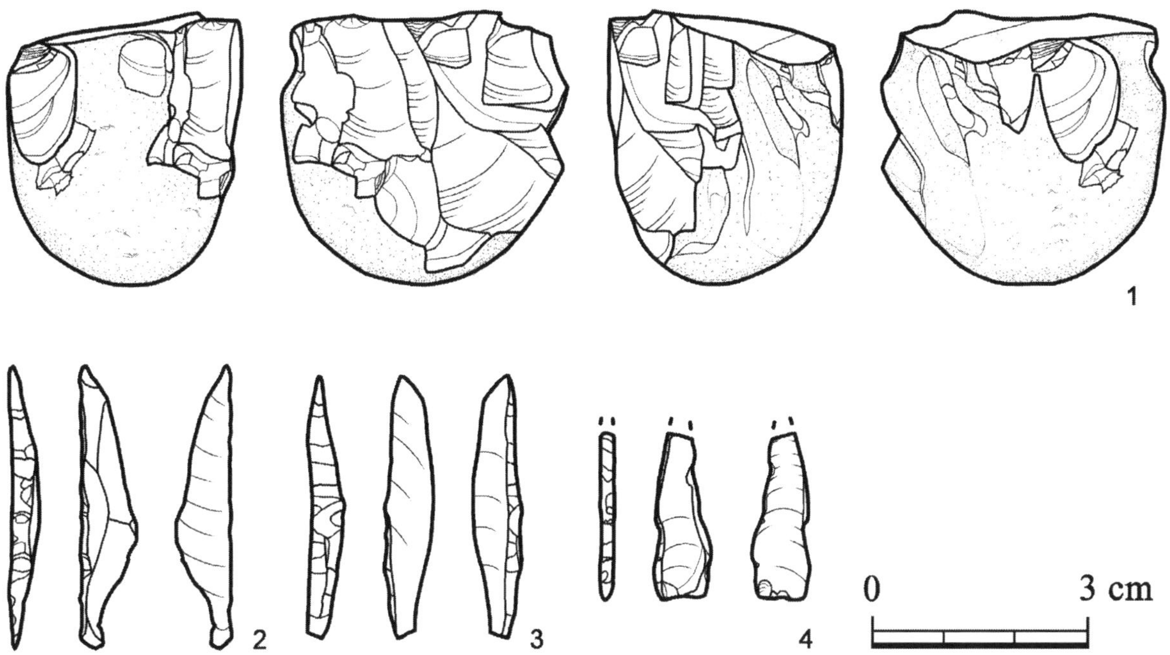

Fig.6.5. A core and tools collected at the Site Z slope

6.4.3.4. Lithic manufacture

There is no refitted specimen for discussing the tool manufacturing process, but the cores and debitage products suggest that toolmakers knapped flint pebbles in a slightly irregular manner according to the different shapes of pebbles. It appears that they tended to use fragments of pebbles or cobbles rather than whole pebbles, and that their major objective was to obtain non-cortical microbladelets and short flakes. Some bladelets from unknown cores were retouched and formed into backed bladelets.

Fig.6.6. Small bifacially-retouched projectile points collected at the Site Z slope

6.4.3.5. Tools

Blades/bladelets amount to 116, including many microbladelets of less than 2 cm long without additional retouch. Other notable tools are backed bladelets (**Fig.6.5**-2, 3 and 4), but their number is only 14. There is one broken double backed bladelet (Tixier's Type 16). It has been known that Epipalaeolithic tool assemblages of the Fayum were dominated by backed bladelets (Mussi *et al.* 1984: 189; Wendorf and Schild 1976: 311), and this seems to be the case with this locality. However, backed bladelets at this locality of Site Z are different from those at Site S4 and Site E29H1. The majority of backed bladelets at this locality are straight-backed ones with slightly convex cutting edge, which are identical to Tixier's Types 45-47. In general, they are approximately 3 cm long.

Other tool classes include three notches made on flakes, three denticulates made on flakes, one endscraper made on a half-split elongated pebble and another endscraper on a flake, and six sidescrapers made on flakes. They have parallels with those in other Epipalaeolithic assemblages of the Fayum and outside the Fayum published so far. However, notched or denticulated blades, perforators, and trapezes which have been abundantly reported in contemporaneous sites in Dakhleh Oasis, the Nabta-Kiseiba region and Elkab as well as Site S4 in the Fayum were not found at this locality of Site Z.

More formal tools include two small bifacially-retouched projectile points. One is leaf-shaped and thoroughly retouched on one face and laterally retouched on another face, and another is a tanged and barbed variety of projectile point (**Fig.6.6**). They are not rare in the Fayum though not securely dated. They are similar to not only those of the (bi)facial techno-complex of the Western Desert in the late 7th-early 6th millennia cal.BC but also those of the Levantine Pottery Neolithic. It is not surprising if such projectile points existed in the later half of the Fayum Epipalaeolithic.

6.4.3.6. Miscellaneous

Apart from the systematic surface collection, some remarkable tools were collected in close proximity to the surface collection square at the same elevation of the slope. One Ounan-Harif point (Close 1984: 276; Wendorf and Schild 1980: 110 and 259; Wendorf and Schild 1984: 304) and two Ounan points (Tixier's Type 107) were found on the surface (**Fig.6.7**). The Ounan-Harif point appears to be associated with a deflated circle of sandstone and limestone cobbles. These typical Epipalaeolithic projectile points of North Africa have been found at sites in Dakhleh Oasis (McDonald 1991b: Fig.6-nos.5 and 23), Kharga Oasis (Caton-Thompson 1952: pl.97-nos.9 and 16, pl.98-no.3, pl.99-no.1; McDonald 2003: Fig.8-a-h), the Nabta-Kiseiba region (Wendorf and Schild 1980: Fig.3.39-x, Fig.3.45-m-p, Fig.3.78-m and Fig.3.102-a) and Elkab (Vermeersch 1978: Fig.33-no.25), but the presence of these types of projectile points in

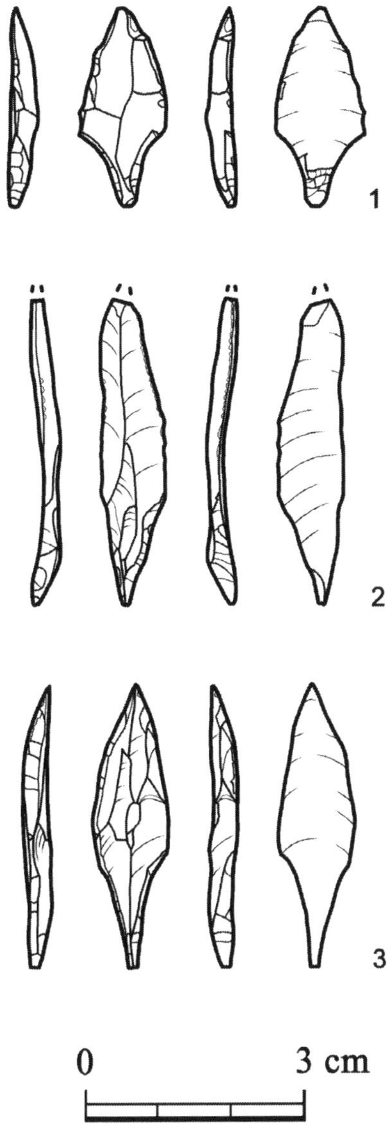

Fig.6.7. An Ounan-Harif point (1) and Ounan points (2 and 3) collected at the Site Z slope

the Fayum has not widely been recognised. The Ounan points have appeared in the collection made by Seton-Karr somewhere probably around Site V or Site Z in the Fayum in the 1900s without being designated these (Currelly 1913: pl.XXXVII), but later visitors to the Fayum have never reported such projectile points at the sites they studied, in spite of similar environmental settings. The online catalogue of Caton-Thompson's Fayum lithic collection which is presently housed in the Petrie Museum of Egyptian Archaeology in London exhibits at least two Ounan Points (UC3435 and UC3436) from Camp II Basin and one Ounan-Harif point (UC3788) from Site N, although she did not publish them. Therefore, new discoveries of these types of projectile points at this locality of Site Z reconfirm that the Fayum Epipalaeolithic has something in common with other Epipalaeolithic industries in Egypt, and that the Fayum Epipalaeolithic is not an isolated culture but is situated in a wider North African Epipalaeolithic context.

Moreover, the presence of the Ounan points in the localities/sites of the Fayum can be used as a chronological marker, because these peculiar projectile points have been dated to around 7500-6500 cal.BC, though some have persisted later than 6500 cal.BC (McDonald 2003; Riemer *et al.* 2004). This time span corresponds to that of the Fayum Epipalaeolithic, and hence this locality of Site Z, which yielded these projectile points, is also securely put within this time span. However, the later date of human occupation at this locality of Site Z suggested by the presence of the projectile points which are reminiscent of those of the Western Desert (bi)facial techno-complex and the Levantine Pottery Neolithic in the late 7th-early 6th millennia cal.BC may contradict the possible occupation span suggested by the presence of the Ounan points. Therefore, it may be assumed that the lithic assemblage obtained on the surface of this locality is the mixture of those from earlier date and later date. It follows that this locality has been visited repeatedly throughout the long span of the Epipalaeolithic period. Alternatively, it can also be assumed that this locality is dated to a transitional period when the Ounan points gradually disappeared and unifacially/bifacially-retouched, tanged or leaf-shaped projectile points appeared in the middle of the 7th millennium cal.BC. As far as the presently-available lithic collections are concerned, it seems that the Ounan points in the Fayum tend to co-occur with unifacially/bifacially-retouched, tanged or leaf-shaped projectile points and do not occur alone. Both Site N and Camp II in particular are known for the concentration of many unifacially/bifacially-retouched, tanged or leaf-shaped projectile points (Caton-Thompson and Gardner 1934: 76-77 and 84-85). This situation suggests that the co-occurrences are not necessarily accidental, and supports the latter assumption that the locality under consideration may perhaps be dated to the middle of the 7th millennium cal.BC.

6.4.4. A lithic debitage concentration

Another particular spot of Site Z was chosen for surface collection. This locality (N29.59021° E30.77433°) is an extremely high density concentration of lithic debitage products (**Fig.6.8**). It is located on the gentle slope at lower elevations of the basin shore near the westernmost part of Site Z. This lithic concentration is approximately 3 m in diameter, and it exhibits a strong contrast to the surrounding area, which is marked by very sparse scatters of lithic artefacts and several strips of colluvial deposits stretching north-south. In this concentration, debitage pieces sit loosely on coarse-grained sand and slightly consolidated silty sediments of the slope.

All debitage products and five unworked natural pebbles in this concentration, which amount to 762 in total, were collected (**Table 6.13**). A number of pieces could be refitted to an extent that the original shape of raw materials

	n
whole pebble	5
single platform core	71
opposed platform core	22
ninety-degree core	5
multiple platform core	6
discoidal core	3
core tablet	2
primary chunk	69
chip/chunk	15
primary flake	51
flake from single platform core	194
flake from opposed platform core	16
flake from ninety-degree core	23
flake from multiple platform core	3
unidentifiable flake	16
primary blade/bladelet	28
blade/bladelet from single platform core	128
blade/bladelet from opposed platform core	8
blade/bladelet from ninety-degree core	3
blade/bladelet	83
backed bladelet	11
total	762

Table.6.13. Inventory of finds at Site Z lithic debitage concentration

Fig.6.8. A lithic debitage concentration in Site Z (looking south)

was understood. Therefore, it is assumed that this was a lithic manufacturing spot, or a debitage dumping spot. However, it is not certain if the debitage products were dumped in a shallow pit dug in sand by toolmakers but the sand was later blown away and heavier debitage products in the deeper parts remained undisturbed and became exposed on the surface, because the spatial extent of the concentration seems to be too wide to be considered as a remnant of a pit for such a purpose.

6.4.4.1. Lithic raw materials

The majority of the raw materials at this locality are subangular or rounded, elongated or tabular, or irregularly-shaped flint pebbles of various colours from light to dark brown. The surface of the pebbles is generally smooth and well polished. These peculiar kinds of flint pebbles do not naturally occur on the surface of this basin environment, but a survey in the vicinity revealed that such flint pebbles were abundantly scattered on escarpments at elevations of more than 30 m asl, which were approximately 1 km to the north of this locality (**Fig.6.9**). These escarpments have been visited by Caton-Thompson, and she found nothing other than thin gravel carpet with some Levallois flakes and a large bifacial arrowhead possibly not of the Neolithic (Caton-Thompson and Gardner 1934: 78). But these gravelly escarpments seem to have been the nearest source of the raw material. Therefore, it can be assumed that the Epipalaeolithic toolmakers of the Z Basin procured lithic raw materials within easy walking distance.

There are only a small number of pieces which may derive from weathered or abraded flint cobbles, some of which have a white calcareous cortex. A further variety of raw material is chert of uncertain original shape and of translucent brown, but there are only two pieces of this raw material. The sources of these materials could not be located in the vicinities of the Z Basin.

6.4.4.2. Cores

Cores are numerous in the collection (**Table 6.14**). They can be divided into four different categories based on their original shape. The first is made on pebbles of various shapes (**Table 6.15**). The second is made on conical or hemispherical chunks with almost 100 % cortex, which derived from elongated or globular pebbles, and the ventral face of the chunks were flaked (**Table 6.16**). The third is made on other fragments of pebbles (**Table 6.17**). The fourth is made on fragments of cobbles (**Table 6.18**). Cores are dominated by single platform cores, which amount to 71. Except for one single platform core made on an angular fragment of a weathered cobble, the rest are made on locally-available pebbles of various shapes (**Fig.6.10**). Most of the single platform cores made on elongated pebbles are for bladelet production. Conical or hemispherical chunks with almost 100 % cortex were also used as cores, and their ventral face was struck for flake and microbladelet production. Most of the 22

Fig.6.9. Scatter of flint pebbles on escarpments to the north of Site Z (looking east)

	n	%
single platform core	71	66.36
opposed platform core	22	20.56
ninety-degree core	5	4.67
multiple platform core	6	5.61
discoidal core	3	2.80
total	107	100.00

Table.6.14. Cores at Site Z lithic debitage concentration

	n	mean (cm)	st.dev
length	80	3.53	0.86
width	80	2.08	0.62
thickness	80	1.72	0.66

Table.6.15. Metrical data of measured cores on pebbles at Site Z lithic debitage concentration

	n	mean (cm)	st.dev
length	8	2.24	0.42
width	8	2.50	0.30
thickness	8	1.61	0.68

Table.6.16. Metrical data of measured cores on conical or hemispherical chunks of pebbles at Site Z lithic debitage concentration

	n	mean (cm)	st.dev
length	17	2.55	0.65
width	17	1.85	0.59
thickness	17	1.26	0.59

Table.6.17. Metrical data of measured cores on fragments of pebbles at Site Z lithic debitage concentration

	n	mean (cm)	st.dev
length	2	3.60	0.70
width	2	3.80	0.50
thickness	2	1.35	0.25

Table.6.18. Metrical data of measured cores on fragments of cobbles at Site Z lithic debitage concentration

Fig.6.10. Single platform cores made on pebbles of various shapes at Site Z lithic debitage concentration

opposed platform cores, five ninety-degree cores and six multiple platform cores are also made on elongated pebbles or their fragments.

6.4.4.3. Debitage products

Debitage products are quite numerous in the collection (**Table 6.19**), and include both small flakes and bladelets (**Table 6.20**). Bladelets are outnumbered.

6.4.4.4. Lithic manufacture

Several successfully refitted pieces show the common pebble knapping sequence (**Fig.6.11**). One end of an elongated pebble is blown off by

	n	%
core tablet	2	0.36
primary chunk	69	12.41
chip/chunk	15	2.70
primary flake	51	9.17
flake from single platform core	194	34.89
flake from opposed platform core	16	2.88
flake from ninety-degree core	23	4.14
flake from multiple platform core	3	0.54
unidentifiable flake	16	2.88
primary blade/bladelet	28	5.04
blade/bladelet from single platform core	128	23.02
blade/bladelet from opposed platform core	8	1.44
blade/bladelet from ninety-degree core	3	0.54
total	556	100.00

Table.6.19. Debitage products at Site Z lithic debitage concentration

	n	mean (cm)	st.dev
length	368	2.18	0.80
width	368	1.38	0.48
thickness	368	0.41	0.27

Table.6.20. Metrical data of measured debitage products at Site Z lithic debitage concentration

one strike, and a striking platform is created, forming an angle of approximately 90 degree or less with the longer axis of pebbles. As a consequence, an unfacetted platform is the most common form of platform preparation. Then several flakes and bladelets were struck off. Some refitted cores may be examples of failure or those handled by unskilful knappers, because the cores and debitage products exhibit irregular fractures. It is probable that the knappers gave up using the cores and discarded them even though the cores are still large enough. One example shows that an elongated pebble was snapped in the middle into two pieces, and the two elongated pieces were used as a single platform core and an opposed platform core respectively.

6.4.4.5. Tools

Bladelets of approximately 3 cm long and microbladelets of less than 2 cm long are the major tools found in this collection, and they

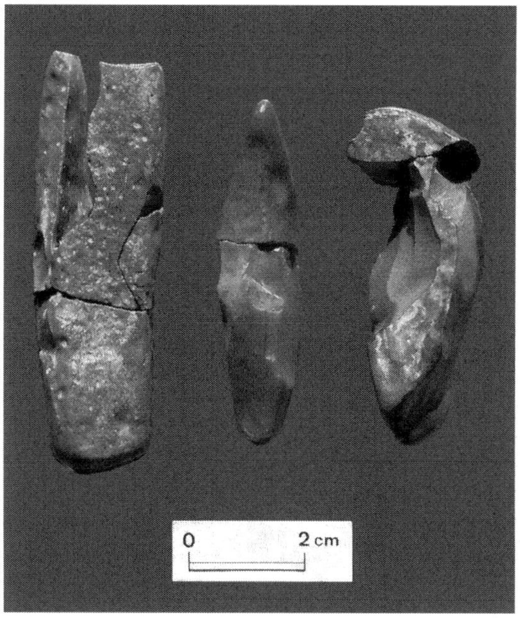

Fig.6.11. Refitted single platform cores made on elongated pebbles at Site Z lithic debitage concentration

Fig.6.12. Site Z hearth field (looking southwest)

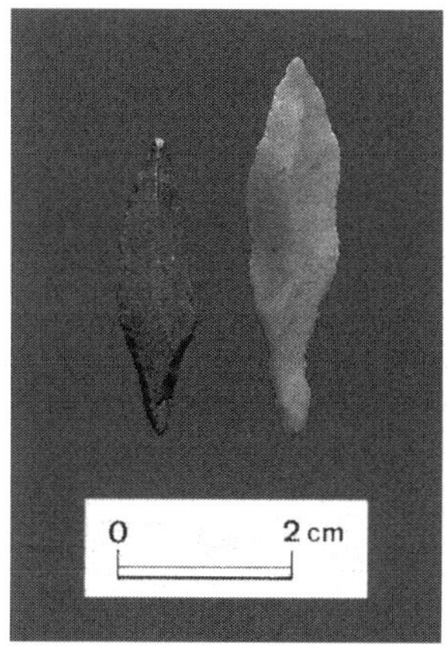

Fig.6.13. Ounan points collected at Site Z hearth field

amount to 83 in total. Backed bladelets are not numerous, and they are only 11, including four broken ones. Five of them are the straight-backed variety which is identical to Tixier's Type 45. Two of the unbroken backed bladelets exhibit unfinished backing retouch. No other kind of retouched tools were found.

6.4.5. Hearth field

Approximately 200 m to the west of the lithic debitage concentration described above, there are a number of concentrations of shell-bearing pale white limestone cobbles on the gentle slope (**Fig.6.12**). The limestone cobbles of some concentrations are burnt, and fragments of charcoal remain beneath the cobbles. The other concentrations of limestone cobbles are accompanied by burnt and fire-cracked flint pebbles, Epipalaeolithic lithic artefacts including backed blades and the Ounan points (**Fig.6.13**), and fish/animal bone fragments. Therefore, it is most likely that these cobble concentrations are stone-built hearths which are dated to the Epipalaeolithic period. Nine discrete concentrations of limestone cobbles were recorded in an area of approximately 50 m by 50 m, though they were not studied in detail due to the lack of time. Four of them are located at the higher elevation of the slope, and they consist of larger limestone cobbles and are less deflated in comparison with the others. It seems obvious that the hearth stones derived from the water/wind-eroded pale limestone bed which is exposed a few metres above this hearth field. The limestone bed stretches east-west approximately 1 km in length on the westernmost part of the northern shore of the Z Basin, and a number of limestone slabs and fragments are scattered downslope. Thus it must have been easy for Epipalaeolithic people to collect them.

6.4.6. Some consideration on life in Site Z

Given the surface structural remains and artefact scatters which do not seem to have been severely tumbled by natural forces, some considerations on how the basin shore was used or inhabited by Epipalaeolithic people may be allowed.

As for the source of the flint pebbles, it was suggested that the gravelly escarpments which are approximately 1 km to the north of the Z Basin were the most likely source. It can be argued that the inhabitants of the westernmost part of Site Z would perhaps have walked to the nearest escarpments with a fine view routinely for monitoring and have transported a whole handful of flint pebbles to the localities on the basin shore. The fact that the people brought pebbles and started to make bladelets on the basin shore rather than made bladelets elsewhere and came with the bladelets suggests that the people could afford to make tools in the proximity of wild food resources there. It follows from this fact that the people would have stayed here for some or a considerable length of time and have exploited resources which did not flee and were not easily depleted. This is certainly how aquatic resources like fish and marsh plants could be most effectively harvested.

In contrast, the situation of the easternmost part of Site Z is fairly different. The lack of clear evidence for mass transport of lithic raw materials and the presence of formal projectile points indicate that people's visit to this part of Site Z was fortuitous and short, and that the aim of the visit was bow-hunting rather than fishing and plant harvesting. Furthermore, this contrasting situation may suggest that even though these two parts of Site Z are located at the almost same elevation, they were occupied at different times of the Epipalaeolithic period. It is possible that the environmental settings such as water level and vegetation cover were different at each time, and accordingly the major focus of subsistence activity shifted from one to the other.

6.5. Epipalaeolithic lithic assemblage at the Camp II Ridge on the eastern shore of the Z Basin

6.5.1. Introduction

Camp II is the place where Caton-Thompson pitched her second camp during her field campaign. It is located at the eastern margin of the Z Basin (**Fig.6.3**). She stayed on the bottom of a narrow cove, which was divided from the main body of the Z Basin by a linear dune, and was named the Camp II Basin by her (Caton-Thompson and Gardner 1934: 76-77). Surface artefact scatters are still quite extensive from the bottom of the Camp II Basin, which is around 7-10 m asl, onto the eastern slope and ridge of the Basin, which is around 15-18 m asl. The Camp II Ridge is actually the eastern shore of the Z Basin, and its surface is marked by an approximately 100 m wide white band of beach sediments, consisting mainly of calcium carbonate pellets.

Artefact scatters are particularly dense around the eastern margin of this white band (**Fig.6.14**), and most noticeable artefacts are lithic cores and tools of the Epipalaeolithic. Scatters of numerous ostrich eggshell fragments were also seen in this area. No pottery sherds are found, and there are no structural remains like hearths. This situation suggests that these beach sediments and artefact

Fig.6.14. Scatter of lithic artefacts at the Camp II Ridge (looking west)

scatter patterns were made by the wave action of oscillating basin water caused by a predominant wind from the west in the Early-Middle Holocene, and hence that the original context of basin shore habitation in the Epipalaeolithic period has been considerably disturbed. Two 5 m x 5 m squares were set up for surface collection at one locality of the densest artefact scatter (surface collection square A) and another locality of relatively sparse artefact scatter (surface collection square B) on the eastern margin of the beach sediments. Surface collection square A is located approximately 90 m southeast of Surface collection square B.

6.5.2. Surface collection square A

At this locality (N29.58528° E30.78867°), 332 artefacts and four unworked flint pebbles were collected in a 5 m x 5 m square (**Table 6.21**). All artefacts were not embedded in the beach sediments but rested on calcium carbonate pellets and coarse-grained loose sand. Large cores made on cobbles as well as pebbles are quite noticeable at this locality.

	n
whole pebble	4
single platform core	39
opposed platform core	5
ninety-degree core	3
discoidal core	2
core tablet	3
primary chunk	6
chip/chunk	1
primary flake	13
flake from single platform core	69
flake from opposed platform core	11
flake from ninety-degree core	21
unidentifiable flake	17
primary blade/bladelet	8
blade/bladelet from single platform core	18
blade/bladelet from opposed platform core	2
unidentifiable blade/bladelet	1
blade/bladelet	95
backed bladelet	11
trihedral rod	1
notch	2
denticulate	4
total	336

Table.6.21. Inventory of finds at Camp II surface collection square A

6.5.2.1. Lithic raw materials

There are two distinct kinds of raw material in this assemblage. One is a subangular or rounded, elongated or irregularly-shaped flint pebble of various colours from light to dark brown. The surface of the pebbles is generally smooth and well polished. Another is a rounded and oval flint cobble of various colours from light to dark brown. The surface of the cobble is weathered or abraded. Many of them have a brown cortex, but some of them have a white calcareous cortex. Both pebbles and cobbles of these kinds do not naturally occur in the beach sediments. Thus it is certain that they have been transported from elsewhere.

	n	%
single platform core	39	79.59
opposed platform core	5	10.20
ninety-degree core	3	6.12
discoidal core	2	4.08
total	49	100.00

Table.6.22. Cores at Camp II surface collection square A

	n	mean (cm)	st.dev
length	29	3.09	0.72
width	29	2.64	0.66
thickness	29	2.64	0.85

Table.6.23. Metrical data of measured cores on pebbles at Camp II surface collection square A

6.5.2.2. Cores

49 cores are included in the collection (**Table 6.22**). Cores can be divided into two different categories based on their original shape. The first is made on pebbles of various shapes (**Table 6.23**) (**Fig.6.15**-1). The second is made on fragments of cobbles (**Table 6.24**) (**Fig.6.15**-2).

	n	mean (cm)	st.dev
length	20	3.27	0.94
width	20	3.35	0.63
thickness	20	2.28	0.78

Table.6.24. Metrical data of measured cores on fragments of cobbles at Camp II surface collection square A

	n	%
core tablet	3	1.76
primary chunk	6	3.53
chip/chunk	1	0.59
primary flake	13	7.65
flake from single platform core	69	40.59
flake from opposed platform core	11	6.47
flake from ninety-degree core	21	12.35
unidentifiable flake	17	10.00
primary blade/bladelet	8	4.71
blade/bladelet from single platform core	18	10.59
blade/bladelet from opposed platform core	2	1.18
unidentifiable blade/bladelet	1	0.59
total	170	100.00

Table.6.25. Debitage products at Camp II surface collection square A

	n	mean (cm)	st.dev
length	107	2.40	0.86
width	107	1.90	0.57
thickness	107	0.57	0.32

Table.6.26. Metrical data of measured debitage products at Camp II surface collection square A

There are 39 single platform cores, and at least 10 of them are made on cobbles. There are five opposed platform cores, four of which are made on cobbles. There are three ninety-degree cores, one of which is made on cobble. There are two discoidal cores made on pebbles. This high rate of cores made on cobbles against cores made on pebbles is quite noticeable. When cores were made on fragments of weathered or abraded flint cobbles, non-cortical parts of the fragments were usually used as striking platforms, and several bladelets of 3-4 cm long were obtained.

6.5.2.3. Debitage products

The number of flakes is much larger than that of blades/bladelets (**Table 6.25**). However, it seems that the production of blades/bladelets was more strongly aimed for, judging from the number of readily-usable blades/bladelets shown in **Table 6.21**. The debitage products at this locality are slightly larger in size than those in Site Z (**Table 6.26**).

6.5.2.4. Lithic manufacture

There is no refitted specimen for discussing the tool manufacturing process, but the cores and debitage products suggest that toolmakers knapped flint pebbles and cobbles in a regular manner. It may be said that debitage production was generally bladelet-oriented.

6.5.2.5. Tools

There are quite numerous bladelets and microbladelets, and they amount to 95. There are 11 backed bladelets including Tixier's Types 45, 52-53, and 95 (**Fig.6.16**-1, 2 and 3). There is one trihedral rod. Other informal tools include four denticulates and two notches.

6.5.3. Surface collection square B

At this locality (N29.58586° E30.78803°), 159 artefacts and five unworked flint pebbles were collected in a 5 m x 5 m square (**Table 6.27**). All artefacts rested on calcium carbonate pellets and coarse-grained loose sand.

6.5.3.1. Lithic raw materials

The raw material use at this locality is almost the same as that at surface collection square A. There are two distinct kinds of raw materials. One is a subangular or rounded, elongated or irregularly-shaped flint pebble of various colours from light to dark brown, and another is a rounded and oval flint cobble of various colours from light to dark brown.

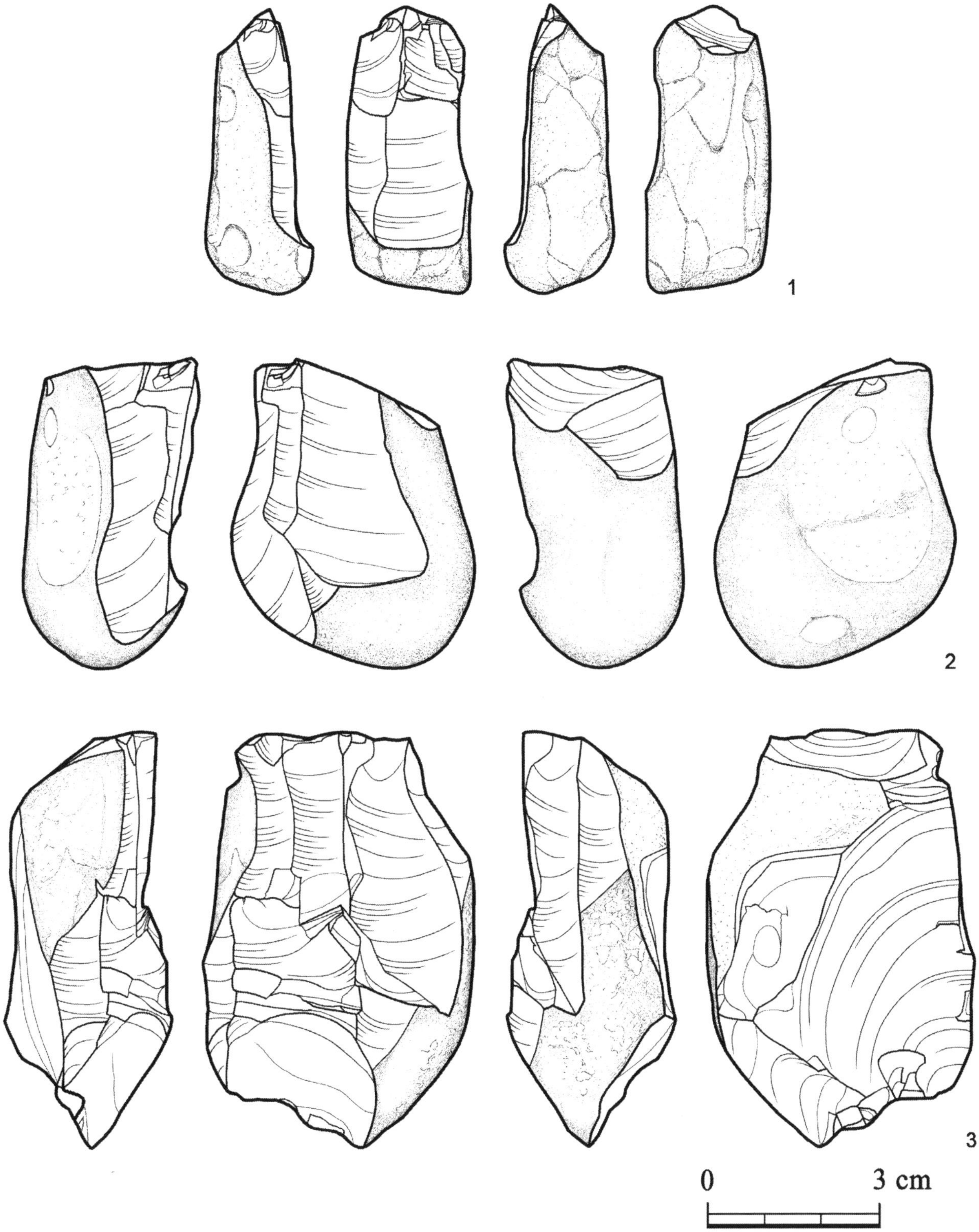

Fig.6.15. Cores collected at Camp II surface collection squares A and B

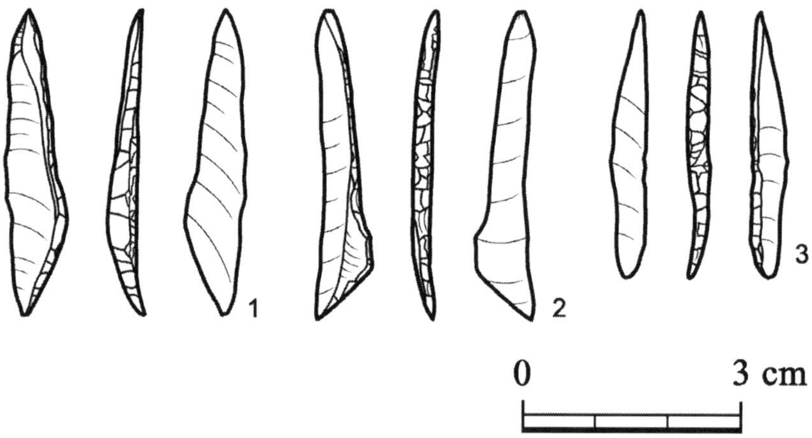

Fig.6.16. Tools collected at Camp II surface collection squares A

	n
whole pebble	5
single platform core	21
opposed platform core	3
ninety-degree core	3
multiple platform core	6
discoidal core	1
core tablet	2
primary chunk	2
primary flake	10
flake from single platform core	58
flake from opposed platform core	3
flake from ninety-degree core	5
flake from multiple platform core	6
unidentifiable flake	5
blade/bladelet from single platform core	4
blade/bladelet	22
backed bladelet	1
trihedral rod	1
notch	1
denticulate	1
scraper	2
retouched flake	2
total	164

Table.6.27. Inventory of finds at Camp II surface collection square B

	n	%
single platform core	21	61.76
opposed platform core	3	8.82
ninety-degree core	3	8.82
multiple platform core	6	17.65
discoidal core	1	2.94
total	34	100.00

Table.6.28. Cores at Camp II surface collection square B

	n	mean (cm)	st.dev
length	17	2.64	1.03
width	17	2.75	0.80
thickness	17	2.33	0.85

Table.6.29. Metrical data of measured cores on pebbles at Camp II surface collection square B

	n	mean (cm)	st.dev
length	7	2.17	0.45
width	7	2.47	0.62
thickness	7	1.49	0.46

Table.6.30. Metrical data of measured cores on conical or hemispherical chunks of pebbles at Camp II surface collection square B

6.5.3.2. Cores

34 cores are included in the collection (**Table 6.28**). Cores are certainly numerous against the total number of all debitage products collected at this locality. Cores can be divided into three different categories based on their original shape. The first is made on pebbles of various shapes (**Table 6.29**). The second is made on conical or hemispherical chunks with almost 100 % cortex,

which derived from elongated or globular pebbles, and the ventral face of the chunks were flaked (**Table 6.30**). The third is made on fragments of cobbles (**Table 6.31**) (**Fig.6.15**-3). All kinds of cores are included, but more than a half of all cores are single platform cores. It is noted that five out of 21 single platform cores and one out of three ninety-degree cores are made on fragments of cobbles. The other cores are made on pebbles. Most cores listed here are for blade/bladelet production. Cores made on conical or hemispherical chunks with almost 100 % cortex were used for flake production.

6.5.3.3. Debitage products

The total number of primary chunks and primary flakes is small against the number of cores (**Table 6.32**). It is likely that this assemblage is distorted to some extent. In general, the size of debitage products at this locality (**Table 6.33**) is slightly larger than those at surface collection square A.

6.5.3.4. Lithic manufacture

There is no refitted specimen for discussing the tool manufacturing process, but the cores and debitage products suggest that toolmakers knapped flint pebbles and cobbles in a regular manner. It seems that debitage production was more flake-oriented.

6.5.3.5. Tools

Tools are not numerous. But considering the small size of the collection, the small number of tools is not surprising. One backed bladelet of an arch-backed and double pointed variety, which is close to Tixier's Type 57, was noted.

6.5.4. A low mound to the east of surface collection squares A and B

Apart from the systematic surface collection at the two localities, one particular location was noticed approximately 40-50 m to the east of these. It is a long, low mound stretching north-

	n	mean (cm)	st.dev
length	10	3.25	1.46
width	10	3.81	0.73
thickness	10	2.75	0.78

Table.6.31. Metrical data of measured cores on fragments of cobbles at Camp II surface collection square B

	n	%
core tablet	2	2.11
primary chunk	2	2.11
primary flake	10	10.53
flake from single platform core	58	61.05
flake from opposed platform core	3	3.16
flake from ninety-degree core	5	5.26
flake from multiple platform core	6	6.32
unidentifiable flake	5	5.26
blade/bladelet from single platform core	4	4.21
total	95	100.00

Table.6.32. Debitage products at Camp II surface collection square B

	n	mean (cm)	st.dev
length	71	2.45	0.89
width	71	2.29	0.73
thickness	71	0.63	0.27

Table.6.33. Metrical data of measured debitage products at Camp II surface collection square B

south along the eastern shore of the Z Basin, and the surface is covered by porous calcrete duricrusts. The western face of the mound is more severely eroded, and laminated calcium carbonate and sand are exposed. It seems that this mound was made and eroded by wave action of oscillating water on the eastern shore of the Z Basin. Lithic artefacts are scattered on and around this low mound, and some artefacts are about to be eroded out of the deposits.

Lithic artefacts include a number of backed bladelets which are quite similar to those seen in Site Z, but the most remarkable artefacts are a side-notched projectile point (**Fig.8.5**-2), a tanged projectile point and a leaf-shaped projectile point (**Fig.8.7**-4 and 5), which are reminiscent of not only those of the (bi)facial techno-complex of the Western Desert in the 7th-

6th millennia cal.BC but also those of the Levantine Pre-Pottery Neolithic and Pottery Neolithic. As Caton-Thompson has reported, Camp II and its vicinity has produced an extremely large number of peculiar projectile points whose dates were uncertain (Caton-Thompson and Gardner 1934: 76-77 and pl.LI), and these new discoveries also reconfirm the uniqueness of Camp II. Although the precise dates of these projectile points remain uncertain, they give some clue for reconsidering the Fayum chronology and cultural connections with neighbouring regions.

6.5.5. Some considerations on life at the Camp II Ridge

Considering the disturbed situation, it is difficult to imagine how the eastern shore of the Z Basin was used or inhabited by Epipalaeolithic people. Nevertheless, the presence of two distinct kinds of lithic raw materials which do not naturally occur on the Z Basin shore suggests that people's stay at Camp II was a regular, planned visit for a considerable length of time, and that the use of the raw materials at Camp II was made possible by either residential moves to and from source areas, or, more likely, logistical moves from Camp II to the source areas by a task group.

The reason why this part of the Z Basin was continuously or repeatedly occupied is not certain because of the paucity of faunal remains. However, the steeply-inclined shore and probably oxygen-rich water due to strong wave action caused by a westerly wind in this part of the Z Basin would have been ideal conditions for the fish and animal species that require or prefer such deep water, and it is possible that this part of the Z Basin was an invaluable resource patch which was not comparable to other places of stagnant water in the surrounding area.

6.6. Epipalaeolithic lithic assemblages on the northeastern shore of the X Basin

6.6.1. Introduction

Site E29H1 in the X Basin has been recognised and reported by Caton-Thompson in the 1920s as an unnamed extensive surface site (Caton-Thompson and Gardner 1934: 74 and pl.CX), and thereafter revisited and studied in more detail by the Combined Prehistoric Expedition in 1969 (Wendorf and Schild 1976: 181-199). The Combined Prehistoric Expedition found vast scatters of Epipalaeolithic lithic artefacts in this site, and studied the lithic assemblage from the surface collection and excavation grids named Areas A, B, and C (Wendorf and Schild 1976: Fig.121). The Combined Prehistoric Expedition published main typological indices of tools from Areas A and C on the basis of the Tixier typology, while dealing with 310 tools in total (Wendorf and Schild 1976: Table 17 and Fig.210). However, only a small number of the tools from Area A were presented (Said *et al.* 1970: Figs.6 and 7; Said *et al.* 1972: Fig.3), and it was only briefly mentioned how the cores in this lithic assemblage looked. Therefore, how the lithic technology was organised remains unknown.

At present, Site E29H1 looks different from that previously described by the Combined Prehistoric Expedition. Although the present topography and spatial extent of the site perfectly match the Combined Prehistoric Expedition's description, its elevation is 10-13 m asl, which is almost the same as described on Caton-Thompson's map but is approximately 5 m lower than that reported by the Combined Prehistoric Expedition (**Fig.6.17**). The Areas A, B and C are not visible on the surface. Not only wide and dense scatters of lithic artefacts but also many concentrations of sandstone/limestone cobbles and fragments, which are apparently hearths, are located on the surface either to the east of the supposed locations of Areas B and C, or between the supposed locations of these two Areas. However, such remains have not been mentioned by the Combined Prehistoric Expedition. In this hearth field, not only several concentrations of

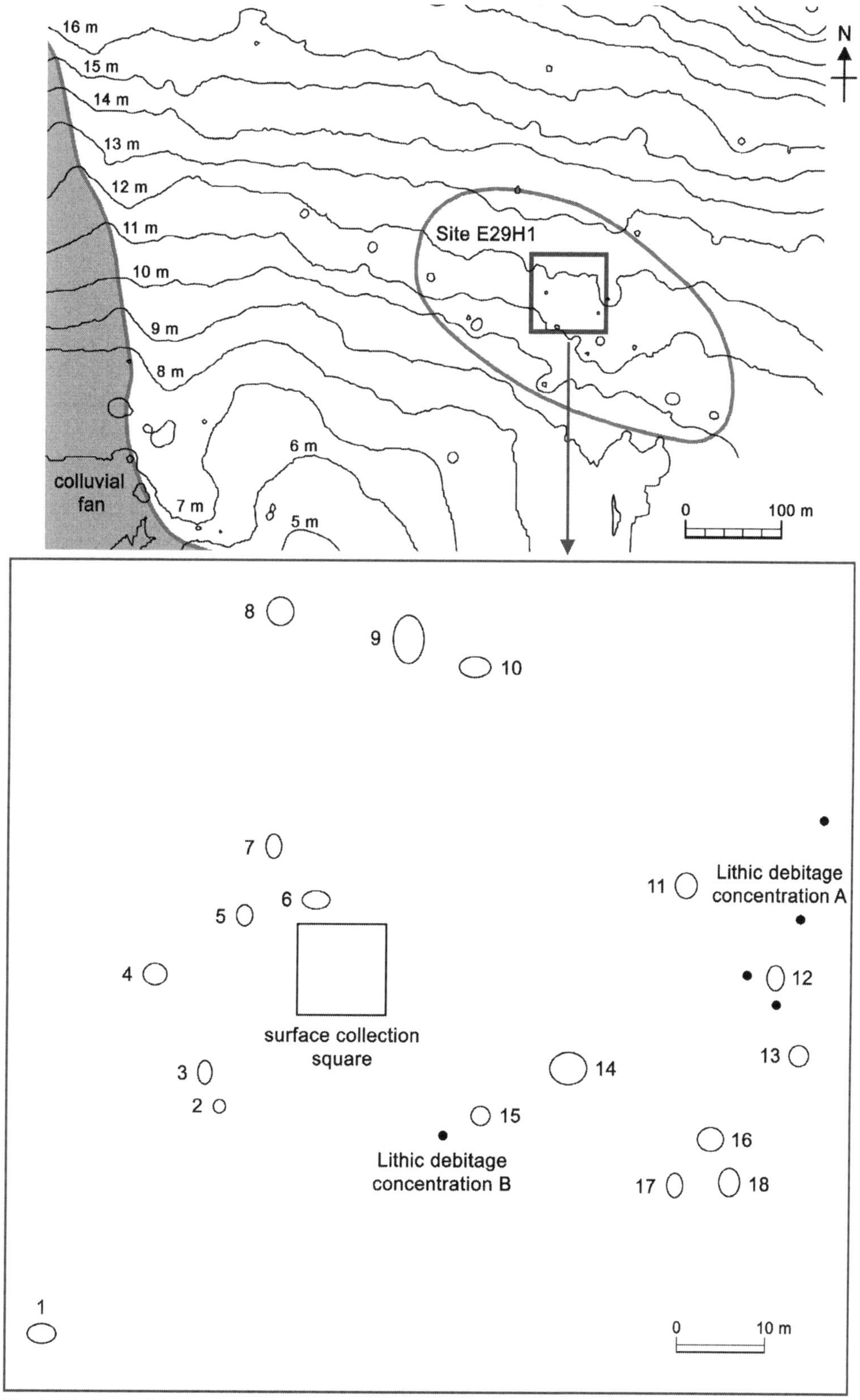

Fig.6.17. Map of Site E29H1 and Area D hearth field

animal and fish bone fragments but also several noticeable concentrations of lithic debitage products, which seem to be lithic debitage dumping spots, were found. This hearth field (N29.58393° E30.83304° in the centre) was named Area D after the Combined Prehistoric Expedition's Areas A, B, and C, and an intensive investigation including mapping and surface artefact collecting was carried out.

6.6.2. Area D

Site E29H1 is located on the gentle slope falling southwards to the bottom of the X Basin. At present, the ground surface is covered by fine-grained aeolian sand, and is devoid of vegetation. A north-south cross section of Site E29H1 has been made by the Combined Prehistoric Expedition (Wendorf and Schild 1976: Fig.140). According to the cross section, the site is located on a levee consisting of fine to medium-grained deltaic sand. This may mean that the Epipalaeolithic people chose a high elevation for their habitation in order to escape inundation. Area D is approximately 80 m (north-south) x 80 m (east-west). Following the typology of hearths by Wright (2005), 18 clearly visible hearths recorded in Area D can be described as stone-filled or stone-lined pit hearths, and four hardly recognisable, deflated ones can be described as fireplaces in a strict sense, or, they had been stone-bordered or stone-filled but the hearth stones had been removed in the past. It is not certain whether there was a pit in the middle of each hearth because no excavation was carried out, but it seems likely that the stones were put together in a shallow depression for distributing heat or supporting items to be heated. It seems that considerable time and energy were expended to construct each hearth, and it is assumed that these hearths represent more than single burning event. The surface on which these hearths were

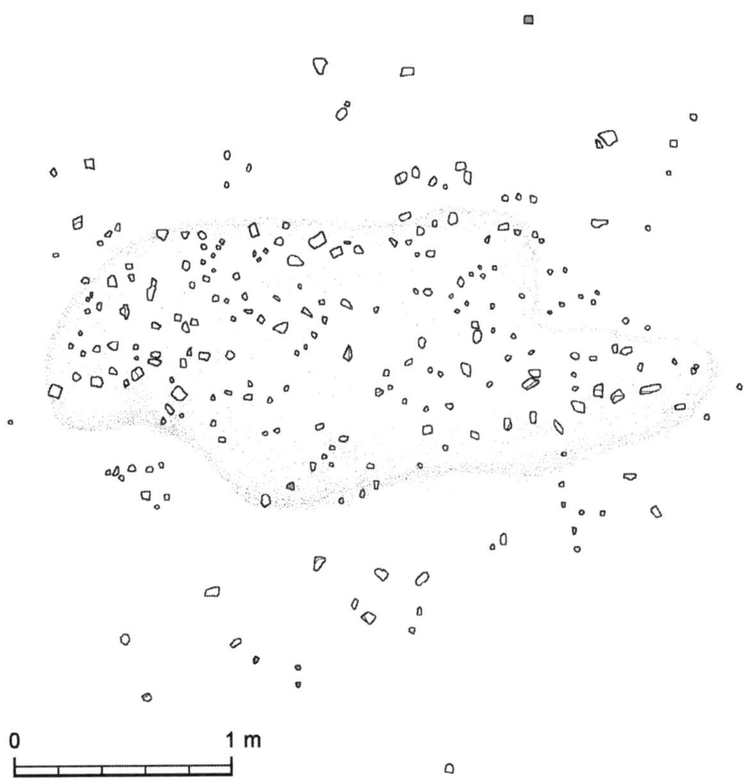

Fig.6.18. Hearth 1 in Site E29H1 Area D

located is generally flat, and the difference of elevation between the hearth on the highest ground and the hearth on the lowest ground is approximately 2 m.

6.6.3. Area D hearths

6.6.3.1. Description of individual hearths

Hearth 1 (Fig.6.18)
It is a dense cluster of limestone cobbles which are approximately 2-6 cm in diameter on a low mound. The mound consists of compacted fine pale yellow sand. The discreteness of the cobble cluster is relatively high, but on the other hand, most cobbles are fragmentary, and the hearth mound seems to be slightly deflated. A few lithic artefacts are scattered on and around the mound. A few pieces of mammal bones are seen 2 m to the south.

Hearth 2 (Fig.6.19)
It consists of subrounded sandstone cobbles of 3-13 cm in diameter and small fragmentary limestone cobbles, but is deflated and flat. Fragments of mammal bones, lacustrine snails, and lithic artefacts are scattered around. Charcoal or swampy sediments were found beneath the surface.

Hearth 3 (Fig.6.20)
It consists of a number of subangular limestone cobbles of 3-15 cm in diameter, but is deflated and flat. Beneath the cobbles is fine compacted pale yellow sand. Fragments of mammal bones, lacustrine snails, and lithic artefacts are scattered around.

Hearth 4 (Fig.6.21)
It is a dense cluster of cobbles on a low mound of fine, compacted pale yellow sand. It consists of subangular limestone and sandstone cobbles of 3-10 cm in diameter. A number of relatively larger, subangular sandstone cobbles are notable. Lithic artefacts are not numerous.

Hearth 5 (Fig.6.22)
It is a dense cluster of cobbles on a low mound of coarse pale yellow aeolian sand. It consists of a number of subangular sandstone cobbles and a few subrounded limestone cobbles of 3-6 cm in diameter. Few lithic artefacts are around.

Hearth 6 (Fig.6.23)
It is a slightly deflated low mound consisting of coarse, aeolian sand. It consists of subangular to subrounded limestone cobbles of 3-8 cm in diameter. Lithic artefacts are scattered in the northern half of the hearth. A few lacustrine snails are notable.

Hearth 7 (Fig.6.24)
It is a sparse cluster of limestone and sandstone cobbles of 2-6 cm in diameter, accompanied by lithic artefacts and some lacustrine snails. It is

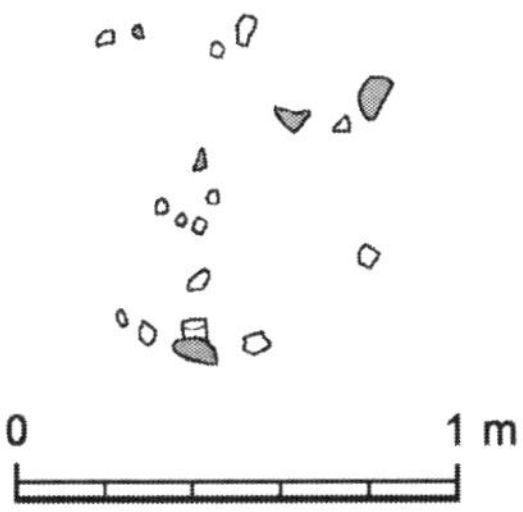

Fig.6.19. Hearth 2 in Site E29H1 Area D (sandstone in grey)

Fig.6.20. Hearth 3 in Site E29H1Area D

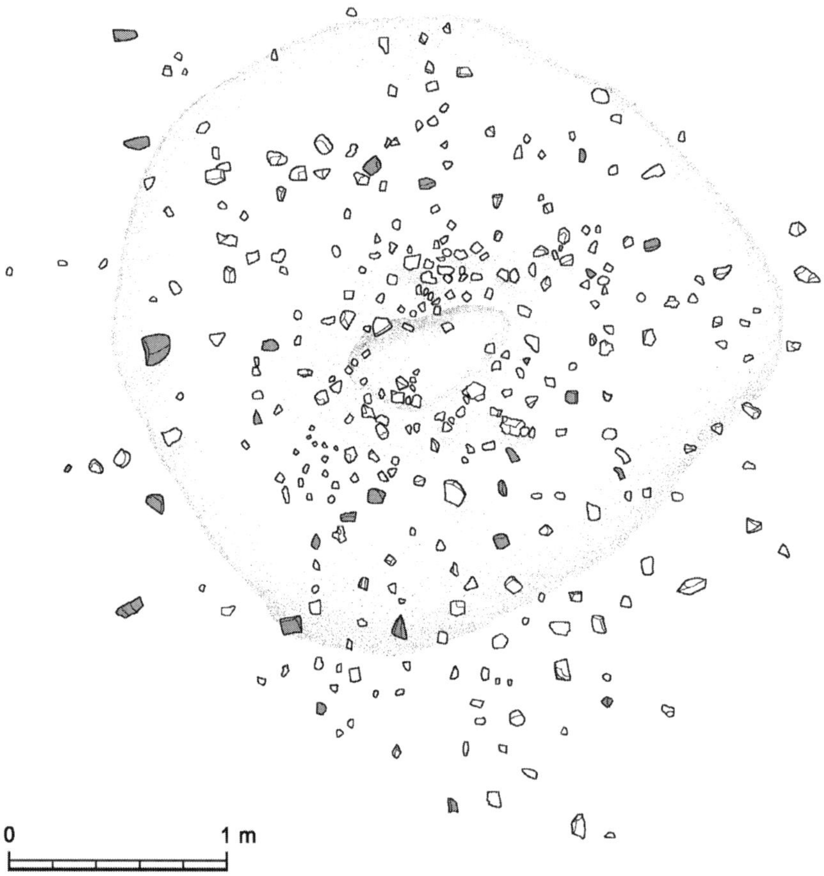

Fig.6.21. Hearth 4 in Site E29H1 Area D (sandstone in grey)

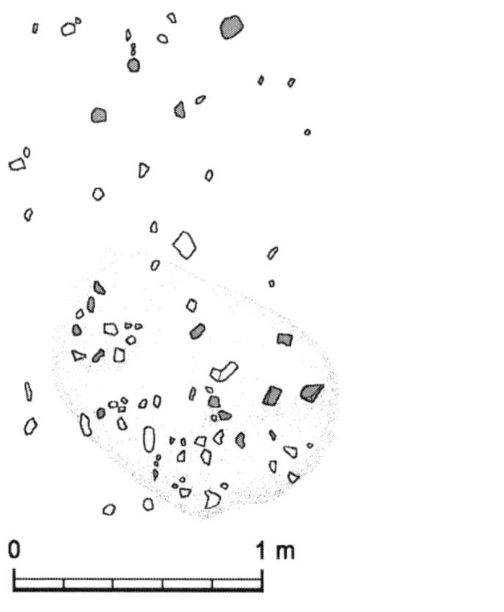

Fig.6.22. Hearth 5 in Site E29H1 Area D (sandstone in grey)

badly deflated and hence looks flat. The surface sand is fine and silty pale yellow sand. It seems to have recently been damaged through holes dug by animals.

Hearth 8 (Fig.6.25)
It is a dense cluster of cobbles on a high mound of fine silty and compacted pale yellow sand. It consists of a large number of subangular to subrounded limestone cobbles of 3-10 cm in diameter and a few subangular sandstone cobbles of similar size. Lithic artefacts are quite few on the mound, but there is a scatter of lithic artefacts to the northeast. Some lacustrine shells are noticeable.

Hearth 9 (Fig.6.26)
Probably a cluster of two or three hearths, but they are deflated and obscured. In particular, the

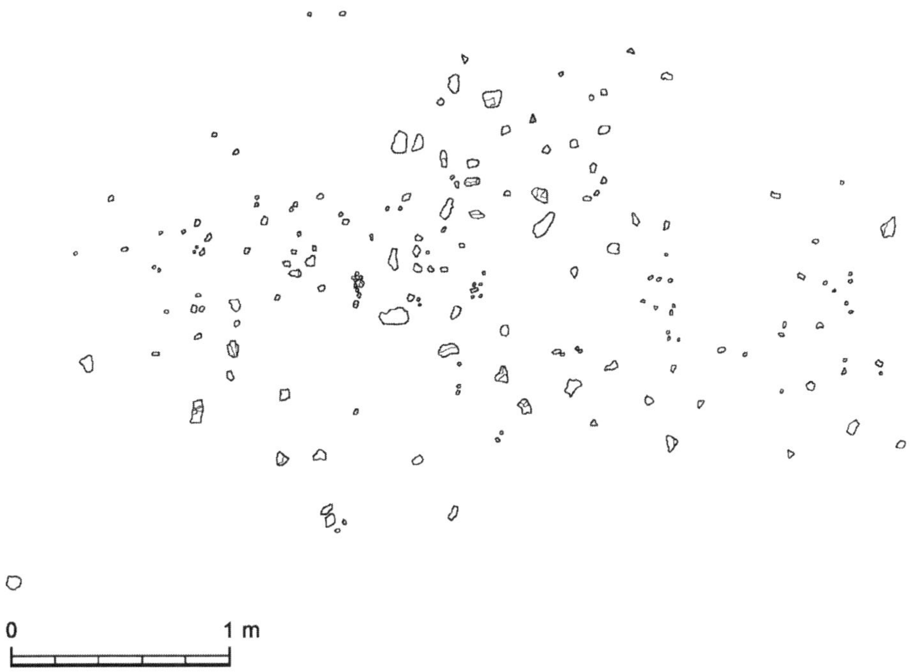

Fig.6.23. Hearth 6 in Site E29H1 Area D

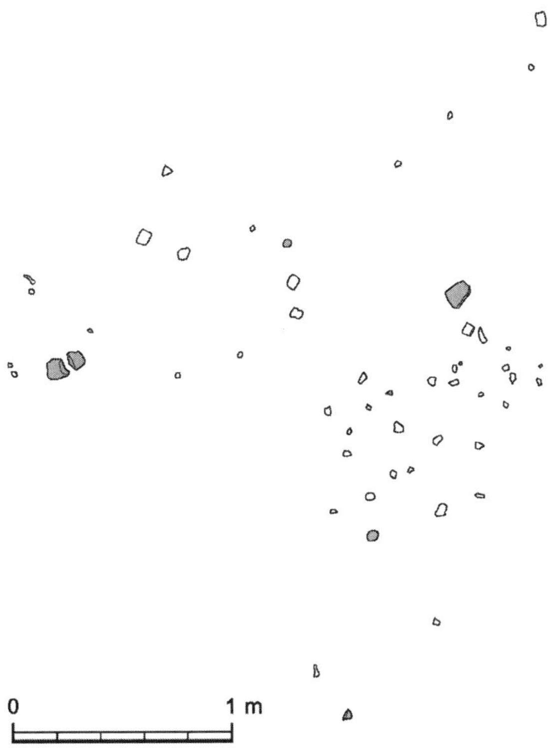

Fig.6.24. Hearth 7 in Site E29H1 Area D (sandstone in grey)

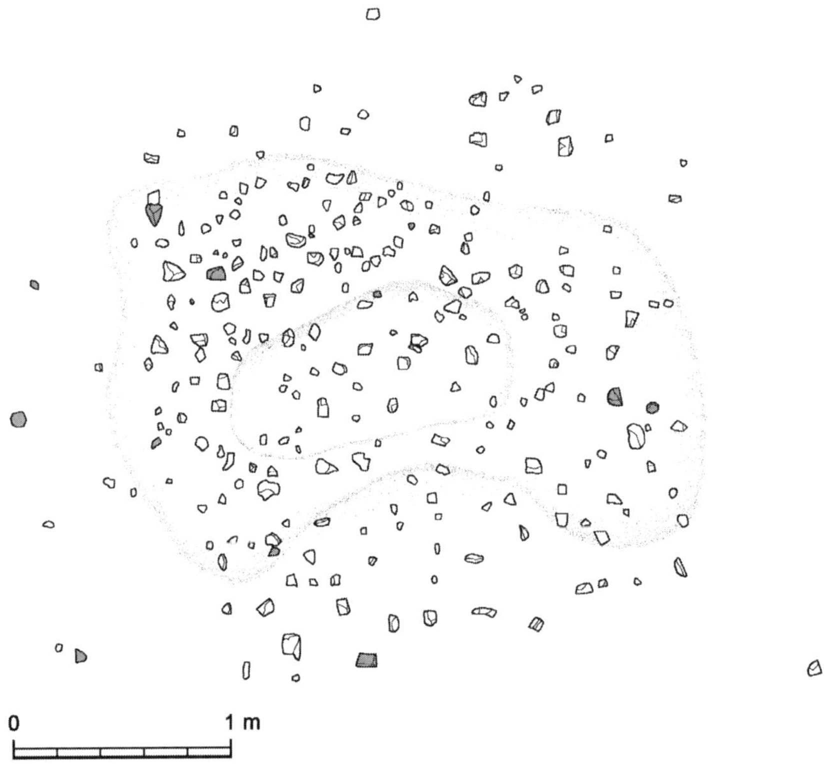

Fig.6.25. Hearth 8 in Site E29H1 Area D (sandstone in grey)

southernmost one is badly deflated. Also they are damaged by animals. Nevertheless, they still remain as low mounds. The mounds consist of fine and silty pale yellow sand. The hearths consist of subangular and subrounded limestone and sandstone cobbles of 2-10 cm in diameter. Lithic artefacts are numerous among the cobble scatters.

Hearth 10 (Fig.6.27)
It is a dense concentration of many subangular to subrounded limestone cobbles and a few angular sandstone cobbles of 2-10 cm in diameter on a mound. The mounds consist of fine and silty pale yellow sand. Lithic artefacts are numerous on and around the mound.

Hearth 11 (Fig.6.28)
Probably there are two hearths side by side, but they seem to have been deflated and hence obscured. Sparse circular clusters of subangular limestone cobbles/fragments and a few sandstone cobbles of 2-12 cm in diameter are on low mounds. Mammal bones and lithic artefacts are scattered on and around the mounds. A pit with charcoal and bones was found beneath the surface of the northwestern one.

Hearth 12 (Fig.6.29)
It is a dense cluster of many angular sandstone cobbles of 2-15 cm in diameter and a few limestone fragments on a low mound. There are many lithic artefacts, lacustrine snail fragments and mammal bones among the cobbles. There is one concentration of lithic artefacts 1.5 m to the south, and another concentration of lithic artefacts and mammal bones 2 m to the west.

Hearth 13 (Fig.6.30)
It consists of subangular limestone cobbles of 3-7 cm in diameter, but is deflated and recently almost destroyed. A very low mound consists of compacted but loose, pale yellow sand. No charcoal was found beneath the surface. A small,

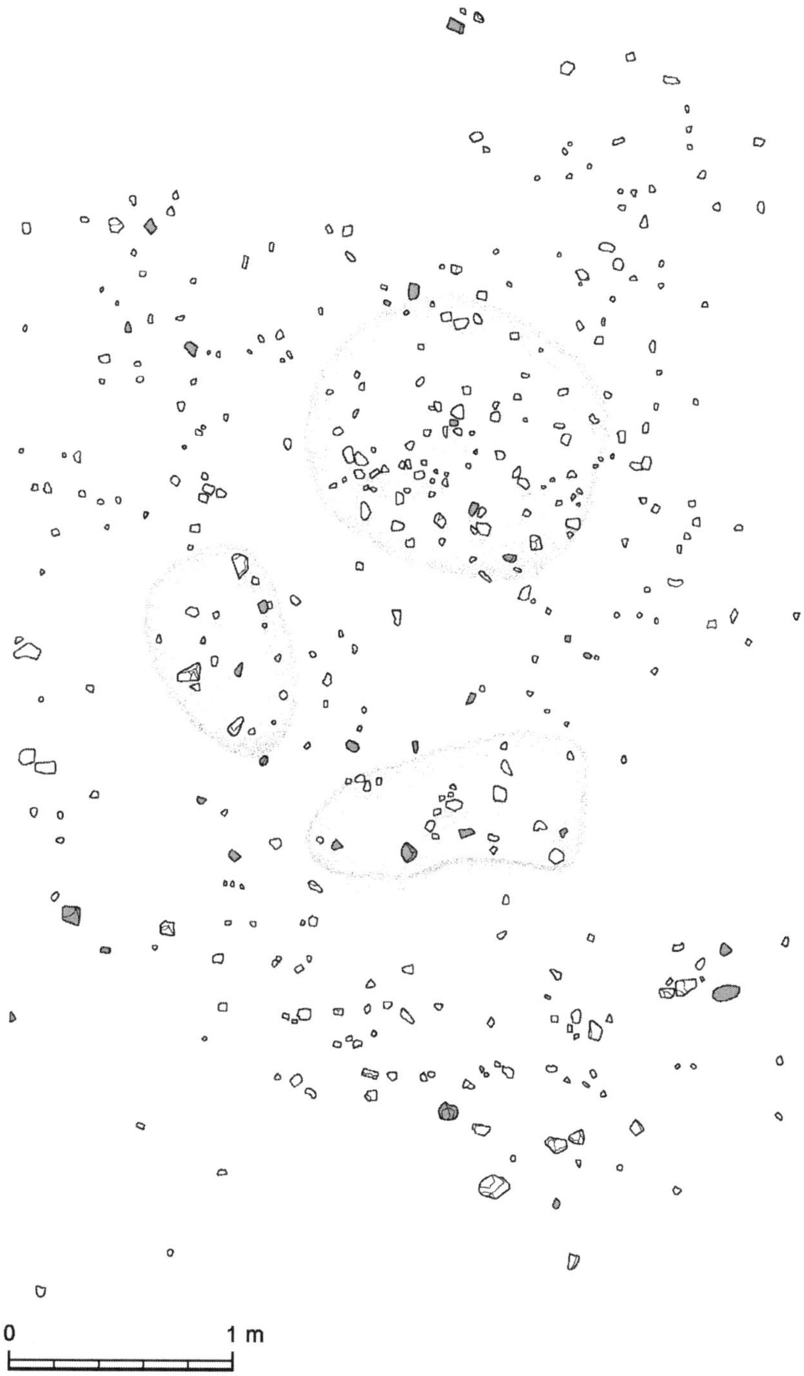

Fig.6.26. Hearth 9 in Site E29H1 Area D (sandstone in grey)

dense cluster of mammal bones are to the south of the hearth.

Hearth 14 (Fig.6.31)

It consists of a wide but sparse scatter of many fragmentary limestone cobbles of 2-6 cm in diameter and a few subangular sandstone

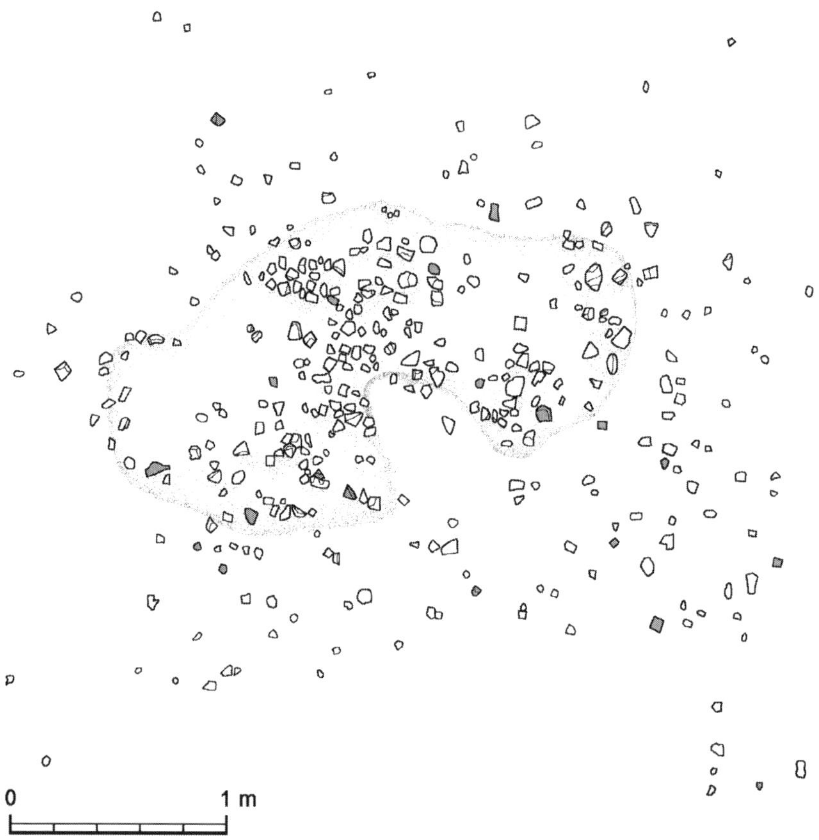

Fig.6.27. Hearth 10 in Site E29H1 Area D (sandstone in grey)

cobbles, but it is heavily deflated. The surface is covered by fine silty and compacted pale yellow sand. Lithic artefacts are numerous among the cobble scatter. There are also a few mammal bones, lacustrine snail fragments, and ostrich eggshell fragments.

Hearth 15 (Fig.6.32)
It is a dense cluster of subangular limestone and sandstone cobbles of 5-8 cm in diameter on a low mound of compacted fine silty pale yellow sand. The ratio of limestone and sandstone is almost 1:1. There are many lithic artefacts and some lacustrine snails among the cobble cluster.

Hearth 16 (Fig.6.33)
It consists of many angular sandstone cobbles and a few limestone cobbles of 3-9 cm in diameter, but it is deflated and flat. Lithic artefacts including cores and bladelets are not numerous.

Hearth 17 (Fig.6.34)
It is a scatter of subangular limestone and sandstone cobbles of 3-7 cm in diameter. It is deflated and flat, and seems to have recently been almost destroyed. Lithic artefacts are extremely numerous among the cobble scatter. The surface is covered by compacted pale yellow sand, and no charcoal was found beneath the surface.

Hearth 18 (Fig.6.35)
The surface is covered by compacted fine, silty, pale yellow sand. The hearths consist of limestone and sandstone cobbles of 3-7 cm in diameter. The surface is deflated and flat, and seems to have recently been destroyed and obscured. Lithic artefacts are not numerous. There are a few pieces of mammal bones to the east.

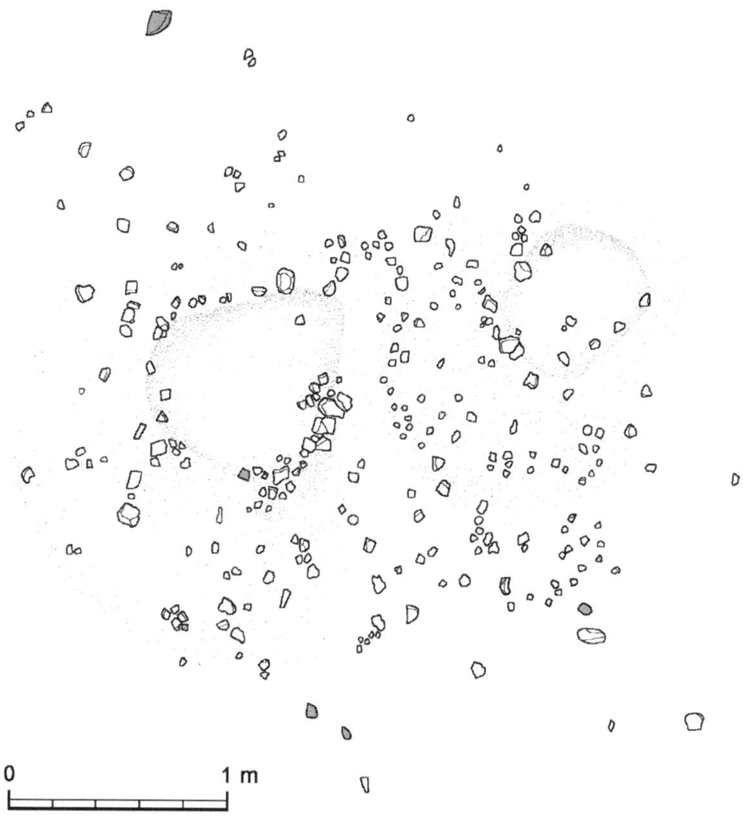

Fig.6.28. Hearth 11 in Site E29H1 Area D (sandstone in grey)

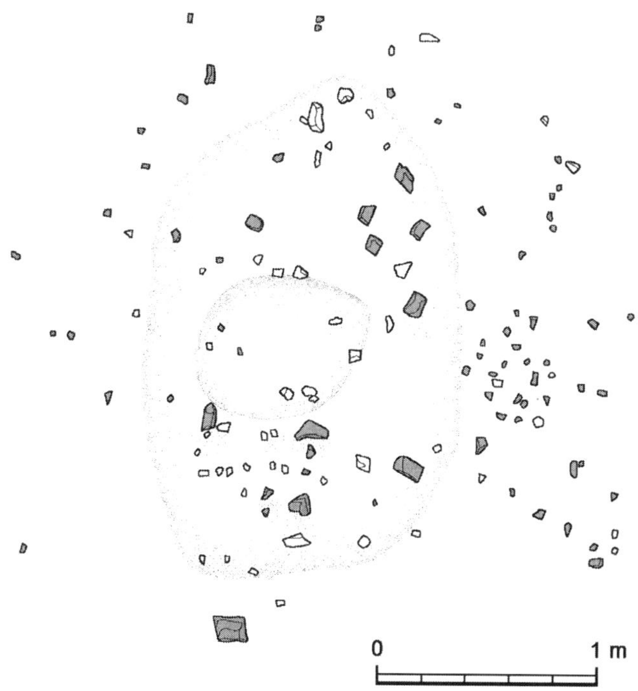

Fig.6.29. Hearth 12 in Site E29H1 Area D (sandstone in grey)

Fig.6.30. Hearth 13 in Site E29H1 Area D

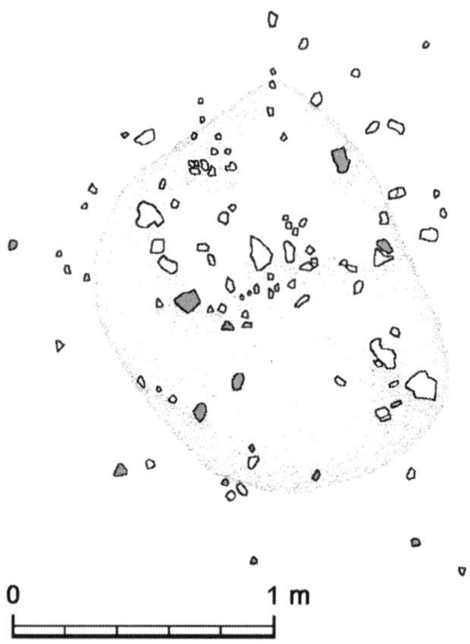

Fig.6.32. Hearth 15 in Site E29H1 Area D (sandstone in grey)

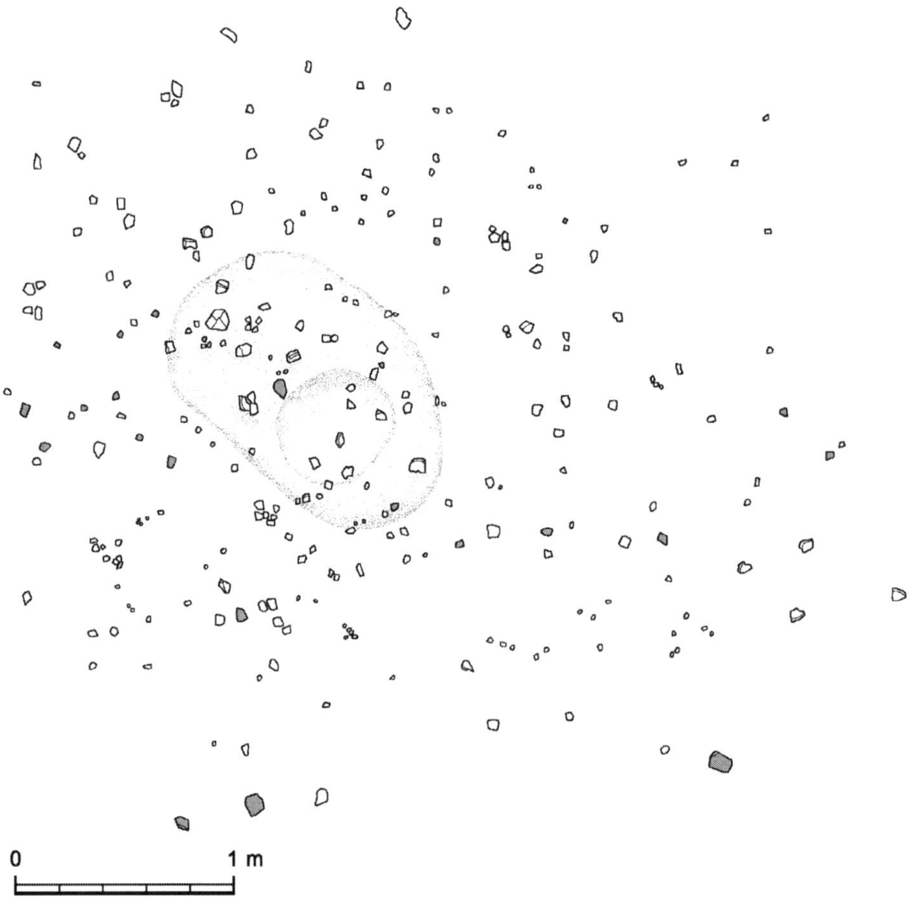

Fig.6.31. Hearth 14 in Site E29H1 Area D (sandstone in grey)

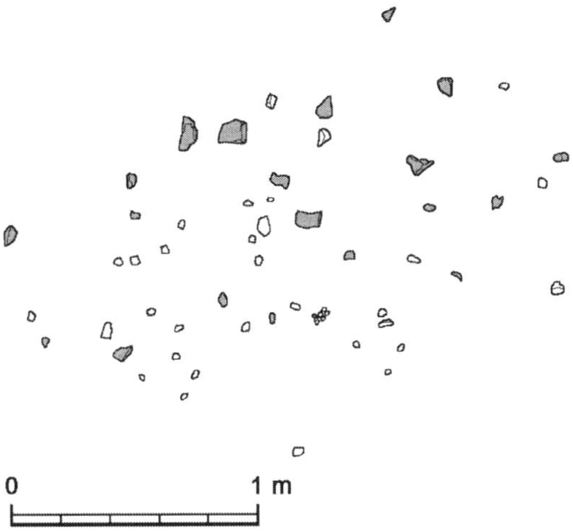

Fig.6.33. Hearth 16 in Site E29H1 Area D (sandstone in grey)

Fig.6.34. Hearth 17 in Site E29H1 Area D (sandstone in grey)

6.6.3.2. Some considerations on the life history of the hearths

Questions arise as to how long or how repeatedly individual hearths were used, and how many hearths were operational at one time. As described in detail, the variety, size, and number of rocks for making hearths are not equal, and the degree of discreteness of features like rock layout and artefact scatter are also not the same. Such various degrees of feature discreteness should be indicators of the duration and repetition of hearth use.

According to Chatters' four-level discreteness measure based on the degree of horizontal displacement among hearths and faunal remains (Chatters 1987: Fig.1), some hearths (9 and 11) should be classified as 'Level 1', which is the least discrete, and represents the result of multiple reuses. Some others (7 and 18) would be classified as 'Level 2', which is the result of a reoccupation of the same site with construction of fires in new places, while obscuring scatter of residues from the previous occupation. Most other hearths (1, 2, 3, 4, 5, 6, 8, 10, 12, 14, 15, 16 and 17) could be classified as 'Level 3', which shows some changes in fire positions and scattering of debris clusters, resulting from a longer-term occupation but still representing a single period of residency. Based on this observation, it is tentatively concluded that this

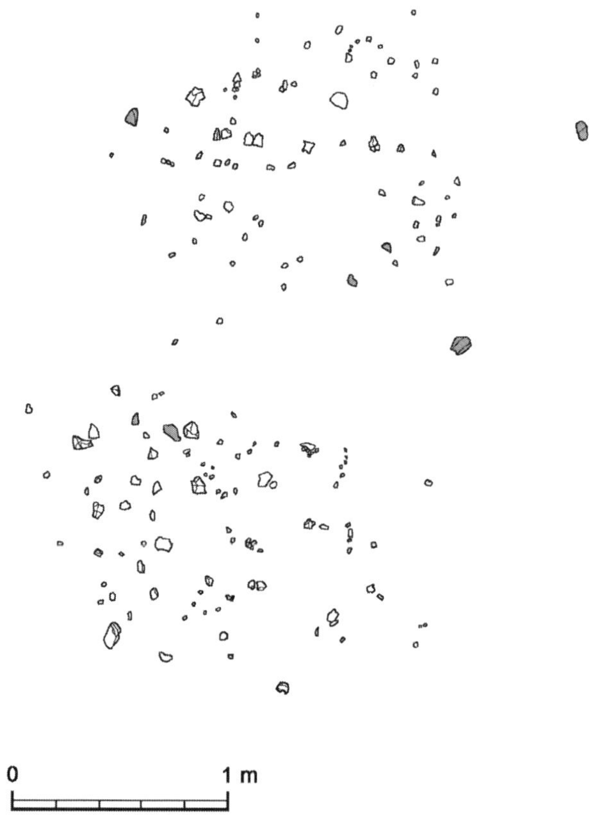

Fig.6.35. Hearth 18 in Site E29H1 Area D (sandstone in grey)

hearth field as a whole represents repeated occupations, and that each occupation was not a brief, undisturbed single event.

One process which has been observed by ethnoarchaeological studies with regard to site furniture is the size effect. Upon arrival at a known site, one generally searches for the furniture and pulls it up out of its matrix for reuse. As a consequence, large items of site furniture get continuously translated upward if a deposit is forming (Binford 1979). If this effect did take place in the hearth field in Area D, it is presumed that cobbles of older hearths would have gradually broken into smaller fragments due to fire cracking and natural erosion and decay, and would have been buried beneath sand. Nevertheless, larger cobbles and their fragments would have tended to remain unburied, and they would have been most likely pulled up and reused. Therefore, it is possible that some hearths (2, 3, 4, 10, 11 and 12) which are characterised by the presence of many larger cobbles are relatively later in date than other hearths consisting of small cobbles and fragments.

6.6.4. Wide scatters of lithic artefacts in the middle of the hearth field

There is a blank area in the middle of the hearth field, and no clear structural remains are visible on the surface, but the surface is covered by a tremendous number of lithic artefacts. Most of them are supposed to be dated to the Epipalaeolithic. It seems that those lithic artefacts are not randomly scattered, but somehow concentrated in a wide meandering band running from the northwest to the southeast. This may be caused by wave action of oscillating basin water on the beach in the past (Morton 2004: 45-54; Rapp and Hill 1998: Fig.2.4). In spite of the possible water rolling, preservation of these lithic artefacts is generally very good, and edges and ridges of the lithic artefacts are still sharp at the macroscopic level. It has been argued that smaller, lighter, and flatter flakes are more easily transported by oscillating water flow than heavy and angular cores, but as described below, a large number of blades/bladelets and flakes are included in these scatters, and their ratio against cores does not seem to be distorted. Hence it may be said that considerable size/weight/shape sorting of artefacts did not take place. This suggests that these lithic artefacts may have been disturbed by a single high energy wave event, and thereafter buried beneath lacustrine sediments for a long time, and have become exposed on the present surface very recently by wind erosion. Also as described below, some concentrations of Epipalaeolithic lithic artefacts in this field exhibit extremely high integrity and no trace of disturbance. Thus it is concluded that successive different wave events caused different degrees of disturbance even within the Epipalaeolithic period.

By contrast, there is a tendency that apparently Neolithic bifacially-retouched tools which are sparsely seen in this hearth field are more heavily rounded. This may support the above-mentioned suggestion that Epipalaeolithic lithic artefacts have been buried intact beneath lacustrine sediments for a long time, but overlying Neolithic lithic artefacts have been subject to water/wind erosion for a longer period.

A 10 m x 10 m square was set up in this blank area, and all lithic artefacts on the surface were collected in order to obtain a general idea about the lithic assemblage of this hearth field. The total number of collected lithic artefacts is 2541, including 31 unused or only partly used whole flint pebbles (**Table 6.34**). As mentioned above, the majority of the pieces are dated to the Epipalaeolithic, but some are dated to the Neolithic on the basis of technological features.

	n
whole pebble	31
single platform core	215
opposed platform core	36
ninety-degree core	13
multiple platform core	78
discoidal core	7
unclassifiable/fragmentary core	20
core tablet	18
primary chunk	134
chip/chunk	196
primary flake	210
flake from single platform core	569
flake from opposed platform core	35
flake from ninety-degree core	9
flake from multiple platform core	186
flake from discoidal core	1
unidentifiable flake	304
primary blade/bladelet	68
blade/bladelet from single platform core	206
blade/bladelet from opposed platform core	14
blade/bladelet from ninety-degree core	1
blade/bladelet from multiple platform core	4
unidentifiable blade/bladelet	58
blade/bladelet	72
backed bladelet	34
notch	2
denticulate	3
endscraper	2
retouched flake	10
winged and tanged projectile point	1
tanged projectile point	1
concave-based arrowhead (Neolithic)	1
unifacially-retouched knife (Neolithic)	1
knife blade (Neolithic)	1
total	2541

Table.6.34. Inventory of finds at Site E29H1 Area D surface collection square

6.6.4.1. Raw materials

The most commonly used raw materials are elongated or globular, subangular or rounded flint pebbles of less than 7 cm long and 4 cm wide. The surface of the pebbles is very smooth and not weathered. The colour of this flint is generally light brown to brown, and darker colour varieties are few. This kind of flint pebble does not naturally occur on the surface of this basin environment, but they are sparsely scattered on the gentle slope of low desert ridges, which extend from a rocky and gravelly summit named Gebel Abyad or El-Qarah el-Kharshah approximately 3 km to the north of the X Basin shore. That area would have been the nearest source of flint pebbles. Therefore, it may be said that the Epipalaeolithic toolmakers of the X Basin procured lithic raw materials within easy walking distance, and it is difficult to believe that they procured flint pebbles at distant sources like the escarpments above Qasr el-Sagha, as has been suggested by previous researchers (Wendorf and Schild 1976: 311).

Another variety of raw material is white chalky flint, and a small number of debitage products and tools from this material was noticed in the collection. Some debitage products deriving from this white chalky flint retain a weathered calcareous cortex, but they are too fragmentary to understand the original shape of the pebble/cobble. Since no whole pebble which has this feature has been found, it is plausible that this flint derives from cobbles or nodules of unknown origin. Other chert which exhibits a translucent brown colour is quite few in this assemblage, and several debitage products from translucent brown chert are too small to understand the original shape of the pebble/cobble.

6.6.4.2. Cores

Cores are quite numerous in the collection (**Table 6.35**). Cores can be divided into four different categories based on their original shape. The first is made on pebbles of various shapes (**Table 6.36**). The second is made on conical or hemispherical chunks with almost 100 % cortex, which derived from elongated or globular pebbles, and the ventral face of the chunks were flaked (**Table 6.37**). The third is made on other fragments of pebbles (**Table 6.38**). The fourth is made on fragments of cobbles (**Table 6.39**). Cores are dominated by single platform cores (**Fig.6.36**-1, 2, 3 and 4), which amount to 215. In most cases, platforms are created on one end of an elongated or globular pebble by one strike, forming an angle of approximately 90 degrees or less with the longer axis of pebbles. As a consequence, an unfacetted platform is the most common form of platform preparation. Dihedral platforms are not numerous. Some dihedral platforms consist of a struck face and a cortical face. A facetted platform is quite rare. In other cases, angular or flat parts of the cortical surface

	n	%
single platform core	215	58.27
opposed platform core	36	9.76
ninety-degree core	13	3.52
multiple platform core	78	21.14
discoidal core	7	1.90
unclassifiable/fragmentary core	20	5.42
total	369	100.00

Table.6.35. Cores at Site E29H1 Area D surface collection square

	n	mean (cm)	st.dev
length	291	2.59	0.89
width	291	2.40	0.52
thickness	291	2.04	0.91

Table.6.36. Metrical data of measured cores on pebbles at Site E29H1 Area D surface collection square

	n	mean (cm)	st.dev
length	31	2.16	0.59
width	31	2.28	0.49
thickness	31	1.86	0.56

Table.6.37. Metrical data of measured cores on conical or hemispherical chunks of pebbles at Site E29H1 Area D surface collection square

	n	mean (cm)	st.dev
length	10	2.97	0.98
width	10	2.60	0.48
thickness	10	1.36	0.47

Table.6.38. Metrical data of measured cores on fragments of pebbles at Site E29H1 Area D surface collection square

	n	mean (cm)	st.dev
length	17	2.65	1.15
width	17	3.35	1.02
thickness	17	2.66	0.93

Table.6.39. Metrical data of measured cores on fragments of cobbles at Site E29H1 Area D surface collection square

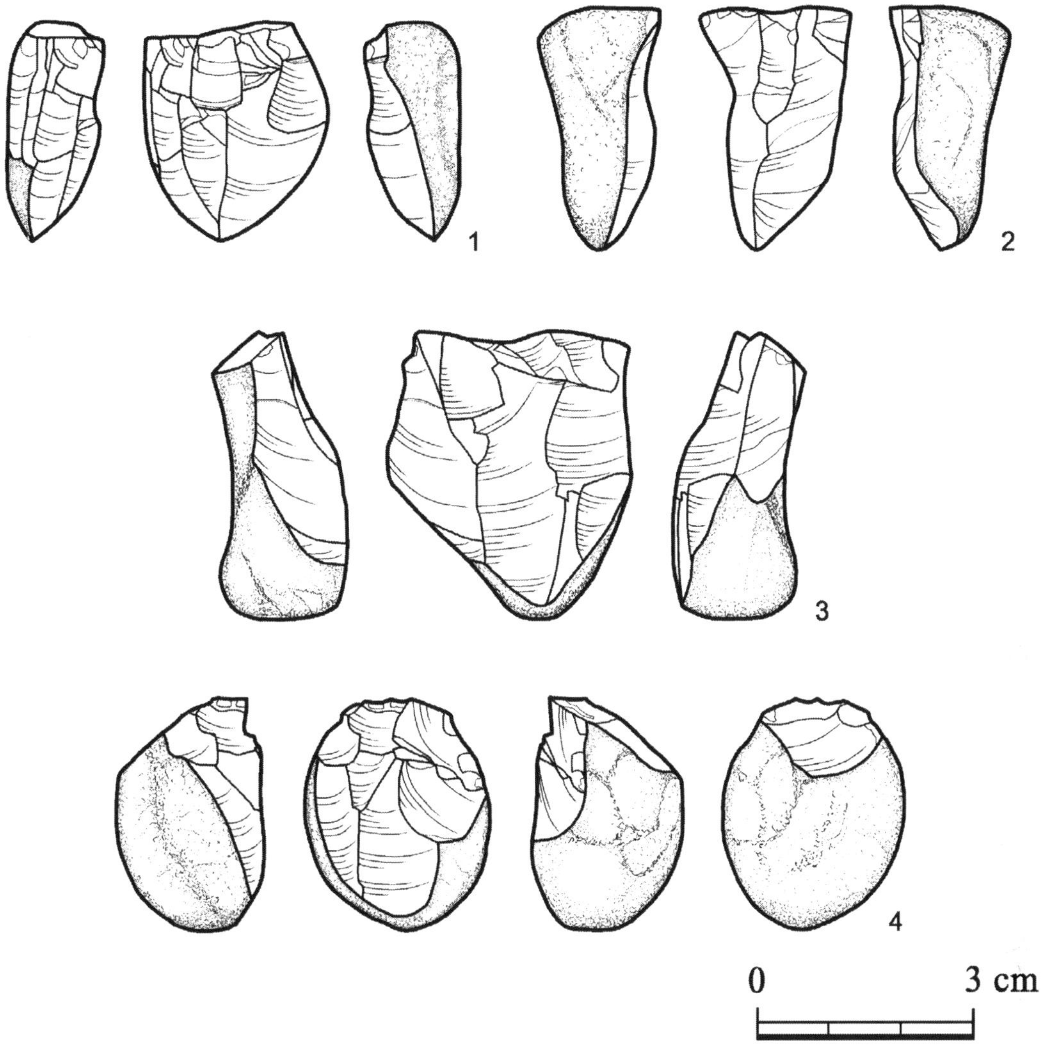

Fig.6.36. Single platform cores collected at Site E29H1 Area D surface collection square

of pebbles were used as platforms. Vertically half-split elongated pebbles were also used as cores, and a few flakes/bladelets were obtained from the ventral face. Pyramidal cores are one type of single platform core. They were made on angular or subangular fragments of weathered or abraded large flint cobbles, and the sources of such larger cobbles are not the same as those of the elongated pebbles described above. This type of core is not numerous in this assemblage.

The second most numerous cores are multiple platform cores, and they amount to 78. It was hard to find any patterned multiple platform preparation, and hence most of them were classified as unpatterned. Opposed platform cores (**Fig.6.37**-1, 2 and 3) and ninety-degree cores are not numerous, and amount to 36 and 13 respectively. There are 20 unclassifiable fragmentary cores. These were so repeatedly struck that it is hard to imagine the original shape of the pebbles, whereas many other cores were discarded after a few flakes or bladelets were obtained, and hence they still retain the original shape.

In some cases, thick primary flakes were also used as cores. Flakes and bladelets were struck off from the dorsal to ventral face, forming an angle of approximately 90 degrees with the

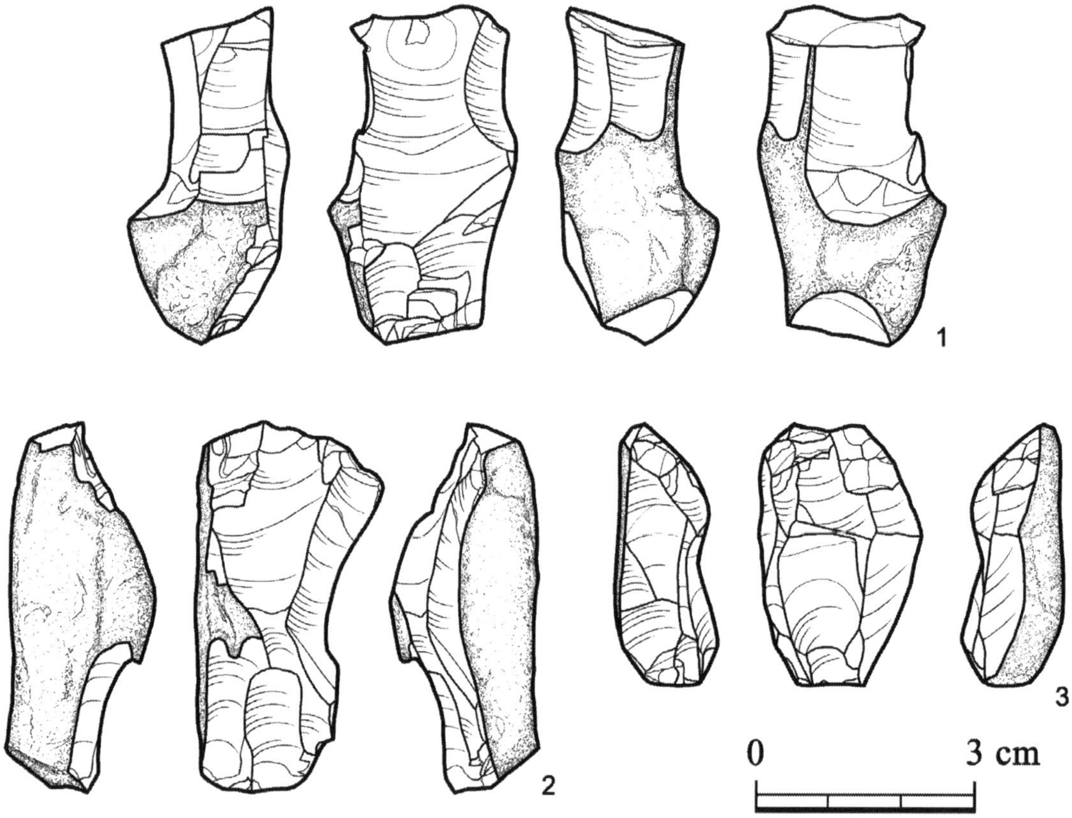

Fig.6.37. Opposed platform cores collected at Site E29H1 Area D surface collection square

	n	%
core tablet	18	0.89
primary chunk	134	6.66
chip/chunk	196	9.74
primary flake	210	10.43
flake from single platform core	569	28.27
flake from opposed platform core	35	1.74
flake from ninety-degree core	9	0.45
flake from multiple platform core	186	9.24
flake from discoidal core	1	0.05
unidentifiable flake	304	15.10
primary blade/bladelet	68	3.38
blade/bladelet from single platform core	206	10.23
blade/bladelet from opposed platform core	14	0.70
blade/bladelet from ninety-degree core	1	0.05
blade/bladelet from multiple platform core	4	0.20
unidentifiable blade/bladelet	58	2.88
total	2013	100.00

Table.6.40. Debitage products at Site E29H1 Area D surface collection square

	n	mean (cm)	st.dev
length	1195	2.40	0.88
width	1195	1.73	0.60
thickness	1195	0.58	0.31

Table.6.41. Metrical data of measured debitage products at Site E29H1 Area D surface collection square

dorsal face. There are single platform, opposed platform, and discoidal platform varieties in these flake cores.

6.6.4.3. Debitage products

The number of debitage products in the collection is 2013 (**Table 6.40**), and they are quite small in size (**Table 6.41**). The predominance of single platform core in the collection is also indicated by a large number of flakes and blades/bladelets from single platform

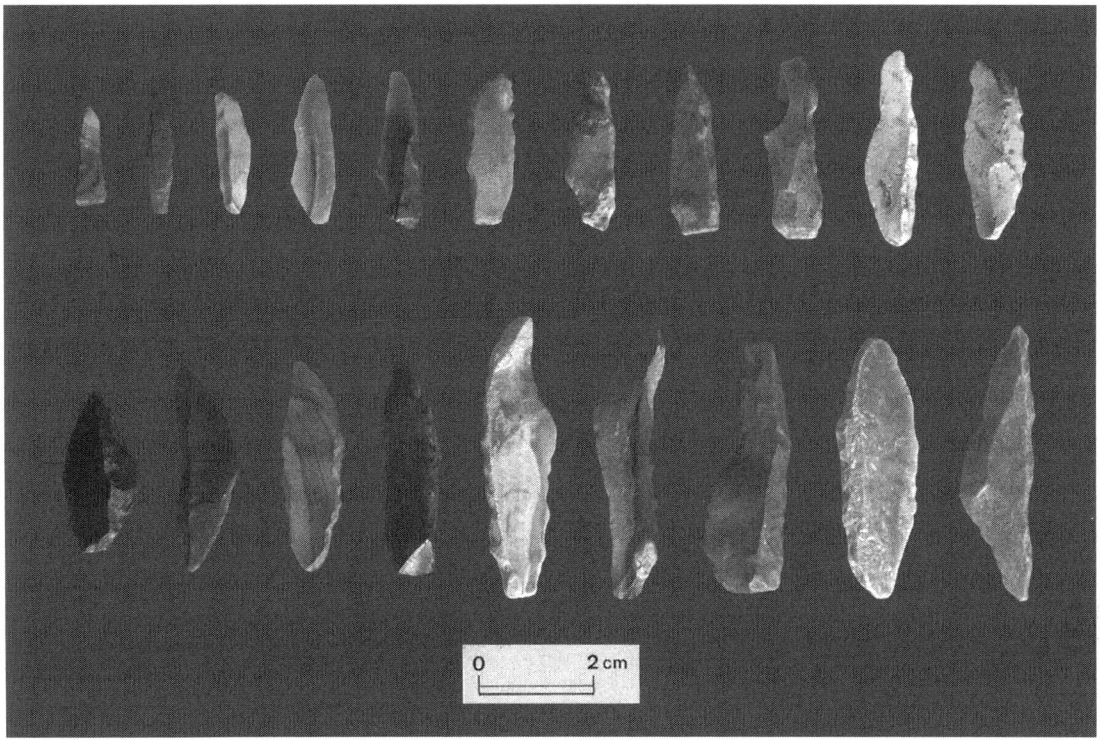

Fig.6.38. Backed bladelets collected at Site E29H1 Area D surface collection square

cores. One notable kind of primary piece is a conical or hemispherical chunk with a complete cortex. The chunk has an impact bulb on the naturally flat proximal end with no platform preparation, and a tiny breakage on the distal end, and the ventral face is flat with few or no surface undulations. This means that a considerable number of whole globular or elongated pebbles were brought here and the primary chunks were produced by bipolar wedging, in order to create a platform on one end of pebbles. Other debitage products are as listed in the table.

6.6.4.4. Tools

Formal retouched tools are not numerous in this assemblage, and the most predominant are bladelets without backing retouch. They are followed by various backed bladelets (**Fig.6.38**), but they amount to only 34, including 24 complete and 10 broken ones. They include a number of straight-backed and pointed examples without basal retouch (Tixier's Type 45) and a few arch-backed ones without basal retouch (Tixier's Type 56). The average length of the complete backed bladelets is 3 cm. Backed bladelets are followed by some retouched flakes. One longer side of primary flakes is retouched continuously from the ventral to the dorsal face, creating a serrated cutting edge. There are only two notches and three denticulates. In addition, there is only one small tanged projectile point whose lateral edges are retouched. On the whole, this tool type frequency is not dissimilar to those of nearby Areas A and C published by the Combined Prehistoric Expedition (Wendorf and Schild 1976: 317-318), though some minor tools like burins and Ouchtata retouched bladelets are absent or may be overlooked in Area D.

6.6.5. Lithic debitage concentrations

Five curious concentrations of lithic artefacts were located in Area D (black dots in **Fig.6.16**). As mentioned, almost the entire surface of the

Fig.6.39. Lithic debitage concentration B at Site E29H1 Area D (looking north)

hearth field is covered by lithic artefacts, but nevertheless, those concentrations were quite noticeable due to their extremely high density and their isolation from other features like hearths. Those lithic concentrations are less than 1 m in diameter, and the accumulation of those debitage concentrations is not thick (**Fig.6.39**). Many debitage pieces sit firmly on slightly consolidated, very fine-grained sand. They look like spots where toolmakers collected debitage products and dumped them. It is probable that the debitage products were originally dumped in a shallow pit dug in the sand by toolmakers, but the light sand was later blown away, and heavier and more solid debitage products in the deeper parts remained intact and became gradually exposed on the surface as a discrete concentration. In order to better understand the nature of these features, two concentrations (lithic debitage concentrations A and B) were selected for the collection of all cores, debitage products and tools. After collecting, all pieces were classified on the basis of the colour and texture of a fresh and weathered surface, and the refitting of the pieces was attempted.

6.6.6. Lithic debitage concentration A

It turned out that this collection included only three tools (two backed bladelets and one denticulate), and the rest of the collection, which amounted to 454 pieces, was cores and debitage products (**Table 6.42**). In addition, although not

	n
single platform core	14
opposed platform core	4
ninety-degree core	1
multiple platform core	4
core tablet	3
primary chunk	31
chip/chunk	37
primary flake	30
flake from single platform core	111
flake from opposed platform core	8
flake from ninety-degree core	5
flake from multiple platform core	7
unidentifiable flake	74
primary blade/bladelet	21
blade/bladelet from single platform core	86
blade/bladelet from opposed platform core	3
blade/bladelet from ninety-degree core	2
blade/bladelet from multiple platform core	1
unidentifiable blade/bladelet	12
backed blade/bladelet	2
denticulate	1
total	457

Table.6.42. Inventory of finds at Site E29H1 Area D lithic debitage concentration A

included in the table, four pebbles of irregular shape with a few breakages were found. They may have been used as hammers.

6.6.6.1. Lithic raw materials

Some unexhausted cores and one very successful refitting of debitage products suggest that the raw material is an elongated or oval flint pebble of 7-8 cm long and 2-3 cm wide. The surface of the pebbles is rounded and not heavily weathered. These characteristics are exactly the same as those of the pebbles found in the surface collection square of Area D. Hence it can be said that this remarkable lithic debitage concentration does not represent any special use of raw material or special toolmaking, but rather a common use of raw materials and toolmaking. The source of this raw material would also be the same as that mentioned before.

	n	%
single platform core	14	60.87
opposed platform core	4	17.39
ninety-degree core	1	4.35
multiple platform core	4	17.39
total	23	100.00

Table.6.43. Cores at Site E29H1 Area D lithic debitage concentration A

	n	mean (cm)	st.dev
length	18	3.13	1.12
width	18	2.52	0.63
thickness	18	2.03	0.99

Table.6.44. Metrical data of measured cores on pebbles at Site E29H1 Area D lithic debitage concentration A

	n	mean (cm)	st.dev
length	4	2.25	0.72
width	4	2.63	0.72
thickness	4	1.28	0.15

Table.6.45. Metrical data of measured cores on conical or hemispherical chunks of pebbles at Site E29H1 Area D lithic debitage concentration A

	n	%
core tablet	3	0.70
primary chunk	31	7.19
chip/chunk	37	8.58
primary flake	30	6.96
flake from single platform core	111	25.75
flake from opposed platform core	8	1.86
flake from ninety-degree core	5	1.16
flake from multiple platform core	7	1.62
unidentifiable flake	74	17.17
primary blade/bladelet	21	4.87
blade/bladelet from single platform core	86	19.95
blade/bladelet from opposed platform core	3	0.70
blade/bladelet from ninety-degree core	2	0.46
blade/bladelet from multiple platform core	1	0.23
unidentifiable blade/bladelet	12	2.78
total	431	100.00

Table.6.46. Debitage products at Site E29H1 Area D lithic debitage concentration A

	n	mean (cm)	st.dev
length	209	2.46	0.90
width	209	1.50	0.52
thickness	209	0.48	0.28

Table.6.47. Metrical data of measured debitage products at Site E29H1 Area D lithic debitage concentration A

6.6.6.2. Cores

Cores are not numerous in the collection (**Table 6.43**). Cores can be divided into two different categories based on their original shape. The first is made on pebbles of various shapes (**Table 6.44**). The second is made on conical or hemispherical chunks with almost 100 % cortex, which derived from elongated or globular pebbles, and the ventral face of the chunks were flaked (**Table 6.45**). The majority are single platform cores (**Fig.6.40**). Platforms are created on one end of an elongated or globular pebble by one strike, forming an angle of approximately 90 degrees or less with the longer axis of pebbles. As a consequence, an unfacetted platform is the most common form of platform preparation.

6.6.6.3. Debitage products

The number of debitage products in the collection is 431 (**Table 6.46**), and they are fairly small in size (**Table 6.47**). The predominance of single platform core in this concentration is also indicated by a large number of flakes and blades/bladelets deriving from single platform cores. One notable kind of primary piece is a conical or hemispherical chunk with a complete cortex. The chunks often have an impact bulb on the naturally flat proximal end with no platform preparation, and a tiny breakage on the distal end, and the ventral face is flat with few or no surface undulations. This means that these primary chunks were produced by bipolar wedging, in order to create a platform on one end of globular or elongated pebbles. Bipolar wedging needs an anvil stone, but it is not certain which kind of stone was used. It is likely that fragments of limestone blocks which are seen on the desert surface could have been expediently used. Since the number of conical or hemispherical chunks reflects the number of

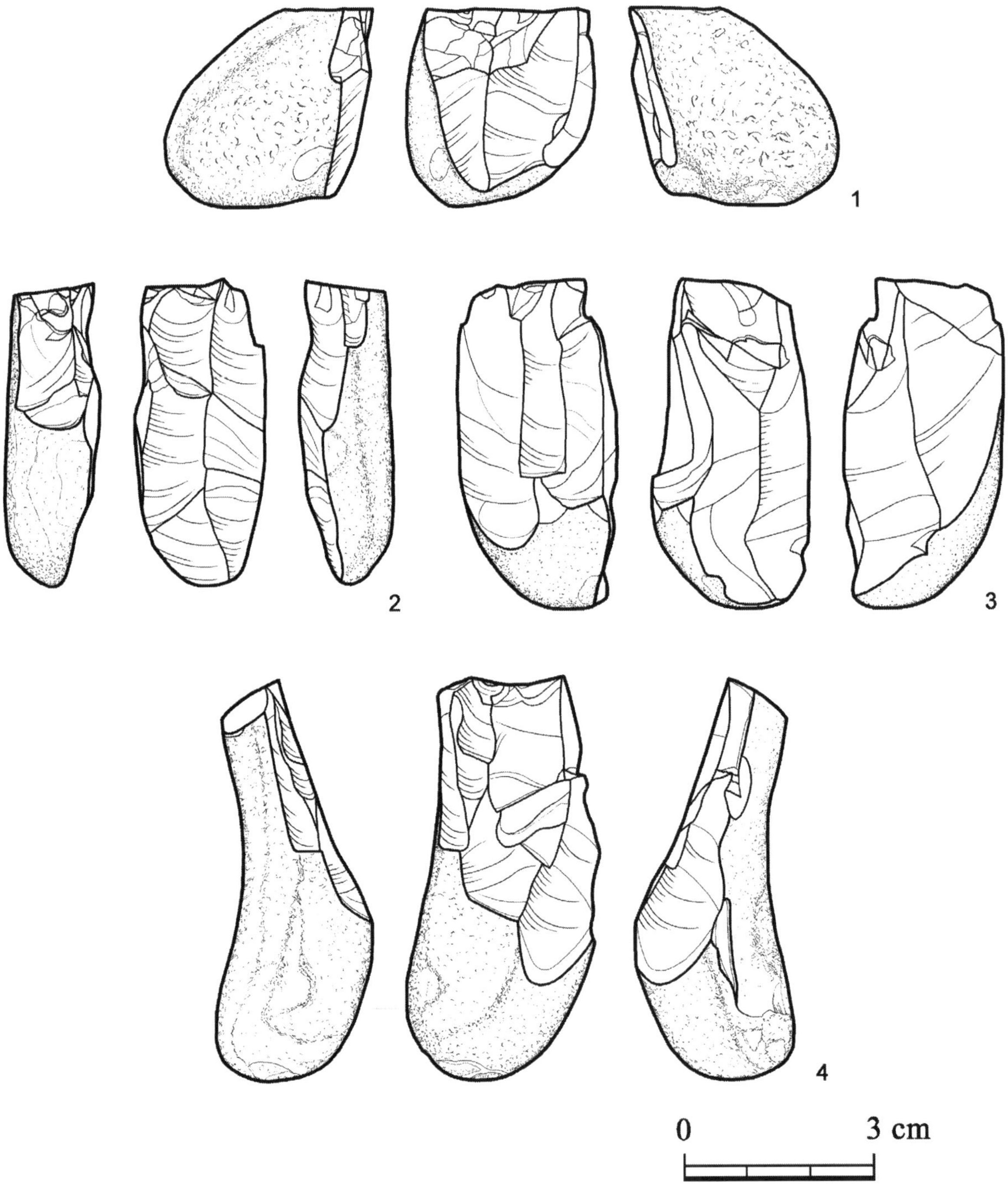

Fig.6.40. Cores collected at Site E29H1 Area D lithic debitage concentration A

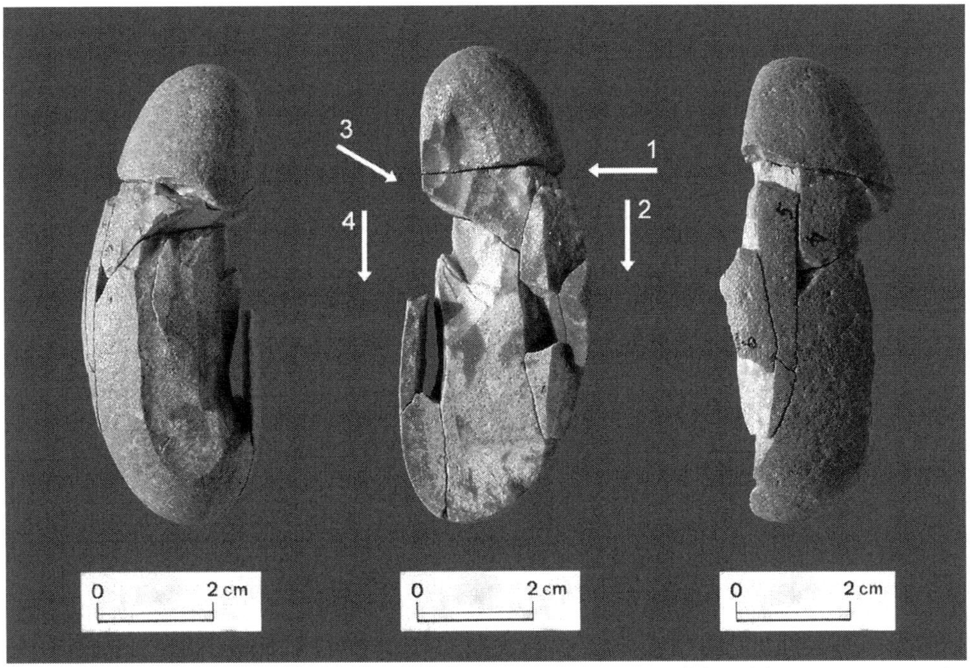

Fig.6.41. A refitted single platform core collected at Site E29H1 Area D lithic debitage concentration A

pebbles, it can tentatively be concluded that there were at least 31 flint pebbles.

6.6.6.4. Lithic manufacture

The manufacturing process which could be reconstructed from a successful example of refitting is as follows (**Fig.6.41**). Firstly, one end of an elongated or oval flint pebble (approximately a quarter of a piece) is struck off by bipolar wedging in order to create a flat, unfacetted platform. Then, cortical flakes and blades/bladelets were taken off continuously along the longer axis of the pebble by striking the edges of the platform. And finally, non-cortical blades/bladelets and flakes were obtained in the same manner of striking the edges of the platform. This example also shows that the platform was rejuvenated by way of removing a core tablet. Other debitage products which could not be refitted also suggest that blade/bladelet production was quite standardised by employing mainly single platform knapping.

6.6.6.5. Tools

The tools which were made from the cores mentioned above are evidently bladelets of 3-4 cm long. There is no complete bladelet of such a size in the collection, and only one complete straight-backed, pointed blade of 5 cm long with no basal retouch (Tixier's Type 45) was found. There was no core which can be associated with this blade, and hence this blade would have been included here by accident. Another broken backed bladelet included in this collection can reasonably be associated with debitage products. One denticulate was made on a non-cortical flake.

6.6.7. Lithic debitage concentration B

It turned out that this collection included only two backed bladelet and one unfinished backed bladelet. Apart from one whole pebble of 5.8 cm long, the rest of the collection, which amounted to 326 pieces, was cores and debitage products (**Table 6.48**). The debitage products could be easily divided into several categories

	n
whole pebble	1
single platform core	11
opposed platform core	2
multiple platform core	1
primary chunk	23
chip/chunk	9
primary flake	23
flake from single platform core	96
flake from opposed platform core	2
flake from ninety-degree core	2
flake from multiple platform core	8
unidentifiable flake	18
primary blade/bladelet	16
blade/bladelet from single platform core	108
blade/bladelet from opposed platform core	3
blade/bladelet from multiple platform core	2
unidentifiable blade/bladelet	2
backed bladelet (including 1 unfinished)	3
total	330

Table.6.48. Inventory of finds at Site E29H1 Area D lithic debitage concentration B

	n	%
single platform core	11	78.57
opposed platform core	2	14.29
multiple platform core	1	7.14
total	14	100.00

Table.6.49. Cores at Site E29H1 Area D lithic debitage concentration B

mentioned above. The success rate of refitting debitage products in this concentration was much higher than that in the other concentration.

6.6.7.1. Lithic raw materials

Some unexhausted cores and several successful refittings of debitage products suggest that the raw material is an elongated to oval or irregularly-shaped subangular flint pebble of 7-8 cm long and 2-3 cm wide. The surface of the pebbles is rounded and not heavily weathered. These characteristics are exactly the same as those of the pebbles in the other concentration.

	n	mean (cm)	st.dev
length	12	3.33	1.04
width	12	2.22	0.41
thickness	12	2.08	0.83

Table.6.50. Metrical data of measured cores on pebbles at Site E29H1 Area D lithic debitage concentration B

	n	mean (cm)	st.dev
length	2	2.10	0.00
width	2	2.25	0.05
thickness	2	2.20	0.50

Table.6.51. Metrical data of measured cores on conical or hemispherical chunks of pebbles at Site E29H1 Area D lithic debitage concentration B

6.6.7.2. Cores

Cores are not numerous in the collection (**Table 6.49**). Cores can be divided into two different categories based on their original shape. The first is made on pebbles of various shapes (**Table 6.50**). The second is made on conical or hemispherical chunks with almost 100 % cortex, which derived from elongated or globular pebbles, and the ventral face of the chunks were flaked (**Table 6.51**). The majority are single platform cores. Platforms are created on one end of an elongated or globular pebble by one strike, forming an angle of approximately 90 degrees or less with the longer axis of pebbles. As a consequence, an unfacetted platform is the most common form of platform preparation.

6.6.7.3. Debitage products

The number of debitage products in the collection is 312 (**Table 6.52**), and they are fairly small in size (**Table 6.53**). The predominance of single platform cores in the collection is also indicated by a large number of flakes and blades/bladelets struck from single platform cores. One notable kind of primary piece is a conical or hemispherical chunk with a complete cortex, which is the same as that seen at another debitage concentration. The chunks often have an impact bulb on the naturally flat proximal end with no platform preparation, and a tiny breakage on the

	n	%
primary chunk	23	7.37
chip/chunk	9	2.88
primary flake	23	7.37
flake from single platform core	96	30.77
flake from opposed platform core	2	0.64
flake from ninety-degree core	2	0.64
flake from multiple platform core	8	2.56
unidentifiable flake	18	5.77
primary blade/bladelet	16	5.13
blade/bladelet from single platform core	108	34.62
blade/bladelet from opposed platform core	3	0.96
blade/bladelet from multiple platform core	2	0.64
unidentifiable blade/bladelet	2	0.64
total	312	100.00

Table.6.52. Debitage products at Site E29H1 Area D lithic debitage concentration B

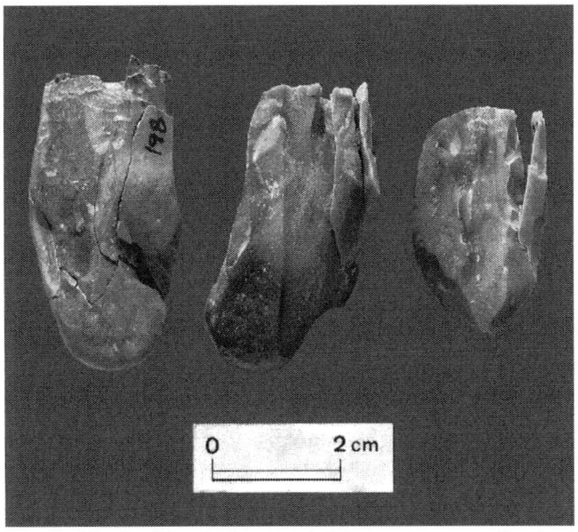

Fig.6.42. Refitted single platform cores collected at Site E29H1 Area D lithic debitage concentration B

	n	mean (cm)	st.dev
length	190	2.18	0.73
width	190	1.28	0.47
thickness	190	0.32	0.23

Table.6.53. Metrical data of measured debitage products at Site E29H1 Area D lithic debitage concentration B

distal end, and the ventral face is flat with few or no surface undulations. This means that these primary chunks were produced by bipolar wedging, in order to create a platform on one end of globular or elongated pebbles. Since the number of hemispherical or conical chunks reflects the number of pebbles, it can tentatively be concluded that there were at least 23 flint pebbles.

6.6.7.4. Lithic manufacture

The manufacturing process which could be reconstructed from some successful examples of refitting (**Fig.6.42**) is the same as described earlier. One end of an elongated or oval flint pebble is struck off in order to create a flat, unfacetted platform. Then, cortical flakes and bladelets were taken off continuously along the longer axis of the pebble by striking the edges of the platform. Finally, non-cortical flakes and bladelets were obtained in the same manner of striking the edges of the platform.

6.6.7.5. Tools

The tools which were made from the cores mentioned above are evidently bladelets of 3-4 cm long. Three backed bladelets including one broken piece and one unfinished piece were all less than 3 cm long. One complete one is a straight-backed, pointed bladelet with no basal retouch (Tixier's Type 45), and another broken one is an arch-backed bladelet with no basal retouch (Tixier's Type 56).

6.6.8. Some considerations on life at Site E29H1

It is significant to consider life at Site E29H1 in terms of the disposal acts of site occupants (Binford 1978). As mentioned, the association of individual hearths with the scatters of lithic debitage products and bone fragments in and around the hearths is not always clear because taphonomic processes must have affected their preservation to some extent. It is not certain whether the present scatter patterns precisely reflect dropping or tossing acts of the site occupants in prehistory.

In many cases, lithic debitage products are sparsely scattered in and around hearths, and they are not refittable to each other. Therefore, it is unlikely that this scatter pattern is a precise reflection of flint knapping and debitage dropping acts of some toolmakers which took place near the fire in the past. In contrast, some cases (Hearths 12 and 15) show clear concentrations of debitage products next to hearths, and such concentrations may perhaps suggest the presence of knapping activity areas. On the other hand, it must be kept in mind that the concentrations of debitage products do not necessarily indicate the exact place of toolmaking, but may indicate a least-used area. Supposedly lithic debitage dumping spots found in Area D seem to be a clear indication of collective dumping acts by toolmakers. Lithic debitage dumping acts are quite normal if people stay at a site continuously, because the scatter of debitage products on the living floor is dangerous to their bare feet. Therefore, lithic debitage dumping acts may be regarded as evidence for the long stay of the site occupants.

As for animal and fish bone fragments around hearths, it is more difficult to interpret their scatter or concentration patterns. Like lithic debitage products, bone fragments would have been dropped or tossed around hearths by people who dined there, or collectively dumped away from hearths. Therefore, concentrations of bone fragments do not necessarily indicate the exact place of butchering, cooking, or eating. While some hearths (Hearths 11, 12, 13 and 14) are accompanied by numerous bone fragments, other hearths are not accompanied by bone fragments. The former situation may suggest that residues of cooking and eating at the hearths remain scattered. The latter situation may mean that bone fragments were collectively dumped away from the hearths in order to keep the hearth area clean and tidy, or, bone fragments which had been scattered around the hearths were later taken away by scavenging animals. Several isolated concentrations of bone fragments found in the hearth field may indicate either dumping acts by site occupants or scavenging acts by carnivores.

It is also important to consider the life of Epipalaeolithic people at Site E29H1 in terms of their adaptive subsistence strategies. The site location strongly suggests that the major subsistence activities were the exploitation of resources on the gently-inclined basin shore and in the shallow water of the X Basin, and this suggestion has been supported by faunal remains obtained at Site E29H1, consisting of mammals like aurochs (wild cattle), hartebeest and hippopotamus, and fish like tilapia, clariid catfish, cyprinid, puffer and Nile perch (Gautier 1976b: Table I-7, Van Neer and Linseele 2007). This suggestion is also supported by the study of the technological organisation of the site occupants. The natural condition of the site, which is devoid of rock materials like flint pebbles suitable for tool making and limestone/ sandstone cobbles suitable for hearth making, suggests that the site occupants recognised it adaptive and optimal to bring all necessary materials to the site from somewhere else and to prepare for food procurement and consumption at the site. This is opposed to making necessary tools in advance of visiting the site, exploiting food resources at the site, and then taking them away immediately back to their residential bases elsewhere. If they had gone hunting on a desperate stalking basis, or if they had been under time stress to exploit available food resources as quickly as possible, they could not have afforded to sit down and to start making tools upon arrival at the site.

The large number of lithic debitage products at the site suggests that the whole lithic reduction sequence took place there, and that this was made possible by a continuous supply of flint pebbles from nearby sources. The fact that people could afford to start making tools at the site suggests that the wild food resources which they exploited were predictable, stable, and not easily depleted, and that their exploiting strategy entailed watching, ambushing and trapping, and not stalking. Fishing and fowling, which have been considered as the major subsistence of Fayum Epipalaeolithic people (Brewer 1989a; 1989b), are surely the activities achieved through watching, ambushing and trapping. As for mammals, it is not surprising if the sedentary mammals listed above were hunted by the Epipalaeolithic people in the same manner.

It is not certain whether their subsistence activities were performed by small groups of people for immediate daily consumption, or the activities were done by more than a few groups of people and included mass production of smoke-dried fish for later consumption, as has been attested at Late Palaeolithic sites in Middle and Upper Egypt (Gautier and Van Neer 1989; Vermeersch *et al.* 1989; Vermeersch *et al.* 2000). The multiple hearths at Area D of Site E29H1 would have been suitable for such mass production at one time, though insufficient faunal data have not supported the possibility of such mass exploitation of fish. It seems reasonable for the large number of flint tools produced at the site that they were made in order to process large amounts of fish as soon as they were caught. Such a demand for tools and probably their quick exhaustion may be one reason for numerous bladelets without backing retouch and a small number of formal tools in the collection. On the other hand, it is also possible that a large number of lithic artefacts in the hearth field are simply a cumulative result of repeated occupations. Based on the present evidence, several different interpretations are possible.

Since the faunal data are not good enough to know the seasonality of site occupation, it is hard to discuss the degree of sedentariness of the site occupants purely on the basis of faunal data. However, the geographic stability of the site and the persistence of a cyclical mobility pattern for some length of time are obvious from the evidence discussed above. In addition, it seems probable that the supply of flint pebbles and limestone/sandstone cobbles which were unavailable in the basin environment was made possible through short-distance return trips by task persons sent off from the site. Therefore, it is almost certain that the hearth field in Area D was continuously and repeatedly occupied, probably several times a year for many years, by Epipalaeolithic people. But referring to controversial discussions on the definition of sedentariness (Chatters 1987: 347-348; Rafferty 1985: 113-116), it is difficult to say that the people who stayed there were sedentary, unless it is revealed that at least part of the site occupants remained there throughout the entire year. As mentioned, the site seems to have experienced inundations even during the Epipalaeolithic period, and therefore, sedentary occupation in a strict sense was physically impossible. However, temporary upward and downward shifts of habitation in this basin environment according to the water level could be one option. If the inhabitants did adopt such shifts and remained there, then their habitation may perhaps be called semi-sedentary.

6.7. Epipalaeolithic lithic assemblage at a watching station in Wadi B

6.7.1. Introduction

It has been revealed by previous research that Epipalaeolithic people were dependent heavily on aquatic resources on the lakeshore. Furthermore, it has been suggested that most Fayum Epipalaeolithic sites might reflect seasonal fishing occupations, and that a very different economic emphasis might possibly be indicated for the same group when they utilised a different microenvironmental situation or in the base camps wherever they were located (Wendorf and Schild 1976: 317). However, this suggestion has never been substantiated by the discovery of base camps and other kinds of sites in different environmental situations.

New discoveries of the remains of Epipalaeolithic human activities were made in a desert wadi which connects the northern rocky terrain of the Fayum Depression and the lakeshore. Some Epipalaeolithic tools were found along the wadi during the survey, and the most important discovery in the wadi was a concentration of Epipalaeolithic lithic artefacts on a high wadi bank, which is approximately 15 km to the north of the Epipalaeolithic lakeshore. The findspot (N29.71137° E30.86858°) is located on an edge of the eastern bank, whose elevation is around 130 m asl, overlooking the wadi floor to the northwest (**Fig.6.43**). There are no structural remains like hearths and no faunal remains in the surroundings. Therefore, the study

Fig.6.43. An Epipalaeolithic watching station in Wadi B (looking north)

Fig.6.44. Scatter of lithic artefacts on the gravelly surface of a watching station in Wadi B

of this isolated concentration of lithic artefacts is the only way of understanding the nature of this locality.

6.7.2. Lithic assemblage at the watching station

The surface of the bank is covered by flint gravel and fine-grained aeolian sand (**Fig.6.44**). On this gravelly surface, 105 pieces of lithic artefacts, including a number of blade/bladelet cores and only a few retouched tools, were concentrated within an approximately 5 m radius. They sit on a slightly consolidated surface, but it is not certain whether more pieces are buried beneath the surface, because no excavation was carried out. All of the surface artefacts were collected and studied (**Table 6.54**).

	n
single platform core	21
multiple platform core	3
core tablet	2
primary chunk	4
chip/chunk	9
primary flake	7
flake from single platform core	22
flake from opposed platform core	1
flake from ninety-degree core	1
flake from multiple platform core	7
primary blade/bladelet	2
blade/bladelet from single platform core	17
blade/bladelet from opposed platform core	1
blade/bladelet from multiple platform core	2
unidentifiable blade/bladelet	1
backed blade/bladelet	1
retouched flake	4
total	105

Table.6.54. Inventory of finds at Wadi B watching station

	n	%
single platform core	21	87.50
multiple platform core	3	12.50
total	24	100.00

Table.6.55. Cores at Wadi B watching station

6.7.2.1. Lithic raw materials

One raw material at this site is a rounded and weathered/abraded flint cobble of light to dark brown. Most cobbles commonly have a brown to dark brown cortex, but some have a calcareous cortex. Although the examples are fragmentary, the whole shape of the cobble seems to be oval with some flat faces. Such cobbles are not seen in the surroundings, and hence it is supposed that they were transported from elsewhere.

Another raw material is an abraded/polished pebble. The pebbles are subangular to rounded, the shape is elongated to oval, but there are flat

	n	mean (cm)	st.dev
length	4	2.43	0.61
width	4	4.00	0.42
thickness	4	2.98	1.29

Table.6.56. Metrical data of measured cores on pebbles at Wadi B watching station

	n	mean (cm)	st.dev
length	2	2.25	0.05
width	2	2.85	0.25
thickness	2	3.30	0.50

Table.6.58. Metrical data of measured cores on conical or hemispherical chunks of pebbles at Wadi B watching station

	n	mean (cm)	st.dev
length	7	2.94	0.76
width	7	3.07	0.77
thickness	7	2.40	1.00

Table.6.57. Metrical data of measured cores on fragments of pebbles at Wadi B watching station

	n	mean (cm)	st.dev
length	11	3.81	1.53
width	11	3.56	0.79
thickness	11	2.25	0.52

Table.6.59. Metrical data of measured cores on fragments of cobbles at Wadi B watching station

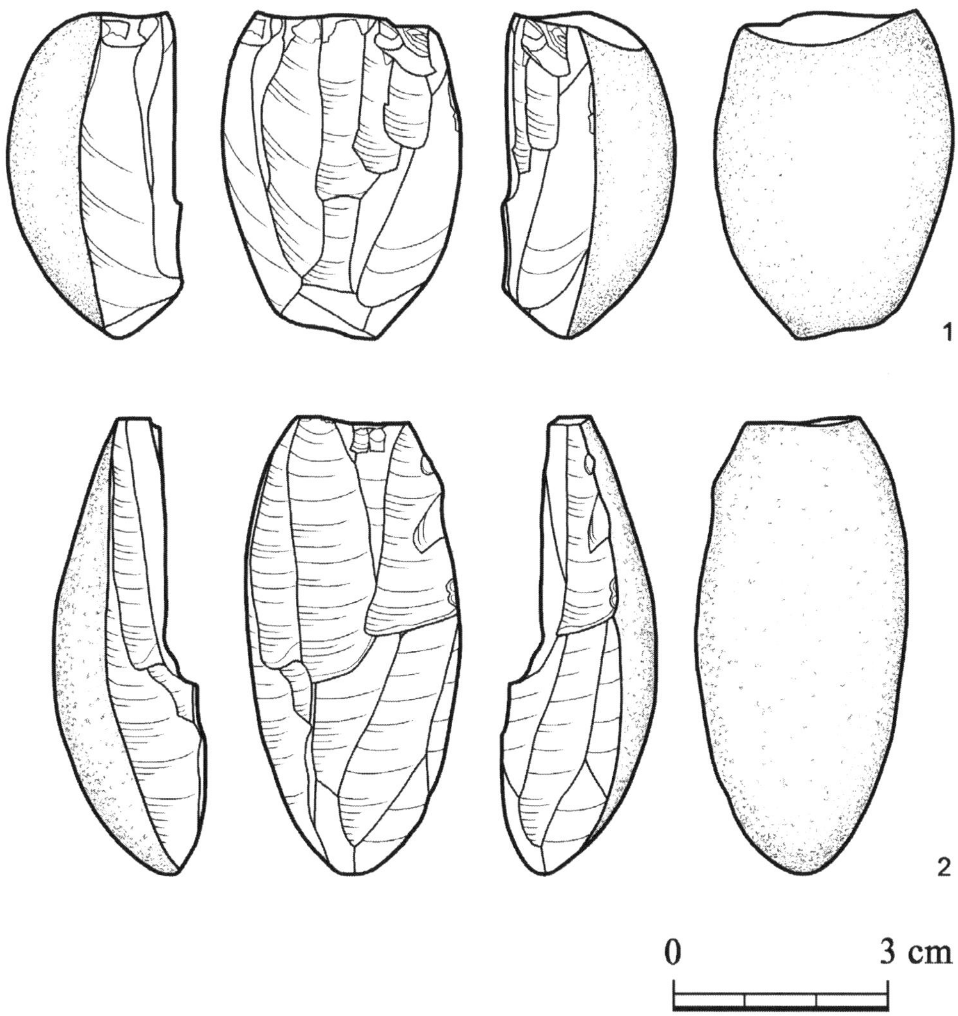

Fig.6.45. Single platform cores collected at Wadi B watching station

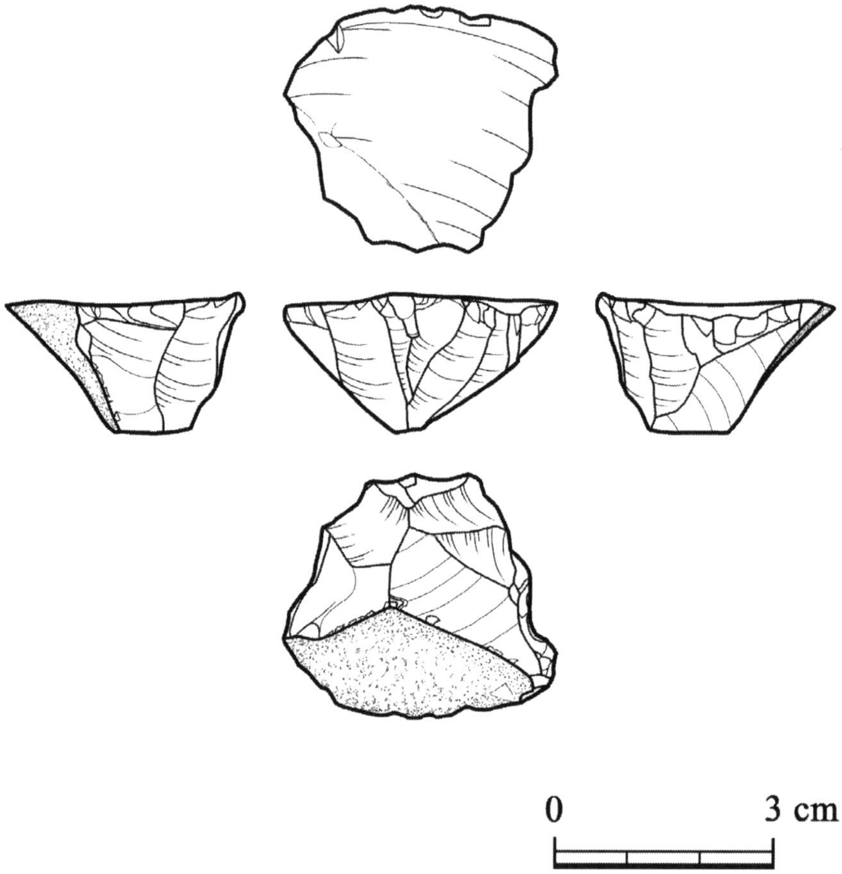

Fig.6.46. A single platform core collected at Wadi B watching station

and irregular-shaped varieties. The surface is generally smooth and not undulated. Such pebbles of 6-7 cm long and 3-4 cm wide are abundantly scattered in this area, and it is highly likely that these were picked up and used.

6.7.2.2. Cores

Cores are numerous against debitage products in the collection (**Table 6.55**). Cores can be divided into four different categories based on their original shape. The first is made on pebbles of various shapes (**Table 6.56**). The second is made on fragments of pebbles (**Table 6.57**). The third is made on conical or hemispherical chunks with an almost 100 % cortex, which derived from elongated or globular pebbles, and the ventral face of the chunks were flaked (**Table 6.58**). The fourth is made on fragments of cobbles (**Table 6.59**). Cores are dominated by single platform cores (**Fig.6.45**-1 and 2, and **Fig.6.46**), amounting to 21. Opposed platform cores (**Fig.6.47**-1 and 2) and multiple platform cores are few. Eight of the 21 single platform cores are made on subangular or rounded fragments of weathered/abraded cobbles. The rest are made on locally-available pebbles of various size and shape and their fragments.

6.7.2.3. Debitage products

The number of debitage products seems to be small against the number of cores (**Table 6.60**). Debitage products also indicate that they derived from two distinct raw materials; abraded/polished flint pebble and weathered/abraded flint

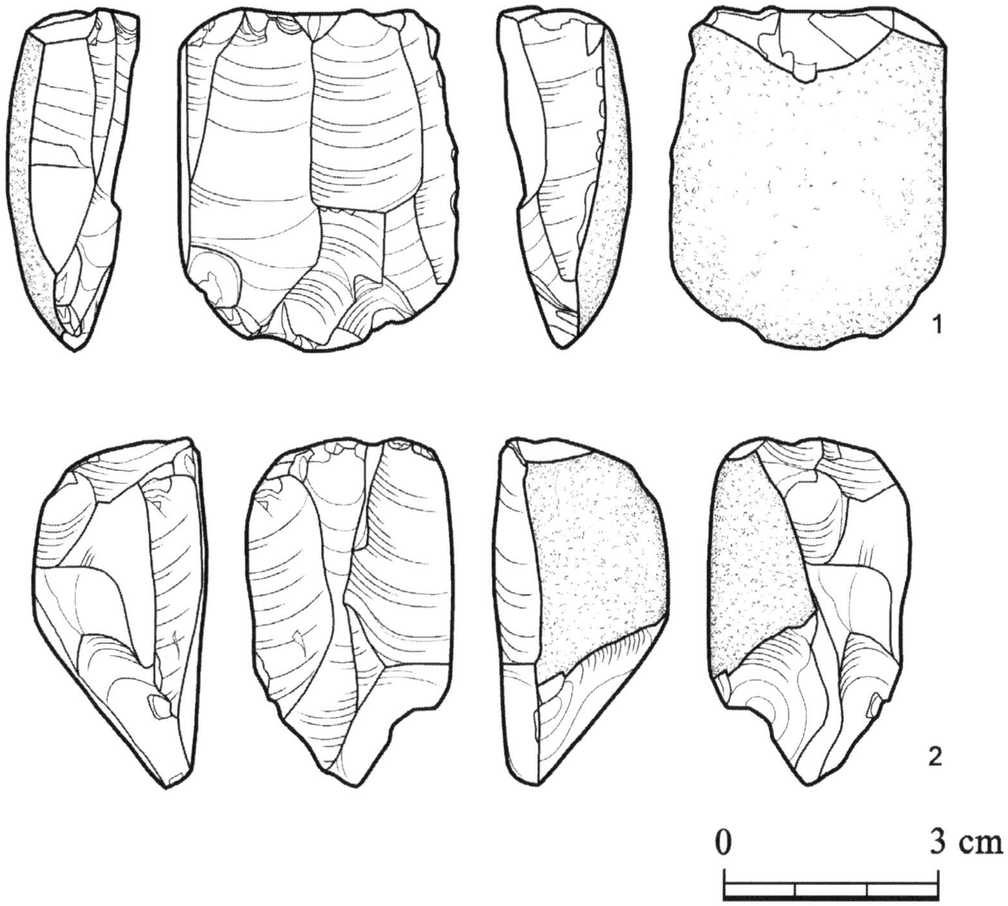

Fig.6.47. Opposed platform cores collected at Wadi B watching station

	n	%
core tablet	2	2.63
primary chunk	4	5.26
chip/chunk	9	11.84
primary flake	7	9.21
flake from single platform core	22	28.95
flake from opposed platform core	1	1.32
flake from ninety-degree core	1	1.32
flake from multiple platform core	7	9.21
primary blade/bladelet	2	2.63
blade/bladelet from single platform core	17	22.37
blade/bladelet from opposed platform core	1	1.32
blade/bladelet from multiple platform core	2	2.63
unidentifiable blade/bladelet	1	1.32
total	76	100.00

Table.6.60. Debitage products at Wadi B watching station

	n	mean (cm)	st.dev
length	38	3.85	0.94
width	38	2.47	0.78
thickness	38	1.00	0.61

Table.6.61. Metrical data of measured debitage products at Wadi B watching station

cobble. The large size of debitage products suggests that they were struck from cobbles rather than pebbles (**Table 6.61**). Non-cortical blades/bladelets, flakes, and chunks are not numerous, and most debitage products have a cortex. Therefore, it is likely that knapping was initiated here from whole pebbles and cobbles. An attempt of refitting these debitage products was not successful, even though it was recognised that several debitage products belonged to particular pebbles or cobbles. This may suggest that this locality was visited briefly but repeatedly, and that the rate of transport of usable flakes and blades/bladelets to other places was high.

6.7.2.4. Lithic manufacture

In the case of cobble use, a cobble is half-split or quarter-split along the longer axis, and the ventral face of a fragment is struck from an unfacetted platform repeatedly to obtain blades/bladelets. Informal large fragments from cobbles were also used as multiple platform cores. In the case of pebble use, the basic knapping technique is quite similar to that observed in the X Basin and Z Basin areas. One end of an elongated or globular pebble is chopped off to make an unfacetted platform, and then several bladelets were flaked from this.

6.7.2.5. Tools

Tools are not numerous in the collection. Only several blades with or without a retouched edge and informally retouched tools made on flakes are included. There is one curious elongated scraper with backing retouch on one lateral margin. The cores suggest that major objectives of the toolmakers were to produce not only blades of approximately 5 cm long but also flakes of approximately 2 cm long.

6.7.3. The mobility and subsistence of Epipalaeolithic people in a wadi

A remarkable thing about these debitage products is that many of them are produced from apparently large cobbles which are not seen in the immediate surroundings. Although rounded and abraded/polished, elongated pebbles which had been commonly used by Epipalaeolithic toolmakers of the X Basin and Z Basin naturally occur on the wadi bank, they were not exclusively used. Many cores are so fragmentary that it is not easy to imagine the original shape of the cobble, but it seems that the most commonly used cobbles are rounded and weathered/abraded, flat and oval cobbles, or irregularly-shaped or subangular cobbles. It is probable that the sources of these cobbles are Pliocene gravel deposits which are to the south and northeast of Ilwet Hialla (Sandford and Arkell 1929: 16-22).

Several isolated Epipalaeolithic finds along a wadi have already indicated that Epipalaeolithic people had passed through the wadi while making and using flint tools, but a concentration of lithic debitage products at a location on the wadi bank very far to the north of the lake substantiates that Epipalaeolithic people did stop and stay at such a distant locality. Considering this odd situation and the location with a fine view, it is most likely that this was a watching station or hunting stand, where Epipalaeolithic hunters sat down and made tools while watching for game animals in the wadi. They stayed there for a while, perhaps overnight. These findings require reconsideration of the subsistence and mobility strategies of Fayum Epipalaeolithic people.

It must be considered that the Epipalaeolithic people who resided on the lakeshore had occasionally organised long distance hunting and monitoring trips to the wadi. A concentration of lithic debitage products at a wadi locality strongly suggests that people did not bring ready-made tools but brought raw materials there from elsewhere and made tools as the occasion arose. As mentioned, provided that sources of the raw materials are located further to the east and northeast of the locality, it can be said that lithic raw material procurement was combined with, or embedded in, hunting and monitoring trips. This means that their hunting did not entail desperate stalking but was on an ambush basis. The rarity of backed blades which must have been made from large cobbles at this locality suggests that finished tools were taken away with the hunters to their lakeshore habitat. This can explain the presence of backed blades and the absence or rarity of large cores for blade production in the X Basin and Z Basin sites.

This wadi locality is approximately 15 km far away from the nearest Epipalaeolithic habitation localities on the lakeshore, and there is no permanent standing water around the wadi locality. Therefore, it is assumed that the people could visit this wadi locality only when sufficient surface water became available by winter rain, and that hunting in the wadi was basically a winter activity and the appearance of game animals was predictable. Since no similar localities were found in the vicinity, it is unlikely that their visit to this wadi locality was the seasonal migration by the entire group of people who usually inhabited the lakeshore. It is more likely that a small task group was sent off to the wadi locality from the lakeshore residential base, and the majority of people remained on the lakeshore. This implies a logistical manner of mobility by basically sedentary people. As an ethnoarchaeological study has suggested, a watching station or hunting stand was primarily an information gathering location, and hence animals were rarely killed directly from such a place, while the place was not necessarily the place for consumption of hunted animals (Binford 1978). Therefore, there may probably be the remains of butchering or camping in the wadi, but large portions of meat must have been transported to the lakeshore residential base.

6.8. The procurement of flint pebbles/cobbles, core reduction techniques, and tool use in the Fayum Epipalaeolithic

Although the sampling method and the size of sample were not consistent between studied localities/sites, the collected data give some new ideas about the similarity and variability in the uses of flint pebbles/cobbles and core reduction techniques in the Fayum Epipalaeolithic. Since tools were not numerous in this study, previous knowledge of the tool assemblages did not have to be revised considerably. Instead, knowledge was surely augmented and strengthened by the information about what kind of flint pebbles/cobbles had preferentially been procured, from which sources, and how they had actually been knapped and discarded.

There is no reason to believe that the Epipalaeolithic people who resided in the X Basin and Z Basin travelled so far westwards as to the Qasr el-Sagha escarpments in order to procure flint pebbles, because the Qasr el-Sagha escarpments are not the sole sources and similar flint pebbles are readily available on the gravelly escarpments to the north of the X Basin and Z Basin. Therefore, contrary to the previous idea about the source of flint in the Fayum (Wendorf and Schild 1976: 311), it must be emphasised that the procurement of most commonly-used raw material in the Fayum Epipalaeolithic did not necessarily entail long distance trips. This may also affect the previous image that Fayum Epipalaeolithic people were highly mobile. People could actually procure lithic raw materials within easy walking distance from their subsistence loci.

The frequency of specific core types in the Fayum Epipalaeolithic is definitely determined by the availability or accessibility of raw materials. As described in detail, the most common raw material in Site Z and Site E29H1 was an elongated flint pebble of less than 7 cm long, and predominant single platform cores were followed in percentages by opposed platform cores. It is obvious that the size and shape of the raw material guided flint knappers to the easiest way of holding by hand and flaking. Creating a platform by breaking off one end or two ends of an elongated pebble and flaking along the longer axis of the pebble is actually the best way of making cutting edges of blades/bladelets as long as possible, though it is difficult to obtain blades of more than 5 cm long from these pebbles. The rarity of microburins in Fayum Epipalaeolithic assemblages is quite reasonable, simply because blades which are long enough to be snapped by the microburin technique are not usually available.

As the successful refitting of debitage products and the presence of unworked pebbles and numerous cortical flakes/bladelets indicate, elongated pebbles were brought from source areas without decortification, and core reduction began at habitation or task localities. Considering the small size and light weight of pebbles and the short distance to the supposed source areas, transporting a whole handful of pebbles repeatedly would not have been burdensome. Most single platform cores made on elongated pebbles were discarded after a few non-cortical bladelets of a certain length were obtained, and hence the use of pebbles seems to have been wasteful. Such seemingly wasteful use of raw material for bladelet production is known in other regions of Egypt. A study in the Nabta-Kiseiba region of the Egyptian Western Desert has revealed that bladelets were almost identical in size even when the cores could have produced longer blanks, and that cores which could no longer produce bladelets of the required size were abandoned even though they were still able to yield smaller blanks and even though the raw material source was far away (Close 1999; 2002a: 36). Therefore, it is possible to argue that the size of bladelets could have been constrained by cultural and functional rather than purely economic reasons, and considerations of hafting and/or composite use were the most likely reasons. In the case of the Fayum, however, the wasteful use of raw materials would have been facilitated by a constant supply from nearby source areas, and the gap between the required size of bladelet and the size of available core was much smaller. On the other hand, in the Fayum Epipalaeolithic, the use of conical or hemispherical chunks which derive from elongated pebbles for obtaining a couple of microbladelets from the ventral face has repeatedly been seen. This manner of chunk use does not seem to be merely expedient raw material use, but may be a kind of habitual economising behaviour to make the most of debitage products (Odell 1996).

It is assumed that making bladelets quickly by using readily-available raw materials wastefully and replacing worn or broken bladelets frequently by new ones would have been recognised by Fayum Epipalaeolithic toolmakers as cost-efficient. This is in contrast to making and maintaining elaborate tools that cost very much in terms of time and labour to procure raw materials and to work on them meticulously but achieve the foraging goals without failure and/or persist for a long time. It has been described that backed bladelets were extremely frequent whereas geometrics and microburins were very rare in the Fayum Epipalaeolithic (Wendorf and Schild 1976: 311). However, in terms of the idea of lithic technological organisation, the extreme frequency of backed bladelets can be regarded as a consequence of the Fayum toolmakers' efforts to optimise their use of the most readily available raw material to meet the technical requirements for their major subsistence activities.

Without microwear analysis, it is difficult to know how the bladelets of the Fayum Epipalaeolithic were actually hafted and used and on what material. A microwear study of similar bladelets from a Late Palaeolithic site in the Nile Valley of Lower Nubia has suggested that the bladelets were most likely used for scraping unknown soft materials (Becker and Wendorf 1993). Another microwear study of similar bladelets from a Late Palaeolithic site in the Nile Valley of Upper Egypt has revealed that they were used for thrusting, cutting and scraping, and on materials including skin, hide, bone and wood (Longo 1997). A further microwear study of blades and bladelets from the Epipalaeolithic sites of Elkab in the Nile Valley of Upper Egypt and Tree Shelter near the Red Sea coast of the Eastern Desert, which are contemporaneous with the Fayum Epipalaeolithic, has also revealed that some of the blades and bladelets were used for meat cutting, hide working and wood working, but that most of the backed bladelets studied had no traces of use (Kweakason 2008). An important insight obtained through these microwear studies of bladelets is that subtle differences in tool morphology are not related to differences in the actual utilisation of the tools. This may also be the case with the bladelets of the Fayum Epipalaeolithic, and the versatility of bladelets must always be kept in mind.

Nonetheless, given the mass production and supposedly frequent replacement of bladelets at use locations as reflected in debitage dumping spots in Site Z and Site E29H1, it is reasonable to presume that the Fayum bladelets may have been used for tasks which caused quick exhaustion or breakage of pointed edges or lateral edges in the short term. Furthermore, given the range of available wild food resources in the circumscribed lacustrine environment of the Fayum, it is assumed that the bladelet-using tasks in question would have been mainly catching and processing fish, which come in large numbers near lakeshores seasonally. The general mobility/residential strategies of Fayum Epipalaeolithic people must also be reconsidered in the light of their raw material procurement and tool making/using activities. It can be assumed that they principally maintained residential bases near lakeshores and relied on lacustrine resources, while procuring additional resources through logistical moves by individuals or small task groups.

As for other tools in the Fayum Epipalaeolithic, notches and denticulates made on large, thick flakes deriving from flint pebbles are noticeable though not numerous. Hence their general paucity in the Fayum can probably be understood in terms of curated/expedient toolmaking. Considering the multifunctionality of bladelets, the only asset of notches and denticulates made on large, thick flakes may be their durability for heavy-duty tasks like whittling or straightening wooden branches and bones for making shafts and handles. Making shafts and handles is generally more time-consuming and labour-intensive than making and replacing hafted stone tools, and hence shafts and handles tend to be more repeatedly used once they are made (Keeley 1982: 800). Therefore, if shafts and handles were not frequently replaced, there might have been relatively fewer occasions on which notches and denticulates were needed.

On the other hand, the occurrence of locally-unavailable flint cobbles in the lithic assemblages at Site Z and the Camp II Ridge suggests that Fayum Epipalaeolithic toolmakers did make extra efforts to procure raw materials from distant sources. It can be said that the lithic technological organisation in the Fayum Epipalaeolithic was not always expediently-oriented, but was adjusted as opportunity or necessity arose. A question is when this might have happened. Since no absolute dates of the studied localities/sites were obtained, it is not certain whether the deviation from the basically expedient technological organisation occurred usually and elsewhere throughout the Epipalaeolithic period depending on seasonal and annual fluctuations of available food resources, or occurred gradually towards a more time-consuming and labour-intensive technological organisation in order to exploit profitable but risky resources and/or depleting resources by all means available. Nonetheless, as already suggested, it is unlikely that Epipalaeolithic people moved their residential bases frequently, but more likely that lithic raw material procurement was achieved logistically and was embedded in foraging or monitoring trips by a task group dispatched from a residential base. Therefore, the occurrence of locally-unavailable cobbles in the lithic assemblages at Site Z and the Camp II Ridge may not reflect a radical change in the general mobility strategy of Epipalaeolithic people, but may suggest the rise in demand for larger raw materials in response to the optimisation of technological investment in subsistence activities. Demands for longer cutting edges for more time-efficient cutting and scraping tasks would be behind the appearance of locally-unavailable cobbles.

6.9. Concluding remarks

Previous studies have suggested that most Fayum Epipalaeolithic sites might represent seasonal encampments mainly for fishing on the grounds that few substantial structural remains have been found. However, given the harsh Fayum environment which has suffered from severe deflation, the lack of substantial structural remains should not necessarily be taken as a lack of evidence for sedentary life in the Fayum Epipalaeolithic. The study of several Fayum Epipalaeolithic sites and lithic technological organisation at the sites has demonstrated that Epipalaeolithic people's stay on lakeshores was not short and that the people were unlikely to move their residential bases frequently over long distances. The lithic technological organisation of the Fayum Epipalaeolithic as revealed through the study of raw material procurement and use suggests that Fayum Epipalaeolithic people principally adopted a logistical mobility strategy, while maintaining residential bases near lakeshores in order to make the most of lacustrine resources. Therefore, it must be stressed again that the transition from the Fayum Epipalaeolithic to Neolithic should not simplistically be supposed as a shift toward sedentism or toward food production, but should rather be investigated as an optimisation in technological investments in subsistence activities under changing environmental and demographic conditions.

7. Lithic technological organisation and mobility in the Fayum Neolithic

7.1. Introduction

The Fayum Neolithic culture has been known not only for its earliest evidence of wheat/barley farming combined with sheep/goat herding in Egypt but also for its elaborate bifacially-retouched flint tools. Antiquarians and scholars have randomly collected Neolithic flint tools at many locations around Lake Qarun in the past hundred years, and nice-looking bifacially-retouched formal tools like axes, arrowheads, sickle blades and knives have tended to be selectively collected and published. As mentioned in Chapter 3, Caton-Thompson, who worked at many Neolithic sites on the northern shore of Lake Qarun, reported a predominance of bifacial tools in her Fayum Neolithic inventory (Caton-Thompson and Gardner 1934). However, other researchers have later undertaken excavations in Qasr el-Sagha as well as surface artefact collection at one site where Caton-Thompson worked, and revealed that she had neglected crude, less-retouched flake tools. Therefore, it became apparent that previously accepted images of the lithic tradition of the Fayum Neolithic were the result of selective collecting, and hence distorted. On the basis of the Qasr el-Sagha lithic assemblage, it has been estimated that 90 percent of the Fayum Neolithic flint tool assemblage must have been composed of flake tools, such as notches, denticulates and sidescrapers, and thus bifacially-retouched tools were quite minor components, even though they certainly existed at most Neolithic sites of the Fayum (Kozlowski and Ginter 1989: 172*ff*).

This revision of the image of the Fayum Neolithic tool assemblage gives rise to another important question about how such a variety of tools was actually made and used. Whereas great attention has been paid to the description of the tool classification in the Fayum Neolithic, toolmaking techniques in the Fayum Neolithic have been poorly studied. Not merely reconstructing the whole sequence of lithic reduction in terms of purely technical aspects but also understanding how this reduction sequence is closely associated with general subsistence and mobility strategies of prehistoric and ethnographic foragers have been popular as the studies of lithic technological organisation since the late 1970s (Binford 1979; Odell 2001: 62-69). This kind of study is definitely relevant to answer the questions as for how Neolithic subsistence activities such as wheat/barley farming and sheep/goat herding were integrated with the tradition of Epipalaeolithic hunting, gathering and fishing in the Fayum, and to what extent Fayum Neolithic people were mobile.

One remarkable thing in the lithic technology of the Fayum Neolithic, which is made clear in this study, is the exploitation of large flint cobbles. Whereas the Fayum Epipalaeolithic people preferred elongated flint pebbles which were readily available within their habitat and did not abundantly use large cobbles, the Neolithic people more abundantly used large cobbles which were not readily available around their lakeshore habitat. There is no doubt that these cobbles were transported to their habitat from distant source areas. Identifying the sources of these cobbles is a key to know the mobility range of Fayum Neolithic toolmakers and to understand the beginning of the lithic reduction sequence.

This study will focus on both unworked cobbles and lithic cores which were collected at selected Neolithic sites in the Fayum, and will discuss not only core reduction techniques and sequence but also raw material procurement and transport, while considering possible sources of raw materials. How the development of bifacial technology was realised in the Fayum Neolithic

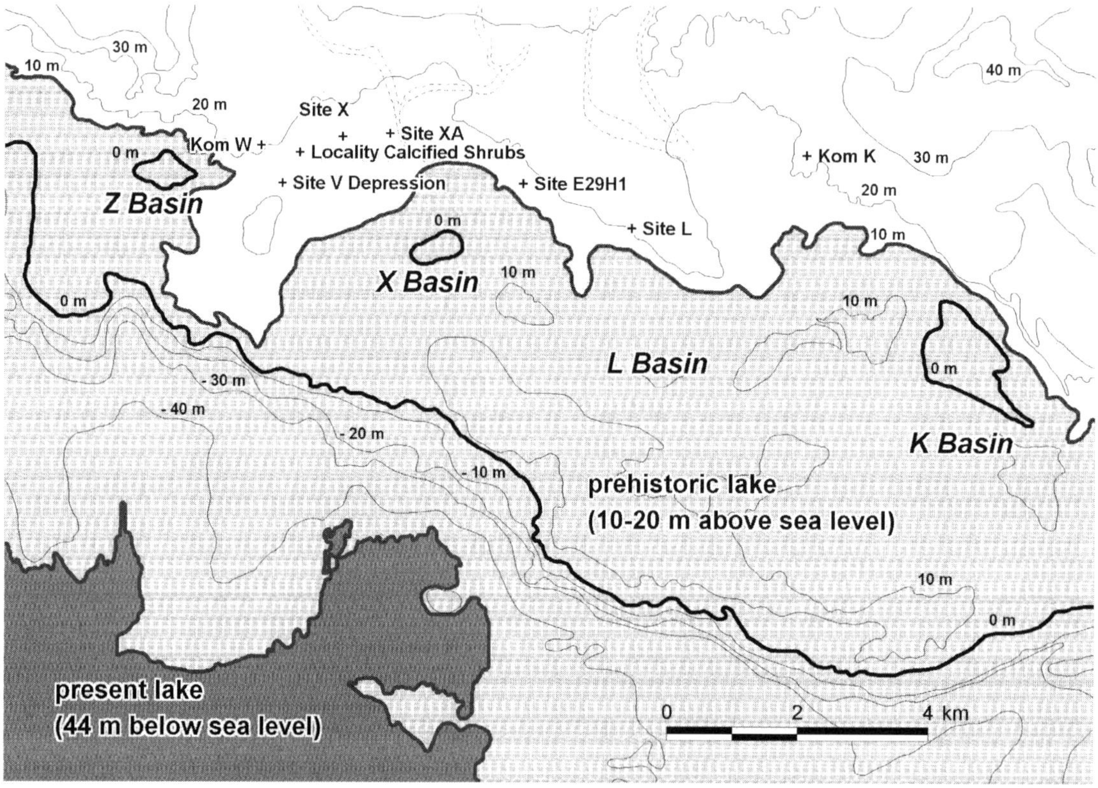

Fig.7.1. Map of the sites studied in this chapter

will also be argued on the basis of this discussion. Based on the lack of evidence for substantial dwellings at any sites, previous scholars have been reluctant to say that Fayum Neolithic people were sedentary, but unexplored features of the Fayum Neolithic culture like the mobility range and strategy of Fayum inhabitants will be revealed by this study. It will help discuss how their subsistence activities and mobility changed or did not change in terms of alternations in their use of raw materials and tools.

7.2. Sites studied

In order to understand the spatial distribution of various lithic raw materials and reduction techniques, eight Neolithic sites on the northeastern shore of Lake Qarun were selected and investigated. They are 1) Kom K, 2) Site L, 3) Site E29H1, 4) Site XA, 5) Site X, 6) Locality 'Calcified Shrubs', 7) Kom W, and 8) the Site V Depression, from the east to the west (**Fig.7.1**). The first four sites are approximately 2 km distant from each other, and the distance between Site XA and Kom W is also approximately 2 km. Site X is approximately 500 m distant from Site XA. Locality 'Calcified Shrubs' is approximately 300 m distant from Kom W. The Site V Depression is approximately 150 m distant from Kom W. Among these sites, Kom K and Kom W are the largest Neolithic sites known in the Fayum. Although no substantial dwelling structure has been found, accumulations of cultural debris as well as many fireholes excavated by Caton-Thompson at these two sites suggest that these two sites were occupied for a considerable length of time. Indeed, the variety of lithic raw materials is particularly wider at Kom K and Kom W than that in other presumably temporary sites. The degree of preservation is different between the sites, and Kom K and Kom W are the most severely disturbed by excavations. Therefore, it was difficult to apply the same method of surface material sampling to all these sites.

7.2.1. Kom K

Kom K (N29.58737° E30.87825° in the centre) is located to the northwest of the K Basin, and its elevation is approximately 20 m asl. Caton-Thompson's excavation at Kom K yielded a number of unifacially/bifacially-retouched, partly-retouched, or ground formal tools mainly made of flint, and they were neatly published. The unifacially/bifacially-retouched formal tools include 28 axes, ten sickle blades, seven concave-based arrowheads, one tanged arrowhead, four triangular arrowheads, one leaf-shaped spearhead, two knife blades, and some halberds. It is noted that a number of egg-shaped or oval quartz pebbles, most of which were battered at the extremities, were found on the surface and *in situ*. However, there is no detailed description of lithic debitage products in her report, and they were mentioned as village debris (Caton-Thompson and Gardner 1934: 38*ff*).

Presently, Kom K is a very low mound which has recently been ploughed heavily (**Fig.7.2**), and hence no trace of the trenches excavated by Caton-Thompson is visible. Nevertheless, there are dense scatters of hammer stones, lithic cores, debitage products, and pottery sherds in between ploughed tracks on top of the mound. This means that such objects were totally neglected and left there during Caton-Thompson's excavation. An important fact revealed by this situation is that some stages of lithic core reduction sequence actually took place on the site during the

Fig.7.2. Plough tracks on Kom K (looking west)

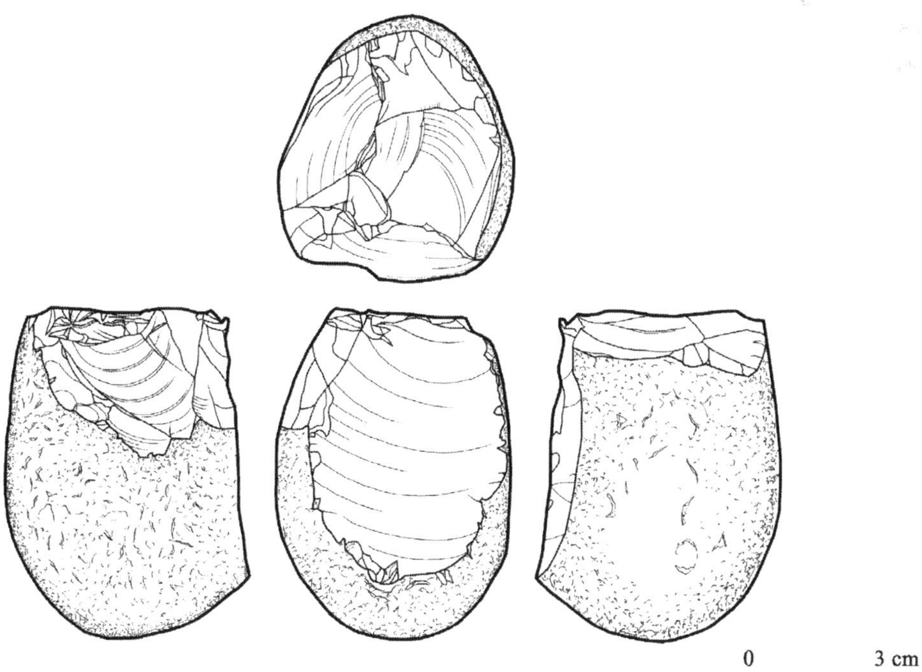

Fig.7.3. A core collected at Kom K

	item	platform preparation	knapping sequence	amount of cortex	L (cm)	W (cm)	T (cm)	cobble type	cortex colour	fresh part colour
1	bifacial platform core, or, chopper	cortical/unfacetted	tertiary	50-75 %	9.1	7.5	3.6	D	brown/cream brown	dark brown
2	bifacial platform core, or, chopper	cortical/facetted	secondary	50-75 %	3.2	7.6	5.9	D	brown/cream brown	brown
3	single platform core	unfacetted	multiple	50-75 %	7.3	5.3	5.7	G	brown	dark brown
4	single platform core	cortical	tertiary	76-99 %	5.3	6.1	8.9	I	brown	brown
5	single platform core	unfacetted	multiple	50-75 %	4.7	10.8	7.0	I	brown	cream
6	single platform core	unfacetted	multiple	50-75 %	4.2	4.2	6.6	G	cream	brown.
7	single platform core	unfacetted	multiple	50-75 %	7.2	6.6	5.5	G	brown/cream brown	mottled brown
8	single platform core	cortical	secondary	76-99%	3.5	6.0	7.9	E	dark brown	dark brown
9	bifacial platform core, or, chopper	unfacetted	multiple	25-49%	3.5	8.6	7.3	D	brown/cream brown	brown
10	single platform core	unfacetted	tertiary	76-99%	7.0	8.4	2.2	A	light brown	brown
11	single platform core	cortical	tertiary	76-99%	3.5	8.8	8.4	K	light brown	light brown
12	single platform core	unfacetted	multiple	25-49%	7.0	8.5	6.4	L	grey	translucent grey
13	single platform core	cortical	secondary	50-75 %	6.8	6.6	4.4	L	grey	translucent grey
14	whole cobble	-	-	-	7.0	7.1	3.3	C	brown	-
	item	**use of circumference**	**percussion sequence**	**amount of cortex**	**L (cm)**	**W (cm)**	**T (cm)**	**cobble type**	**cortex colour**	**fresh part colour**
1	longitudinal hammer	at one end (fractures on both faces)	less than multiple	76-99%	6.6	5.3	3.4	E	dark brown	brown
2	longitudinal hammer	at one end (fractures on both faces)	less than multiple	76-99%	7.6	4.7	3.7	E	dark brown/cream brown	brown
3	longitudinal hammer	at one end (fractures on both faces)	less than multiple	50-75 %	7.7	6.4	3.9	E	brown	light brown
4	longitudinal hammer	one quarter of circumference	multiple	76-99%	7.1	6.8	3.8	F	brown	cream brown
5	transverse hammer	three quarter of circumference	multiple	76-99%	6.3	7.2	3.4	F	brown	light brown
6	transverse hammer	three quarter of circumference	multiple	50-75 %	6.1	8.3	5.3	F	dark brown	dark brown
7	longitudinal hammer	at one end	multiple	76-99%	6.2	4.4	2.8	N	translucent white/grey	translucent white
8	longitudinal hammer	at opposed ends	multiple	76-99%	6.6	4.5	2.6	N	translucent white/grey	white
9	longitudinal hammer	at opposed ends	multiple	76-99%	8.0	5.4	3.4	N	translucent white/grey	white

Table 7.1. Items collected at Kom K

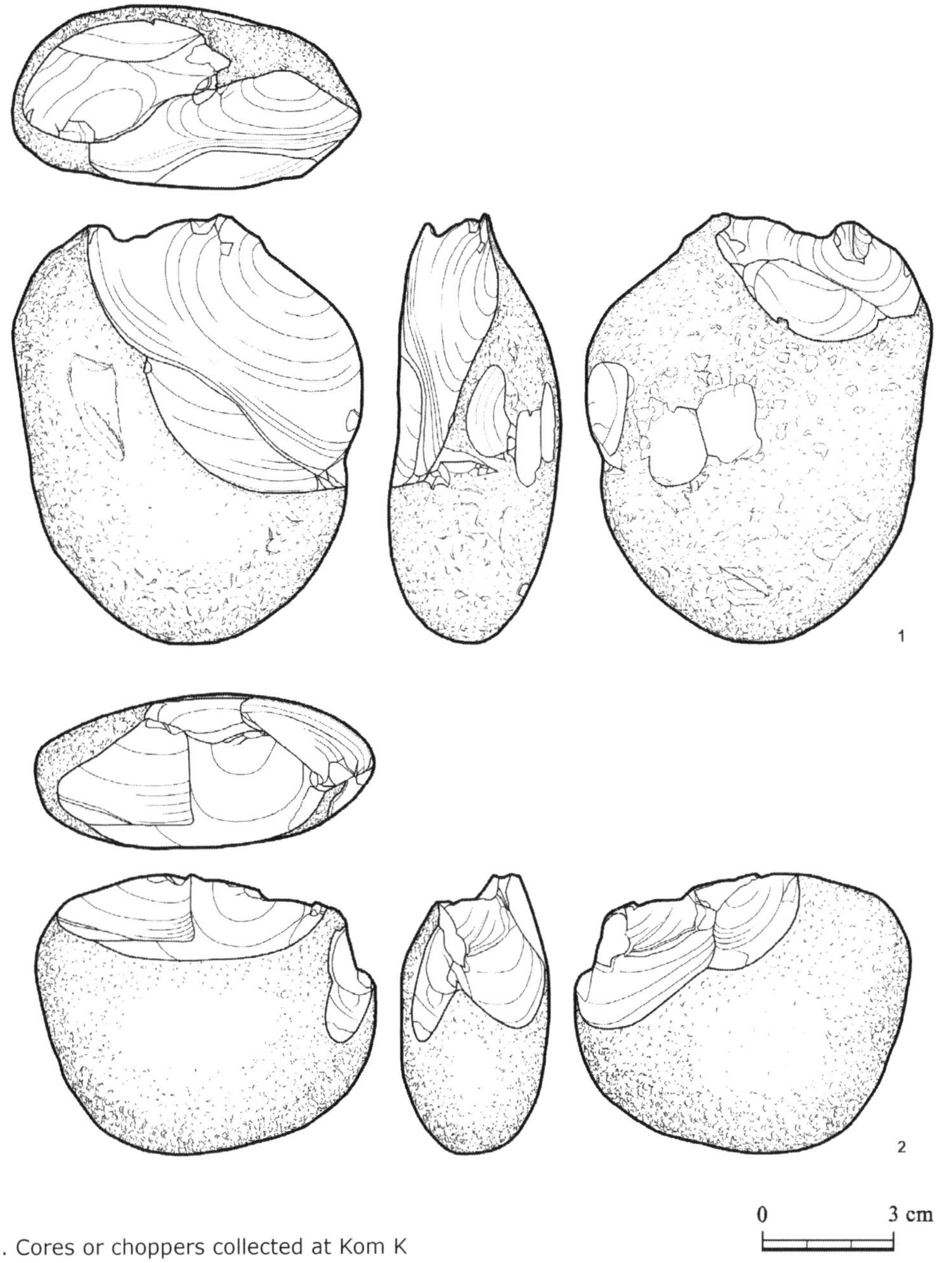

Fig.7.4. Cores or choppers collected at Kom K

Neolithic period. A surface collection of quite visible hammer stones and lithic cores was carried out in this artefact scatter in a grab sample manner (**Table 7.1** and **Fig.7.3** and **Fig.7.4**).

7.2.2. Site L

Site L is located on a slope overlooking the L Basin to its southeast. Small surface archaeological features like hearths and artefact concentrations distributed over a wide area on the slope were recognised and collectively designated as Site L by Caton-Thompson, but no detailed description of individual archaeological features was presented (Caton-Thompson and Gardner 1934: 73-74). One of such archaeological features dealt with here is located on a plain of approximately 20 m asl in

Fig.7.5. Scatter of cores at Site L (looking west)

the middle of Site L. The locality (N29.57819° E30.85024° in the centre) consists of a cluster of four stone-built hearths accompanied by a number of lithic artefacts and pottery sherds. The spatial extent of the hearth cluster surrounded by artefact scatters is 20 m wide. Therefore, it is assumed that this hearth cluster was a temporary field camp which may have been occupied several times. A concentration of large, oval lithic cores to the east of this hearth cluster was particularly remarkable (**Fig.7.5**), and hence all the lithic cores were collected (**Table 7.2** and **Fig.7.6**).

7.2.3. Site E29H1

Site E29H1 is located on the northeastern shore of the X Basin, and its elevation is approximately 10-13 m asl. The site has been recorded as an unnamed 'Fayum B Culture' site by Caton-Thompson (Caton-Thompson and Gardner 1934: Pl.CIX), and has been re-investigated later by Wendorf and Schild in more detail, and recognised as a huge Epipalaeolithic artefact cluster overlain by wide but sparse Neolithic artefact scatters (Wendorf and Schild 1976: 182*ff*). It has been known that most of the

	item	platform preparation	knapping sequence	amount of cortex	L (cm)	W (cm)	T (cm)	cobble type	cortex colour	fresh part colour
1	half-split discoidal core	cortical	multiple	25-49%	8.0	5.8	2.5	D	brown	light brown
2	bifacial discoidal core	unfacetted	multiple	25-49%	9.8	6.8	3.4	D	dark brown	mottled brown
3	half-split bifacial discoidal core	unfacetted	multiple	25-49%	10.2	8.5	2.5	D	dark brown	mottled brown
4	half-split discoidal core	cortical	multiple	25-49%	12.3	6.8	4.0	J	dark brown	grey
5	bifacial platform core, or, chopper	unfacetted	multiple	50-75 %	3.5	8.4	8.5	D	dark brown	dark brown
6	single platform core	cortical	multiple	50-75 %	10.7	8.2	3.2	C	dark brown	brown
7	bifacial discoidal core	cortical/unfacetted	multiple	50-75 %	10.6	10.0	3.0	A	brown/cream brown	mottled brown
8	single platform core	unfacetted	secondary	25-49%	3.8	7.4	6.8	G	brown/cream brown	mottled brown
9	unused half-split discoidal core	cortical	primary	76-99%	9.6	7.0	2.3	D	dark brown	mottled brown
10	unused half-split discoidal core	cortical	primary	76-99%	11.0	8.1	2.1	D	brown/cream brown	mottled brown
11	whole cobble	-	-	76-99%	8.2	8.9	2.6	A	brown/cream brown	mottled brown
12	whole cobble	-	-	complete (100%)	10.1	8.1	2.6	C	dark brown	-

Table 7.2. Items collected at Site L

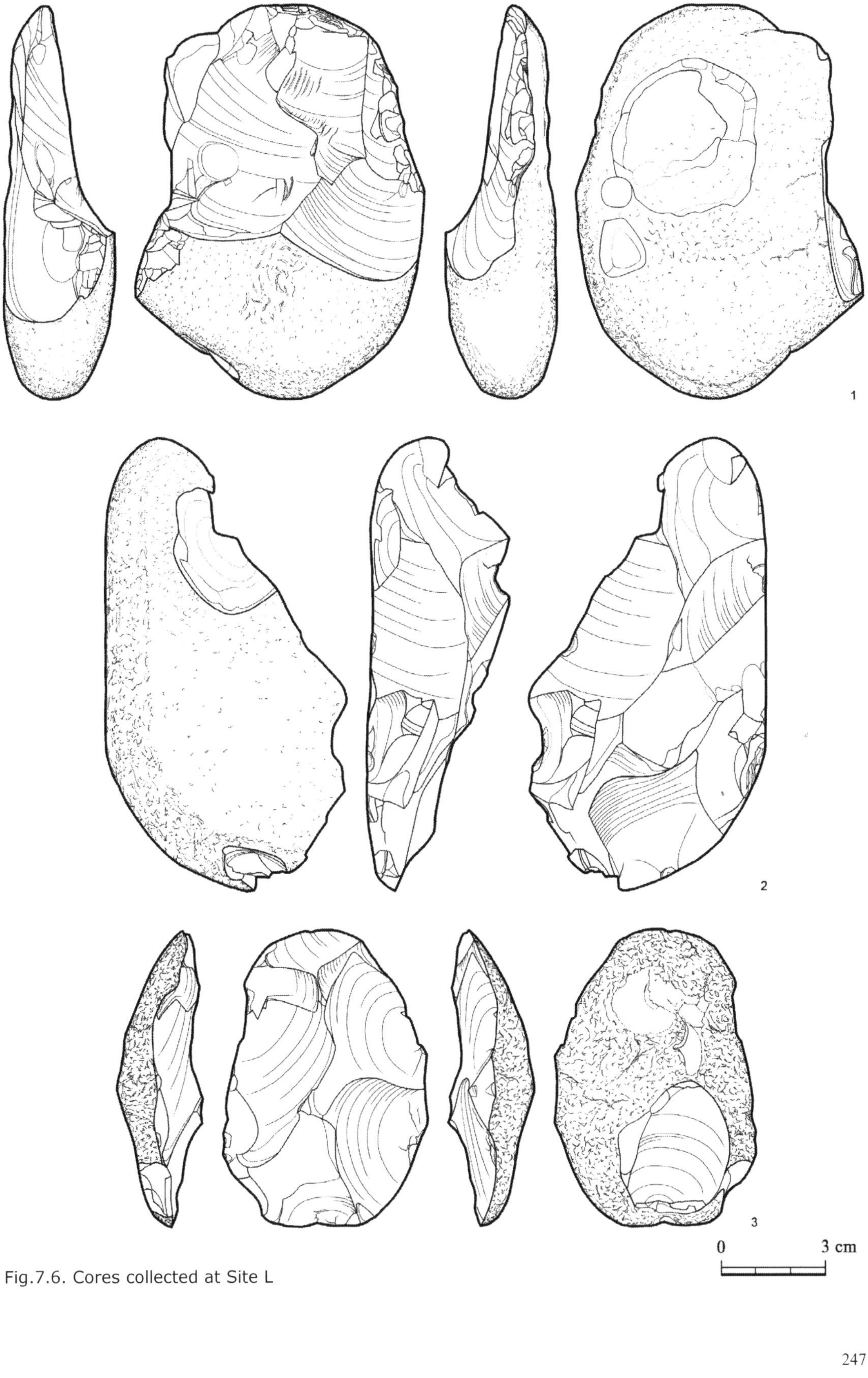

Fig.7.6. Cores collected at Site L

	item	platform preparation	knapping sequence	amount of cortex	L (cm)	W (cm)	T (cm)	cobble type	cortex colour	fresh part colour
1	bifacial platform core, or, chopper	unfacetted	secondary	76-99%	13.9	11.1	3.7	B	brown	brown
2	single platform core	unfacetted	quarternary	50-75%	5.8	10.6	5.1	E	brown	mottled brown
3	single platform core	cortical/unfacetted	multiple	50-75%	4.2	15.2	7.0	J	brown	light brown
4	half-split single platform core	unfacetted	tertiary	50-75 %	4.0	9.8	6.2	H	brown	light brown
5	multiple platform core	unfacetted	multiple	0-24%	5.0	5.8	4.4	H	cream brown	dark brown
6	opposed platform core, or, chopper	cortical	tertiary	50-75%	2.5	7.8	11.0	A	brown	light brown
7	bifacial discoidal core	cortical	multiple	25-49%	9.9	10.2	2.2	A	brown/cream brown	brown
8	half-split bifacial discoidal core, or, chopper	unfacetted	multiple	25-49%	12.5	9.5	4.2	G	brown/cream brown	mottled brown

Table 7.3. Items collected at Site E29H1

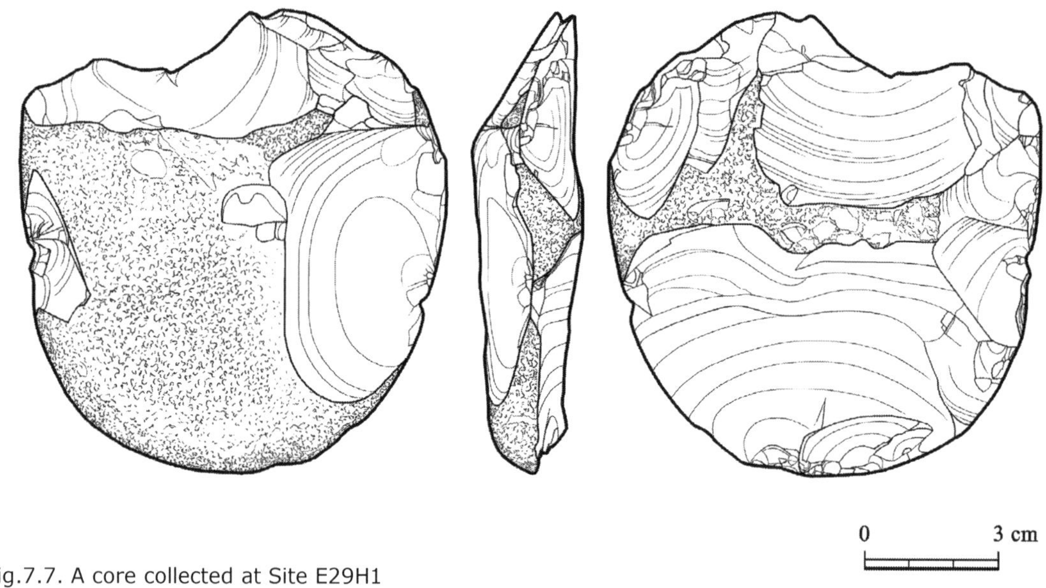

Fig.7.7. A core collected at Site E29H1

Epipalaeolithic lithic cores in the Fayum were made of rounded elongated pebbles of less than 5 cm long (Wendorf and Schild 1976: 311), and my investigation found that slightly larger pebbles of less than 7 cm long readily available in the surroundings were commonly used.

During the surface collection of lithic artefacts in the hearth field of Site E29H1 Area D, a certain number of unusually large unworked/worked cobbles and large debitage products deriving from the cobbles were noticed. Their presence in an Epipalaeolithic assemblage looks quite odd in light of the predominance of elongated pebbles, and hence it is assumed that such unusually large cobbles were brought here by Neolithic people and were mixed up with Epipalaeolithic artefact scatters. Besides the surface collection square, several large cores of apparently not the Epipalaeolithic were concentrated at the southwestern corner of the hearth field (E29.58383° E30.83260°), and all of them were collected (**Table 7.3** and **Fig.7.7**).

7.2.4. Site XA

Site XA (N29.58978° E30.81465° in the centre) is located on the terrace of a large meandering wadi running into the X Basin, and its elevation is approximately 15 m asl. This site has not been reported by previous visitors to the Fayum. The site is marked by several hillocks of less than two metres high, and the surface is covered by a crust of light yellow silty sediments which is broken into polygons. There are scatters of transparent gypsum crystals on and around this crust surface. These suggest that the site has been inundated in the past.

A dense concentration of lithic artefacts was observed on the crust surface around the hillocks (**Fig.7.8**). The number of unworked/worked cobbles as well as large and thick, primary or secondary flakes with wide unfacetted platforms, which must have been produced by hard hammer percussion, is enormous, while there are relatively few small chips/chunks which would be produced in later stages of the lithic reduction sequence. Apart from the obviously accidental occurrence of some Epipalaeolithic backed bladelets, few retouched tools of the Neolithic period were seen in this site. This situation suggests that initial core reduction took place here, but further reduction for tool making was done at other places. Or, this situation may simply be a result of taphonomic processes, by which small, thin, light-weight lithic artefacts may have been washed away by water. If the present situation of the site is to some extent the reflection of past reality, it may be argued that a number of cobbles were brought here and roughly knapped for making blanks for the ease of further transport. There are no other occupational features like hearths, scatters of pottery sherds, and clusters of animal bone fragments in the middle of this debitage product concentration, but such features are seen in the vicinity. This may suggest that this particular locality was a kind of flint knapping workshop.

Fig.7.8. Scatter of cores at Site XA (looking south)

All the lithic cores, debitage products, and supposedly hammers and anvils were collected on the surface in a 10 m x 10 m square while recording their spatial distribution. An attempt at refitting these debitage products was not at all successful. Therefore, it is assumed that this particular spot of debitage product concentration was occupied only for a little while but repeatedly. Only cores which are made on identifiable types of cobbles are listed (**Table 7.4**).

7.2.5. Site X

Site X (N29.58924° E30.80651° in the centre) is located in a shallow depression of approximately 150 m in diameter, which is surrounded on the north and west by sand dunes and hence looks like a cove. Its elevation is slightly below 15 m asl. The surface is covered by a crust of light yellow silty sediments which is broken into polygons, and there are scatters of transparent gypsum crystals on and around this crust surface. It was noticed that several intact lacustrine bivalves (*Aspatharia rubens*) of approximately 10 cm wide were embedded in the silty sediments. These suggest the presence of water for a considerable length of time in the past. The site was recognised by Caton-Thompson as a large surface site, and a number of Neolithic formal tools were collected by her. According to her report, amongst 111 unifacially/

	item	platform preparation	knapping sequence	amount of cortex	L (cm)	W (cm)	T (cm)	cobble type	cortex colour	fresh part colour
50	fragmentary multiple platform core	unfacetted	multiple	25-49%	7.5	6.0	3.0	E	brown	brown
204	fragmentary single platform core	unfacetted	multiple	50-75%	2.3	5.2	7.2	G	brown	light brown
265	fragmentary discoidal core	unfacetted	multiple	50-75%	5.3	6.1	2.4	E	dark brown	brown
322	bifacial discoidal core, or, chopper	unfacetted	multiple	50-75%	7.8	7.0	2.8	E	brown	brown
379	bifacial platform core, or, chopper	unfacetted	multiple	50-75%	3.2	8.6	8.4	C	dark brown	light brown
380	multiple platform core	cortical/unfacetted	multiple	50-75%	7.2	6.0	4.0	H	brown	mottled brown
391	bifacial discoidal core	unfacetted	multiple	50-75%	7.5	7.5	3.5	E	brown	brown
408	fragmentary multiple platform corc	unfacetted	multiple	50-75%	3.3	5.3	5.3	G	brown	light brown
410	multiple platform core	unfacetted	multiple	25-49%	7.8	6.2	3.5	J	light brown	light brown
433	fragmentary multiple platform core	unfacetted	multiple	25-49%	5.2	4.5	2.4	E	brown	brown
434	fragmentary multiple platform core	unfacetted	multiple	25-49%	7.3	4.4	3.3	E	brown	mottled brown
444	single platform core	cortical	secondary	76-99%	6.1	3.1	5.6	J	brown	brown
466	multiple platform core	unfacetted	multiple	25-49%	6.2	5.7	2.6	H	brown	mottled brown
488	multiple platform core	unfacetted	multiple	50-75%	8.1	6.9	4.6	K	cream grey	cream
491	multiple platform core	cortical	multiple	50-75%	6.0	7.7	11.8	J	dark brown	dark brown
493	single platform core	unfacetted	tertiary	76-99%	6.8	12.5	5.5	D	brown	brown
497	multiple platform core	unfacetted	multiple	50-75%	4.5	5.8	3.9	H	brown/cream brown	brown
505	multiple platform core	unfacetted	multiple	50-75%	4.2	8.2	6.8	J	brown	brown
538	single platform core	unfacetted	multiple	25-49%	3.3	6.3	6.6	H	brown	mottled brown
540	multiple platform core	unfacetted	multiple	76-99%	4.0	8.2	6.5	G	brown/cream brown	brown
542	bifacial platform core, or, chopper	unfacetted	multiple	50-75%	10.1	6.5	3.6	E	brown	brown
550	single platform core	unfacetted	multiple	50-75%	7.6	4.7	2.8	H	brown	light brown
576	bifacial platform core, or, chopper	unfacetted	multiple	76-99%	9.7	7.6	3.6	D	dark brown	dark brown
577	single platform core	unfacetted	multiple	50-75%	3.6	8.1	5.5	D	brown	light brown

Table 7.4. Items collected at Site XA

	item	platform preparation	knapping sequence	amount of cortex	L (cm)	W (cm)	T (cm)	cobble type	cortex colour	fresh part colour
1	single platform core	unfacetted	multiple	24-49%	5.4	6.2	4.7	H	light brown	mottled brown
2	single platform core	unfacetted	tertiary	50-75%	5.5	5.3	4.2	G	brown/cream brown	translucent brown
3	multiple platform core	unfacetted	multiple	25-49%	8.3	6.0	3.9	D	brown	mottled brown
4	multiple platform core	unfacetted	multiple	25-49 %	9.4	7.6	4.6	E	brown	mottled brown
5	single platform core	unfacetted	multiple	50-75%	10.8	7.9	4.4	H	brown	brown
6	multiple platform core	unfacetted	multiple	25-49%	9.8	8.8	4.5	J	brown	mottled brown
7	bifacial platform core, or, chopper	cortical/unfacetted	secondary	76-99%	10.5	8.9	3.4	B	brown	mottled brown
8	bifacial platform core, or, chopper	unfacetted	multiple	76-99%	10.7	8.6	2.3	B	brown	brown
9	bifacial platform core, or, chopper	unfacetted	multiple	50-75%	10.3	7.4	2.9	C	brown	brown
10	bifacial opposed platform core	cortical/unfacetted	multiple	76-99%	10.6	7.9	2.2	A	brown/cream brown	brown
11	bifacial opposed platform core	unfacetted	multiple	50-75%	9.4	7.6	2.8	B	light brown	mottled brown
12	bifacial platform core, or, chopper	unfacetted	multiple	50-75%	9.9	9.5	2.7	B	brown	brown
13	half-split bifacial discoidal core	cortical/unfacetted	multiple	25-49%	8.6	6.5	2.9	E	brown	mottled brown
14	sidescraper made on half-split cobble	one side retouched from ventral to dorsal face	primary	76-99%	11.1	8.8	2.7	D	brown/cream brown	mottled brown
15	bifacial sidescraper made on flat cobble	two sides forming 90 degrees retouched from both faces	multiple	50-75%	8.8	7.9	2.3	C	brown	light brown
16	bifacial platform core, or, chopper	unfacetted	multiple	50-75%	8.1	8.3	2.1	B	brown	mottled brown
17	bifacial platform core, or, chopper	unfacetted	primary	50-75%	10.1	7.4	4.0	D	brown/cream brown	brown
18	bifacial platform core, or, chopper	unfacetted	tertiary	50-75%	9.2	8.2	3.1	E	brown/cream brown	mottled brown
19	single platform core	unfacetted	secondary	50-75%	10.3	8.5	4.8	E	brown	light brown
20	bifacial platform core, or, chopper	unfacetted	multiple	50-75%	3.0	9.9	6.4	A	brown	light brown
21	single platform core	cortical	multiple	76-99%	2.7	14.0	9.0	B	brown/cream brown	light brown
22	multiple platform core	unfacetted	multiple	25-49 %	8.6	9.5	6.5	J	brown/cream brown	brown
23	multiple platform core	unfacetted	multiple	1-24 %	4.3	10.4	7.8	L	grey	translucent light brown
24	longitudinal hammer?	at one end (fractures on both faces)	primary	50-75%	7.5	5.8	2.5	D	brown	light brown

Table 7.5. Items collected at Site X

Fig.7.9. Scatter of cores at Site X (looking south)

Fig.7.11. Scatter of unworked and worked cobbles at Locality Calcified Shrubs (looking southwest)

bifacially-retouched formal tools collected in Site X, there were eight axes, seven concave-based arrowheads, six triangular arrowheads, and 15 sickle blades (Caton-Thompson and Gardner 1934: 74-75). Although there are no structural remains at the site, the scatter of lithic artefacts and pottery sherds on and around the crust surface is still enormous (**Fig.7.9**), and in particular, a number of large lithic cores were quite noticeable in its northern half. A random collection of notable items was carried out (**Table 7.5** and **Fig.7.10**).

7.2.6. Locality 'Calcified Shrubs'

Approximately 300 m to the east of Kom W, there is a wide scatter of calcified plant roots (N29.58880° E30.79805° in the centre). It is 50 m long at most and approximately 200 m wide. Its elevation is slightly below 20 m asl. In contrast to its surroundings characterised by wind-blown fine-grained sand sheet and well-developed sand ripples, this dense scatter of calcified plant roots is quite visible. At many places in this calcified plant field, the bottom parts of the trunks still remain standing. A large number of unworked and worked cobbles and flakes deriving from the cobbles are scattered only on and around this calcified plant field (**Fig.7.11**). Many worked globular cobbles are undoubtedly single platform cores. Other flat and oval cobbles often have a worked edge at one end and look like choppers. Except for one presumably Neolithic bifacially-retouched knife, no formal tools were encountered.

There is no concrete clue to determine how old these calcified plant roots are and what species they are, but the scatters of choppers on and around this field may suggest that these plants are not common reeds or sedges but shrubs, and these tools were used for cutting the shrubs in the Neolithic period by the inhabitants of Kom W. Hundreds of fireholes excavated at Kom W by Caton-Thompson suggest the high demand of fuel at this site, and the pottery production on and around Kom W must also have required a stable supply of fuel. Therefore, sources of firewood in close proximity to Kom W must have been essential, and it is likely that this calcified plant field was one of the sources. Alternatively, considering that common reeds which thrive along the lakeshore and sheep/goat dung could also have been used as fuel, the primary aim of cutting wood may have been to obtain long branches for making arrow/spear shafts, bows, sickle handles and axe handles. Random collecting of quite visible lithic cores was carried out (**Table 7.6**).

7.2.7. Kom W

Kom W (N29.58894° E30.79248° in the centre) is located to the northeast of the Z Basin, and its elevation is approximately 22 m asl. Surface artefacts on this low mound and its vicinity have

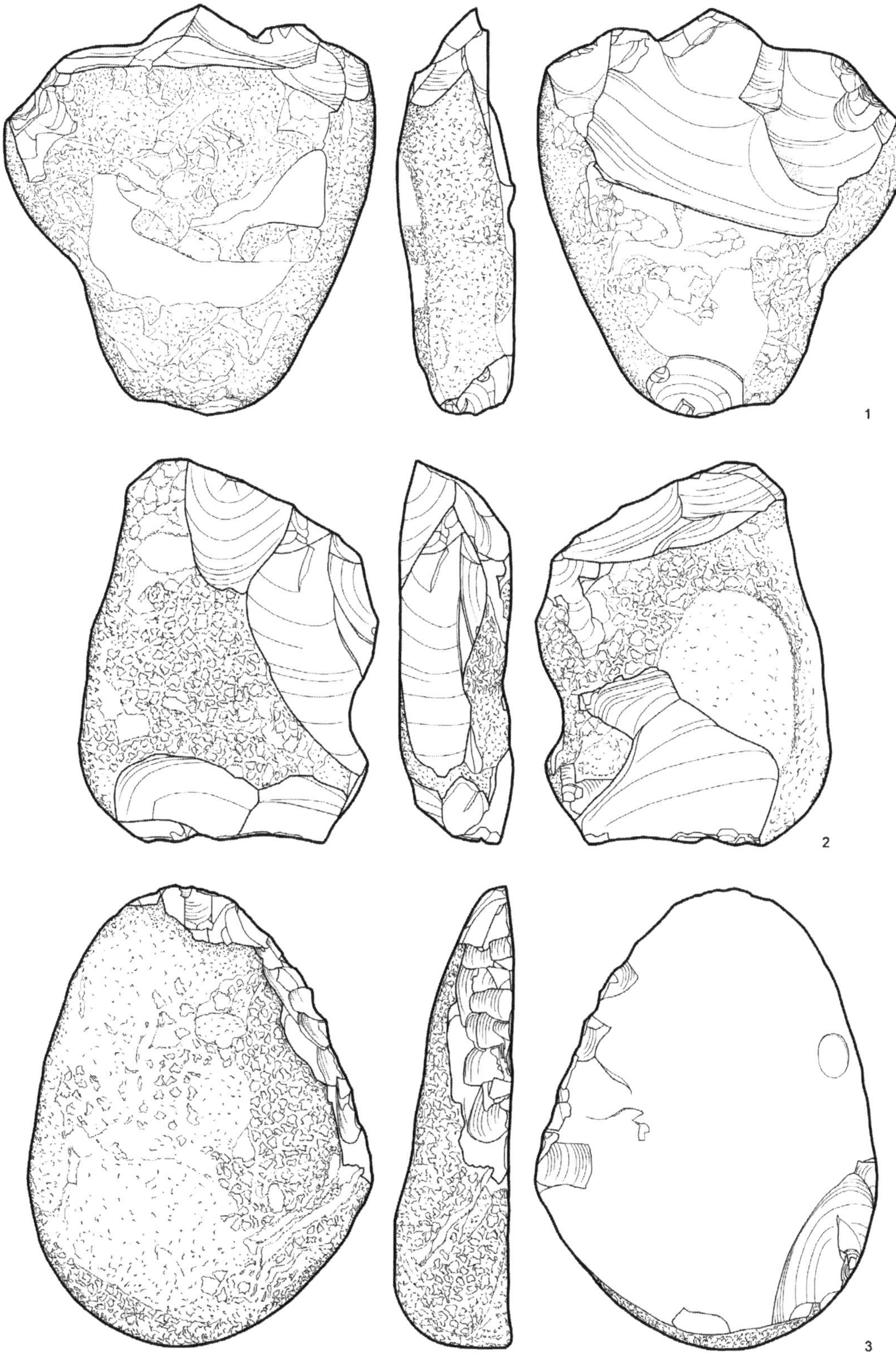

0 3 cm

Fig.7.10. Items collected at Site X

	item	platform preparation	knapping sequence	amount of cortex	L (cm)	W (cm)	T (cm)	cobble type	cortex colour	fresh part colour
1	discoidal core	cortical/unfacetted	multiple	50-75%	6.9	5.9	1.8	B	brown	brown
2	single platform core	unfacetted	multiple	50-75%	11.8	9.7	4.9	J	brown/cream brown	cream brown
3	single platform core	unfacetted	tertiary	50-75%	10.6	9.5	4.4	E	brown	mottled brown
4	single platform core	unfacetted	secondary	50-75%	11.2	8.5	4.3	E	brown/cream brown	mottled brown
5	single platform core	unfacetted	tertiary	50-75%	8.5	6.8	3.4	D	brown/cream brown	brown
6	single platform core	unfacetted	multiple	76-99%	8.1	6.4	4.1	G	brown	cream brown
7	ninety-degree core	unfacetted	multiple	76-99%	3.8	9.8	11.4	J	brown	mottled brown
8	single platform core, or, chopper	unfacetted	multiple	76-99%	2.9	7.4	10.4	B	brown/cream brown	mottled brown
9	bifacial platform core, or, chopper	unfacetted	multiple	50-75%	3.4	9.1	8.3	B	brown/cream brown	mottled brown
10	bifacial platform core, or, chopper	cortical/unfacetted	multiple	76-99%	2.9	11.1	8.2	B	brown/cream brown	cream brown
11	whole cobble	-	-	76-99%	11.7	7.6	2.4	B	brown	brown
12	single platform core	unfacetted	multiple	25-49 %	4.9	6.4	5.5	I	brown/cream brown	brown

Table 7.6. Items collected at Locality Calcified Shrubs

been known and plundered by antiquarians since the late 19th century. The first archaeological excavation by Caton-Thompson yielded a number of Neolithic lithic artefacts including unifacially/bifacially-retouched, partly-retouched or ground formal tools made of flint, limestone, basalt, and exotic stones. These findings were thoroughly described in her publication. Unifacially/bifacially-retouched formal tools include 75 axes, 17 concave-based arrowheads, six triangular arrowheads, one tanged arrowhead, and 31 sickle blades among others. Axes constitute more than 40 percent of all formal tools collected by her at Kom W. However, the presence of lithic debitage products was not mentioned in her report (Caton-Thompson and Gardner 1934: 22-31). It is also noted that she found 548 hammer stones, which were oval and spherical pebbles of flint, quartz and fossil wood and showed bruised areas, as well as a heap of 22 rounded flint cobbles and a quartz pebble which lay not far above bedrock (Caton-Thompson and Gardner 1934: 32).

Kom W is presently a huge excavation dump, and the traces of excavation trenches and backfills are still quite visible on the low mound (**Fig.7.12**). Each excavation trench has been

Fig.7.12. Caton-Thompson's excavation strips on Kom W (looking east)

designated by Caton-Thompson as 'Strip', and there are 20 strips, named Strip A to T from the east to the west. Since she collected only unifacially/bifacially-retouched and partly-retouched formal tools from her excavation trenches, while ignoring lithic cores and debitage products, an enormous amount of lithic cores and debitage products are still left on the site. A random surface collection of notable lithic cores was carried out between Strip D and Strip J (**Table 7.7** and **Fig.7.13**). This is the eastern half of Kom W.

According to Kozlowski and Ginter's study on Neolithic cores collected in the neighbourhood of Strip E, most cores are very small (approximately 3 cm long and 3 cm wide), and several small flakes were struck off from the cores. Thus, they concluded that the lithic industry at Kom W was principally flake-oriented (Kozlowski and Ginter 1989: 170-174). This conclusion must be partly true. However, a strange thing is that the flake tools which they collected are larger than the cores they collected, though some of their cores are not fragmentary, and hence there seems to be no direct relation between the flake tools and the cores. Some of the flake tools collected by them obviously derive from much larger cores, and indeed, many large unworked cobbles and worked cores are presently seen on Kom W.

More importantly, a puzzling thing is that the small cores which they collected and published (Kozlowski and Ginter 1989: fig.6) are similar to Epipalaeolithic cores which were described in Chapter 6. The presence of a small number of Epipalaeolithic tools at Kom W has been reported by Caton-Thompson (Caton-Thompson and Gardner 1934: 30-31), and hence, it is not surprising if Epipalaeolithic cores are present at Kom W. A number of small cores resembling

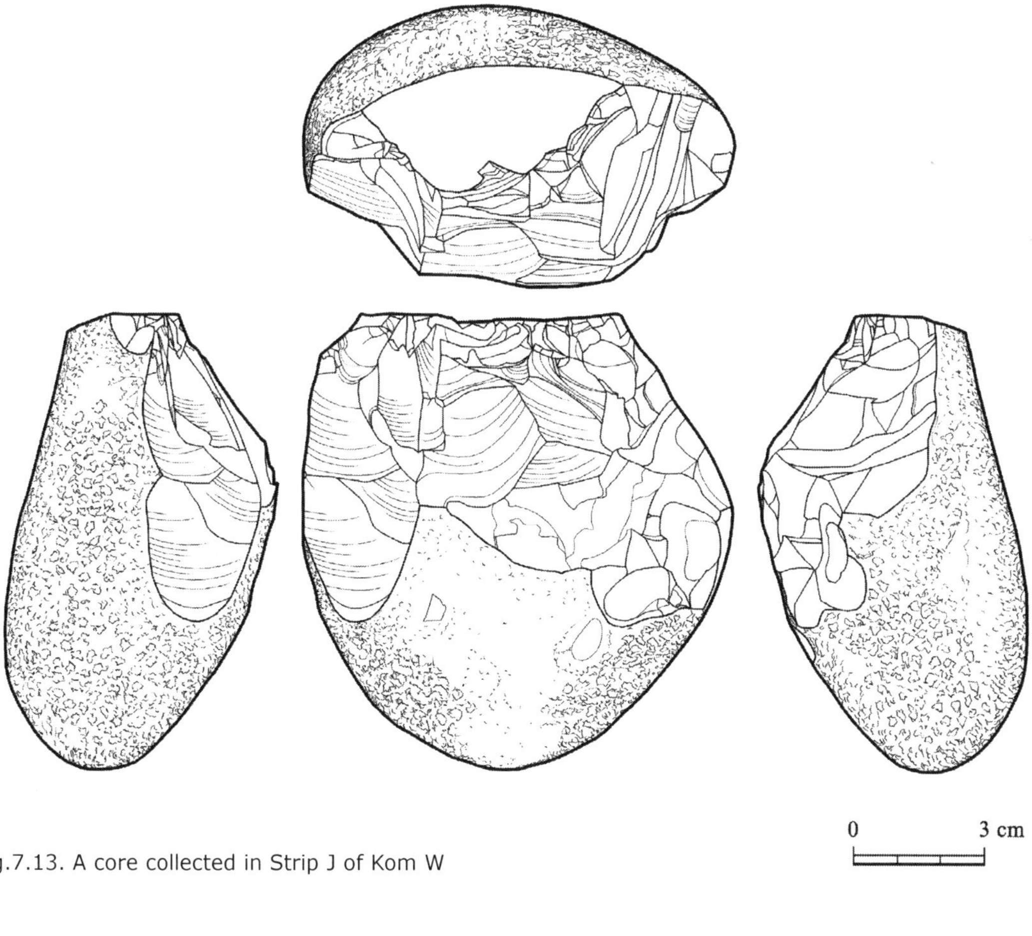

Fig.7.13. A core collected in Strip J of Kom W

	core type	platform preparation	knapping sequence	amount of cortex	L (cm)	W (cm)	T (cm)	cobble type	cortex colour	fresh part colour
D 1	single platform core	unfacetted	multiple	25-49%	4.1	8.6	6.9	D	brown	brown/cream brown
D 2	ninety-degree core	cortical/unfacetted	multiple	25-49%	6.7	4.5	3.7	H	brown	brown
D 3	discoidal core	cortical	multiple	76-99 %	5.7	4.1	4.2	G	brown/cream brown	translucent brown
D 4	fragment of multiple platform core	cortical/unfacetted	multiple	50-75%	3.2	6.5	4.2	E	brown	brown
D 5	multiple platform core	unfacetted	multiple	25-49%	2.7	4.2	3.1	G	brown	mottled brown
E 1	multiple platform core	unfacetted	multiple	25-49%	5.2	7.2	5.5	H	brown	mottled brown
E 2	bifacial platform core, or, chopper	unfacetted	multiple	76-99%	8.3	5.3	3.1	D	brown	mottled brown
E 3	multiple platform core	cortical/unfacetted	multiple	50-75%	7.2	3.6	5.0	E	brown	brown
E 4	opposed platform core	cortical/unfacetted	multiple	50-75%	5.6	10.0	8.6	J	brown	light brown
F 1	single platform core	cortical/unfacetted	quaternary	76-99 %,	9.6	6.6	3.0	C	brown	mottled brown
F 2	single platform core, or, chopper	unfacetted	tertiary	50-75%,	9.8	8.5	4.3	K	light brown	light brown
F 3	multiple platform core	unfacetted	multiple	none	7.0	5.2	2.0	-	unidentifiable	brown
F 4	multiple platform core	unfacetted	multiple	1-24 %	6.8	7.4	4.9	L	grey	translucent green
H 1	bifacial platform core, or, chopper	unfacetted	multiple	50-75 %	9.1	5.6	2.5	B	brown	brown
H 2	bifacial platform core	cortical/unfacetted	multiple	50-75 %	6.6	7.5	3.2	A	brown	light brown
H 3	single platform core	unfacetted	multiple	50-75 %	6.0	7.1	3.9	D	brown/cream brown	brown
H 4	single platform core	unfacetted/dihedral	secondary	76-99 %	9.2	5.4	4.8	I	brown	light brown
H 5	multiple platform core	unfacetted	multiple	1-24 %	6.1	6.5	4.0	L	grey	translucent cream brown
H 6	discoidal core	unfacetted	multiple	50-76 %	11.4	10.8	5.3	L	grey	translucent green
H 7	multiple platform core	cortical/unfacetted	quaternary	50-76 %	9.9	7.4	4.3	D	brown	brown
H 8	multiple platform core	unfacetted	multiple	25-49 %	5.6	6.5	6.0	L	grey	translucent green
H 9	single platform core	unfacetted	multiple	50-76 %	5.1	9.2	10.2	L	grey	translucent green
I 1	half-split bifacial discoidal core	cortical/unfacetted	secondary	76-99 %	8.8	8.9	2.7	D	brown	mottled brown
I 2	multiple platform core	cortical/unfacetted	multiple	50-75 %	8.2	6.2	3.0	C	brown	light brown

Table 7.7. Items collected at Kom W

	core type	platform preparation	knapping sequence	amount of cortex	L (cm)	W (cm)	T (cm)	cobble type	cortex colour	fresh part colour
I 3	multiple platform core	unfacetted	multiple	1-24 %	8.8	7.5	4.9	L	green	translucent light green
I 4	multiple platform core	unfacetted	multiple	none	9.1	5.1	3.0	L	green	translucent green
I 5	multiple platform core	unfacetted	multiple	25-49 %	4.5	5.5	5.0	H	cream	brown
I 6	single platform core	unfacetted	multiple	50-75 %	4.1	4.2	7.8	J	cream brown	mottled brown
I 7	single platform core	unfacetted	quaternary	50-75 %	3.5	4.5	6.8	J	brown	mottled brown
I 8	opposed platform core	cortical/unfacetted	multiple	25-49 %	4.2	3.1	1.9	-	brown/cream brown	light brown
I 9	single platform core	cortical/unfacetted	multiple	25-49 %	2.8	3.3	3.2	-	brown/cream brown	light brown
I 10	multiple platform core	cortical/unfacetted	multiple	25-49 %	3.4	3.4	2.9	-	brown	brown
I 11	multiple platform core	unfacetted	multiple	25-49 %	3.7	3.8	3.0	-	brown	brown
I 12	multiple platform core	cortical/unfacetted	multiple	25-49 %	3.1	3.9	2.2	-	brown	translucent green
I 13	multiple platform core	unfacetted	multiple	1-24 %	3.1	3.0	3.8	-	brown	mottled brown
I 14	multiple platform core	unfacetted	multiple	1-24 %	2.1	2.4	2.7	-	calcareous white	brown
I 15	multiple platform core	unfacetted	multiple	1-24 %	2.2	2.7	2.1	-	calcareous white	light brown
J 1	multiple platform core	unfacetted	multiple	1-24 %	3.9	3.7	2.6	-	brown	cream brown
J 2	single platform core	unfacetted	tertiary	50-75 %	5.4	4.4	3.5	J	dark brown	brown
J 3	single platform core	cortical	multiple	76-99 %	4.0	5.8	8.8	I	brown/cream brown	brown
J 4	multiple platform core	unfacetted	multiple	50-75 %	7.5	5.5	3.5	D	brown/cream brown	brown
J 5	single platform core	unfacetted	multiple	76-99 %	9.4	9.8	5.4	D	brown/cream brown	mottled brown
J 6	multiple platform core	unfacetted	multiple	1-24 %	4.9	6.0	4.4	L	cream	grey
J 7	multiple platform core	unfacetted	multiple	1-24 %	3.5	7.0	3.3	L	grey	grey
J 8	multiple platform core	unfacetted	multiple	25-49 %	2.9	3.7	3.5	-	brown	light brown
J 9	ninety degree core	unfacetted	multiple	25-49 %	3.3	2.8	3.1	-	brown	mottled brown
J 10	single platform core	unfacetted	multiple	25-49 %	2.6	3.4	2.6	-	brown/cream brown	green

Table 7.7. Items collected at Kom W (continued)

Fig.7.14. Small cores on pebbles and cobble fragments collected in Strip J of Kom W

those collected by Kozlowski and Ginter could easily be collected by me on the Strips (**Fig.7.14**). The cores can be divided into those made on flint pebbles and those made on fragments of rounded or subangular large cobbles. Both of them exhibit the same platform preparation and flaking patterns as those of the cores collected by me at Epipalaeolithic sites in the X Basin and Z Basin. However, considering the abundance of similar examples of cores at the Predynastic site of Maadi (Rizkana and Seeher 1988: pls.1 and 2), it is probable that such cores did actually exist in the Neolithic. Nevertheless, it must be kept in mind that some of the small cores at Kom W may be dated to the Epipalaeolithic. In other words, it must be supposed that Kozlowski and Ginter's collection of cores was a mixture of Epipalaeolithic and Neolithic ones, but was misrepresented as merely Neolithic.

7.2.8. The Site V Depression

The Site V Depression (N29.58354° E30.79358° in the centre) is located approximately 150 m to the south of Kom W, and its elevation is between 15 m and 20 m asl. The area is a large, oval-shaped, shallow depression of approximately 500 m north-south and 300 m east-west. The surface of this depression is covered by white calcareous clay sediments and scatters of transparent gypsum crystals. Beneath the clay surface, there is a thin layer of dark grey fine-grained sand. A number of lacustrine snails of approximately 2 cm long are scattered on this surface, and also many lacustrine bivalves (*Aspatharia rubens*) of more than 10 cm wide remain intact and embedded in these sediments. This suggests that this depression had been filled with water permanently in certain periods of time. Caton-Thompson speculated that this

Fig.7.15. Scatter of worked cobbles at the Site V Depression (looking northwest)

depression with marginal loams had been used as an agricultural field by the inhabitants of Kom W (Caton-Thompson and Gardner 1934: 75).

Although there are no clear structural remains like hearths, scatters of lithic artefacts and pottery sherds are seen on and around this depression. Particularly dense scatters of artefacts are seen on slightly higher mounds to the west. The surface of these higher mounds is also covered by silty sediments and tiny fragments of indurated calcium carbonate, but no lacustrine snail and bivalve are seen. This may mean that inundations of the mounds were not long enough for lacustrine snails and bivalves to inhabit them and to grow up. As for the dense scatters of artefacts on the mounds, the pottery sherds are undoubtedly dated to the Neolithic, and except for some apparently Old Kingdom knives, most lithic artefacts seem to be dated to the Neolithic. A concentration of flint cobbles was seen in these artefact scatters (**Fig.7.15**), and all the cobbles were collected (**Table 7.8** and **Fig.7.16**).

7.3. Identifying and distinguishing Neolithic cobbles and lithic cores from Epipalaeolithic and Old Kingdom examples

Before discussing unworked and worked rocks used by Neolithic people in detail, one problem which the sites studied bore must be solved. Overlapping occupations of the same sites by people from different periods are quite natural,

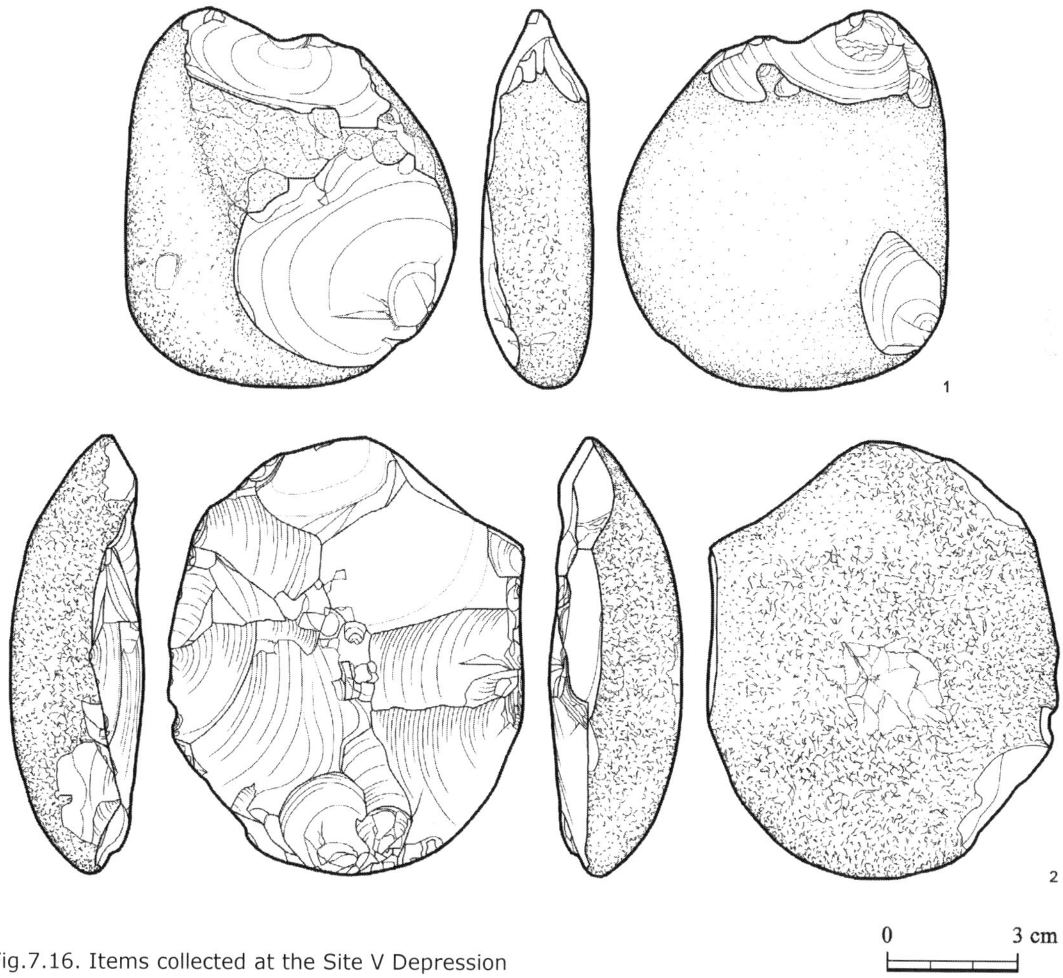

Fig.7.16. Items collected at the Site V Depression

	item	platform preparation	knapping sequence	amount of cortex	L (cm)	W (cm)	T (cm)	cobble type	cortex colour	fresh part colour
1	bifacial discoidal core	cortical	multiple	50-75 %	9.7	9.3	2.1	A	brown/cream brown	brown
2	bifacial discoidal core	cortical	multiple	25-49 %	9.3	9.1	2.3	A	brown/cream brown	mottled brown
3	bifacial platform core, or, chopper	cortical/unfacetted	secondary	50-75 %	8.3	7.3	2.2	A	brown/cream brown	brown
4	discoidal core	cortical	multiple	50-75 %	9.2	7.4	2.1	B	brown	brown
5	bifacial discoidal core	cortical/unfacetted	multiple	25-49 %	8.1	6.5	2.2	A	brown	brown
6	half-split bifacial discoidal core	cortical/unfacetted	multiple	25-49 %	9.2	7.7	1.6	D	brown/cream brown	brown
7	half-split discoidal core	cortical/unfacetted	multiple	25-49 %	9.3	7.7	2.7	D	brown/cream brown	brown
8	endscraper made on half-split cobble	cortical	primary	76-99%	10.3	6.6	2.3	D	brown/cream brown	mottled brown
9	sidescraper made on half-split discoidal core	cortical/unfacetted	multiple	25-49 %	9.8	6.4	2.1	I	brown	brown
10	half-split discoidal core	cortical	multiple	25-49 %	10.6	6.0	2.5	J	brown	light brown
11	single platform core	cortical	multiple	50-75 %	6.8	8.5	2.8	D	brown	light brown

Table 7.8. Items collected at the Site V Depression

and have actually been observed at many sites in the Fayum. As long as one is dealing with artefacts collected on the surface, there is always a problem of the mixing up of artefacts from different periods and the misunderstanding of a mixed assemblage as an undisturbed single assemblage of one specific period. Caton-Thompson could recognise some diagnostic Predynastic and Old Kingdom formal tools found among Neolithic formal tools on the surface of Kom K and Kom W based on her knowledge (Caton-Thompson and Gardner 1934: 23-24, 38). Similar careful examination of surface artefacts has to be done for the studied sites.

It was not difficult for me to distinguish the Neolithic lithic cores from the Epipalaeolithic cores, because uncontaminated collections of Fayum Epipalaeolithic cores are at my disposal for reference. Not only at Kom W but also at other sites studied like Site L, Site XA and the Site V Depression, the presence of a very small number of Epipalaeolithic cores and tools was recognised, and these were carefully eliminated from this study.

Moreover, through my survey, it was concluded that the area near Site L and particularly the area around Kom W had been occupied during the Old Kingdom as well, and a number of odd lithic cores were found. Hence, it was suspected that Old Kingdom people not only brought flint cobbles there by themselves, but also reused flint cobbles left by Neolithic people. Therefore, distinguishing Neolithic cobbles and lithic cores from Old Kingdom examples was the first step.

For this purpose, unworked and worked cobbles at gypsum quarrying workshops in Umm es-Sawan (N29.71340° E30.87966° at a workshop in the middle), which is located 14 km to the north of Kom K, were referred to. Umm es-Sawan is known for extensive outcrops of gypsum, and it was exploited exclusively in the Old Kingdom period. When Caton-

Fig.7.17. Scatter of cobbles around the gypsum quarrying workshop A in Umm es-Sawan (looking north)

Fig.7.18. Scatter of cobbles on the flint chipping floor in Umm es-Sawan (looking southeast)

	item	platform preparation	knapping sequence	amount of cortex	L (cm)	W (cm)	T (cm)	cobble type	cortex colour	fresh part colour
1	single platform core	unfacetted	primary	50-75 %	10.2	9.7	6.1	J	brown	light brown
2	conical chunk	cortical	primary	76-99%	9.7	7.8	6.1	J	brown/cream brown	mottled brown
3	multiple platform core	cortical/unfacetted	multiple	50-75 %	5.5	7.8	9.9	H	brown/cream brown	dark brown/ dark grey
4	hemispherical chunk	cortical	secondary	50-75 %	9.4	7.8	4.8	H	brown/cream brown	mottled brown
5	single platform core	unfacetted	multiple	25-49 %	5.0	6.9	5.3	H	brown	light brown
6	single platform core	unfacetted	primary	50-75 %	7.2	7.2	5.6	H	brown/cream brown	brown
7	single platform core	unfacetted	multiple	50-75 %	7.8	6.9	7.2	I	brown/cream brown	cream brown
8	single platform core	unfacetted	multiple	25-49 %	6.0	8.4	7.9	J	brown	brown
9	single platform core	cortical	primary	76-99%	5.0	8.4	11.8	J	mottled brown	mottled brown
10	single platform core	cortical	multiple	76-99%	4.9	10.0	5.5	E	mottled brown	mottled brown
11	single platform core	unfacetted	primary	76-99%	5.5	10.4	8.6	J	brown	cream brown
12	single platform core	cortical	multiple	76-99%	5.3	9.2	6.7	J	light brown	mottled brown
13	ninety-degree core	cortical	secondary	76-99%	3.0	9.3	7.2	C	brown	brown
14	chopper	cortical	multiple	76-99%	2.8	9.8	9.2	A	light brown	light brown
15	chopper	cortical	multiple	76-99%	3.1	9.5	10.1	C	brown	mottled brown
16	chopper	cortical	quarternary	76-99%	2.5	12.5	10.3	C	brown	brown

Table 7.9. Items collected on the flint chipping floor in Umm es-Sawan

Thompson visited and studied the gypsum quarrying workshops there, she found near the workshops the flint chipping floor, where a large amount of unworked and worked flint cobbles were scattered. Since flint cobbles do not naturally occur in this terrain, it was obvious that they had been brought there by Old Kingdom workers as raw materials for toolmaking (Caton-Thompson and Gardner 1934: 104, pl.LVIII and pl.LXIII-3). This flint chipping floor still exists (**Fig.7.17** and **Fig.7.18**). Worked cobbles were collected there for a comparative study (**Table 7.9**).

It is probable that the original sources of cobbles visited by Neolithic and Old Kingdom people were the same. However, it was realised through the observation of the Umm es-Sawan specimens that the cobbles chosen and the knapping techniques employed by Old Kingdom people are apparently different from those by Neolithic people. The general characteristics of the unworked and worked cobbles of the Old Kingdom are; 1) the preference for weathered/abraded, globular/egg-shaped or irregularly-shaped/subangular flint cobbles, which are identical to the cobble types H and J described below, but are much larger and heavier than Neolithic specimens, 2) splitting the cobble

Fig.7.19. An Old Kingdom single platform core collected on the flint chipping floor in Umm es-Sawan

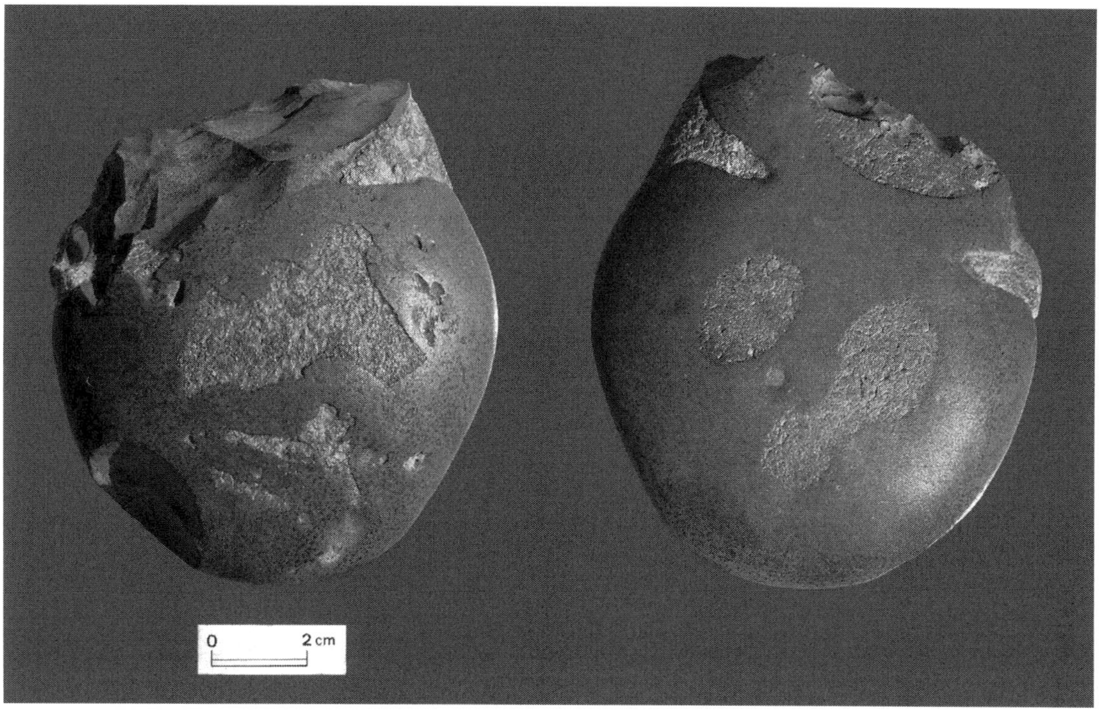

Fig.7.20. An Old Kingdom chopper collected on the flint chipping floor in Umm es-Sawan

around the half part of the body by a very hard, poorly-controlled blow as is indicated by peculiar ripples on the scar, and obtaining conical or hemispherical pieces which were utilised as single platform cores by using the scar as a striking platform (**Fig.7.19**), and 3) making choppers by striking repeatedly one end of oval and flat cobbles, which are identical to the cobble types A and C described below, from one face only without preparing an unfacetted platform (**Fig.7.20**). As a result, one face of the cutting edge of the chopper remains cortical. Based on these characteristics, suspicious worked cobbles collected at the Neolithic sites studied could carefully be eliminated. It was revealed that problematic cobble collections from Site L, Locality 'Calcified Shrubs' and Kom W certainly included some presumably Old Kingdom worked cobbles, whereas the other sites did not.

A remaining problem is the possible presence of Predynastic people in the sites studied. According to Caton-Thompson's publication and my field observations, a very small number of formal retouched blades of the Predynastic period seem to be present at Kom K, Site E29H1 and the Site V Depression. However, it is not certain whether tool making took place at these sites in the Predynastic period, due to the paucity of reliable references for Predynastic lithic cores except for those from Maadi (Rizkana and Seeher 1998). It can only be said that the lack of flint cores or nodules for the production of large blades, which are the hallmarks of Predynastic lithic artefacts, and the raw materials of the long blades which are apparently different from any types of flint cobbles found in the sites studied, may suggest that Predynastic blade production was probably not undertaken there. On the other hand, it is known that bifacially-retouched arrowheads and knives which flourished in the Neolithic did persist into the Predynastic period, though few in number. Therefore, it is difficult to exclude completely the possibility of the occurrence of Predynastic tool making.

7.4. The description of the rock types collected at Neolithic sites

It was recognised through the surface collection that a variety of rock types in different forms were used in the Neolithic sites. Almost all of them do not naturally occur in the lakeshore habitats of the Neolithic period, and hence it is certain that they were transported from elsewhere. Since Kom W yielded the highest variety of rock types and the other sites lack some or many of the various types, the following description of rock types relies mainly on those from Kom W. Flint is the commonest raw material, and many different forms of flint were recognised. They were classified on the basis of shape, surface weathering and abrasion.

A) rounded and weathered, flat flint cobbles
The surface is rough due to weathering, and is covered by clefts. The circumference is well-rounded. The shape is not always oval, but there are triangular and rectangular varieties. It is very flat and thin. The cortex has a dark brown to brown colour, but some parts are faded into cream brown.

B) rounded and abraded, flat flint cobbles
These cobbles are different from the cobbles mentioned just above in terms of the degree of surface abrasion. There is little or no surface undulation, and it is abraded. The circumference is well-rounded. The shape is not always oval but there are triangular and rectangular varieties. It is very flat and thin. The colour of the surface is generally dark brown to brown.

C) rounded and polished, flat flint cobbles
These cobbles are different from the cobbles mentioned just above in terms of the degree of surface abrasion. There is definitely no surface undulation, and it is naturally polished. The circumference is well-rounded. The shape is not always oval but there are triangular and rectangular varieties. It is very flat and thin. The colour of the surface is generally dark brown to brown.

D) rounded and weathered, oval and flat flint cobbles
The surface is rough due to weathering, and is covered by clefts. The circumference is well-rounded. The shape is oval and flat. The colour of the cortex is generally dark brown to brown, but some parts are faded into cream brown.

E) rounded and abraded, oval and flat flint cobbles
Undulated but not porous surface is abraded. The circumference is well-rounded. The shape is oval and flat. The colour of the cortex is generally dark brown to brown.

F) rounded and polished, oval and flat flint cobbles
Due to a considerable degree of abrasion, the surface undulation is almost gone, and the surface looks smooth, and it is naturally polished. The circumference is well-rounded. The shape is oval and flat. The colour of the cortex is generally dark brown to brown.

G) rounded and weathered, globular or egg-shaped flint cobbles
The surface is rough due to weathering and is covered by clefts. The circumference is well-rounded. The colour of the cortex is generally dark brown to brown, but some parts are faded into cream brown.

H) rounded and abraded, globular or egg-shaped flint cobbles
Due to abrasion, the surface is undulated but not porous. The circumference is well-rounded. The colour of the cortex is generally dark brown to brown, but there are examples which have a white to cream calcareous cortex.

I) rounded and weathered, irregularly-shaped or subangular flint cobbles
The surface is rough due to weathering, and is covered by clefts. The circumference is well-rounded, but the entire shape is irregular and subangular. The colour of the cortex is generally dark brown to brown, but some parts are faded into cream brown.

J) rounded and abraded, irregularly-shaped or subangular flint cobbles
Due to abrasion, the surface is undulated but not porous. The circumference is well-rounded, but the entire shape is irregular and subangular. The colour of the cortex is generally dark brown to brown.

K) rough, porous and abraded, irregularly-shaped flint cobbles
The surface is quite rough and porous, and it is abraded. The entire shape is irregular. The colour of the cortex is generally dark brown to brown, but there are lighter varieties.

L) rough and porous, angular translucent chert nodules
This nodule looks similar to that described above, but it is more angular, and its surface is very rough and porous like lava. Its colour is apparently different from that of common flint described above, and is translucent brown to grey. Since the size of collected fragmentary samples is various, it is difficult to imagine the original size of the nodule before reduction.

M) rough and porous flint/sandstone hexahedrons/balls
The entire surface is very rough and exhibits traces of repetitive percussion which resemble those seen on the circumferences of hammer stones. The entire shape is hexahedron to ball. In many examples, there is no clear trace of use, but some examples from Kom K and Kom W have a small part of surface abrasion, suggesting that they were used as rubbers.

N) quartz cobbles
The entire surface is very smooth, and the circumference is well-rounded. The shape is flat and oval, and the colour is white to translucent white. Quartz cobbles are often found scattered not only at the sites studied mentioned above but also at other Neolithic surface sites surveyed by me. Many examples have traces of repetitive percussion and resultant fractures on several parts of their circumference, suggesting that they were used as hammers. This kind of quartz cobble use has been recognised by Caton-Thompson (Caton-Thompson and Gardner 1934: 87). There is no evidence for other kind of use.

O) limestone nodules and cobbles
There are two distinct kinds of limestone. One is pale and coarse-grained and bears many fossil shells. Another is white and fine-grained, and bears no visible inclusions. The first kind of limestone is too coarse and too fragile to be used for manufacturing, and indeed, it was observed through my survey that they had often been used without modification for making hearths at Neolithic surface sites in the L Basin, X Basin and Z Basin. The second kind of limestone is fine enough for manufacturing. One example of a limestone cobble (approximately 8 cm in length, 4 cm in width, and 3 cm in thickness) collected at Kom K is grooved longitudinally against the longer axis, suggesting that it was used as a weight. It was often observed during the survey that fine-grained limestone slabs were used as querns, judging from a shallow depression on them. It is also likely that some fine-grained limestone slabs seen at Site E29H1 and Site XA were used as anvils for flint knapping.

Water/wind-eroded pale limestone slabs and fragments are scattered on extensive linear outcrops of limestone beds on the northern shore of the L Basin and Z Basin, and also on around the 0-10 m asl contour line more than 2 km away from the present lakeshore. Fine-grained limestone blocks must have been exploited at scarps which are sparsely seen at higher elevations to the north.

P) sandstone nodules and cobbles
There are two distinct kinds of sandstone. One is fine-grained, and cream to white. Another is coarse-grained, and has a dark grey to black colour. It was often observed during my survey that slabs and blocks of the fine-grained one had been used as querns, judging from a shallow depression on the slabs and blocks. It is likely that some fine-grained slabs seen at Site E29H1 and Site XA were used as anvils for flint

knapping. It was also observed through my survey that sandstone cobbles of slightly larger than fist size had often been used without modification for making hearths at Neolithic surface sites in the L Basin, X Basin and Z Basin. But it is noticeable that these hearths rarely consist of sandstone cobbles only. In most cases, the majority of hearth stones are pale and coarse-grained limestone cobbles, and sandstone cobbles are only minor components. Those sandstone cobbles often have a flat face, and therefore, it is probable that they had actually been used as rubbers. Similar supposedly querns and rubbers made on coarse-grained sandstone were also seen during my survey.

Q) conglomerate nodules and cobbles
Grains of this rock are much coarser than those of sandstone. The shape of this specimen is flat and oval to hexahedron/ball. Traces of use are hardly seen in most examples collected and observed in the field.

R) basalt nodules and cobbles
Basalt seems quite homogeneous, and no difference is seen between specimens collected or observed at different places in the field. Querns and rubbers made on basalt were rarely seen during my survey. Other kinds of basalt use were not found.

It has been argued that basalt was abundantly available in Gebel Qatrani, approximately 8 km to the northwest of Qasr el-Sagha, and indeed, this Gebel Qatrani basalt is known to have been intensively quarried in the Old Kingdom period. However, basalt occurs naturally on top of sandstone escarpments not only in Gebel Qatrani but also along the entire northern fringe of the Fayum Depression, and hence it is reasonable to think that Neolithic people did not necessarily go to exploit the Gebel Qatrani basalt, but rather procured basalt from sources closer to their habitat.

S) elongated petrified wood fragments
There are various shapes and sizes of this raw material. The largest examples are quite angular or tabular, and they tend to be broken longitudinally along old 'fibres' into elongated fragments. Most of such fragments are subrounded. The colour is light brown to dark grey.

T) hexagonal petrified wood cobbles
As described above, petrified wood naturally occurs in angular and tabular forms, but this specimen is hexagonal in shape. In many examples, there is no clear trace of use, but some examples from Kom K and Kom W have a small part of surface abrasion, suggesting that they were used as rubbers. One or two faces of some other examples from Kom W have one or two grooves which are parallel to old 'fibres', suggesting that they were used as sharpeners.

7.5. Remarks on the various uses of cobbles and core reduction techniques

A number of unworked flint cobbles seen at the sites studied suggest that flint cobbles were usually brought to habitation sites without decortification for reducing carrying weight and/or for insuring quality. The presence of primary and secondary cortical flakes at habitation sites and task locations means that the decortification of flint cobbles was done at habitation sites and task locations, and not at source areas. This may suggest that the cobble collectors were quite sure of the quality of cobbles procured at specific sources, and that the sources are not very far from the habitation sites, because transporting heavy cobbles must have been a big burden.

Removing low-utility portions of resources prior to their transport back to the residential base is known as field processing in the central place foraging models of human behavioural ecology, and lithic raw materials can also be field-processed (Metcalfe and Barlow 1992: 352). It has been argued that when the travel distance between a residential base and a source of lithic raw materials is long, reduction of the materials would proceed further at the source than when the travel distance is short, in order to reduce carrying weight. However, it is difficult to predict precisely the travel distance at which field processing becomes an optimal solution to carry the heavy load efficiently, without the estimates of load capacities and processing costs and the calculation of the low/high-utility parts of the raw materials. Actually, no ethnographic and experimental data exist on optimal load size for a single lithic raw material procurement event by an individual (Beck *et al.* 2002: 489-490). Therefore, what the lack of decortification of flint cobbles at source areas in the Fayum case really implies is not certain, without examining the manner of cobble use in more detail.

7.5.1. Cobble shapes

In general, there are four distinct shapes of flint cobbles for core reduction. The first is a flat cobble of circular or irregular shape. The second is an oval and flat cobble of 7-12 cm in length, 6-10 cm in width, and 3-5 cm in thickness. The third is a globular or egg-shaped cobble of 5-6 cm in diameter and 7-8 cm in height. The fourth is an irregularly-shaped or subangular cobble. The surface of these four shapes of cobbles is rounded, weathered or abraded. The shape and size of the cobble and the extent of surface weathering and abrasion must depend on the extent to which the cobble has suffered from water rolling, sandblasting and chemical action. In other words, the differences are related to which geological deposits they derived from.

7.5.2. Core reduction techniques

Different techniques were employed for the four distinct shapes of flint cobbles mentioned above. Five different kinds of core reduction techniques were used for the flat cobbles and the oval and flat cobbles (**Fig.7.21**). The first kind of core reduction technique is to strike one end of a cobble from one face repeatedly without making a platform, thereby obtaining several cortical flakes (**Fig.7.6**-1: Site L-6). The resultant core can be called a single platform core. The second kind of core reduction technique is to strike the cobble at one end along the shorter axis, in order to create a flat platform. Then, flakes were taken off continuously by striking the edges of the platform (**Fig.7.13**: Kom W- J5). The resultant core can also be called a single platform core.

The third kind of core reduction technique is to strike one end of a cobble from both faces repeatedly, thereby obtaining several cortical flakes. One or more flake scars made on one end of one face were used as platforms for obtaining flakes from the reverse face (**Fig.7.4**-1: Kom K-1, **Fig.7.4**-2: Kom K-2, **Fig.7.10**-1: Site X-12, and **Fig.7.16**-1: the Site V Depression-3). The resultant platform can be called a 'bifacial platform'. It is also highly probable that some or many of 'bifacial platform cores' were actually made as choppers. Cores or choppers of the same size have been reported as abundant at sites QS VIA/79, QS VI/79, QS V/79, QS VII H/80 and an unnamed surface site in Qasr el-Sagha (Caneva 1970: Fig.2; Dagnan-Ginter *et al.* 1984: Fig.35; Ginter *et al.* 1980: Figs. 24, 26, 27 and 28), and they are collectively dated to the Middle Kingdom. One noticeable characteristic of the Middle Kingdom cores or choppers is that they rarely have the 'bifacial platform'. This is the same characteristic as that of the Old Kingdom specimens from Umm es-Sawan described earlier. Bifacial platform cores or choppers similar to the Fayum examples are seen in the Predynastic assemblage at Maadi (Rizkana and Seeher 1988: pl.9-1). Therefore, it can be said that a 'bifacial platform' is definitely a characteristic of the Neolithic-Predynastic cores or choppers.

The fourth kind of core reduction technique is to strike one or more ends of a cobble from both faces, thereby obtaining a number of cortical flakes. Platforms are not necessarily made (**Fig.7.7**: Site E29H1-7 and **Fig.7.10**-2: Site X-11). The resultant cores can be called either bifacial opposed platform cores, bifacial multiple platform cores, or bifacial discoidal cores. No blade cores are formed from these cobbles.

The fifth and the most unique core reduction technique is to wedge the cobble along the long axis, producing two discoids, and then, non-cortical flakes were taken off continuously from the edges of the dorsal face to the ventral face of a discoid, while rotating it (**Fig.7.6**-3: Site L-1). This can be called a 'half-split unifacial

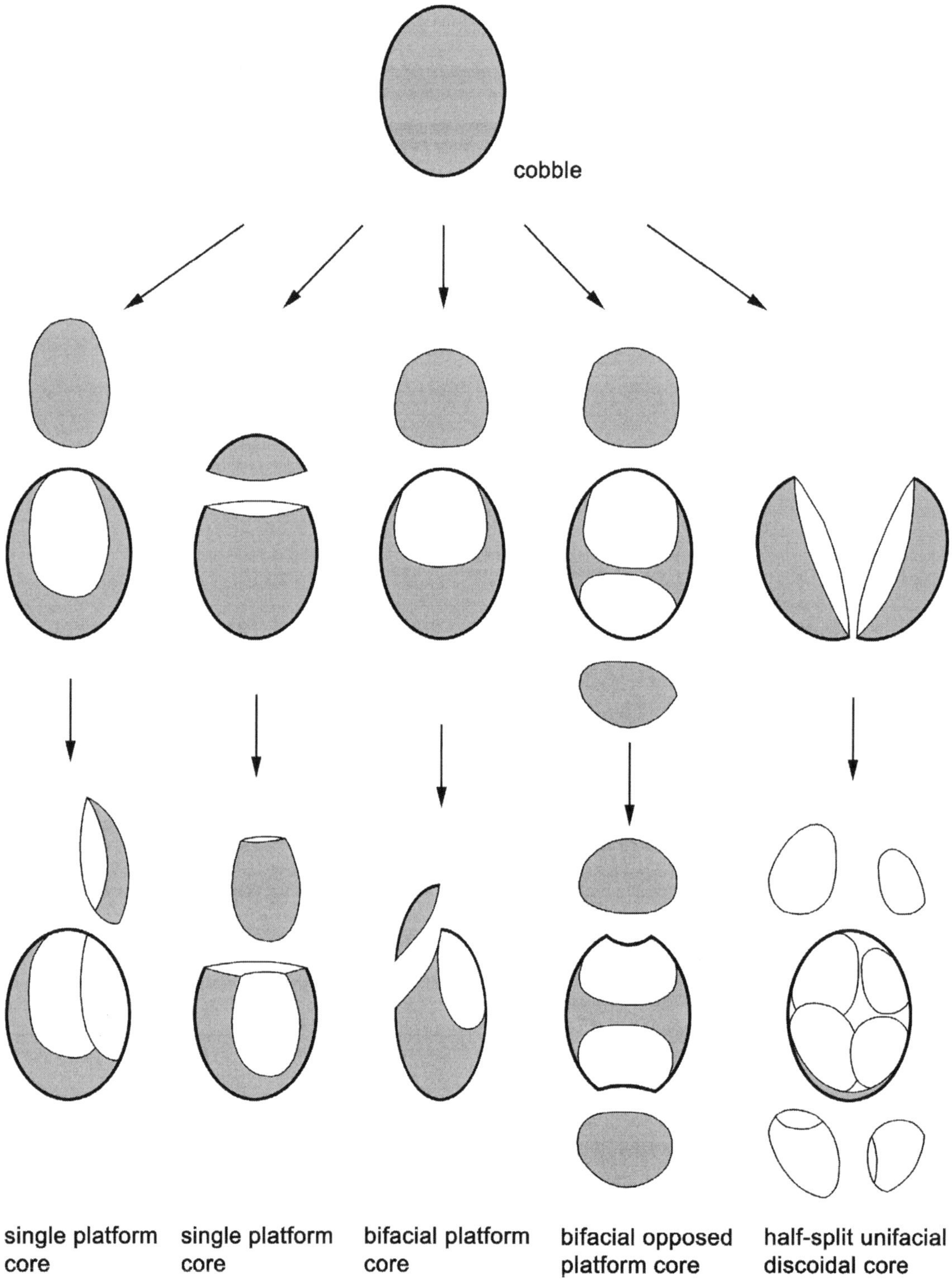

Fig.7.21. Core reduction techniques employed in the Fayum Neolithic

discoidal core'. And when the discoid is thick enough, cortical flakes were also taken off continuously from the edges of the ventral face to the dorsal face. The resultant core can be called a 'half-split bifacial discoidal core'. It is not sure how this splitting of oval and flat cobbles was done. However, traces of a hard blow such as an unusually large compression bulb on one end and a bad fracture on the opposite end of unused discoids from Site L (**Fig.7.22**: Site L-9 and **Fig.7.23**: Site L-10) and of a discoidal core from the Site V Depression (**Fig.7.16**-2: the Site V Depression-7) suggest that both the bipolar percussion technique, by which a straight blow wedges a cobble rested on a hard anvil, and the split cone technique, by which a very hard blow at right angles splits a cobble rested on a yielding surface like sand or a padded leg (Whittaker 1994: 113*ff*), were employed.

These five different core reduction techniques were employed for the globular or egg-shaped cobbles and the irregularly-shaped or subangular cobbles as well. However, it seems that the first technique by which one end of a cobble is struck in order to create a flat platform and to take off flakes while striking the edges of the platform (**Fig.7.3**: Kom K-3) and the fifth technique by which cobbles were split into two pieces in order to flake the ventral face of the pieces (**Fig.7.6**-2: Site L-4 and **Fig.7.24**: the Site V Depression-10) are the most suitable for the globular or egg-shaped cobbles and the irregularly-shaped or subangular cobbles which have no good striking platforms for initial flaking in a natural state.

7.5.3. Flakes

As for flakes struck off from these cores, the size of flakes is already determined by the size of cores, and hence the flakes cannot be larger than 9-12 cm in length and 7-10 cm in width. Except for flakes from unifacial discoidal cores, most flakes from the other cores are primary flakes, because the cores are not exhaustively reduced. How these primary flakes were actually used is another interesting topic, which will be discussed later in more detail.

7.5.4. Hammers

It was often observed that one end or opposed ends of oval quartz cobbles of approximately 6-

Fig.7.22. An unused discoid collected at Site L (half-split along the long axis of a cobble)

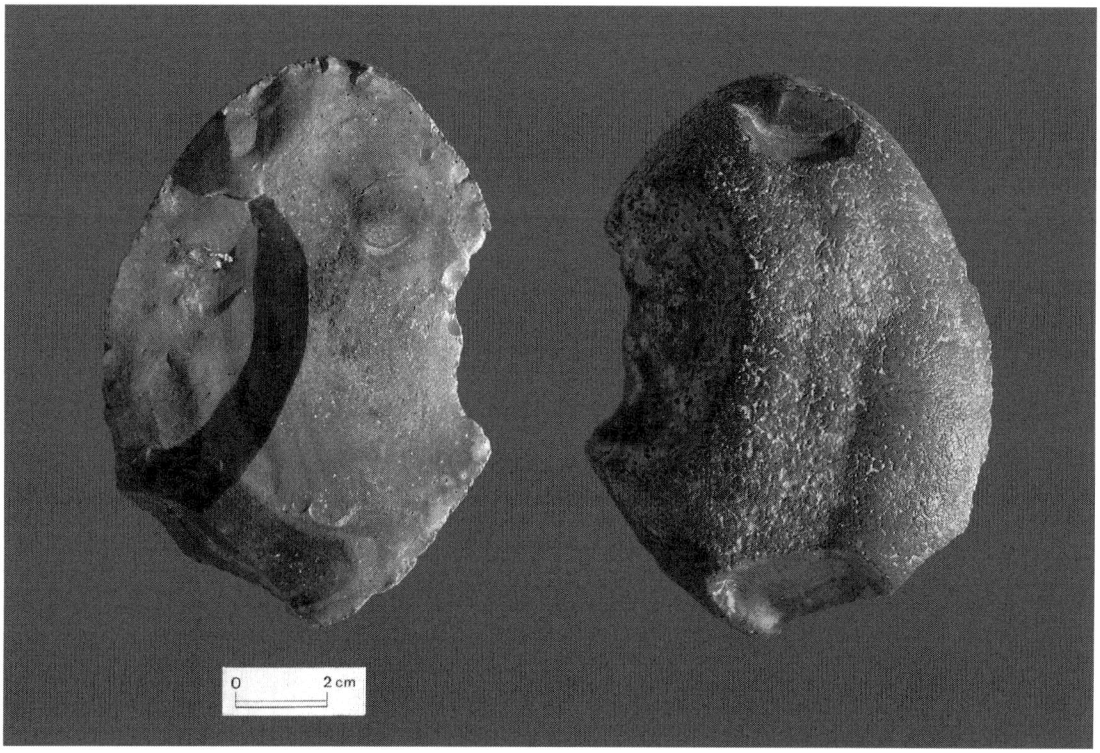

Fig.7.23. An unused discoid collected at Site L (half-split along the short axis of a cobble)

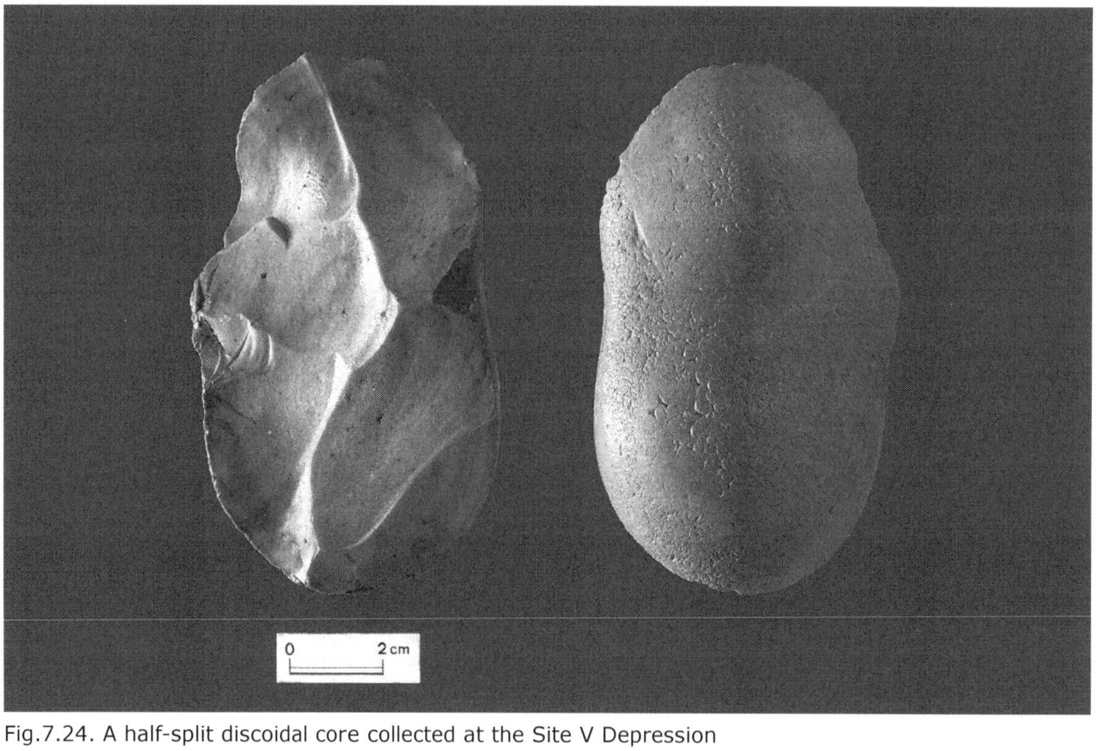

Fig.7.24. A half-split discoidal core collected at the Site V Depression

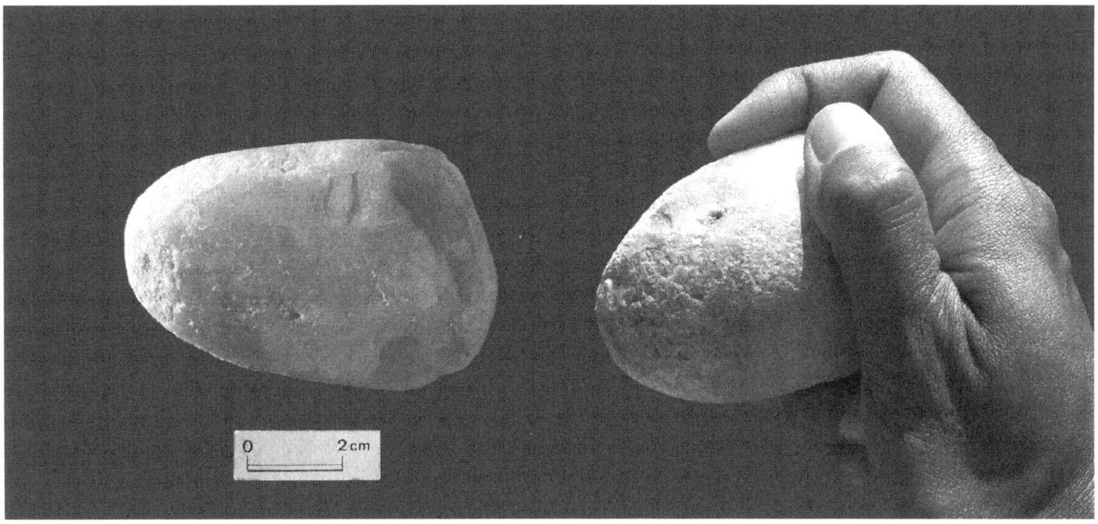

Fig.7.25. A quartz hammer collected at Kom K

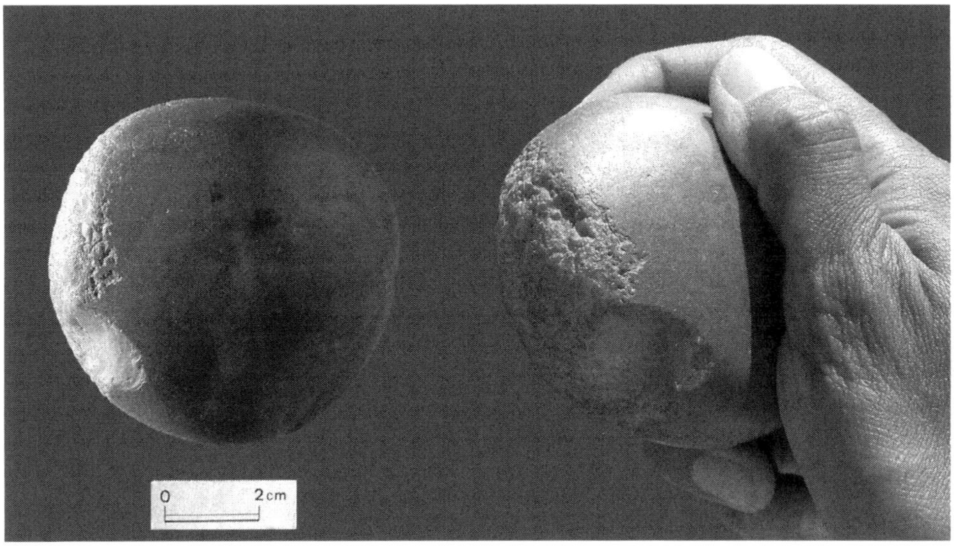

Fig.7.26. A flint hammer collected at Kom K

8 cm long and 4-5 cm wide had numerous percussion marks and fractures, indicating that they were used as hammers (**Fig.7.25**: Kom K-7). Similar examples of quartz cobble hammers have been found at the Neolithic site of Merimde Beni Salama (Eiwanger 1992: pl.105-IV.1225, III.188 and OF.87). Since quartz cobbles are relatively light and brittle, it is assumed that they were not used for hard percussion practised in the early stages of a knapping sequence.

Flint cobbles of the same size and the same shape or more circular shape were also used as hammers, judging from numerous percussion marks on one end or opposed ends of the cobbles (**Fig.7.26**: Kom K-4) or in a ring on the circumference of the cobbles (**Fig.7.27**: Kom K-6) as well as large fractures on one end of the cobbles (**Fig.7.28**: Kom K-1). Similar examples of flint cobble hammers have been reported at the Neolithic sites of Merimde Beni Salama (Eiwanger 1992: pl.105-IV.1226) and El Omari (Debono and Mortensen 1990: pl.32-2 and 3)

Fig.7.27. A flint hammer collected at Kom K

Fig.7.28. A flint hammer collected at Kom K

and at the Predynastic site of Maadi (Rizkana and Seeher 1998: pl.11-1), and there is no doubt that the Fayum cobbles were also used as hard hammers. Several samples from Kom K show that the type E (rounded and abraded, oval and flat flint cobbles) and type F (rounded and polished, oval and flat flint cobbles) of approximately 6-8 cm long and 5-7 cm wide are usually used as hammers. This is reasonable, given the ease of holding by hand.

A curious thing is that elongated petrified wood fragments seem to have been used as soft hammers. Such a use had already been guessed by Caton-Thompson at the Old Kingdom gypsum quarrying workshops in Umm es-Sawan. Near these workshops, there was a flint knapping ground, and roughly-knapped flint cobbles which were no doubt used for quarrying

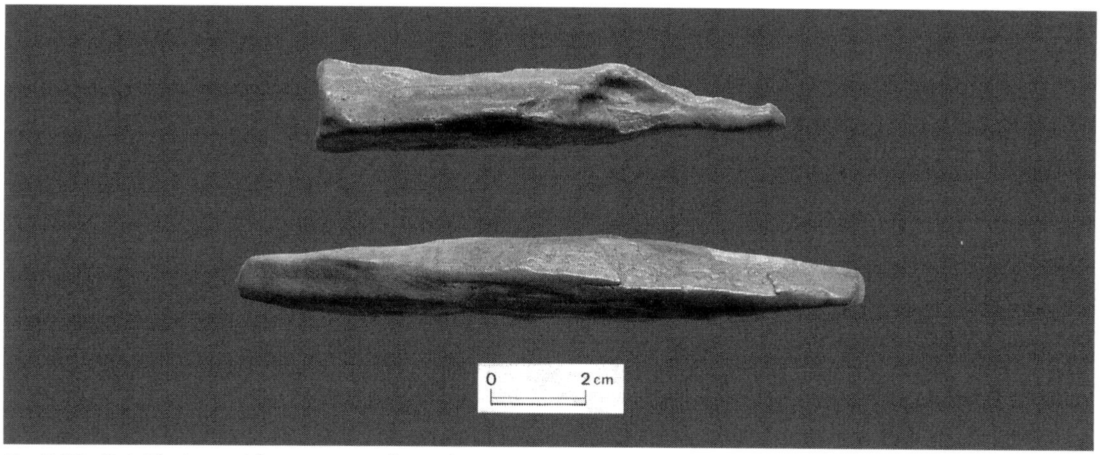

Fig.7.29. Petrified wood hammers collected at Site XA (above) and Site X (below)

gypsum were accompanied by splintered petrified wood (Caton-Thompson and Gardner 1934: 104). During my survey, elongated and slightly pointed fragments of petrified wood of hand-held size and length were often found with lithic cores and debitage products not only at the Neolithic surface sites studied but also at many other localities not intensively studied (**Fig.7.29**). These petrified wood fragments could have been used as a soft hammer (billet) or pressure flaker, though it seems difficult to use them as indirect percussion punches because experimental use demonstrates that they easily shatter. It is possible that animal horn and bone were used as soft hammers, but such examples have never been reported at Neolithic sites in Egypt. There is no example of the use of a petrified wood nodule as a lithic core in the Fayum Neolithic sites. Petrified wood does not naturally occur at lower elevations close to the lakeshore, and therefore, it is certain that they were brought from elsewhere.

7.5.5. Wasteful and thorough uses of flint cobbles

It seems that many flint cobbles were abandoned after a small number of flakes were obtained. In some cases, this is obviously because of the failure of knapping such as hinged termination of flake scars and obtuse platform angle, but it is not certain whether this could also be because of other problems such as the bad knapping quality of the cobbles. In many cases, cobbles and prepared cores were discarded even though they were still in good shape and large enough to provide more flakes of a certain size. Therefore, it gives the impression that Neolithic people used flint cobbles in a rather wasteful manner. Unless cobbles were abundant and readily available, people would have had to make the most of scarce cobbles by various economising behaviours (Odell 1996), and the cobbles must have been more carefully selected at the sources and the core reduction must have been more exhaustive. This Fayum Neolithic case may suggest that flint cobbles were so abundant and so readily available that toolmakers tended to waste the material. In other words, this may indicate that people did not mind wasting raw materials and were sure of procuring more materials again without trouble. Flint cobbles may have been procured through regular trips to specific source locations and stockpiled at habitation sites. Or, the lithic cores which seem to be wastefully discarded should be regarded as de facto refuse rather than primary refuse (Schiffer 1976: 33), and may actually have been stockpiled at the sites for future reuse.

On the other hand, there are small fragmentary cores which seem to have been used thoroughly. Because of different sampling methods, such small fragmentary cores were collected only at Site L, Site XA and Kom W.

The fragmentary cores apparently derive from rounded or subangular large cobbles, and the fragments could probably be obtained by shattering the cobbles. Several flat faces of the fragments which form an angle of less than 90 degrees were used as striking platforms in an unpatterned manner, whereas some cortical parts were left untouched. This fragmentary cobble use stands in strong contrast to the seemingly wasteful use of whole cobbles mentioned above. It is probable that the use of fragments of cobbles as cores was the last resort to utilise large cores which were already used partly but were of no more use due to dull platform angle and bad flake scars caused by previous flaking. This manner of cobble fragment production and use has been argued as a kind of economising behaviour under conditions where lithic raw materials are scarce (Odell 1996). However, the situation at Site L, Site XA and Kom W in terms of the availability of lithic raw materials does not seem to have been very difficult. Therefore, it is more likely that shattering of cobbles has habitually been done in an expedient manner for obtaining small non-cortical flakes at these sites.

7.5.6. Enigmatic stone balls

Lastly, as for the rough and porous flint/sandstone balls collected at Kom K and Kom W (**Fig.7.30**), since there are few visible traces of wear, it is not certain how they were used. Some balls were broken into two pieces, but these hemispherical pieces do not seem to have been used as lithic cores. Therefore, one possible use of these enigmatic objects is that the balls were thrown by hand or by using a sling at game animal for hunting. Such balls cannot kill the animal instantly by one throw, but it can immobilise or weaken the animals, which are afterwards killed with spears and clubs. This kind of stone ball use was already suggested by

Fig.7.30. Enigmatic stone balls collected at Kom K

Caton-Thompson (Caton-Thompson and Gardner 1934: 39), and has recently been argued in the Neolithic and later periods in the Near East (Mazurowski 1994). It is significant to consider this possibility, since this gives an insight into the development of an unprecedented hunting tactic in the Fayum Neolithic.

7.5.7. Differences in the use of cobbles and the core reduction techniques between the sites studied

As mentioned earlier, due to the different preservation of the sites studied, the sampling method and the number of samples were not consistent. Therefore, any statistical analysis of flint cobble assemblages is quite difficult. Nevertheless, the collected data give some tentative ideas about the similarities and differences of flint cobble assemblages between sites.

It seems that apart from the extent of surface weathering, flat flint cobbles (types A, B and C) and oval and flat flint cobble (types D, E and F) are the most prevalent cobbles in the studied sites. It may be said that the cobbles of this size and shape were the most versatile cobbles and were the easiest to transport and handle.

As for the general size of cobbles, it is difficult to find any significant differences between sites, partly because of the sampling bias. Both large and small cobbles are unevenly distributed, and it does not seem that either are concentrated at specific sites. Therefore, it is hard to determine whether there is an increase or decrease of cobble size according to the distance between source areas and the sites, as has been negatively discussed in the Early Ceramic sites in the Egyptian Western Desert (Close 1999). This may perhaps suggest that this entire Neolithic habitat in the northeast of Lake Qarun belonged to one technological organisation based on some distribution centres, and that the procurement and distribution of cobbles were logistically organised.

The general absence of unifacial/bifacial discoidal cores made on the A, B and C types of cobbles at Kom K, Site XA, Site X and Kom W exhibits a striking contrast to their presence at Site L, Site E29H1, Locality 'Calcified Shrubs' and the Site V Depression. Considering that Site L, Site E29H1, Locality 'Calcified Shrubs' and the Site V Depression look like field camps or locations for subsistence activities, it is presumed that this core reduction technique employed for flat cobbles was related to the immediate need for fresh thin flakes at task locations. It seems that half-split unifacial/bifacial discoidal cores made on the D, E, G, H, I, and J types of cobbles are substitutes for discoidal cores made on flat cobbles mentioned above, but it is not certain whether half-wedging of cobbles was usually done upon arrival at task locations. The complete lack of half-wedging techniques at Kom K, Site XA and Locality 'Calcified Shrubs' does not necessarily mean that half-wedging of cobbles were never done there, but may be that half-split cobbles were rarely left there. This possibility may support the assumption that they were related to the immediate need for fresh thin flakes at task locations for specific subsistence activities. As described below, given the fact that half-split cobbles were sometimes partly retouched and transformed into large scrapers, it may be said that half-split cobbles were quite versatile raw materials comparable to unworked flat cobbles of the A, B and C types.

Kom K and Kom W are remarkable in terms of the presence of the type F (rounded and polished, oval and flat flint cobbles). These cobbles have not been seen at the other sites studied. Even at Kom K, these cobbles seem to have been used almost exclusively as hard hammers. This may perhaps reflect a unique preference of toolmakers at Kom K. Kom K and Kom W are also remarkable in terms of the presence of the type L (rough and porous, angular translucent chert nodules). These nodules have not been seen at the other sites studied.

In summary, these observed differences in the use of cobbles and the core reduction techniques between the sites studied may reflect the different functions of the sites or different durations of occupation. It seems probable that Kom K, Site XA and Kom W were residential bases and logistical centres for subsistence activities, and that Site L, Site E29H1, Site X, Locality 'Calcified Shrubs' and the Site V Depression were field camps or locations occupied or visited temporarily for some specific tasks. This topic will be discussed later in more detail.

7.6. Sources of lithic raw materials in the Fayum Depression and its vicinity

Although several scholars have discussed the possible sources of flint used by Neolithic toolmakers in the Fayum and its vicinity, no one has pinpointed exact locations. Citing Beadnell's suggestion, Caton-Thompson considered that the flint used by Neolithic people might have derived from outside the Fayum Depression in nodular or tabular form: one type from the Middle Eocene limestone to the south like that observed in Wadi Rayan and another type from the Cretaceous limestone to the north of Abu Roash. As for the possibility of the use of local materials, she mentioned the material available at Gebel Qatrani (Caton-Thompson and Gardner 1934: 87).

Considering the huge amount of cobbles found at Neolithic sites, it is unlikely that all of them came from such distant places as Abu Roash, which is located more than 100 km to the north of the Fayum. It seems more likely that the major source was much closer to the Fayum Neolithic habitats. The rocky terrain of Qasr el-Sagha and Gebel Qatrani, which are approximately 15-20 km to the northwest of Kom W, has been argued by several scholars as a possible source. However, my visit to this terrain revealed that on the limestone escarpments above Qasr el-Sagha, there is no surface scatter of large flint cobbles like those described at length (**Fig.7.31**). Since Gebel Qatrani is a sandstone plateau and does not yield tabular or nodular flint, it is not clear where at Gebel Qatrani Caton-Thompson found flint sources. No flint cobble is scattered at Gebel Qatrani, and only small pebbles which are not suitable for tool making are sparsely scattered (**Fig.7.32**). Therefore, the sources of flint cobbles must be sought somewhere else. In search of flint sources within the Fayum Depression, some explorations were carried out (**Fig.7.33**).

7.6.1. The northern fringe of the Fayum Depression

The northern fringe of the Fayum Depression is approximately 22 km to the north of the present lakeshore and is higher than 100 m asl. It is dominated by a sandstone plateau capped by a thin layer of basalt, and there is no natural outcrop of flint. Some outcrops of quartzitic sandstone, which was commonly used for tool making in southern Egypt in prehistory, were observed in this area, but this material has never been used for tool making in the prehistory of

Fig.7.31. Escarpments above Qasr el-Sagha (looking southeast)

Fig.7.32. Gebel Qatrani (looking northwest)

the Fayum. Some scatters of rough and porous, angular translucent chert nodules found only at Kom K and Kom W are seen in this area. Their size and shape are quite similar to those found at these sites, and it is probable that this place is one of the sources of this peculiar raw material.

In the desert wadis which stretch north-south and connect the rocky fringe of the Fayum Depression to the lakeshore, a survey was carried out to see whether flint cobbles and artefacts are scattered along the wadis. Scatters of flint pebbles were actually seen on wadi levees and banks, but again, they are too small to be used for tool making. A number of Middle Palaeolithic, Epipalaeolithic and Neolithic lithic artefacts were collected during this survey, but they are made of flint cobbles which are not seen in these wadis. Therefore, it is concluded that the rocky terrain on the northern fringe of the Fayum Depression is not the source of flint cobbles, even though basalt and sandstone blocks could probably have been exploited there by prehistoric people.

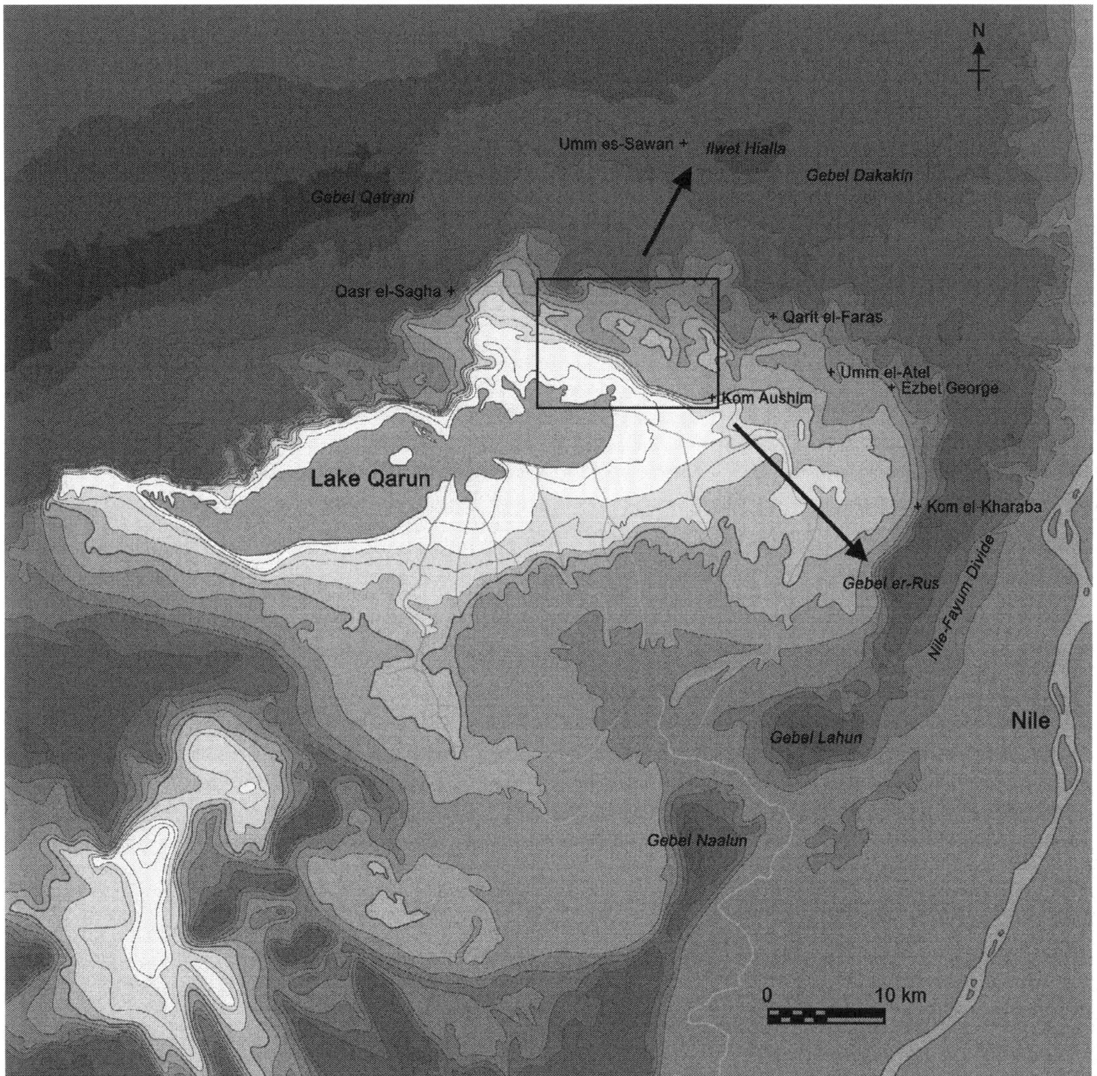

Fig.7.33. Locations of possible sources of lithic raw materials in the Fayum

Fig.7.34. Limestone outcrop near the present lakeshore (looking south)

7.6.2. Rocky terrains close to the present lakeshore

The rocky terrains around the 10-15 m asl contour line close to the present lakeshore is formed of Upper Eocene limestone of the Qasr el-Sagha Formation. There are a number of linear outcrops of limestone bedrock which stretch northwest-southeast and mark ancient shorelines. This flat limestone bed extends southwards and is gradually replaced by sandstone beds of the Birket Qarun Formation. They gently fall, and form steep cliffs at some places. The sandstone beds are replaced by another limestone bed, which reaches the present lakeshore (**Fig.7.34**). These successive limestone and sandstone beds do not contain flint layers, and no flint cobbles are scattered in these terrains.

In summary, there is no possible source of flint cobbles to the north, south, and northwest of the major Fayum Neolithic habitation sites within the Fayum Depression. Therefore, remaining areas to be explored are to the east and the northeast of the Fayum.

7.6.3. The Nile-Fayum Divide

The nearest potential source of flint cobbles is the area between Lake Qarun and the Nile Valley, or, the Nile Valley itself. This area, which is called the Nile-Fayum Divide, has not been sufficiently investigated by Caton-Thompson, because of trouble with another archaeological mission regarding the research area concession. Therefore, it is no wonder that she overlooked this area as a potential source of flint cobbles in the Neolithic period. However, when she investigated Old Kingdom gypsum quarrying workshops at Umm es-Sawan, she discovered a flint knapping ground on which thousands of unworked flint cobbles and cobble hand-picks were scattered. The cobbles were trimmed down to a rough point by careless free flaking, though a rounded butt of the cortex were retained, and the points were undoubtedly used for quarrying gypsum. She was amazed by the fact that there was no flint of comparable size in the surroundings and concluded that those cobbles must have been transported from elsewhere by Old Kingdom quarry workers. She guessed that the sources of those flint cobbles might be to the north, or might be the Quaternary deposit at Gebel er-Rus on the Nile-Fayum Divide to the southeast (Caton-Thompson and Gardner 1934: 104; 129). Strangely, she did not mention the possibility that Gebel er-Rus was visited by Neolithic people, but it is not surprising if Gebel er-Rus was one source of flint cobbles in the Neolithic period.

Sandford and Arkell (1929) investigated the Nile-Fayum Divide and made a detailed geological map. They located the extent of Middle-Upper Eocene limestone escarpments and Pleistocene gravel beaches containing Middle and Late Palaeolithic artefacts eroded out and washed by the wave action of the Pleistocene lake, which was much larger than the Neolithic Moeris Lake. Such Pleistocene gravel beaches are located within my survey area to the north of the lake around the contour line of approximately 30-40 m asl, but the gravels consist of rolled pebbles and subangular fragments of flint, which are much smaller than the flint cobbles under consideration, and hence they are obviously not the source areas of the cobbles.

More substantial information about the possible sources of flint cobbles has been provided not only by Sandford and Arkell but also by Little, who mapped many locations of Pliocene/Plio-Pleistocene gravel deposits in the Nile-Fayum Divide (Sandford and Arkell 1929: 11-27 and folding map; Little 1936: pl.IX). The Pliocene/Plio-Pleistocene gravel deposits have been found on top of high escarpments at many places in the region between the Fayum and the south of Cairo, and have been known to contain well-rounded flint cobbles of fist-size (Mori and Iryu 2001: 78-81). The contents of the Pliocene/Plio-Pleistocene deposits in the Nile-Fayum Divide must be the same. Sandford and Arkell did not mention the exact size and characteristics of flint cobbles seen in the Pliocene/Plio-Pleistocene deposits in the Nile-Fayum Divide and instead preferred to use the term 'gravels' when they described the contents of the deposits. When one sees the photographs in their publication, their Pliocene/Plio-Pleistocene 'gravels' seem to be larger than clastic Pleistocene beach gravels. However, according to Cagle (1994), who has investigated some of Plio-Pleistocene deposits around the Fayum, only a few of them contained flint cobbles adequate for tool making, though he did not mention exactly where they were. It seems that he did collect good samples of flint cobbles near Gebel Dakakin, which is approximately 25 km to the northeast of Kom K and is beside the modern Cairo-Fayum Road No.22.

Based on the assumption that the Pliocene/Plio-Pleistocene deposits in the Nile-Fayum Divide provide some types of large flint cobbles described earlier and that Neolithic people visited some of these Pliocene/Plio-Pleistocene deposits on high escarpments, a survey was carried out at 1) Kom el-Kharaba (the ancient Philadelphia of the 3rd century BC to the 3rd century AD), which is approximately 27 km to the southeast of Kom K, 2) Fag el-Gamous and Seila, which are located on Gebel er-Rus and are approximately 28 km to the southeast of Kom K and approximately 7 km to the southwest of Kom el-Kharaba, and 3) Gebel Lahun, which is approximately 14 km to the southwest of Gebel er-Rus. There was no time to visit Gebel Naalun, which is the highest plateau in the Nile-Fayum Divide and is located approximately 2 km to the southwest of Gebel Lahun across the Hawara Channel.

As is known from unpublished Fayum lithic collections presently housed in the Egyptian Museum in Cairo, stray Neolithic tools like bifacially-retouched concave-based arrowheads and knife blades have been collected by de Prorok and Caton-Thompson at such sites as Kom Aushim (the ancient Karanis of the 3rd century BC to the 5th century AD), Qarit el-Faras, and Umm el-Atel (the ancient Bacchias of the 3rd century BC to the 4th century AD), all of which are approximately 10-20 km to the east of the present lake but were actually located on the northern shore of the Neolithic Moeris Lake. It has also been reported that there were Neolithic artefact scatters and hearths at Ezbet George, which is supposed to be around the northeast corner of the Neolithic Moeris Lake and is located between Umm el-Atel and Kom el-Kharaba (Caton-Thompson *et al.* 1937). All of them can be indirect evidence for the movement of Neolithic people between the Fayum Depression and the Nile Valley.

The site of Kom el-Kharaba (N29.44145° E31.09347° in the approximate centre) is located on plain desert, and the southeastern end of the site is marked by a high plateau which stretches east-west along Darb Gerzeh (**Fig.7.35**) and is dated to the Pliocene. Rounded and weathered flint cobbles of larger than fist size are sparsely scattered on and around the plateau of approximately 100 m asl at the highest point (**Fig.7.36**). Unexpectedly, a number of seemingly Neolithic, but more likely, Predynastic partly-retouched and bifacially-retouched spearheads and blades were collected on one of the plateau, which is approximately 60 m asl. However, the raw material of some of the tools and the flint cobbles collected are not similar to those which are commonly seen in the Neolithic sites in the northeast of Lake Qarun, in terms of shape, colour and surface weathering. Therefore, even though it is probable that Neolithic people passed by Kom el-Kharaba, it must be said that Kom el-Kharaba is not the major source area of the flint cobbles used by Neolithic people.

Gebel er-Rus (N29.39869° E31.04626° in the

Fig.7.35. Kom el-Kharaba (looking southeast)

Fig.7.37. Gebel er-Rus (looking north)

Fig.7.36. A high plateau near Kom el-Kharaba (looking southwest)

Fig.7.38. Scatter of cobbles at lower elevations of Gebel er-Rus (looking east)

approximate centre) is marked by the third highest plateau in the Nile-Fayum Divide (**Fig.7.37**), and flint cobbles of various sizes and shapes are widely scattered on and around the plateau. The plateau is sandstone of the Upper Eocene Birket Qarun Formation, overlying a limestone bed of the Middle Eocene Gehannam Formation. The flint cobble deposits are dated to the Pliocene. The cobbles at lower elevations are very dirty and muddy (**Fig.7.38**), and hence, at first glance, they do not look similar to those which are commonly seen in the Neolithic sites in the northeast of Lake Qarun, in terms of colour and surface weathering. However, once they are cleaned, they exhibit a remarkable similarity to some types of cobbles which have been used by Neolithic people in the northeast of Lake Qarun. The cobbles collected at lower elevations of Gebel er-Rus, which are approximately 50 m asl, include the type B (rounded and abraded, flat flint cobbles), type C (rounded and polished, flat flint cobbles), type D (rounded and weathered, oval and flat flint cobbles), type I (rounded and weathered, irregularly-shaped or subangular flint cobbles), and type N (quartz cobbles) (**Table 7.10**). Specimens of the types B, D and I are actually knapped in the manner quite similar to those have been repeatedly observed on Neolithic cores in the northeast of Lake Qarun.

Only the highest point of the plateau of Gebel er-Rus, on which the Pyramid of Seila, a step pyramid of the Old Kingdom is located (N29.38239° E31.05152° in the centre), is dated to the Plio-Pleistocene. Flint cobbles of various sizes and shapes are quite extensively scattered there (**Fig.7.39**). The composition of various flint

	item	platform preparation	knapping sequence	amount of cortex	L (cm)	W (cm)	T (cm)	cobble type	cortex colour	fresh part colour
1	bifacial platform core, or, chopper	unfacetted	multiple	50-75 %	9.7	11.3	3.0	B	brown/cream brown	brown
2	whole cobble	-	-	76-99%	11.8	8.7	2.4	C	mottled brown	light brown
3	discoidal core	cortical	tertiary	50-75 %	10.2	9.4	4.0	D	cream brown	mottled brown
4	single platform core	unfacetted	quaternary	76-99%	2.7	6.8	6.5	D	dark brown	brown
5	single platform core	unfacetted	primary	76-99%	4.0	8.7	11.9	I	mottled brown/ cream brown	mottled brown
6	whole cobble	-	-	complete (100%)	6.9	6.2	3.9	D	brown/cream brown	-
7	whole cobble	-	-	complete (100%)	9.4	8.1	3.3	D	brown	-
8	whole cobble	-	-	complete (100%)	6.2	4.5	2.1	N	translucent white	-
9	whole cobble	-	-	complete (100%)	7.1	4.5	2.0	N	translucent white	-

Table 7.10. Items collected at lower elevations of Gebel er-Rus

	item	platform preparation	knapping sequence	amount of cortex	L (cm)	W (cm)	T (cm)	cobble type	cortex colour	fresh part colour
1	bifacial discoidal core	cortical	tertiary	50-75 %	8.9	10.1	1.6	A	brown	mottled brown
2	bifacial discoidal core	cortical	multiple	50-75 %	10.4	10.8	2.1	B	brown	mottled brown
3	single platform core, or, chopper	cortical	multiple	76-99%	3.1	9.1	8.4	C	brown	light brown
4	whole cobble	-	-	76-99%	11.8	7.7	11.5	A	brown/cream brown	brown
5	whole cobble	-	-	complete (100%)	10.2	9.5	2.6	A	brown/cream brown	-
6	whole cobble	-	-	complete (100%)	10.8	8.4	3.0	B	brown	-
7	whole cobble	-	-	complete (100%)	9.3	6.6	2.2	C	brown	-
8	whole cobble	-	-	complete (100%)	9.1	6.4	3.1	D	dark brown	-
9	single platform core	-	multiple	50-75 %	10.9	9.2	6.1	J	brown	brown
10	whole cobble	-	-	complete (100%)	7.3	4.6	2.2	N	translucent white	-
11	whole cobble	-	-	76-99%	10.0	9.4	3.0	A	cream brown	brown

Table 7.11. Items collected at higher elevations of Gebel er-Rus

Fig.7.39. Scatter of cobbles at higher elevations of Gebel er-Rus (looking west)

Fig.7.40. Scatter of cobbles on Gebel Lahun (looking southeast)

cobbles in this Plio-Pleistocene deposit resembles that in the Pliocene deposit at the base of Gebel er-Rus. The cobbles collected at higher elevations of Gebel er-Rus, which is approximately 100 m asl, include the type A (rounded and weathered, flat flint cobbles), type B (rounded and abraded, flat flint cobbles), type C (rounded and polished, flat flint cobbles), type D (rounded and weathered, oval and flat flint cobbles), type J (rounded and abraded, irregularly-shaped or subangular flint cobbles), and type N (quartz cobbles) (**Table 7.11**). Specimens of the types A, B, C and J are actually knapped in a manner quite similar to what has been observed on Neolithic cores in the northeast of Lake Qarun.

Gebel Lahun (N29.27099° E30.98967° in the approximate centre) is marked by the second highest plateau in the Nile-Fayum Divide, and flint cobbles of various sizes and shapes are quite extensively scattered on the plateau (**Fig.7.40**). The plateau is sandstone of the Upper Eocene Birket Qarun Formation, overlying a limestone bed of the Middle Eocene Gehannam Formation. The flint cobble deposits are dated to the Pliocene. The cobbles collected at higher elevations of Gebel Lahun, which is approximately 140 m asl, include the type A (rounded and weathered, flat flint cobbles), type B (rounded and abraded, flat flint cobbles), type C (rounded and polished, flat flint cobbles), type D (rounded and weathered, oval and flat flint cobbles), type G (rounded and weathered, globular or egg-shaped flint cobbles), type H (rounded and abraded, globular or egg-shaped flint cobble), type J (rounded and abraded, irregularly-shaped or subangular flint cobbles), and type N (quartz cobbles) (**Table 7.12**). Specimens of the types A, B, D and H are knapped in a manner similar to what has been observed on Neolithic cores in the northeast of Lake Qarun.

Therefore, it can be concluded that these Pliocene/Plio-Pleistocene deposits on the plateaus of Gebel er-Rus and Gebel Lahun are the sources of flint cobbles and quartz cobbles used by Neolithic people.

Fig.7.41. Ilwet Hialla (looking northeast)

	core type	platform preparation	knapping sequence	amount of cortex	L (cm)	W (cm)	T (cm)	cobble type	cortex colour	fresh part colour
1	single platform core, or side scraper	unfacetted	quarternary	25-49 %	1.9	8.6	5.7	D	brown	mottled brown
2	bifacial discoidal core	cortical	multiple	25-49 %	7.9	6.8	2.1	A	brown	brown
3	discoidal scraper	unfacetted	multiple	25-49 %	8.8	6.6	1.2	A	brown	mottled brown
4	end scraper	cortical	multiple	50-75 %	8.4	8.2	2.4	A	brown	brown
5	bifacial platform core, or chopper	unfacetted	multiple	50-75 %	9.4	8.6	2.6	A	brown	brown
6	bifacial platform core, or chopper	unfacetted	quarternary	50-75 %	11.6	8.3	2.9	A	brown	brown
7	side scraper	unfacetted	multiple	25-49 %	11.8	9.2	3.2	B	brown	brown
8	single platform core, or chopper	cortical	multiple	50-75 %	12.8	8.2	3.9	D	brown	brown
9	single platform core, or chopper	cortical	tertiary	76-99%	16.0	8.5	2.0	C	brown	brown
10	single platform core	unfacetted	quarternary	50-75 %	3.8	8.6	4.0	J	brown	brown
11	single platform core, or natural break	cortical	tertiary	50-75 %	4.2	10.1	4.3	D	brown	brown
12	single platform core	unfacetted	tertiary	50-75 %	6.7	8.1	5.4	H	brown	brown
13	single platform core, or natural break	unfacetted	quarternary	50-75 %	5.8	12.1	5.7	H	brown	brown
14	whole cobble	-	-	complete (100%)	9.4	5.8	4.2	G	brown	brown
15	whole cobble	-	-	complete (100%)	9.9	8.5	1.6	C	brown	brown
16	whole cobble	-	-	complete (100%)	8.3	7.7	2.1	A	brown	brown
17	whole cobble	-	-	50-75 %	8.1	7.8	2.1	A	brown	mottled brown
18	quartz cobble	-	-	complete (100%)	8.5	4.9	3.0	N	cream	-
19	quartz cobble	-	-	complete (100%)	6.0	3.6	2.7	N	cream	-

Table 7.12. Items collected at Gebel Lahun

7.6.4. Ilwet Hialla and Umm es-Sawan

In addition, another survey was carried out at Ilwet Hialla and its vicinity, approximately 14 km to the northeast of Kom K. Ilwet Hialla is a sandstone plateau of the Oligocene Gebel Qatrani Formation which marks the northeastern boundary of the Fayum Depression and stretches east-west (**Fig.7.41**). It is above 200 m asl, and forms steep cliffs. The surface on top of this plateau is covered by scatters of petrified wood fragments and coarse-grained black sandstone slabs as well as flint pebbles of elongated or irregular shape. However, a few kilometres farther to the northeast of the plateau and close to the modern Cairo-Fayum Road No.22, the

Fig.7.42. Scatter of cobbles on Ilwet Hialla Northeast (looking northeast)

Fig.7.44. Scatter of sandstone slabs and cobbles on top of Umm es-Sawan (looking east)

Fig.7.43. Scatter of cobbles in the south of Ilwet Hialla (looking north)

landscape is more hilly, and the surface is covered by extensive scatters of flint cobbles of various sizes and shapes (**Fig.7.42**), which are similar to those found in Pliocene deposits in Gebel er-Rus. These high elevations (N29.74523° E30.97495° in the approximate centre) can be understood as western extensions or patches of the Pliocene deposits of Gebel Dakakin.

The cobbles collected at high elevations to the northeast of Ilwet Hialla, which are approximately 205 m asl, include the type B (rounded and abraded, flat flint cobbles), type C (rounded and polished, flat flint cobbles), type D (rounded and weathered, oval and flat flint cobbles), type E (rounded and abraded, oval and flat flint cobbles), type F (rounded and polished, oval and flat flint cobbles), type G (rounded and weathered, globular or egg-shaped flint cobbles), type H (rounded and abraded, globular or egg-shaped flint cobble), type J (rounded and abraded, irregularly-shaped or subangular flint cobbles), type K (rough, porous and abraded, irregularly-shaped flint cobbles), and type N (quartz cobbles) (**Table 7.13**). Whereas quartz cobbles seen at these high elevations are much smaller than those commonly used by Neolithic people and hence are not usable as hammers, other flint cobbles listed are quite similar to those which are seen in Neolithic sites to the northeast of Lake Qarun, in terms of size, shape, colour and surface weathering. Specimens of the types B, D, E and F are actually knapped in the manner similar to those which were observed on Neolithic cores to the northeast of Lake Qarun. Therefore, it is highly probable that this area was also visited by Neolithic cobble collectors.

The southern edge of Ilwet Hialla is severely disturbed by a modern military base, which seems to have been abandoned many years ago, but nevertheless, scatters of flint cobbles are still visible on the surface. The area to the south of the Ilwet Hialla plateau is dominated by Upper Eocene limestone, and the flat surface of the lowest area is covered by extensive scatters of fossil shells which derive from the limestone bed. In contrast, parts of this area are quite undulated, which seem to be caused by water/wind erosion, and the surface is covered by fragments of petrified wood, limestone slabs, black and white

	item	platform preparation	knapping sequence	amount of cortex	L (cm)	W (cm)	T (cm)	cobble type	cortex colour	fresh part colour
1	whole cobble	-	-	76-99%	11.3	7.9	1.6	B	brown	light brown
2	bifacial discoidal core	cortical	multiple	25-49 %	8.4	6.7	2.1	B	brown	light brown
3	single platform core	unfacetted	multiple	50-75 %	3.1	7.4	9.3	B	brown/cream brown	light brown
4	whole cobble	-	-	complete (100%)	9.1	7.5	2.7	C	brown	-
5	single platform core	cortical	multiple	50-75 %	3.8	8.8	8.0	E	brown	mottled brown
6	half-split opposed platform core	unfacetted	multiple	25-49 %	8.5	6.1	2.7	E	brown	light brown
7	whole cobble	-	-	50-75 %	8.1	6.9	3.0	E	brown	light brown
8	whole cobble	-	-	76-99%	8.2	6.9	3.8	E	brown	light brown
9	multiple platform core	unfacetted	tertiary	76-99%	9.9	7.3	4.2	E	brown/cream brown	brown
10	whole cobble	-	-	76-99%	9.1	6.5	4.2	E	brown	brown
11	single platform core	cortical	primary	76-99%	9.0	6.7	3.6	F	brown	mottled brown
12	multiple platform core	cortical/unfacetted	multiple	50-75 %	10.8	8.4	5.2	G	brown	brown
13	single platform core	unfacetted	multiple	50-75 %	6.5	4.7	3.7	J	brown/cream brown	brown
14	bifacial platform core	unfacetted	multiple	50-75 %	8.7	6.0	4.6	J	brown/cream brown	light brown
15	whole cobble	-	-	complete (100%)	8.3	5.5	3.8	J	dark brown	-
16	single platform core	unfacetted	multiple	76-99%	10.7	8.1	3.9	J	brown	mottled brown
17	whole cobble	-	-	complete (100%)	13.7	8.1	6.6	J	brown	-
18	whole cobble	-	-	complete (100%)	11.4	7.6	4.6	K	brown	-

Table 7.13. Items collected at Ilwet Hialla Northeast

sandstone slabs, chert cobbles and flint pebbles (**Fig.7.41**). One peninsular high elevation is covered by an enormous amount of fine-grained black sandstone blocks. According to a geological map (**Fig.3.2**), there are several patches of Pliocene deposits in this area, and indeed, some wadi-like traces of surface water flow, which come downslope from the plateau (**Fig.7.43**), contain oval or irregularly-shaped flint cobbles and flint balls, both of which are characterised by a calcareous cortex. These types of flint cobbles have not been seen in the Neolithic sites studied, but flint balls are similar to those found at Kom K and Kom W in terms of size and shape, and hence it is probable that this area (N29.69149° E30.91022° in the approximate centre) was a source of such flint balls. It seems that more patches of Pliocene deposits are distributed in this geologically complex area.

The northwestern extension of Ilwet Hialla is covered by remarkably extensive scatters of large petrified wood nodules and their fragments, fine-grained black sandstone slabs and cobbles, and conglomerate slabs and cobbles (**Fig.7.44**). The downslope of the western end of this Oligocene plateau is Umm es-Sawan, and its gypsum deposits are quite visible on rock walls and on the surface of the plain in the south. Considering that Umm es-Sawan must have been visited by Old Kingdom gypsum quarry workers via a wadi which runs from around the X Basin and that an Epipalaeolithic locality was found on the wadi bank approximately 1 km to the southwest of Umm es-Sawan, it is not surprising if the Neolithic people who inhabited the lakeshore visited Umm es-Sawan and its vicinity for exploiting these rock materials.

7.6.5. Summary

Although one would tend to assume that different types of flint cobbles must have derived from different source areas, it was revealed through visits to some Pliocene/Plio-Pleistocene deposits to the east and northeast of the Neolithic habitats of the Fayum, that flint cobbles included in these deposits are definitely not homogeneous but are quite various in terms of size, shape, colour and surface weathering. Thus, it seems to have been possible for Neolithic cobble collectors to procure easily more than several types of cobbles at one source area. These source areas actually have more types of cobbles which were not used by Neolithic people. This means that Neolithic people did not collect cobbles randomly but rather chose cobbles suitable for their needs. Moreover, it is likely that Neolithic cobble collectors checked the quality of cobbles at the source areas by knapping cobbles by way of trial once or twice, but that such trial cobbles with poor fractures and internal cracks were discarded there immediately, and whole cobbles collected nearby were taken away.

7.7. Lithic raw material procurement and its embeddedness in mobility and subsistence strategies

The question arises as to how Neolithic inhabitants of the northern shore of the lake organised lithic raw material procurement trips to such distant source areas as Gebel er-Rus and Ilwet Hialla. This question is related to another important question as to how the Fayum Neolithic people integrated lithic raw material procurement into their general mobility and subsistence strategies on a daily, seasonal, and yearly basis. It has been argued on the basis of ethnoarchaeological studies that lithic raw material procurement was normally embedded in routine movement for subsistence activities and that special trips for lithic raw materials were very rarely organised (Binford 1979: 259). If this argument was the case with the Fayum Neolithic people, they must have had economic reasons for visiting the area between the lake and the Nile Valley or the Nile Valley itself, other than lithic raw material procurement. Therefore, it is useful to start first by considering the basic mobility and subsistence strategies of the Fayum Neolithic people.

It is assumed in terms of human behavioural ecology that the people adopted central place foraging, and attempted to maximise the foraging return rate through monitoring and exploiting several resource patches, by means of logistical trips as well as occasional residential moves (Kaplan and Hill 1992). Given the dense accumulations of flint cobbles at some large sites and the supposedly low sedentariness of site occupations observed on the Fayum Neolithic lakeshore, two possibilities on a yearly basis must be examined, while following the well-debated dichotomy of foragers' residential mobility and collectors' logistical mobility. Furthermore, the possibility of territorial mobility which encompasses cyclical movement of people among a series of territories on a long-term basis must also be taken into account (Binford 1980; 1982; Kelly 1992).

7.7.1. Residential mobility

The first possibility is that Fayum Neolithic people are classified as foragers who move their residential bases seasonally, and that the entire population regularly moved to the Nile Valley in seasons of bad harvests of plants and fish and poor hunting of terrestrial mammals due to low or high lake water, and then returned to the Fayum while collecting flint cobbles on their way after the lake water came back to a moderate level. Alternatively, this move might occur on a long-term basis, and thus people moved out in lean years, and eventually returned to a previously occupied place. This manner of move may probably explain how the accumulation of flint cobbles at some Neolithic sites in the Fayum was made possible by the efforts of many people who transported a large number of heavy flint cobbles at one time. It also explains why Neolithic sites in the Fayum do not show clear evidence for fully sedentary occupations.

A problem in this possible mobility strategy is that a stable supply of flint cobbles throughout a year would be difficult, and there would always be a risk of the depletion of flint cobbles at residential bases for unexpected reasons before new materials become available by the next return residential move. The accumulation of cobbles at some sites and the supposedly wasteful manner of cobble use mentioned earlier do not seem to reflect such a risky situation. In addition, another problem is the feasibility of the residential mobility strategy in relation to socioeconomic factors like territoriality and lean season/year economy. This mobility strategy is a possible option only in the case that the fluctuations in resource availability differ between adjacent or distant regions, and that the region which one group of people want to move into is not occupied by another group. Otherwise, staying at the present location and stabilising food supply by increasing diet breadth and storing food are inevitable options (Kelly 1991).

In the case of the Fayum and the Nile Valley, the variety and seasonality of available wild food resources in both regions must have been the same. Essential resources in the Fayum such as fish and waterfowl were quite seasonal, and this was also the case in the Nile Valley (Hassan 1984b). There are some data about the seasonality of subsistence activities in the Fayum Neolithic (Brewer 1989a; 1989b). The most popular fish caught by Fayum Neolithic people was clariid catfish. Clariid catfish inhabit shallow water all the year around, but according to the study of the growth pattern of fish spines, Fayum people caught the fish most intensively when the lake level was rising in late summer, and when the lake level was lowering in late spring. Late summer is the spawning season of clariid catfish, and they are highly aggregated. Therefore, people could catch them abundantly. In late spring, clariid catfish must have been trapped in residual shallow pools of receding water, and people could catch them easily. Migratory waterfowl come to the Fayum in winter, and thus waterfowl hunting was basically a winter activity. The fluctuation of resource availability in the Fayum and the Nile Valley must have been almost identical, because both regions are fed by the same, sole water source, namely, the Nile. Even if spring water at particular locations in the desert and some rain water in winter were available, the success of subsistence activities in both regions was ultimately dependent on the Nile water. The Fayum resources may have been more vulnerable to droughts, because the water level of the lake has been subject to the annual influx of Nile floodwater through the Hawara Channel in the Nile-Fayum Divide and the water supply to the lake might be cut off during particularly low floods (Hassan 1986b: 494). Therefore, a residential move from the Fayum to the Nile Valley could have been an option to mitigate food resource shortages caused by the failure of annual Nile floods.

However, it is doubtful that the Nile Valley was an entirely uninhabited area where 'refugees' from the Fayum came in to exploit wild food resources freely, though there are no demographic data for these regions in this period. The original inhabitants of the Nile Valley must have claimed the ownership of particular resource-rich locations, and the outsiders would not have been allowed to exploit the resources without socioeconomic relations. Ethnographic studies have shown that hunter-gatherers maintain a network of kin ties across wide regions and use a variety of mechanisms to reinforce reciprocity between particular partners in different geographic locations and to allow mutual territorial access in order to buffer temporal local resource scarcity (Cashdan 1992: 248 and 259*ff*). Even if there were peaceful, risk-sharing ties between the Fayum and Nile Valley inhabitants, given the general parallelism of resource fluctuations in both regions, it is likely that the Nile Valley inhabitants tended to try to limit the access which the Fayum inhabitants wanted to essential food resources, especially as population increased in both regions. This must have encouraged or forced the Fayum inhabitants to stay within the Fayum and to look for other solutions to survive occasional lean periods. It has been argued that the Fayum people resided in the Fayum for most if not all of the year, because wild food resources were almost constantly available even though they were seasonal (Wetterstrom 1993: 209-210), but this could also be because the Fayum people had no freedom to exploit wild food resources in the Nile Valley. In fact, wheat/barley farming and grain storage started in the Fayum in the Neolithic period, and this is a more reasonable solution in the face of seasonal resource shortages and restricted residential moves.

7.7.2. Logistical mobility

The second possibility is that the Fayum inhabitants are classified as collectors who do not move their residential bases frequently, and that extra resource procurement was logistically organised by dispatching small task groups from residential bases on the lakeshores in the Fayum in the direction of the Nile Valley routinely and perhaps frequently. The logistical mobility strategy may have ensured a stable supply of flint cobbles no matter where the residential base was moved. However, from a viewpoint of human behavioural ecology, it must be explained if the cost of taking long distance trips for lithic raw materials really met the benefit of making flint tool-using activities more efficient, thereby achieving a high return rate (Kelly 2000: 69-72). Therefore, embedding lithic raw material procurement in other routine movements for subsistence activities could be an optimal solution to reduce opportunity costs. The question is whether this was feasible in the Fayum situation.

When Fayum Neolithic people collected some types of flint cobbles from the nearest Plio-Pleistocene deposits on top of Ilwet Hialla and Gebel Dakakin, they had to walk a distance of 15-20 km from their habitat on the northern shore of the Neolithic Moeris Lake, and to walk back the same distance. When they collected flint cobbles from the Plio-Pleistocene deposits at places like Gebel er-Rus in the Nile-Fayum Divide, then they had to walk a distance of 30-40 km from their habitat, and to walk back the same distance. Since it has been known in ethnography that a 20-30 km round trip was the maximum distance that hunter-gatherers could walk comfortably in a day in a variety of habitats (Kelly 1995: 133), it may have been possible for Neolithic cobble collectors to leave at dawn for Ilwet Hialla and Gebel Dakakin and to come back before dusk. On the other hand, there is little doubt that the Neolithic cobble collectors walking to Gebel er-Rus from the habitat on the northern shore had to stay overnight somewhere between the Fayum and the Nile Valley during their trips. Thus it seems unreasonable that during resource-rich years/seasons some task groups took trips to the Nile Valley in order to exploit similar wild food resources, and then came back to the Fayum while collecting flint cobbles on their way in addition to carrying a heavy load of food items. Therefore, it may be more likely that lithic raw material procurement was embedded in animal herding trips.

In spite of numerous bones of sheep and goats found at Fayum Neolithic sites (Brewer 1989b: table 4; Gautier 1976b: table I-7; von den Driesch 1986: table 1; Wenke *et al.* 1988: table 1), there is no information about how these newly-introduced domestic animals were actually tended by Fayum Neolithic people.

However, it is logically assumed that the people must have kept sheep and goats away from farming plots which were supposed to be near the lakeshore residential bases, particularly while crops were growing. If people often took pastoral grazing trips, they may have had a good reason to visit hilly and gravelly terrains of the Fayum Depression like Qasr el-Sagha and Gebel Qatrani as well as the Nile-Fayum Divide. Since these gravelly terrains are not good places for foraging and flint cobbles are almost inexhaustible, these gravelly terrains would have been beyond the territorial claims of any other group of people, and the cobble collectors would have had no difficulty in accessing the sources, and they could collect flint cobbles there and could even carry the cobbles on the backs of sheep and goats.

The use of sheep and goats for carrying things has not been known in ethnographic records, but the use of cattle for transporting heavy rocks to task locations for expedient toolmaking has been suggested at Early Ceramic sites in the Western Desert of Egypt (Close 1996a). Hence, it is possible that flint cobbles were transported on the backs of sheep and goats, and that cattle were used in the same manner in the Fayum Neolithic. This practice may probably explain how a large amount of flint cobbles could easily be transported long distances by herdsmen. This may also have been the case with the procurement of basalt blocks and petrified wood nodules in the rocky terrains 12-20 km to the north and northwest of the Neolithic lakeshore.

Another probable optimal lithic raw material procurement may be embedded in boat/raft fishing in the lake. According to the reconstruction of lake level fluctuations in prehistory (Wendorf and Schild 1976: 222-226), Gebel er-Rus abutted the eastern shore of the Neolithic Moeris Lake (**Fig.3.4**). The use of boats/rafts by people in this period has not been substantiated by archaeological evidence, but it has been argued that the appearance and dramatic increase in number of deep water fish in the faunal assemblages of Early Holocene sites in the Nile Valley might suggest the beginning of deep water fishing on boats/rafts in the Nile (Van Neer 1989: 54-55; 2004: 257). In the case of the Fayum, the presence of a certain number of deep water fish like Nile perch in both Epipalaeolithic and Neolithic faunal assemblages has been revealed, and it has been suggested that deep water fish might have been caught by netting or angling in the open, deeper water of the lake (Brewer 1989b: 113). However, most of the Nile perch found through recent excavations at Kom K and Kom W are not large-sized adults that surely inhabit the deeper waters of the lake but are juveniles that can inhabit shallow water (Wim Van Neer, personal communication 2007). Therefore, it is unlikely that the inhabitants of Kom K and Kom W practised deep water fishing with the aid of boats/rafts. However, this does not necessarily mean that boats/rafts were never used at all in the Fayum Neolithic. It is still possible that they were used by the inhabitants of other locations in the Fayum to enable occasional deep water fishing during trips on the water from the northern shore to Gebel er-Rus on the eastern shore, and this must have made the transport of procured flint cobbles much easier.

If lithic raw materials were really collected by herdsmen or fishermen and not by the toolmakers themselves, it is possible to assume that the cost of obtaining raw materials was virtually zero for the toolmakers and hence the use of the raw materials by the toolmakers tended to be expedient and even wasteful. Such division of labour in the sequence of core reduction is worth considering, especially when the costs and benefits are supposed to be important determinants of which materials are chosen and which techniques are employed.

The next question as to how frequently or at what time the Fayum Neolithic people moved between the Fayum Depression and the Nile Valley for lithic raw material procurement is a key to consider further their basic mobility and subsistence strategies. Considering the dense accumulations of flint cobbles at some sites, it is unlikely that trips for lithic raw material procurement were planned and carried out during emergencies or at times when the raw materials became scarce or depleted at the residential bases, but more likely that procurement occurred frequently, regardless of the abundance of materials at residential bases, as exemplified by ethnographic records (Gould and Saggers 1985: 120). This situation in the Fayum may support the above-mentioned assumption that lithic raw material procurement might be embedded in routine animal herding or boat/raft fishing trips.

7.7.3. Eclectic mobility

In terms of the possible embeddedness of lithic raw material procurement in the basic mobility and subsistence strategies, it is argued that flint cobble procurement could have normally been achieved by small task groups, through logistical trips from residential bases. A problem with this possibility is that there is no evidence for substantial dwellings at large sites like Kom K and Kom W, which are supposed to be residential bases. Hence it is not certain whether the Neolithic people really maintained any central place while adopting a logistical mobility strategy in a strict sense, as expected in the central place foraging model. Since the geographic stability of the sites is obvious even though they may not have been occupied throughout the year due to inundation or desiccation, it is presumed that the Neolithic people adopted an eclectic mobility strategy depending on the fluctuating situation, instead of choosing one from the two extreme strategies and sticking to it.

It is probable that the Fayum Neolithic people maintained several residential bases on the lakeshore and moved between them, or repeatedly aggregated and dispersed within the Fayum Depression. During certain seasons or years, people stayed at a particular residential base, and from there, they organised logistical trips for foraging and herding, depending on necessity. When the essential resources within an easy walking radius of the residential base were depleted and/or the residential base became less comfortable due to the accumulation of trash or due to changing conditions of wind, sunlight and shade, people decided to move their residential base to other resource-rich locations or more comfortable locations, and continued similar logistical trips for additional resources. The people could return to the original place when the essential resources became available again or the living condition became better again.

7.7.4. Non-embedded lithic raw material procurement

It has so far been argued that lithic raw material procurement was embedded in general mobility and subsistence strategies. But it may be worthwhile to consider lithic raw material procurement in terms of a lack of such embeddedness, because the wide variety of lithic raw materials may have derived from more than the several sources which were accessible by routine herding trips, and because there are actually examples of, and arguments about, lithic raw material procurement being disembedded from regular subsistence activities. Contrary to the optimal foraging model, it has been argued that optimal exploitation of food resources and lithic raw materials at specific sites might co-occur but that this would not always be the case for other sites, and in many cases, procuring lithic raw materials would involve a significant extra expenditure in time and effort, and would create scheduling conflicts (Hayden 1989: 9).

Ethnographic studies have shown that people make special efforts to visit distant places for obtaining lithic raw materials which are known to have superior technical properties, and avail themselves of any edibles along the way (Andrefsky 1994: 23; Gould and Saggers 1985: 120). In such cases, people clearly state that their primary aim is to procure lithic raw materials even though they do other things on their way. This means that other activities were embedded in lithic raw material procuring trips. Since such ethnographic records come from people who are no longer in the habit of making and using stone tools, it is not certain that special trips for lithic raw materials were common among prehistoric people whose primary material for toolmaking was stone. Nevertheless, it must be taken into account that lithic raw material procurement could be carried out in the same manner as foraging trips for food resources, apart from the general mobility and subsistence patterns. In other words, it may be assumed that lithic raw material procurement was made possible by the toolmakers' primary concern with, and accessibility to, source areas, and not induced by their pre-existing mobility/settlement and subsistence patterns (Andrefsky 1994; Bamforth 1986). Therefore, even in the Fayum Neolithic, it can be said that people may have organised small task groups and took long distance trips especially for procuring lithic raw materials, or that pastoral grazing may have habitually been embedded in the lithic raw material procurement trips and herdsmen intentionally took the herds of sheep and goats close to lithic raw material sources.

Moreover, lithic raw material procurement is not necessarily embedded in purely subsistence-oriented activities, but can be embedded in other non-foraging activities. It has been known in ethnography that foragers make information-acquiring or monitoring trips specifically to determine the location of resources or resource patches and when and where to move camp in the near future, and travel very long distances (Kaplan and Hill 1992: 186-187; Kelly 1995: 97-98). Furthermore, it has been recorded in ethnography that people regularly visit their families and relatives in remote areas in order to maintain close ties and to find mates, and also travel to exotic locations of symbolic or religious importance regularly or occasionally, in order to maintain links with important locations (Gould and Saggers 1985; MacDonald and Hewlett 1999; Whallon 2006). It is possible that lithic raw material procurement may have habitually been embedded in these kinds of mobility. Such a manner of lithic raw material procurement must also be taken into account in the Fayum Neolithic.

Lastly, although this is beyond the argument on mobility strategies, it must be mentioned that Fayum Neolithic lithic raw materials could have been obtained through long distance exchange as well. Since exotic materials like Red Sea shells, Mediterranean Sea shells and Nubian diorite did actually begin to come into the Fayum in the Neolithic period (Caton-Thompson and Gardner 1934: 87-88), it is certain that long distance exchange networks existed in this period. It would be no great surprise if some types of lithic raw materials were also obtained from distant regions through exchange.

7.8. Mobility pattern and lithic raw material economy

How flint cobbles were distributed from place to place within the Fayum is a key to understand the mobility pattern and lithic raw material economy of the Fayum Neolithic people. Remarkably dense concentrations of a wide variety of unworked/worked cobbles at Kom K, Site XA and Kom W, and concentrations of less various unworked/worked cobbles at Site L, Site E29H1, Site X, Locality 'Calcified Shrubs' and the Site V Depression may possibly imply that the cobbles were first brought to large residential bases and stockpiled there, and then, several cobbles were selectively transported to other small, temporary field camps or locations without reduction, and tools were made at the task locations according to arising needs.

This presumed logistical manner of cobble transportation seems to contradict the well-debated idea of curated technology. This states that special-purpose tools are made at residential bases in advance of going to achieve expected tasks at distant specific sites in an environment where lithic raw materials are not readily available, and then the tools can be repaired and recycled at the task locations if necessary (*e.g.*, Bamforth 1986; Binford 1979; Odell 1996). Moreover, such cobble transportation seems to be inconsistent with the argument regarding the concept of mobile toolkits, which defines that optimising the utility of artefacts relative to their weight is the single most important consideration in making up assemblages of artefacts which mobile people forage around with, and that it is most rational to remove unusable parts of cobbles and to reduce the cobbles to tool blanks of portable small size and light weight prior to departure (Kuhn 1994: 436*ff*; Shott 1986).

However, if curation is more generally defined as the preparation of raw materials in anticipation of inadequate conditions (materials, time, or facilities) for tool-using activities at the time and place of use, or, as the mitigation of the incongruity between availability of tools or raw materials and the location of tool-using activities (Nelson 1990: 63), then, the logistical manner of cobble transportation in the Fayum Neolithic habitat may be called a kind of curatorial behaviour. It can be said that transported and stockpiled cobbles facilitated not only making tools expediently but also making elaborate tools in anticipation of future needs, namely, in a curatorial manner, according to different conditions.

One reason for such lithic raw material transportation in the Fayum may be that the tasks at the sites like Site L, Site E29H1, Site X and the Site V Depression did not entail desperate stalking but rather ambushing, watching or waiting. Therefore, the task performers could afford to sit down and to spend time making tools from cobbles according to needs, without being bothered by an idea that time should be invested in toolmaking in advance of arriving at the task locations, in order to maximise food procuring time (Torrence 1983). It is presumed that their subsistence activities were not under time-stress, and that the availability of food resources was more or less predictable. Such activities must be a combination of more promising and predictable fishing and wild plant harvesting and less predictable game hunting and waterfowl hunting on an encounter basis and trap hunting on a fortuitous basis. Another reason for cobble transportation may be that the unique functional properties of whole cobbles as tools were highly appreciated. Large cobbles with thick edges can be very useful and efficient for a variety of heavy-duty tasks, for which smaller flake tools are entirely inadequate and inefficient (Kuhn 1994; Morrow 1996). The task performers must have found it more economical and flexible to transport unworked cobbles rather than tool blanks and/or finished tools and to leave them at the task locations, no matter how burdensome the transportation of heavy cobbles was. This behaviour suggests long occupation or regular reuse of the sites in order to take advantage of the stockpile.

It is difficult to interpret the enormous accumulation of unworked/worked flint cobbles at Site XA with little clear evidence of tool-using activities. This site is located close to a large meandering wadi which runs from the north, and there may have been some strategic reasons for stockpiling cobbles there. Considering that the meandering wadi runs in the direction of Ilwet Hialla via Umm es-Sawan, it is likely that the accumulation of flint cobbles at Site XA was left by the people who returned from trips to the flint source area. It is assumed that the site may have functioned as a cache of lithic raw materials for those who passed by for foraging. As has been argued on the basis of ethnoarchaeological studies (Binford 1979), logistical operations for foraging trips are supported by a wide-ranging caching strategy ensuring the dispersion in the habitat of goods and materials which might be needed later. When people dropped in at the lithic raw material caches during foraging trips, it may have been most optimal for them to pick up at least one or two cobbles in addition to smaller and lighter tool blanks and/or finished tools, thereby realising the versatility and lightweight of overall mobile toolkits for any contingent event.

7.9. Expedient toolmaking and curation

How flakes obtained from the cores described earlier were actually used is not easy to demonstrate due to the paucity of collected samples. Nevertheless, tools collected along with cores at the sites studied and their vicinities provide some ideas about how flakes were dealt with by toolmakers at task locations.

7.9.1. Uses of half-split discoids

The largest flake which could be obtained from a cobble is a half-split discoid. Interesting examples from Site X and the Site V Depression show that a half-split cortical discoid could be shaped into a sidescraper or endscraper by retouching one long or short margin of the discoid continuously from the ventral to dorsal face (**Fig.7.10**-3: Site X-14 and **Fig.7.45**: the Site V Depression-8). It is not certain whether this way of use was common. It is probable that half-split discoids were normally used as unifacial/ bifacial discoidal cores to obtain non-cortical flakes. However, one example from the Site V Depression shows that a half-split unifacial discoidal core was shaped into a sidescraper by retouching one long convex margin of the discoid continuously from the already exhausted ventral face to the dorsal face (**Fig.7.46**: the Site V Depression-9). In other words, an exhausted half-split unifacial discoidal core was recycled as a sidescraper.

Half-split unifacial discoidal cores were collected not only at the sites studied but also in an isolated situation. These discoids are already knapped from the margin of the dorsal face to the ventral face in their entire circumference to an exhaustive extent and became thin (**Fig.7.47** and **Fig.7.48**). Therefore, they look like unifacial axes or scrapers. However, since there is no clear trace of such uses on the edges of the discoids, it can be considered that they were actually cores, and that they were discarded there because of exhaustion. These examples seem to suggest that people on the move did not always bring whole cobbles but took half-split cobbles probably for reducing weight, and obtained non-cortical flakes from the discoids when necessity arose.

7.9.2. Uses of primary flakes

The size of flakes obtained from any kinds of cores used in the Fayum Neolithic is already determined by the size of cores, and hence the flakes cannot be larger than 9-12 cm in length and 7-10 cm in width. Actually, many of the previously collected and published Fayum Neolithic bifacial tools like arrowheads and sickle blades are shorter than this size. Except for flakes from unifacial discoidal cores, most flakes from the other cores are primary flakes, because many cores are not reduced to an exhaustive extent. Primary flakes obtained from flat cobbles are naturally flat, and hence are suitable for making straight tools.

How these primary flakes were actually utilised is a key to understand tool making in the Fayum Neolithic. The tools made on primary flakes have been classified by Caton-Thompson as 'pebble-backed knives and scrapers' (Caton-Thompson and Gardner 1934: 21, pl.XLI). It has also been observed that even relatively small bifacially-retouched tools in the Fayum Neolithic still retained cortex in the middle of the dorsal face (Shirai *in press*). This means that these tools were made on primary flakes, and that primary flakes were absolutely not waste products but rather the most favoured pieces for making tools. A number of interesting examples of the various uses of flakes and the various stages of tool making were collected at the Site V Depression. They will be used for a discussion about expedient and curated tool making.

The first examples are the simplest uses of primary flakes as denticulates and sidescrapers with partial retouch at an acute angle of less than 45 degrees. In the case of a denticulate (**Fig.7.49**-1) and a sidescraper (**Fig.7.49**-2), one long margin of an oval or elongated primary flake was continuously retouched from the ventral to dorsal face, thereby making a slightly convex cutting edge. There is no retouch on the ventral face. In the case of an endscraper (**Fig.7.49**-3), one long margin and one short margin of a rectangular or trapezoidal primary flake was continuously retouched from the ventral to dorsal face, thereby making a cutting edge which forms a corner at an angle of approximately 90 degrees. There is no retouch on the ventral face. Primary flakes could be shaped into denticulates in a different way. One denticulate (**Fig.7.50**-1) shows that one long margin of an elongated primary flake was continuously retouched from the dorsal to ventral face at an obtuse angle of more than 45 degrees, thereby making a denticulated cutting edge. There is no retouch on the dorsal face. In the case of denticulates, flake scars on either the dorsal face or the ventral face tend to be wider and longer, suggesting the use of a hard hammer, whereas in the case of scrapers, flake scars on the dorsal face tend to be narrower and shorter, suggesting the use of a

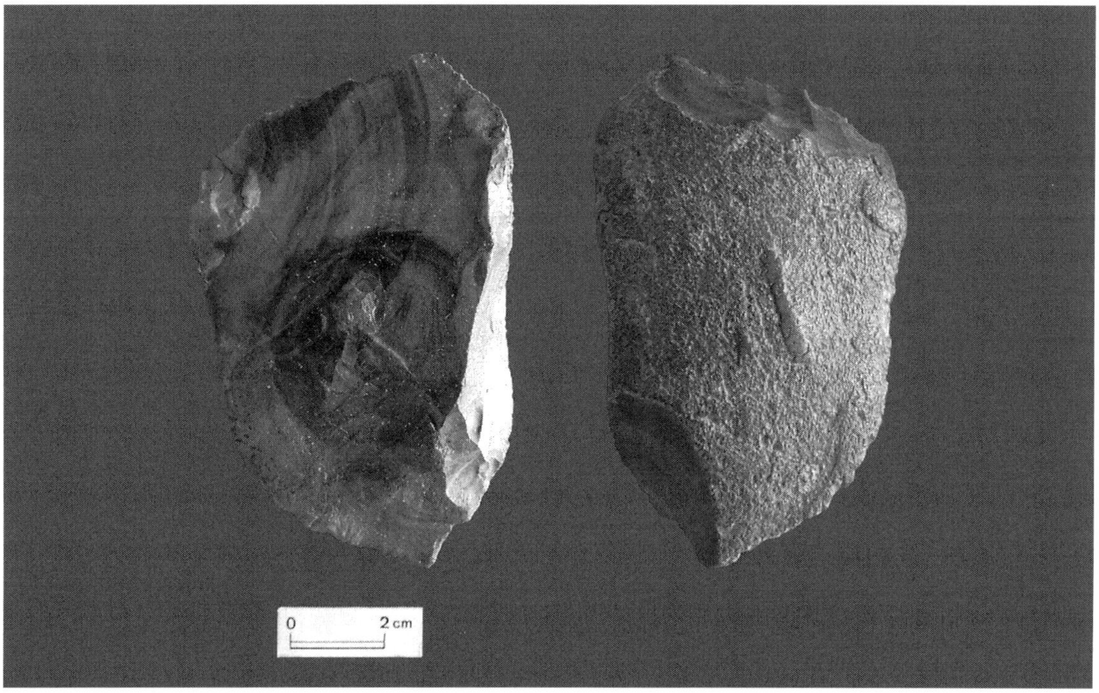

Fig.7.45. Endscraper made on a half-split discoid collected at the Site V Depression

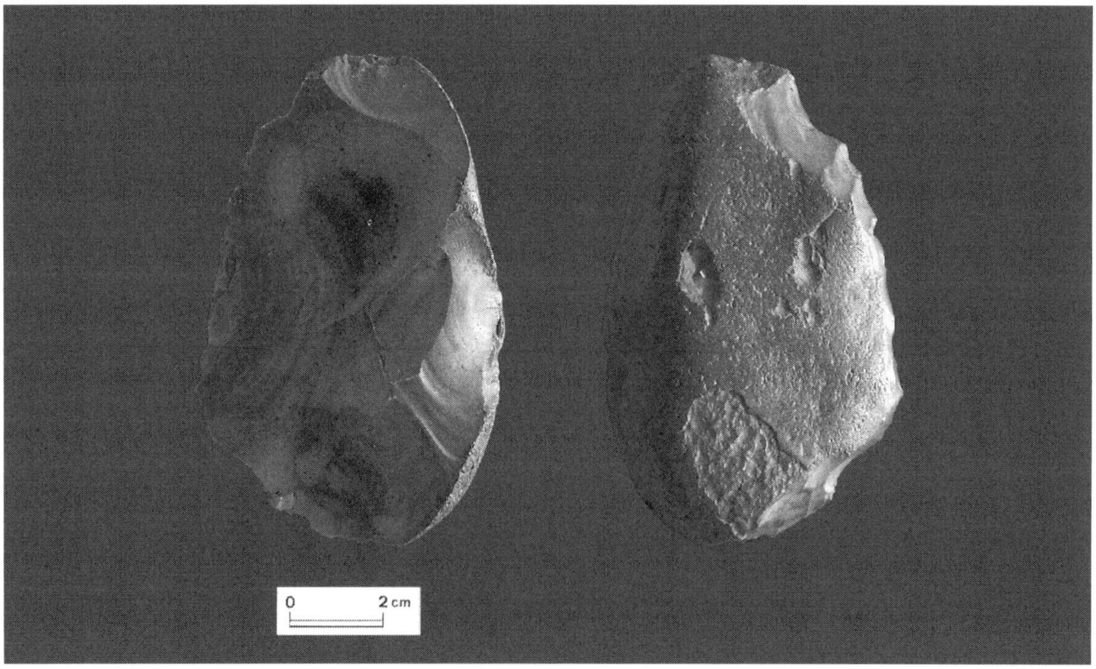

Fig.7.46. Sidescraper made on a half-split unifacial discoidal core collected at the Site V Depression

Fig.7.47. A half-split unifacial discoidal core collected 500 m to the northeast of Kom W

Fig.7.48. A half-split unifacial discoidal core collected 500 m to the northeast of Kom W

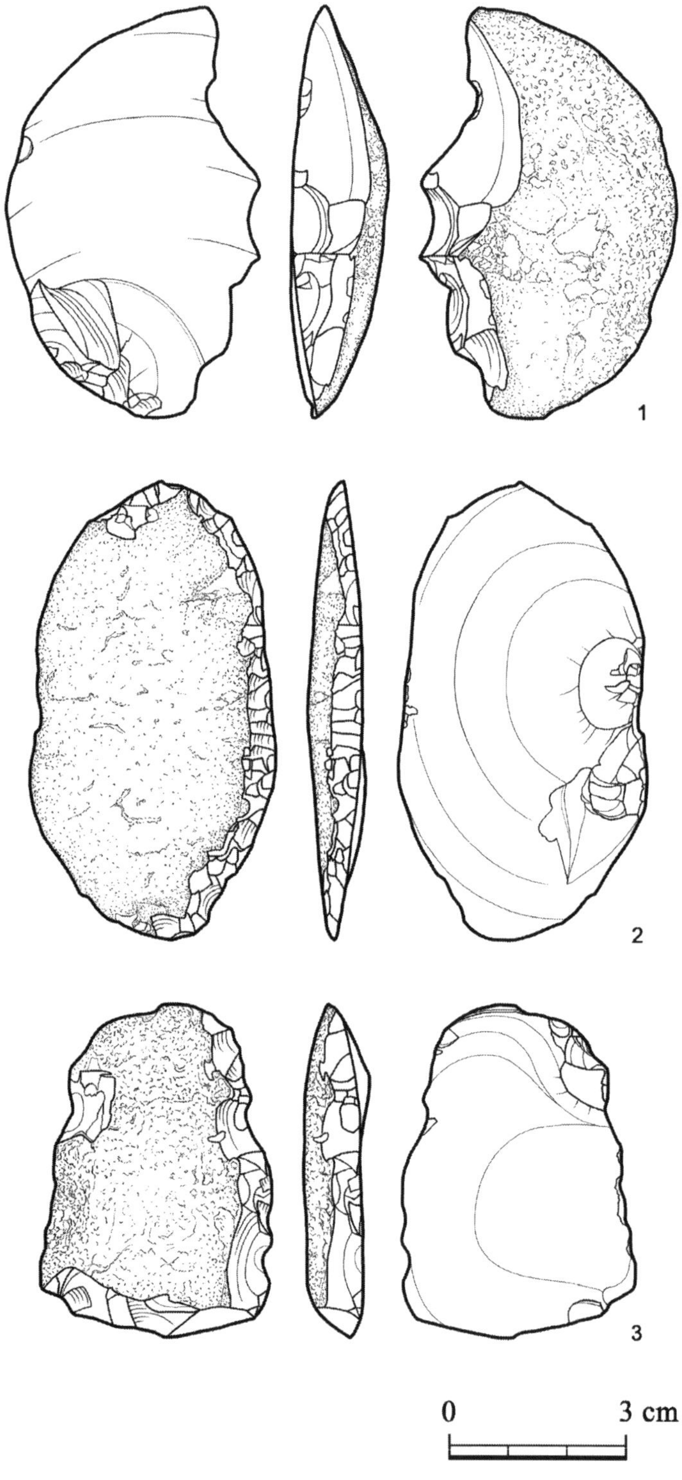

Fig.7.49. Tools collected at the Site V Depression

soft hammer. In these cases, there would be no considerable difference in time and energy expended for retouching, and this seem to be literally expedient tool making.

The second example (**Fig.7.50**-2) is an advanced version of the denticulates or scrapers made on a primary flake described above. The primary flake with retouch on one convex margin of the dorsal face was turned over, and then another convex margin of the primary flake was retouched continuously from the dorsal to ventral face. As a result, the entire circumference of a leaf-shaped flake is retouched either from the ventral to dorsal face or from the dorsal to ventral face.

The third example (**Fig.7.50**-3) is different from the second example described above in terms of the treatment of the ventral face. The ventral face of a primary flake was continuously knapped from the circumference of the dorsal face, while rotating the flake in the same manner as that of a discoidal core. Then, one longer convex margin of the flake was continuously retouched from the ventral to the dorsal face, but more than 90 % of cortex remains on the dorsal face. The resultant tool can be called a unifacial denticulate or scraper. However, a strange thing is that the thorough removal of flakes from the ventral face is absolutely unnecessary work for creating one cutting edge on one long margin of the primary flake. Therefore, it is probable that the toolmaker recycled discoidal cores and trimmed them into denticulates or scrapers, or that these items were still in the middle of the production of bifacially-retouched, leaf-shaped tools, even though they may have actually been used.

The fourth example (**Fig.7.51**-1) is different from the third example described above in terms of the treatment of the dorsal face. The dorsal face of a primary flake was continuously knapped from the circumference of the ventral face, while rotating the flake in the same manner as that of a discoidal core, and the cortex was mostly removed by large scars which covered the dorsal face. And then, one long margin of the flake was minimally retouched from the dorsal to ventral face, and the ventral face was left almost unretouched. The resultant tool can also be called a unifacial denticulate or scraper. But again, the thorough removal of cortex from the dorsal face looks absolutely unnecessary for creating one cutting edge on one long margin or two cutting edges on two long margins of the primary flake. Therefore, it is highly likely that these items were still in the middle of the production of bifacially-retouched, leaf-shaped tools, even though they may have actually been used.

The third and fourth examples strongly suggest that making bifacially-retouched tools was not necessarily an undisturbed, straightforward process which was immediately fulfilled in a given moment for specific purposes, but instead was a gradual process, and must be regarded as a part of a long reduction sequence. In other words, these examples demonstrate that the border between supposedly expedient, partly-retouched tools and supposedly curated, bifacially-retouched tools is not always clear, and there are a number of 'transitional' tools between them. Such 'transitional' tools could be used and abandoned before the completion of the final elaborate form. It may be said that seemingly 'finished' bifacial tools are merely contingent end products of a long reduction sequence, and that they could become different from those originally designed in the mind of toolmakers. This observation is consistent with an argument regarding a re-definition of curation as a continuous variable and a property of individual tools, and not of entire tool assemblages (Shott 1996).

It can be said that most bifacially-retouched tools were actually made by removing cortex on the dorsal face of unifacial denticulates or scrapers in the third example as much as possible, while rotating the unifacial items in the same manner as that of a discoidal core. The resultant bifacial items can be finally shaped into axes (**Fig.7.51**-2), knives, and leaf-shaped, triangular, or concave-based arrowheads. As mentioned earlier, well-debated ideas of curated technology have referred to special-purpose tools which were made at residential bases in advance of going to achieve expected tasks at distant

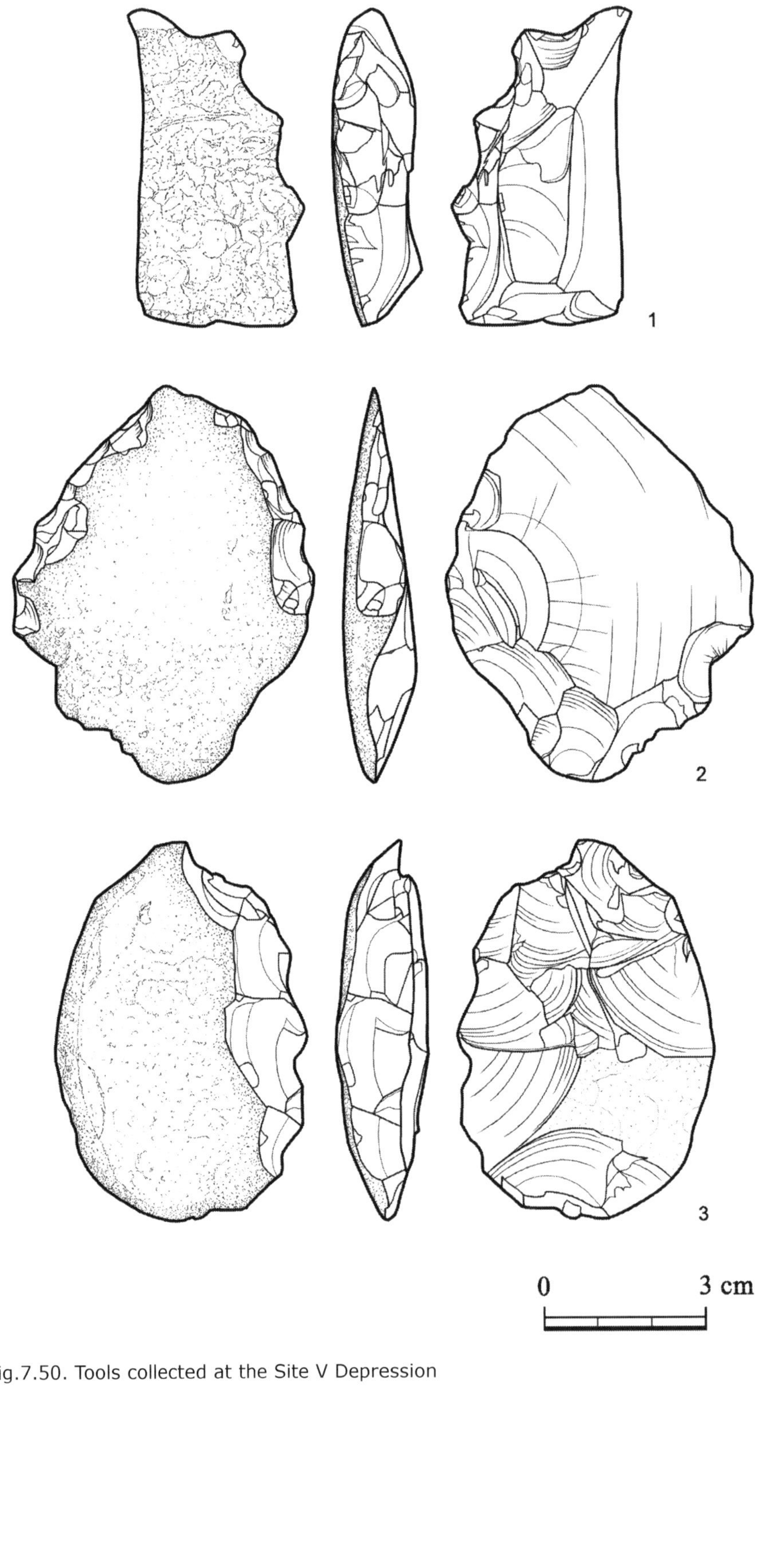

Fig.7.50. Tools collected at the Site V Depression

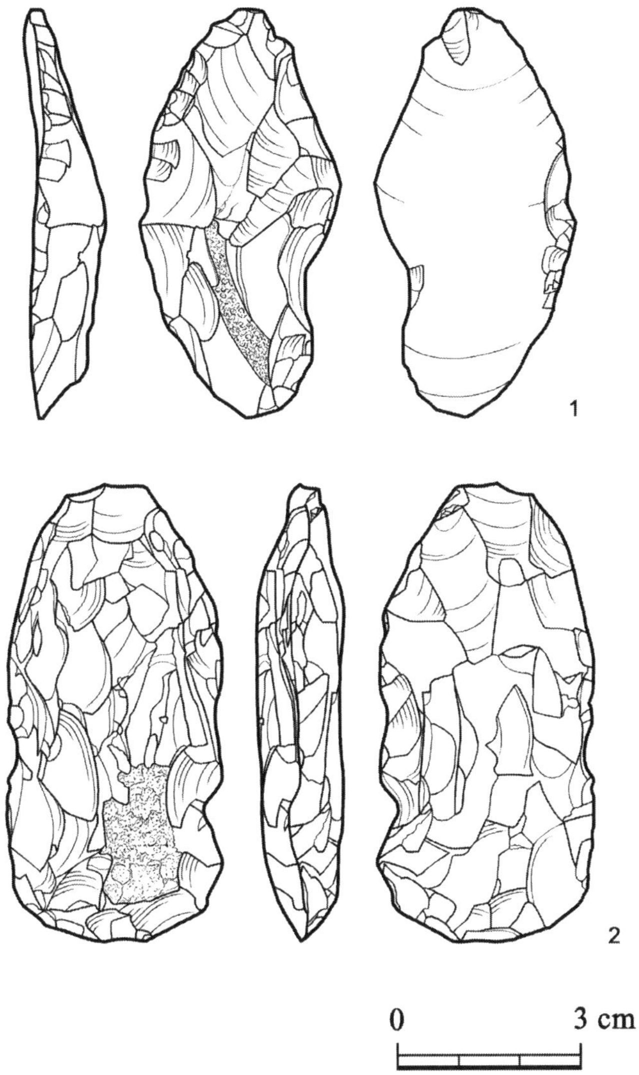

Fig.7.51. Tools collected at the Site V Depression

specific sites and were repaired or recycled there. However, the manner of tool making observed at the Site V Depression suggests that bifacially-retouched tools were actually being made at task locations. Moreover, it is probable that the making of bifacially-retouched tools was initiated at task locations presumably under a relaxed condition, because if the toolmakers had been under severe time-stress when they had been engaged in food procuring and processing, they should have finished making tools in advance of arriving at the site. As has been discussed, it appears that the major food procuring activities of the Fayum Neolithic people did not entail desperate stalking but rather ambushing, watching or waiting. Therefore, it is quite possible that they made or initiated to make formal tools not only for immediate needs but also for future needs, in order to relieve boredom while ambushing, watching or waiting.

It must be stressed that primary flakes were not the sole materials used for making tools which could eventually develop into elaborate bifacial ones, but this popularity of primary flakes in the Fayum Neolithic must be the reason for not only the transportation of whole cobbles without decortification from source areas to habitation sites and from the habitation sites to task locations, but also the discard of cobbles in the early stages of core reduction.

7.9.3. Uses of other cortical flakes

Another unique types of flakes which were probably often used for making formal thin tools are the oval flakes which have curved cortical parts on the margin but have no cortex on the dorsal face (**Fig.7.52**-1 and **Fig.7.52**-2). These curved cortical parts on the margin of the flakes are apparently parts of the circumference of a discoidal core, because the cortical parts form an angle of approximately 90 degrees against both the ventral and dorsal faces. Hence it can be understood that these flakes were obtained from the ventral face of a discoidal core made on a half-split cobble, or a bifacial discoidal core made on a flat cobble by striking the cortical margin of the discoid. In the case of the first example (**Fig.7.52**-1), a striking platform and a percussion bulb on the proximal end and a hinged or stepped distal end of the flake seem to have been taken off, and consequently, a flat and nearly rectangular flake with cortex on the short lateral margins is formed. Then, this flake is rotated at an angle of 90 degrees, and one cortical lateral margin becomes the basal part of an elongated flake, and the long lateral margins can be retouched. The final form of the elongated flake can be a projectile point or a knife. In the case of the second example (**Fig.7.52**-2), a cortical part remains on one lateral margin, and another lateral margin is thoroughly retouched from both faces.

The tools made on these types of flakes have already been classified by Caton-Thompson as 'pebble-butted points and knives' and 'pebble-backed knives and scrapers', and have been recognised as the largest and most various tool classes (Caton-Thompson and Gardner 1934: 21, pl.XLI). It is likely that flat flakes without percussion bulbs on the ventral face and ridges of flake scars on the dorsal face were favoured by makers of pebble-butted points and knives, because removing them in the process of bifacial thinning is sometimes difficult. An example of pebble-backed knife made on this type of flake (**Fig.7.52**-2) shows that the toolmaker made a special effort to remove a percussion bulb at the proximal end of the ventral face, even though such an effort seems to be unnecessary, because the feathered distal end of the flake has a long, sharp cutting edge, and hence it can be used as a pebble-backed knife without additional retouch. Instead of removing a percussion bulb on the cortical proximal end of an oval flake, the ventral face is repeatedly flaked from the cortical margin of the dorsal face, thereby a percussion bulb was removed, and the flake was made thinner. Then, the distal end of the dorsal face was flaked from the ventral face, whereby a cutting edge was made. Therefore, these examples of the preparation of cortical flakes are definitely not that of expedient tool making, but must be regarded as a kind of curated technology.

The generally known prevalence of pebble-backed/butted tools in the Fayum Neolithic tool assemblage and the reconstructed sequence of bifacial tool making may suggest that the size, shape and thickness of primary flakes obtained from flat cores and flakes with marginal cortex obtained from discoidal cores were the easiest for Neolithic toolmakers to handle. In other words, these facts may reflect the cultural preference of the Fayum Neolithic toolmakers, because in other cultures, non-cortical flakes and blades are the most preferred raw materials for making formal tools, and primary flakes and other cortical flakes are waste products.

7.9.4. Uses of non-cortical flakes

The last but the commonest and hardest-to-define type of flakes which could have been used for tool making in the Fayum Neolithic were all kind of flakes other than the flakes described above. At Site XA, where all lithic artefacts were collected in a 10 m x 10 m square, flakes and chunks of various sizes and shapes with various extent of cortex were produced (**Tables 7.14, 7.15** and **7.16**), though they are generally characterised by an unfacetted platform and hard hammer percussion bulb. It is difficult to

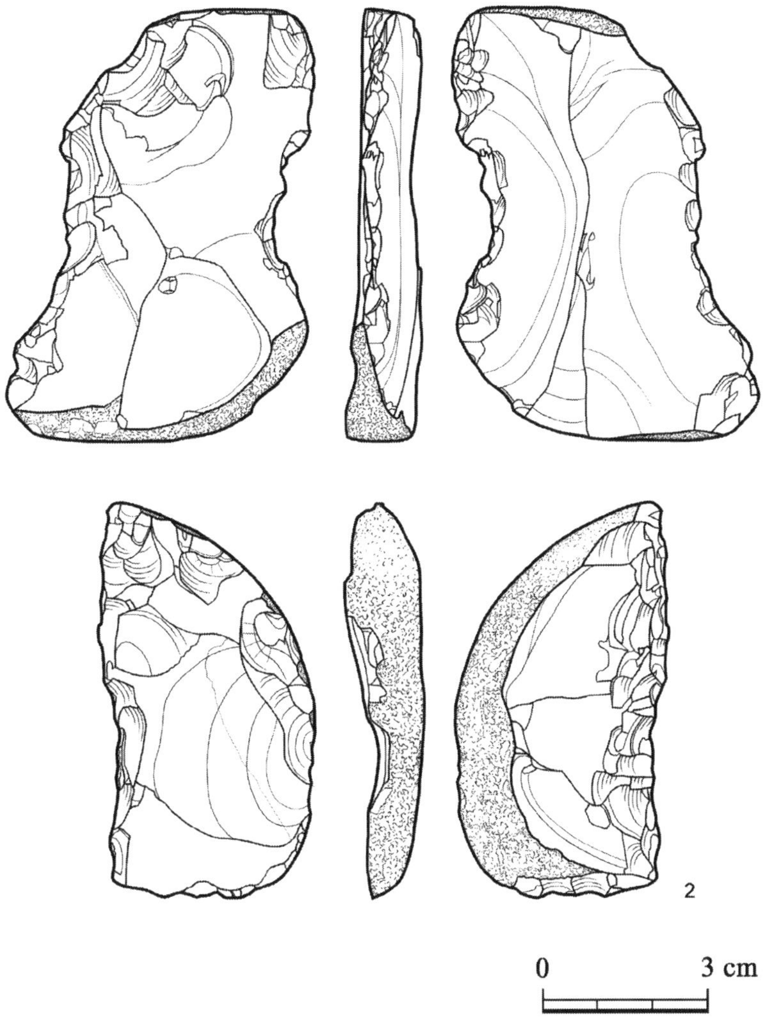

Fig.7.52. Tools collected at the Site V Depression

interpret the abundance of large and thick flakes of various extent of cortex, which would be usable for further reduction, left unused at Site XA. It may suggest that cobble knappers had an intention to produce such flakes in large number for use, but it is also possible that those flakes are actually waste products and hence left unused.

A successfully refitted core made on a flat and oval cobble, which was collected at Site L, shows that after a large primary flake was obtained from one flat face of the cobble and was taken away, the flake scar was used as a striking platform and three quarters of the circumference of the cobble were knapped off by hard blows, whereby several thick cortical flakes were produced (**Fig.7.53**). These thick cortical flakes were left unused, and instead, two thick non-cortical flakes were knapped off from the resultant cubic core and were taken away. It is not certain how such non-cortical flakes were utilised. But no matter how wasteful this manner of knapping is, obtaining such non-cortical flakes may also be the reason why cobbles at Site XA were knapped so roughly to produce numerous unused thick cortical flakes.

	n	%
primary chunk	4	0.76
chip/chunk	64	12.14
primary flake	44	8.35
flake from single platform core	217	41.18
flake from opposed platform core	15	2.85
flake from ninety-degree core	7	1.33
flake from multiple platform core	89	16.89
flake from discoidal core	13	2.47
unidentifiable flake	29	5.50
primary blade/bladelet	5	0.95
blade/bladelet from single platform core	31	5.88
blade/bladelet from opposed platform core	3	0.57
blade/bladelet from ninety-degree core	1	0.19
blade/bladelet from multiple platform core	2	0.38
unidentifiable blade/bladelet	3	0.57
total	527	100.00

Table 7.14. Debitage products collected in a collection square at Site XA

	n	mean (cm)	st.dev
length	40	3.23	1.36
width	40	2.93	1.30
thickness	40	0.89	0.50

Table 7.15. Metrical data of measured primary flakes collected in a collection square at Site XA

	n	mean (cm)	st.dev
length	376	3.25	1.37
width	376	2.81	1.30
thickness	376	0.86	0.49

Table 7.16. Metrical data of measured debitage products other than primary flakes collected in a collection square at Site XA

7.9.5. The progressive manner of making bifacially-retouched tools

The co-existence of a number of cobbles, debitage products, finished bifacial tools and broken bifacial tools at Kom K and Kom W, as revealed by Caton-Thompson's excavations and my research, can certainly fit the concept of curation. One could assume that the inhabitants of Kom K and Kom W transported flint cobbles from distant sources, and stockpiled them, making formal tools in anticipation of special tasks at distant sites. Upon return from those tasks, they resharpened and recycled broken tools as well as complete ones. On the other hand, one previous study at Kom W demonstrated that the majority of Neolithic tools were expediently-made, informal flake tools such as notches, denticulates and scrapers, and that bifacially-retouched formal tools were quite minor components of the assemblage (Kozlowski and Ginter 1989: 170*ff*). The manner of tool making observed at the Site V Depression also suggests that expedient tool making and curated tool making could always co-exist sequentially according to need and spare time, and that originally expedient tools could develop into highly-curated elaborate tools.

There is no doubt that making bifacial tools is more labour-intensive and time-consuming than making partly-retouched flake tools. When a toolmaker decides to make a flint tool, he/she has a choice among various kinds of tools and ways to make tools. Which is chosen may depend on how much time it takes to make the tool and on the expected return from using the tool. In terms of human behavioural ecology, given the invested labour and time, it is not cost-effective if bifacial tools do not ensure higher returns or more efficient tool-using activities. Therefore, it has been argued that tool makers/users had to make a decision whether to spend less time getting raw material and making tools and to forage with the less effective, short-lived flake tools, or, to spend more time getting raw materials and making elaborate tools which would enable more efficient foraging and hence maximise returns. If a resource could be obtained or processed with a simple flake tool just as easily as with a bifacial tool, then flake tool production would probably be chosen over bifacial tool production, especially if raw materials suitable for bifacial tools were not readily available. One benefit of making bifacial tools would be that they could be used for a longer period of time (Kelly 2000: 70-72). But the progressive manner of bifacial tool making as described above can also average the cost of procuring raw material. Considering that the border between expedient tools and highly-curated elaborate tools is ambiguous, arguments

Fig.7.53. A refitted single platform core collected at Site L

such as which sites were more or less 'intensively' or 'sedentarily' occupied, on the basis of the presence or absence of supposedly expedient and curated tool assemblages, may not be significant.

7.9.6. Expedient toolmaking reconsidered

Another question is what the abundant fragmentary cores and informal flake tools observed at Kom W imply, in terms of expedient and curated tool making and the costs and benefits of technologies. It is probable that people at residential bases had less time to spare for meticulous tool making than those who got bored at field camps or watching locations, and that the people at residential bases had fewer opportunities of being required to respond to unanticipated needs. Therefore, it is likely that they tended to be satisfied with minimal technological preparation of tools for an expected range of household and communal tasks, but instead they had to take care of other things.

If an enormous amount of large and small debitage products, which were produced by knapping whole cobbles, were left scattered on the floor of household and communal areas in residential bases, razor-sharp edges of the debitage products would have been dangerous to barefoot residents and particularly for young children, who tend to pick up small things and to take them into their mouths. When people stayed at one residential base continuously, collective dumping of debitage products as well as other food refuse must have been really necessary and inevitable, in order to keep the living floor safe and tidy (Hardy-Smith and Edwards 2004). It is reasonable to think that even if tool making was performed at residential bases, debitage products would have been collected immediately and dumped away from the major household area of the residential bases, or deeply buried beneath the surface of the living floor, as has been observed at Epipalaeolithic sites in the X Basin and Z Basin.

Alternatively, it is plausible that reduction of whole cobbles, which would produce a large amount of debitage products at one time, was principally avoided at household areas of residential bases, and that recycling already exhausted cores collected from debitage middens in dumping area or workshop area by shattering was the common way of making tools. Fragmentary cores and informal tools at Kom W may reflect such economising behaviour. As has been suggested in a discussion about the definition of expediency (Bousman 1993: 69-70; Nelson 1991: 64-65), expedient tool making at presumably residential bases must be viewed as a planned response to expected tasks with least technological effort, and is different from opportunistic tool making as an unplanned technological response to unanticipated tasks.

7.10. Development of bifacial technology in terms of design theory and behavioural ecology

A remarkable feature of the lithic technology of the Fayum Neolithic is the emergence of bifacially-retouched, formal tools. A number of beautifully-shaped arrowheads, knife blades, sickle blades and axes found at Kom K and Kom W by Caton-Thompson were made by bifacial technology. One major reason for the emergence of bifacial tools in the Neolithic would be that good quality large cobbles, which provided fine-grained durable flakes, became available. This causality has not yet been substantiated by meticulous lithic refitting studies, but is assumed on the basis of the coincidence of unprecedented cobbles and bifacial tools in Neolithic sites and the possible reduction sequence demonstrated so far, as well as the fact that bifacial tools of longer than the average cobble size are rare.

A question arises as to whether the needs of bifacial formal tools required toolmakers to look for good quality large cobbles, or the discovery of good quality large cobbles enabled toolmakers to think about developing elaborate bifacial tools. It is true that raw material procurement and the organisation of technology are mutually co-dependent (Odell 2001: 67), and thus, this way of questioning may lead to a chicken-and-egg argument. However, according to the principles of design theory, a tool must exist to solve a given problem, and tool design is a means of creating or adapting the tool form to meet functional needs within the context of given environmental, technological, social and economic conditions. Different kinds of constraints operate in the development of solutions for each problem, and elimination of one constraint may enable a new design (Hayden 1998: 3*ff*; Hayden *et al.* 1996). Therefore, it is significant to consider tool design and technological organisation by analysing each tool type in its own terms, identifying the constraints and design strategies represented by each, and combining them, and then to reach a better understanding of the entire assemblage.

7.10.1. Arrowheads and knives

Given the faunal data showing that both Epipalaeolithic and Neolithic Fayum people exploited the same species of fish and waterfowl in similar relative abundance, while using similar strategies during the same time of year (Brewer 1989a; 1989b), it is difficult to think that Neolithic people were particularly eager to increase the yield of fishing and fowling grounds or to improve the efficiency of fishing and fowling by technological innovation. However, most Fayum Neolithic arrowheads and knives made by bifacial technology are relatively large and heavy (**Fig.7.54** and **Fig.7.55**), and thus are apparently not suitable for fishing and fowling, but more suitable for large game hunting and butchering. Therefore, it must be assumed that these tools were first and foremost invented according to arising needs for hunting large animals that were dangerous but could provide a large amount of meat. Indeed, two bifacially-retouched, concave-based arrowheads have been found among the bones of a hippopotamus and an alleged elephant respectively (Caton-Thompson and Gardner 1934, 72 and 84). These findings clearly indicate at what kinds of target animals such arrowheads were shot. It has also been revealed that animals like hippopotamus and crocodile are less commonly found in Epipalaeolithic assemblages but are found more in the assemblages of the Neolithic and later periods in the Fayum (Gautier 1976b: table I-7; Wenke *et al.* 1988: table 1). These facts suggest that new hunting weapons and butchering tools were invented especially for such large, aggressive and thick-skinned animals.

The appearance of enigmatic flint balls at Kom K and Kom W in the Neolithic period, as discussed earlier, may be put into this context and can be argued as a part of a new tactic for hunting dangerous animals. Namely, Fayum Neolithic hunters threw flint balls at these animals and immobilised them, and then delivered the fatal spear shot. In other words, it may be said that a new adaptive strategy for hunting previously less-exploited animals required reliable tool systems in which tools were specially designed to accomplish risky tasks at the time of use without failure in predictable situations, at the expense of multifunctionality or maintainability, which are the optimal design alternatives for tool systems needed in unpredictable situations (Bettinger 2001; Bleed 1986; Torrence 1989).

The reliable tool systems would be realised through taking mainly material, technological, and socioeconomic constraints into consideration. As already discussed, regular access to the sources of large flint cobbles which have better flaking quality and provide better and longer cutting edges was somehow made possible in the Fayum Neolithic, and this eliminated at least a material constraint on the development of elaborate tools of a certain size. It can be argued that elaborate, adaptive tools emerged as a consequence of the elimination of this constraint, but after a long evolutionary process in which many attempts of technological innovation were made and one of many, more or less equally acceptable solutions was selected according to variable circumstances (Fitzhugh 2001).

It is apparent that large and robust knives made by bifacial technology are more useful for butchering thick-skinned large animals than tiny bladelets, and the resharpening potential of bifacial knives under intensive use conditions must also have been highly appreciated. In contrast, the value of large bifacial arrowheads is not as apparent as bifacial knives. According to experimental studies, although bifacial technology, and pressure flaking in particular, can make a sharp, thin, formal projectile tip, it is not robust and fractures easily during manufacture and use (Whittaker 1994: 161-166). It has also been argued that projectile points would have rarely been designed with durability in mind because projectile points of any size and shape tend to break so easily under any use conditions that durability beyond a few shots or throws is not an achievable goal (Cheshier and Kelly 2006). Moreover, the possibility of reusing bifacially-retouched projectile points, with or without modification, is not much higher than that of reusing unretouched flake projectile points (Odell and Cowan 1986: 205*ff*).

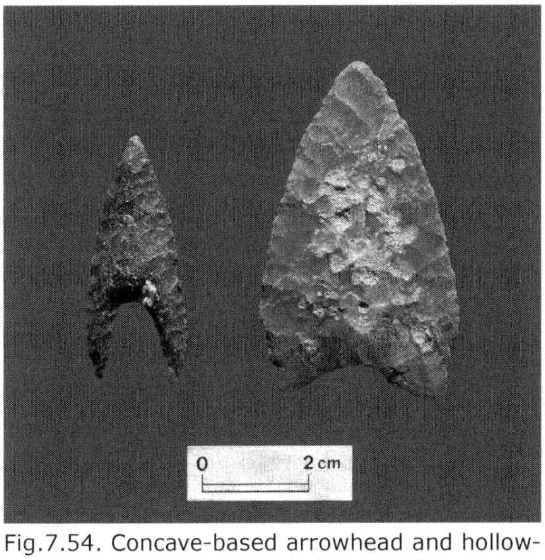

Fig.7.54. Concave-based arrowhead and hollow-based arrowhead collected at Camp II

Fig.7.55. Knife blades collected at Site LX

Therefore, the relative merits of a bifacial spearhead must be evaluated by whether it can make a fatal wound on a target animal by the first shot. Another experimental study has demonstrated that bifacially-retouched thin projectile points penetrated more deeply into animal bodies than informal flake points did, and are less likely to bounce off a target animal especially if hafted onto shafts (Odell and Cowan 1986: 203 and 208-209). It is probable that compared with microlithic or flake equivalents, large bifacial arrowheads proved their better killing power and higher reliability when they were used for hippopotamus and crocodile, and thus were selected for.

The costs of procuring good quality flint cobbles from distant source areas and making reliable, specialised tools for hunting and butchering hippopotamus and crocodile are certainly very high. However, according to a prediction of optimal foraging models that foragers employing costly technology need to exploit resources whose return rates are high (Bousman 1993: 64), it is presumed that the benefits of obtaining a large amount of meat from these animals met these costs. It can be said that the development of reliable tool systems in the Fayum Neolithic, as shown by elaborate bifacial arrowheads and knives, suggests the addition of a high cost and high return exploitation or resource maximisation strategy in predictable resource patches to the low cost and low-to-high return exploitation or time minimisation strategy of the preceding Epipalaeolithic period. Or, if the procurement of cobbles was not so costly due to its embeddedness in herding or fishing trips taken by non-toolmakers, the development of elaborate bifacial arrowheads and knives should better be regarded as a part of a risk minimisation strategy.

7.10.2. Axes, gouges, and planes

The development of reliable tool systems would also be the case with bifacially-retouched and ground axes, gouges and planes (**Fig.7.56**). These new tools, which first appeared in the Neolithic period, could not be realised without cobbles of fist size, and hence, getting access to the sources of large cobbles was essential. It must be better to assume that arising needs for new activities in the Neolithic period like tilling soil, and cutting, whittling, and carving wood required specialised toolkits, and that those bifacially-retouched and ground tools proved not only their advantage compared with microlithic tools or flake tools but also their cost-effectiveness in terms of their resharpening possibility under intensive use conditions.

The coincidence of the emergence of bifacially-retouched and ground tools with an increasing wood-cutting requirement has been reported elsewhere (Hayden 1989: 14-15), and this may also be the case in the Fayum Neolithic. Considering that most of the Fayum Neolithic bifacial tools are not hand-held tools and cannot be used without being hafted, the development of various bifacial tools would not have been realised without the extra costs of getting wood branches and making shafts and handles, which are generally more time-consuming and labour-intensive than making hafted stone tools (Keeley 1982: 800). Therefore, it is quite likely that bifacially-retouched gouges and planes were preferred due to their high resharpening possibilities under intensive use conditions. Furthermore, the beginning of pottery production in the Fayum Neolithic period must also have required a large amount of firewood for firing pottery vessels in bonfire, and this may have led to the invention of handy wood-cutting tools.

However, as mentioned, there seem to have been choppers made of cobbles in the Fayum Neolithic. The scatter of many choppers found around calcified plants in Locality 'Calcified Shrubs' suggests that they were used for cutting wood very roughly. It is assumed that they were made under relaxed conditions which did not necessitate frequent resharpening and that they were used expediently, because making and resharpening choppers by hard hammer percussion is the least labour-intensive but is wasteful of raw materials, and tends to create progressively steeper edge angles with every resharpening, thereby preventing effective continued use (Hayden 1989: 11*ff*). Therefore,

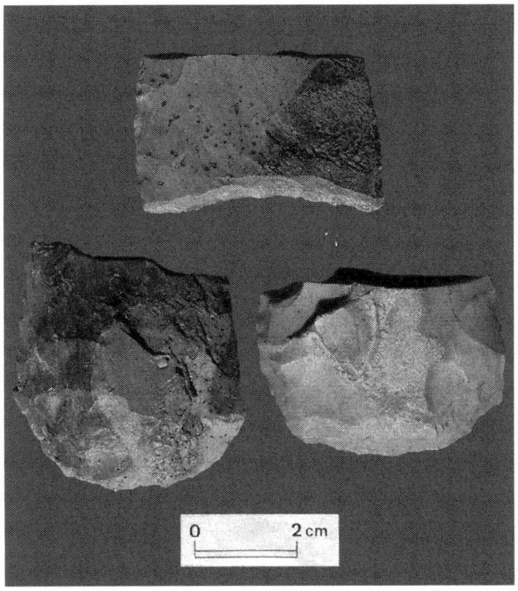

Fig.7.56. Gauge, axe and plane collected 500 m to the north of Kom W

Fig.7.57. Sickle blades collected at the Upper K Pits (left) and in Wadi A (right)

it may be said that the choice of curated and expedient technologies in the Fayum Neolithic was not always dependent on available raw materials but was subject to use conditions. Since such choppers have been found around the concentrations of large animal bone fragments at surface sites of supposedly Neolithic date around Kom W, it may be said that the choppers were also used for breaking hard bones.

7.10.3. Sickle blades

On the other hand, it is difficult to explain why Neolithic sickle blades were also made by bifacial technology. In the Fayum Neolithic culture as well as other contemporary Neolithic cultures in Lower Egypt, both faces of elongated and often pointed sickle blades were finely retouched, and one lateral margin of the blades was usually serrated. Bilaterally-serrated bifacial sickle blades are extremely rare (Caton-Thompson and Gardner 1934: 21) (**Fig.7.57**). A well-preserved sickle found in a Neolithic granary pit in the Fayum shows that three blades, which are 4.7 cm long due to being snapped short, 7.8 cm long, and 8.2 cm long respectively, are inserted in line into a centrally-placed longitudinal groove on a slightly curved wooden shaft of 51 cm long and are held in position by resin (Caton-Thompson and Gardner 1934: 45, pls.XXVIII and XXX). This way of use means that the blades were expendable and were replaced by new ones when their cutting edges became worn and dull.

It has been argued on the basis of experiments and ethnographic observations, that sickle harvesting was the most productive when wheat and barley grew very densely in hard soil and when they were at the green or half-green stage of maturity, whereas hand harvesting like picking or stripping seed heads without tools could be as efficient as sickle harvesting, when wheat and barley grew sparsely in sandy soil, and when they were at the half-green or ripe stage of maturity (Anderson 1999; Simms and Russell 1997). Therefore, the use of a long sickle in the Fayum Neolithic suggests quite intensified harvesting for high productivity as well as low cutting on the stems to obtain a long straw. It must be assumed that the cost of making such bifacially-retouched sickle blades as described above met the benefits of increasing productivity of harvesting tasks at the expense of efficiency.

Given that threshing and milling harvested grains to render them edible are also time-consuming and labour-intensive tasks, which require suitable facilities or tools, it must also be assumed that making sickle blades would have been optimised in relation to the costs of processing harvested grains against the benefits of obtaining sufficient nutrition.

From this cost-benefit perspective, relevant questions are why the entire surface of sickle blades had to be finely retouched before one cutting edge was serrated, and why the distal end of sickle blades had to be pointed. Retouching the entire surface seems to be an unnecessary effort, because the most important element of a sickle blade is a sharp and long cutting edge. One serrated cutting edge of a simple blade without further bifacial thinning or retouching sufficiently meets the functional need to cut siliceous plants, as exemplified by Levantine Neolithic sickle blades (Quintero *et al.* 1997). It seems that the pointed distal end of a sickle blade has no utility, because this part is covered by the wooden shaft and does not contact the materials being cut.

One possible explanation about these bifacial sickle blades is that such blades could be wedged into the groove of a wooden shaft more easily and be fitted better to a slightly-curved shaft. In terms of the aims and effects of hafting, the advantage of wedged hafts is that the attachment of blades to its handle is speedy and simple, and hence the replacement of blades is also easy. Better fitting of bifacially-retouched tools to a pre-existing haft has been emphasised as the reason why the tools are shaped in such a manner (Keeley 1982: 801; Kelly 1988: 718-719, 721*ff*). But the disadvantage is that such hafts allow movement of blades in the haft, which increases breakage and lowers the precision of work (Keeley 1982: 799). However, as mentioned, one example of the Fayum sickle shows that blades were actually held in position by resin. Therefore, unless this mastic haft example is exceptional, and unless the use of resin was uncommon in the Fayum Neolithic, it does not seem that bifacial retouching and a pointed distal end were intended to increase fitness to the shaft considerably without being assisted by mastic.

Another possible explanation is that bifacially-retouched sickle blades were intended to double the possibility of serrating cutting edges, by using two lateral margins of a blade one after another. However, bilaterally-serrated bifacial sickle blades are extremely rare in the Fayum Neolithic, and thus it seems likely that such a manner of blade use was not habitually intended, but rather was expediently attempted. Given that sickle blades were held firmly in a groove of a wooden shaft by resin, it is quite unlikely that blades were frequently replaced by new ones during a sickle-using task at the location of their use, because blade replacement requires a fire to melt resin, and this is complicated and time-consuming work (Keeley 1982: 799-800). As mentioned in Chapter 5, sickle blades have been found most abundantly at Kom W by Caton-Thompson, whereas they have been found elsewhere in isolation during my survey. As is often the case with hafted tools discussed in a study of the distributional effects of hafting (Keeley 1982: 802*ff*), tools may be resharpened or replaced when it is convenient to do so rather than when it is necessary. It can be said that worn sickle blades in the Fayum Neolithic were more frequently discarded and replaced at residential bases than they were at use locations, and that worn sickle blades were rarely resharpened to an exhaustive extent. Therefore, the high possibility of resharpening and recycling is apparently not a good explanation for the bifacial sickle blades in the Fayum Neolithic.

A further possible explanation about the seemingly unreasonable bifacial sickle blades is that those sickle blades were actually secondary products, and that other bifacial items like arrowheads and knives were habitually recycled and transformed into sickle blades, by making one lateral margin serrated. It is not easy to substantiate this explanation by demonstrating the reduction sequence or life history of a bifacial item, but it is significant to keep this possibility in mind, for shedding further light on the curatorial behaviour of Neolithic people. A unilaterally-serrated, concave-based sickle blade found in Merimde Beni Salama (Eiwanger 1992: pl.B-E) may be considered as an example for transforming a concave-based spearhead into a sickle blade.

7.11. Development of a unique technological organisation in the Fayum Neolithic

It has been argued that the mobility frequency and magnitude of foragers significantly affected the size and diversity of their technological inventory (Shott 1986). It has also been discussed that bifacial tools might be associated with frequent long-distance mobility in the environment, where good lithic raw materials were not always available, because bifacial tools were superior in terms not only of portability but also of maintainability that refers to the possibility of resharpening and recycling (Bleed 1986; Kelly 1988). However, there is no simple relationship between curated/expedient technology and residential/logistical mobility, and the Fayum Neolithic case seems to suggest that the organisation of bifacial technology was actually associated with a logistical type of mobility, supported by a caching or stockpiling strategy, in generally predictable resource patches. Given the lack of flint cobbles and the richness of food resources in the Neolithic habitat of the Fayum, it is understandable that Neolithic people developed bifacial technology with a basically logistical mobility strategy. Even though no substantial dwellings were found, it is considered on the basis of such lithic raw material use that the Fayum people have principally maintained residential bases in several essential resource locations at water margins and have procured additional resources from remote places by sending task persons routinely rather than moving the residential bases to those places. It is probable that routine visit to lithic raw material sources was embedded in pastoral grazing trip.

Another remarkable feature of the lithic technology of the Fayum Neolithic is the great reliance on locally-unavailable flint cobbles. In the Fayum Epipalaeolithic period, the toolkit included formal backed bladelets and arrowheads as well as informal flake tools like scrapers, notches and denticulates, and they were made not only on flakes obtained from elongated flint pebbles, which were abundantly available within an easy walking radius of their habitat, but also on flakes obtained from large flint cobbles, which were not locally available but must have been procured from distant sources. The division between formal tools and informal tools does not seem to derive from different raw materials, but the size difference of tools is certainly affected by the different size of raw materials, and large tools could not be made on locally-available pebbles.

In the Neolithic period, by contrast, it seems that toolmakers stopped relying heavily on locally-available elongated flint pebbles, but started to use locally-unavailable flint cobbles even for making small expedient tools, which could otherwise be made easily on locally-available flint pebbles. One previous study at Kom W has found that the majority of Neolithic tools were actually informal flake tools such as notches, denticulates and scrapers, and that bifacially-retouched formal tools were quite minor components of the assemblage (Kozlowski and Ginter 1989: 170*ff*). According to my observation at Kom W, those informal tools are apparently made on flakes from large cobbles and not on flakes from elongated pebbles. Therefore, it may be concluded that a new demand for large lithic raw materials required for new subsistence activities in the Neolithic period triggered more intensive exploitation of locally-unavailable large flint cobbles, and that this gradually affected the entire Neolithic technological organisation, and eventually led to the great reliance on large flint cobbles. In other words, it can be said that the Fayum Neolithic lithic technological organisation on the whole is characterised by its inclination toward a high cost and high return resource exploitation strategy, departed from a previous low cost, time minimising resource exploitation strategy.

7.12. Concluding remarks

It must be stressed that the Neolithic lithic artefacts studied record patterns in prehistoric human behaviour as they are manifested over large areas and long spans of time, and hence reflect the cumulative results of decisions made and actions taken by many generations of people. These patterns may not necessarily represent the ways which individual cobble collectors and toolmakers took in order to meet immediate needs in one particular situation during the Neolithic period. Moreover, the contemporaneity of the sites studied, which should be measured ideally in decades at least, is not adequately substantiated. Nevertheless, this study could illustrate that the lithic technological organisation in the Neolithic period was significantly different from that in the preceding Epipalaeolithic period, and that it represented a unique adaptation to the Fayum environment. Although the lack of substantial dwelling remains at any sites studied is puzzling, other circumstantial evidence strongly suggests that Fayum Neolithic people decreased residential moves by groups but increased logistical foraging moves by individuals considerably. The success of a farming-herding lifeway in the Fayum Neolithic was probably not possible without the decrease of residential moves, but was not realised without a supply of external resources enabled by the increase of logistical moves by individuals.

8. The diffusion of material culture and domesticates from the Levant to Egypt

8.1. Introduction

As discussed in chapter 2, the late diffusion of wheat/barley farming and sheep/goat herding from the Levant to Egypt can be explained in terms of the historical contingency of the process of domestication and diffusion within the Levant and the climatic events in the 7th millennium cal.BC. However, it is still not clear exactly how and from where in the Levant domesticates came to Egypt. It has been recognised that domesticated sheep/goats arrived on the Red Sea coast of Egypt in the early 6th millennium cal.BC (Marinova *et al.* 2008; Vermeersch *et al.* 1994; 1996; 2002; 2008), but they were not accompanied by wheat/barley farming. As described in Chapter 3 and Chapter 5, the earliest evidence for wheat/barley farming in Egypt was found in the Fayum Neolithic, and it was accompanied by sheep/goat herding from the beginning. The Fayum wheat/barley and sheep/goat are associated with sites which are radiocarbon-dated to no earlier than 4600 cal.BC, though the Neolithic human habitation began no later than 5700 cal.BC. Research in the Fayum has revealed that there was a hiatus of human habitation in the early 6th millennium cal.BC, and it looks as if domesticated wheat/barley and sheep/goat appeared suddenly in the Fayum at some time between the hiatus and 4600 cal.BC. Therefore, exactly when and how a package of domesticated plants and animals arrived in the Fayum remains unclear. This chapter aims to answer these questions.

8.2. Means of contact

Since domesticates do not move by themselves, humans must have existed behind such a movement. It is necessary to examine how and where Egyptian people could meet farmer-herders who were based in the southern Levant or hunter-herders who wandered in the Negev and Sinai, or could obtain access to Levantine domesticates and technical knowledge of farming and herding. There are two possible means of contact between these people. One is exchange, and another is migration.

Exchange can take place in many different ways. The simplest ways are either that one visits another's residential base or that people meet at a common territorial boundary, and then they exchange information, material items, food resources, and mates that each of them controls. The territorial boundary area is beyond the so-called extended range, which is regularly monitored through logistical moves by individuals who are dispatched from a residential base in the centre of one residential group's economic zone. The nature of contact can be friendly and reciprocal, competitive, or unidirectional, depending on whether one is subordinate to the other or the two are equal. Furthermore, an exchange at a residential base or a territorial boundary can be reduplicated by successive exchanges in different directions, and as a consequence, exchanged things may travel across successive territories. In addition, it is also probable that the two visit, not necessarily simultaneously, a central place, where there is a central person or a market, and exchanges take place with or without direct contact of persons who bring things to be exchanged there (Renfrew and Bahn 2000: 351-384).

Migration is an interregional long distance residential move by a group. Migration does not take place at random, but is usually well-planned on the basis of cost-benefit considerations as well as information about potential destination areas obtained through monitoring trips by scouts. The presence of kinsmen in the destination areas is also very important in the decision for migration.

In short, migrants are not likely to move to areas about which they have no information. Migrants tend to proceed along well-defined routes toward a destination, and significant expanses of less desirable areas may be leapfrogged. Therefore, migrants may move over great distances quickly, without leaving any sign in the middle of the routes. Particularly, farmers who depend on a narrow range of highly productive but localised resources are considered to be more likely to migrate long distances quickly in streams toward a destination, than foragers who depend on a broad array of wild food resources. Moreover, migration is not a single event but a process which is often recurrent and bidirectional. Migration streams can continue to flow in a given direction, in spite of considerable change in the circumstances that prompted the initial residential move of people. Kinship linkages and the reduction of obstacles may attract a secondary flow, that is different in goals and composition from the first migrants, and may also cause a counterstream moving back to the migrants' place of origin (Anthony 1990: 899-905; 1997: 22-27).

Given these two possibilities, it can be assumed either that technical knowledge of farming and herding and domesticates were passed on to Egyptian people somewhere in the border area between Egypt and the Levant, or that farmer-herders undertook long distance residential moves from the Levant to Egypt, due to negative stresses in the place of origin, or due to positive attractions in the destination area. It may be that Levantine people immigrated into Egypt with their domesticates and dominated local people or intermingled with them, or that Egyptian people emigrated into the Levant and learnt farming and herding, whereupon they or their descendants returned to Egypt with Levantine domesticates. A problem is that it is difficult to substantiate how these people have contacted and moved, as long as domesticates are the sole focus of study.

Another way of examining the contacts between Egypt and the Levant in the Early-Middle Holocene is to focus on the material culture in both regions. Archaeology has long discussed, while referring to ethnological data, what kinds of human activities are reflected in the distribution of an archaeological material culture. It has been cautiously argued that the uniformity or uniqueness of a material culture in a region is not necessarily a result of a cultural group's isolation or autonomy, and that interregional similarities in material culture are not necessarily a result of frequent human interaction and intermingling or human migration between the regions, even though the movements and contacts of human groups could certainly bring about change and diffusion of material culture (*e.g.*, Clark 1994; David and Kramer 2001: 360-377; Hegmon 1998; Stark 1998). Therefore, it is necessary to know the characteristics, distribution, and changes of material culture in Egypt and the Levant, in order to reconstruct portions of the possible interregional networks which may have enabled migration and to examine whether the diffusion of knowledge and domesticates or the migration of farmer-herders led to the beginning of farming and herding in Egypt. In the following, Neolithic pottery and stone tools in Egypt and the southern Levant will be overviewed, and the chronological relationship between material items of Egypt and the southern Levant will be considered (**Table 8.1**).

8.3. A brief overview of diagnostic Neolithic material items in Egypt and the southern Levant

8.3.1. Pottery

As for pottery, the Neolithic pottery of Lower Egypt as represented at the Fayum and Merimde Beni Salama is rather different from contemporaneous Levantine pottery in terms of shape, surface treatment, and decoration. The earliest pottery-bearing Neolithic culture in the southern Levant is the Yarmukian, and it is dated to around 6500-5700 cal.BC according to the latest data (Garfinkel 2008). The spatial distribution of the Yarmukian spans all the topographical units of the southern Levant

	Dakhleh Oasis	Fayum	Lower Egypt	Negev & Sinai	southern Levant
4000 cal.BC	Sheikh Muftah (Ceramic pastoral)	Moerian (Predynastic)	Maadi-Buto (Predynastic)	Timnian	Ghassulian (Chalcolithic)
5000 cal.BC	Bashendi B (Ceramic pastoral)	Fayumian (Fayum Neolithic)	Merimde Neolithic		Qatifian (Late Pottery Neolithic)
	Late Bashendi A (Ceramic pastoral)			Early Pottery Neolithic	Lodian (Jericho IX)
6000 cal.BC	Early Bashendi A (Ceramic pastoral)				Yarmukian (Early Pottery Neolithic)
		Qarunian (Fayum Epipalaeolithic)		Tuwailan	PPNC
7000 cal.BC					LPPNB
	Masara (Epipalaeolithic)		?Helwan Epipalaeolithic?	Desert PPNB	MPPNB
8000 cal.BC					EPPNB
9000 cal.BC				PPNA	PPNA
				Harifian (Epipalaeolithic)	Final Natufian (Epipalaeolithic)
10000 cal.BC				Late Natufian (Epipalaeolithic)	Late Natufian (Epipalaeolithic)

Table 8.1. Chronology of the regions mentioned in this chapter

including the Mediterranean coastal plain, the mountainous ridges and valleys, the Lower and Middle Jordan Valley and the Jordanian Plateau, but there is no evidence for the Yarmukian in the Negev (Gopher 1995; Gopher and Gophna 1993; Kafafi 1993; 1998). Although a considerable number of undecorated pottery vessels are present in the Yarmukian, the most conspicuous vessels are bowls and necked and loop-handled jars of various sizes with red-painted and incised decoration. The incised decoration is composed of horizontal lines, zigzag lines, and herringbone patterns. Parallel horizontal lines forming a frame are incised around the neck of jars and close to the rim of bowls, and parallel zigzag lines forming a frame are incised beneath the two horizontal lines along the perimeter of the vessel, and then the frames are filled with short incisions of the herringbone pattern, while leaving the incised areas unpainted (Garfinkel 1993: 118-120; 1999: 16-96; Gopher and Gophna 1993: 307-317). In the Neolithic of Lower Egypt, such elaborately decorated pottery vessels are absent and the majority are undecorated and handleless. A limited number of pottery sherds from the earliest level (*Urschicht*) of Merimde Beni Salama do have large incised herringbone pattern decoration, loop handles, and lug handles (Eiwanger 1984: 30-31, 32, 38, and pls.18-21 and 36), suggesting some cultural connection to the Yarmukian. However, due to a problematic radiocarbon date of the earliest level (*Urschicht*) of Merimde Beni Salama as mentioned in Chapter 2, its chronological relationship with the Yarmukian is unclear.

In Egypt, as described in Chapter 2, there had been a long tradition of pottery making in the Saharo-Sudanese culture in the Nabta-Kiseiba region since the 9th millennium cal.BC, and in the Bashendi culture in the Dakhleh Oasis region since the 7th millennium cal.BC. Whereas the pottery in the Nabta-Kiseiba region is generally characterised by dotted wavy line decoration, the pottery in Dakhleh Oasis and adjacent regions in the late 7th - 6th millennia cal.BC includes thin-walled vessels with rocker stamp decoration, red-polished vessels, and red-polished vessels with black rims as well as undecorated simple vessels. Notably, undecorated vessels are a new variety which appeared in these regions in this period, and it is argued that they did not spread to the north of these regions (Hope 2002; Kuper 1995; Riemer and Kindermann 2008; Riemer and Schönfeld 2007). Such wide varieties in surface treatment and decoration are not known in the Neolithic pottery of Lower Egypt. Either red/black-polished or not is the variety which is usually seen in the surface treatment of pottery in the Lower Egyptian Neolithic. Given that the general crudeness of undecorated vessels is a common characteristic, the Neolithic pottery of Lower Egypt may have partially originated from this Egyptian Western Desert tradition, but a variety of body shapes and sizes seen in the Neolithic pottery of Lower Egypt are dissimilar to those in Dakhleh Oasis and adjacent regions (Warfe 2003: 190-191). In terms of a variety of body shapes and sizes, the Neolithic pottery of Lower Egypt resembles that of the Yarmukian in the southern Levant. For instance, flat plates, bowls/jars with flat bases, and miniature vessels with pedestals seen in the Fayum Neolithic are absent in Dakhleh Oasis and adjacent regions but are not uncommon in the Yarmukian (Garfinkel 1999: 16-96).

8.3.2. Stone tools

As for stone tools, bifacially-retouched, concave-based projectile points, which are particular to the Lower Egyptian Neolithic culture, have been found in the contemporaneous Egyptian Western Desert though in limited numbers, and in the Egyptian Nile Valley in the subsequent Predynastic period, but have never been found in the Levant, Negev and Sinai. Therefore, previous scholars have concluded that Levantine influence on the material culture of the earliest Neolithic farming-herding community in the Fayum was very slight, even though a package of Levantine domesticates was attested there. It has been believed that the Fayum Neolithic material culture developed autonomously somewhere in the Nile Valley or the Western Desert and that the indigenous people would have been willing to adopt foreign domesticates (Wenke *et al.* 1988: 47).

However, it is more important to know whether Egyptian and Levantine Neolithic stone tools which are closely related to farming activities share common characteristics. Flint sickle blades in Egypt and the Levant are quite remarkable due to their unique morphology and visible use wear, whereas it is not easy to identify hoes. Hence, hoe-like items have often been described as axes. Some use wear analyses have demonstrated that a considerable number of Neolithic flint axes found at different sites in the southern Levant were indeed for wood working and none of them were used as hoes

(Barkai 2005; Barkai and Yerkes 2008). Therefore, it is possible that flint hoes did not exist at all. Nonetheless, since flint axes appeared in the southern Levant and Egypt when farming began, axes are considered to be related to farming activities like shrub clearance.

Egyptian Neolithic sickle blades, as represented by those found in the Fayum, Merimde Beni Salama, and El Omari, are deeply and densely serrated blades made from bifacially-retouched leaf-shaped points or rectangles. It is not certain exactly when they first appeared in Egypt. In Merimde Beni Salama, bifacially-retouched, serrated sickle blades started to appear in the second earliest level (*Schicht II*) of the stratigraphy (Eiwanger 1988: 37 and pls.37-38), and increased in the subsequent levels (*Schichten III*, *IV* and *V*) (Eiwanger 1992: 48-49, fig.15, and pls.69-73). Since the earliest level (*Urschicht*) is radiocarbon-dated to around 4900-4500 cal.BC and the latest level (*Schicht V*) is radiocarbon-dated to around 4500-4000 cal.BC (Hendrickx 1999: 60), these sickle blades would fall in the 5th millennium cal.BC. El Omari, which produced 13 bifacially-retouched, serrated sickle blades (Debono and Mortensen 1990: 45 and pl.18), is radiocarbon-dated to around 4700-4200 cal.BC (Hendrickx 1999: 61). As mentioned in Chapter 5, now that Kom W and Kom K in the Fayum, which produced the largest number of bifacially-retouched, serrated sickle blades, are radiocarbon-dated to around 4600-4200 cal.BC, these sickle blades should also fall in the middle of the 5th millennium cal.BC at least. It is known that such sickle blades persisted in the Predynastic Maadi culture of Lower Egypt and the Badarian and Naqada cultures of Middle and Upper Egypt until the early 4th millennium cal.BC, though they were not numerous (Holmes 1989; Rizkana and Seeher 1988: 35, 99-100 and pl.73). Besides these sickle blades of the 5th-4th millennia cal.BC, two fragments of bifacially-retouched, serrated sickle blades have been found at a site in Abu Gerara, which is approximately 80 km to the northeast of Dakhleh Oasis and gives no evidence of farming, and the site is radiocarbon-dated to around 5600-5500 cal.BC (Riemer 2003). Therefore, although the dating clues are not sufficient, it may be assumed that the first appearance of bifacially-retouched, serrated sickle blades in the Fayum would be no later than the middle of the 6th millennium cal.BC, which is around the beginning of the Neolithic human occupation in the Fayum.

On the other hand, sickle blades in the southern Levant have a much longer tradition since the Natufian. According to some synthetic studies of the development of sickle blades (Gopher *et al.* 2001; Rosen 1997: 134-140) (**Fig.8.1**), it was not until the PPNC and the Yarmukian in the 7th millennium cal.BC that sickle blades in the southern Levant were coarsely serrated bifacially on one or two lateral edges. It was in the Lodian (Jericho X) culture, which would probably be regarded as the later phase of the Yarmukian and is dated to the early 6th millennium cal.BC (Garfinkel 1999: 101-102; 2008: 15-21; Gopher and Gophna 1993: 339-343), that the body surface of deeply and densely serrated sickle blade was thoroughly retouched bifacially. However, such bifacially-retouched serrated sickle blades disappeared in the subsequent Wadi Raba culture and Qatifian culture of the southern Levant, which are roughly dated to the late 6th - early 5th millennia cal.BC (Gopher 1995; Gopher and Gophna 1993). Considering this trend in sickle blade production in the Pottery Neolithic of the southern Levant and its possible influence on Egypt, it is natural to assume that the first appearance of bifacially-retouched, serrated sickle blades in the Fayum would be no later than the middle of the 6th millennium cal.BC, and that bifacially-retouched, serrated sickle blades or the idea of making such sickle blades would have diffused to Egypt together with Levantine wheat and barley. It follows that such sickle blades persisted for a longer period in Egypt despite the fast disappearance of their Levantine counterparts.

It is not easy to posit a similar sequence of development for Neolithic axes. As described in Chapter 3, Fayum Neolithic bifacial axes are divided into ground and polished ones, polished and flaked ones, and flaked ones. It is assumed on the basis of similar examples in the

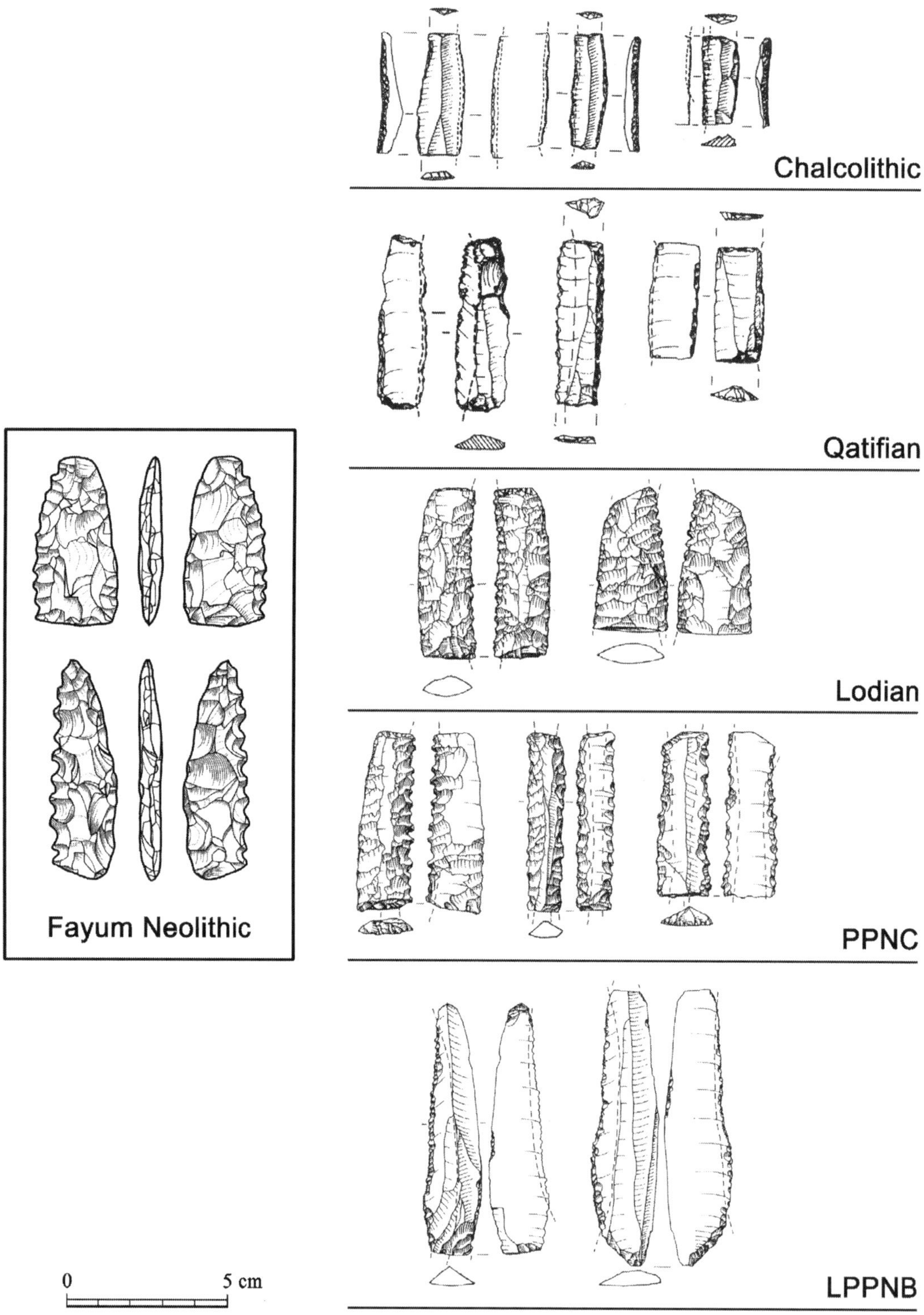

Fig.8.1. Development of sickle blades in the southern Levant (from Gopher *et al.* 2001: figs.4, 6, 7 and 8; Rosen 1997: figs.6.5 and 6.6; Shirai *in press*)

neighbouring region that they would have first appeared in the Fayum in the middle-late 6th millennium cal.BC, even though they were most numerously found at Kom W and Kom K, which are now surely dated to the middle of the 5th millennium cal.BC. In the southern Levant, both bifacially-polished axes and bifacially-flaked axes of rectangular or triangular shape have existed since the 9th millennium cal.BC until the end of the Chalcolithic in the 4th millennium cal.BC (Barkai 2002; 2005; Barkai and Yerkes 2008; Kozlowski and Aurenche 2005: 22-25, figs.1.3.3.1 and 2.2.5.2; Rosen 1997: 93-98). The cutting edges of bifacially-flaked axes in the PPNA period were produced with transverse or tranchet blows, whereas the cutting edges of most axes after the PPNB period were ground and polished, and the tranchet technique was abandoned (Barkai 2002; 2005; Barkai and Yerkes 2008). Therefore, it is not certain exactly when Levantine influence reached Egypt and affected local axe making, if it did. Nonetheless, the bifacially-flaked and partially-polished axes of triangular shape in the Yarmukian/Lodian (*e.g.*, Gopher and Gophna 1993: figs.3 and 7) look particularly similar to Egyptian Neolithic examples.

Even if this possible connection between Egyptian and Levantine sickle blades and axes is really the case, Levantine influence on Egyptian material culture in the period under consideration still looks slight and temporary. Although I have been doubtful about the slight and temporary Levantine influence on the Fayum material culture, I could not clear up my doubt as long as I depended on limited information. The best-known publication about the prehistoric archaeology of the Fayum is Caton-Thompson's report entitled *The Desert Fayum* (Caton-Thompson and Gardner 1934), and most scholars have relied on this report as the most authentic information. However, she did not publish all available data. Another problem is that she was a late visitor to the Fayum, and antiquarians had already collected a large number of prehistoric stone tools. Although parts of such antiquarians' collections were published a long time ago (Currelly 1913; Seton-Karr 1904), they have scarcely drawn the attention of serious scholars, despite the existence of peculiar types of stone tools which were not thoroughly reported by Caton-Thompson.

Re-reading such old publications and my study not only of unpublished Fayum lithic artefacts which were collected by Seton-Karr and Caton-Thompson and presently housed in museums in Egypt and Britain but also of new lithic artefacts collected during my fieldwork in the Fayum revealed that a considerable number of small projectile points, which were comparable to Pre-Pottery Neolithic and Pottery Neolithic small projectile points of the southern Levant, Negev and Sinai, existed in the Fayum. In addition, as already described in Chapter 4, recent research has revealed that the distribution of such small projectile points was not confined to the Fayum alone, although they were not very widespread in the Egyptian Western Desert and Nile Valley. In the following, these unique varieties of projectile points will be described in more detail, and the overall form of contacts between Egypt and the southern Levant, Negev and Sinai in the Early-Middle Holocene will be discussed. There seem to have been two successive waves of diffusion of Levantine projectile points since no later than the 7th millennium cal.BC. The first one is represented by the Helwan points of the Pre-Pottery Neolithic, and the second one is represented by the Nizzanim point, the Haparsa point, and the Herzliya point of the Pottery Neolithic. They are dealt with separately.

8.4. The first wave of diffusion of Levantine material culture to Egypt: The Helwan point

8.4.1. Introduction

The so-called Helwan point is a type of stone projectile point which has been roughly defined by the presence of side notches and a tang. It is assumed that side notches would not only prevent the ligature from interfering with the penetration power of the projectile point but also ensure the projectile point to be firmly attached to the shaft. In so doing, the projectile point would penetrate deeper and could be retrieved without being detached for reuse. However, since experiments suggest that notching itself would interfere with penetration, notching may possibly be intended to cause easy breakage at the point of the notch and to cause severe wounds (Christenson 1997). The Helwan point was named after the site of Helwan on the east bank of the Nile near modern Cairo, but such projectile points are not numerous in northeastern Africa. Many Helwan points have actually been found in the Levant. Consequently, the Helwan points have been a focus of study in Near Eastern archaeology and have played an important role as cultural and chronological markers in the Levant. In contrast, the study of such projectile points has been neglected in the archaeology of northeastern Africa.

From the African side, Eiwanger has shown that several side-notched and tanged projectile points found at Helwan as well as a side-notched and tanged projectile point found at his excavation site in Merimde Beni Salama in the western Nile Delta were similar to those of the Pre-Pottery Neolithic in the Levant. However, he did not present a clear chronological relationship between northeastern Africa and the Levant (Eiwanger 1983: 63-64). From the Levantine side, Gopher has analysed the geographical and chronological distribution of the Helwan points in the Levant, and argued that the Helwan points first appeared in the northern Levant in the PPNA period and thereafter dispersed southwards to the Negev in the Early PPNB period, eventually diffusing into northeastern Africa across Sinai (Gopher 1994: fig.8.2). However, when and which types of Helwan points appeared in northeastern Africa, and whether Levantine Helwan points actually diffused to northeastern Africa or were somehow imitated there by local people using local raw materials, have not been made clear, because Gopher's quest for the Helwan points stopped in the Negev in the Early PPNB period (Gopher 1989; 1994). No Helwan point has ever been found in northern Sinai, where the route of diffusion is posited.

Therefore, it is significant to re-study information about side-notched and tanged projectile points found in northeastern Africa, in order to complete Gopher's quest and to answer remaining questions. This part of the chapter will present some new data and ideas regarding such projectile points found in northeastern Africa including the Fayum, and will consider whether the diffusion of Levantine Helwan points to northeastern Africa really took place.

8.4.2. Definition and division of Helwan points

As already mentioned, the so-called Helwan point has been defined as the projectile point bearing side notches and a tang (Bar-Yosef 1981: 559; Brézillon 1968: 252), but it actually occurs in a variety of body forms and sizes, and the extent of the retouch on the body surface varies (Gopher 1994: 34-36). Because of this variability, it was argued as early as the 1970s that a single name like the Helwan point to represent so many variants had better be abandoned (Cauvin 1974: 316).

It is presently understood that the variations of the so-called Helwan points depend on time period and region. While middle-sized and elongated Helwan points made on blades or bladelets were prevalent around the middle reaches of the Euphrates in earlier periods, small-sized and wide Helwan points made on blades or flakes were prevalent on the Mediterranean coastal plain and around the Dead Sea later (Gopher 1994: 190*ff*). For this reason, the Helwan point has been divided into the earlier Sheikh Hassan type and the later Nahal Lavan type, named after the centres of their distribution (Adachi 1997). Alternatively, it has recently been argued that the former type, which is regarded as the northern variant of the Helwan point and is roughly dated to the 10th-9th millennia cal.BC, should be named the Sheikh Hassan point, and that the latter type, which is regarded as the southern variant of the Helwan point and is roughly dated to the 9th-8th millennia cal.BC, should be named the Abu Salem point (Kozlowski and Aurenche 2005: 110 and 117). Furthermore, the geographically and

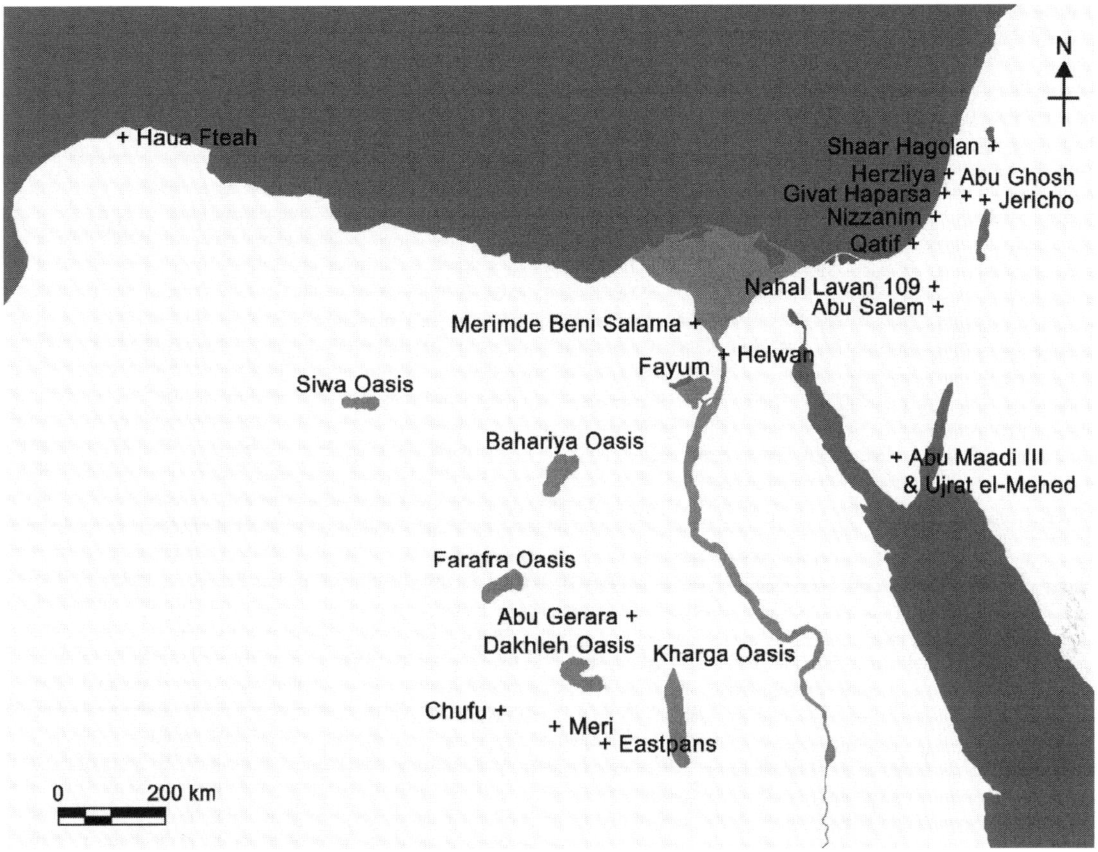

Fig.8.2. Map of the sites mentioned in this chapter

chronologically transitional type between the Sheikh Hassan point and the Abu Salem point is called the Aswad point (Kozlowski and Aurenche 2005: 113). A clear difference between the Sheikh Hassan point and the Aswad point is the presence of barbs in the latter.

This division of the so-called Helwan points is useful to describe apparent variations, but abandoning and re-naming the Helwan point may cause some confusion for those who prefer the conventional name. Therefore, in the following, the name Helwan point remains unchanged and is referred to as the side-notched and tanged projectile point which persisted in the 10th-8th millennia cal.BC in the Levant and Negev, but is divided into the Sheikh Hassan type, the Aswad type, and the Abu Salem type, which correspond to the Sheikh Hassan point, the Aswad point, and the Abu Salem point respectively as described above. On the other hand, side-notched and tanged projectile points found in northeastern Africa will not be called the Helwan point but will merely be described in comparison with these three types. This is because the name Helwan point carries a connotation for Near Eastern archaeologists that it *should* have existed in the 10th-8th millennia cal.BC in the Levant and Negev.

8.4.3. The present state of knowledge regarding the spatial and chronological distribution of side-notched projectile points in northeastern Africa

In northeastern Africa, the findspots of side-notched and tanged projectile points are confined to a few regions (**Fig.8.2**). Merimde Beni Salama is located on the western edge of the Nile Delta, whereas Helwan is located on the east bank of the Nile, and both of these two sites are within a

20 km radius of modern Cairo. The Fayum is a large depression containing Lake Qarun which is fed by the nearby Nile, and is approximately 60 km to the southwest of Cairo. Dakhleh Oasis, Abu Gerara, Chufu, and Eastpans are located in the middle of the desert far to the west of the Nile Valley and are approximately 500-600 km to the southwest of Cairo. No side-notched and tanged projectile points have so far been found to the south of the latitude of Chufu and Eastpans despite extensive research. Haua Fteah is located on the Mediterranean coast of Cyrenaica, and is approximately 1000 km to the northwest of Cairo. It is not certain whether such projectile points have spread further westwards.

Only one side-notched and tanged projectile point has been reported in Merimde Beni Salama (Eiwanger 1983; 1984), and at least eight side-notched projectile points are known in Helwan (Debono and Mortensen 1990; de Morgan 1896; Schmidt 1996). It is presently not certain how many side-notched and tanged projectile points in total have been collected in the Fayum. According to some publications and my museum research (Currelly 1913; Seton-Karr 1904), at least ten side-notched and tanged projectile points have been collected in the Fayum by Seton-Karr and Caton-Thompson. In addition, during my recent field survey in the Fayum, two more side-notched and tanged projectile points were found. A side-notched projectile point has been reported in Dakhleh Oasis (McDonald 1991a), and a side-notched and tanged projectile point has been reported in the vicinities of Dakhleh Oasis, such as Abu Gerara, Chufu, and Eastpans respectively (Gehlen *et al.* 2002; Reimer 2003; 2007). Haua Fteah in Cyrenaica also yielded only one side-notched and tanged projectile point (McBurney 1967).

There are many uncertainties about the context of discovery and possible date of individual artefacts. The site of Helwan has been visited and plundered by antiquarians since the late 19th century, and the site itself has been destroyed by the expansion of the modern town and roads. Many lithic artefacts have been collected on the surface, and the majority of artefacts are microlithic bladelets, dominated by arch-backed and scalene forms. On the basis of this technological feature, the Helwan industry has been approximately related to the Epipalaeolithic Mushabian/Ramonian of the Negev and Sinai, and the so-called Helwan points have been argued as resembling those of the Sinai PPNB (Schmidt 1996). However, no radiocarbon dates which support these arguments have been obtained in Helwan. Moreover, it is not certain whether more types of projectile points other than the side-notched projectile points existed in Helwan.

The side-notched and tanged projectile point at Merimde Beni Salama has been obtained through trench excavation. The layer in which the projectile point was found was dated to approximately 4900-4500 cal.BC by radiocarbon dating, but the excavator has argued that this radiocarbon date was unacceptably young because the majority of artefacts from this layer were microlithic, which is not consistent with the lithic industries of the 5th millennium cal.BC known in other parts of northeastern Africa. Accordingly, it has been suggested that the layer in question should be dated to the 6th millennium cal.BC (Eiwanger 1988: 53-54). Besides this radiocarbon dating problem, it seems odd that the layer in question does not contain any other formal projectile points at all despite the presence of thousands of lithic artefacts. Therefore, one must wonder if the only one side-notched and tanged projectile point in this layer was a stray artefact which was accidentally included in this layer.

As far as I know, the Fayum has produced the largest number of side-notched and tanged projectile points in northeastern Africa. As described in previous chapters, two distinct cultures in the Early-Middle Holocene are known in the Fayum. The earlier is the Epipalaeolithic (*ca.* 7500-6100 cal.BC), which is characterised by the predominance of backed bladelets, and the later is the Neolithic (*ca.* 5700-4200 cal.BC), which is characterised by the presence of various unifacially/bifacially-retouched, formal tools. Some diagnostic artefact types of each culture found by excavations have been securely dated. On the other hand, many types of lithic artefacts remain undated, because they have been collected only on the deflated desert surface, and because it is common in the Fayum that artefacts from different periods are found mixed up on the surface. Therefore, it is difficult to determine whether such undated surface artefacts belong to the Epipalaeolithic or Neolithic industry. All side-notched and tanged projectile points found in the Fayum are also such undated types of artefacts. Undated small projectile points which are similar in body size and body surface retouch to the side-notched and tanged ones are generally abundant in the Fayum (Currelly 1913: pl.XXVIII), and are particularly numerous at some sites in the Fayum like Site V and Camp II (Caton-Thompson and Gardner 1934: 75-77 and pl.LI), and actually, side-notched and tanged projectile points have been found at these sites. The rarity of side-notched and tanged projectile points in contrast to the general abundance of other types of small formal projectile points in the Fayum is quite remarkable.

A side-notched projectile point reported in Dakhleh Oasis is approximately dated to the Bashendi A period (ca.6400-5700 cal.BC) (McDonald 1991a). A side-notched and tanged projectile point reported at Abu Gerara may be dated to around 5600-5500 cal.BC (Riemer 2003: 86-88), and a side-notched and tanged projectile point reported at Chufu may be dated to the first half of the 6th millennium cal.BC (Riemer 2007a: 521-522). A side-notched and tanged projectile point reported at Eastpans may be dated to approximately 5100-4950 cal.BC, but some associated artefacts seem to suggest that the assemblage can be dated slightly earlier (Gehlen *et al.* 2002: 96-97). The rarity of side-notched and tanged projectile points in contrast to the abundance of other types of small formal projectile points is also the case in this region.

A side-notched and tanged projectile point from Haua Fteah in Cyrenaica may probably be dated to as late as 5800-5400 cal.BC by radiocarbon dating of the layer in which it was found (McBurney 1967: 274). The rarity of side-notched and tanged projectile point in the lithic assemblage of the layer is noted there as well.

8.4.4. The manufacture and form of the side-notched projectile points in northeastern Africa

As for the manufacture and form of the side-notched and tanged projectile points found in northeastern Africa, there is some variation between sites.

Among the eight complete or nearly-complete side-notched projectile points in Helwan (**Fig.8.3**) (originally Schmidt 1996: fig.2), six of eight (points 2, 3, 4, 6, 7, and 8 in **Fig.8.3**) are apparently made on bladelets, and apart from notches on lateral edges, there is few or no facial retouch. These are the features of the Sheikh Hassan type and the Aswad type. On the contrary, two of the eight points (points 1 and 5 in **Fig.8.3**) look different in terms of the extent of facial retouch. They are thoroughly retouched on at least one face of the body. Such facial retouch is unusual in the Sheikh Hassan type and the Aswad type. One of the eight (point 3 in **Fig.8.3**) seems to lack a tang and has side notches close to its base. Hence it looks more like the El-Khiam point, which is defined as the projectile point with side notches close to its concave- or straight-retouched base (Bar-Yosef 1981: 559; Brézillon 1968: 319-320; Gopher 1994: 32-34).

The Merimde specimen [I.1106] (**Fig.8.4**) (originally Eiwanger 1984: 111 and pl.57) shows the characteristics of the Abu Salem type. The body is well retouched not only on one face but also around the projectile edge and tang, and has pointed barbs fashioned by a pair of notches that form the tang. A long tang of the Merimde specimen is the only unusual thing in comparison with the Abu Salem type. Despite this difference, as the excavator of Merimde has shown (Eiwanger 1983: fig.2), the Merimde specimen is certainly comparable to those found at Nahal Lavan 109 and Abu Ghosh.

Concerning the Fayum specimens, among the four side-notched and tanged projectile points (**Fig.8.5**-1: UC 3264 from Site V, **Fig.8.5**-3: UC3265 from Site V, **Fig.8.5**-4: UC3781 from Dimai and **Fig.8.5**-6: UC3759 from Site N) which were collected by Caton-Thompson and are presently housed in the Petrie Museum of

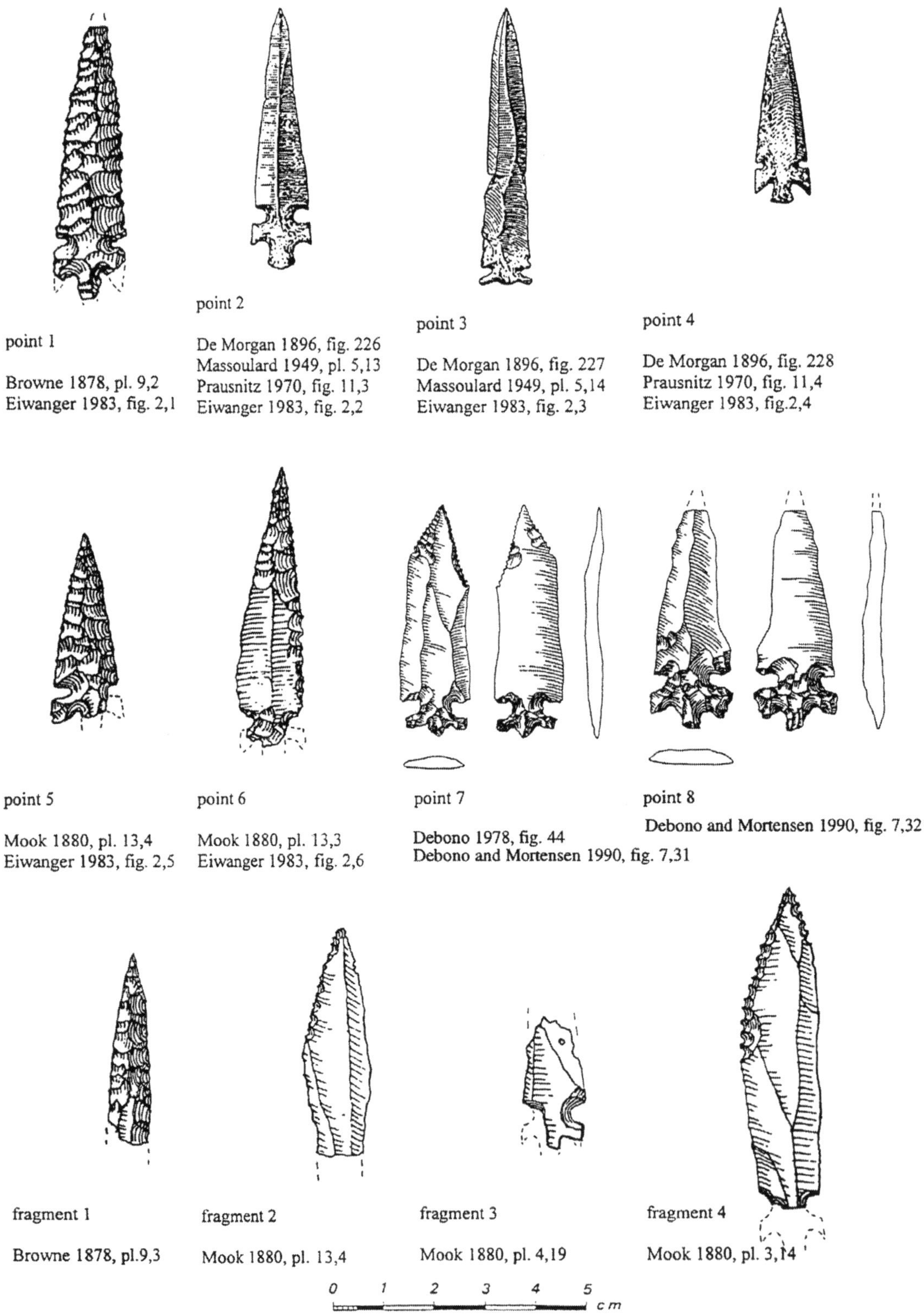

Fig.8.3. Side-notched projectile points from Helwan (from Schmidt 1996: fig.2)

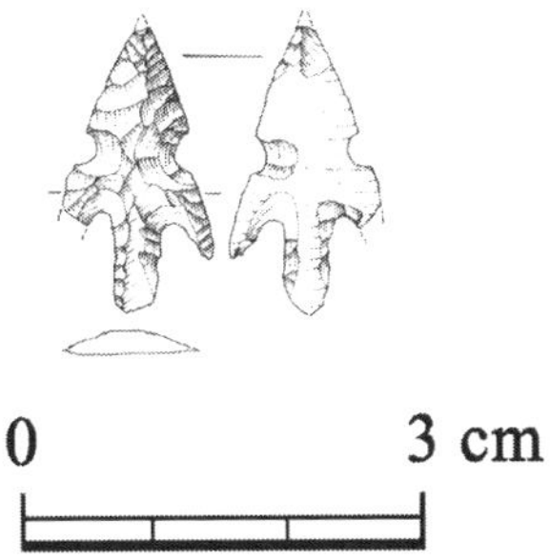

Fig.8.4. A side-notched and tanged projectile point from Merimde Beni Salama (from Eiwanger 1984: pl.57)

Egyptian Archaeology in University College London, two (**Fig.8.5**-4 and -6) are thoroughly retouched on both faces, and the rest (**Fig.8.5**-1 and -3) are well retouched on lateral edges. Poorly-made barbs and well-made tang of two elongated points (**Fig.8.5**-3 and -4) give an impression that they are similar to the Sheikh Hassan type. In contrast, one (**Fig.8.5**-6) is close to the Aswad type in terms of body form and barbs fashioned by a pair of notches that form the tang, and resembles Helwan specimens (points 1 and 5 in **Fig.8.3**). It also seems to resemble two side-notched projectile points (CG63875 and CG63876) which were collected by Seton-Karr and are presently housed in the Egyptian Museum in Cairo (Currelly 1913: pl.XXVIII), though CG63875 has a long tang.

A side-notched and tanged projectile point found at Caton-Thompson's Camp II during my recent field survey in the Fayum (**Fig.8.5**-2) closely resembles the Merimde specimen in terms of manufacture, body form, and the extent of surface retouch. Another side-notched and tanged projectile point found at Site XA during the recent survey in the X Basin area (**Fig.8.5**-5) closely resembles one of Caton-Thompson's Fayum specimens mentioned above (**Fig.8.5**-6). It is closer to the Aswad type in terms of body form, but is different from the Aswad type in terms of thorough bifacial retouch.

Most of the Fayum specimens are made on local flint. Its colour ranges from dark brown to

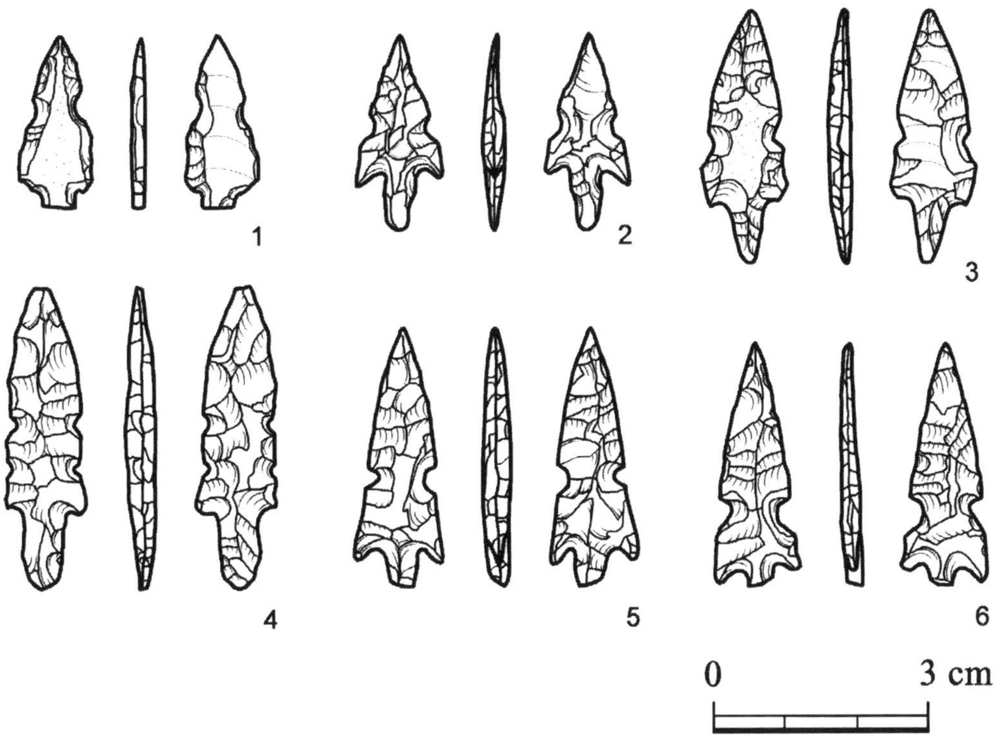

Fig.8.5. Side-notched and tanged projectile points from the Fayum

light brown. In the Fayum, such flint is found scattered in the form of elongated pebbles of approximately 5-7 cm long in Pleistocene gravels on rocky escarpments which are within an easy walking distance from Epipalaeolithic and Neolithic habitats. Only one of the Fayum specimens (**Fig.8.5**-5) is made on white chalky flint, and its source area is still unknown.

It is not certain that a side-notched projectile point reported in Dakhleh Oasis (McDonald 1991a: fig.3-e) had a tang, but another side-notched and tanged projectile point reported at Abu Gerara (Riemer 2003: fig.8-no.8) resemble the Dakhleh specimen in terms of body form and thorough facial retouch, and they are very similar to the Abu Salem type. On the other hand, a side-notched and tanged projectile point reported at Chufu (Riemer 2007a: fig.9-no.3) and another side-notched and tanged projectile point reported at Eastpans (Gehlen *et al.* 2002: fig.7-no.3) resemble each other in terms of body form, thorough facial retouch, and presence of barbs. Their elongated body form is closer to that of the Aswad type. A side-notched and tanged projectile point found at Haua Fteah (McBurney 1967: fig.IX.15-no.10) also has an elongated body and well-made barbs, and thus resembles the Chufu and Eastpans specimens.

In summary, although the sample size is very small, it seems that the Aswad type and Abu Salem type of side-notched projectile point are more widely spread in northeastern Africa than the Sheikh Hassan type. As mentioned earlier, given that the Abu Salem type was widespread in the southern Levant and the Aswad type was widespread in the central Levant, whereas the Sheikh Hassan type was distributed mainly in the northern Levant, it is no surprise that the Aswad type and the Abu Salem type spread farther in northeastern Africa.

8.4.5. The time gap between Levantine Helwan points and African side-notched projectile points

The dates of the side-notched and tanged projectile points found in northeastern Africa and their sporadic occurrence are really problematic, if their cultural connection to those of the southern Levant and Negev is assumed. Many of the side-notched and tanged projectile points in northeastern Africa have been surface-collected and undated. The side-notched projectile points found in isolation in remote places like Dakhleh Oasis and its vicinities and Haua Fteah are all roughly dated to the first half of the 6th millennium cal.BC. This seems to be rather later in date than those found in the Levant and Negev, even if the long distances to be traversed for the diffusion of artefact or technique/knowledge between the Levant/Negev and the lower latitude of northeastern Africa and between the Levant/Negev and Cyrenaica are taken into account. Therefore, a considerable time gap between the Helwan points of the Levant/Negev and some dated African side-notched and tanged projectile points must be explained, while considering undated side-notched and tanged projectile points found in Helwan and the Fayum.

It is probable that the undated side-notched and tanged projectile points found in Helwan and the Fayum are relatively earlier than the first half of the 6th millennium cal.BC, if they originated from the southern Levant and Negev. Indeed, some of the side-notched and tanged projectile points with few or no facial retouch found in Helwan (points 2 and 4 in **Fig.8.3**) have no comparable example at other sites in northeastern Africa. A side-notched projectile point in Helwan (point 2 in **Fig.8.3**) resembles the El-Khiam point, which is considered to be earlier in date than the Helwan point in the southern Levant (Bar-Yosef 1981: fig.3; Gopher 1994: fig.6.6). These facts may suggest that the Helwan specimens are earlier in date than most other bifacially-retouched ones. Furthermore, as mentioned earlier, the time span of the Fayum occupation is known to be between 7500 cal.BC and 4200 cal.BC, and hence it is possible that the undated Fayum side-notched and tanged projectile points fall in the late 8th or early 7th millennium cal.BC. If these assumptions regarding the dates of side-notched projectile points found in Helwan and the Fayum are right, then a time gap between the side-notched and tanged projectile points of the Levant/Negev and some dated African side-notched and tanged projectile points found at other sites in northeastern Africa can be filled.

The timing of the disappearance of the Helwan points in the southern Levant and Negev may also have to be reconsidered. It has been argued that the Helwan point disappeared from the southern Levant and Negev during the Middle PPNB and did not persist until the Late PPNB (Gopher 1994: 190*ff*), and this argument seems to be widely accepted at present. However, there are still ambiguities in the argument on the spatial and chronological distribution of the Helwan points. Many sites in the southern Levant and Negev which have produced the Helwan points have not been securely radiocarbon-dated (Gopher 1994: 231-232). Moreover, sites like Abu Maadi III and Ujrat el-Mehed in Sinai, which are most likely to be dated to the Late PPNB, have yielded side-notched and tanged projectile points, but they have been treated as a derivative of the Helwan point or the Jericho point and given a different type name (Gopher 1994: 57-62, 133-135, and 202-204). These facts may allow another proposition that the Helwan points possibly persisted well into the Late PPNB in the Negev and Sinai, and this proposition sounds more reasonable in the light of the situation in northeastern Africa.

8.5. The Ounan points and unifacially/bifacially-retouched projectile points in northeastern Africa, Sinai, the Negev and southern Levant

In order to better understand the appearance and development of side-notched and tanged projectile points in northeastern Africa, the presence of other types of projectile points in northeastern Africa and their possible connection to Levantine projectile points must be mentioned here. As described in Chapter 6, tanged projectile points made on bladelets in the Epipalaeolithic cultures of North Africa in the Early Holocene have been defined as the Ounan points (Tixier 1963). According to the latest research, the chronological distribution of the Ounan points in northeastern Africa is between 8000 cal.BC and 6500 cal.BC or somewhat later (McDonald 2003: 57*ff*; Riemer *et al.* 2004: 14).

On the other hand, the southern Levant, Negev and Sinai had a longer tradition of making projectile points on blades or bladelets. Tanged projectile points similar to the African Ounan points existed in the Epipalaeolithic Harifian industry of the Negev and Sinai in the 10th millennium cal.BC, and these points were also named the Ounan points by an archaeologist who had worked in the Sudanese Nile Valley and hence had good knowledge of the Epipalaeolithic of north Africa (Marks and Scott 1976), even though there is a considerable time gap between the African examples and the Harifian ones. Despite this problem, the name Ounan point was adopted by other Near Eastern archaeologists when the Harifian industry was dealt with (Goring-Morris 1987; 1991; Kozlowski and Aurenche 2005: 106). Such Ounan point-like projectile points existed in the PPNA of the southern Levant, and they were named the Jordan Valley point (Kozlowski and Aurenche 2005: 112; Nadel *et al.* 1991). From the end of the 9th millennium cal.BC onwards, projectile points made on blades or bladelets became morphologically more elaborate by the application of further edge retouch. The projectile points of the PPNB include the Jericho point, which is characterised by a pair of down-turned barbs and a tang of a triangular, trapezoid, or elliptical form, the Byblos point, which is characterised by a tang set off from the body by two shoulders at an obtuse angle, and the Amuq point, which is characterised by its elongated leaf-shape. Their smaller variants, which have been named the Haparsa point, the Nizzanim point and the Herzliya point respectively, appeared in the subsequent Pottery Neolithic from the late 7th millennium cal.BC onwards. These small projectile points are often unifacially or bifacially retouched (Baird 2001: 320*ff*; Bar-Yosef 1981: 559-561 and fig.3; Gopher 1994: 36-41 and fig.4.9).

There seem to be few morphological differences between the Byblos point and the contemporaneous African Ounan point. Furthermore, in the late 7th - early 6th millennia cal.BC, the region to the north of Dakhleh and Kharga Oases saw the appearance of unifacially/bifacially retouched small projectile points (*e.g.*, Barich and Lucarini 2002; 2005; Kindermann 2002; 2004), which are reminiscent of the Levantine Pottery Neolithic small projectile points, and they are collectively called the '(bi)facial techno-complex' (Riemer 2007a; 2007b). Therefore, it is probable that the development of tanged projectile points since the 10th-9th millennia cal.BC were actually almost synchronous across the southern Levant, Negev, Sinai, and northeastern Africa, and that the barbs seen in the Jericho point and the side-notches seen in the Helwan points as well as the bifacial retouch commonly seen in small projectile points of the Pottery Neolithic were major technological innovations in the course of the 8th and 7th millennia cal.BC.

As described, the side-notched and tanged projectile points in northeastern Africa certainly share some features with the Aswad type and the Abu Salem type in the southern Levant and Negev, but the African side-notched and tanged projectile points are not precise copies of the Aswad type and the Abu Salem type. Bifacial retouch is generally more common in the African side-notched and tanged projectile points, and their appearance was much later in date. Side-notched and tanged projectile points in the region around Dakhleh Oasis seem to belong to the assemblage of the unifacially/bifacially-retouched, tanged or leaf-shaped small projectile points that appeared and developed in the same region in the late 7th - early 6th millennia cal.BC. The sequence of the appearance of individual innovations suggests that northeastern Africa has always been slow to adopt these innovations but has developed unique variants autonomously by adopting and combining these innovations. In other words, it is suggested that technological innovations and the production of unique variants in northeastern Africa have been realised or stimulated by indirect, slightly delayed influences from the southern Levant, Negev and Sinai.

8.6. The second wave of diffusion of Levantine material culture to Egypt: The Pottery Neolithic projectile points

8.6.1. Introduction

As mentioned not only in this chapter but also in Chapter 3 and Chapter 4, in the late 7th - early 6th millennia cal.BC, the regions to the north of Dakhleh and Kharga Oases saw the appearance of unifacially/bifacially retouched, leaf-shaped or tanged small projectile points, which replaced the African Ounan points, and this new technological tradition is named the (bi)facial techno-complex. Such small projectile points are extremely abundant at some sites in the Fayum like Site V, Camp II and the Z Basin slopes (Caton-Thompson and Gardner 1934: 75-79 and pl.LI), but it has been difficult to date them to either the Fayum Epipalaeolithic or Neolithic, because they were collected on the desert surface. As a consequence, they have not drawn much attention from scholars. However, considering the increasing information about the appearance of such small projectile points in the surrounding regions of the Fayum, numerous Fayum examples must be put in this wider geographical context, and their possible date should also be deduced from the sequence of technical and morphological development across these regions.

This part of the chapter will present some new data and will re-evaluate the importance of unifacially/bifacially retouched, leaf-shaped or tanged small projectile points found in the Fayum, which are comparable to those of the Levantine Pottery Neolithic and those of the Egyptian Western Desert (bi)facial techno-complex. Then it will be considered that the (bi)facial techno-complex of the Egyptian Western Desert may actually have spread from the Fayum to the west and the south rather than from the west and the south to the Fayum. It will further be argued that the southward and westward spread of the small projectile points could indicate the dispersal of domesticated sheep and goats from the Fayum in the early 6th millennia cal.BC.

8.6.2. The study of small projectile points in the Levantine Pottery Neolithic and the Egyptian Western Desert (bi)facial techno-complex

Small projectile points in the Levantine Pottery Neolithic have often been collectively called 'the Late Neolithic points', including the Haparsa point, the Nizzanim point, and the Herzliya point. As already mentioned, they have been defined as the smaller variants of the Jericho point, the Byblos point and the Amuq point, and are usually less than 4 cm in length (**Fig.8.6**). The Haparsa point is characterised by pointed barbs fashioned by a pair of notches that also form a tang, and the shape and length of the tang vary considerably. The Nizzanim point has a tang set off from the body by two shoulders, but the tang is not much narrower than the body and forms a natural continuation of its contour. The Herzliya point is leaf-shaped and has no conspicuous tang (Bar-Yosef 1981: 561; Gopher 1994: 41). The relative frequencies of these three types of projectile points in the lithic assemblages between different sites in the Levant are difficult to understand, but it has been suggested that the Haparsa point tends to increase whereas the Nizzanim point tends to decrease through the Pottery Neolithic period, though the Herzliya point does not seem to follow any clear course (Gopher 1994: 211-220).

Small projectile points similar to these three types certainly existed in the northern half of the Egyptian Western Desert. However, since there are not much quantitative data about the relative frequencies of these three types, it is difficult to know the trend in their appearance in Egypt. For instance, some reports with illustrations of representative artefacts show that the Siwa Oasis region, which is almost on the same latitude of the Fayum, yielded these three types of small projectile points, but no quantitative data have been presented (Cziesla 1989: fig.1; Hassan and Gross 1987: fig.5.4). This is also the case with other regions like Farafra Oasis, Dakhleh Oasis, Kharga Oasis, and

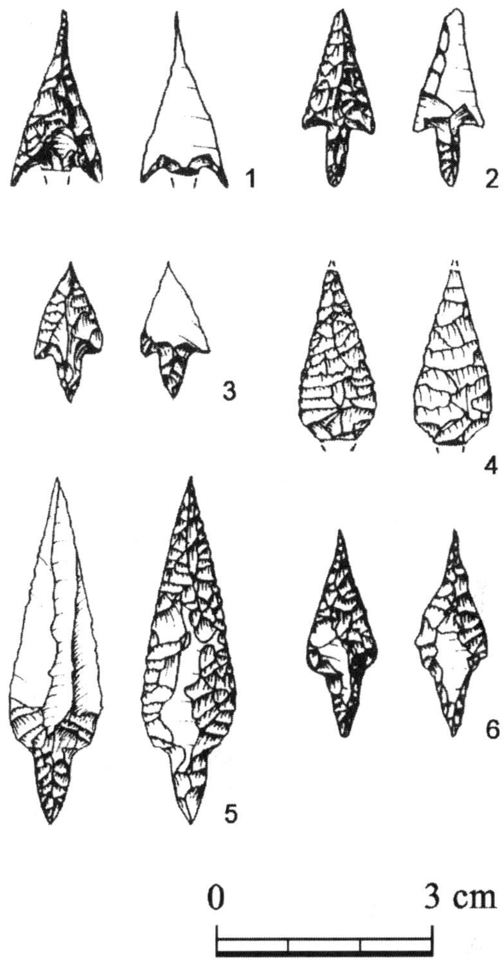

Fig.8.6. Small projectile points of the Pottery Neolithic collected at Nahal Issaron in the Negev. 1-3: Haparsa points, 4-6: Nizzanim points (from Gopher *et al.* 1994: fig.6)

Djara (Barich and Lucarini 2002; 2005; Caton-Thompson 1952; Gehlen *et al.* 2002; Kindermann 2002; 2003; 2004; McDonald 2008), which are considered to belong to the (bi)facial techno-complex.

As for the small projectile points which were selectively collected by Caton-Thompson in extremely large numbers at Site V, Camp II and the Z Basin slopes in the Fayum but have remained to be published and dated, there are some quantitative data (Caton-Thompson and Gardner 1934: 75-77 and 84-85). Among 343 small projectile points in her collection, tanged ones, which are not subdivided into the barbed variety and the shouldered variety in her description, predominate, whereas leaf-shaped ones are apparently very few (**Table 8.2**). I studied parts of Caton-Thompson's collection of the Fayum small projectile points which are distributed to the Egyptian Museum in Cairo, the Petrie Museum in London, the Ashmolean Museum in Oxford, and the Allard Pierson Museum in Amsterdam. Although the projectile points which I studied amount to only one quarter of 343 projectile points, they show that the tanged and barbed variety is slightly outnumbered by the tanged and shouldered variety (**Table 8.3**). The variety of the small projectile points which I collected at Site V, Camp II, Camp II Basin and the Z Basin slopes (**Fig.8.7**-4, 5 and 6, **Fig.8.8** and **Fig.8.9**) as well as those which I studied in the unpublished Caton-Thompson's collection in the Petrie Museum (**Fig.8.7**-1: UC3262 from Site V, **Fig.8.7**-2: UC3407 from Camp II, and **Fig.8.7**-3: UC3412 from Camp II) is comparable to that illustrated by Caton-Thompson (Caton-Thompson and Gardner 1934: pl.LI).

In contrast, in the so-called Bedouin Microlithic assemblages of Kharga Oasis, although the sample is small and surface-collected, leaf-shaped points are predominant, whereas tanged and barbed projectile points are few (Caton-Thompson 1952: 159-164). In addition, in Chufu and Meri to the south of Dakhleh Oasis, although the sample size is very small, leaf-shaped projectile points predominate, whereas tanged projectile points are rare to absent (Riemer 2007a: fig.8).

Therefore, it is understandable that because of the inconsistency in datasets, previous studies have had no other way but to focus on the common technique of unifacial/bifacial retouch on small flakes or bladelets, rather than the detailed morphology of projectile points. Nonetheless, the extreme predominance of tanged projectile points in the Fayum assemblage can be noted as a unique regional feature within the Egyptian Western Desert (bi)facial techno-complex.

	Site V	Camp II	Z Basin slopes	total
tanged	52	189	53	294
leaf-shaped	7	38	4	49

Table.8.2. Number of small projectile points found in three Fayum sites

Site V	those found in museum collection
tanged and barbed	6
tanged and shouldered	8
Camp II	those found in museum collection
tanged and barbed	34
tanged and shouldered	36
Z Basin slopes	those found in museum collection
tanged and barbed	2
tanged and shouldered	8

Table.8.3. Number of small projectile points found in Caton-Thompson's collection in several museums

8.6.3. The possible date of unifacially/bifacially retouched, tanged or leaf-shaped small projectile points in the Fayum

Given the dates of small projectile points in the Egyptian Western Desert (bi)facial techno-complex, the question is whether the Fayum small projectile points are earlier or later in date than the Western Desert examples. One possibility is that the small projectile points under consideration appeared in the Fayum as early as the second half of the Fayum Epipalaeolithic period, which is contemporaneous with the Pottery Neolithic of the southern Levant and the Negev as well as the earliest period of the (bi)facial techno-complex of the Egyptian Western Desert. Another possibility is that they appeared in the Fayum around the beginning of Neolithic human habitation, and hence are later in date than the Western Desert examples.

One negative fact affecting the first possibility is that such small projectile points

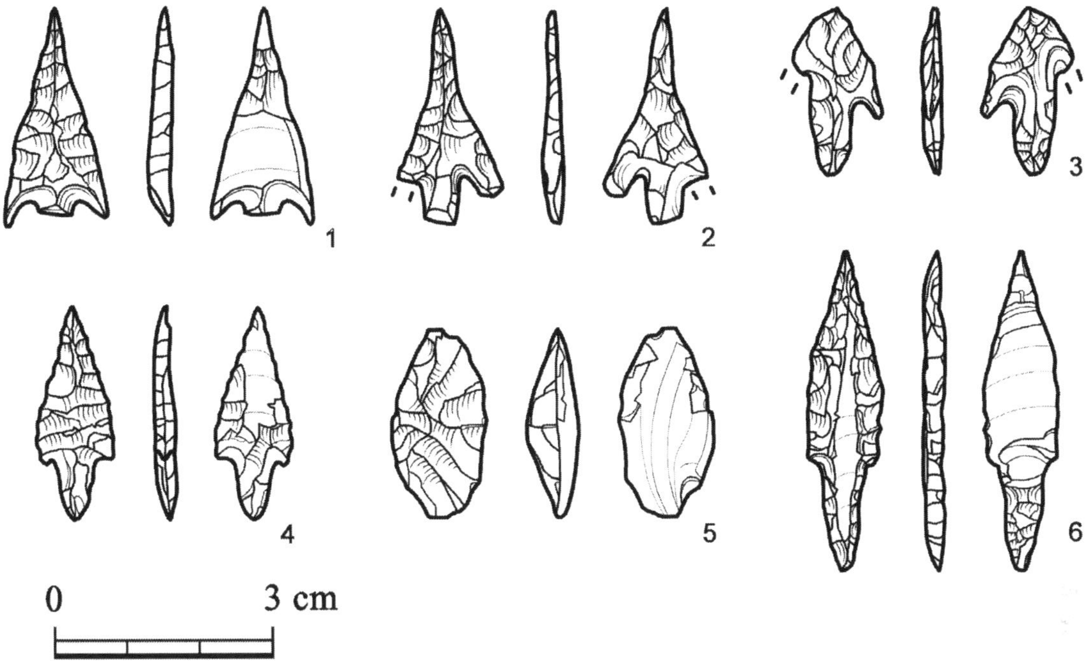

Fig.8.7. Small projectile points from the Fayum (1 from Site V, 2-5 from Camp II, 6 from the Camp II Basin)

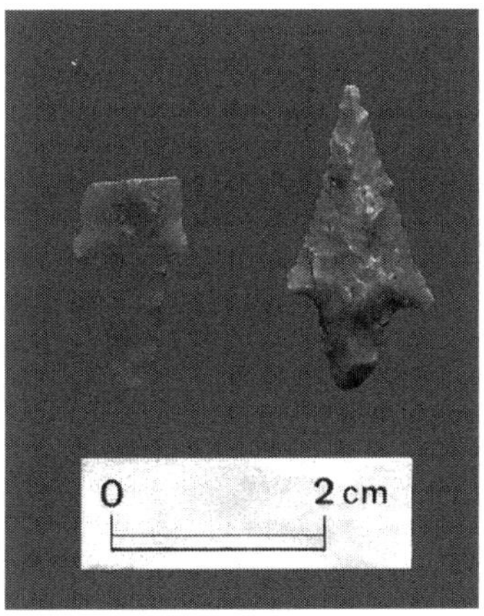

Fig.8.8. Small projectile points from Site V

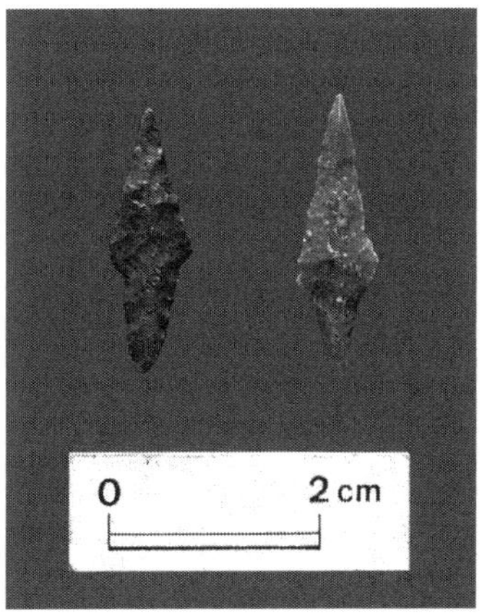

Fig.8.9. Small projectile points from the Z Basin slopes

have not been found in the Epipalaeolithic sites of Helwan, which are located on the east bank of the Nile to the northeast of the Fayum and thus closer to Sinai. However, as mentioned earlier, the sites of Helwan have not been radiocarbon-dated, and the presence of a projectile point which is comparable to the El-Khiam point suggests that Helwan should be much earlier in date than the Epipalaeolithic sites of the Fayum. Therefore, it may be no surprise if the small projectile points have not been found in Helwan. In the light of the trend in the appearance and disappearance of the three types of small projectile points in the Levantine Pottery Neolithic mentioned above, the predominance of tanged and barbed projectile points in the

Fayum suggests that the Fayum assemblage certainly reflects its geographical and chronological proximity to the southern Levant rather than the Egyptian Western Desert, which has not yielded tanged and barbed projectile points in large numbers. It is probable that the Fayum assemblage is earlier in date than the other assemblages in the Western Desert.

As for the second possibility, it must be noted that only one small tanged projectile point has been found *in situ* at Kom K and Kom W respectively (Caton-Thomson and Gardner 1934: 22, 29 and 39), which are surely dated to the second half of the Fayum Neolithic in the middle 5th millennium cal.BC, and that such projectile points have not been found in any layers of Merimde Beni Salama, which are contemporaneous with Kom K and Kom W. It should be assumed that those projectile points are dated much earlier than the second half of the Fayum Neolithic.

On the whole, it is natural to conclude that the Fayum small projectile points under consideration could be dated between the second half of the Fayum Epipalaeolithic and the first half of the Fayum Neolithic in the late 7th and early 6th millennia cal.BC. This conclusion is significant when the circumstances behind the diffusion of Levantine domesticates to the Fayum are considered, because without this material clue, the discussion would keep going around the problem that Levantine domesticates appear suddenly at Kom K and Kom W in the Fayum in the middle 5th millennium cal.BC. Given this material clue, the diffusion of Levantine domesticates to the Fayum can be reconsidered in the context of possibly almost synchronous developments of peculiar projectile points across the southern Levant, Negev, Sinai and northeastern Africa in the late 7th and early 6th millennia cal.BC.

8.7. The spread of Levantine influence to northeastern Africa in the 7th - 6th millennia cal.BC

In that there may have been almost synchronous developments of similar projectile points across the southern Levant, Negev, Sinai and northeastern Africa since no later than the 7th millennium cal.BC, some considerations must be given to the questions as to how and for what reasons these synchronous developments took place and what kind of human behaviour caused the current distribution of the projectile points under consideration.

8.7.1. The timing of the spread of Levantine influence to northeastern Africa

Regarding the timing of the spread of Levantine influence to northeastern Africa, climatic and environmental changes and demographic changes in the southern Levant in the 7th millennium cal.BC may have played a great role. The 7th millennium cal.BC in the Levant has been known as the time of turmoil called 'the PPNB collapse', and this collapse is said to have started around 6900 cal.BC, which marks the end of the Late PPNB period (Rollefson and Köhler-Rollefson 1989). It has been argued that overaggregation of population and overexploitation of natural resources in the central and southern Levant may have caused unprecedented social stress and environmental degradation, leading to the fission and subsequent restructuring of Neolithic communities (Kuijt 2000; Simmons 2000; Bar-Yosef 2003). As mentioned in Chapter 3, it has also been revealed on the basis of various climatic data in the Eastern Mediterranean that there was a remarkable cooling and drying event in the Levant between 6700 cal.BC and 5900 cal.BC, centring around 6200 cal.BC (Robinson *et al.* 2006; Rohling *et al.* 2002; Rohling and Pälike 2005; Rossignol-Strick 1999). The water level of the Dead Sea dropped and fluctuated radically (Migowski *et al.* 2006), and precipitation in the Negev seems to have decreased around this period (Goodfriend 1991). Therefore, it is probable that this cooling and drying event drove people in the southern Levant and adjacent regions to better places like the Nile Delta.

In contrast, such dramatic changes in the size and distribution of occupation sites have not been seen in the archaeological record of northeastern Africa in this period. The sites in the Fayum are actually the only well-studied places which are in close proximity to the southern Levant and are surely dated to the 7th millennium cal.BC, but the Fayum sites are not as large nor as sedentary as contemporaneous southern Levantine sites. Therefore, Bar-Yosef's suggestion that the PPNB collapse could have triggered the dispersal of Levantine people and their subsequent colonisation of the Nile Delta (Bar-Yosef 2003: 122) is presently an unsubstantiated assumption, because no site of the 7th millennium cal.BC has been found there.

If the undated side-notched and tanged projectile points found in Helwan and the Fayum can be dated to the 7th millennium cal.BC, and if they were not locally made in Helwan and the Fayum, then it is possible to argue that Levantine farmer-herders, armed with the Helwan points, came to colonise the Nile Delta and Nile Valley in order to obtain more arable lands or pastures. However, this colonisation assumption is very difficult to support, firstly because no evidence for wheat/barley farming and sheep/goat herding has been found in Merimde Beni Salama and the Fayum before the 6th millennium cal.BC, and secondly because no evidence of conflict and violent death has been found in any part of northeastern Africa in the 7th millennium cal.BC, though such evidence may be buried deeply in the alluvium plain of the Nile Delta and Nile Valley.

Furthermore, as described earlier, the side-notched and tanged projectile points in northeastern Africa are not precise copies of those of the southern Levant and Negev, and are extremely rare at most known sites in northeastern Africa. In the case of the southern Levant and Negev, where both side-notched and unnotched projectile points existed, the reason for their existence may be attributed to a difference in function. In the case of northeastern Africa, by contrast, side-notched and tanged projectile points had never become prevalent despite the assumed assets of side notches, and do not seem to have been an option for functionally different uses. It is suggested that the side-notched and tanged projectile points in northeastern Africa were foreign in origin, and that they were not necessarily selected and evolved because of their functional assets, in comparison with other types of projectile points, but rather were made and used as a kind of novelty item.

8.7.2. The stylistic behaviour of foragers

It is difficult to say why side-notched projectile points were so special unless they were functionally superior. Therefore, stylistic and symbolic aspects of projectile points must be considered for a better understanding of the background to the appearance and development of new types of projectile points in northeastern Africa. An observation that the Helwan points in the southern Levant tended to be made by using translucent chalcedony or other fine-grained materials, which might reflect aesthetic and symbolic concerns (Goring-Morris and Belfer-Cohen 2001: 259), is of particular interest in this context. In addition, based on the fact that about 1000 nearly identical, high quality Helwan points of the Abu Salem type were found at Nahal Lavan 109 in the Negev, it has been argued that there was a workshop of a small group of persons or a single craftsman for the production of the Helwan points (Gopher 1994: 159 and 193). Such an extraordinary concentration of the Helwan points suggests that they were in great demand and something special. It sounds likely that this site may have served as an aggregation locality for exchange and redistribution (Kuijt and Goring-Morris 2002: 385). It is possible that some unknown stylistic properties or symbolic meanings which the Helwan points bore were appreciated in northeastern Africa.

As described in Chapter 4, an ethnological

study has demonstrated that it was not uncommon for projectile points to move over 100 km by exchange as well as through movement of the owner (Wiessner 1983). Although the physical distance between the Negev and Lower Egypt is far more than 100 km, it is possible that projectile points travelled these areas in prehistoric times. Using Wiessner's terms, while the projectile points of the emblemic style would disperse in a limited area in order to solidify the ties between kin groups, the projectile points of the assertive style may possibly disperse beyond the territorial boundary independently of the maker, or the style itself could be adopted in different places as a fashion. Hunters' desire to obtain skilled makers' projectile points, which are believed to enable good hunting, can be regarded as a kind of assertive stylistic behaviour. Therefore, it should be considered that the existence of side-notched and tanged projectile points in northeastern Africa does not necessarily indicate the intrusion of Levantine people, but rather suggests the advent of a new assertive style. In other words, the highly appreciated Helwan points or their style may have somehow been adopted, and thereafter the modified imitation of the Helwan points would have been made and spread sporadically across northeastern Africa.

A similar consideration can be given to the spread of small bifacially-retouched projectile points in northeastern Africa, which would have most likely derived from Levantine Pottery Neolithic projectile points. The much wider spread of the small bifacially-retouched projectile points in larger numbers in northeastern Africa in the late 7th - early 6th millennia cal.BC may suggest that this part of the continent was more densely occupied than before. The so-called extended range of one residential group's economic zone would have overlapped others' extended range more often than before, and the flows of material items as well as technical knowledge, stylistic information and symbolic beliefs could have increased, diverged and became faster, though it is not certain whether interregional residential moves of people were behind such flows.

8.7.3. The territories of Levantine farmer-herders and the boundaries between Levantine farmer-herders and Egyptian foragers

The suggestion regarding the wide spread of common types of small projectile points across the southern Levant, Negev, Sinai and northeastern Africa in the late 7th - early 6th millennia cal.BC still does not answer the questions concerning the territories of southern Levantine farmer-herders and the social boundaries between them and the people in the Negev, Sinai, Nile Delta, and Nile Valley. In other words, the remaining questions are whether and to what extent southern Levantine farmer-herders penetrated into the territories of foragers in these regions, and at which point Levantine domesticates were passed on to local foragers.

Defining sociocultural boundaries between different people by looking at the spatial distribution of diagnostic material cultures is common in ethnology as well as archaeology (*e.g.*, David and Kramer 2001: 168-224). Ethnological studies have also revealed that physical and sociocultural boundaries certainly exist between mobile foragers and sedentary farmer-herders, but that the long physical distance between them is not necessarily the reason for foragers' not introducing farming and herding. In some cases, occasional or frequent contacts between foragers and farmer-herders have resulted in the foragers' adoption of farming-herding products by exchange or introduction of farming and herding, whereas in other cases, such contacts did not lead to the diffusion of farming and herding even though foragers knew such a way of subsistence very well (*e.g.*, Bellwood 2005: 28-42; Headland and Reid 1989; Spielmann and Eder 1994). In addition, as mentioned in Chapter 2, archaeological studies have also revealed that the diffusion of farming and herding across sociocultural boundaries was not always fast and straightforward, like a wave of advance sweeping across large regions. The rates of advance varied in different frontier situations, and a phase of foragers' encounter with a new

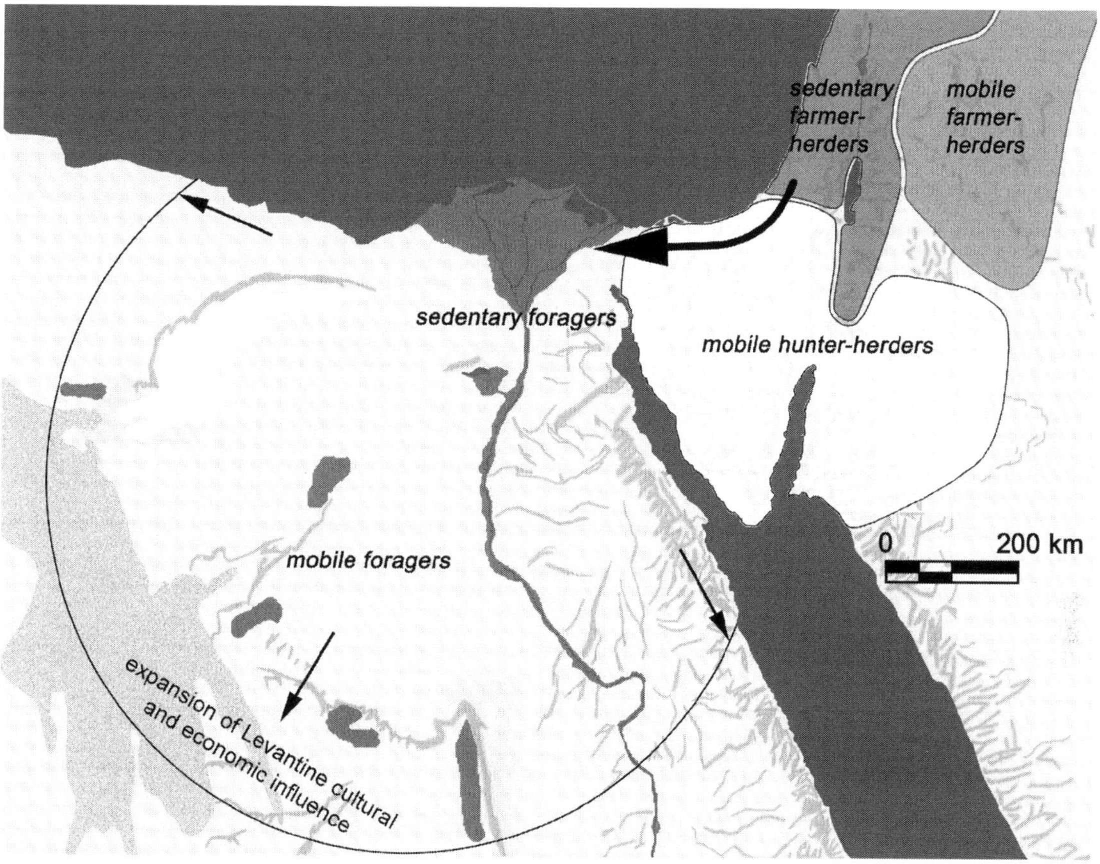

Fig.8.10. The situation of Egypt, Sinai, the Negev and southern Levant in the late 7th - early 6th millennia cal.BC

subsistence before it started to substitute for the existing subsistence tended to last for many centuries or even a millennium (Zvelebil 1986a; 1986b; Zvelebil and Rowley-Conwy 1984).

Based on various archaeological and ecological data, it has been attempted to delineate the territories of farmer-herders, hunter-herders, and foragers in the Levant and adjacent regions during the Pre-Pottery Neolithic and Pottery Neolithic, and to model how they interacted over territorial boundaries (Bar-Yosef 2001; 2003; Bar-Yosef and Meadow 1995; Bar-Yosef and Bar-Yosef Mayer 2002). According to this attempt, during the PPNB, the Negev and northern Sinai are defined as one territory of mobile foragers, whereas southern Jordan and southern Sinai are defined as another territory of mobile foragers, and these foragers actively contacted farmer-herders of the southern Levant in the border areas which are termed interaction zones. The large territories of foragers in the Negev and Sinai intervene between the territory of farmer-herders in the southern Levant and the territory of sedentary foragers in Lower Egypt, but there is no mention of an interaction zone between Sinai and Lower Egypt.

I suggested in Chapter 2 that people in the Negev and Sinai who started sheep/goat herding after the PPNC or Tuwailan may have played an important role as mediators in the diffusion of Levantine wheat and barley as well as sheep and goat to Lower Egypt. However, given the almost synchronous development of similar projectile points across these wide regions for millennia as well as the appearance of peculiar sickle blades in a particular period of the 6th millennium cal.BC in the southern Levant which are comparable to Lower Egyptian Neolithic ones, a further interpretation can be proposed (**Fig.8.10**). That is, even if hunter-herders in the Negev and Sinai played a role not only in relaying the latest information about potential migration destinations in Lower Egypt to farmer-herders in the southern Levant but also in passing on sheep and goat to people on the Red Sea coast of the Egyptian Eastern Desert, it is more probable that a certain groups of the farmer-herders depended on kin linkages outside their territory and migrated to somewhere in Lower Egypt in the early 6th millennium cal.BC, while leapfrogging the Negev and northern Sinai and leaving no sign of their moves there.

The appearance of bifacially-retouched serrated sickle blades in the Neolithic of Lower Egypt and their persistence in the Predynastic of Lower and Middle Egypt, despite their fast disappearance in the southern Levant, can be regarded as a founder's effect, which constrained the subsequent morphological change from what had been a narrowly defined pool of variability in their place of origin. Those Neolithic sickle blades in Lower Egypt seem to suggest that Levantine domesticates and technical knowledge of farming were soon passed onto local foragers in Lower Egypt by the migrants of the Lodian culture in the southern Levant during the first half of the 6th millennium cal.BC. More importantly, the long persistence of such peculiar sickle blades in Lower Egypt suggests that after the middle 6th millennium cal.BC, further inflows of migrants, who should have brought new types of sickle blades or new ideas about making sickle blades from the southern Levant, stopped.

Little evidence for cultural contacts with the southern Levant is known in Lower Egypt in the 5th millennium cal.BC, and it was not until the beginning of the 4th millennium cal.BC that apparent southern Levantine cultural influence started to appear in Lower Egypt (Braun and Van den Brink 2008; Guyot 2008; Levy and Van den Brink 2002; Maczynska 2008; Watrin 1998). In Buto in the western Nile Delta, diagnostic pottery of the Chalcolithic Beersheba-Ghassulian culture in the southern Levant/ northern Negev appeared in the early 4th millennium cal.BC, and made up approximately one third of the total pottery assemblage there. The fact that the pottery under consideration was made of local Nile clay but with remarkable techniques unknown in Egypt suggests that a group of Levantine potters immigrated to Buto (Faltings 2002). Furthermore, unique dwelling structures, which are not known anywhere else in Egypt but are comparable to those of the Chalcolithic Beersheba-Ghassulian culture in the southern Levant/northern Negev, appeared in Maadi, and these suggest that Levantine immigrants settled there (Haltung 2004; Rizkana and Seeher 1989: 49-56). Slightly later, not only the pottery and copper artefacts but also the lithic artefacts like the Canaanean blades of the Early Bronze Age Ia in the southern Levant appeared in Maadi, and bifacially-retouched serrated sickle blades declined there (Rizkana and Seeher 1988: 35-36, 99-101 and pls.73-76). In turn, a limited number of Egyptian products started to appear in many sites in the southern Levant (Braun and Van den Brink 2008; Guyot 2008; Levy and Van den Brink 2002; Maczynska 2008; Watrin 1998). It is interesting to note that the contacts between Lower Egypt and the southern Levant in the 4th millennium cal.BC started from the migration of Levantine people to the habitats of indigenous people in Lower Egypt, and it was followed by the establishment of an exchange relationship. In other words, the contacts were initially not induced by a mutual interest in the acquisition of exotic products.

It is not certain whether such a development of contacts was also the case in the 6th millennium cal.BC, but it is probable that the relationship between the people of Lower Egypt and the southern Levant have not been hostile, and that Levantine people have been allowed to cross the geographical boundaries and to intermingle with people in Lower Egypt in times of some kind of emergency. In the light of the sedimentary record of the Dead Sea, which demonstrates the lowest water level between 6200 and 5600 cal.BC (Migowski *et al.* 2006), it is possible that some people of the Lodian culture resorted to migration at the driest time but stopped migration after the climate in their region became wet again, as suggested by the rapid rise of the Dead Sea water level around 5600 cal.BC onward.

8.8. Concluding remarks

The southward diffusion of the Helwan points from the Levant to northeastern Africa and the colonisation of the Nile Delta by Levantine immigrants in the 8th-7th millennia cal.BC have been argued by Near Eastern archaeologists but have not been demonstrated with sound archaeological evidence. Even in the light of some new finds in northeastern Africa, it is still difficult to argue the direct diffusion of Levantine Helwan points to northeastern Africa and the population movement from the southern Levant to northeastern Africa in this period.

It is certainly surprising that there is no clear evidence of contacts between the southern Levant and the Nile Valley during the Pre-Pottery Neolithic period, given the distance which could easily have been traversed in a matter of days (Kuijt and Goring-Morris 2002: 428). This is one reason why it has been argued that the diffusion of barley farming and sheep herding from the northern Levant to the Nile Delta might have taken place by sea and not by land (Bar-Yosef 2002a: 54-55). However, the sporadic occurrence of the side-notched and tanged projectile points in northeastern Africa seems to indicate that there were some contacts by land but that these contacts were definitely other than colonisation. No matter what kind of contacts, it is probable that some Levantine cultural influence reached at least Helwan no later than the 7th millennium cal.BC. Continual contacts must have become the basis of the diffusion of domesticated wheat/barley and sheep/goat to Lower Egypt, because it is unlikely that the diffusion was realised by only a single contact event in the 6th millennium cal.BC. It is suggested by the side-notched, tanged and often unifacially/bifacially-retouched projectile points found in northeastern Africa that there would probably have been a steady flow of technical knowledge, stylistic information or symbolic beliefs from the southern Levant to northeastern Africa, long before the advent of wheat/barley and sheep/goat in Lower Egypt.

The widespread appearance of small projectile points comparable to Levantine Pottery Neolithic ones in the northern half of the Egyptian Western Desert including the Fayum suggests that socioeconomic contacts across the southern Levant, Negev, Sinai and northeastern Africa became frequent and fast in the late 7th - early 6th millennia cal.BC. Through these contacts and probably the establishment of dense kin networks during this period, information about arable land in Egypt would have accumulated sufficiently on the side of Levantine farmer-herders, and an idea about wheat/barley farming and sheep/goat herding would have been acquired on the side of Egyptian foragers. Levantine farmer-herders would have had little reluctance to migrate, once the information about potential destinations was acquired, and routes were defined following kinship connections. It may be concluded that the diffusion of farming and herding to Egypt was not so unreasonably late and slow as previously discussed, but was probably a consequence of increasing population and expanding kin networks across regions through the 8th - 6th millennia cal.BC, as well as of a contingent cooling and drying event in the 7th millennium cal.BC. It is difficult to know how fast was the diffusion of wheat/barley and sheep/goat to the Fayum after their first arrival somewhere in Lower Egypt, but it can be said that they were within the reach of the Fayum inhabitants no later than the early 6th millennium cal.BC.

9. Synthesis

9.1. Research background and aim

The beginning of farming and herding in human prehistory has been an important research topic in archaeology, but apart from the fact that major domesticates like wheat, barley, sheep and goats have diffused from the Levant to Egypt, the beginning of farming and herding in Egypt has not been sufficiently studied. The Fayum is the region in northern Egypt where the earliest evidence of farming and herding was found by previous researchers in the last century, but the situation in which Levantine domesticates were employed in the Fayum looks different from that in the Levant. Whereas the appearance of sedentary settlements have certainly preceded the beginning of farming and herding in the Levant, no substantial dwellings have been found in the Fayum, even after the appearance of Levantine domesticates. The primary aim of my research is thus to consider when, how and why farming and herding started in Egypt, and special attention was paid to the Fayum in order to achieve this aim. A major question is whether the situation in the Fayum should be explained as a matter of preservation or as a reflection of past reality. If the latter was the case, then it must be explained why Levantine domesticates were introduced to the Fayum and how a farming-herding lifeway without sedentism was realised.

9.2. Research results

9.2.1. Revision of the Early-Middle Holocene chronology of the Fayum

As described in Chapter 3, previous research in the Fayum in the last century has already revealed the basic sequence of cultural development in the Early-Middle Holocene. Holocene human occupation in the Fayum was supposed to have started in the 7th millennium cal.BC, and the culture of this period is designated as Epipalaeolithic. Epipalaeolithic people lived on hunting and fishing, and their culture is characterised by the predominance of microlithic artefacts and a lack of pottery. The next major human occupation in the Fayum was supposed to have started in the middle 6th millennium cal.BC, and the culture of this period is designated as Neolithic. Neolithic people lived on farming and herding as well as hunting and fishing, and their culture is characterised by the appearance of pottery and bifacially-retouched elaborate flint tools. It has been argued on the basis of insufficient data that there was no human habitation in the Fayum around 6000-5400 cal.BC. During this time, a significant change in subsistence and material culture, which is recognised as the transition from the Fayum Epipalaeolithic to Neolithic, took place. This transition has been considered to have occurred due to the abandonment of the Fayum by Epipalaeolithic foragers and the arrival of farmer-herders from outside the Fayum.

However, research in the surrounding regions of the Fayum in the last decades has revealed that there were certainly recurrent climatic and environmental deteriorations in the Early-Middle Holocene but a desiccation event in the first half of the 6th millennium cal.BC was around 6000-5800 cal.BC, as reflected by the abandonment and subsequent reoccupation of human settlements in the Western Desert. Furthermore, recent research in the Western Desert has also found many lithic artefacts which are very similar to those found in the Fayum, and these new finds are radiocarbon-dated to the first half of the 6th millennium cal.BC. In the light of such situations in the surroundings of the Fayum, it is unlikely that the Fayum was uninhabited until 5400 cal.BC. Therefore, it was expected that new field research could find evidence to reduce the chronological gap between the Fayum Epipalaeolithic and Neolithic.

As mentioned in Chapter 3 and Chapter 5, radiocarbon dates obtained by new field research as well as re-calibration of all the radiocarbon dates obtained through past research demonstrate that the Fayum Neolithic is dated to around 5700-4200 cal.BC, whereas the Fayum Epipalaeolithic is dated to around 7100-6000 cal.BC. Although the time span of both cultures must be further attested by more data, it suggests that the break of human habitation in the Fayum in the first half of the 6th millennium cal.BC was shorter than previously believed, and that the blank period corresponds to that known in other parts of the Western Desert.

9.2.2. The origins of the Fayum Neolithic material culture

As described in Chapters 2, 3 and 4, recent research in the Western Desert has found many lithic artefacts which are very similar to those found in the Fayum, and these new finds are radiocarbon-dated to the first half of the 6th millennium cal.BC. In addition, as noted in Chapter 8, the development of research on Neolithic cultures in the Levant has also given more accurate dates to characteristic lithic artefacts which resemble the Fayum ones, thereby making more sound comparisons possible. Furthermore, it has been recognised that some peculiar projectile points were quite widespread from the southern Levant to northeastern Africa since no later than the 7th millennium cal.BC. My research in the field and in museums also found that such peculiar projectile points in the Fayum, which have not drawn much attention from previous researchers, are quite notable and significant in understanding the origins and development of Fayum material culture in the Early-Middle Holocene. Firstly, the Ounan point, which is typical in northeastern Africa in the 8th - 7th millennia cal.BC but has not been explicitly reported in the Fayum, certainly existed in the Fayum. Secondly, bifacially-retouched small projectile points, which are reminiscent of those of the Pre-Pottery Neolithic and Pottery Neolithic cultures in the southern Levant, Negev and Sinai in the 7th - 6th millennia cal.BC, also existed and were numerous in the Fayum. The fact that the sequence of the development of projectile points was almost synchronous in these regions suggests that there were steady flows of technical knowledge, stylistic information and symbolic beliefs across these regions. It is considered that the establishment of such a sociocultural network in this period was definitely the background to the diffusion of farming and herding from the southern Levant to Egypt.

The timing of the advent of farming in the Fayum can be specified by focusing on peculiar sickle blades. Neolithic sickle blades in Lower Egypt are thoroughly bifacially-retouched and deeply and coarsely serrated on a lateral side. Sickle blades which share these characteristics are known only in the Lodian culture of the southern Levant in the early 6th millennium cal.BC, and such sickle blades declined in the southern Levant after this period. Therefore, it is reasonable to consider that the technical knowledge of farming as well as domesticated wheat and barley was certainly diffused by migrants to Lower Egypt no earlier or later than the early 6th millennium cal.BC.

A remaining question is; what was the driving force for the diffusion of farming and herding from the southern Levant to Egypt. Even though the establishment of a sociocultural network across the southern Levant and Egypt no later than the 7th millennium cal.BC is suggested by the spatial distribution of archaeological cultures, this does not necessarily mean that farming and herding should have diffused from the southern Levant to Egypt simultaneously. In the course of sociocultural contacts, there would have been a push factor on the Levantine side or a pull factor on the Egyptian side for the diffusion of farming and herding to take place at a particular time. Field research in the Fayum serves to understand the situation on the recipients' side when the diffusion took place.

9.2.3. Land use and resource scheduling in the Fayum Epipalaeolithic and Neolithic in terms of lithic technological organisation

Field research in the Fayum aimed to understand how Epipalaeolithic and Neolithic people exploited a circumscribed lacustrine environment and adapted their subsistence to changing climatic and environmental situations. The research achieved its aim firstly by surveying the northeastern part of the Fayum Depression and studying the spatial distribution of human occupation loci and resource patches, and secondly by studying lithic artefacts collected at the occupation loci and locating the sources of lithic raw material.

As described in detail in Chapter 5, due to severe surface deflation, the preservation of surface archaeological remains is generally bad, and no evidence of substantial dwellings was found on the surface by the new survey. Nonetheless, there is an apparent pattern in the spatial distribution of Epipalaeolithic and Neolithic remains. They tend to concentrate near past water margins like lakeshores and wadi terraces, suggesting that people's life heavily depended on water and such aquatic resources as marsh plants, fish, and waterfowl. In other words, people were tethered to water margins. The spatial distribution of artefacts such as sickle blades and grinding stones suggests that harvesting and grinding/pounding activities also took place near water margins.

Previous researchers have suggested on the basis of the lack of substantial dwelling remains that Fayum people were nomadic and moved seasonally. However, considering their need to maintain a close link to drinking water and rich aquatic resources in a harsh desert environment, it seems unrealistic that all the people moved their residential bases far away from lakeshores, even temporarily. As discussed in Chapter 3, the seasonality of all the available wild food resources in the Fayum also suggests that there was probably no season of severe food shortage in the year, and hence Fayum people would have had no reason to leave for other remote places in order to look for food. Therefore, it must be understood that the lack of substantial dwellings in the Fayum is probably due to perishable building material and bad preservation, and hence is not the evidence for the absence of sedentism. It must also be considered that a water-tethered life since the Epipalaeolithic period was a good precondition for the introduction of farming and herding in the Fayum.

Although no substantial dwellings were found at the occupation loci which were recorded and investigated through the new survey, dense scatters of lithic artefacts were seen at most occupation loci. These lithic artefacts do not tell how long a locus was actually occupied, but they give a clue as to how Epipalaeolithic and Neolithic people made, used, and discarded tools in relation to their subsistence and residential/mobility strategies.

As described in Chapter 6, the study of lithic artefacts collected at several Epipalaeolithic localities/sites near former lakeshores revealed that the majority of tools were made on flint pebbles which were readily available within easy walking distances from the localities/sites. Flint pebbles were transported to the localities/sites and knapped there, as indicated by collective dumping of lithic debitage products there. Besides the localities/sites near former lakeshores, one interesting Epipalaeolithic remain was found at a place which is far away from the former lakeshores. It is an isolated concentration of lithic artefacts on a wadi terrace close to the northeastern rocky fringe of the Fayum Depression, and is considered to be a watching station where Epipalaeolithic hunters observed game animals while making tools by using flint cobbles scattered in the surroundings. It can be considered that some people routinely took hunting trips to the rocky terrain, whereas the majority of people remained near lakeshores.

On the other hand, as described at length in Chapter 7, the study of lithic artefacts collected at several Neolithic localities/sites near the former lakeshores revealed that the majority of tools were made on flint cobbles which were not readily available around there. Flint cobbles were transported over long distances, which cannot be walked in a day, from the gravelly terrain of the Fayum Depression to the localities/sites near former lakeshores and stockpiled there. A study of the distribution of different types of flint cobbles and cores suggests that there were at least two types of localities/sites. One is a residential base, and another is a task location. It seems that tools were made at residential bases and transported to task locations, or cobbles were transported to task locations and tools were made there according to arising needs. Cobbles tended to be used wastefully at task locations and thoroughly at residential bases. It is considered on the basis of this observation that Fayum Neolithic people principally employed a logistical mobility strategy, while maintaining residential bases in several essential resource patches near water margins and have procured additional resources from remote places by dispatching task persons routinely, rather than moving their residential bases to those places. Since cobble sources are in barren terrain, it is probable that routine visits to the cobble sources were embedded in other activities like pastoral grazing trips.

In summary, despite the lack of substantial dwellings, other circumstantial evidence strongly suggests that the Fayum people through the Epipalaeolithic and Neolithic periods were not nomadic but were tethered to water margins, even though they cannot be called sedentary in a strict sense. A simplistic dichotomy between either nomadic or sedentary does not explain precisely the situation of the Fayum people. As mentioned in Chapter 4, sedentism does not emerge as people move less and less until they do not move at all, and a reduction in movement as a group generally requires increased movement as individuals. Considering the Fayum ecology, which is different from that of the original habitat of Levantine domesticates, it can be said that a farming-herding lifeway in the Fayum Neolithic was probably not possible without the protection of the domesticates from local predators by lakeshore-tethered if not fully sedentary people. On the other hand, it can also be said that increasing dependence on farming and herding was not possible without a constant supply of external resources like flint cobbles for toolmaking, which was enabled by an increase of individual logistical moves.

Given these situations in the Fayum, it is still unclear why Levantine domesticates were introduced when they became available to Fayum inhabitants, even though wild food resources seem to have been constantly available and more cost-efficient than domesticates. As discussed in Chapter 4, according to optimal foraging models, it is assumed that domesticates were added to the diet of Fayum Neolithic people when some of the higher-ranked profitable wild food resources or resource patches became temporarily or perpetually unavailable. This could have been caused by either unusual weather conditions and environmental disturbances, or the loss of access to the higher-ranked profitable resources or resource patches due to population increase and overcrowding in a circumscribed area like the Fayum. Therefore, it is important to put the beginning of farming and herding in the Fayum in a wider geographical and chronological context.

9.3. Contextualising the beginning of farming and herding in the Fayum into the Neolithisation of the Levant and northeastern Africa

As mentioned in Chapter 2 and Chapter 8, a driving force for the diffusion of farming and herding from the southern Levant to Egypt would be climatic and environmental changes in the 7th millennium cal.BC centring around 6200 cal.BC. A particularly important event is probably the southward shift of the Intertropical Convergence Zone, which has reached the southernmost part of the southern Levant during the Early Holocene climatic optimum. The effects of the southward shift of the Intertropical Convergence Zone and the northward shift and subsequent return of the polar front would have been not only the desiccation of the southern Levant, Negev and Sinai, but probably also the transition from a summer and winter rain regime to a winter rain regime in the Negev, Sinai and northern Egypt. This would have enabled winter crops like Levantine wheat and barley to thrive in these regions. In other words, it can be assumed that no matter how close and frequent the sociocultural contacts between the southern Levant and Egypt had been in the Early Holocene, the diffusion of Levantine winter crops could not have occurred before climatic conditions became favourable for them. It was not until the early 6th millennium cal.BC that the diffusion of farming to Egypt became possible.

Previous researchers have asserted that the beginning of farming and herding in Egypt was unreasonably later than that in the Levant, without taking the ecology of Levantine domesticates into account. The possible diffusion of Levantine domesticates and technical knowledge of farming and herding from the southern Levant to Lower Egypt in the early 6th millennium cal.BC suggests that it took place soon after the remarkable climatic and environmental change around 6200 cal.BC. It must be reconsidered that the late beginning of farming in Egypt is definitely not a reflection of Egyptian people's unreasonable reluctance or resistance to adopting a new subsistence for a long time, but would merely have been due to an ecological reason.

On the other hand, farming and herding in the Fayum Neolithic seem to have been minor additions to the major subsistence forms of hunting and fishing for a millennium, and essential tools for farming like sickle blades did not exhibit a notable technological improvement for such a long period. These facts seem to suggest that Fayum Neolithic people passed through the initial phase of encounter with exotic new food resources quickly by knowing their relative profitability in advance and adding them to the diet, but did not immediately place them in a high rank, probably because they had more profitable wild food resources. An intriguing question here is not why Levantine domesticates were added to the diet of Fayum Neolithic people, but rather why those domesticates retained their minor position in the diet for such a long time, without dropping out of the diet. If farming and herding had turned out to be unsuitable in the Fayum environment after an initial attempt, they would have dropped out of the Fayum subsistence. However, as discussed in Chapter 7, Fayum Neolithic people made unprecedented time and labour investments in lithic raw material procurement and toolmaking for a series of new activities, and it is obvious that they kept making special efforts to maximise the yield of farming and herding. Therefore, social reasons for such a situation must be considered.

As described in Chapter 3 and Chapter 4, the social circumstances of the Fayum Neolithic are not well known, and no new information about these aspects of the Fayum Neolithic was obtained in the field. Although competitive aestheticism is assumed in the manner of toolmaking in the Fayum Neolithic, there is no clear archaeological evidence to support the model that socioeconomic competition between ambitious individuals for higher status drove them to produce surplus food to be served on special occasions like feasts in order to attract their followers. Increasing demographic pressure from around the Fayum and growing population/ resource imbalances within the Fayum in the 7th - 6th millennia cal.BC would be more likely reasons for adopting domesticates and attempting to intensify farming and herding.

As described in Chapter 3 and Chapter 5, the number and density of Neolithic localities/sites are much larger and higher than Epipalaeolithic ones, and population increase in the Fayum Neolithic is evident, although how and why it occurred in this period are not certain. As discussed in Chapter 8, it is quite possible that the influx of migrants from the southern Levant to Lower Egypt occurred in the early 6th millennium cal.BC, but their spatial extent and demographic impact on population in Lower Egypt are still unclear and probably small. On the other hand, as mentioned in Chapter 2 and Chapter 8, general population increase in the Egyptian Western Desert in the Early Holocene is attested by the wide distribution of human occupation loci and the fast spread of similar material cultures. The recurrence of depopulation in arid regions and population aggregation in well-watered regions in the Western Desert is also known throughout the Early-Middle Holocene. Therefore, it is likely that such a demographic trend in the Western Desert affected the Fayum to some or a large extent. Even if the Fayum was very rich in wild food resources, and even if the balance between human population size and available food resource amount was maintained well below the carrying capacity of the Fayum in a natural state, inflows of migrants from outside the Fayum must have sooner or later upset this balance, and Fayum inhabitants would have had to increase the carrying capacity of their habitat by producing food. This would be the reason why Fayum inhabitants did not give up farming and herding in spite of the supposed difficulties in taking care of domesticates in the Fayum environment, as described in Chapter 4. Their efforts did not result in the complete replacement of traditional hunting and fishing by farming and herding, and probably as a result of this, farming and herding in the Fayum Neolithic look as if they retained a minor position for such a long time.

9.4. Conclusion

In conclusion, the beginning of farming and herding in the Fayum can be considered as a consequence of human population increase during the Early Holocene climatic optimum and the subsequent population dispersal and aggregation during severe desiccation events in the 7th - 6th millennia cal.BC across the southern Levant, Negev, Sinai and northeastern Africa. The beginning of farming and herding would not have been motivated by socioeconomic competition between ambitious individuals through using surplus food, but by a purely economic need for increasing yields in order to improve the imbalance between human population size and available food resources in a circumscribed lacustrine environment, which may have been caused by population inflows from outside the Fayum. A role played by individuals in adopting and intensifying farming and herding may not be ignored, but should not be overestimated. The development of farming and herding in the Fayum were realised by many generations of hardworking people at the conjuncture of rare climatic events and unprecedented population increases in the Early-Middle Holocene.

References

Adachi, T., 1997. Typological analysis of the arrowheads of the Neolithic Levant, *Aoyama Historical Review* 15, 55-97.

Alexandrowicz, S. W., 1986. Holozäne Molluskengemeinschaften von Qasr el-Sagha, *Mitteilungen des Deutschen Archäologischen Instituts, Abteilung Kairo* 42, 25-34.

Allen, M. J., 1991. Analysing the Landscape: A Geographical Approach to Archaeological Problems, in A. J. Schofield (ed.), *Interpreting Artefact Scatters: Contributions to Ploughzone Archaeology*, Oxbow Books, Oxford, 39-57.

Anderson, P. C., 1999. Experimental Cultivation, Harvest, and Threshing of Wild Cereals: Their Relevance for Interpreting the Use of Epipalaeolithic and Neolithic Artefacts, in P. C. Anderson (ed.), *Prehistory of Agriculture: New Experimental and Ethnographic Approaches*, UCLA Institute of Archaeology, Los Angeles, 118-144.

Anderson, P. C. (ed.), 1999. *Prehistory of Agriculture: New Experimental and Ethnographic Approaches*, UCLA Institute of Archaeology, Los Angeles.

Andrefsky, W., Jr., 1994. Raw material availability and the organization of technology, *American Antiquity* 59/1, 21-34.

Andrefsky, W., Jr., 1998. *Lithics: Macroscopic approaches to analysis*, Cambridge University Press, Cambridge.

Anthony, D. W., 1990. Migration in Archaeology: The Baby and the Bathwater, *American Anthropologist* 92, 895-914.

Anthony, D. W., 1997. Prehistoric migration as social process, in J. Chapman and H. Hamerow (eds.), *Migrations and Invasions in Archaeological Explanation*, Archaeopress, Oxford, 21-32.

Aref, M. A. M., 2003. Classification and depositional environments of Quaternary pedogenic gypsum crusts (gypcrete) from east of the Fayum Depression, Egypt, *Sedimentary Geology* 155, 87-108.

Arnold, J. E., 1993. Labor and the Rise of Complex Hunter-Gatherers, *Journal of Anthropological Archaeology* 12, 75-119.

Arnold, J. E., 1996. The Archaeology of Complex Hunter-Gatherers, *Journal of Archaeological Method and Theory* 3, 77-126.

Arz, H. W., F. Lamy, J. Pätzold, P. J. Müller and M. Prins, 2003. Mediterranean moisture source for an early-Holocene humid period in the northern Red Sea, *Science* 300, 118-122.

Asouti, E., 2006. Beyond the Pre-Pottery Neolithic B interaction sphere, *Journal of World Prehistory* 20, 87-126.

Atta, G. A. K., and W. J. Verheugt, 1992. Chapter 8: Fauna, in H. C. J. van Zon and K. W. Jeanes (eds.), *Environmental Profile Fayoum Governorate, Egypt*, Euroconsult/Darwish Consulting Engineers, Arnhem, 24-32.

Baines, J., and J. Marek, 2000. *Cultural Atlas of Ancient Egypt*, Andromeda Books, Abingdon.

Baird, D., 2001. Explaining technological change from the 7th to the 6th millennium bc in the southern Levant, in I. Caneva, C. Lemorini, D. Zampetti and P. Biagi (eds.), *Beyond Tools: Redefining the PPN Lithic Assemblages of the Levant*, ex oriente, Berlin, 319-331.

Baker, P., and A. Gautier, 1997. Site E71K12 and the Late Palaeolithic Annual Round along the Nile in Upper Egypt, in F. Wendorf and R. Schild (eds.), *A Late Paleolithic Kill-Butchery Camp in Upper Egypt*, Southern Methodist University and Polish Academy of Sciences, 43-56.

Ball, J., 1939. *Contributions to the Geography*

of Egypt, The Survey of Egypt, Cairo.

Bamforth, D. B., 1986. Technological efficiency and tool curation, *American Antiquity* 51/1, 38-50.

Banning, E. B., 2002. *Archaeological Survey*, Kluwer Academic/Plenum Publishers, New York.

Barakat, H., 1990. Plant remains from El Omari, in F. Debono and B. Mortensen (eds.), *El Omari: A Neolithic settlement and other sites in the vicinity of Wadi Hof, Helwan*, Philipp von Zabern, Mainz am Rhein, 109-114.

Barakat, H. N., 2002. Regional pathways to agriculture in Northeast Africa, in F. A. Hassan (ed.), *Droughts, Food and Culture: Ecological change and food security in Africa's later prehistory*, Kluwer Academic/Plenum Publishers, New York, 111-122.

Barakat, H. N., and A. G. Fahmy, 1999. Wild grasses as 'Neolithic' Food Resources in the Eastern Sahara: A Review of Evidence from Egypt, in M. Van der Veen (ed.), *The Exploitation of Plant Resources in Ancient Africa*, Kluwer Academic/Plenum Publishers, New York, 33-46.

Bard, K. A., 1989. Predynastic Settlement Patterns in the Hu-Semaineh Region, Egypt, *Journal of Field Archaeology* 16, 475-478.

Bard, K. A., 2007. *An Introduction to the Archaeology of Ancient Egypt*, Blackwell Publishing, Oxford.

Barich, B. E., 1996. Archaeology of Farafra (Western Desert, Egypt): Settlement patterns and implications for food production in the El Bahr-El Obeiyid Region, in G. Pwiti and R. Soper (eds.), *Aspects of African Archaeology: Papers from the 10th Congress of the Pan African Association for Prehistory and Related Studies*, University of Zimbabwe Publications, Harare, 401-409.

Barich, B. E., and F. A. Hassan, 1987. The Farafra Oasis Archaeological Project (Western Desert, Egypt), *Origini* 8, 117-191.

Barich, B. E., and F. A. Hassan, 2000. A stratified sequence from Wadi el-Obeiyd, Farafra: new data on subsistence and chronology of the Egyptian Western Desert, in L. Krzyzaniak, K. Kroeper and M. Kobusiewicz (eds.), *Recent Research into the Stone Age of Northeastern Africa*, Poznan Archaeological Museum, Poznan, 11-20.

Barich, B., F. A. Hassan and A. Stoppiello, 1996. Farafra Oasis between the Sahara and the Nile, in L. Krzyzaniak, K. Kroeper and M. Kobusiewicz (eds.), *Interregional Contacts in the Later Prehistory of Northeastern Africa*, Poznan Archaeological Museum, Poznan, 71-79.

Barich, B. E., and G. Lucarini, 2002. Archaeology of Farafra Oasis (Western Desert, Egypt): A Survey of the most recent research, *Archéo-Nil* 12, 101-108.

Barich, B. E., and G. Lucarini, 2005. L'interazione pastori/agricoltori e le dinamiche del deserto occidentale egiziano, *Origini* 27, 51-77.

Barich, B. E., and G. Lucarini, 2008. The Nile Valley seen from the oases: The contribution of Farafra, in B. Midant-Reynes and Y. Tristant (eds.), *Egypt at Its Origins 2*, Peeters, Leuven, 569-584.

Barkai, R., 2002. Toward a methodology of Neolithic and Chalcolithic bifacial tool analysis, *Neo-Lithics* 1/02, 3-8.

Barkai, R., 2005. *Flint and Stone Axes as Cultural Markers: Socio-Economic Changes as Reflected in Holocene Flint Industries of the Southern Levant*, ex oriente, Berlin.

Barkai, R., and R. Yerkes, 2008. Stone axes as cultural markers: technological, functional and symbolic changes in bifacial tools during the transition from hunter-gatherers to sedentary agriculturalists in the southern Levant, in L. Longo and N. Skakun (eds.), *'Prehistoric Technology' 40 years later: Functional Studies and the Russian Legacy*, Archaeopress, Oxford, 159-167.

Barker, G., 2003. Transition to Farming and Pastoralism in North Africa, in P. Bellwood and C. Renfrew (eds.), *Examining the farming/language dispersal hypothesis*, McDonald Institute for Archaeological Research, Cambridge, 151-162.

Barker, G., 2006. *The Agricultural Revolution in Prehistory: Why did foragers become farmers?* Oxford University Press, Oxford.

Bar-Yosef, O., 1981a. The Pre-Pottery Neolithic period in the southern Levant, in J. Cauvin and P. Sanlaville (eds.), *Préhistoire du Levant: Chronologie et organisation de l'espace depuis les origines jusqu'au VIe millénaire*, Éditions du CNRS, Paris, 555-569.

Bar-Yosef, O., 1981b. Pre-Pottery Neolithic Sites in Southern Sinai, *Biblical Archaeologist* 45, 9-12.

Bar-Yosef, O., 1984. Seasonality among Neolithic hunter-gatherers in Southern Sinai, in J. Clutton-Brock and C. Grigson (eds.), *Animal and Archaeology 3: Early Herders and Their Flocks*, BAR, Oxford, 145-160.

Bar-Yosef, O., 2001. Lithics and the social geographic configurations identifying Neolithic tribes in the Levant, in I. Caneva, C. Lemorini, D. Zampetti and P. Biagi (eds.), *Beyond Tools: Redefining the PPN Lithic Assemblages of the Levant*, ex oriente, Berlin, 437-448.

Bar-Yosef, O., 2002a. Early Egypt and the Agricultural Dispersals, in H. G. K. Gebel, B. D. Hermansen and C. H. Jensen (eds.), *Magic Practices and Ritual in the Near Eastern Neolithic*, ex oriente, Berlin, 49-65.

Bar-Yosef, O., 2002b. The Role of the Younger Dryas in the Origin of Agriculture in West Asia, in Y. Yasuda (ed.), *The Origins of Pottery and Agriculture*, Roli Books, New Delhi, 39-54.

Bar-Yosef, O., 2003. The Natufian Culture and the Early Neolithic: Social and Economic Trends in Southwestern Asia, in P. Bellwood and C. Renfrew (eds.), *Examining the farming/language dispersal hypothesis*, McDonald Institute for Archaeological Research, Cambridge, 113-126.

Bar-Yosef, O., 2004. Targets of Current Neolithic Research in Southwestern Asia, *Neo-Lithics* 1/04, 24-27.

Bar-Yosef Mayer, D. E., 1997. Neolithic Shell Bead Production in Sinai, *Journal of Archaeological Science* 24/2, 97-111.

Bar-Yosef, O., and D. E. Bar-Yosef Mayer, 2002. Early Neolithic Tribes in the Levant, in W. A. Parkinson (ed.), *The Archaeology of Tribal Societies*, International Monographs in Prehistory, Ann Arbor, 340-371.

Bar-Yosef, O., and A. Belfer-Cohen, 1989. The Levantine PPNB Interaction Sphere, in I. Hershkovitz (ed.), *People and Culture in Change: Symposium on Upper Palaeolithic, Mesolithic and Neolithic Populations of Europe and the Mediterranean Basin*, BAR International, Oxford, 59-72.

Bar-Yosef, O., and A. Belfer-Cohen, 2002. Facing environmental crisis: Societal and cultural changes at the transition from the Younger Dryas to the Holocene in the Levant, in R. T. J. Cappers and S. Bottema (eds.), *The Dawn of Farming in the Near East*, ex oriente, Berlin, 55-66.

Bar-Yosef, O. and R. H. Meadow, 1995. The Origin of Agriculture in the Near East, in T. D. Price and A. B. Gebauer (eds.), *Last Hunters, First Farmers: New perspectives on the prehistoric transition to agriculture*, School of American Research Press, Santa Fe, 39-94.

Beadnell, H. J. L., 1905. *The Topography and Geology of the Fayum Province of Egypt*, National Printing Department, Cairo.

Beck, C., A. K. Taylor, G. T. Jones, C. M. Fadem, C. R. Cook and S. A. Millward, 2002. Rocks are heavy: transport costs and Paleoarchaic quarry behavior in the Great Basin, *Journal of Anthropological Archaeology* 21, 481-507.

Beck, F., and P. Amiet (eds.), 1982. *Archeìologie compareìe: Afrique et Europe occidentale et centrale. Catalogue sommaire illustreì des collections du Museìe des antiquités nationales de Saint-Germain-en-Laye, 1*, Reìunion des museìes nationaux, Paris.

Becker, M., and F. Wendorf, 1993. A Microwear Study of a Late Pleistocene Qadan Assemblage from Southern Egypt, *Journal of Field Archaeology* 20, 389-398.

Bellwood, P., 2005. *First Farmers: The Origin of Agricultural Societies*, Blackwell, Oxford.

Bender, B., 1978. Gatherer-hunter to farmer: A social perspective, *World Archaeology* 10, 204-222.

Bettinger, R. L., 1991. *Hunter-Gatherers: Archaeological and Evolutionary Theory*, Plenum Press, New York.

Bettinger, R. L., 2001. Holocene Hunter-Gatherers, in G. M. Feinman and T. D. Price (eds.), *Archaeology at the Millennium: A Sourcebook*, Kluwer Academic/Plenum Publishers, New York, 137-195.

Bettinger, R. L., 2006. Agriculture, Archaeology, and Human Behavioral Ecology, in D. J. Kennett and B. Winterhalder (eds.), *Behavioral Ecology and the Transition to Agriculture*, University of California Press, Berkeley, 304-322.

Betts, A., 2008. Things to do with sheep and goats: Neolithic hunter-forager-herders in North Arabia, in H. Barnard and W. Wendrich (eds.), *The Archaeology of Mobility: Old World and New World Nomadism*, Cotsen Institute of Archaeology at UCLA, Los Angeles, 25-42.

Binford, L. R., 1978. Dimensional Analysis of Behavior and Site Structure: Learning from an Eskimo Hunting Stand, *American Antiquity* 43/3, 330-361.

Binford, L. R., 1979. Organization and Formation Processes: Looking at curated technologies, *Journal of Anthropological Research* 35, 255-273.

Binford, L. R., 1980. Willow smoke and dogs' tails: hunter-gatherer settlement systems and archaeological site formation, *American Antiquity* 45/1, 4-20.

Binford, L. R., 1982. The Archaeology of Place, *Journal of Anthropological Archaeology* 1, 5-31.

Bintliff, J., 1991. The contribution of an *Annaliste*/structural history approach to archaeology, in J. Bintliff (ed.), *The Annales School and Archaeology*, Leicester University Press, London, 1-33.

Bintliff, J., 2000. The concepts of 'site' and 'offsite' archaeology in surface artefact survey, in M. Pasquinucci and F. Trément (eds.), *Non-Destructive Techniques Applied to Landscape Archaeology*, Oxbow Books, Oxford, 200-215.

Bintliff, J., 2003. Searching for Structure in the Past – or Was it 'One Damn Thing after Another'? in R. A. Bentley and H. D. G. Maschner (eds.), *Complex Systems and Archaeology: Empirical and Theoretical Applications*, The University of Utah Press, Salt Lake City, 79-83.

Bintliff, J., 2004. Time, Structure and Agency: The Annales, Emergent Complexity and Archaeology, in J. Bintliff (ed.), *A Companion to Archaeology*, Blackwell Publishing, Oxford, 174-194.

Bird, D. W., and J. F. O'Connell, 2006. Behavioral Ecology and Archaeology, *Journal of Archaeological Research* 14, 143-188.

Bleed, P., 1986. The optimal design of hunting weapons: maintainability or reliability, *American Antiquity* 51/4, 737-747.

Bliege Bird, R., and E. A. Smith, 2005. Signaling Theory, Strategic Interaction, and Symbolic Capital, *Current Anthropology* 46/2, 221-248.

Bloxam, E., and T. Heldal, 2007. The industrial landscape of the Northern Faiyum Desert as a World Heritage Site: modelling the 'outstanding universal value' of third millennium bc stone quarrying in Egypt, *World Archaeology* 39/3, 305-323.

Boessneck, J., 1969. Osteological differences between sheep (*Ovis aries Linneì*) and goats (*Capra hircus Linneì*), in D. Brothwell and E. Higgs (eds.), *Science in archaeology: a survey of progress and research*, Themes and Hudson, London, 331-358.

Boessneck. J., and A. von den Driesch, 1990. Tierreste aus der vorgeschichtlichen Siedlung von El-Omari bei Heluan/Unterägypten, in F. Debono and B. Mortensen (eds.), *El Omari: A Neolithic settlement and other sites in the vicinity of Wadi Hof, Helwan*, Philipp von Zabern, Mainz am Rhein, 99-107.

Bogucki, P., 1999. *The Origins of Human Society*, Blackwell, Oxford.

Bolten, A., and O. Bubenzer, 2007. Watershed analysis in the Western Desert of Egypt, in O. Bubenzer, A. Bolten and F. Darius (eds.), *Atlas of Cultural and Environmental Change in Arid Africa*, Heinrich Barth Institut, Köln, 22-23.

Bornkamm, R., and H. Kehl, 1990. The plant communities of the Western Desert of Egypt, *Phytocoenologia* 19/2, 149-231.

Boulos, S. T., 1992. Chapter 7: Flora, in H. C. J.

van Zon and K. W. Jeanes (eds.), *Environmental Profile Fayoum Governorate, Egypt*, Euroconsult/Darwish Consulting Engineers, Arnhem, 20-24.

Bousman, C. B., 1993. Hunter-gatherer adaptations, economic risk and tool design, *Lithic Technology* 18, 59-86.

Braun, E., and E. C. M. van den Brink, 2008. Appraising South Levantine-Egyptian interaction: Recent discoveries from Israel and Egypt, in B. Midant-Reynes and Y. Tristant (eds.), *Egypt at Its Origins 2*, Peeters, Leuven, 643-688.

Brewer, D. J., 1989a. A model for resource exploitation in the prehistoric Fayum, in L. Krzyzaniak and M. Kobusiewicz (eds.), *Later Prehistory of the Nile Basin and the Sahara*, Poznan Archaeological Museum, Poznan, 127-137.

Brewer, D. J., 1989b. *Fishermen, Hunters and Herders: Zooarchaeology in the Fayum, Egypt (ca. 8200-5000 bp)*, BAR International, Oxford.

Brézillon, M. N., 1968. *La dénomination des objets de pierre taillée: Matériaux pour un vocabulaire des préhistoriens de langue française*, CNRS, Paris.

Bright, J., A. Ugan and L. Hunsaker, 2002. The effect of handling time on subsistence technology, *World Archaeology* 34/1, 164-181.

Bronk Ramsey, C., 1995. Radiocarbon calibration and analysis of stratigraphy: The OxCal program, *Radiocarbon* 37(2), 425-430.

Bronk Ramsey, C., 2001. Development of the radiocarbon calibration program OxCal, *Radiocarbon* 43(2A), 355-363.

Brookes, I. A., 2003. Geomorphic indicators of Holocene winds in Egypt's Western Desert, *Geomorphology* 56, 155-166.

Bubenzer, O., A. Hilgers and H. Riemer, 2007. Luminescence dating and archaeology of Holocene fluvio-lacustrine sediments of Abu Tartur, Eastern Sahara, *Quaternary Geochronology* 2, 314-321.

Bubenzer, O., and H. Riemer, 2007. Holocene climatic change and human settlement between the central Sahara and the Nile Valley: Archaeological and geomorphological results, *Geoarchaeology* 22/6, 607-620.

Bussemer, S., K. Rögner, T. Mayer and J. Michel, 2006. Gypsum and gypsum crusts (gypcretes) at the rims of the Faiyum Depression (Egypt): Results concerning matter and paleoclimatic conditions, in *Proceedings of the International Conference: Soil and Desertification -Integrated Research for the Sustainable Management of Soils in Drylands, 5-6 May 2006, Hamburg, Germany*, http://www.desertnet.de/proceedings/start.htm.

Butzer, K. W., 1976. *Early Hydraulic Civilization in Egypt: A Study in Cultural Ecology*, University of Chicago Press, Chicago.

Butzer, K. W., 1984. Long-term Nile flood variation and political discontinuities in Pharaonic Egypt, in J. D. Clark and S. A. Brandt (eds.), *From Hunters to Farmers: The Causes and Consequences of Food Production in Africa*, University of California Press, Berkeley, 102-112.

Butzer, K. W., 1998. Late Quaternary problems of the Egyptian Nile: Stratigraphy, environments, prehistory, *Paleorient* 23/2, 151-173.

Byrd, B. F., 1992. The dispersal of food production across the Levant, in A. B. Gebauer and T. D. Price (eds.), *Transition to Agriculture in Prehistory*, Prehistory Press, Madison, 49-61.

Cagle, A., 1994. *University of Washington 1994 Fayum Project: NARCE Report*, The American Research Center in Egypt, http://www.acagle.net/fayum94/narce.html.

Caneva, I., 1970. I crescenti litici del Fayum, *Origini* 4, 161-204.

Cappers, R. T. J., 2006. The reconstruction of agricultural practices in Ancient Egypt: An ethnoarchaeobotanical approach, *Palaeohistoria* 47/48, 429-446.

Cappers, R. T. J., and S. Bottema (eds.), 2002. *The Dawn of Farming in the Near East*, ex oriente, Berlin.

Casey, J., 1998. Just a Formality: The Presence of Fancy Projectile Points in a Basic Tool

Assemblage, in S. Kent (ed.), *Gender in African Prehistory*, AltaMira Press, Walnut Creek, 83-103.

Cashdan, E., 1992. Spatial Organization and Habitat Use, in E. A. Smith and B. Winterhalder (eds.), *Evolutionary Ecology and Human Behavior*, Aldine de Gruyter, New York, 237-266.

Casini, M., 1984. Neolithic and Predynastic in the Fayum, in L. Krzyzaniak and M. Kobusiewicz (eds.), *Origin and Early Development of Food-Producing Cultures in North-Eastern Africa*, Poznan Archaeological Museum, Poznan, 199-204.

Caton-Thompson, G., 1952. *The Kharga Oasis in Prehistory*, The Ashlone Press, London.

Caton-Thompson, G., and E. W. Gardner, 1934. *The Desert Fayum*, The Royal Anthropological Institute of Great Britain and Ireland, London.

Caton-Thompson, G., E. W. Gardner and S. A. Huzayyin, 1937. Lake Moeris: Re-investigations and some comments, *Bulletin de l'Institut Égypte* 19, 243-303.

Cauvin, M. C., 1974. Haches à encoches de Syrie: essai d'interprétation culturelle, *Paléorient* 2/2, 311-322.

Cauvin, J., 2000a. *The Birth of the Gods and the Origins of Agriculture*, Cambridge University Press, Cambridge.

Cauvin, J., 2000b. The Symbolic Foundations of the Neolithic Revolution in the Near East, in I. Kuijt (ed.), *Life in Neolithic Farming Communities: Social Organization, Identity, and Differentiation*, Kluwer Academic/ Plenum Publishers, New York, 235-251.

Chatters, J. C., 1987. Hunter-Gatherer Adaptations and Assemblage Structure, *Journal of Anthropological Archaeology* 6, 336-375.

Cheshier, J., and R. L. Kelly, 2006. Projectile point shape and durability: The effect of thickness: length, *American Antiquity* 71/2, 353-363.

Christenson, A. L., 1997. Side-Notched and Unnotched Arrowpoints: Assessing Functional Differences, in H. Knecht (ed.), *Projectile Technology*, Plenum, New York, 131-142.

Churcher, C. S., 1999a. The Neolithic fauna from archaeological contexts in Dakhleh Oasis, Egypt, in I. Plug (ed.), *Archaeozoology in Africa*, Editions La Pensée Sauvage, Grenoble, 47-54.

Churcher, C. S., 1999b. Holocene Faunas of the Dakhleh Oasis, in C. S. Churcher and A. J. Mills (eds.), *Reports from the Survey of the Dakhleh Oasis, Western Desert of Egypt 1977-1987*, Oxbow Books, Oxford, 133-151.

Churcher, C. S., M. R. Kleindienst and H. P. Schwarcz, 1999. Faunal remains from a Middle Pleistocene lacustrine marl in Dakhleh Oasis, Egypt: palaeoenvironmental reconstructions, *Palaeogeography, Palaeoclimatology, Palaeoecology* 154, 301-312.

Churcher, C. S., M. R. Kleindienst, M. F. Wiseman and M. M. A. McDonald, 2008. The Quaternary Faunas of Dakhleh Oasis, Western Desert of Egypt, in M. F. Wiseman (ed.), *The Oasis Papers 2: Proceedings of the Second International Conference of the Dakhleh Oasis Project*, Oxbow Books, Oxford, 1-24.

Clark, G. A., 1994. Migration as an explanatory concept in Paleolithic archaeology, *Journal of Archaeological Method and Theory* 1/4, 305-343.

Clark, J. D., 1971. A Re-examination of the Evidence for Agricultural Origins in the Nile Valley, *Proceedings of the Prehistoric Society* 37, 34-79.

Clark, J. D., 1980. Human populations and cultural adaptations in the Sahara and Nile during prehistoric times, in M. Williams and H. Faure (eds.) *The Sahara and the Nile: Quaternary Environments and Prehistoric Occupation in Northern Africa*, Balkema, Rotterdam 527-582.

Close, A. E., 1984. Report on Site E-80-1, in F. Wendorf, R. Schild and A. E. Close (eds.), *Cattle-Keepers of the Eastern Sahara: The Neolithic of Bir Kiseiba*, South Methodist University Press, Dallas, 251-297.

Close, A. E., 1990. Living on the edge: Neolithic herders in the eastern Sahara, *Antiquity* 64, 79-96.

Close, A. E., 1992. Holocene Occupation of the Eastern Sahara, in F. Klees and R. Kuper (eds.), *New Light on the Northeast African Past*, Heinrich Barth Institut, Köln, 156-183.

Close, A. E., 1995. Few and far between: early ceramics in North Africa, in W. K. Barnett and J. W. Hoopes (eds.), *The Emergence of Pottery: Technology and Innovation in Ancient Societies*, Smithsonian Institution Press, Washington DC, 23-37.

Close, A. E., 1996a. Carry that weight: The use and transportation of stone tools, *Current Anthropology* 37/3, 545-553.

Close, A. E., 1996b. Plus Ça Change: The Pleistocene-Holocene Transition in Northeast Africa, in L. G. Straus, B. V. Eriksen, J. M. Erlandson and D. R. Yesner (eds.), *Humans at the End of the Ice Age: The Archaeology of the Pleistocene-Holocene Transition*, Plenum Press, New York, 43-60.

Close, A. E., 1999. Distance and decay: an uneasy relationship, *Antiquity* 73, 24-32.

Close, A. E., 2002a. Backed bladelets are a foreign country, in R. G. Elston and S. L. Kuhn (eds.), *Thinking Small: Global Perspectives on Microlithization*, American Anthropological Association, Arlington, 31-44.

Close, A. E., 2002b. Sinai, Sahara, Sahel: The introduction of domestic caprines to Africa, in Jennerstrasse 8 (eds.), *Tides of the Desert: Contributions to the Archaeology and Environmental History of Africa in Honour of Rudolph Kuper*, Heinrich Barth Institut, Köln, 459-469.

Close, A. E., and F. Wendorf, 1992. The Beginnings of Food Production in the Eastern Sahara, in A. B. Gebauer and T. D. Price (eds.), *Transitions to Agriculture in Prehistory*, Prehistory Press, Madison, 63-72.

Cohen, M., 1977. *The Food Crisis in Prehistory: Overpopulation and the Origins of Agriculture*, Yale University Press, New Haven.

Colledge, S., J. Conolly and S. Shennan, 2004. Archaeobotanical Evidence for the Spread of Farming in the Eastern Mediterranean, *Current Anthropology* 45, 35-58.

Cordova, C. E., 2007. *Millennial Landscape Change in Jordan: Geoarchaeology and Cultural Ecology*, The University of Arizona Press, Tucson.

Cowan, C. W., and P. J. Watson (eds.), 1992. *The Origins of Agriculture: An International Perspective*, Smithsonian Institution Press, Washington.

Cremaschi, M., and S. Di Lernia, 1999. Holocene Climatic Changes and Cultural Dynamics in the Libyan Sahara, *African Archaeological Review* 16/4, 210-238.

Currelly, C. T., 1913. *Catalogue Général des Antiquités Égyptiennes du Musée du Caire Nos. 63001-64906: Stone Implements*, Imprimerie de l'Institut Français d'Archéologie Orientale, Le Caire.

Cziesla, E., 1989. Sitra and related sites at the western border of Egypt, in L. Krzyzaniak and M. Kobusiewicz (eds.), *Late Prehistory of the Nile Basin and the Sahara*, Poznan Archaeological Museum, Poznan, 205-214.

Dagnan-Ginter, A., B. Ginter, J. K. Kozlowski, M. Pawlikowski and J. Sliwa, 1984. Excavations in the region of Qasr el-Sagha, 1981: Contribution to the Neolithic period, Middle Kingdom settlement and chronological sequences in the northern Fayum desert, *Mitteilungen des Deutschen Archäologischen Instituts, Abteilung Kairo* 40, 33-102.

Darius, F., and S. Nussbaum, 2007. In search of the bloom: plants as witnesses to the humid past, in O. Bubenzer, A. Bolten and F. Darius (eds.), *Atlas of Cultural and Environmental Change in Arid Africa*, Heinrich Barth Institut, Köln, 78-81.

David, N., and C. Kramer, 2001. *Ethnoarchaeology in Action*, Cambridge University Press, Cambridge.

Dayan, T., E. Tchernov, O. Bar-Yosef and Y. Yom-Tov, 1986. Animal exploitation in Ujrat el-Mehed, a Neolithic site in Southern Sinai, *Paléorient* 12/2, 105-116.

Debono, F., and B. Mortensen, 1990. *El Omari: A Neolithic Settlement and Other Sites in the Vicinity of Wadi Hof, Helwan*, Philipp von Zabern, Mainz am Rhein.

de Morgan, J. J. M., 1896. *Recherches sur les origines de l'Eìgypte: l'age de la pierre et les meìtaux*, Leroux, Paris.

de Morgan, J. J. M., 1926. *La preìhistoire orientale, tome II: L'Eìgypte et l'Afrique du Nord*, Geuthner, Paris.

Dobres, M-A., and C. Hoffman, 1994. Social Agency and the Dynamics of Prehistoric Technology, *Journal of Archaeological Method and Theory* 1, 211-258.

Donahue, R., 1992. Desperately Seeking Ceres: A Critical Examination of Current Models for the Transition to Agriculture in Mediterranean Europe, in A. B. Gebauer and T. D. Price (eds.), *Transitions to Agriculture in Prehistory*, Prehistory Press, Madison, 73-80.

Dorst, J., and P. Dandelot, 1970. *A Field Guide to the Larger Mammals of Africa*, Collins, London.

Ducassou, E., T. Mulder, S. Migeon, E. Gonthier, A. Murat, M. Revel, L. Capotondi, S. M. Bernasconi, J. Mascle and S. Zaragosi, 2008. Nile floods recorded in deep Mediterranean sediments, *Quaternary Research* 70, 382-391.

Dunnell, R. C., and W. S. Dancey, 1983. The Siteless Survey: A Regional Scale Data Collection Strategy, *Advance in Archaeological Method and Theory* 6, 267-287.

Dyson-Hudson, R., and E. A. Smith, 1978, Human Territoriality: An Ecological Reassessment, *American Anthropologist* 80, 21-41.

Eiwanger, J., 1983. Die Entwicklung der vorgeschichtlichen Kultur in Ägypten, in J. Assmann and G. Burkard (eds.), *5000 Jahre Ägypten: Genese und Permanenz Pharaonischer Kunst*, IS Edition, Heidelberg, 61-74.

Eiwanger, J., 1984. *Merimde-Benisalâme I: Die Funde der Urschicht*, Philipp von Zabern, Mainz am Rhein.

Eiwanger, J., 1987. Die Archäologie der späten Vorgeschichte: Bestand und Perspektiven, in J. Assmann and G. Burkard (eds.), *Problems and Priorities in Egyptian Archaeology*, Kegan Paul, London, 81-103.

Eiwanger, J., 1988. *Merimde-Benisalâme II: Die Funde der mittleren Merimdekultur*, Philipp von Zabern, Mainz am Rhein.

Eiwanger, J., 1992. *Merimde-Benisalâme III: Die Funde der jüngeren Merimdekultur*, Philipp von Zabern, Mainz am Rhein.

El-Moslimany, A. P., 1994. Evidence of Early Holocene summer precipitation in the continental Middle East, in O. Bar-Yosef and R. S. Kra (eds.), *Late Quaternary Chronology and Paleoclimates of the Eastern Mediterranean*, Braun-Brumfield, Ann Arbor, 121-130.

Ellis, C. J., 1997. Factors Influencing the Use of Stone Projectile Tips: An Ethnographic Perspective, in H. Knecht (ed.), *Projectile Technology*, Plenum, New York, 37-74.

Fahmy, A. G. E., 2001. Palaeoethnobotanical studies of the Neolithic settlement in Hidden Valley, Farafra Oasis, Egypt, *Vegetation History and Archaeobotany* 10, 235-246.

Fahmy, A. G. E., 2005. Missing plant macro remains as indicators of plant exploitation in Predynastic Egypt, *Vegetation History and Archaeobotany* 14, 287-294.

Faltings, D. A., 2002. The Chronological Frame and Social Structure of Buto in the Fourth Millennium BCE, in E. C. M. van den Brink and T. E. Levy (eds.), *Egypt and the Levant: Interrelations from the 4th through the Early 3rd Millennium B.C.E.*, Leicester University Press, London, 163-170.

Fitzhugh, B., 2001. Risk and Invention in Human Technological Evolution, *Journal of Anthropological Archaeology* 20, 125-167.

Flannery, K., 1973. The Origins of Agriculture, *Annual Review of Anthropology* 2, 271-310.

Fontugne, M., M. Arnold, L. Labeyrie, M. Paterne, S. E. Calvert and J.-C. Duplessy, 1994. Paleoenvironment, sapropel chronology and Nile river discharge during the last 20000 years as indicated by deep-sea sediment record in the Eastern Mediterranean, in O. Bar-Yosef and R. S. Kra (eds.), *Late Quaternary Chronology and Paleoclimates of the Eastern Mediterranean*, Braun-Brumfield, Ann Arbor, 75-88.

Gabriel, B., 1987. Palaeoecological evidence from Neolithic fireplaces in the Sahara, *The*

African Archaeological Review 5, 93-103.

Gabriel, B., 2002. Neolithic Camp Sites in the Sahara: Anticipation of Future Research, in Jennerstrasse 8 (eds.), *Tides of the Desert: Contributions to the Archaeology and Environmental History of Africa in Honour of Rudolph Kuper*, Heinrich Barth Institut, Köln, 27-40.

Galili, E., M. Weinstein-Evron and A. Ronen, 1988. Holocene sea-level changes based on submerged archaeological sites off the northern Carmel coast in Israel, *Quaternary Research* 29, 36-42.

Galili, E., D. Zviely and M. Weinstein-Evron, 2005. Holocene sea-level changes and landscape evolution on the northern Carmel coast (Israel), *Méditerranée* 104, 79-86.

Garcea, E. A. A., 2004. An Alternative Way towards Food Production: The Perspective from the Libyan Sahara, *Journal of World Prehistory* 18/2, 107-154.

Garcea, E. A. A., 2006. Semi-permanent foragers in semi-arid environments of North Africa, *World Archaeology* 38/2, 197-219.

Gardner, E. W., 1932. *Some Lacustrine Mollusca from the Faiyum Depression: A Study in Variation*, L'Institut Français d'Archeiologie Orientale, Cairo.

Garfinkel, Y., 1993. The Yarmukian Culture in Israel, *Paléorient* 19/1, 115-134.

Garfinkel, Y., 1999. *Neolithic and Chalcolithic Pottery of the Southern Levant*, Keterpress Enterprises, Jerusalem.

Garfinkel, Y., 2008. The chronology of the eighth millennium BP, in Y. Garfinkel and D. Dag (eds.), *Neolithic Ashkelon*, Old City Press, Jerusalem.

Garrard, A. N., 1998. Environment and cultural adaptations in the Azraq Basin: 24,000-7,000 BP, in D. O. Henry (ed.), *The Prehistoric Archaeology of Jordan*, Archaeopress, Oxford, 139-148.

Garrard, A., S. Colledge and L. Martin, 1996. The emergence of crop cultivation and caprine herding in the Marginal Zone of the southern Levant, in D. R. Harris (ed.), *The origins and spread of agriculture and pastoralism in Eurasia*, UCL Press, London, 204-226.

Gasse, F., 2000. Hydrological changes in the African tropics since the Last Gracial Maximum, *Quaternary Science Reviews* 19, 189-211.

Gautier, A., 1976a. Freshwater mollusks and mammals from Upper Palaeolithic sites near Idfu and Isna, in F. Wendorf and R. Schild (eds.), *Prehistory of the Nile Valley*, Academic Press, New York, 349-364.

Gautier, A., 1976b. Animal remains from archaeological sites of Terminal Paleolithic to Old Kingdom age in the Fayum, in F. Wendorf and R. Schild (eds.), *Prehistory of the Nile Valley*, Academic Press, New York, 369-381.

Gautier, A., 1978. La faune de vertébrés des sites épipaléolithiques d'Elkab, in P. M. Vermeersch (ed.), *Elkab II: Epipaléolithique de la vallée du Nil égyptien*, Leuven University Press, Leuven, 103-114.

Gautier, A., 1984. Archaeozoology of the Bir Kiseiba region, Eastern Sahara, in F. Wendorf, R. Schild and A. E. Close (eds.), *Cattle-Keepers of the Eastern Sahara: The Neolithic of Bir Kiseiba*, South Methodist University Press, Dallas, 49-72.

Gautier, A., 1988. L'exploitation saisonnière des ressources animales pendant le paléolithique supérieur dans la vallée du Nil égyptien, *Anthropozoologica*, numéro spécial 2, 23-26.

Gautier, A., 1989. A general review of the known prehistoric faunas of the Central Sudanese Nile Valley, in L. Krzyzaniak and M. Kobusiewicz (eds.), *Later Prehistory of the Nile Basin and the Sahara*, Poznan Archaeological Museum, Poznan, 353-357.

Gautier, A., 1993a. The Middle Paleolithic archaeofaunas from Bir Tarfawi (Western Desert, Egypt), in F. Wendorf, R. Schild and A. E. Close (eds.), *Egypt during the Last Interglacial: The Middle Paleolithic of Bir Tarfawi and Bir Sahara East*, Plenum Press, New York, 121-143.

Gautier, A., 1993b. The faunal spectrum of the Middle Paleolithic in Bir Tarfawi (Western Desert, Egypt), in L. Krzyzaniak, M. Kobusiewicz and J. Alexander (eds.), *Environmental Change and Human Culture in the Nile Basin and Northern Africa until the Second Millennium B.C.*, Poznan Archaeological Museum, Poznan, 123-127.

Gautier, A., 2001. The Early to Late Neolithic Archeofaunas from Nabta and Bir Kiseiba, in F. Wendorf and R. Schild (eds.), *Holocene Settlement of the Egyptian Sahara, volume 1: The Archaeology of Nabta Playa*, Kluwer Academic/Plenum Publishers, New York, 609-635.

Gautier, A. 2002. The Evidence for the Earliest Livestock in North Africa: Or adventures with large bovids, ovicaprids, dogs and pigs, in F. A. Hassan (ed.), *Droughts, Food and Culture: Ecological change and food security in Africa's later prehistory*, Kluwer Academic/ Plenum Publishers, New York, 195-207.

Gautier, A., 2007. Animal domestication in North Africa, in M. Bollig, O. Bubenzer, R. Vogelsang and H.-P. Wotzka (eds.), *Aridity, Change and Conflict in Africa*, Heinrich Barth Institut, Köln, 75-89.

Gautier, A., and W. Van Neer, 1989. Animal Remains from the Late Palaeolithic Sequence at Wadi Kubbaniya, in F. Wendorf, R. Schild and A. E. Close (eds.), *The Prehistory of Wadi Kubbaniya, vol.2: Stratigraphy, Paleoeconomy and Environment*, Southern Methodist University Press, Dallas, 119-161.

Gebauer, A. B., and T. D. Price, 1992. Foragers to Farmers: An Introduction, in A. B. Gebauer and T. D. Price (eds.), *Transitions to Agriculture in Prehistory*, Prehistory Press, Madison, 1-10.

Gebauer, A. B., and T. D. Price (eds.), 1992. *Transitions to Agriculture in Prehistory*, Prehistory Press, Madison.

Gebel, H. G. K., 2002. The Neolithic of the Near East: An essay on a 'Polycentric Evolution' and other current research problems, in A. Hausleiter, S. Kerner and B. Müller-Neuhof (eds.), *Material Culture and Mental Spheres*, Ugarit Verlag, Münster, 313-324.

Gebel, H. G. K., 2004. There was no center: The polycentric evolution of the Near Eastern Neolithic, *Neo-Lithics* 1/04, 28-32.

Gehlen, B., K. Kindermann, J. Linstädter and H. Riemer, 2002. The Holocene Occupation of the Eastern Sahara: Regional Chronologies and Supra-regional Developments in Four Areas of the Absolute Desert, in Jennerstrasse 8 (eds.), *Tides of the Desert: Contributions to the Archaeology and Environmental History of Africa in Honour of Rudolph Kuper*, Heinrich Barth Institut, Köln, 85-116.

Gifford-Gonzalez, D., 1991. Bones are not enough: Analogues, Knowledge, and Interpretive Strategies in Zooarchaeology, *Journal of Anthropological Archaeology* 10, 215-254.

Gifford-Gonzalez, D., K. M. Stewart and N. Rybczynski, 1999. Human Activities and Site Formation at Modern Lake Margin Foraging Camps in Kenya, *Journal of Anthropological Archaeology* 18, 397-440.

Gingerich, P. D., 1993. Oligocene age of the Gebel Qatrani Formation, Fayum, Egypt, *Journal of Human Evolution* 24, 207-218.

Ginter, B., and J. K. Kozlowski, 1983. Investigations on Neolithic settlement, in J. K. Kozlowski (ed.), *Qasr el-Sagha 1980*, Panstwowe Wydawnictwo Naukowe, Warszawa, 37-71.

Ginter, B., and J. K. Kozlowski, 1986. Kulturelle und paläoklimatische Sequenz in der Fayum-Depression: eine zusammenfassende Darstellung der Forschungsarbeiten in den Jahren 1979-1981, *Mitteilungen des Deutschen Archäologischen Instituts, Abteilung Kairo* 42, 9-23.

Ginter, B., W. Heflik, J. K. Kozlowski and J. Sliwa, 1980. Excavations in the region of Qasr el-Sagha, 1979: Contribution to the Holocene Geology, the Predynastic and Dynastic settlement in the northern Fayum desert, *Mitteilungen des Deutschen Archäologischen Instituts, Abteilung Kairo* 36, 105-169.

Goldberg, P., 1995. The changing landscape, in T. E. Levy (ed.), *The Archaeology of Society in the Holy Land*, Facts on File, New York, 40-57.

Goldberg, P., and R. I. Macphail, 2006. *Practical and Theoretical Geoarchaeology*, Blackwell, Oxford.

Goodfriend, G. A., 1990. Rainfall in the Negev Desert during the Middle Holocene, based on

^{13}C of organic matter in land snail shells, *Quaternary Research* 34, 186-197.

Goodfriend, G. A., 1991, Holocene trends in ^{18}O in land snail shells from the Negev Desert and their implications for changes in rainfall source areas, *Quaternary Research* 35, 417-426.

Goodfrined, G. A., 1999. Terrestrial stable isotope records of Late Quaternary paleoclimates in the eastern Mediterranean region, *Quaternary Science Reviews* 18, 501-513.

Gopher, A., 1989. Diffusion processes in the Pre-Pottery Neolithic Levant: the case of the Helwan point in I. Hershkovitz (ed.), *People and Culture in Change: Symposium on Upper Palaeolithic, Mesolithic and Neolithic Populations of Europe and the Mediterranean Basin*, BAR International, Oxford, 91-106.

Gopher, A. 1994. *Arrowheads of the Neolithic Levant: A seriation analysis*, Eisenbrauns, Winona Lake.

Gopher, A., 1995. Early pottery-bearing groups in Israel - the Pottery Neolithic period, in T. E. Levy (ed.), *The Archaeology of Society in the Holy Land*, Facts on File, New York, 205-221.

Gopher, A., S. Abbo and S. Lev-Yadun, 2001. The "when", the "where" and the "why" of the Neolithic Revolution in the Levant, *Documenta Praehistorica* 28, 49-61.

Gopher, A., R Barkai and A. Asaf, 2001. Trends in sickle blades production in the Neolithic of the Hula Valley, Israel, in I. Caneva, C. Lemorini, D. Zampetti and P. Biagi (eds.), *Beyond Tools: Redefining the PPN Lithic Assemblages of the Levant*, ex oriente, Berlin, 411-425.

Gopher, A., and R. Gophna, 1993. Cultures of the Eighth and Seventh Millennia BP in the Southern Levant: A Review for the 1990s, *Journal of World Prehistory* 7/3, 297-353.

Gopher, A., N. Goring-Morris and D. Gordon, 1994. Nahal Issaron: The Lithics of the Late PPNB Occupation, in H. G. Gebel and S. K. Kozlowski (eds.), *Neolithic Chipped Stone Industries of the Fertile Crescent*, ex oriente, Berlin, 479-494.

Goring-Morris, A. N., 1987. *At the Edge: Terminal Pleistocene Hunter-Gatherers in the Negev and Sinai*, BAR International, Oxford.

Goring-Morris, A. N., 1991. The Harifian of the Southern Levant, in O. Bar-Yosef and F. R. Villa (eds.), *The Natufian Culture in the Levant*, International Monographs in Prehistory, Ann Arbor, 173-216.

Goring-Morris, A. N., 1993. From foraging to herding in the Negev and Sinai: the early to late Neolithic transition, *Paléorient* 19/1, 65-89.

Goring-Morris, A. N., and A. Belfer-Cohen, 2001. The symbolic realms of utilitarian material culture: the role of lithics, in I. Caneva, C. Lemorini, D. Zampetti and P. Biagi (eds.), *Beyond Tools: Redefining the PPN Lithic Assemblages of the Levant*, ex oriente, Berlin, 257-271.

Goring-Morris, N., and A. Belfer-Cohen, 2002. Symbolic Behaviour from the Epipalaeolithic and Early Neolithic of the Near East: Preliminary Observations on Continuity and Change, in H. G. K. Gebel, B. D. Hermansen and C. H. Jensen (eds.), *Magic Practices and Ritual in the Near Eastern Neolithic*, ex oriente, Berlin, 67-79.

Goring-Morris, N., and P. Goldberg, 1990. Late Quaternary dune incursions in the southern Levant: Archaeology, chronology and palaeoenvironments, *Quaternary International* 5, 115-137.

Goring-Morris, N., and A. Gopher, 1983. Nahal Issaron, a Neolithic settlement in the southern Negev: preliminary report on the excavation in 1980, *Israel Exploration Journal* 33, 149-162.

Goring-Morris, A. N., A. Gopher and S. A. Rosen, 1994. The Neolithic Tuwailan Cortical Knife Industry of the Negev, Israel, in H. G. Gebel and S. K. Kozlowski (eds.), *Neolithic Chipped Stone Industries of the Fertile Crescent*, ex oriente, Berlin, 511-524.

Gould, R. A., 1985. 'Now Let's Invent Agriculture...': A Critical Review of Concepts of Complexity among Hunter-Gatherers, in T. D. Price and J. Brown (eds.), *Prehistoric Hunter-Gatherers: The*

Emergence of Cultural Complexity, Academic Press, Orlando, 427-434.

Gould, R. A., and S. Saggers, 1985. Lithic procurement in Central Australia: A closer look at Binford's idea of embeddedness in archaeology, *American Antiquity* 50/1, 117-136.

Greiss, E. A. M., 1955. Anatomical identification of plant remains and other materials from: 1. El Omari excavations at Helwan from the Neolithic period. 2. The excavations at Helwan from the 1st Dynasty, *Bulletin de l'Institut d'Egypte* XXVI, 227-235.

Greiss, E. A. M., 1957. *Anatomical Identification of Some Ancient Egyptian Plant Materials*, Costa Tsoumas & Co., Cairo.

Gremillion, K. J., 1996. Diffusion and Adoption of Crops in Evolutionary Perspective, *Journal of Anthropological Archaeology* 15, 183-204.

Guyot, F., 2008. The origins of the 'Naqadan Expansion' and the interregional exchange mechanisms between Lower Nubia, Upper and Lower Egypt, the south Levant and north Syria during the first half of the 4th millennium B.C., in B. Midant-Reynes and Y. Tristant (eds.), *Egypt at Its Origins 2*, Peeters, Leuven, 707-740.

Haltung, U., 2004. Rescue excavations in the Predynastic settlement of Maadi, in S. Hendrickx, R. F. Friedman, K. M. Cialowicz and M. Chlodnicki (eds.), *Egypt at Its Origins*, Peeters, Leuven, 337-356.

Hames, R., 1992. Time Allocation, in E. A. Smith and B. Winterhalder (eds.), *Evolutionary Ecology and Human Behavior*, Aldine de Gruyter, New York, 167-201.

Hardy-Smith, T., and P. C. Edwards, 2004. The Garbage Crisis in prehistory: artefact discard patterns at the Early Natufian site of Wadi Hammeh 27 and the origins of household refuse disposal strategies, *Journal of Anthropological Archaeology* 23, 253-289.

Harris, D. R., 1989. An evolutionary continuum of people-plant interaction, in D. R. Harris and G. C. Hillman (eds.), *Foraging and Farming: The Evolution of Plant Exploitation*, Unwin Hyman, London, 11-26.

Harris, D. R. (ed.), 1996. *The Origins and Spread of Agriculture and Pastoralism in Eurasia*, UCL Press, London.

Hassan, F. A., 1974. *The Archaeology of the Dishna Plain, Egypt: A Study of a Late Palaeolithic Settlement*, The Geological Survey of Egypt, Cairo.

Hassan, F. A., 1981. *Demographic Archaeology*, Academic Press, Orlando.

Hassan, F. A., 1984a. Toward a model of agricultural developments in Predynastic Egypt, in L. Krzyzaniak and M. Kobusiewicz (eds.), *Origin and Early Development of Food-Producing Cultures in North-Eastern Africa*, Poznan Archaeological Museum, Poznan, 221-224.

Hassan, F. A., 1984b. Environment and subsistence in Predynastic Egypt, in J. D. Clark and S. A. Brandt (eds.), *From Hunters to Farmers: The Causes and Consequences of Food Production in Africa*, University of California Press, Berkeley, 57-64.

Hassan, F. A., 1985. Radiocarbon Chronology of Neolithic and Predynastic sites in Upper Egypt and the Delta, *The African Archaeological Review* 3, 95-116.

Hassan, F. A., 1986a. Desert Environment and Origins of Agriculture in Egypt, *Norwegian Archaeological Review* 19, 63-76.

Hassan, F. A., 1986b. Holocene Lakes and Prehistoric Settlements of the Western Faiyum, Egypt, *Journal of Archaeological Science* 13, 483-501.

Hassan, F. A., 1988. The Predynastic of Egypt, *Journal of World Prehistory* 2, 135-185.

Hassan, F. A., 1996. Abrupt Holocene climatic events in Africa, in G. Pwiti and R. Soper (eds.), *Aspects of African Archaeology: Papers from the 10th Congress of the Pan African Association for Prehistory and Related Studies*, University of Zimbabwe Publications, Harare, 83-89.

Hassan, F. A., 1997a. Holocene Palaeoclimates of Africa, *African Archaeological Review* 14, 213-230.

Hassan, F. A., 1997b. The dynamics of a riverine civilization: a geoarchaeological perspective on the Nile Valley, Egypt, *World Archaeology* 29/1, 51-74.

Hassan, F. A., 1999. Population Dynamics, in G. Barker (ed.), *Companion Encyclopedia of Archaeology*, Routledge, London, 672-713.

Hassan, F. A., 2002a. Palaeoclimate, Food and Culture Change in Africa: An overview, in F. A. Hassan (ed.), *Droughts, Food and Culture: Ecological change and food security in Africa's later prehistory*, Kluwer Academic/Plenum Publishers, New York, 11-26.

Hassan, F. A., 2002b. Holocene Environmental Change and the Transition to Agriculture in South-west Asia and North-east Africa, in Y. Yasuda (ed.), *The Origins of Pottery and Agriculture*, Roli Books, New Delhi, 55-68.

Hassan, F. A., 2003. Archaeology and Linguistic Diversity in North Africa, in P. Bellwood and C. Renfrew (eds.), *Examining the farming/ language dispersal hypothesis*, McDonald Institute for Archaeological Research, Cambridge, 127-133.

Hassan, F. A., B. E. Barich, M. Mahmoud and M. A. Hemdan, 2001. Holocene Playa Deposits of Farafra Oasis, Egypt, and Their Palaeoclimatic and Geoarchaeological Significance, *Geoarchaeology* 16/1, 29-46.

Hassan, F. A., and G. T. Gross, 1987. Resources and subsistence during the Early Holocene at Siwa Oasis, Northern Egypt, in A. E. Close (ed.), *Prehistory of Arid North Africa: Essays in Honor of Fred Wendorf*, Southern Methodist University Press, Dallas, 85-103.

Hassan, F. A., G. Tassie, R. Flower, M. Hughes and M. Hamden, 2006. Modelling environmental and settlement change in the Fayum, *Egyptian Archaeology: The Bulletin of the Egypt Exploration Society* 29, 37-40.

Hawkes, K., and R. Bliege Bird, 2002. Showing off, handicap signalling, and the evolution of men's work, *Evolutionary Anthropology* 11, 58-67.

Hawkes, K., and J. O'Connell, 1992. On optimal foraging models and subsistence transitions, *Current Anthropology* 33/1, 63-66.

Hayden, B., 1989. From chopper to celt: the evolution of resharpening techniques, in R. Torrence (ed.), *Time, energy and stone tools*, Cambridge University Press, Cambridge, 7-16.

Hayden, B., 1990. Nimrods, Piscators, Pluckers and Planters: The emergence of food production, *Journal of Anthropological Archaeology* 9, 31-69.

Hayden, B., 1992. Models of Domestication, in A. B. Gebauer and T. D. Price (eds.), *Transitions to Agriculture in Prehistory*, Prehistory Press, Madison, 11-19.

Hayden, B., 1995a. A New Overview of Domestication, in T. D. Price and A. B. Gebauer (eds.), *Last Hunters-First Farmers: New Perspectives on the Prehistoric Transitions to Agriculture*, School of American Research Press, Santa Fe, 273-299.

Hayden, B., 1995b. Pathways to Power: Principles for creating socioeconomic inequalities, in T. D. Price and G. M. Feinman (eds.), *Foundations of Social Inequality*, Plenum Press, New York, 15-86.

Hayden, B., 1998. Practical and Prestige Technologies: The evolution of material systems, *Journal of Archaeological Method and Theory* 5, 1-55.

Hayden, B., 2001. Richman, Poorman, Beggarman, Chief: The Dynamics of Social Inequality, in G. M. Feinman and T. D. Price (eds.), *Archaeology at the Millennium: A Sourcebook*, Kluwer Academic/Plenum Publishers, New York, 231-272.

Hayden, B., N. Franco and J. Spafford, 1996. Evaluating Lithic Strategies and Design Criteria in G. H. Odell (ed.), *Stone Tools: Theoretical Insights into Human Prehistory*, Plenum Press, New York, 9-45.

Haynes, C. V., 1987. Holocene Migration Rates of the Sudano-Sahelian Wetting Front, Arba'in Desert, Eastern Sahara, in A. E. Close (ed.), *Prehistory of Arid North Africa: Essays in Honor of Fred Wendorf*, Southern Methodist University Press, Dallas, 69-84.

Haynes, C. V., 2001. Geochronology and Climate Change of the Pleistocene-Holocene Transition in the Darb el Arba'in Desert, Eastern Sahara, *Geoarchaeology* 16/1, 119-141.

Headland, T., and L. A. Reid, 1989. Hunter-Gatherers and Their Neighbors from

Prehistory to the Present, *Current Anthropology* 30/1, 43-66.

Hegmon, M., 1998. Technology, Style, and Social Practices: Archaeological approaches, in M. Stark (ed.), *The Archaeology of Social Boundaries*, Smithsonian Institution Press, Washington, 264-279.

Heldal, T, E. Bloxam, P. Degryse, P. Storemyr and A. Kelany, 2006. Old Kingdom gypsum quarries at Umm es-Sawan, Northern Faiyum Quarry Landscape, Egypt, in *Conservation of Ancient Stone Quarry Landscapes in the Eastern Mediterranean: QuarryScapes First Symposium*, Antalya, 11-14.

Hendrickx, S., 1999. La chronologie de la préhistoire tardive et des débuts de l'histoire de l'Egypte, *Archéo-Nil* 9, 13-81.

Hendrickx, S., and P. Vermeersch, 2000. Prehistory from the Palaeolithic to the Badarian culture (c.700,000-4,000 BC), in I. Shaw (ed.), *The Oxford History of Ancient Egypt*, Oxford University Press, Oxford, 17-43.

Henneberg, M, M. Kobusiewicz, R. Schild and F. Wendorf, 1989. The Early Neolithic, Qarunian burial from the Northern Fayum Desert, in L. Krzyzaniak and M. Kobusiewicz (eds.), *Later Prehistory of the Nile Basin and the Sahara*, Poznan Archaeological Museum, Poznan, 181-196.

Henry, D. O., 1989. *From Foraging to Agriculture: The Levant at the End of the Ice Age*, University of Pennsylvania Press, Philadelphia.

Hershkovitz, I., O. Bar-Yosef and B. Arensburg, 1994. The Pre-Pottery Neolithic populations of south Sinai and their relations to other circum-Mediterranean groups: An anthropological study, *Paléorient* 20/2, 59-84.

Hitchcock, R., and P. Bleed, 1997. Each According to Need and Fashion: Spear and Arrow Use among San Hunters of the Kalahari, in H. Knecht (ed.), *Projectile Technology*, Plenum, New York, 345-368.

Hillman, G. C., 1989. Late Palaeolithic plant foods from Wadi Kubbaniya in Upper Egypt: dietary diversity, infant weaning, and seasonality in a riverine environment, in D. R. Harris and G. C. Hillman (eds.), *Foraging and Farming: The Evolution of Plant Exploitation*, Unwin Hyman, London, 205-239.

Hillman, G. C., E. Madeyska and J. Hather, 1989. Wild plant foods and diet at Late Palaeolithic Wadi Kubbaniya: The evidence from charred remains, in F. Wendorf, R. Schild and A. E. Close (eds.), *The Prehistory of Wadi Kubbaniya, vol.2: Stratigraphy, Paleoeconomy and Environment*, Southern Methodist University Press, Dallas, 162-242.

Hitchcock, R., and P. Bleed, 1997. Each according to need and fashion: Spear and arrow use among San hunters of the Kalahari, in H. Knecht (ed.), *Projectile Technology*, Plenum Press, New York, 345-368.

Hodder, I., 1990. *The Domestication of Europe: Structure and Contingency in Neolithic Societies*, Blackwell, Oxford.

Hole, F., 2003. Centers in the Neolithic? *Neo-Lithics* 2/03, 33-35.

Holmes, D. L., 1989. *The Predynastic Lithic Industries of Upper Egypt: A comparative study of the lithic traditions of Badari, Nagada and Hierakonpolis*, BAR International, Oxford.

Holmes, D. L., 1992a. Analysis and Comparison of Some Prehistoric Projectile Points from Egypt, *University College London Institute of Archaeology Bulletin* 28, 99-131.

Holmes, D. L., 1992b. Archaeological Cultural Resources and Modern Land-use Activities: Some Observations made during a Recent Survey in the Badari Region, Egypt, *Journal of the American Research Center in Egypt* 29, 67-80.

Hope, C. A., 2002. Early and Mid-Holocene Ceramics from Dakhleh Oasis: Traditions and Influences, in R. Friedman (ed.), *Egypt and Nubia: Gifts of the Desert*, British Museum Press, London, 39-61.

Horwitz, L. K., 2003. Temporal and spatial variation in Neolithic caprine exploitation strategies: A case study of fauna from the site of Yiftah'el (Israel), *Paléorient* 29/1, 19-58.

Horwitz, L. K., and P. Ducos, 1998. An investigation into the origins of domestic sheep in the southern Levant, in H. Buitenhuis, L. Bartosiewicz and A. M. Choyke (eds.), *Archaeozoology of the Near East III*, ARC Publication, Groningen, 80-94.

Horwitz, L. K., E. Tchernov, P. Ducos, C. Becker, A. von den Driesch, L. Martin and A. Garrard, 2000. Animal domestication in the southern Levant, *Paléorient* 25/2, 63-80.

Huyge, D., 1998. Egypt's oldest 'art'? The petroglyph of El-Hosh, *Egyptian Archaeology: The Bulletin of the Egypt Exploration Society* 13, 34-36.

Huyge, D., 2002. Dating the El-Hosh rock art, *Egyptian Archaeology: The Bulletin of the Egypt Exploration Society* 20, 34-35.

Huyge, D., A. Watchman, M. De Dapper and E. Marchi, 2001. Dating Egypt's oldest 'art': AMS ^{14}C age determinations of rock varnishes covering petroglyphs at El-Hosh (Upper Egypt), *Antiquity* 75, 68-72.

Huyge, D., M. Aubert, H. Barnard, W. Claes, J. C. Darnell, M. De Dapper, E. Figari, S. Ikram, A. Lebrun-Nélis and I. Therasse, 2007. 'Lascaux along the Nile': Late Pleistocene rock art in Egypt, http://antiquity.ac.uk/ProjGall/huyge/index.html.

Issawi, B., 1976. Geology of the Fayum Depression, in F. Wendorf and R. Schild (eds.), *Prehistory of the Nile Valley*, Academic Press, New York, 151-153.

Jesse, F., 2003. Early ceramics in the Sahara and the Nile Valley, in L. Krzyzaniak, K. Kroeper and M. Kobusiewicz (eds.), *Cultural Markers in the Later Prehistory of Northeastern Africa and Recent Research*, Poznan Archaeological Museum, Poznan, 35-50.

Junker, H., 1928. *Bericht über die von der Akademie der Wissenschaften in Wien nach dem Westdelta entsendete Expedition*, Hölder-Pichler Tempsky A.-G, Wien.

Junker, H., 1930. Vorläufiger Bericht über die Grabung der Akademie der Wissenschaften in Wien auf der neolithischen Siedelung von Merimde-Benisalâme (Westdelta) vom 1. bis 30. März 1929, *Anzeiger Akademie der Wissenschaften in Wien, Philosophisch-historische Klasse* 66, 156-250.

Junker, H., 1931. Vorläufiger Bericht über die zweite Grabung der Akademie der Wissenschaften in Wien auf der vorgeschichtlichen Siedelung von Merimde-Benisalâme vom 7. Februar bis 8. April 1930, *Anzeiger Akademie der Wissenschaften in Wien, Philosophisch-historische Klasse* 67, 21-83.

Junker, H., 1933, Vorbericht über die von der Akademie der Wissenschaften in Wien in Verbindung mit dem Egiptiska Museet in Stockholm unternommenen Grabungen auf der neolithischen Siedelung von Merimde-Benisalâme vom 6. November 1931 bis 20. Jänner 1932, *Anzeiger Akademie der Wissenschaften in Wien, Philosophisch-historische Klasse* 69, 36-100.

Junker, H., 1934. Vorläufiger Bericht über die von der Akademie der Wissenschaften in Wien in Verbindung mit dem Egiptiska Museet in Stockholm unternommenen Grabungen auf der neolithischen Siedelung von Merimde-Benisalâme vom 2. Jänner bis 20. Februar 1933, *Anzeiger Akademie der Wissenschaften in Wien, Philosophisch-historische Klasse* 70, 53-97.

Junker, H., 1935. Vorbericht über die fünfte von der Akademie der Wissenschaften in Wien und dem Egiptiska Museet in Stockholm unternommenen Grabung auf der neolithischen Siedelung von Merimde-Benisalâme vom 13. Februar bis 26. März 1934, *Anzeiger Akademie der Wissenschaften in Wien, Philosophisch-historische Klasse* 71, 118-132.

Junker, H., 1941. Vorbericht über die siebente Grabung der Akademie der Wissenschaften in Wien auf der vorgeschichtlichen Siedelung Merimde-Benisalâme vom 25. Januar bis 4. April 1939, *Anzeiger Akademie der Wissenschaften in Wien, Philosophisch-historische Klasse* 77, 3-25.

Kafafi, Z., 1993. The Yarmoukians in Jordan, *Paléorient* 19/1, 101-114.

Kafafi, Z., 1998. The Late Neolithic in Jordan, in D. O. Henry (ed.), *The Prehistoric Archaeology of Jordan*, Archaeopress, Oxford, 127-138.

Kaplan, H., and K. Hill, 1992. The Evolutionary

Ecology of Food Acquisition, in E. A. Smith and B. Winterhalder (eds.), *Evolutionary Ecology and Human Behavior*, Aldine de Gruyter, New York, 167-201.

Keeley, L. H., 1982. Hafting and retooling: Effects on the archaeological record, *American Antiquity* 47/4, 798-809.

Keeley, L. H., 1988. Hunter-Gatherer Economic Complexity and 'Population Pressure': A Cross-Cultural Analysis, *Journal of Anthropological Archaeology* 7, 373-411.

Keeley, L. H., 1995. Protoagricultural practices among hunter-gatherers, in T. D. Price and A. B. Gebauer (eds.), *Last Hunters, First Farmers: New perspectives on the prehistoric transition to agriculture*, School of American Research Press, Santa Fe, 243-272.

Keeley, L. H., 1999. Use of Plant foods among Hunter-Gatherers: A Cross-cultural Survey, in P. C. Anderson (ed.), *Prehistory of Agriculture: New Experimental and Ethnographic Approaches*, UCLA Institute of Archaeology, Los Angeles, 6-14.

Kelly, R. L., 1988. The three sides of a biface, *American Antiquity* 53/4, 717-734.

Kelly, R. L., 1991. Sedentism, sociopolitical inequality, and resource fluctuations, in S. A. Gregg (ed.), *Between Bands and States*, Southern Illinois University Press, Carbondale, 135-158.

Kelly, R. L., 1992. Mobility/Sedentism: Concepts, Archaeological Measures, and Effects, *Annual Review of Anthropology* 21, 43-66.

Kelly, R. L., 1995. *The Foraging Spectrum: Diversity in Hunter-Gatherer Lifeways*, Smithsonian Institution Press, Washington.

Kelly, R. L., 2000. Elements of a behavioral ecological paradigm for the study of prehistoric hunter-gatherers, in M. B. Schiffer (ed.), *Social Theory in Archaeology*, The University of Utah Press, Salt Lake City, 63-78.

Kent, S., 1993. Variability in Faunal Assemblages: The Influence of Hunting Skill, Sharing, Dogs, and Mode of Cooking on Faunal Remains at a Sedentary Kalahari Community, *Journal of Anthropological Archaeology* 12, 323-385.

Kindermann, K., 2002. Djara: Prehistoric Links between the Desert and the Nile, in Z. Hawass (ed.), *Egyptology at the Dawn of the Twenty-First Century: Proceedings of the Eighth International Congress of Egyptologists Cairo 2000*, American University in Cairo Press, Cairo, 272-279.

Kindermann, K., 2003. Investigations of the Mid-Holocene settlement of Djara (Abu Muhariq Plateau, Western Desert of Egypt), in L. Krzyzaniak, K. Kroeper and M. Kobusiewicz (eds.), *Cultural Markers in the Later Prehistory of Northeastern Africa and Recent Research*, Poznan Archaeological Museum, Poznan, 51-72.

Kindermann, K., 2004. Djara: Excavations and surveys of the 1998-2002 seasons, *Archéo-Nil* 14, 31-50.

Kindermann, K., and O. Bubenzer, 2007. Djara: humans and their environment on the Egyptian limestone plataeu around 8,000 years ago, in O. Bubenzer, A. Bolten and F. Darius (eds.), *Atlas of Cultural and Environmental Change in Arid Africa*, Heinrich Barth Institut, Köln, 26-29.

Kindermann, K., O. Bubenzer, S. Nussbaum, H. Riemer, F. Darius, N. Pöllath and U. Smettan, 2006. Palaeoenvironment and Holocene land use of Djara, Western Desert of Egypt, *Quaternary Science Reviews* 25, 1619-1637.

Klees, F., 1989. Lobo: a contribution to the prehistory of the eastern Sand Sea and the Egyptian oases, in L. Krzyzaniak and M. Kobusiewicz (eds.), *Late Prehistory of the Nile Basin and the Sahara*, Poznan Archaeological Museum, Poznan, 223-231.

Knecht, H., 1997. The History and Development of Projectile Technology Research, in H. Knecht (ed.), *Projectile Technology*, Plenum, New York, 3-35.

Kobusiewicz, M., 1984. Report on Site E-79-4: The Archaeology of El Ghorab Playa, in F. Wendorf, R. Schild and A. E. Close (eds.), 1984. *Cattle-Keepers of the Eastern Sahara: The Neolithic of Bir Kiseiba*, South Methodist University Press, Dallas, 135-164.

Kobusiewicz, M., 1996. Early Holocene Lithic

Industries of Northeastern Africa, in S. K. Kozlowski and H. G. Gebel (eds.), *Neolithic Chipped Stone Industries of the Fertile Cresent, and Their Contemporaries in Adjacent Regions*, ex oriente, Berlin, 23-36.

Kobusiewicz, M., 2003. Neolithic wells of the Western Desert of Egypt, in L. Krzyzaniak, K. Kroeper and M. Kobusiewicz (eds.), *Cultural Markers in the Later Prehistory of Northeastern Africa and Recent Research*, Poznan Archaeological Museum, Poznan, 95-104.

Kohn, M., and S. Mithen, 1999. Handaxes: products of sexual selection? *Antiquity* 73, 518-526.

Kozlowski, J. K., 1983. Proto-Dynastic and Early Dynastic settlement, in J. K. Kozlowski (ed.), *Qasr el-Sagha 1980: Contribution to the Holocene geology, the Predynastic and Dynastic settlements in the northern Fayum desert*, Panstwowe Wydawnictwo Naukowe, Warszawa, 72-79.

Kozlowski, J. K., and B. Ginter, 1989. The Fayum Neolithic in the light of new discoveries, in L. Krzyzaniak and M. Kobusiewicz (eds.), *Later Prehistory of the Nile Basin and the Sahara*, Poznan Archaeological Museum, Poznan, 157-179.

Kozlowski, J. K., and B. Ginter, 1993. Holocene changes in the Fayum: Lake Moeris and the evolution of climate in Northeastern Africa, in L. Krzyzaniak, M. Kobusiewicz and J. Alexander (eds.), *Environmental Change and Human Culture in the Nile Basin and Northern Africa until the Second Millennium B.C.*, Poznan Archaeological Museum, Poznan, 327-336.

Kozlowski, S. K., and O. Aurenche, 2005. *Territories, Boundaries and Cultures in the Neolithic Near East*, Archaeopress, Oxford.

Krzyzaniak, L., 1992. Again on the earliest settlement at Minshat Abu Omar, in E. C. M. van den Brink (ed.), *The Nile Delta in Transition: 4th-3rd Millennium B.C.*, Pinkhas, Tel Aviv, 151-155.

Krzyzaniak, L., 1993. New data on the late prehistoric settlement at Minshat Abu Omar, Eastern Nile Delta, in L. Krzyzaniak, M. Kobusiewicz and J. Alexander (eds.), *Environmental Change and Human Culture in the Nile Basin and Northern Africa until the Second Millennium B.C.*, Poznan Archaeological Museum, Poznan, 321-325.

Kuhn, S. L., 1994. A formal approach to the design and assembly of mobile toolkits, *American Antiquity* 59/3, 426-442.

Kuhn, S. L., and R. G. Elston, 2002. Thinking small globally, in R. G. Elston and S. L. Kuhn (eds.), *Thinking Small: Global Perspectives on Microlithization*, the American Anthropological Association, Arlington, 1-7.

Kuijt, I., 2000. People and Space in Early Agricultural Villages: Exploring Daily Lives, Community Size, and Architecture in the Late Pre-Pottery Neolithic, *Journal of Anthropological Archaeology* 19, 75-102.

Kuijt, I., 2004. Cyprus as a regional Neolithic entity: Do researchers need to revisit the concept of the Levantine PPNB interaction sphere? *Neo-Lithics* 1/04, 8-9.

Kuijt, I., and N. Goring-Morris, 2002. Foraging, Farming, and Social Complexity in the Pre-Pottery Neolithic of the Southern Levant: A Review and Synthesis, *Journal of World Prehistory* 16/4, 361-440.

Kuper, R., 1995. Prehistoric Research in the Southern Libyan Desert: A Brief Account of the B.O.S. Project, *Cahier de Recherches de l'Institut de Papyrologie et d'Égyptologie de Lille* 17, 123-140.

Kuper, R., 1996. Between the Oases and the Nile – Djara: Rohlfs' cave in the Western Desert, in L. Krzyzaniak, K. Kroeper and M. Kobusiewicz (eds.), *Interregional Contacts in the Later Prehistory of Northeastern Africa*, Poznan Archaeological Museum, Poznan, 81-91.

Kuper, R., 2002. Routes and Roots in Egypt's Western Desert: The Early Holocene Resettlement of the Eastern Sahara, in R. Friedman (ed.), *Egypt and Nubia: Gifts of the Desert*, The British Museum Press, London, 1-12.

Kuper, R., 2007. An attempt at structuring the Holocene occupation of the Eastern Sahara, in K. Kroeper, M. Chlodnicki and M.

Kobusiewicz (eds.), *Archaeology of Early Northeastern Africa*, Poznan Archaeological Museum, Poznan, 261-272.

Kuper, R., and S. Kröpelin, 2006. Climate-Controlled Holocene Occupation in the Sahara: Motor of Africa's Evolution, *Science* 313, 803-807.

Kuper, R., W. Möhlig, M. Bollig and O. Bubenzer, 2007. Environmental change and cultural history in northeastern and southwestern Africa, in O. Bubenzer, A. Bolten and F. Darius (eds.), *Atlas of Cultural and Environmental Change in Arid Africa*, Heinrich Barth Institut, Köln, 8-11.

Kweakason, A. P., 2008. Microwear analysis of some artefacts from Archaeological Horizon 5, in Vermeersch, P. M. (ed.), *A Holocene Prehistoric Sequence in the Egyptian Red Sea Area: The Tree Shelter*, Leuven University Press, Leuven, 63-72.

Layton, R., 1999. The human evolutionary time-scale and the transition between hunting and gathering, and farming, in J. Bintliff (ed.), *Structure and Contingency: Evolutionary Processes in Life and Human Society*, Leicester University Press, London, 102-117.

Layton, R., 2003. Agency, Structuration, and Complexity, in R. A. Bentley and H. D. G. Maschner (eds.), *Complex Systems and Archaeology: Empirical and Theoretical Applications*, The University of Utah Press, Salt Lake City, 103-109.

Layton, R., R. Foley and E. Williams, 1991. The Transition between Hunting and Gathering and the Specialized Husbandry of Resources, *Current Anthropology* 32/3, 255-274.

Lee, R., 1968. What hunters do for a living, or how to make out on scarce resources, in R. Lee and I. Devore (eds.), *Man the Hunter*, Aldine, New York, 30-48.

Lemonnier, P., 1992. *Elements for an Anthropology of Technology*, University of Michigan, Ann Arbor.

Lev-Yadun, S., A. Gopher and S. Abbo, 2000. The Cradle of Agriculture, *Science* 288, 1602-1603.

Levy, T. E., and E. C. M. van den Brink, 2002. Interaction Models, Egypt and the Levantine Periphery, in E. C. M. van den Brink and T. E. Levy (eds.), *Egypt and the Levant: Interrelations from the 4th through the Early 3rd Millennium B.C.E.*, Leicester University Press, London, 3-38.

Little, O. H., 1936. Recent geological work in the Faiyum and in the adjoining portion of the Nile Valley, *Bulletin de l'Institut Égypte* 18, 201-240.

Longo, L., 1997. Functional Analysis, in F. Wendorf and R. Schild (eds.), *A Late Paleolithic Kill-Butchery Camp in Upper Egypt*, Southern Methodist University and Polish Academy of Sciences, 43-56.

Lucarini, G., 2007. The use and exploitation of sorghum and wild plants in the Hidden Valley village (Farafra Oasis, Egypt), in K. Kroeper, M. Chlodnicki, and M. Kobusiewicz (eds.), *Archaeology of Earliest Northeastern Africa*, Poznan Archaeological Museum, Poznan, 463-478.

Lupo, K. D., 1995. Hadza Bone Assemblages and Hyena Attrition: An Ethnographic Example of the Influence of Cooking and Mode of Discard on the Intensity of Scavenger Ravaging, *Journal of Anthropological Archaeology* 14, 288-314.

Lupo, K. D., 2006. What Explains the Carcass Field Processing and Transport Decisions of Contemporary Hunter-Gatherers? Measures of Economic Anatomy and Zooarchaeological Skeletal Part Representation, *Journal of Archaeological Method and Theory* 13/1, 19-66.

MacDonald, D. H., and B. S. Hewlett, 1999. Reproductive Interests and Forager Mobility, *Current Anthropology* 40/4, 501-523.

Maczynska, A., 2008. Some remarks on Egyptian-southern Levantine interrelations in the first half of the 4th millennium BC, in B. Midant-Reynes and Y. Tristant (eds.), *Egypt at Its Origins 2*, Peeters, Leuven, 763-781.

Marks, A. E., and T. R. Scott, 1976. Abu Salem: Type Site of the Harifian Industry of the Southern Levant, *Journal of Field Archaeology* 3/1, 43-60.

Marshall, F., and E. Hildebrand, 2002. Cattle before Crops: The Beginnings of Food

Production in Africa, *Journal of World Prehistory* 16/2, 99-143.

Marinova, E., V. Linseele and P. Vermeersch, 2008. Holocene environment and subsistence patterns near the Tree Shelter, Red Sea Mountains, Egypt, *Quaternary Research* 70, 392-397.

Martin, L., 2000. Mammal Remains from the Eastern Jordanian Neolithic and the Nature of Caprine Herding in the Steppe, *Paléorient* 25/2, 87-104.

Mazurowski, R. F., 1994. Flint bolas balls and chopper/chopping tools from Nemrik 9 and Tell M'lefaat, in H. G. Gebel and S. K. Kozlowski (eds.), *Neolithic Chipped Stone Industries of the Fertile Crescent: Proceedings of the First Workshop on PPN Chipped Lithic Industries*, ex oriente, Berlin, 173-188.

McBurney, C. B. M., 1967. *The Haua Fteah (Cyrenaica) and the Stone Age of the South-east Mediterranean*, Cambridge University Press, Cambridge.

McCorriston, J., 2006. Breaking the Rain Barrier and the Tropical Spread of Near Eastern Agriculture into Southern Arabia, in D. J. Kennett and B. Winterhalder (eds.), *Behavioral Ecology and the Transition to Agriculture*, University of California Press, Berkeley, 217-236.

McCorriston, J., and F. Hole, 1991. The ecology of seasonal stress and the origin of agriculture in the Near East, *American Anthropologist* 93, 46-69.

McDonald, M. M. A., 1991a. Origins of the Neolithic in the Nile Valley as seen from Dakhleh Oasis in the Egyptian Western Desert, *Sahara* 4, 41-52.

McDonald, M. M. A., 1991b. Technological organization and sedentism in the Epipalaeolithic of Dakhleh Oasis, Egypt, *African Archaeological Review* 9, 81-109.

McDonald, M. M. A., 1996. Relations between Dakhleh Oasis and the Nile Valley in the Mid-Holocene: A discussion, in L. Krzyzaniak, K. Kroeper and M. Kobusiewicz (eds.), *Interregional Contacts in the Later Prehistory of Northeastern Africa*, Poznan Archaeological Museum, Poznan, 93-99.

McDonald, M. M. A., 1998. Early African Pastoralism: View from Dakhleh Oasis (South Central Egypt), *Journal of Anthropological Archaeology* 17, 124-142.

McDonald, M. M. A., 2001. The Late Prehistoric Radiocarbon Chronology for Dakhleh Oasis within the Wider Environmental and Cultural Setting of the Egyptian Western Desert, in C. Marlow and A. Mills (eds.), *The Oasis Papers 1: The Proceedings of the First Conference of the Dakhleh Oasis Project*, Oxbow Books, Oxford, 26-42.

McDonald, M. M. A., 2003. The Early Holocene Masara A and Masara C Cultural Sub-Units of Dakhleh Oasis, within a Wider Cultural Setting, in G. E. Bowen and C. A. Hope (eds.), *The Oasis Papers 3: Proceedings of the Third International Conference of the Dakhleh Oasis Project*, Oxbow Books, 43-69.

McDonald, M. M. A., 2008. Emerging Social Complexity in the Mid-Holocene Egyptian Western Desert: Site 270 and its Neighbours in South-Eastern Dakhleh Oasis, in M. F. Wiseman (ed.), *The Oasis Papers 2: Proceedings of the Second International Conference of the Dakhleh Oasis Project*, Oxbow Books, Oxford, 83-106.

Menghin, O., 1933a. Die Primitivtypen des Neolithikums von Merimde-Benisalame, *Anzeiger Akademie der Wissenschaften in Wien, Philosophisch-historische Klasse* 69, 83-88.

Menghin, O., 1933b. Paläolithische Funde in der Umgebung von Benisalame, *Anzeiger Akademie der Wissenschaften in Wien, Philosophisch-historische Klasse* 69, 89-97.

Metcalfe, D., and K. R. Barlow, 1992. A model for exploring the optimal trade-off between field processing and transport, *American Anthropologist* 94, 340-356.

Midant-Reynes, B., 2000. *The Prehistory of Egypt: From the First Egyptians to the First Pharaohs*, Blackwell, Oxford.

Migowski, C., M. Stein, S. Prasad, J. F. W. Negendank and A. Agnon, 2006. Holocene climate variability and cultural evolution in the Near East from the Dead Sea sedimentary record, *Quaternary Research* 66, 421-431.

Millett, M., 2000. The comparison of surface and stratified artefact assemblages, in M. Pasquinucci and F. Trément (eds.), *Non-Destructive Techniques Applied to Landscape Archaeology*, Oxbow Books, Oxford, 216-222.

Mithen, S., 1996. *The Prehistory of Mind: A search for the origins of art, religion and science*, Thames and Hudson, London.

Moeyersons, J., P. M. Vermeersch, H. Beeckman and P. Van Peer, 1999. Holocene environmental changes in the Gebel Umm Hammad, Eastern Desert, Egypt, *Geomorphology* 26, 297-312.

Mohamed, A., 2003. *Die Krusten der Ränder der Fayoum Depression: Geomorphologische Untersuchungen*, Dissertation der Fakultät für Geowissenschaften der Ludwig Maximilians Universität München, München.

Mohammed-Ali, A. S., and A. M. Khabir, 2003. The Wavy Line and the Dotted Wavy Line Pottery in the Prehistory of the Central Nile and the Sahara-Sahel Belt, *African Archaeological Review* 20/1, 25-58.

Moore, A. M. T., 1989. The transition from foraging to farming in Southwest Asia: present problems and future directions, in D. R. Harris and G. C. Hillman (eds.), *Foraging and Farming: The Evolution of Plant Exploitation*, Unwin Hyman, London, 620-631.

Moore, A. M. T., and G. C. Hillman, 1992. The Pleistcene to Holocene transition and human economy in Southwest Asia: The impact of the Younger Dryas, *American Antiquity* 57, 482-494.

Mori, K., and Y. Iryu, 2001. Geological Survey, in the Institute of Egyptology at Waseda University (ed.), *Abusir South I*, Kakuzando, Tokyo, 78-81.

Morrow, T. A., 1996. Bigger is better: Comments on Kuhn's formal approach to mobile toolkits, *American Antiquity* 61/3, 581-590.

Morton, A. G. T., 2004. *Archaeological Site Formation: Understanding Lake Margin Contexts*, Archaeopress, Oxford.

Mussi, M., I. Caneva and A. Zarattini, 1984. More on the Terminal Palaeolithic of the Fayum Depression, in L. Krzyzaniak and M. Kobusiewicz (eds.), *Origin and Early Development of Food-Producing Cultures in North-Eastern Africa*, Poznan Archaeological Museum, Poznan, 185-191.

Nadel, D., O. Bar-Yosef and A. Gopher, 1991. Early Neolithic Arrowhead Types in the Southern Levant: A Typological Suggestion, *Paléorient* 17/1, 109-119.

Nelson, M. C., 1991. The Study of Technological Organization, *Archaeological Method and Theory* 3, 57-100.

Nelson, M. C., 1997. Projectile Points: Form, Function, and Design, in H. Knecht (ed.), *Projectile Technology*, Plenum, New York, 371-384.

Nelson, M. C., and H. Lippmeier, 1993. Grinding-tool design as conditioned by land-use pattern, *American Antiquity* 58/2, 286-305.

Nesbitt, M., 2002. When and where did domesticated cereals first occur in southwest Asia? in R. T. J. Cappers and S. Bottema (eds.), *The Dawn of Farming in the Near East*, ex oriente, Berlin, 113-132.

Neumann, K., 1989a. Zur Vegetationsgeschichte der Ostsahara im Holozän: Holzkohlen aus prähistorischen Fundstellen, in R. Kuper (ed.), *Forschungen zur Umweltgeschichte der Ostsahara*, Heinrich Barth Institut, Köln, 13-181.

Neumann, K., 1989b. Holocene vegetation of the Eastern Sahara: charcoal from prehistoric sites, *African Archaeological Review* 7, 97-116.

Nicholson, S. E., 2000. The nature of rainfall variability over Africa on time scales of decades to millennia, *Global and Planetary Change* 26, 137-158.

Nicholson, S. E., and H. Flohn, 1980. African environmental and climatic changes and the general atmospheric circulation in Late Pleistocene and Holocene, *Climate Change* 2, 313-348.

Nicoll, K., 2001. Radiocarbon Chronologies for Prehistoric Human Occupation and Hydroclimatic Change in Egypt and Northern

Sudan, *Geoarchaeology* 16, 47-64.

Nicoll, K., 2004. Recent environmental change and prehistoric human activity in Egypt and Northern Sudan, *Quaternary Science Review* 23, 561-580.

O'Brien, M., and H. Wilson, 1988. A Paradigmatic Shift in the Search for the Origin of Agriculture, *American Anthropologist* 90, 958-965.

O'Connell, J. F., K. Hawkes and N. Blurton Jones, 1988. Hadza hunting, butchering, and bone transport and their archaeological implications, *Journal of Anthropological Research* 44, 113-161.

O'Connor, D., 1997. Ancient Egypt: Egyptological and Anthropological Perspective, in J. Lustig (ed.), *Anthropology and Egyptology: A Developing Dialogue*, Sheffield Academic Press, Sheffield, 13-24.

Odell, G. H., 1996. Economizing Behavior and the Concept of Curation, in G. H. Odell (ed.), *Stone Tools: Theoretical Insights into Human Prehistory*, Plenum Press, New York, 51-80.

Odell, G. H., 2001. Stone Tool Research at the End of the Millennium: Classification, Function, and Behavior, *Journal of Archaeological Research* 9, 45-100.

Odell, G. H., and F. Cowan, 1986. Experiments with Spears and Arrows on Animal Targets, *Journal of Field Archaeology* 13, 195-212.

Osborn, D. J., 1998. *The Mammals of Ancient Egypt*, Aris and Phillips, Warminster.

Pachur, H.-J., 1991. Tethering stones as palaeoenvironmental indicators, *Sahara* 4, 13-32.

Parry, W. J., and R. L. Kelly, 1987. Expedient Core Technology and Sedentism, in J. K. Johnson and C. A. Morrow (eds.), *The Organization of Core Technology*, Westview Press, Boulder, 285-304.

Pawlikowski, M., 1983. The evolution of Lake Moeris in the region of Qasr el-Sagha, in J. K. Kozlowski (ed.), *Qasr el-Sagha 1980: Contribution to the Holocene geology, the Predynastic and Dynastic settlements in the northern Fayum desert*, Panstwowe Wydawnictwo Naukowe, Warszawa, 9-36.

Pazdur, M. F., 1983. Radiocarbon dating of organic samples, in J. K. Kozlowski (ed.), *Qasr el-Sagha 1980: Contribution to the Holocene geology, the Predynastic and Dynastic settlements in the northern Fayum desert*, Panstwowe Wydawnictwo Naukowe, Warszawa, 114-117.

Peltenburg, E., 2004. Cyprus: A regional component of the Levantine PPN, *Neo-Lithics* 1/04, 3-7.

Peters, J., 1990. Late Palaeolithic Ungulate Fauna and Landscape in the Plain of Kom Ombo, *Sahara* 3, 45-52.

Peters, J., 1996. New light on Mesolithic resource scheduling and site inhabitation in Central Sudan, in L. Krzyzaniak, K. Kroeper and M. Kobusiewicz (eds.), *Interregional Contacts in the Later Prehistory of Northeastern Africa*, Poznan Archaeological Museum, Poznan, 381-394.

Peters, J., D. Helmer, A. von den Driesch and S. Segui, 2000. Early animal husbandry in the northern Levant, *Paléorient* 25/2, 27-48.

Peters, J., A. von den Driesch and D. Helmer, 2005. The upper Euphrates-Tigris basin: cradle of agro-pastoralism? in J.-D. Vigne, J. Peters and D. Helmer (eds.), *First Steps of Animal Domestication: New archaeozoological approaches*, Oxbow Books, Oxford, 96-124.

Pfaffenberger, B., 1992. Social Anthropology of Technology, *Annual Review of Anthropology* 21, 491-516.

Price, T. D. (ed.), 2000. *Europe's First Farmers*, Cambridge University Press, Cambridge.

Price, T. D., and A. B. Gebauer, 1995. New Perspectives on the Transition to Agriculture, in T. D. Price and A. B. Gebauer (eds.), *Last Hunters, First Farmers: New perspectives on the prehistoric transition to agriculture*, Santa Fe, 3-19.

Price, T. D., and A. B. Gebauer (eds.), 1995. *Last Hunters-First Farmers: New Perspectives on the Prehistoric Transition to Agriculture*, School of American Research Press, Santa Fe.

Puglisi, S., 1967. Missione per Ricerche Preistoriche in Egitto, *Origini* 1, 301-312.

Quintero, L. A., P. J. Wilke and J. G. Waines,

1997. Pragmatic Studies of Near Eastern Neolithic Sickle Blades, in H. G. K. Gebel, Z. Kafafi and G. O. Rollefson (eds.), *The Prehistory of Jordan II*, ex oriente, Berlin, 263-286.

Rafferty, J., 1985. The Archaeological Record on Sedentariness: Recognition, Development, and Implications, *Advances in Archaeological Method and Theory* 8, 113-156.

Rapp, Jr., G., and C. L. Hill, 1998. *Geoarchaeology: The Earth-Science Approach to Archaeological Interpretation*, Yale University Press, New Haven.

Redding, R., 1988. A General Explanation of Subsistence Change: From Hunting and Gathering to Food Production, *Journal of Anthropological Archaeology* 7, 56-97.

Renfrew, C., and P. Bahn, 2000. *Archaeology: Theories, Methods and Practice*, Thames and Hudson, London.

Richerson, P., R. Boyd and R. L. Bettinger, 2001. Was agriculture impossible during the Pleistocene but mandatory during the Holocene? A climate change hypothesis, *American Antiquity* 66, 387-411.

Riemer, H., 2003. Abu Gerara: Mid-Holocene sites between Djara and Dakhla Oasis (Egypt), in L. Krzyzaniak, K. Kroeper and M. Kobusiewicz (eds.), *Cultural Markers in the Later Prehistory of Northeastern Africa and Recent Research*, Poznan Archaeological Museum, Poznan, 73-93.

Riemer, H., 2005. Pastoralism and the 'absolute' desert: A view from the southern Great Sand Sea, Egypt, in B. E. Barich, T. Tillet and K. H. Striedter (eds.), *Hunters vs. Pastoralists in the Sahara: Material Culture and Symbolic Aspects*, Archaeopress, Oxford, 57-65.

Riemer, H., 2006. Archaeology and environment of the Western Desert of Egypt: 14C-based human occupation history as an archive for Holocene palaeoclimatic reconstruction, in S. A. A. Youssef (ed.), *Geology of the Tethys: Proceedings of the First International Conference on the Geology of the Tethys*, Geology Department, Faculty of Science, Cairo University, Giza, 553-564.

Riemer, H., 2007a. Out of Dakhla: Cultural diversity and mobility between the Egyptian Oases and the Great Sand Sea during the Holocene humid phase, in K. Kroeper, M. Chlodnicki and M. Kobusiewicz (eds.), *Archaeology of Earliest Northeastern Africa*, Poznan Archaeological Museum, Poznan, 491-526.

Riemer, H., 2007b. When hunters started herding: Pastro-foragers and the complexity of Holocene economic change in the Western Desert of Egypt, in M. Bollig, O. Bubenzer, R. Vogelsang and H.-P. Wotzka (eds.), *Aridity, Change and Conflict in Africa*, Heinrich Barth Institut, Köln, 105-144.

Riemer, H., K. Kindermann and S. Eickelkamp, 2004. Dating and production technique of Ounan points in the Eastern Sahara: New archaeological evidence from Abu Tartur, Western Desert of Egypt, *Nyame Akuma* 61, 10-16.

Riemer, H., and K. Kindermann, 2008. Contacts between the oasis and the Nile: A résumé of the Abu Muhariq plateau survey 1995-2002, in B. Midant-Reynes and Y. Tristant (eds.), *Egypt at Its Origins 2*, Peeters, Leuven, 609-633.

Riemer, H., and P. Schönfeld, 2007. The prehistoric pottery of Abu Tartur, Western Desert of Egypt, in K. Kroeper, M. Chlodnicki and M. Kobusiewicz (eds.), *Archaeology of Earliest Northeastern Africa*, Poznan Archaeological Museum, Poznan, 335-354.

Rindos, D., 1980. Symbiosis, Instability, and the Origin and Spread of Agriculture: A New Model, *Current Anthropology* 21, 751-772.

Rindos, D., 1984. *The Origins of Agriculture: An Evolutionary Perspective*, Academic Press, Orlando.

Rizkana, I., and J. Seeher, 1987. *Maadi I: The Pottery of the Predynastic Settlement*, Philipp von Zabern, Mainz am Rhein.

Rizkana, I., and J. Seeher, 1988. *Maadi II: The Lithic Industries of the Predynastic Settlement*, Philipp von Zabern, Mainz am Rhein.

Rizkana, I., and J. Seeher, 1988. *Maadi III: The Non-lithic Small Finds and the Structural Remains of the Predynastic Settlement*,

Philipp von Zabern, Mainz am Rhein.

Robinson, S. A., S. Black, B. W. Sellwood and P. J. Valdes, 2006. A review of palaeoclimates and palaeoenvironments in the Levant and Eastern Mediterranean from 25,000 to 5000 years BP: setting the environmental background for the evolution of human civilisation, *Quaternary Science Reviews* 25, 1517-1541.

Rohling, E., J., Casford, R. Abu-Zied, S. Cooke, D. Mercone, J. Thompson, I. Croudace, F. J. Jorissen, H. Brinkhuis, J. Kallmeyer and G. Wefer, 2002. Rapid Holocene Climate Changes in the Eastern Mediterranean, in F. A. Hassan (ed.), *Droughts, Food and Culture: Ecological change and food security in Africa's later prehistory*, Kluwer Academic/ Plenum Publishers, New York, 35-46.

Rohling, E. J., and H. Pälike, 2005. Centennial-scale climate cooling with a sudden cold event around 8,200 years ago, *Nature* 434, 975-979.

Rollefson, G. O., and H. G. K. Gebel, 2004. Short note on a 4ICAANE workshop held in Berlin, 1-2 April 2004, *Neo-Lithics* 1/04, 21-22.

Rollefson, G. O., and I. Köhler-Rollefson, 1989. The Collapse of the Early Neolithic Settlements in the Southern Levant, in I. Hershkovitz (ed.), *People and Culture in Change: Symposium on Upper Palaeolithic, Mesolithic and Neolithic Populations of Europe and the Mediterranean Basin*, BAR International, Oxford, 73-89.

Rollefson, G. O., and I. Köhler-Rollefson, 1993. PPNC adaptations in the first half of the 6th millennium B.C., *Paléorient* 19/1, 33-42.

Ronen, A., S. Milstein, M. Lamdan, J. C. Vogel, H. K. Mienis and S. Ilani, 2001. Nahal Reuel, a MPPNB site in the Negev, Israel, *Quartär* 51/52, 115-156.

Rosen, S. A., 1988. Notes on the Origins of Pastoral Nomadism: A Case Study from the Negev and Sinai, *Current Anthropology* 29, 498-506.

Rosen, S. A., 1997. *Lithics after the Stone Age: A Handbook of Stone Tools from the Levant*, Altamira Press, Walnut Creek.

Rosen, S. A., 2002. The Evolution of Pastoral Nomadic Systems in the Southern Levantine Periphery, in E. van den Brink and E. Yannai (eds.), *In Quest of Ancient Settlements and Landscapes: Archaeological Studies in honour of Ram Gophna*, Ramot Publishing, Tel Aviv, 23-44.

Rosen, S. A., 2008a. Desert pastoral nomadism in the *longue durée*, in H. Barnard and W. Wendrich (eds.), *The Archaeology of Mobility: Old World and New World Nomadism*, Cotsen Institute of Archaeology at UCLA, Los Angeles, 115-140.

Rosen, S. A., 2008b. Desert Landscapes in Archaeology: A Case Study from the Negev, in B. David and J. Thomas (eds.), *Handbook of Landscape Archaeology*, Berg, Oxford, 409-423.

Rosen, S. A., A. B. Savinetsky, Y. Plakht, N. K. Kisseleva, B. F. Khassanov, A. M. Pereladov and M. Haiman, 2005. Dung in the Desert: Preliminary Results of the Negev Holocene Ecology Project, *Current Anthropology* 46/ 2, 317-327.

Rosenberg, M., 1990. The Mother of Invention: Evolutionary Theory, Territoriality, and the Origins of Agriculture, *American Anthropologist* 92, 399-415.

Rosenberg, M., 1998. Cheating at Musical Chairs: Territoriality and Sedentism in an Evolutionary Context, *Current Anthropology* 39, 653-681.

Rossignol-Strick, M., 1999. The Holocene climatic optimum and pollen records of sapropel 1 in the eastern Mediterranean, 9000-6000 BP, *Quaternary Science Reviews* 18, 515-530.

Rossignol-Strick, M., 2002. Holocene Climatic Changes in the Eastern Mediterranean and the Spread of Food Production from Southwest Asia to Egypt, in F. A. Hassan (ed.), *Droughts, Food and Culture: Ecological change and food security in Africa's later prehistory*, Kluwer Academic/Plenum Publishers, New York, 157-169.

Sahlins, M., 1972. *Stone Age Economics*, Aldine, New York.

Said, R., 1990. Chapter 24: Cenozoic, in R. Said (ed.), *The Geology of Egypt*, A.A.Balkema, Rotterdam, 451-486.

Said, R., 1993. *The River Nile: Geology, Hydrology and Utilization*, Pergamon Press, Oxford.

Said, R., C. C. Albritton, F. Wendorf, R. Schild and M. Kobusiewicz, 1970. A Preliminary Report on the Holocene Geology and Archaeology of the Northern Fayum Desert, http://www.lib.ttu/playa/text/playa6.htm.

Said, R., C. C. Albritton, F. Wendorf, R. Schild and M. Kobusiewicz, 1972. Remarks on the Holocene Geology and Archaeology of Northern Fayum Desert, *Archaeologia Polona* 13, 7-22.

Sandford, K. S., and W. J. Arkell, 1929. *Paleolithic man and the Nile-Faiyum divide: A Study of the Region during Pliocene and Pleistocene times*, The University of Chicago Press, Chicago.

Schepers, M., R. Cappers, and I. Heijen, 2006. Neolithische graanopslag in de Fayum, *Paleo-Aktueel* 17, 55-62.

Schiffer, M. B., 1976. *Behavioral Archaeology*, Academic Press, New York.

Schild, R., M. Chemielewska and H. Wieckowska, 1968. The Arkinian and Shamarkian Industries, in F. Wendorf (ed.), *The Prehistory of Nubia, Volume II*, South Methodist University Press, Dallas, 651-767.

Schild, R., and F. Wendorf, 2002. Palaeo-ecologic and Palaeo-climatic Background to Socio-economic Changes in the South Western Desert of Egypt, in R. Friedman (ed.), *Egypt and Nubia: Gifts of the Desert*, The British Museum Press, London, 21-27.

Schmidt, K., 1980. Paläolithische Funde aus Merimde-Benisalame, *Mitteilungen des Deutschen Archäologischen Instituts, Abteilung Kairo* 36, 411-435.

Schmidt, K., 1993. Comments to the lithic industry of the Buto-Maadi culture in Lower Egypt, in L. Krzyzaniak, M. Kobusiewicz and J. Alexander (eds.), *Environmental Change and Human Culture in the Nile Basin and Northern Africa until the Second Millennium B.C.*, Poznan Archaeological Museum, Poznan, 267-277.

Schmidt, K., 1996. Helwan in Egypt - a PPN site? in S. K. Kozlowski and H. G. K. Gebel (eds.), *Neolithic Chipped Stone Industries of the Fertile Crescent, and Their Contemporaries in Adjacent Regions*, ex oriente, Berlin, 127-135.

Seton-Karr, H. W., 1904. Fayoom Flint Implements, *Annales du Service des Antiquites de l'Egypte* 5, 145-186.

Seton-Karr, H. W., 1905. Discovery of a Neolithic settlement in the Western Desert North of the Fayoum, *Annales du Service des Antiquites de l'Egypte* 6, 185-187.

Sherratt, A., 1997. Climatic cycles and behavioural revolutions: the emergence of modern humans and the beginning of farming, *Antiquity* 71, 271-287.

Shirai, N., *in press*. A Missing Chapter of *THE DESERT FAYUM*: Fayum prehistoric lithic artefact collection in the Allard Pierson Museum, Amsterdam, *Archéo-Nil*.

Shott, M. J., 1986. Technological organization and settlement mobility: an ethnographic examination, *Journal of Anthropological Research* 42/1, 15-51.

Shott, M. J., 1996. An exegesis of the curation concept, *Journal of Anthropological Research* 52/3, 259-280.

Simmons, A. H., 1997. Ecological Changes during the Late Neolithic in Jordan: A Case Study, in H. G. K. Gebel, Z. Kafafi and G. O. Rollefson (eds.), *The Prehistory of Jordan II: Perspectives from 1997*, ex oriente, Berlin, 309-318.

Simmons, A. H., 2000. Villages on the Edge: Regional Settlement Change and the End of the Levantine Pre-Pottery Neolithic, in I. Kuijt (ed.), *Life in Neolithic Farming Communities: Social Organization, Identity, and Differentiation*, Kluwer Academic/Plenum Publishers, New York, 211-230.

Simmons, A. H., and R. D. Mandel, 1986. *Prehistoric Occupation of a Marginal Environment: An Archaeological Survey near Kharga Oasis in the Western Desert of Egypt*, BAR, Oxford.

Simms, S. R., and K. W. Russell, 1997. Bedouin Hand Harvesting of Wheat and Barley: Implications for Early Cultivation in Southwestern Asia, *Current Anthropology* 38/

4, 696-702.

Sinclair, A., 1990. Technology as Phenotype? An extended look at Time, Energy and Stone Tools, *Archaeological Review from Cambridge* 9/1, 71-81.

Sinclair, A., 1995. The technique as a symbol in Late Glacial Europe, *World Archaeology* 27/1, 50-62.

Sinclair, A., 2000. Constellations of Knowledge: Human agency and material affordance in lithic technology, in M-A. Dobres and J. Robb (eds.), *Agency in Archaeology*, Routledge, London, 196-212.

Sinclair, P., T. Shaw and B. Andah, 1993. Introduction, in T. Shaw, P. Sinclair, B. Andah and A. Okpoko (eds.), *The Archaeology of Africa: Food, Metals and Towns*, Routledge, London, 1-31.

Smith, A. B., 1989. The Near Eastern connection: Early to Mid-Holocene relations between North Africa and the Levant, in L. Krzyzaniak and M. Kobusiewicz (eds.), *Late Prehistory of the Nile Basin and the Sahara*, Poznan Archaeological Museum, Poznan, 69-77.

Smith, A. B., 1996. The Near Eastern connection II: cultural contacts with the Nile Delta and the Sahara, in L. Krzyzaniak, K. Kroeper and M. Kobusiewicz (eds.), *Interregional Contacts in the Later Prehistory of Northeastern Africa*, Poznan Archaeological Museum, Poznan, 29-35.

Smith, A. B., 2005. The concepts of 'Neolithic' and 'Neolithisation' for Africa? *Before Farming* 2005/1, 29-34.

Smith, B. D., 2001. Low-Level Food Production, *Journal of Archaeological Research* 9/1, 1-43.

Smith, E. A., and B. Winterhalder, 1992. Natural Selection and Decision-Making: Some Fundamental Principles, in E. A. Smith and B. Winterhalder (eds.), *Evolutionary Ecology and Human Behavior*, Aldine de Gruyter, New York, 25-60.

Smith, E. A., R. Bliege Bird and D. W. Bird, 2003. The benefits of costly signalling: Meriam turtle hunters, *Behavioral Ecology* 14/1, 116-126.

Smith, J. R., R. Giegengack, H. P. Schwarcz, M. M. A. McDonald, M. R. Kleindienst, A. L. Hawkins and C. S. Churcher, 2004. A Reconstruction of Quaternary Pluvial Environments and Human Occupations Using Stratigraphy and Geochronology of Fossil-Spring Tufas, Kharga Oasis, Egypt, *Geoarchaeology* 19/5, 407-439.

Soliman, M. M., and R. K. Koopmans, 1992. Chapter 2: Climate, in H. C. J. van Zon and K. W. Jeanes (eds.), *Environmental Profile Fayoum Governorate, Egypt*, Euroconsult/Darwish Consulting Engineers, Arnhem, 5-7.

Spielmann, K. A., and J. F. Eder, 1994. Hunters and Farmers: Then and Now, *Annual Review of Anthropology* 23, 303-323.

Stanley, J. D., 2002. Configuration of the Egypt-to-Canaan Coastal Margin and North Sinai Byway in the Bronze Age, in E. C. M. van den Brink and T. E. Levy (eds.), *Egypt and the Levant: Interrelations from the 4th through the Early 3rd Millennium B.C.E.*, Leicester University Press, London, 98-117.

Stark, M. T., 1998. Technical Choices and Social Boundaries in Material Culture Patterning: An Introduction, in M. T. Stark (ed.), *The Archaeology of Social Boundaries*, Smithsonian Institution Press, Washington, 1-11.

Staubwasser, M., and H. Weiss, 2006. Holecene climate and cultural evolution in late prehistoric-early historic West Asia, *Quaternary Research* 66, 372-387.

Stiner, M. C., and N. D. Munro, 2002. Approaches to Prehistoric Diet Breadth, Demography, and Prey Ranking Systems in Time and Space, *Journal of Archaeological Method and Theory* 9/2, 181-214.

Sultan, M., N. Sturchio, F. A. Hassan, M. A. R. Hamdan, A. M. Mahmood, Z. El-Alfy and T. Stein, 1997. Precipitation source inferred from stable isotopic composition of Pleistocene groundwater and carbonate deposits in the Western Desert of Egypt, *Quaternary Research* 48, 29-37.

Täckholm, V., 1990. Botanical Examination, in F. Debono and B. Mortensen (eds.), *El Omari:*

A Neolithic settlement and other sites in the vicinity of Wadi Hof, Helwan, Philipp von Zabern, Mainz am Rhein, 115-116.

Tainter, J. A., 2004. Persistent Dilemmas in American Cultural Resource Management, in J. Bintliff (ed.), *A Companion to Archaeology*, Blackwell, Oxford, 435-453.

Tchernov, E, 1998. An attempt to synchronize the faunal changes with the radiometric dates and the cultural chronology in Southwest Asia, in H. Buitenhuis, L. Bartosiewicz and A. M. Choyke (eds.), *Archaeozoology of the Near East III*, ARC Publication, Groningen, 7-44.

Tchernov, E., and O. Bar-Yosef, 1982. Animal exploitation in the Pre-Pottery Neolithic B period at Wadi Tbeik, Southern Sinai, *Paléorient* 8/2, 17-37.

Testart, A., 1982. The significance of food storage among hunter-gatherers: residence patterns, population densities and social inequalities, *Current Anthropology* 23-5, 523-537.

Thomas, J., 1999. Culture and Identity, in G. Barker (ed.), *Companion Encyclopedia of Archaeology*, Routledge, London, 431-469.

Thorpe, I., 1996, *The Origins of Agriculture in Europe*, Routledge, London.

Tixier, J., 1963. *Typologie de l'épipaléolithique du Maghreb*, Arts et Métiers Graphiques, Paris.

Trigger, B., 1979. Anthropology and Egyptology: Egypt and the Comparative Study of Early Civilizations, in K. Weeks (ed.), *Egyptology and the Social Sciences*, The American University in Cairo Press, Cairo, 23-56.

Trigger, B., 1997. Ancient Egypt in Cross-cultural Perspective, in J. Lustig (ed.), *Anthropology and Egyptology: A Developing Dialogue*, Sheffield Academic Press, Sheffield, 137-143.

Torrence, R., 1983. Time budgeting and hunter-gatherer technology, in G. Bailey (ed.), *Hunter-Gatherer Economy in Prehistory: A European Perspective*, Cambridge University Press, Cambridge, 11-22.

Torrence, R., 1989. Retooling: towards a behavioural theory of stone tools, in R. Torrence (ed.), *Time, energy and stone tools*, Cambridge University Press, Cambridge, 57-66.

Uerpmann, H-P., 1987. *The Ancient Distribution of Ungulate Mammals in the Middle East: Fauna and Archaeological Sites in Southwest Asia and Northeast Africa*, Dr. Ludwig Reichert Verlag, Wiesbaden.

Ugan, A., J. Bright and A. Rogers, 2003. When is technology worth the trouble? *Journal of Archaeological Science* 30, 1315-1329.

Van Couvering, J. A., and J. A. Harris, 1991. Late Eocene age of Fayum mammal faunas, *Journal of Human Evolution* 21, 241-260.

Van den Brink, E. C. M., 1987. A Geo-Archaeological Survey in the North-Eastern Nile Delta, Egypt: the First Two Seasons, A Preliminary Report, *Mitteilungen des Deutschen Archäologischen Instituts, Abteilung Kairo* 43, 7-24.

Van Neer, W., 1989. Fishing along the prehistoric Nile, in L. Krzyzaniak and M. Kobusiewicz (eds.), *Later Prehistory of the Nile Basin and the Sahara*, Poznan Archaeological Museum, Poznan, 49-56.

Van Neer, W., 2004. Evolution of Prehistoric Fishing in the Nile Valley, *Journal of African Archaeology* 2/2, 251-269.

Van Neer, W., A. Ervynck, L. J. Bolle and R. S. Millner, 2004. Seasonality only works in certain parts of the year: the reconstruction of fishing seasons through otolith analysis, *International Journal of Osteoarchaeology* 14: 457-474.

Van Neer, W., and V. Linseele, 2007. *Fayum faunal report 2006 season.* Unpublished internal report.

Van Neer, W., L. Lougas and A. D. Rijnsdorp, 1999. Reconstructing age distribution, season of capture and growth rate of fish from archaeological sites based on otoliths and vertebrae, *International Journal of Osteoarchaeology* 9, 116–130.

Van Neer, W., E. Paulissen and P. M. Vermeersch, 2000. Chronology, subsistence and environment of the Late Palaeolithic fishing sites of Makhadma 2 and 4, in P. M.

Vermeersch (ed.), *Palaeolithic Living Sites in Upper and Middle Egypt*. Leuven University Press, Leuven, 271-287.

Van Neer, W., and H-P. Uerpmann, 1989. Palaeoecological Significance of the Holocene Faunal Remains of the B.O.S.-Missions, in R. Kuper (ed.), *Forschungen zur Umweltgeschichte der Ostsahara*, Heinrich Barth Institut, Köln, 309-341.

Van Zeist, W., and S. Bottema, 1991. *Late quaternary vegetation of the Near East*, Dr. Ludwig Reichert Verlag, Wiesbaden.

Van Zeist, W., and G. J. de Roller, 1993. Plant remains from Maadi, a Predynastic site in Lower Egypt, *Vegetation History and Archaeobotany* 2, 1-14.

Van Zeist, W., G. J. de Roller and A. G. E. Fahmy, 2003. An archaeobotanical study of Maadi, a Pre-Dynastic site in Lower Egypt, in W. van Zeist (ed.), *Reports on Archaeobotanical Studies in the Old World*, Groningen Institute of Archaeology, Groningen, 167-202.

Verhoeven, M., 2004. Beyond Boundaries: Nature, Culture and a Holistic Approach to Domestication in the Levant, *Journal of World Prehistory* 18/3, 179-282.

Vermeersch, P. M., 1978. *Elkab II: Epipaléolithique de la vallée du Nil égyptien*, Leuven University Press, Leuven.

Vermeersch, P. M., 1984. Subsistence Activities on the Late Palaeolithic Sites of Elkab (Upper Egypt), in L. Krzyzaniak and M. Kobusiewicz (eds.), *Origin and Early Development of Food-Producing Cultures in North-Eastern Africa*, Poznan Archaeological Museum, Poznan, 137-142.

Vermeersch, P. M., 1992. The Upper and Late Palaeolithic of Northern and Eastern Africa, in F. Klees and R. Kuper (eds.), *New Light on the Northeast African Past: Current Prehistoric Research*, Heinrich Barth Institut, Köln, 100-153.

Vermeersch, P. M., 1994. L'homme et le Nil au paléolithique final, *Archéo-Nil* 4, 5-16.

Vermeersch, P. M., (ed.), 2000. *Palaeolithic Living Sites in Upper and Middle Egypt*, Leuven University Press, Leuven.

Vermeersch, P. M., 2002. The Egyptian Nile Valley during the Early Holocene, in Jennerstrasse 8 (eds.), *Tides of the Desert: Contributions to the Archaeology and Environmental History of Africa in Honour of Rudolph Kuper*, Heinrich Barth Institut, Köln, 27-40.

Vermeersch, P. M. (ed.), 2008. *A Holocene Prehistoric Sequence in the Egyptian Red Sea Area: The Tree Shelter*, Leuven University Press, Leuven.

Vermeersch, P. M., E. Paulissen and W. Van Neer, 1989. The Late Palaeolithic Makhadma Sites (Egypt): Their Environment and Subsistence in L. Krzyzaniak and M. Kobusiewicz (eds.), *Late Prehistory of the Nile Basin and the Sahara*, Poznan Archaeological Museum, Poznan, 87-114.

Vermeersch, P. M., E. Paulissen and D. Huyge, 2000. Makhadma 4, A Late Palaeolithic fishing site, in P. M. Vermeersch (ed.), *Palaeolithic Living Sites in Upper and Middle Egypt*, Leuven University Press, 227-270.

Vermeersch, P. M., W. Van Neer and F. Gullentops, 2007. El Abadiya 3, Upper Egypt, a Late Palaeolithic site on the shore of a large Nile lake, in K. Kroeper, M. Chlodnicki and M. Kobusiewicz (eds.), *Archaeology of Early Northeastern Africa*, Poznan Archaeological Museum, Poznan, 375-424.

Vermeersch, P. M., P. Van Peer, J. Moeyersons and W. Van Neer, 1994. Sodmein cave site, Red Sea Mountains (Egypt), *Sahara* 6, 31-40.

Vermeersch, P. M., P. Van Peer, J. Moeyersons and W. Van Neer, 1996. Neolithic occupation of the Sodmein area, Red Sea Mountains, Egypt, in G. Pwiti and R. Soper (eds.), *Aspects of African Archaeology: Papers from the 10th Congress of the Pan African Association for Prehistory and Related Studies*, University of Zimbabwe Publications, Harare, 411-419.

Vermeersch, P. M., P. Van Peer, J. Moeyersons and W. Van Neer, 2002. The Tree Shelter, a Holocene Site in the Red Sea Mountains, *Archéo-Nil* 12, 123-137.

Vermeersch, P. M., P. Van Peer and V. Rots, 2005a. A Survey of the Bili Cave and its surroundings in the Red Sea Mountains, El

Gouna, Egypt, *Journal of African Archaeology* 3, 267-276.

Vermeersch, P. M., P. Van Peer, V. Rots, L. Van Kerckhoven and W. Van Neer, 2005b. The Middle Holocene Shell Mound of El Gouna on the Red Sea (Egypt), *Journal of Field Archaeology* 30, 435-442.

Von den Driesch, A., 1986. Tierknochenfunde aus Qasr el-Sagha/Fayum, *Mitteilungen des Deutschen Archäologischen Instituts, Abteilung Kairo* 42, 1-8.

Von den Driesch, A., and J. Boessneck, 1985. *Die Tierknochenfunde aus der neolithischen Siedlung von Merimde-Benisalâme am westlichen Nildelta*, Institut für Palaeoanatomie, Domestikationsforschung und Geschichte der Tiermedizin der Universität München, München.

Wagstaff, M., 1991. The Archaeological 'Site' from a Geographical Perspectives, in A. J. Schofield (ed.), *Interpreting Artefact Scatters: Contributions to Ploughzone Archaeology*, Oxbow Books, Oxford, 9-10.

Wanas, H. A., 2008. Calcite-cemented concretions in shallow marine and fluvial sandstones of the Birket Qarun Formation (Late Eocene), El-Faiyum depression, Egypt: Field, petrographic and geochemical studies: Implications for formation conditions, *Sedimentary Geology* 212, 40-48.

Warburton, D. A., 2004. Towards new frameworks: Supra-regional concepts in Near Eastern Neolithization, *Paléorient* 30/1, 183-188.

Warfe, A. R., 2003. Cultural Origins of the Egyptian Neolithic and Predynastic: An Evaluation of the Evidence from the Dakhleh Oasis (South Central Egypt), *African Archaeological Review* 20/4, 175-202.

Wasylikowa, K., J. Harlan, J. Evans, F. Wendorf, R. Schild, A. E. Close, H. Krolik and R. Housley, 1993. Examination of botanical remains from early Neolithic houses at Nabta Playa, Western Desert, Egypt, with special reference to sorghum grains, in T. Shaw, P. Sinclair, B. Andah and A. Okpoko (eds.), *The Archaeology of Africa: food, metals and towns*, Routledge, London, 154-164.

Wasylikowa, K., J. Mitka, F. Wendorf and R. Schild, 1997. Exploitation of wild plants by the early Neolithic hunter-gatherers of the Western Desert, Egypt: Nabta Playa as a case-study, *Antiquity* 71, 932-941.

Wasylikowa, K., and J. Dahlberg, 1999. Sorghum in the Economy of the Early Neolithic Nomadic Tribes at Nabta Playa, Southern Egypt, in M. Van der Veen (ed.), *The Exploitation of Plant Resources in Ancient Africa*, Kluwer Academic/Plenum Publishers, New York, 11-31.

Wasylikowa, K., H. N. Barakat, L. Boulos, A. Butler, J. A. Dahlberg, J. Hather and J. Mitka, 2001. Site E-75-6: Vegetation and Subsistence of the Early Neolithic at Nabta Playa, Egypt, Reconstructed from Charred Plant Remains, in F. Wendorf and R. Schild (eds.), *Holocene Settlement of the Egyptian Sahara, volume 1: The Archaeology of Nabta Playa*, Kluwer Academic/Plenum Publishers, New York, 544-591.

Watkins, T., 2003. Developing socio-cultural networks, *Neo-Lithics* 2/03, 36-37.

Watkins, T., 2006. Neolithisation in southwest Asia- the path to modernity, *Documenta Praehistorica* 33, 71-88.

Watrin, L., 1998. The relationship between the Nile Delta and Palestine during the Fourth Millennium: From early exchanges (Naqada I-II) to the colonisation of southern Palestine (Naqada III)," in C. J. Eyre (ed.), *Proceedings of the Seventh International Congress of Egyptologists*, Peeters, Leuven, 1215-1226.

Watrin, L., 2003. Lower-Upper Egyptian interaction during the Pre-Naqada period: From initial trade contacts to the ascendancy of southern chiefdoms, in Z. Hawass and L. Pinch Brock (eds.), *Egyptology at the Dawn of the Twenty-first Century vol.2*, American University in Cairo Press, Cairo, 566-581.

Wendorf, F., 1968. *The Prehistory of Nubia*, Southern Methodist University Press, Dallas.

Wendorf, F., and R. Schild, 1976. *Prehistory of the Nile Valley*, Academic Press, New York.

Wendorf, F., and R. Schild, 1980. *Prehistory of the Eastern Sahara*, Academic Press, New York.

Wendorf, F., and R. Schild, 1984. Report on Site E-80-2, in F. Wendorf, R. Schild and A. E. Close (eds.), *Cattle-Keepers of the Eastern Sahara: The Neolithic of Bir Kiseiba*, South Methodist University Press, Dallas, 298-306.

Wendorf, F., and R. Schild, 1986. *The Prehistory of Wadi Kubbaniya Volume 1. The Wadi Kubbaniya Skeleton: A Late Paleolithic Burial from Southern Egypt*, Southern Methodist University Press, Dallas.

Wendorf, F., and R. Schild, 1989. Summary and Synthesis, in F. Wendorf, R. Schild and A. E. Close (eds.), *The Prehistory of Wadi Kubbaniya, vol.3: Late Paleolithic Archaeology*, Southern Methodist University Press, Dallas, 768-824.

Wendorf, F., and R. Schild, 1994. Are the early Holocene cattle in the eastern Sahara domestic or wild? *Evolutionary Anthropology* 3, 118-128.

Wendorf, F., and R. Schild, 1998. Nabta Playa and Its Role in Northeastern African Prehistory, *Journal of Anthropological Archaeology* 17, 97-123.

Wendorf, F., and R. Schild, 1998. Nabta Playa and Its Role in Northeastern African Prehistory, *Journal of Anthropological Archaeology* 17, 97-123.

Wendorf, F., and R. Schild, 2002a. Implications of Incipient Social Complexity in the Late Neolithic in the Egyptian Sahara, in R. Friedman (ed.), *Egypt and Nubia: Gifts of the Desert*, The British Museum Press, London, 13-20.

Wendorf, F., and R. Schild, 2002b. The Role of Storage in the Neolithic of the Egyptian Sahara, in Jennerstrasse 8 (eds.), *Tides of the Desert: Contributions to the Archaeology and Environmental History of Africa in Honour of Rudolph Kuper*, Heinrich Barth Institut, Köln, 41-49.

Wendorf, F., and R. Schild, 2003. Food economy and settlement system during the Neolithic in the Egyptian Sahara, in L. Krzyzaniak, K. Kroeper and M. Kobusiewicz (eds.), *Cultural Markers in the Later Prehistory of Northeastern Africa and Recent Research*, Poznan Archaeological Museum, Poznan, 145-157.

Wendorf, F., and R. Schild, 2004. The Western Desert during the 5th and 4th millennia BC: The Late and Final Neolithic in the Nabta-Kiseiba Area, *Archéo-Nil* 14, 13-30.

Wendorf, F., R. Schild and A. E. Close (eds.), 1984. *Cattle-Keepers of the Eastern Sahara: The Neolithic of Bir Kiseiba*, Southern Methodist University, Dallas.

Wendorf, F., R. Schild and Associates, 2001. *Holocene Settlement of the Egyptian Sahara, volume 1: The Archaeology of Nabta Playa*, Kluwer Academic/Plenum Publishers, New York.

Wendrich, W., and R. Cappers, 2005. Egypt's earliest granaries: evidence from the Fayum, *Egyptian Archaeology: The Bulletin of the Egypt Exploration Society* No.27, 12-15.

Weninger, B., E. Alram-Stern, E. Bauer, L. Clare, U. Danzeglocke, O. Jöris, C. Kubatzki, G. Rollefson, H. Todorova and T. Van Andel, 2006. Climate forcing due to the 8200 cal yr BP event observed at Early Neolithic sites in the eastern Mediterranean, *Quaternary Research* 66, 401-420.

Wenke, R., 1984. Early agriculture in the Southern Fayum Depression: some test survey results and research implications, in L. Krzyzaniak and M. Kobusiewicz (eds.), *Origin and Early Development of Food-Producing Cultures in North-Eastern Africa*, Poznan Archaeological Museum, Poznan, 193-198.

Wenke, R., 1989. Egypt: Origins of Complex Societies, *Annual Review of Anthropology* 18, 129-155.

Wenke, R. J., 1990. *Patterns in Prehistory: Humankind's First Three Million Years (3rd ed.)*, Oxford University Press, Oxford.

Wenke, R., P. Buck, J. Hanley, M. Lane, J. Long and R. Redding, 1983. The Fayyum Archaeological Project: Preliminary Report of the 1981 Season, *Newsletter of the American Research Center in Egypt* 122, 25-40.

Wenke, R. J., J. E. Long and P. E. Buck, 1988. Epipaleolithic and Neolithic Subsistence and Settlement in the Fayyum Oasis of Egypt,

Journal of Field Archaeology 15, 29-51.

Wenke, R., and M. Casini, 1989. The Epipaleolithic-Neolithic transition in Egypt's Fayum Depression, in L. Krzyzaniak and M. Kobusiewicz (eds.), *Later Prehistory of the Nile Basin and the Sahara*, Poznan Archaeological Museum, Poznan, 140-155.

Wenke, R., and D. Brewer, 1992. The Neolithic-Predynastic Transition in the Fayum Depression, in R. Friedman and B. Adams (eds.), *The Followers of Horus: Studies dedicated to Michael Allen Hoffman*, Oxbow Books, Oxford, 175-184.

Wetterstrom, W., 1993. Foraging and farming in Egypt: the transition from hunting and gathering to horticulture in the Nile Valley, in T. Shaw, P. Sinclair, B. Andah and A. Okpoko (eds.), *The Archaeology of Africa: Food, Metals and Towns*, Routledge, London, 165-226.

Wetterstrom, W., 1996. La chasse-cueillette et l'agriculture en Égypte: la transition de la chasse et de la cueillette a l'horticulture dans la vallée du Nil, *Archéo-Nil* 6, 27-49.

Wetterstrom, W., 1998. The Origins of Agriculture in Africa: With Particular Reference to Sorghum and Pearl Millet, *The Review of Archaeology* 19/2, 30-46.

Whallon, R., 2006. Social networks and information: Non-"utilitarian" mobility among hunter-gatherers, *Journal of Anthropological Archaeology* 25, 259-270.

Whittaker, J. C., 1994. *Flintknapping: Making and understanding stone tools*, University of Texas Press, Austin.

Wiessner, P., 1983. Style and social information in Kalahari San projectile points, *American Antiquity* 48/2, 253-276.

Wiessner, P., 1996. Introduction: Food, Status, Culture, and Nature, in P. Wiessner and W. Schiefenhovel (eds.), *Food and Status Quest: An Interdisciplinary Perspective*, Berghahn Books, Oxford, 1-18.

Willcox, G., 2002. Geographical variation in major cereal components and evidence for independent domestication events in Western Asia, in R. T. J. Cappers and S. Bottema (eds.), *The Dawn of Farming in the Near East*, ex oriente, Berlin, 133-140.

Willcox, G., 2005. The distribution, natural habitats and availability of wild cereals in relation to their domestication in the Near East: multiple events, multiple centres, *Vegetation History and Archaeobotany* 14, 534-541.

Wilson, P., 2006. Prehistoric settlement in the western Delta: A regional and local view from Sais (Sa el-Hagar), *Journal of Egyptian Archaeology* 92, 75-126.

Wilson, P., and G. Gilbert, 2002. Pigs, Pots and Postholes, *Egyptian Archaeology: The Bulletin of the Egypt Exploration Society* 21, 12-13.

Wilson, P., and G. Gilbert, 2003. The Prehistoric Period at Sais, *Archéo-Nil* 13, 65-72.

Winterhalder, B., and D. J. Kennett, 2006. Behavioral Ecology and the Transition from Hunting and Gathering to Agriculture, in D. J. Kennett and B. Winterhalder (eds.), *Behavioral Ecology and the Transition to Agriculture*, University of California Press, Berkeley, 1-21.

Winterhalder, B., and E. A. Smith, 1992. Evolutionary Ecology and the Social Sciences, in E. A. Smith and B. Winterhalder (eds.), *Evolutionary Ecology and Human Behavior*, Aldine de Gruyter, New York, 3-23.

Winterhalder, B., and E. A. Smith, 2000. Analyzing adaptive strategies: Human behavioral ecology at twenty-five, *Evolutionary Anthropology* 9, 51-72.

Wright, H., 1993. Environmental Determinism in Near Eastern Prehistory, *Current Anthropology* 34, 458-469.

Wright, K., 2005. The emergence of cooking in Southwest Asia, *Archaeology International* 2004/05, 33-37.

Wright, K., and A. Garrard, 2003. Social identities and the expansion of stone bead-making in Neolithic Western Asia: new evidence from Jordan, *Antiquity* 77, 267-284.

Zahran, M. A., and A. J. Willis, 1992. *The Vegetation of Egypt*, Chapman & Hall, London.

Zeder, M. A., 2000. Animal domestication in the

Zagros: a review of past and current research, *Paléorient* 25/2, 27-48.

Zeder, M. A., 2005. A View from the Zagros: new perspectives on livestock domestication in the Fertile Crescent, in J.-D. Vigne, J. Peters and D. Helmer (eds.), *First Steps of Animal Domestication: New archaeozoological approaches*, Oxbow Books, Oxford, 125-146.

Zeder, M. A., 2008. Domestication and early agriculture in the Mediterranean Basin: Origins, diffusion, and impact, *Proceedings of the National Academy of Sciences* 105/33, 11597-11604.

Zohary, D., 1989. Domestication of the Southwest Asian Neolithic crop assemblage of cereals, pulses, and flax: the evidence from the living plants, in D. R. Harris and G. C. Hillman (eds.), *Foraging and Farming: The Evolution of Plant Exploitation*, Unwin Hyman, London, 358-373.

Zohary, D., and M. Hopf, 1993. *Domestication of Plants in the Old World: The Origin and Spread of Cultivated Plants in West Asia, Europe, and the Nile Valley*, Clarendon Press, Oxford.

Zvelebil, M., 1986a. Mesolithic prelude and Neolithic revolution, in M. Zvelebil (ed.), *Hunters in Transition: Mesolithic Societies of Temperate Eurasia and Their Transition to Farming*, Cambridge University Press, Cambridge, 5-15.

Zvelebil, M., 1986b. Mesolithic societies and the transition to farming: problems of time, scale and organisation, in M. Zvelebil (ed.), *Hunters in Transition: Mesolithic Societies of Temperate Eurasia and Their Transition to Farming*, Cambridge University Press, Cambridge, 167-188.

Zvelebil, M., and P. Rowley-Conwy, 1984. Transition to farming in northern Europe: A hunter-gatherer perspective, *Norwegian Archaeological Review* 17, 104-128.

English Summary

The Archaeology of the First Farmer-Herders in Egypt: New Insights into the Fayum Epipalaeolithic and Neolithic

The beginning of food production by means of crop farming and animal herding in human prehistory is an important research topic in archaeology, but this topic has not been sufficiently studied in the archaeology of Egypt. It is important to understand how and why farming and herding started in a particular time period in a particular region of Egypt. Food production began in Egypt at the transition from the Epipalaeolithic to Neolithic in the 6th millennium cal.BC owing to the arrival of Levantine domesticates. The earliest Neolithic farming in combination with herding in Egypt is known in the Fayum, which is a large oasis with a permanent lake in the Egyptian Western Desert.

The earliest Neolithic farmer-herders in the Fayum relied heavily on hunting and fishing, which had been the major subsistence activities since the Epipalaeolithic period. There are no remains of substantial dwellings to indicate that these farmer-herders lived a sedentary way of life. Previous researchers have thus asserted that the Fayum people were nomadic and moved seasonally. A major research question is whether such an assertion is really supported by other archaeological data. Considering the harsh desert environment, it seems unrealistic that all the people moved far away from drinking water and rich wild food resources at a permanent water source, even temporarily.

Research on lithic artefacts used by the Epipalaeolithic hunter-fishers and Neolithic farmer-herders in the Fayum reveals where lithic raw material was exploited and where and how tools were produced. This gives a clue as to the mobility and residential strategy of the Fayum people. Fayum Neolithic farmer-herders preferentially procured larger lithic raw material from far more distant sources than Epipalaeolithic hunter-fishers did. In addition, the Neolithic people invented much larger and more elaborate hunting weapons than their Epipalaeolithic predecessors by using large raw material. Questions are why Neolithic people took such longer distance trips, and why they invested more time and labour in making such weapons despite the arrival of domesticated animals. Furthermore, although the data are scarce, the number of hippopotamus and crocodile seem to have increased in the Neolithic faunal assemblage compared with the Epipalaeolithic one. A question is why such an increase occurred in the Neolithic.

These changes in the Neolithic indicate people's adaptation to new subsistence activities. It is plausible that the Neolithic people had to take the herd of domesticated animals for grazing, particularly when crops were growing in farming plots which would have probably been located around lakeshores. Collecting lithic raw material would have been embedded in the pastoral grazing trips. The appearance of new hunting weapons and the increase in the number of hippopotamus and crocodile in the Neolithic would be due to a new predator-prey relationship in the Fayum ecological system caused by the arrival of Levantine domesticates. Farming and herding in the Fayum lakeshore environment would not have been possible without the protection of farming plots and herds from hippopotamus and crocodile by the people who inhabited lakeshores. On the other hand, increasing dependence on these new subsistence activities was not possible without a constant supply of larger raw material for toolmaking, which was probably enabled by an increase of logistical moves of individual members from a residential group.

Despite the lack of substantial dwellings, other circumstantial evidence strongly suggests that the Fayum people were not nomadic but were tethered to lakeshores. The introduction of farming and herding would not have taken place in the Fayum without a lakeshore-tethered if not fully sedentary lifeway. However, the success of a farming-herding lifeway in the Fayum would not have been possible without the reorganisation of mobility, which led to decreased moves of residential bases and increased logistical moves of individuals. A simplistic dichotomy between either sedentary or nomadic does not precisely describe the situation of the Fayum Neolithic farmer-herders.

The last question is why Levantine domesticates were introduced in the Fayum, even though wild food resources seem to have been constantly available and more efficiently exploited than domesticates. If farming and herding had turned out to be unsuitable in the Fayum environment after an initial attempt, they would have dropped out of the Fayum subsistence. However, Fayum Neolithic people made unprecedented time and labour investments in lithic raw material procurement and toolmaking for new activities. It is obvious that the people kept making special efforts to maximise the yield of farming and herding. It is assumed that domesticates were added to the diet of Fayum Neolithic people when some essential wild food resources became temporarily or perpetually unavailable. This could have been caused by either unusual weather conditions and environmental disturbances, or the loss of access to the essential resources due to population increase and overcrowding in a circumscribed area like the Fayum. Therefore, it is important to consider the social context of the beginning of farming and herding in the Fayum in a wider geographical and chronological framework.

In the Fayum Neolithic, the number and density of sites are much larger and higher than those in the Epipalaeolithic, and population increase in the Neolithic is evident. General population increase in the Egyptian Western Desert since the 8th millennium cal.BC is attested by the wide distribution of human occupation loci and the fast spread of similar material cultures. The recurrence of depopulation in arid regions and population aggregation in well-watered regions of the Western Desert is also well documented. It is likely that such a demographic trend in the Western Desert affected the Fayum. The Fayum was very rich in wild food resources, and the balance between human population size and available food resource amount would have been maintained well below the carrying capacity of the Fayum in a natural state. However, the influx of migrants from outside the Fayum must have sooner or later upset this balance, and Fayum people would have had to increase the carrying capacity of their habitat by means of food production. This would be the reason why the Fayum people did not give up farming and herding in spite of the supposed difficulties in taking care of domesticates in this specific environment.

Nederlandse samenvatting

De Archeologie van de Eerste Boeren-Herders in Egypte: Nieuwe Inzichten in het Fajoem Epipaleolithicum en Neolithicum

Het begin van de voedselproductie door middel van landbouw en veeteelt is een belangrijk onderzoeksthema in de archeologie. Dit onderwerp is echter onvoldoende bestudeerd voor wat betreft Egypte. Het is belangrijk om te begrijpen hoe en waarom landbouw en veeteelt begon in een bepaalde periode en regio van Egypte. Voedselproductie in Egypte wordt gedateerd in de overgang van het Epipaleolithicum naar het Neolithicum in het 6e millennium v.Chr., wanneer voor het eerst sprake is van de komst van gedomesticeerde gewassen en dieren uit de Levant. De vroegste Neolithische landbouw in combinatie met veeteelt in Egypte is bekend uit de Fajoem, een grote oase in de Egyptische Westelijke Woestijn, met een permanent meer.

De vroegste Neolithische boeren-herders in de Fajoem leunden nog zwaar op jacht en visserij, die sinds de Epipaleolithische periode de belangrijkste bronnen van bestaan vormden. Er zijn geen resten van substantiële woningen die erop duiden dat deze boeren-herders een sedentair bestaan hadden. Eerdere onderzoekers hebben daarom beweerd dat de bewoners van de Fajoem een nomadisch bestaan leidden en zich seizoensmatig verplaatsten. Een belangrijke onderzoeksvraag is of deze bewering ondersteund wordt door andere archeologische data. Het is namelijk onwaarschijnlijk dat de mensen van de Fajoem een woonplek nabij water en rijke voedselbronnen zouden verlaten, zelfs niet tijdelijk, gezien de zeer droge omstandigheden in de woestijn.

Onderzoek naar de lithische artefacten van de Epipaleolithische jager-vissers en Neolithische boeren-herders in de Fajoem kan aanwijzingen geven over de wijze waarop de grondstofbronnen werden geëxploiteerd en waar en hoe de werktuigen werden geproduceerd. Dergelijke gegevens kunnen in verband gebracht worden met mobiliteitspatronen en de locatiekeuze voor de nederzettingen. De Neolithische boeren-herders gaven de voorkeur aan lithische grondstoffen van grotere omvang en uit veel verder gelegen bronnen dan de Epipaleolithische jager-vissers. Het gebruik van grotere uitgangsmaterialen maakte het voor de Neolithische mensen mogelijk veel grotere en complexere jachtwapens te maken dan hun Epipaleolithische voorgangers. Belangrijke vragen zijn waarom de Neolithische mensen de moeite namen om lange afstanden af te leggen voor het verkrijgen van grondstoffen en waarom ze zoveel meer tijd en arbeid investeerden in de productie van wapens, ondanks de komst van gedomesticeerde dieren. Hoewel de gegevens schaars zijn, lijkt bovendien het aantal nijlpaarden en krokodillen in het Neolithische faunaspectrum te zijn toegenomen in vergelijking met het Epipaleolithische. Een vraag is waarom deze toename optrad in het Neolithicum.

Deze veranderingen in het Neolithicum duiden op aanpassing van de mensen aan de nieuwe bestaanswijzen. Het is aannemelijk dat de Neolithische mensen met hun kudde gedomesticeerde dieren hebben rondgetrokken. Vooral tijdens de periode dat de gewassen op de, waarschijnlijk rond het meer gelegen, velden stonden, moet beweiding elders hebben plaatsgevonden. Het verzamelen van de lithische grondstoffen zou dan zijn ingebed in de trektochten die men maakte met het vee. De verschijning van nieuwe jachtwapens en de toename van de jacht op nijlpaarden en krokodillen in het Neolithicum zou het gevolg zijn van een nieuwe *predator-prey* relatie in het ecologisch systeem van de Fajoem veroorzaakt door de komst van Levantijnse gewassen en dieren. Landbouw en veeteelt langs de oevers van het Fajoem meer was niet mogelijk zonder de velden en kudden te beschermen tegen krokodillen en nijlpaarden. Aan de andere kant, de toenemende afhankelijkheid van de nieuwe bestaanswijze was niet mogelijk zonder een constante aanvoer van grotere grondstoffen voor werktuigproductie, mogelijk gemaakt door een toename van de logistieke bewegingen van individuele leden van de gemeenschap.

Ondanks de afwezigheid van substantiële woningen, wijzen andere, indirecte gegevens erop dat de

Fajoem mensen niet nomadisch waren, maar aan de meeroevers verbleven. De introductie van landbouw en veeteelt is in de Fajoem niet mogelijk zonder een aan het meer gebonden bestaan, hoewel dit niet volledig sedentair hoeft te zijn geweest. Sterker, het succes van een agrarisch bestaan in de Fajoem zou niet mogelijk zijn geweest zonder een reorganisatie van de mobiliteit van overwegend residentiële verplaatsingen naar een toename van het aantal logistieke bewegingen. Een simplistische tweedeling in sedentair of nomadisch is daarom niet van toepassing op de situatie van de Neolithische boerenherders in de Fajoem.

De laatste vraag is waarom gedomesticeerde gewassen en dieren uit de Levant werden ingevoerd in de Fajoem terwijl wilde voedselbronnen beschikbaar waren die efficiënter geëxploiteerd konden worden dan gedomesticeerde gewassen en dieren. Als landbouw en veeteelt niet mogelijk waren gebleken in het milieu van de Fajoem, dan zou men hier waarschijnlijk verder van hebben afgezien. De Neolithische bewoners van de Fajoem hebben echter heel veel tijd en arbeid geïnvesteerd in de verwerving van lithische grondstoffen van hoge kwaliteit en de productie van werktuigen voor nieuwe activiteiten. Het is duidelijk dat men tot bijzondere inspanningen bereid was om de opbrengst van landbouw en veeteelt te maximaliseren. Er wordt verondersteld dat gedomesticeerde gewassen en dieren werden toegevoegd aan het dieet van de Neolithische mensen toen enkele van de essentiële wilde voedselbronnen tijdelijk of permanent niet beschikbaar waren. Dit kan veroorzaakt zijn door ofwel ongewone weersomstandigheden en veranderingen in het milieu, ofwel door het verlies van toegang tot de essentiële wilde voedselbronnen als gevolg van populatiegroei en overbevolking in een beperkt bewoonbaar gebied als dat van de Fajoem. Daarom is het belangrijk om de sociale context van het begin van landbouw en veeteelt in de Fajoem in een ruimer geografisch en chronologisch kader te plaatsen.

In het Fajoem Neolithicum is het aantal sites groter en de dichtheid hoger dan in het Epipaleolithicum. Dit wijst op een populatiegroei in het Neolithicum. Een algemene populatiegroei in de Egyptische Westelijke Woestijn sinds het 8e millennium v.Chr blijkt uit de brede verspreiding van menselijke bewoningsresten en de snelle verspreiding van materiële cultuurelementen. Ook de herhaaldelijke ontvolking van droge gebieden en de populatie aggregatie in goed bewaterde regio's van de Westelijke Woestijn is goed gedocumenteerd. Het is waarschijnlijk dat deze demografische trends in de Westelijke Woestijn ook hun invloed hebben gehad in de Fajoem. De Fajoem was zeer rijk aan wilde voedselbronnen en normaliter moet de balans tussen menselijke populatiegrootte en beschikbare hoeveelheid voedsel ver onder de draagkracht van de Fajoem zijn gebleven. De instroom van migranten van buiten de Fajoem moet echter vroeger of later dit evenwicht hebben verstoord en de Fajoem mensen hebben gedwongen om de draagkracht van hun woongebied te verhogen door middel van voedselproductie. Dit zou de reden kunnen zijn geweest waarom de bewoners van de Fajoem niet zijn gestopt met landbouw en veeteelt, in weerwil van de moeilijkheden bij het verzorgen van gedomesticeerde gewassen en dieren in dit specifieke milieu.

List of figures

All photographs were taken and improved by the author.
All illustrations were made by the author, and several of them were made on the basis of those in other publications. They are;
Fig.2.3 (on the basis of Said 1993: Fig.1.37)
Fig.2.4 (on the basis of McCorriston 2006: Fig.10.1)
Fig.3.1 (on the basis of Ball 1939: folding map)
Fig.3.2 (on the basis of Bussemer *et al.* 2006: Fig.2 and Wanas 2008: Fig.1)
Fig.3.6 (on the basis of Caton-Thompson and Gardner 1934: pls.III and V)
Fig.3.7 (on the basis of Caton-Thompson and Gardner 1934: pl.XXI)
Fig.3.9 (on the basis of Kuper and Kröpelin 2006: Fig.3)
Fig.4.4 (on the basis of Binford 1982: Fig.2)

List of tables

Acknowledgements

This dissertation was completed thanks to many people.

First of all, I would like to thank Willeke Wendrich and René Cappers for allowing me to join the UCLA-RUG Fayum Project. Without their understanding and tolerance, my work would not have been completed. I would also like to thank all people in the Fayum Project for their help on different occasions.

Secondly, I would like to thank Mahmoud El-Halwagy, Stephen Quirke, Willem Van Haarlem and Helen Whitehouse for giving me permission to study and publish Fayum lithic artefacts in their museums. Research on the museum collections greatly enriched my ideas.

Thirdly, in the process of writing up the dissertation chapters, parts of which have been presented at international meetings or published in books and journals in the past years, I have greatly benefited from many people's encouragement, suggestions and criticism. I am particularly indebted to Ofer Bar-Yosef, Bleda Düring, Hans Georg Gebel, Avi Gopher, Nigel Goring-Morris, Fekri Hassan, Robert Kelly, Mary McDonald, Heiko Riemer, Avraham Ronen, Steven Rosen, Romuald Schild, Klaus Schmidt, and Wim Van Neer. I truly appreciate their taking the time to read my manuscript and/or to answer my inquiries. My ideas would not have taken the present shape without their valuable input. But I stress that I am solely responsible for any errors and misunderstandings found in this dissertation.

Lastly, I would like to express my sincere gratitude to my promoters, referent and the other members of the promotion committee. Over the years, they have taken care of a stranger from the Far East. As well as reading my dissertation thoroughly and critically, they have taught me how to behave and study in the European academic community. Under their comprehensive guidance and careful supervision, I have spent the most stimulating time in my life.

Curriculum Vitae

Noriyuki Shirai was born in Kyoto, and grew up in Kobe, Hiroshima, and Saitama. He studied archaeology at Waseda University in Tokyo and gained experience of archaeological fieldwork and artifact study at several sites in Egypt. After finishing his BA and MA studies on the prehistory of Egypt, he worked at the Waseda University Museum as a research associate. Then he came to Leiden University in order to do PhD research, for which he obtained a four-year research grant of the Netherlands Organisation of Scientific Rescarch. He is currently teaching prehistoric archaeology of Egypt at Leiden University.

Printed in the United States
by Baker & Taylor Publisher Services